# Lecture Notes in Computer Science 13106

More information about this subseries at https://link.springer.com/bookseries/7410

Sokratis Katsikas · Costas Lambrinoudakis ·
Nora Cuppens · John Mylopoulos ·
Christos Kalloniatis · Weizhi Meng · Steven Furnell ·
Frank Pallas · Jörg Pohle · M. Angela Sasse ·
Habtamu Abie · Silvio Ranise · Luca Verderame ·
Enrico Cambiaso · Jorge Maestre Vidal ·
Marco Antonio Sotelo Monge (Eds.)

# Computer Security

## ESORICS 2021 International Workshops

CyberICPS, SECPRE, ADIoT, SPOSE, CPS4CIP, and CDT&SECOMANE
Darmstadt, Germany, October 4–8, 2021
Revised Selected Papers

Springer

*Editors*
Sokratis Katsikas
Norwegian University of Science and Technology
Gjøvik, Norway

Costas Lambrinoudakis
University of Piraeus
Piraeus, Greece

Nora Cuppens
Polytechnique Montréal
Montréal, QC, Canada

John Mylopoulos
University of Toronto
Toronto, ON, Canada

Christos Kalloniatis
University of the Aegean
Mytilene, Greece

Weizhi Meng
Technical University of Denmark
Kongens Lyngby, Denmark

Steven Furnell
University of Nottingham
Nottingham, UK

Frank Pallas
Technische Universität Berlin
Berlin, Germany

Jörg Pohle
Alexander von Humboldt Institut für Internet und Gesellschaft GmbH
Berlin, Germany

M. Angela Sasse
Ruhr-Universität Bochum
Bochum, Germany

Silvio Ranise
University of Trento and Fondazione Bruno Kessler
Trento, Italy

Habtamu Abie
Norwegian Computing Center
Oslo, Norway

Enrico Cambiaso
Consiglio Nazionale delle Ricerche (CNR)
Genoa, Italy

Luca Verderame
Università degli Studi di Genova
Genoa, Italy

Marco Antonio Sotelo Monge
Indra
Alcobendas, Spain

Jorge Maestre Vidal
Indra
Alcobendas, Spain

ISSN 0302-9743 ISSN 1611-3349 (electronic)
Lecture Notes in Computer Science
ISBN 978-3-030-95483-3 ISBN 978-3-030-95484-0 (eBook)
https://doi.org/10.1007/978-3-030-95484-0

LNCS Sublibrary: SL4 – Security and Cryptology



This Springer imprint is published by the registered company Springer Nature Switzerland AG
The registered company address is: Gewerbestrasse 11, 6330 Cham, Switzerland

# Preface

The 26th edition of the European Symposium on Research in Computer Security (ESORICS 2021) was held as an online event in Darmstadt, Germany, during October 4–8, 2021. In addition to the main conference, 11 workshops were organized and held in the same time period.

This volume includes the accepted contributions, in total 31 full papers and one short paper, to six of these workshops, as follows:

- 7th Workshop on the Security of Industrial Control Systems and of Cyber-Physical Systems (CyberICPS 2021);
- 5th International Workshop on Security and Privacy Requirements Engineering (SECPRE 2021);
- 4th International Workshop on Attacks and Defenses for Internet-of-Things (ADIoT 2021);
- 3rd Workshop on Security, Privacy, Organizations, and Systems Engineering (SPOSE 2021);
- 2nd International Workshop on Cyber-Physical Security for Critical Infrastructures Protection (CPS4CIP 2021); and
- 1st International Workshop on Cyber Defence Technologies and Secure Communications at the Network Edge (CDT&SECOMANE 2021).

While each of the workshops had a high-quality program of its own, the organizers opted to publish the proceedings jointly; these are included in this volume. The authors improved and extended these papers based on the reviewers' feedback as well as the discussions at the workshops.

We would like to thank each and every person who was involved in the organization of the ESORICS 2021 workshops. Special thanks go to the ESORICS 2021 Workshops Chairs and to all the workshop organizers and their respective Program Committees who contributed to making the ESORICS 2021 workshops a real success. We would also like to thank the Organizing Committee for supporting the day-to-day operation and execution of the workshops.

December 2021

Sokratis Katsikas
Costas Lambrinoudakis
Nora Cuppens
John Mylopoulos
Christos Kalloniatis
Weizhi Meng
Steven Furnell
Frank Pallas
Jörg Pohle
Angela Sasse
Habtamu Abie
Silvio Ranise
Luca Verderame
Enrico Cambiaso
Jorge Maestre Vidal
Marco Antonio Sotelo Monge

# Contents

# 7th Workshop on the Security of Industrial Control Systems and of Cyber-Physical Systems (CyberICPS 2021)

# CyberICPS 2021 Preface

This part contains revised versions of the papers presented at the 7th Workshop on Security of Industrial Control Systems and Cyber-Physical Systems (CyberICPS 2021). The workshop was co-located with the 26th European Symposium on Research in Computer Security (ESORICS 2021) and was held online as a virtual event on October 8, 2021.

Cyber-physical systems (CPSs) are physical and engineered systems that interact with the physical environment, whose operations are monitored, coordinated, controlled, and integrated by information and communication technologies. These systems exist everywhere around us, and range in size, complexity, and criticality, from embedded systems used in smart vehicles to SCADA systems in smart grids, control systems in water distribution systems, smart transportation systems, plant control systems, engineering workstations, substation equipment, programmable logic controllers (PLCs), and other industrial control systems (ICSs). These systems also include the emerging trend of the Industrial Internet of Things (IIoT) that will be the central part of the fourth industrial revolution. As ICSs and CPSs proliferate, and increasingly interact with us and affect our lives, their security becomes of paramount importance.

CyberICPS 2021 brought together researchers, engineers, and governmental actors with an interest in the security of ICSs and CPSs in the context of their increasing exposure to cyberspace by offering a forum for discussion on all issues related to their cyber security. CyberICPS 2021 attracted 18 high-quality submissions, each of which was assigned to three referees for review; the review process resulted in seven papers being accepted to be presented and included in the proceedings. These cover topics related to threats, vulnerabilities, and risks that cyber-physical systems and industrial control systems face; cyber attacks that may be launched against such systems; and ways of detecting and responding to such attacks.

We would like to express our thanks to all those who assisted us in organizing the event and putting together the program. We are very grateful to the members of the Program Committee for their timely and rigorous reviews. Thanks are also due to the event's Organizing Committee and to the ESORICS Organizing Committee. Last but by no means least, we would like to thank all the authors who submitted their work to the workshop and contributed to an interesting set of proceedings.

November 2021

Costas Lambrinoudakis
Nora Cuppens
Sokratis Katsikas
Frédéric Cuppens

# CyberICPS 2021 Organization

## General Chairs

| | |
|---|---|
| Sokratis Katsikas | Norwegian University of Science and Technology, Norway |
| Frédéric Cuppens | Polytechnique Montréal, Canada |

## Program Committee Chairs

| | |
|---|---|
| Costas Lambrinoudakis | University of Piraeus, Greece |
| Nora Cuppens | Polytechnique Montréal, Canada |

## Program Committee

| | |
|---|---|
| Habtamu Abie | Norwegian Computing Centre, Norway |
| Cristina Alcaraz | University of Malaga, Spain |
| Marios Anagnostopoulos | Aalborg University, Denmark |
| Mauro Conti | University of Padua, Italy |
| David Espes | University of Brest, France |
| Joaquin Garcia-Alfaro | Institut Polytechnique De Paris, France |
| Dieter Gollmann | Hamburg University of Technology, Germany |
| Michail Maniatakos | NYU Abu Dhabi, UAE |
| Sjouke Mauw | University of Luxembourg, Luxembourg |
| Weizhi Meng | Technical University of Denmark, Denmark |
| Pankaj Pandey | Norwegian University of Science and Technology, Norway |
| Nikos Pitropakis | Edinburgh Napier University, UK |
| Indrakshi Ray | Colorado State University, USA |
| Rodrigo Roman | University of Malaga, Spain |
| Andrea Saracino | Consiglio Nazionale delle Ricerche, Italy |
| Georgios Spathoulas | University of Thessaly, Greece |
| Nils Ole Tippenhauer | CISPA Helmholtz Center for Information Security, Germany |
| Stefano Zanero | Politecnico di Milano, Italy |
| Jianying Zhou | Singapore University of Technology and Design, Singapore |

# Communication and Cybersecurity Testbed for Autonomous Passenger Ship

Ahmed Amro(✉) and Vasileios Gkioulos

Norwegian University of Science and Technology, Gjøvik, Norway
{ahmed.amro,vasileios.gkioulos}@ntnu.no

**Abstract.** Many industrial sectors are undergoing a digital transformation, including maritime. New technological advancements and modes of operations are being introduced to maritime infrastructure, which includes ships, ports, and other facilities. Digital transformation in maritime has among its goals reducing human involvement and improving remote connectivity. The achievement of these goals hinges on several components, including communication technologies and cybersecurity. Consequently, maritime-related communication and cybersecurity solutions are in high demand. This paper targets the development of a maritime-themed testbed utilized to evaluate and analyze several maritime use cases, including autonomous passenger ships (APS) with a prime focus on the communication and cybersecurity aspects. We have proposed abstraction of processes guiding the utilization of the testbed capabilities. Also, we proposed an approach for replicating the target system of analysis which facilitates the analysis and evaluation activities. The proposed testbed and its processes have been evaluated by discussing some of the projects that utilized it, including evaluating communication and cybersecurity architectures for an APS use case. Additionally, after comparison with the state-of-the-art in cybersecurity testbeds, the testbed was found to be supporting the majority of the concepts and properties observed in the literature while the missing elements were highlighted and designated as suggestions for future work. Moreover, we provide a discussion of the challenges in cybersecurity evaluation in maritime in general and autonomous ships in particular.

**Keywords:** Cybersecurity · Communication · Testbed · Autonomous passenger ship · ICS

## 1 Introduction

In the modern era, technological advancements are enriching several aspects of our lives. Innovations in the maritime domain have found their application in passenger transportation in inland waterways. Several projects are undergoing aiming to develop autonomous passenger ships or ferries in three regions in Norway [6] including a project named Autoferry which aims to develop an Autonomous all-electric Passenger Ship (APS) for inland water transport in the


S. Katsikas et al. (Eds.): ESORICS 2021 Workshops, LNCS 13106, pp. 5–22, 2022.
https://doi.org/10.1007/978-3-030-95484-0_1

city of Trondheim [2]. The new APS operates within a new operational mode called autoremote, this entails that the APS will be mainly autonomous, with human supervision from a remote control center (RCC) [9]. Although this unconventional mode of operation is expected to improve the provisioning of navigational services, it introduces a wide range of cyber threats with possible safety impacts as it relies on a group of interconnected Industrial Control Systems (ICS) as well as several communication technologies.

Communication and cybersecurity are considered among the biggest challenges for the advancement of the autonomous shipping concept [9]. This is based on the fact that improper communication is the main factor for maritime casualties [1] and cybersecurity has been considered among the most significant challenges in the usage of unmanned ships according to seafarers [23]. Therefore, there is a growing interest in the development of communication and cybersecurity-related solutions for autonomous ships. Cyber ranges and testbeds are commonly utilized for the evaluation of the developed solution as well as for training and awareness [26,27]. However, during this study, we have observed a lack in the literature regarding the utility of cyber ranges or testbeds for the evaluation of cybersecurity solutions in the maritime domain in general and in autonomous shipping in particular. In the remainder of this paper, we use the terms cyber range and testbed interchangeably.

This paper proposes a testbed suitable for the analysis and evaluation of several maritime use cases focusing on cybersecurity and communication aspects. Initially, a literature review is conducted to identify relevant artifacts and approaches utilized in similar testbeds. Then the testbed is developed following the ISO 15288 standard [17]. Finally, the identified state-of-the-art is utilized to evaluate the testbed focusing on the comprehensiveness and utility of the included capabilities. Our contributions in this work can be summarised as follow:

- We propose a communication and cybersecurity testbed for several maritime use cases. The testbed capabilities are comprehensive compared to the state-of-the-art and provide a novel introduction for such testbed in the maritime domain.
- We propose an abstraction of three processes that can be followed during the utilization of cybersecurity testbeds namely, system replication, system analysis, and technical management.
- We propose an approach for the system replication process based on standardized system elements. The system elements can be utilized as guidelines for replicating the target system for analysis.

## 2 Background and Related Work

In this section, we provide a brief background regarding the motivation for this study as well as several relevant works regarding cybersecurity testbeds in general and in maritime in particular. Regarding the motivation, the testbed proposed in this paper is mainly developed to evaluate artifacts that were designed based on a group of established communication and cybersecurity requirements for an autonomous passenger ship or ferry (APS). The requirements were collected from several APS stakeholders, analyzed, and adopted in our earlier work [9]. The communication requirements were utilized to define and design a communication architecture for the APS that allows it to communicate with its operational context and support several navigational services such as autonomous navigation and autonomous engine monitoring and control [10]. On the other hand, the cybersecurity requirements in addition to a group of risk analysis processes for the APS as a cyber physical system [8,11] were utilized to define and design a cybersecurity architecture for the APS [7]. Additionally, the testbed capabilities enable the exploration of additional use cases allowing the advancement of cybersecurity research in maritime. Moreover, the testbed is evaluated using qualitative functional evaluation and through comparison with the state-of-the-art. The captured state-of-the-art of cybersecurity testbeds relies on the works summarized in the remainder of this section since a comprehensive literature survey is outside the scope of this paper.

Yamin et al. [27] conducted a systematic literature survey (SLR) and presented the state-of-the-art in cyber ranges and cybersecurity testbeds by highlighting several aspects such as environment building, scenarios, monitoring, learning, teaming, and management. Moreover, the authors discussed the observed approaches for testbed evaluation. We mapped our testbed capabilities, processes, and evaluation based on the artifacts highlighted in this work.

Kavak et al. [19] surveyed several works and presented the state-of-the-art related to the utility of simulation in the cybersecurity domain. The authors have highlighted the efforts observed in the literature during the construction of the testing environment which is referred to as "Representative environment building" and the utility of both physical equipment as well as virtual equipment in both simulating or emulating cyber exercises in security evaluation and testing.

Tam et al. [26] have discussed the concept of cyber ranges in the maritime context. The authors aimed to enhance the state-of-the-art by discussing cyber ranges in a maritime context, scalability, and the coordination of cyber ranges (i.e. federation). Regarding inserting the maritime context into cyber ranges, the authors have presented a layer representation of ships and ports components in maritime to aid the development of cyber ranges. This demonstrates the utility of the concept of facilities in cyber ranges in maritime, which refers to the separation of the different arrangement of components based on their geographical location or functionality. Regarding scalability, the authors have discussed the utilization of both simulation/emulation components in addition to real equipment in an attempt to maintain a balance between cost, scalability, repeatability, and realism. Finally, the authors have highlighted the utility of cyber ranges for generating data that can be used to enhance other processes such as risk assessment and machine learning algorithms.

## 3 Testbed Architecture

The testbed is aimed to include a group of capabilities that allow the analysis and evaluation of design and implementation artifacts for several maritime use cases focusing on communication and cybersecurity aspects. These use cases currently include an autonomous passenger ship and traditional integrated bridge systems. Considering the undergoing digitalization in maritime, the testbed is aimed to have a flexible design in order to accommodate several traditional and futuristic ship models and operational modes. The testbed model is a hybrid; consisting of both physical and virtual components. Moreover, the testbed provides both remote and on-site testing capabilities in addition to having a mobility feature.

### 3.1 Concepts and Processes

Figure 1 reflects a view of the testbed processes. It includes three main processes inspired from the ISO 15288 standard [17], namely, system replication, system analysis, and technical management.

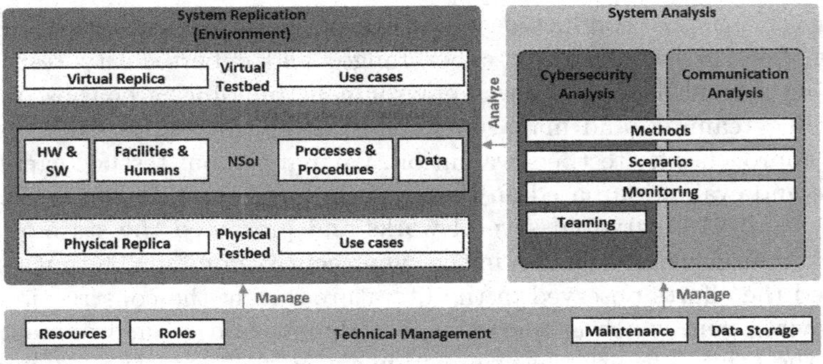


**Fig. 1.** Process view of the testbed

**System Replication:** Also referred to as "Representative environment building" [19] during this process, the Narrowest System of Interest (NSoI) is constructed utilizing physical and/or virtual components emulating and or simulating the real system under investigation. The system description is intended to be comprehensive to facilitate the system analysis process. The ISO 15288 standard [17] details the different system elements that can describe the manner in which a system is configured. As a guideline for capturing each NSoI, we propose using this system element abstraction. The outcome of this process is a constructed replica of the NSoI as well as an architecture description of it. The different system elements and their replication mechanisms are depicted in Table 1.

The use of simulation and emulation in cybersecurity testbeds and exercises is widely common as indicated in the literature [19,26,27]. Such tools can be utilized to replicate several system elements such as hardware or data streams. Yamin et al. [27] highlighted the utilization of traffic generation and behavior

**Table 1.** Replication mechanisms for the different system elements

| System element | Replication mechanism | Example |
|---|---|---|
| Hardware | - Simulation/Emulation tool<br>- Physical equipment | Automatic Identification System (AIS) replicated using physical equipment or a AIS simulator software |
| Software | - Tool | *OpenCPN* chart plotter software |
| Data | - Simulation/Emulation tool<br>- Physical equipment<br>- Traffic generation tools (e.g. stubs, fuzzing, replay) | Captured sensor data (e.g. lidar) transmitted through a traffic generation tool (e.g. *Tcpreplay*) |
| Humans | - Human<br>- User behavior generation tool | A Remote operator role emulated using a human or a user behavior generation tool |
| Processes, and procedures | - Scenarios<br>- Tools<br>- Physical equipment<br>- Human<br>- User behavior generation tool<br>- Facilities | Ship-to-Ship communication emulated using a group of physical equipment with relevant technology (e.g. VHF), people at another ship (i.e. facility), following a certain scenario for collision avoidance |
| Facilities | - Physical location<br>- Arrangement of physical equipment and tools | Sites 1 and 2 shown in Fig. 2 |

generation tools. The traffic generation tools are utilized for generating realistic data streams for creating different attack and normal operational scenarios while the user behavior generation tools are utilized to emulate human behavior. Additionally, Tam et al. [26] have highlighted the different types of data generated in cyber ranges, particularly, data needed to meet minimum requirements and allow services to function (i.e. stubs), data simulating all types of input to systems without applying logic (i.e. fuzzing), more realistic data based on simulation, and date that is replayed after being captured. Our testbed aims to provide data replication capabilities based on the data generation mechanisms discussed in [26,27] and focus on data streams that are relevant to the maritime domain.

Additionally, several maritime processes and procedures are addressed including the different communication functions specified in the APS communication architecture [10], namely, Ship-to-Shore, Ship-to-Ship, and Internal Communication. Ship-to-Shore communication targets the communication links between the ship and the shore for remote monitoring, control, and maintenance. Ship-to-Ship communication focuses on the communication channels between the ship and other ships for safe navigation. Internal communication focuses on the communication between internal ship systems. The ship systems include Information Technology (IT) as well as Operational Technology (OT). Examples of such systems are control servers (e.g. Dynamic Positioning System), and Programmable Logic Controllers (PLC) for controlling several safety systems. More details can be found in our earlier work [10]. Moreover, the representation of system's facilities in maritime has been observed to provide improved system analysis capabilities.

Materials and naturally occurring entities are other physical system elements discussed in the ISO 15288 standard [17]. Nevertheless, they have been found to be irrelevant to the current objectives of our testbed as the later focuses on cybersecurity and communication aspects of maritime use cases.

**System Analysis.** This process consists of a group of activities to analyze the constructed replica of the NSoI. In our testbed, the system analysis can follow two main directions, particularly, communication or cybersecurity analysis. Different aspects are relevant for each direction. Brief discussion for each aspect is provided below:

- **Methods**: Several methods for communication analysis are observed in the literature such as wireless coverage analysis [18] and performance analysis [22]. On the other hand, cybersecurity analysis methods include; among others, risk assessment, adversary emulation, and evaluation of security solutions [7]. Additionally, the cybersecurity analysis approaches; depending on the use case under analysis, can be conducted using black box, grey box, or white box analysis techniques [20].
- **Scenarios**: a scenario describes the storyline which specifies the steps for conducting a test or training exercise [27]. Scenario definitions should include a purpose, environment, storyline, type, domain, and tools. For the cybersecurity analysis, scenario types should include both normal operation scenarios (e.g. navigational scenario) as well as attack scenarios.
- **Monitoring**: this includes the methods, tools, and focus of the real-time monitoring of the exercise. In our testbed, this is mostly related to documentation and data collection. Network traffic capture, screen capture, and manual documentation are among the supported monitoring methods.
- **Teaming**: Cybersecurity analysis can be conducted through the utilizing of the concept of teaming. Several teaming formations have been observed in the literature including red teams conducting offensive security testing, blue teams conducting defensive security, white teams responsible for scenario creation, green teams involved in monitoring the scenarios, and autonomous teams utilized for automating the roles of other teams [27]. Additionally, a recent teaming concept, namely purple teaming [24], integrates the activities of red and blue teams extending the exercises toward further evaluation and improvement of the security posture of the target system. In our testbed, we aim to include several formations of such teams within different cybersecurity operations, namely, offensive security, defensive security, and offensive defense. Moreover, these cybersecurity operations are supported by white teams and autonomous teams for creating and automating the analysis process.
  - **Offensive Security**: This includes the identification and implementation of attack scenarios within the testbed components by conducting various

penetration testing activities (i.e. red team activities). The *ATT&CK* framework [25] is utilized to structure and formalize the description of these activities. *ATT&CK* was chosen based on our earlier works [7,8] due to its comprehensive threat model and updated common knowledge. Additionally, the utility of the ICS matrix in *ATT&CK* has been demonstrated in our earlier work [8] and resulted in several ICS specific attack scenarios which are target for analysis in our testbed. For instance, the manipulation of view [5] and denial of view [3] are two identified attack techniques with considerable risk against the APS system. Their risk is being evaluated in one of the project utilizing the testbed (refer to Sect. 4.2). The testbed provides capabilities to conduct attack techniques across the different cyber kill chain phases, including; among others, reconnaissance, initial access, discovery, impair process control, and inhibit response function. Performing these activities within the maritime context is expected to identify and evaluate novel and relevant attack techniques.
- **Defensive Security**: This includes the identification and implementation of defensive capabilities within the testbed (i.e. blue team activities). The NIST framework as well as the defense-in-depth strategies are both considered for mapping and updating the defensive capabilities to facilitate defensive operations. For instance, the testbed includes defensive capabilities allowing for threat identification, protection, and detection as well as capabilities for incident response and recovery from cyber-attacks. The choice for NIST and defense-in-depth is based on our previous work [7] which identified both among the most referenced risk management strategies. Performing these activities within the maritime context is expected to identify and evaluate novel and relevant defensive capabilities.
- **Offensive Defense**: This includes the implementation and analysis of the purple teaming concept in which red team and blue team activities are intertwined toward improving the security posture of a target system [24]. To the best of our knowledge, the introduction of this concept in the maritime domain is novel.

The outcome of this process is data and information for understanding the technical aspects of the NSoI. This allows for informed decision-making regarding the system development throughout its life cycle as well as support research activities in maritime communication and cybersecurity.

**Technical Management.** This process includes several management activities related to both the system replication and the system analysis processes for each project (i.e. test), such as; among others, resource management, maintenance, role management, and data storage. Brief discussion for each activity is provided below:

- **Resource Management**: this entails the identification and allocation of computational resources (e.g. memory), disk storage, and required components for conducting tests [27].

- **Role Management**: this entails the specification and distribution of roles during the different tests. For instance, during an attack scenario targeting a certain navigational operation, an attacker role is expected as well as a navigational role (e.g. Officer on Watch OOW).
- **Maintenance**: management of the testbed equipment such as inventory, licensing, and support.
- **Data Storage**: the management of any data related to the testbed. This includes the generated data during the analysis process, the different software binaries as well as backups of the different devices.

### 3.2 Tools and Equipment

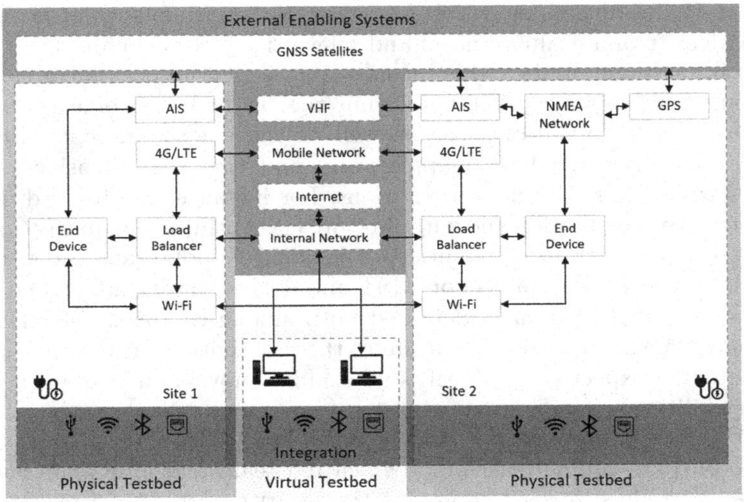


**Fig. 2.** Layout view of the testbed

Figure 2 depicts a layout view of the testbed reflecting the different physical and logical components that are utilized during the different processes discussed in Sect. 3.1. The components can be organized in different configurations in order to emulate several use cases. Overall, the testbed is organized into three main sections, a physical testbed, a virtual testbed, and an integration of both. The virtual testbed consists of a group of workstations with several tools providing different capabilities. A summary of the included tools is depicted in Table 2 highlighting their categories and the process during which they are mainly utilized. On the other hand, the physical testbed consists of a group of hardware equipment providing different capabilities. A summary of the included equipment is depicted in Table 3. Finally, both the physical and virtual testbeds have advantages and disadvantages which are depicted in Table 4. Therefore, an integration between the two sections is proposed to enrich the system replication and analysis processes. The virtual and physical testbeds are integrated through a group of interfaces utilizing different technologies such as USB, Wi-Fi, Bluetooth, and Ethernet.

**Table 2.** Tools utilized in the virtual testbed

| Process | Category | Tools | Description |
|---|---|---|---|
| System replication | Emulation/ Simulation | *Bridgecommand* | Customizing and building cooperative navigational scenarios |
| | | *NMEASimulator* | Customization of navigational scenarios |
| | | *GNS3* | Generation of complex networks and functional component through virtualization technology. It can be used to emulate the network and configuration of the NSoI |
| | | *VMWare* | Utilized alone or along with the GNS3 simulator to create virtual machines |
| | | *Virtualbox* | |
| | Navigation | *OpenCPN* | A chart plotter software |
| | Traffic generation | *Tcpreplay* | Replay recorded packet capture containing sensor data or other types of traffic |
| | | Python Scripts | |
| | | *IMU + GPS* | Generate and transmit Inertia measurements and GPS information from a mobile app |
| | | *PacketSender* | Transmit data or recorded packet capture over the network |
| | Cybersecurity controls | *Snort* | Open-source Intrusion Detection System (IDS) |
| | | *Wazuh* | Open-source Security Information and Event Management (SIEM) |
| | | *Duo* | Two Factor Authentication (2FA) software from Cisco |
| | | *OpenLDAP* | Role-Based Access Control (RBAC) software for access management |
| | | *ClamAV* | Antivirus software |
| | | *BorgBackup* | Backup software supporting encryption and compression as well as remote storage |
| System analysis | Monitoring | *Wireshark* | Packet capture and analysis |
| | | Screen Recorder | Record video and snapshots during experiments |
| | Cybersecurity testing | Ettercap | Man-in-the-middle tool |
| | | Kali Linux | Utilized as an attacker node |
| | | *Nmap* | Network scanner tools |
| | | *Caldera* | Breach and attack simulation platform for automating and emulating adversarial behavior (i.e. autonomous team) |
| | | Scikit-learn | Machine learning library for python programming. Utilized for model building, training, and evaluation toward anomaly detection solutions |
| | Communication testing | *Iperf* | Network performance measurements |
| | | *NetAnalyzer* | App for analyzing Wi-Fi signals and LAN networks |
| | | *WiFiAnalyzer* | App for analyzing Wi-Fi signals |

**Table 3.** Equipment utilized in the physical testbed

| Process | Category | Equipment (Quantity) | Description |
|---|---|---|---|
| System replication | Maritime equipment | AIS A200 (1) | Class A Automatic Identification System with external GNSS and VHF antenna |
| | | AIS B921 (1) | Class B Automatic Identification System with internal GNSS and VHF antenna |
| | | Furunu GP 170 (1) | Marine GPS with external GPS antenna |
| | | Garmin NMEA 2000 network starter kit (1) | NMEA 2000 network |
| | | Garmin NMEA 2000 Network Updater (1) | |
| | | Maretron IPG100 (2) | NMEA Internet Protocol Gateway |
| | Network equipment | Cisco Aironet 1532E (3) | Wi-Fi outdoor lightweight access points with external directional and Omni antennas |
| | | Cisco Wireless Controller 3504 (1) | For the management of the Wi-Fi network |
| | | Netgear Nighthawk Mobile Hotspot Router (3) | LTE/4G router |
| | | Cisco RV042G (2) | Load balancer, VPN router, and firewall |
| | Portable power sources | Omnicharge Ultimate (7) | Portable power source with 38400 mAh. Providing DC, AC, and USB output. |
| | | 9V power bank (3) | Additional power sources |
| System analysis | Software Defined Radio (SDR) | SDRplay RSPdx (1) | Wideband SDR |
| | | ADALM-PLUTO (4) | Active SDR learning module |
| Technical management | Data backup | LaCie 2TB (1) | 2TB External Hard drive |

## 4 Evaluation

In this section, we present a qualitative functional evaluation for our testbed through the discussion of some of the past and ongoing use cases utilizing it, namely, the analysis of communication and a cybersecurity architecture for an APS as well as an analysis of the security of sensor data in NMEA message format. Additionally, we provide a comparison of our testbed with the several aspects observed in the state of the art in cybersecurity testbeds. We demonstrate the utility of the testbed capabilities utilized during the system replication, system analysis, and technical management processes (refer to Sect. 3.1)

**Table 4.** Advantages and disadvantages of our physical and virtual testbeds

| | Advantages | Disadvantages |
|---|---|---|
| Physical | Wireless communication testing is possible using several technologies | Security attacks emulation is restricted due to limited possible configurations |
| | Built as mobile units to capture real measurements in different environments (e.g. marine traffic) | Wired communication testing is limited due to the lack of ethernet switches |
| | | cost of testing autonomous navigation and control components is high due to expensive physical components (e.g. radar, lidar, cameras, etc.) |
| Virtual | Security attack emulation is flexible due to virtualization | No capabilities for wireless communication testing |
| | Wired communication testing is possible with advanced capabilities | Real measurements (e.g.marine traffic) cannot be effectively captured during experiments |
| | Autonomous navigation and control components can be simulated | |

### 4.1 APS Communication and Cybersecurity Architecture

As discussed in Sect. 2, the main motivation for this testbed is the evaluation of a communication architecture [10] and a cybersecurity architecture [7] proposed in our earlier works based on a group of predefined communication and cybersecurity requirements in [9] for an autonomous passenger ship (APS). The testbed in both works was utilized for the evaluation of the proposed architectures to demonstrate their fulfillment of the stakeholders' requirements and concerns. Table 5 summarizes the processes and the different aspects regarding the evaluation of both proposed architectures. A prototype of the communication architecture was implemented using the GNS3 simulator consisting of several emulated network devices with network protocols to support ship-to-ship and internal communication functions. The implementation included two networks representing both a remote control center and an APS. The role of the human operator was emulated to evaluate the provisioning of the required capabilities. Then, the implementation was subject to a test scenario to evaluate the implementation performance considering aspects such as redundancy, fault tolerance, and remote access. More details can be found in [10]. On the other hand, a prototype of cybersecurity architecture was implemented extending the implemented communication architecture. Additional equipment included two workstations emulating the two facilities for improved resource management in addition to two physical gateways (RV042G). Moreover, a group of required cybersecurity controls was implemented (see Table 2) to evaluate their integration feasibility. Also, some sensor data was emulated using traffic generation tools. Then, the implemented architecture was evaluated using adversary emulation following 3 attack scenarios including red and blue team activities. The attack included several techniques including network sniffing, service scanning, ARP cache poisoning, gather victim information, and internet accessible devices using valid accounts. Although the attacks are not unique to the APS network, they were intended to evaluate the concept of layered defences within the context of the autoremote operational mode.

The testbed was found to be sufficient in evaluating the feasibility of integrating several architectural components and adequate in providing offensive security and defensive security analysis capabilities. However, the GNS3 simulator was found to be unsuitable for comprehensive performance analysis due to high latency related to virtualization.

**Table 5.** Use case 1: architecture evaluation

| Process | Aspect | Communication architecture | Cybersecurity architecture |
|---|---|---|---|
| System replication | Hardware | Workstation, GNS3, VMWare | Workstation, GNS3, VMWare, Virtualbox, Cisco RV042G |
| | Software | | Cyber security Controls |
| | Data | | Python scripts, IMU+GPS, Packet Sender |
| | Humans | Human (e.g. operator) | Human |
| | Processes, and Procedures | Ship-to-Shore, internal communication | Ship-to-Shore, internal communication, cybersecurity functions and protocols, sensor data collection. |
| | Facilities | Remote Control Center, APS | Remote Control Center, APS |
| System analysis | Tools | | Kali Linux, Nmap, Iperf |
| | Methods | Performance analysis | Feasibility of security solutions, Adversary Emulation, Performance Analysis |
| | Scenarios | 1 Scenario | 3 Scenarios |
| | Teaming | | Red team, Blue team |
| Technical management | Resource management | | Each facility at a dedicated workstation |
| | Role management | Human | Human, attacker |
| | Maintenance | ✓ | ✓ |
| | Data Storage | Local, Cloud | Local, Cloud and External HDD |

## 4.2 NMEA Security

Several maritime-related protocols operate within the testbed components such as the National Marine Electronics Association (NMEA) protocol which is a standard for the communication among marine equipment including sensor data. A study is being conducted to analyze the security of NMEA messages in two use cases, the APS as well as Integrated Navigation Systems (INS) in traditional vessels [12]. Initially, a system emulating the INS and its equivalent in the APS is constructed using several tools that emit NMEA messages including the *bridgecommand*[1] simulator, *NMEA simulator*[2], and a physical GPS or Automatic Identification System (AIS) device. Additionally, the *OpenCPN* chart plotter software[3] is used and configured to receive the transmitted NMEA messages. Additional scripts are utilized to transmit NMEA messages in certain

[1] https://www.bridgecommand.co.uk (accessed July 2021).
[2] https://cutt.ly/NMEASimulator (accessed July 2021).
[3] https://opencpn.org (accessed July 2021).

scenarios. Several navigational procedures are emulated such as collision avoidance. Then the developed system is used to study the NMEA messages, their structure, behavior, and security. Several attack scenarios are carried as well as normal operational scenarios. This allowed for the generation of both normal and attack traffic for the application of machine learning techniques utilizing several modules in the Scikit-learn including some pre-processing modules and classifiers (e.g. decision trees) [21]. The analysis included offensive security, defensive security as well as a offensive defense by interchanging the red team and blue team activities toward an improved anomaly detection solution. The offensive security activities included several attacks among them are attacks against maritime sensor data including variations of Manipulation of View [5] and Denial of View [3] attack techniques. Table 6 depicts a summary of the processes and the different aspects related the activities in this project.

**Table 6.** Use case 2: NMEA security

| Process | Aspect | APS, INS |
|---|---|---|
| System replication | Hardware | Workstation, Virtualbox, Bridgecommand Simulator, NMEA Simulator, Furunu GP 170 |
| | Software | OpenCPN chart plotter |
| | Data | Simulated GPS, Python scripts |
| | Humans | Officer on Watch (OOW) |
| | Processes, and procedures | Navigation status, route planning, collision avoidance, internal communication |
| | Facilities | Vessel |
| System analysis | Tools | Kali Linux, ettercap, Scikit-learn |
| | Methods | Adversary emulation, anomaly detection, risk analysis |
| | Scenarios | Many navigational scenarios, many attack scenarios |
| | Monitoring | Wireshark, Screen recorder |
| | Teaming | Red, blue, and purple teaming |
| Technical management | Resource management | |
| | Role management | Attacker, OOW |
| | Maintenance | ✓ |
| | Data Storage | Local, cloud, external HDD |

### 4.3 Relevance to the State-of-the-Art

Table 7 depicts a summary of the comparison between our testbed and the concepts and properties observed in the state-of-the-art of cybersecurity testbeds captured by the literature discussed in Sect. 2. The comparison highlights the comprehensive nature of our testbeds capabilities as it supports most of the common concepts and properties. However, this comparison points to the areas of limitations. First of all, our testbed does not include components dedicated to cybersecurity learning; which is adopted by 25% of the surveyed works by Yamin et al. [27], this is because no requirements for such component have been communicated by the stakeholders. This also justifies the lack of education-related scenarios, scoring tools, and a green team. Additionally, no user behavior generation tools or dedicated or special management tools are utilized in our testbed. The management process is supported by several general-purpose tools such as Microsoft office word, excel, as well as commercial data backup software.

**Table 7.** Comparison between our proposed testbed and the concepts and properties observed in the state-of-the-art

| Concepts and properties | | | Our testbed | Concepts and properties | | Our testbed |
|---|---|---|---|---|---|---|
| Scenario | Purpose | Testing | ✓ | Environment | Emulation | ✓ |
| | | Education | ✗ | | Simulation | ✓ |
| | | Experiment | ✓ | | Real Equipment | ✓ |
| | Type | Dynamic | ✓ | | Hybrid | ✓ |
| | | Static | ✗ | Tools | Emulation tools | ✓ |
| | Domain | Hybrid network applications | ✓ | | Simulation tools | ✓ |
| | | Networking | ✓ | | Management tools | ✗ |
| | | SCADA systems | ✗ | | Monitoring tools | ✓ |
| | | Social engineering | ✗ | | Traffic generation | ✓ |
| | | IoT systems | ✗ | | User behavior generation | ✗ |
| | | Critical infrastructure | ✗ | | Scoring tools | ✗ |
| | | Cloud based systems | ✗ | | Security testing tools | ✓ |
| | | Autonomous systems | ✓ | Teaming | Red team | ✓ |
| Management | | | ✓ | | Blue team | ✓ |
| Learning | | | ✗ | | White team | ✓ |
| Monitoring | | | ✓ | | Green team | ✗ |
| Remote access | | | ✓ | | Autonomous team | ✓ |
| Mobility | | | ✓ | | Purple teaming | ✓ |
| Scalability | | | Restricted | | | |

The state-of-the-art captured by Yamin et al. [27] does not capture the concept of testbed mobility. Additionally, purple teaming and remote access are discussed as concepts but the number of works that implement them were not tracked. Moreover, scalability is discussed only as a direction for future work. However, Tam et al. [26] discussed testbed mobility and its utility in maritime testbeds. Also, the authors addressed scalability as a main direction for developing maritime-specific cyber ranges. Our testbed includes solutions for remote access, mobility, scalability, as well as activities implementing purple teaming. The remote access component is carried using the *TeamViewer* software configured with the roles defined during the role management process (Sect. 3.1). The utility of *TeamViewer* for remote laboratories and collaborative learning has been discussed in the literature (e.g. [15,16]) and is found adequate in our testbed especially during the pandemic. Our testbed includes a mobility feature allowing it to be relocated to other indoor and outdoor locations. The mobility is supported through portable power sources allowing for extended experimentation periods, compact workstations in addition to specialized suite cases and mountable equipment, as well as certain waterproof equipment. Regarding scalability, our virtual testbed includes elements supporting scalabilities such as the GNS3 simulator, virtualization technology, and other simulation tools. This allows for the expansion, replication, and exportation of test scenarios. However, the scalability is restricted by the resources allowed by the testbed and identified during the resource management process (Sect. 3.1). The integration of a cloud-based component for the generation and execution of test scenarios is a future research direction. Lastly, the purple teaming concept has been applied in our testbed in a project targeting NMEA security (Sect. 4.2). This is supported by the integration of capabilities supporting red teams activities (e.g. Kali, Caldera, etc.) as well as blue team activities through the different security controls.

## 5 Challenges and Future Work

The testbed proposed in this paper aims to support research regarding communication and cybersecurity of an autonomous passenger ship (APS) and other related maritime use cases. The novelty of the autonomous shipping domain introduces both temporal and contextual complexity that impacts our research. The contextual complexity is related to the lack of legal framework governing the technology while the temporal complexity is related to the lack of a unified industrial vision regarding the technology. The International Maritime Organization (IMO) has just recently completed a regulatory scoping exercise for the Maritime Autonomous Surface Ship (MASS); the ship class under which the APS falls. Plans for the next steps are yet undecided [4]. Moreover, several projects are undergoing regarding the development of autonomous passenger ships or ferries [6] including the Autoferry project [2] which is the prime focus of this testbed. This means that the current envisaged technology posture is subject to change because most of the components governing and supporting autonomous operations are yet under development. This leads to the possibility that certain communication and cybersecurity testing capabilities supported by the testbed might not be of relevance in the future. The contextual complexity can be addressed in the same manner when addressing the temporal complexity, particularly by using a divide and conquer approach [14]. This entails the formulation of a specific operational context (i.e. use case) containing several design alternatives to be analyzed. Then, the data generated by the analysis can lead to the generation of new possible use cases or technology adaptation of the analyzed technology. For this sake, our testbed included several components from several providers, using several technologies, and providing several capabilities. This flexible design aims to circumvent the challenges inflected by the aforementioned complexity aspects.

Additional challenges are related to the usage of licensed communication frequencies for ship-to-ship, and ship-to-shore communication. Our testbed includes two AIS devices for supporting ship-to-ship communication. AIS operates over Very High Frequency (VHF) which requires a license to operate in Norway. Thus, restricted testing capabilities. We have deferred to other means for getting AIS and NMEA data through utilizing simulators and previously captured data. On the other hand, the LTE routers supporting ship-to-shore communication requires monthly data subscription which adds additional management cost.

In maritime, safety and cybersecurity are inter-related aspects, recently, IMO has issued resolution MSC.428(98) dictating that ship owners and operators must address cybersecurity in their safety management system [13]. Integrating capabilities for safety management within the testbed is a future direction. This is intended to support the efforts of integrating cybersecurity capabilities in such management systems toward the development of an Integrated Ship Safety and Security Management System (IS3MS). In addition to this, several use cases are expected to be utilized in the testbed including AIS security and Breach and Attack Simulation (BAS) platforms in the maritime context. Finally, the testbed is still under development and not available for public access at this moment. However, we can provide demonstrations of certain scenarios and capabilities.

## 6 Conclusion

The maritime domain is undergoing major digitization through the integration of technology and new operational aspects. Communication and cybersecurity are considered crucial aspects that could impact this major change in the industry. Therefore, in this paper, we proposed a testbed that can be utilized for the evaluation of several maritime use cases including the autonomous passenger ships (APS), and focusing on the communication and cybersecurity aspects. The testbed development is based on the observed state-of-the-art in cybersecurity testbeds and is inspired by several processes from the ISO 15288 system development standard. Our proposition includes an abstraction of three processes that can be followed for the utilization of the testbed namely, system replication, system analysis, and technical management. Moreover, we propose a system engineering approach for the system replication process that relies on standardized system elements. The three processes were followed during two projects (Sects. 4.1 and 4.2) and found to help guide the progress throughout the projects. Additionally, the utilization of standardized system elements as guidelines during the system replication process led to the development of a realistic replica of the systems targeted for analysis.

Also, after comparing our testbed to the state-of-the-art it was found to be comprehensive in the inclusion of a set of capabilities covering most of the observed concepts and properties. In addition to that, the testbed includes additional less observed features such as remote access, mobility, and purple teaming. Nevertheless, the testbed was found to be lacking some of the observed aspects such as having a learning component, user behavior generation tools, automated environment building tools, and dedicated management system tools in addition to restricted scalability. However, such limitations can induce future research directions.

## References

1. Norwegian maritime authority - focus on risks (2018). http://bit.ly/sdirRisks2018 (Sep 2017)

2. Autonomous all-electric passenger ferries for urban water transport, July 2021. https://www.ntnu.edu/autoferry
3. Denial of view - ATT and CK ICS (2021). https://cutt.ly/DoV
4. Imo completes regulatory scoping exercise for autonomous ships, May 2021. http://bit.ly/IMOMASS
5. Manipulation of view - ATT and CK ICS (2021). https://cutt.ly/MoV
6. Nfas - norwegian projects (2021). https://cutt.ly/NFAS
7. Amro, A., Gkioulos, V.: Securing autonomous passenger ship using threat informed defense-in-depth (2021, preprint). https://doi.org/10.13140/RG.2.2.33308.62083. Submitted for review to Computers & Security
8. Amro, A., Gkioulos, V., Katsikas, S.: Assessing cyber risk in cyber-physical systems using the ATT and CK ICS framework (2021, Preprint). Submitted for review to ACM Transactions on Privacy and Security (TOPS)
9. Amro, A., Gkioulos, V., Katsikas, S.: Connect and protect: requirements for maritime autonomous surface ship in urban passenger transportation. In: Katsikas, S., et al. (eds.) CyberICPS/SECPRE/SPOSE/ADIoT -2019. LNCS, vol. 11980, pp. 69–85. Springer, Cham (2020). https://doi.org/10.1007/978-3-030-42048-2_5
10. Amro, A., Gkioulos, V., Katsikas, S.: Communication architecture for autonomous passenger ship. Proc. Inst. Mech. Eng. Part O J. Risk Reliab. 1748006X211002546 (2021)
11. Amro, A., Kavallieratos, G., Louzis, K., Thieme, C.A.: Impact of cyber risk on the safety of the milliampere2 autonomous passenger ship. In: IOP Conference Series: Materials Science and Engineering, vol. 929, p. 012018. IOP Publishing (2020)
12. Amro, A., Oruc, A., Gkioulos, V., Katsikas, S.: Navigation data anomaly analysis and detection. 2022010322 (2022). Preprints. https://doi.org/10.20944/preprints202201.0322.v1
13. Committee, T.M.S.: Maritime cyber risk management in safety management systems (2017)
14. Gaspar, H.M., Ross, A.M., Rhodes, D.H., Erikstad, S.O.: Handling complexity aspects in conceptual ship design. In: International Maritime Design Conference, Glasgow, UK (2012)
15. Gravano, D.M., Chakraborty, U., Pesce, I., Thomson, M.: Solutions for shared resource lab remote quality control and instrument troubleshooting during a pandemic. Cytometry Part A **99**(1), 51–59 (2021)
16. Hubalovsky, S.: Remote desktop access us a method of learning of programming in distance study. In: 2011 14th International Conference on Interactive Collaborative Learning, pp. 450–455. IEEE (2011)
17. ISO, I: IEC/IEEE 15288: 2015. Systems and software engineering-Content of systems and software life cycle process information products (Documentation), International Organization for Standardization/International Electrotechnical Commission: Geneva, Switzerland (2015)
18. Jo, S.W., Shim, W.S.: LTE-maritime: high-speed maritime wireless communication based on LTE technology. IEEE Access **7**, 53172–53181 (2019)
19. Kavak, H., Padilla, J.J., Vernon-Bido, D., Diallo, S.Y., Gore, R., Shetty, S.: Simulation for cybersecurity: state of the art and future directions. J. Cybersecurity **7**(1), tyab005 (2021)
20. Khan, M.E., Khan, F., et al.: A comparative study of white box, black box and grey box testing techniques. Int. J. Adv. Comput. Sci. Appl. **3**(6) (2012)
21. Komer, B., Bergstra, J., Eliasmith, C.: Hyperopt-Sklearn. In: Hutter, F., Kotthoff, L., Vanschoren, J. (eds.) Automated Machine Learning. TSSCML, pp. 97–111. Springer, Cham (2019). https://doi.org/10.1007/978-3-030-05318-5_5

22. Mir, Z.H., Filali, F.: LTE and IEEE 802.11p for vehicular networking: a performance evaluation. EURASIP J. Wirel. Commun. Netw. **2014**(1), 89 (2014)
23. Norwegian Shipowners' Association: Maritime outlook 2018. Technical report, Norwegian Shipowners' Association (2018)
24. Oakley, J.G.: Purple teaming. In: Professional Red Teaming, pp. 105–115. Apress, Berkeley (2019). https://doi.org/10.1007/978-1-4842-4309-1_8
25. Strom, B.E., Applebaum, A., Miller, D.P., Nickels, K.C., Pennington, A.G., Thomas, C.B.: Mitre att&ck: Design and philosophy. Technical report (2018)
26. Tam, K., Moara-Nkwe, K., Jones, K.: The use of cyber ranges in the maritime context: assessing maritime-cyber risks, raising awareness, and providing training. Marit. Technol. Res **3**(1) (2021). Manuscript-Manuscript
27. Yamin, M.M., Katt, B., Gkioulos, V.: Cyber ranges and security testbeds: scenarios, functions, tools and architecture. Compute. Secur. **88**, 101636 (2020)

# A Cybersecurity Ontology to Support Risk Information Gathering in Cyber-Physical Systems

Christos Grigoriadis(✉), Adamantios Marios Berzovitis, Ioannis Stellios, and Panayiotis Kotzanikolaou

University of Piraeus, Piraeus Athens, 185 34 Piraeus, Greece
cgrigoriadis@unipi.gr

**Abstract.** The goal of this paper is to define an extended cybersecurity ontology, which may be used to assist in targeted information gathering and risk assessment procedures applied on complex cyber-physical systems. The proposed ontology unifies information from an extensive collection of known cybersecurity datasets, semi-structured or unstructured (text) data from public security reports, environmental security information gathered from network security tools that may be applied in networks and systems under assessment, as well as information about threat actors and valid users of existing infrastructures. In order to demonstrate the efficiency and the applicability of the proposed cybersecurity ontology, we have implemented part of the ontology as a knowledge graph using Python and Neo4J. To validate the efficacy of such a security ontology in practical security assessments of complex cyber-physical systems, two practical application and validation scenarios are presented. In the first case we apply our ontology to fill in some gaps into the National Vulnerability Database, by utilizing a logistic classifier trained by a subset of the NVD, with the purpose of predicting missing values for recorded vulnerabilities. In the second validation scenario, we demonstrate how to extract additional connections and relationships between known security catalogues and databases such as NVD, CWE, CAPEC and Intel-TAL.

**Keywords:** Security ontology · Cyber threat intelligence · Risk knowledge graph

## 1 Introduction

In our era, IT infrastructures and cyber-physical systems are continuously expanded and integrated by adding new layers of equipment and software in an

This work has been supported by the EU H2020-SU-ICT-03-2018 Project No. 830929 CyberSec4Europe (http://cybersec4europe.eu). This research has been co-financed by the European Union and Greek national funds through the Operational Program Competitiveness, Entrepreneurship and Innovation, under the call RESEARCH-CREATE-INNOVATE (project code: T1EDK-01958).


S. Katsikas et al. (Eds.): ESORICS 2021 Workshops, LNCS 13106, pp. 23–39, 2022.
https://doi.org/10.1007/978-3-030-95484-0_2

effort to increase automation, productivity and efficiency. This integration however raises numerous security issues, since unique combinations of software and hardware occur daily, which can produce previously unobserved attack paths in the underlying infrastructures. To explore existing risks in such complex cyber-physical systems, security specialists must gather security related information from various sources and feed them in targeted risk assessment tools, in an effort to proactively mitigate potential risks against their organizations. Procuring and combining all relevant threat and vulnerability information is a strenuous task that stretches along numerous knowledge fields like security controls, security policies, threat agent libraries and taxonomies, vulnerability databases, network monitoring data and open source cyber threat intelligence reports (OSCTI) [21].

Each knowledge field presents different challenges since the available information can be either vast or limited depending on the case. For a comprehensive view, a top to bottom architecture is required, ranging from a high level view of human actors, IT infrastructures, devices and networks, to a low level technical view, where all entities are decomposed to smaller entities and all possible connections residing in the available information map are calculated. This procedure will allow us to view existing connections between interacting entities from a cyber-security perspective, and possibly unveil new types of interactions between those entities, with the end goal of automating the calculation of security risks, threats and vulnerability scores in specific environments at a specific time.

*Motivation.* In our previous work [20], a risk assessment methodology is developed to identify and assess attack paths against critical components of complex cyber-physical systems. The algorithm uses CVSSv3.1[1] scores as input for the vulnerability assessment and threat agent libraries for the threat assessment. However, although various catalogues and databases do exist, such as CPE [2] , CVE [7], CWE [4] and CAPEC [1] along with their interconnections [13], which may be utilized to support the assessment of the risk produced by a vulnerability found in an asset, multiple false positives might be produced, if such input is not properly modified in the context of a specific system under examination. As stated in the CVSS documentation [3], the CVSS base score only sets a paradigm for a vulnerability, but does not fully characterize it. Therefore it is the researcher's job to specify *environmental* and *temporal* metrics depending on the specific application environment the vulnerability resides in, and the time of vulnerability identification respectively. Indeed, as proposed by the CVSS framework, the security experts should define the environmental and temporal modifications for the systems under examination and apply them to the base score already provided by the NIST National Vulnerability Database (NVD). Such work is usually a manual, expert-driven and timely process. And although some efforts exist in the literature to automate this process [10,13,15] none of the existing works propose a holistic security ontology along with a knowledge extraction process, that may be used to automate this process with high accuracy.

---

1 https://nvd.nist.gov/vuln-metrics/cvss/v3-calculator.

*Contribution.* Towards this direction, our main goal in this paper is to design a cybersecurity ontology that will integrate and correlate information that may be utilized in assessing the security risk of systems. The ontology will model information related with all the phases of a risk assessment such as: (i) vulnerability information (including base, environmental and temporal metrics as defined in CVSS); (ii) threat information such as threats categories (e.g. CAPEC, CWE), threat agents (such as INTEL-TAL [9]); (iii) information related with temporal characteristics and security impact for various environments, sectors and application domains based on Open Source Cyber Threat Intelligence (OSCTI) reports. To cover the security characteristics of complex cyber-physical systems, we utilize low-level entities such as devices and networks, and attempt to connect them to relevant data sources, such as:

- *DS1:* Vulnerability Databases & Related Catalogues.
- *DS2:* Security Policies & Controls.
- *DS3:* Threat Agent Libraries-Geolocation & Crime types.
- *DS4:* Network Security Configurations & Monitoring Data.
- *DS5:* Temporal Data-Open Source Cyber Threat Intelligence Reports.

This approach supports the mapping of additional characteristics for cyber and physical entities that reside in infrastructures undergoing assessment procedures. Such an ontology would be an important step towards automating existing risk assessment methodologies, thus enabling their continuous implementation.

To validate the applicability of the proposed ontology in solving real problems, we design and apply two application scenarios. In the first case we utilize the ontology by implementing a machine learning classification pipeline that helps us predict missing values for older CVE's. Utilizing this pipeline we produced a custom NVD dataset that we filled with CVSS v3.1 values for CVEs that were previously catalogued only with CVSS v2 values. In the second test case, we implement and validate a knowledge graph containing the NVD, the CPE, CWE and CAPEC catalogues along with the Threat Agent Library (TAL) from Intel.

*Paper Structure.* The rest of this paper is structured as follows: In Sect. 2 we ponder upon existing state-of-the-art security ontologies, and we consider the main challenges identified in the literature. In Sect. 3 we present the architecture and background of our security ontology, while in Sect. 4 we present our knowledge graph and machine learning implementations. In Sect. 5 we present two application scenarios that were utilized to validate the knowledge graph. Finally, Sect. 6 concludes this paper.

## 2 Related Work

In the literature, several research efforts related with the definition of security ontologies are found, although they may differ in their goal and scope. Depending on the investigated problem, each ontology might focus on subjects as specific as security entities like threats [1,4], vulnerabilities [7], threat agents [9], intrusion detection systems, attacks [6] and countermeasures [5], or as broad as security policies, network security and network management, information security management systems etc.

One of the most recent security ontologies presented in [10] emphasizes on information derived from existing OSCTI gathering and management platforms, which they focus on low level indicators of compromise (IOC). To bridge the existing gap of higher level IOCs, a knowledge graph called SecurityKG is presented in [10], which is essentially a system for automated OSCTI gathering and management. SecurityKG is capable of extracting information from semi-structured text reports through the use of AI and NLP.

In [13] a security ontology that connects known security databases such as NVD, CVE, CWE and ATT&CK [6] is presented. An aggregate data graph called BRON is presented, which enables the bi-directional, relational path tracing within entities. BRON is then used to identify attack patterns, tactics, and techniques that exploit CVEs. Furthermore, BRON is able to support a hypothesis expressed in plaintext that refers to information that can be indexed through the data graph.

Another recent approach presented in [17] provides a framework that enables access control policy updating within the Cloud infrastructure using Cyber Threat Intelligence. Furthermore, it considers updating access control policies using collaborative knowledge in the latest cyber activities of an infrastructure. To describe the correlation between security policies and security reports a combination of the DOLCE-spray ontology [16] and STIX[2] is utilized.

In [11] the steady growth in IoT as a rising threat to security is assessed, since security in IoT is not a mature field yet. They present DS4IoT, a data security ontology that covers the representation of data-security concepts. Another research effort presented in [15] underlines the importance of constructing knowledge graphs as a cybersecurity knowledge base. Their approach entails a knowledge base along with a set of deduction rules supporting a quintuple model. A strong relation towards NVD, MITRE and the known Asset-Vulnerability-Threat model is observed in this paradigm. In [21] various network security ontologies are identified and structured under eight distinct categories: Threats, IDS, Alerts, Attacks, Vulnerabilities, Countermeasures, Security policies and Network Management.

The Exploit Prediction Scoring System (EPSS) presented in [14] is an open, data-driven framework for assessing vulnerabilities, in the context of calculating the probability that a vulnerability will be exploited in the wild within the first twelve months after public disclosure. This scoring system is designed to be simple and flexible, while providing accurate estimates of exploitation. Moreover, the implementation is intended for scalability, so it can be updated while more and better data becomes available, in this context it already allows users to either search the probability of exploitation for recorded CVEs, or to create a custom vulnerability by setting the corresponding attributes manually. A functional version of the EPSS calculator[3] resides in the kenna research website.

[2] https://docs.oasis-open.org/cti/stix/v2.0/stix-v2.0-part2-stix-objects.html.

[3] https://www.kennaresearch.com/tools/epss-calculator/.

Finally in [19] a security ontology for modeling enterprise level risk assessment is defined. The ontology contains entities for core risk assesment elements such as Threats, Vulnerabilities, Security Mechanisms and Assets along with their interconnections. However, the model is only conceptual and it is not supported by any implementation or data sources of either structured or unstructured format. The security ontology presented in this paper integrates and extends the above related work by proposing a holistic security ontology that combines information derived from (see Table 1): (a) known security taxonomies and vulnerability databases, as in [13]; (b) network security information gathering tools, which are able to collect environmental information regarding the network and software security state and connect them to known taxonomies; and (c) semi-structured and unstructured text derived from OSCTI reports and relevant sources, as in [10].

**Table 1.** Related work, data sources and applications.

| | Related work | | | | | | |
|---|---|---|---|---|---|---|---|
| | [17] | [13] | [10] | [14] | [15] | [21] | Our ontology |
| Data sources | | | | | | | |
| DS1 | X | X | | X | X | X | X |
| DS2 | X | X | | | X | X | X |
| DS3 | X | | X | | | | X |
| DS4 | | | | | | X | X |
| DS5 | X | X | X | X | X | | X |
| Applications | | | | | | | |
| Security ontology | X | X | X | | X | X | X |
| Integration of vulnerability+threat databases | X | X | | | | | X |
| Risk assessment | X | | | X | | | X |
| Integration of security policy elicitation | X | X | | | | X | |
| Integration of temporal data | X | X | X | X | | | |
| Integration of environmental data | | | | | | X | |

## 3 Security Ontology

The first step towards defining and implementing our security ontology is to specify the knowledge fields that will be involved into its construction. We define two layers of information: In the fist layer we define all the core elements that may be used to model complex cyber-physical systems. The core elements of this layer are: *devices*, *networks* and *human actors*. The data sources for the entities defined in this layer are unstructured security-related data like reports and policies, as well as organization specific cyber physical information, which can be harvested through monitoring tools, scanners, implants and other sources.

In the second layer we express the information related with vulnerabilities, threats, exploits and threat agents, derived from public sources of structured information, as well as in relation to the first layer. In a sense we utilize the structure of the CVSS model that characterizes vulnerabilities utilizing Base, Environmental and Temporal vectors of characteristics, along with known interconnections to shape this layer. In particular, environmental characteristics for vulnerabilities residing in a specific environment can be filled in through Device and Network Information harvested from the corresponding infrastructures. Furthermore, threat agents that might be active throughout the infrastructure undergoing risk assessment, can be connected to information about human entities recorded in the upper layer, which are acting in the same environment. Further information related to temporal characteristics of vulnerabilities like the state of exploit or patch as well as the report confidence can be pulled from open sources.

We attempt to create a detailed sub-graph for each element and create end-nodes that may ultimately be interconnected in various ways, and finally procure ways to automatically produce CVSS environmental and temporal metrics. Following this approach we aim to establish a knowledge base that will enhance the detail-orientation and provide automation to our previous risk assessment approach.

### 3.1 Architecture

Each of the core elements mentioned above present different sources of information that require targeted handling; through our ontology we present the sources we identify along with an implementation for a subset of them.

*Devices.* In our paradigm, devices act as containers for further entities; one device may contain multiple interconnected assets that fall under the categories of hardware, or software, while the latter may be defined in sub-categories such as operating systems or application software. Attributes of devices that should also be taken into account are their type, which might range from single use device to composite, along with their physical location and the access controls tied to it. The device's attributes can be used as anchors to define *physical interactions* among devices, which in turn may be used to define and assess the risk of cyber-physical attack paths as in [20].

Devices may also contain specific slots for *network interfaces* that enable connectivity among devices and networks, while *users* can utilize functionality based on their privileges on specific components of a device. We utilize the CPE catalogue to detect the various components of devices since multiple scanning tools can identify an asset and connect it to a CPE identifier. Then, the connection between the CPE and the NVD catalogues can be used to enumerate the vulnerabilities of a particular asset. A final step here is to enumerate the relationships of assets contained in a single device.

*Networks.* Networks act as enablers for device connectivity, by providing communication channels that allow devices to exchange traffic. At the same time networks act as filtering entities that implement network security controls, that entail access controls, authentication controls and other rules derived from high level security policies. The network security controls are implemented through the use of systems like firewalls, Intrusion Detection Systems, monitoring applications and other network traffic management systems. Physical attributes of networks that should be taken into account include their access type in the essence of being internal or external, the technology or protocol they utilize, the frequency they broadcast and receive and finally their specific physical location along with the corresponding access controls.

*Human Entities.* Human entities are utilized in our ontology to express entities having access, authentication and execution rights to devices and more specifically towards components contained in devices. For example, consider a user having specific execution rights (user or admin) on an application that is installed on an operating system running on the hardware of a desktop or laptop computer. By mapping human actors this way, it is possible to catalogue user roles and to extend threat modeling in risk assessment approaches. Essentially, user roles may be used to represent an additional layer of abstraction in the identification of potential attack paths (e.g. [20]).

### 3.2 Data Sources and Challenges

In order to feed the security ontology we use various existing data sources. We identify the following challenges for the relevant data sources:

- *DS1: Vulnerability databases and other related catalogues.* While NVD contains abundant information for a wide set of security vulnerabilities, a significant portion of the dataset is not complete. More specifically a significant subset of the NVD, containing vulnerabilities published before 2016 is incomplete, since it procures the CVSS base score in CVSS v2.0 format, which is considered deprecated, and not the current CVSS v3.1 format.
- *DS2: Security Policies and Controls.* There is a direct line between security policies containing access controls, user roles/user execution rights and threat agents that can activate certain attack paths by compromising certain accounts. This connection should be investigated.
- *DS3: Threat Agent Libraries, Geolocation and Crime types.* Depending on the location and type of an organization, various threat agent profiles conducting divergent crime types can be encountered. The question that arises here is which threat agent profiles have the motive and the resources to target critical structures and assets inside organizations.
- *DS4: Network Security-Network Traffic and Monitoring Data.* Another vast challenge is to produce a way to define the security states of networks and translate them to the corresponding CVSS environmental vectors. This can be implemented by analyzing Network Traffic and by parsing active Firewall and Intrusion Detection System rulesets (Fig. 1).

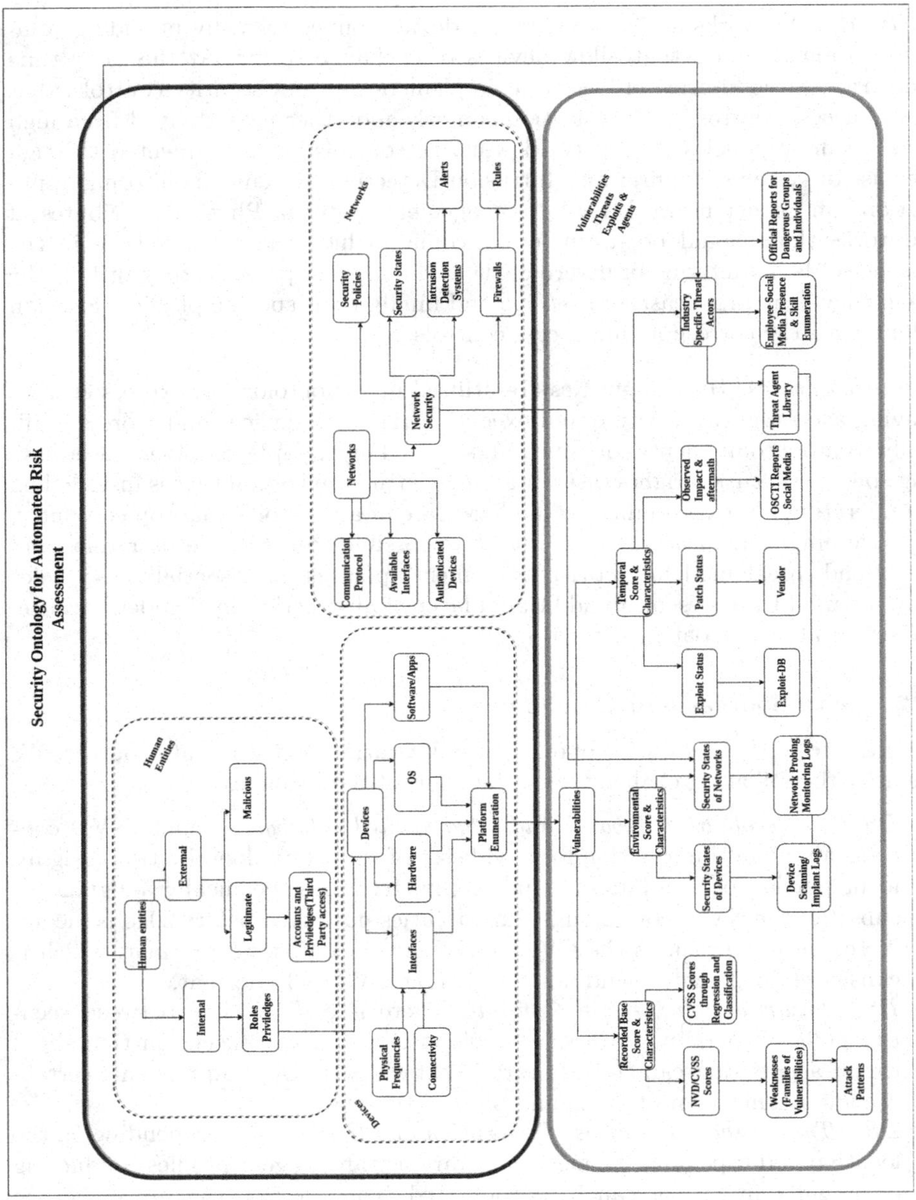


**Fig. 1.** Security ontology for automated risk assessment.

– *DS5: Temporal Data-Open Source Cyber Threat Intelligence Reports.* Finally a resource that can be found in abundance for further analysis are OSCTI reports. We recognize three types of reports that require three different approaches to achieve information extraction and transformation:
  - *Structured Reports* like the information found in exploit db.
  - *Semi Structured Reports* as produced by Nessus, OWASP ZAP and other similar tools.
  - *Unstructured Reports* that usually refers to plaintext, like posts found in blogs etc.
  - *Exploits Prediction.* Exploit prediction can be implemented through the analysis of reports about vulnerabilities being exploited in the wild, and the parsing of exploit catalogues for proof of concept code and working exploits. EPSS [14] is a characteristic example of exploit prediction (Table 2).

**Table 2.** Data sources connected to ontology elements.

| Data sources | Devices | Networks | Human entities |
|---|---|---|---|
| DS1: Vulnerability Databases & Related Catalogues | X | X | |
| DS2: Security Policies and Controls | X | X | X |
| DS3: Threat Agent Libraries-Geolocation and Crime types | | | X |
| DS4: Network Security-Network Traffic and Monitoring Data | X | X | |
| DS5: Temporal Data-Open Source Cyber Threat Intelligence Reports | X | X | X |

For the blocks we build, a variety of options is presented for information harvesting; structured information from public catalogues like NVD can be directly inserted into our knowledge base, while semi-structured or unstructured text based documents like OSCTI reports, relevant blog posts and information harvested from social media require further filtering and analysis. Going into environmental information we suggest the use of multiple monitoring and scanning tools that can recover information and represent it based on the attack vectors of malicious users.

## 4 Knowledge Graph Implementation

The security ontology presented in Sect. 3 has been partially implemented as a Knowledge Graph containing specific blocks of the ontology, based on open sources. A visual demonstration of the implemented knowledge graph can be found in [12], while an open repository of the alpha version of our tool can be found in [8].

### 4.1 Implementation Architecture

We present an initial knowledge graph, which incorporates a subset of the presented security ontology. Our implementation is based on known catalogues, similar to the work presented in [13]. The implemented blocks include: (i) CPE, (ii) vulnerabilities, (iii) recorded base score and characteristics, (iv) NVD/CVSS scores, (v) weaknesses, (vi) attack patterns, (vii) CVSS scores through regression and classification and finally (viii) the threat agent library block. The blocks 'CVSS scores through regression and classification' and 'threat agent library' are produced by properly addressing the attributes contained in the assessed open sources. Our implementation consists of a set of functionalities implemented through a set of modules (scripts) as shown in Fig. 2.

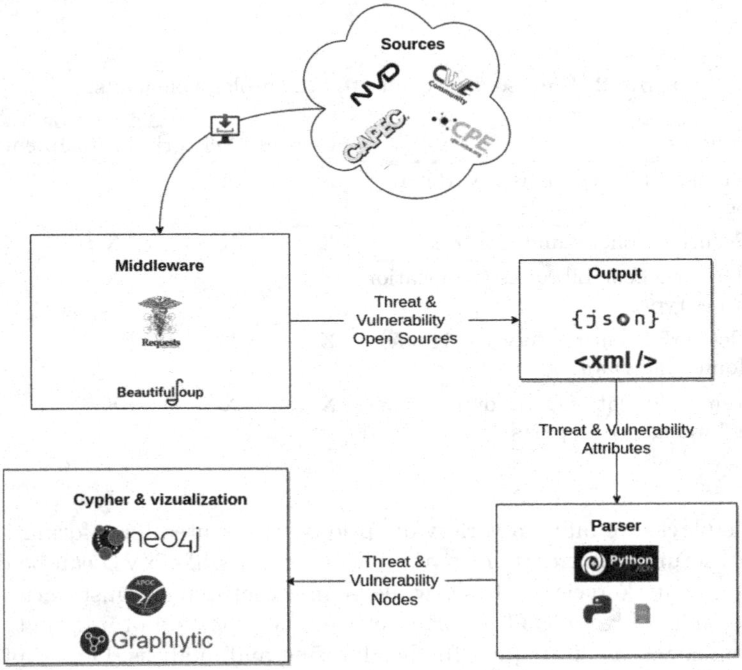


**Fig. 2.** Implementation architecture: workflow of the knowledge graph implementation components

- A *middleware script* that collects datasets from known API's. In this case python's requests[4] and beautiful soup[5] libraries are utilized to collect data from NIST's API that contains the National Vulnerability Database along with the CPE catalogue and MITRE's website that contains the CWE and CAPEC catalogues.

[4] https://docs.python-requests.org/en/latest/.
[5] https://www.crummy.com/software/BeautifulSoup/bs4/doc/.

- A *parsing script* that gathers a set of attributes from each collected dataset. In this case two python libraries are utilized in order to access and adjust the attributes, xml2dict[6] and json[7].
- A *cypher script* that takes as input the parsed attributes and inserts them into a neo4j graph database. In this case the APOC library[8] is utilized for the cypher functions it contains, since they enable faster insert times for the graph database entries.
- Finally the neo4j *graphlytic extension*[9] is utilized in order to apply further graphics to the already implemented knowledge graph.

The source, the format and the number of entries included in the files downloaded by our middleware are presented in Table 3. Our parser component utilizes multiple components to handle the various formats found in different repositories successfully.

**Table 3.** Number of entries per parsed catalogue

| Catalogue | Number of entries | Source format |
|---|---|---|
| NVD | 169.388 | JSON |
| CPE | 719.072 | XML |
| CWE | 1.298 | CSV/XML |
| CAPEC | 667 | CSV/XML |

### 4.2 Building Custom Blocks Based on Machine Learning

Besides the publicly available data sources, custom blocks were also generated for specific cases. In order to create custom blocks for the implemented knowledge graph, the datasets mentioned in the previous section are pulled and appropriately modified, to produce the vectors required for machine learning applications.

- A *middleware script* that collects datasets from known API's. In this case python's requests and beautiful soup libraries are utilized to collect data from NIST's API that contains the National Vulnerability Database. Utilizing python's json, zipfile[10] and bytesIO[11] libraries the set of json files provided for the vulnerabilities disclosed every year by NIST are combined into a single json file (Fig. 3).

[6] https://pypi.org/project/XML2Dict/.
[7] https://docs.python.org/3/library/json.html.
[8] https://neo4j.com/developer/neo4j-apoc/.
[9] https://graphlytic.biz/.
[10] https://docs.python.org/3/library/zipfile.html.
[11] https://docs.python.org/3/library/io.html.

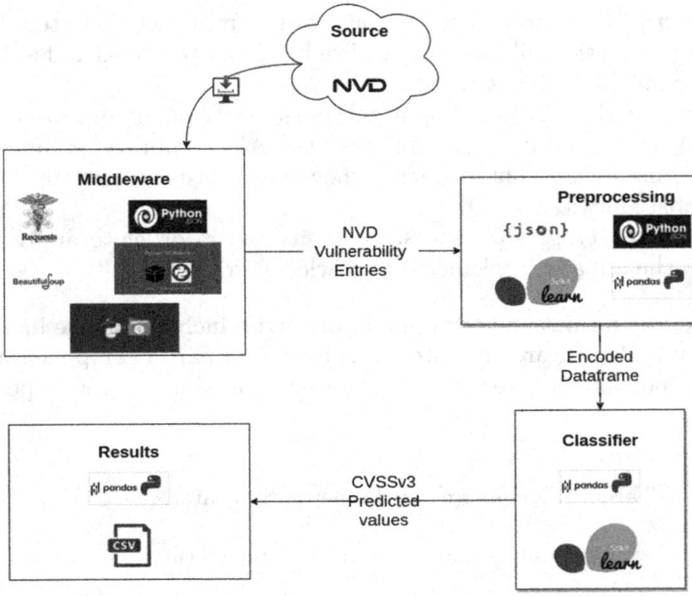


**Fig. 3.** Implementation architecture: workflow of the machine learning implementation components

- A *conversion script* that takes as input the json file produced by the middleware script and provides a flattened version containing all characteristics in different columns. This script utilizes python's pandas library which contains the function json.normalize, that takes as input a json file and outputs a dataframe that contains a flattened format of the json attributes.
- A *filtering script* that gathers all the NVD entries from the created dataframe that have no CVSSv2 and CVSSv3 missing values in order to create a complete training subset from the initial dataset.
- A *transformer script/preprocessor* to bring the dataset in the required format called OneHotEncoder[12]; OHE takes as input an array-like of integers or strings, denoting the values taken on by categorical features. The features are encoded using a 'one-of-K' or 'dummy' encoding scheme. This creates a binary column for each category, in this case each available option for the existing CVSS attributes, and returns a sparse matrix or dense array.
- A *logistic regression classifier*[13] provided by python's scikit-learn library, which utilizes the one-vs-rest (OvR) scheme in its training algorithm for the multi-class problem we tackle. It implements regularized logistic regression for our classes using the 'lbfgs' solver.

[12] https://scikit-learn.org/stable/modules/generated/sklearn.preprocessing.OneHotEncoder.html.

[13] https://scikit-learn.org/stable/modules/generated/sklearn.linear_model.LogisticRegression.html.

### 4.3 Deducing Relationships Between Existing Blocks

For most of the ontology blocks, their relationships can be directly pulled from the catalogued open sources, extracted from the corresponding datasets and inserted into our knowledge graph. This for example holds for the Vulnerability, Weakness, and Attack Patterns blocks. For other blocks however, such as the Threat Agent Profiles, their relationships with the rest of the ontology entities are not directly extractable. To enable the implementation of those relationships we examine their attributes and attempt to discover common characteristics with other entities that can be successfully compared. Furthermore, we look into multiple approaches to expressing threat agent profiles, with the purpose of extending the initial attribute vectors that broadly describe the entries. Following this approach the scope of relationship extraction is also broadened, making it more likely to yield accurate results for specific instances. A practical scenario of relationship extraction between threat agents, CWEs, CVEs and CPEs by utilizing CAPEC as a stepping stone, is presented in Sect. 5.2.

## 5 Application Scenarios – Validation

To validate the functionality of the implemented knowledge graph we test it with two application scenarios. In our first validation scenario, we will utilize the catalogued information that resides in the implemented knowledge graph in order to produce an extended version of NVD, where we supplement older vulnerabilities with CVSSv3.1 vectors. This approach can be utilized to support Risk Assessment methodologies that rely only on a specific version of the CVSS scoring system, such as MITIGATE [18].

In our second scenario, we were able to unveil previously unregistered connections between threat agent profiles and attack patterns, while utilizing open sources to find real world examples of threat agents executing attacks. We derive this connection from background work [20], where threat agents were expressed as CVSS capability vectors and from some common characteristics between CAPEC and TAL.

### 5.1 Using the Ontology to Predict CVSS Scores

We used a similar approach to the one used to insert the CVEs pulled from NIST's NVD into our knowledge graph, to create a pandas Dataframe. By applying filtering rules we derive that while almost 170.000 CVEs are catalogued, only a subset of them is characterized by CVSSv3.1 vectors, while older entries are in many cases characterized only by CVSSv2. To complete the missing values we utilized a subset of NVD that contains vectors for both versions of the CVSS as a training set for a logistic regression classification model.

The first step towards implementing our pipeline is to adjust our dataset for the logistic regression model; Considering the format of the CVSS vector it becomes apparent that we are dealing with a multiclass, multilabel classification

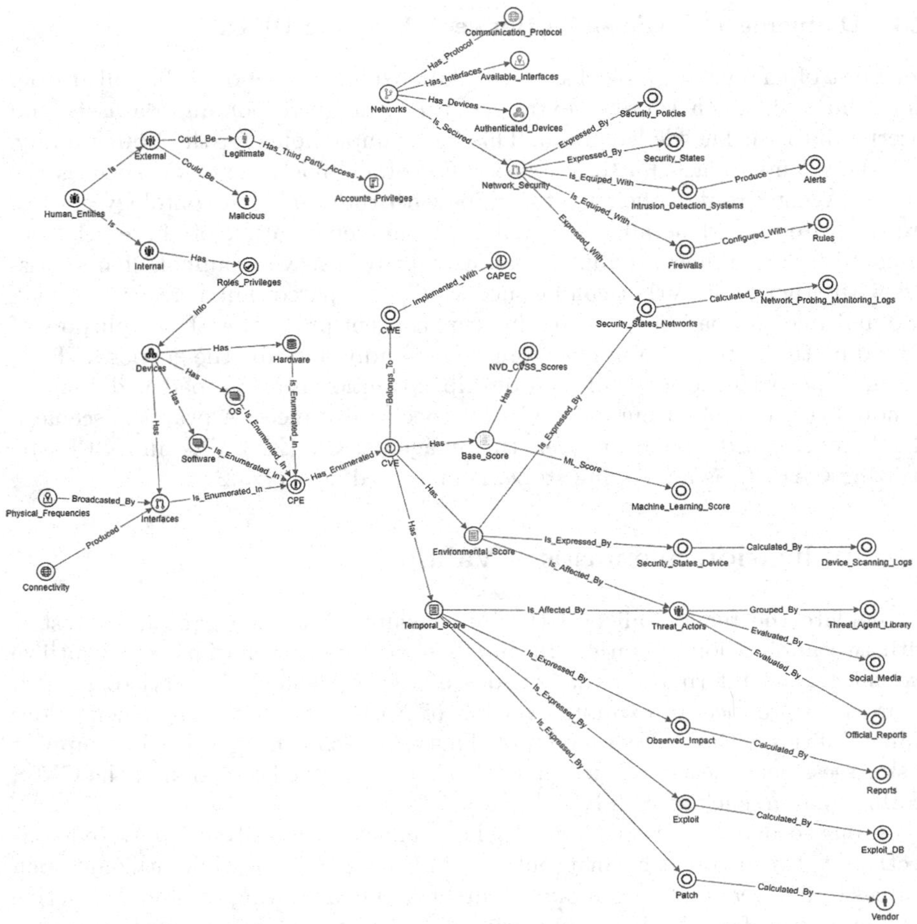


**Fig. 4.** Security ontology knowledge graph.

problem. To bring the dataset in the required format we utilize the transformer script mentioned in Sect. 4.2. By default, the encoder derives the categories based on the unique values in each feature. Having brought the training subset of NVD in the appropriate format we instantiate our model for all the characteristics of the CVSSv3 except for the Attack Vector which remains the same across different versions of the scoring system, while CVSSv3 provides an extra option for physical vectors. We achieved an accuracy rate of over 90% for all metrics while testing the classifiers, which we later used to predict the missing values. The accuracy per characteristic is shown in Table 4. We achieved different results in each metric due to the changes in the CVSS vectors across versions and due to the changes in the security analyst perspective throughout the years. More specifically (Fig. 4):

- We achieve very high accuracy results on the prediction of the *Attack Complexity* metric, while the scale itself changed from a three tier `[Low, Medium, High]` to a two tier `[Low, High]` for CVSSv2 and CVSSv3 respectively, we observe that most values set as `High` in the three tier system kept their status while `Low` and `Medium` mostly became `Low` in the predicted dataset.
- *Authentication* can be considered the equivalent metric from CVSSv2 for *Privileges Required* used in CVSSv3. We yield a lower accuracy of 91,7% for the Privileges Required predicted values. Both the Authentication and the Privileges Required metrics present three options, `[None, Single, Multiple]` and `[None, Low, High]` respectively. Since the metrics do not represent identical paradigms in both versions a small decline is expected to occur.
- *User interaction* while not catalogued as part of the CVSSv2 vector, it was listed in CVSSv2 entries in the NVD as an extra attribute. In CVSSv2 the metric User Interaction Required could be `True` or `False` while in the CVSSv3 User Interaction is either `Required` or `Not Required`.
- *Scope* can be considered the ability of a vulnerability in one software component to impact resources beyond its means and privileges. While not catalogued as part of the CVSSv2 vector, we identify and utilize three CVSSv2 attributes derived from NVD entries to predict if the scope is changed or unchanged: *(a) obtainAllPrivilege*, *(b) obtainUserPrivilege*, and *(c) obtainOtherPrivilege.* Since the metrics do not represent identical para-digms in both versions a small decline is expected to occur.
- For the *Impact (CIA)* metrics, while the usage in the different CVSS versions is almost identical we observe lower prediction accuracy, especially for the Confidentiality Impact. This decline occurs due to the nature of the dataset, which contains vulnerability entries recorded between 1999 to 2021. From this we derive that the perception of vulnerabilities and their impact that were initially catalogued in CVSSv2 possibly changed until their CVSSv3 characterization, thus introducing some inconsistent patterns into the datasets.

**Table 4.** Achieved accuracy of prediction for CVSS metrics.

| CVSSv3.1 metrics | Attack complexity | Privileges required | User interaction | Scope | Confidentiality impact | Integrity impact | Availability impact |
|---|---|---|---|---|---|---|---|
| Accuracy of prediction | 98.44% | 91,7% | 99.19% | 93.42% | 90.29% | 93.01% | 95.12% |

### 5.2 Using the Ontology to Correlate Threat Agents with Attacks and Vulnerabilities

In order to map threat agents in our methodology, our initial approach is to replicate the matrix presented in Intel's TAL. Furthermore, we extend the attribute vectors of TAL profiles with CVSS capability vectors as in [20]. The attributes provided by Intel for threat agents include resources, skills and objectives. Similar characteristics are observed in the CAPEC dataset, as illustrated in Table 5 to express the requirements for the execution of recorded attack patterns. The required skills to activate an attack pattern can be tied directly to the skills an attacker may have. The other attributes presented in Table 5 require further processing in order to be matched, due to their descriptive nature. This especially holds for attributes like the 'resources required' and the 'consequences', which also include a description along with their scope. Utilizing this common ground, we extract further relationships between the 'threat agents' we have inherited in our knowledge graph from TAL and individual CAPEC entries.

**Table 5.** Similar attributes of Intel's TAL and CAPEC

| TAL | | | CAPEC | | | |
|---|---|---|---|---|---|---|
| Skills | Resources | Objective | Skills required | Resources required | Typical severity | Consequences scope |
| None | Individual | Copy | None | Description | Very low | Confidentiality |
| Minimal | Club | Deny | Low | – | Low | Integrity |
| Operational | Contest | Destroy | Medium | – | Medium | Availability |
| Adept | Team | Damage | High | – | High | – |
| – | Organization | Take | – | – | Very high | – |
| – | Government | All/None | – | – | – | – |

In [20] similar characteristics are presented for threat agent profiles specific to the healthcare environment, with a slight twist. Instead of utilizing a `[Low, High]` scale for the capabilities of an attacker, in this case the skills are presented as a CVSS *capability vector* that can be directly compared to the CVSS vulnerability vectors of recorded vulnerabilities. This approach is utilized to extend TAL's threat agent profiles, thus enabling the deduction of relationships between the catalogued threat agents and vulnerabilities in our knowledge graph.

## 6 Conclusions

In this paper we present our approach for a holistic cyber security ontology to support risk assessment processes and relevant methodologies. The proposed ontology is built and filled in as a knowledge graph consisting of a plethora of modules. Such a knowledge graph may assist a risk assessor to harvest further information in a semi-autonomous manner by extracting knowledge and relations between the entities, and thus enhance current risk assessment procedures. Through our application scenarios we proved both paradigms by applying knowledge extraction in the already catalogued CVEs from NIST and relationship extraction by connecting CAPEC and Intel's TAL through common characteristics. Such approaches can enhance already existing risk assessment schemes by presenting extra layers of calculation complexity, by adjusting vulnerability characteristics based on environmental and temporal factors and by providing complete datasets for existing tools that utilize one out of the two versions of

CVSS. In future work we would like to extend our knowledge graph towards environmental and temporal characteristics which we plan to harvest and translate through multiple data sources.

## References


1. Common attack pattern enumeration and classification. https://capec.mitre.org/
2. Common platform enumeration. https://nvd.nist.gov/products/cpe
3. Common vulnerability scoring system. https://www.first.org/cvss/
4. Common weakness enumeration. https://cwe.mitre.org/
5. D3FEND matrix: Mitre d3fend. https://d3fend.mitre.org/
6. Mitre ATT&CK. https://attack.mitre.org/
7. Common vulnerabilities and exposures (2021). https://cve.mitre.org/
8. Berzovitis, A.: Security ontology tool-graphker. https://github.com/amberzovitis/GraphKer
9. Casey, T.: Threat agent library helps identify information security risks. Intel White Paper 2 (2007)
10. Gao, P., et al.: A system for automated open-source threat intelligence gathering and management. In: Proceedings of the 2021 International Conference on Management of Data, pp. 2716–2720 (2021)
11. Gonzalez-Gil, P., Martinez, J.A., Skarmeta, A.F.: Lightweight data-security ontology for IoT. Sensors **20**(3), 801 (2020)
12. Grigoriadis, C., Kotzanikolaou, P.: Security ontology knowledge graph video demonstration, https://youtu.be/EPK9HI9-ZI0
13. Hemberg, E., et al.: Linking threat tactics, techniques, and patterns with defensive weaknesses, vulnerabilities and affected platform configurations for cyber hunting. arXiv preprint arXiv:2010.00533 (2020)
14. Jacobs, J., Romanosky, S., Edwards, B., Roytman, M., Adjerid, I.: Exploit prediction scoring system (EPSS). arXiv preprint arXiv:1908.04856 (2019)
15. Jia, Y., Qi, Y., Shang, H., Jiang, R., Li, A.: A practical approach to constructing a knowledge graph for cybersecurity. Engineering **4**(1), 53–60 (2018)
16. Oltramari, A., et al.: Senso comune: a collaborative knowledge resource for Italian. In: Gurevych, I., Kim, J. (eds.) The People's Web Meets NLP. TANLP, pp. 45–67. Springer, Heidelberg (2013). https://doi.org/10.1007/978-3-642-35085-6_2
17. Osliak, O., Saracino, A., Martinelli, F., Dimitrakos, T.: Towards collaborative cyber threat intelligence for security management. In: ICISSP, pp. 339–346 (2021)
18. Papastergiou, S., Polemi, N.: MITIGATE: a dynamic supply chain cyber risk assessment methodology. In: Yang, X.-S., Nagar, A.K., Joshi, A. (eds.) Smart Trends in Systems, Security and Sustainability. LNNS, vol. 18, pp. 1–9. Springer, Singapore (2018). https://doi.org/10.1007/978-981-10-6916-1_1
19. Singhal, A., Singapogu, S., et al.: Security ontologies for modeling enterprise level risk assessment. In: Proceedings of the 2012 Annual Computer Security Applications Conference, Orlando, FL, USA, pp. 3–7 (2012)
20. Stellios, I., Kotzanikolaou, P., Grigoriadis, C.: Assessing IoT enabled cyber-physical attack paths against critical systems. Comput. Secur. **107**, 102316 (2021)
21. Velasco, D., Rodriguez, G.: Ontologies for network security and future challenges. arXiv preprint arXiv:1704.02441 (2017)

# GLASS: Towards Secure and Decentralized eGovernance Services Using IPFS

Christos Chrysoulas[1(✉)], Amanda Thomson[1], Nikolaos Pitropakis[1(✉)], Pavlos Papadopoulos[1(✉)], Owen Lo[1], William J. Buchanan[1], George Domalis[2], Nikos Karacapilidis[2], Dimitris Tsakalidis[2], and Dimitris Tsolis[2]

[1] Blockpass ID Lab, School of Computing, Edinburgh Napier University, Edinburgh EH10 5DT, UK
{C.chrysoulas,N.Pitropakis,pavlos.papadopoulos}@napier.ac.uk
[2] Computer Engineering and Informatics Department, University of Patras, Patras, Greece

**Abstract.** The continuously advancing digitization has provided answers to the bureaucratic problems faced by eGovernance services. This innovation led them to an era of automation, broadened the attack surface and made them a popular target for cyber attacks. eGovernance services utilize the internet, which is a location addressed system in which whoever controls its location controls not only the content itself but also the integrity and the access of that content. We propose GLASS, a decentralized solution that combines the InterPlanetary File System with Distributed Ledger Technology and Smart Contracts to secure eGovernance services. We also created a testbed environment where we measure the system's performance.

**Keywords:** eGovernance · Security · DLT · IPFS · DHT · Kademlia

## 1 Introduction

The rapid evolution of digital technologies, including mobile communications, cloud computing infrastructures, and distributed applications, has created an extended impact on society while also enabling the establishment of novel eGovernance models. The need for an inclusive eGovernance model with integrated multi-actor governance services is apparent and a key element towards a European Single Market. Digital transformation of public services can remove existing digital and physical barriers, reduce administrative burdens, enhance governments' productivity, minimize the extra cost of traditional means to increase capacity, and eventually improve the overall quality of interactions with (and within) public administrations.

eGovernance includes novel and digital by default public services aiming for administrative efficiency and minimization of bureaucratic processes, enabling


S. Katsikas et al. (Eds.): ESORICS 2021 Workshops, LNCS 13106, pp. 40–57, 2022.
https://doi.org/10.1007/978-3-030-95484-0_3

open government capabilities, behavior and professionalism, improved trust and confidence in governmental transactions. Towards the modernization of public services, public administrations need to transform their manual business flows and upgrade their existing internal processes and services.

However, the digitization of eGovernance services has also expanded the attack surface, thus making them attractive to malicious third parties. In 2017 the National Health Service of the United Kingdom suffered from the WannaCry ransomware, which resulted in missed appointments, deaths, and fiscal costs [1]. Recently, in May 2021 the American oil pipeline system suffered a ransomware cyberattack that impacted all the computerized equipment managing the pipeline. The company paid a ransom of 75 Bitcoins, approximately $5 million, to the hackers in exchange for a decryption tool which eventually proved so slow that Colonial's own backups were used to bring the system back to service [2].

As the need for privacy-preserving and secure solutions in eGovernance services is imminent, our decentralized solution, namely GLASS, moves towards that direction by examining the effectiveness and efficiency of distributed cutting edge technologies, demonstrating the capacity of a public, distributed infrastructure, based on the InterPlanetary File System (IPFS). Our contributions can be summarised as follows:

- We analyze the threat landscape in the context of an eGovernance use case.
- We create a distributed testbed environment based on IPFS and detail our methodology.
- We analyze and critically evaluate the runtime performance of our implementation.

The structure of the rest of the paper is organized as follows: Sect. 2 builds the background on distributed models and presents the related literature, while Sect. 3 details the GLASS architecture while briefly explaining the threat landscape in the context of an eGovernance services use case scenario. Section 4 consists of our methodology and implementation used to conduct the main experimental activity of our work, while Sect. 5 presents and evaluates the performance results of our experimental activity. Finally, Sect. 6 draws the conclusions, giving some pointers for future work.

## 2 Background and Related Literature

### 2.1 Kademlia

In 2001 Maymounkov and Mazières published Kademlia, a Distributed Hash Table (DHT) that offered multiple features that were currently not available simultaneously in any other DHT [3]. The paper introduced a novel XOR metric to calculate the distance between nodes in the key space and a node Id routing algorithm that enabled nodes to locate other nodes close to a given target key efficiently. The presented single routing algorithm was more optimal compared to other algorithms such as Pastry [4], Tapestry [5] and Plaxton [6] that all required secondary routing tables. Kademlia was outlined as easily optimised with a base other than 2 with no need for secondary routing tables. The k-bucket table was configured so as to approach the target $b$ (initial implementation was b = 5) bits per hop. With one bucket being used for nodes within distance range of $[j2^{160-(i+1)b)}, (j+1)2^{160-(i+1)b}]$ from the initial node for each $0 < j < 2^b$ and $0 \leq i < 160/b$ based on a SHA1 160 bit address space. At any point, it is expected that there would be no more than $(2^b - 1)log_{2^b}$ buckets with entries. The k-buckets were described as being resistant to certain DoS attacks [3] due to the inability to flood the system with new nodes, as Kademlia only inserts new nodes once old ones leave.

In 2008 Baumgart and Mies introduced S/Kademlia [7] which offered several further security enhancements designed to improve on the original specification. They examined various attacks that peer-to-peer (P2P) networks were vulnerable to and offered practical solutions to protect against them. The key attacks identified by them were: a) Eclipse Attack, b) Sybil Attack, and c) Adversarial Routing. In 2020 Prünster et al. [8] highlighted the need for further implementation of S/Kademlia mitigations by demonstrating an effective eclipse attack. They were able to generate a large number of ephemeral identities and poison multiple nodes routing tables for very little expense, and *CVE-2020-10937* was assigned to the demonstrated attack.

### 2.2 IPFS

The IPFS is a distributed system based on a P2P protocol that provides public data storage services to transform the web into a new decentralized and more efficient tool. Its primary purpose is to replace the HTTP protocol for document transactions by solving HTTP's most limiting problems like availability, cost, and centralization of data in data centers.

IPFS is based on a Merkle Directed Acyclic Graph (DAG) [9], the data structure to keep track of the location its data chunks are stored and the correlation between them. Each data block has a unique content identifier (CID) fabricated by hashing its content in this peculiar data structure. In case the content of a node's child changes, the CID of the parent node changes as well. For someone to access a file, knowing its unique Content Identifier, constructed by the hash of the data contained within it, is essential. Each participating node (user) keeps a list of the CIDs it hosts in a Distributed Hash Table (DHT) implemented using the Kademlia protocol [10]. Each user "advertises" the CIDs they store in the DHT, resulting in a distributed "dictionary" used for looking up content. When a user tries to access a specific file, IPFS crawls the DHTs to locate the file by matching the unique content identifier. Using content-based addressing instead of location-based addressing serves in preventing saving duplicate files in the network and tracking down a file by its content rather than by its address.

IPFS enables its users to store and distribute data globally in a secure, resilient and efficient way. Each file uploaded on IPFS is fragmented into chunks of 256 KB and hashed before being scattered in participating nodes around the globe. Following the aforementioned methodology, data integrity is ensured since no one can tamper with a data block without affecting its unique hash. Furthermore, data resilience is ensured by placing the same data block in more than one participating node.

Mukne et al. [11] are using IPFS and Hyperledger Fabric augmented to perform secure documentation of land record management. Andreev and Daskalov [12] are using IPFS to keep students' personal information off-chain in a solution that manages students' data through blockchain. Singh [13] created an architecture for open government data where proof-of-concept uses Ethereum for decentralized processing and BigchainDB and IPFS for storage of large volumes of data and files, respectively.

### 2.3 Distributed Ledger

A Distributed Ledger is a distributed database architecture that enables multiple members to maintain their own identical copy of information without the need for validation from a central entity while ensuring data integrity. Transaction data are scattered among multiple nodes using the P2P protocol principles and are synchronized simultaneously in all nodes. By providing Identification Management through DLTs, it is ensured that the user has control of their identity records since the information is stored publicly on the ledger instead of the systems of a central authority. Furthermore, since editing information on past transactions on a blockchain system is not supported, protection against unauthorized alteration of the identity records is established. Finally, having a single record of identity information that the user can utilize on multiple occasions minimizes the data duplication on multiple databases [14]. The second generation of blockchain technologies introduced the smart contracts that act as mini-programs used to automate code deployment when some pre-defined terms are met.

Our solution, GLASS, combines the advantages of IPFS with those offered by the Distributed Ledgers and Smart Contracts, thus creating a distributed scalable and secure eGovernance infrastructure. Moving towards the first steps of our implementation, we create an IPFS based testbed environment and empirically evaluate its runtime performance.

## 3 Architecture

We propose a combination of IPFS with Distributed Ledger and Smart Contracts which are proven to be beneficial for recording massive volumes of transactions. Extracting helpful information efficiently has significant computational challenges, such as analysing, aggregating, visualising, and storing data collected in distributed ledgers. More specifically, the volume and velocity of the data make it difficult for typical algorithms to scale while querying the ledger might come at high computation costs. State-of-the-art efforts seek to introduce new models that deal with such large-scale, distributed data queries to reduce data volume transferred over the network via adaptive sampling that maintains certain accuracy guarantees [15]. As the ledgers (and thus the data) keep getting bigger, a challenge is to make sense of the collected data for the users and perform analytics leveraging big data processing engines (i.e., Spark) that can deliver results quickly and efficiently. In order to adequately protect data resources, it is paramount to encrypt data in such a way that no one other than intended parties should be able to get the original data.

A simple use case presenting a European Union's citizen, Alice, getting a job abroad from Greece to another member state, Portugal, using GLASS ecosystem, is presented in Algorithm 1. The current practice compared to our approach can be seen in Fig. 1. The entities of the figure represent governmental departments such as the Ministry of Digital Governance (MoDG), Ministry of Justice (MoJ), University of Patras (UoP), a Bank, and a Company.

---

**Algorithm 1.** Alice getting a job to Portugal

---

1: Starting from Greece, Alice finds a vacant job position in Portugal. She applies for the job, and thankfully she gets hired.
2: In Portugal, she has to deal with a series of bureaucratic processes (ID card, social security number, open a bank account).
3: To obtain a Portuguese Residence title, rent an apartment and open a bank account, Alice needs to present at least a validated ID documentation, birth certificate, nationality certification validated by a Greek Authority and proof that she works in Portugal.
4: Adopting the GLASS solution, Alice can request the proof of ID and the validated data from the Ministry of Digital Governance (MoDG).
5: The MoDG can issue the document, and after Alice's permission, the document can be forwarded to the Ministry of Justice (MoJ).
6: After this transaction is completed, Alice can access and securely share her Portuguese social security number through her Wallet.
7: Then Alice's employer in Portugal can directly get the validated social security number from the MoJ, after her approval, to register her credentials to their internal payroll system.
8: Using a decentralized application of the GLASS ecosystem, Alice can use her validated digital identity to request remotely the required documentation from the respective Greek Authority (MoDG), the Portuguese authority (MoJ) and her employer.
9: MoDG can digitally issue and validate the documentation and transmit the encrypted data into the distributed network while the transaction among the users is being recorded.
10: All the transactions, including requests, notifications, and permissions, can be monitored and stored, protecting Alice's (and each participant's) privacy.

---

### 3.1 Threat Landscape

Distributed file systems, such as IPFS, need to solve several challenges related to the security and privacy of the stored data, the infrastructure's scalability, the decentralized applications and big data complexities. However, there is a number of promising solutions that aim to settle some of these hurdles.

**Security and Privacy Challenges.** The key challenge of distributed file systems, including IPFS, is that when new peers participate in the system, they can access any stored file, including sensitive documents. Hence, the security and privacy of the system remain an open question, especially due to General Data Protection Regulation (GDPR) [17] in the European Union. A prominent solution to that is the application of smart contract-based Access Control (AC) policies [18–21], and further encryption mechanisms [22].

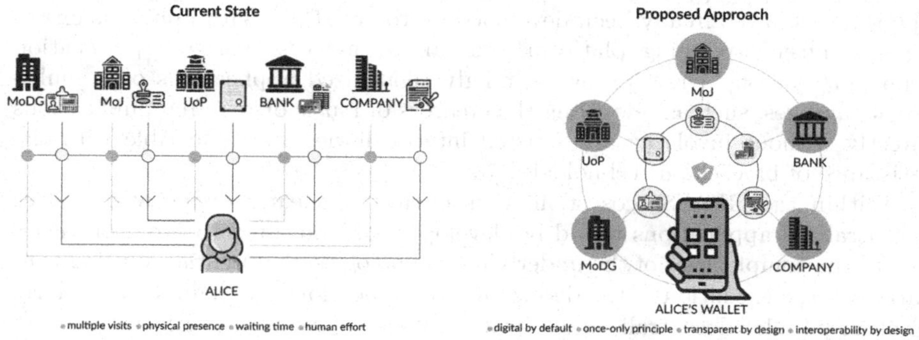


**Fig. 1.** Current practice compared to our approach [16].

Another security and privacy challenge is related to file erasure. By their nature, distributed file systems distribute all the stored files and documents among their participating peers. Hence, when data owners transmit "erasure commands" to the distributed network, it is not clear if all the peers would obey this command and delete their version of the "deleted" file or document. A solution to this data replication issue can be a common technique commonly present in data centers, such as *Reed-Solomon Coding* [23,24].

**Scalability Challenges.** Since GLASS aims to create an eGovernance framework to be followed by all European Union's member states, the infrastructure's scalability poses a real threat. According to [25,26], one of the scalability issues on IPFS is the bandwidth limit in each IPFS instance due to the P2P nature of the system. Each participant needs to connect to another IPFS node to read or download the data objects. [27] proposed a combination of IPFS and blockchain technology, namely BlockIPFS, to improve the traceability of all the occurred access events on IPFS. The authors measured the latency of each event, such as storing, reading, downloading, by varying the number of IPFS nodes and presented that even incorporating large numbers of IPFS nodes does not significantly improve the latency of all the IPFS actions. However, the authors' experiments were limited to a maximum of 27 nodes; hence, the latency measurement on a vast scale remains an open question.

For the storage optimization, two prominent solutions can be applied:

- **Storing data off-chain**. The concept of utilising smart contracts off-chain and use IPFS as a storage database is storage efficient since the IPFS nodes need to exchange only hash values of the data [28–30].
- **Utilize erasure codes**. In erasure codes, a file is divided into smaller batches and these batches are encoded [31–33]. Following that, each batch can be decoded and reconstruct the full file. [34] utilized erasure codes in a scenario combining blockchain and IPFS.

**Decentralized Applications Complexities.** Multiple novel decentralized applications have already been developed on top of IPFS, with luminous examples, a music streaming platform, and an open-access research publication repository [35,36]. Distributing seemingly centralized applications offer multiple advantages, such as rewarding the creators of music or research publications directly without involving any trusted intermediaries and is feasible with the assistance of blockchain technologies [37].

Within the GLASS ecosystem, it is critical to clearly define where these decentralized applications would be developed and executed to avoid obstacles due to the complexities of the underlying technologies. A potential solution is to carry out the execution of the decentralized applications off-chain [37], similarly to other popular decentralized applications ecosystems, such as Blockstack [38].

## 4 Methodology and Implementation

As seen in the previous sections, IPFS comes with its own complexities and characteristics. Hence, a detailed presentation of each used feature within our implementation is required for a sufficient understanding of our work.

IPFS uses Libp2p[1] library as it's base. Originally Libp2p was part of the IPFS project but has since become standalone. This library provides all of the transport abstractions and the Kad-DHT functionality. The main release is written in Go, with ports to Rust and JavaScript. To look at the implementation of the DHT, JavaScript was chosen as it natively would not rely on a multi-threading approach but instead asynchronous I/O and an event-driven programming model.

For the local testing of the DHT, a Libp2p node was created 40 times[2] to monitor the host machine[3], and the associated ports differentiate each node. The

[1] Lib2p: https://github.com/libp2p/js-libp2p.

[2] Code can be found at: https://github.com/aaoi990/ipfs-kad-dht-evaluation.

[3] The host machine was a VM which ran on Ubuntu 20.04 x64 OS, with 4 CPU cores, 8 GB of RAM, and a 40 GB HDD.

DHT configuration[4] is the standard recommended Libp2p Kad-DHT configuration with all standard defaults applied. The exception being the DHT random walk - which is not enabled by default but does allow for random host discovery. The connection encryption used is Noise protocol[5].

When a new node is initialized, it knows no peers. Typically in IPFS, this issue is solved by bootstrapping the node - providing it with a set of long-serving core nodes that have fully populated routing tables ready to share. In this case, to provide some basic routing entries, the initial node is populated by the address of the next created node, ensuring that each node knows of at least one other but only the next node. Although enabled, the random walk would be an untenable solution to peer discovery in such a small set of nodes given that the Libp2p implementation of the random walk involves dialling a random peerId created from a sha256 multi hash of 16 random bytes.

The last node initialized is then chosen to host the content. To transform the content into a CID, it is first hashed with the standard sha256 algorithm, and then a multi hash is created from this. As we are using CIDv0, the multi hash is then base 58 encoded (CIDv1 is base 32 encoded)and provided to the js-cids library to create the CID.

Once the CID is created, the final node starts providing it to the network. The content routing class of the Kad-DHT will then distribute the pointer to the nodes closest to the key itself. Each node DHT will then begin searching for other nodes and populating its routing table entries. The peer discovery process is best witnessed by examining the debug log for the Kad-DHT by starting the program with the following: `DEBUG="libp2p:dht:*" node index.js`.

Each instance of the Kad-DHT is initialized with an instance of the Providers class that manages all known providers - a peer known to have the content for a given CID. The providers class is initialized with an instance of the datastore, which houses the records of providers in the format of a key-value pair, with the key being created from the array of the CID and PeerID and the value being the time the record was entered into the store.

When the class is created, it spawns its own cleanup service. The service is a set interval clean up that runs and keeps the list of providers healthy. It is important to note at this point that although a list of providers are stored in the datastore, to ensure access is fast, there is an LRU (least recently used) cache in front of it which speeds up the process of not only cleaning up expired providers but accessing active ones as well. The default constant for the LRU size is 256, and the default cleanup interval is one hour. The cleanup service retrieves all provider entries from the datastore, checks the time of entry against the current time, and batch deletes any which have been in the store for longer than the one-hour window.

The *getClosestPeers* query is a direct query of the peers taken from the DHT's RoutingTable class, which is responsible for managing the kBuckets. The query looks through all nodes in the kBuckets and returns the closest 20 (as the

---

[4] DHT configuration: https://github.com/libp2p/js-libp2p-kad-dht.

[5] Noise Protocol: https://noiseprotocol.org/.

default bucket size in IPFS is 20). Libp2p uses the javascript implementation k-bucket[6] to handle the management of the buckets. The function does a raw calculation of the XOR distances by comparing each PeerId in the bucket as a unit8aray to the CID as a uint8array and then orders them from nearest to furthest.

With a populated routing table, it is now possible to query the network to find any provider of the created CID. In this instance, the very first initialised node - who only had contact details for the second initialised node - can query the DHT using the built-in *findProviders* function. The result of the promise is an array containing the details of any node providing the requested content. More details on the system's configuration can be found in Appendix A.

## 5 Evaluation

To evaluate the runtime performance of the JavaScript implementation of the Kad-DHT, we can examine the flame graph of the running processes. Figure 2 shows the performance of the entire program from start to finish. Each rectangle represents a stack frame, with the y-axis showing the number of frames on the stack - the stack depth. The bottom of each icicle shows the function on-CPU, with everything above it being the function ancestry. The x-axis spans the entirety of the sample population grouped alphabetically. The total width of each rectangle is the total time it was on-CPU or part of the ancestry that was on-CPU; the wider the rectangle, the more CPU consumed per execution. It is worth noting that time is not represented in flame graphs. The Graphs and the logs used to generate them can be found in the corresponding git repo[7].

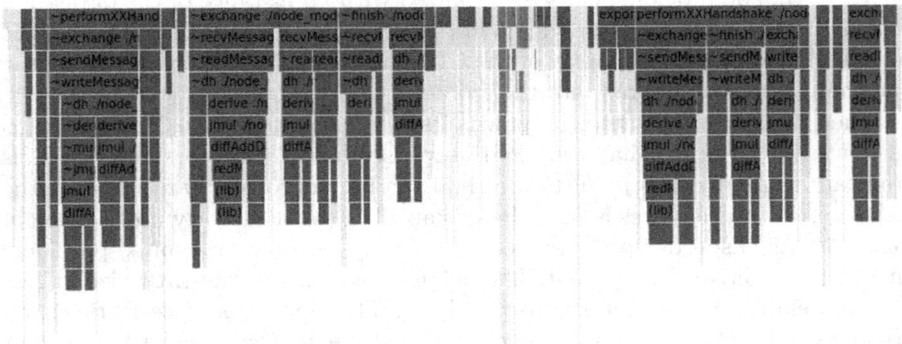

**Fig. 2.** All processes - with Kad-DHT processes shown in green (Color figure online)

[6] K-bucket: https://github.com/tristanls/k-bucket.
[7] Code can be found at: https://github.com/aaoi990/ipfs-kad-dht-evaluation/tree/main/perf.

Table 1 and Fig. 2 illustrate that unsurprisingly the vast majority of CPU usage was spent in the crypto functions, either performing handshakes between nodes or in the functions that support the key generation process.

**Table 1.** CPU time by package based on Fig. 2.

| Package | Function | Percentage |
|---|---|---|
| libp2p-noise | performXXhandshake | 28.9 |
| libp2p-noise | exchange | 18.87 |
| libp2p-noise | finish | 10.07 |
| peer-id | createFromPubKey | 4.86 |
| libp2p | encryptOutbound | 2.43 |
| libp2p | encryptInbound | 2.005 |

The key generation for a basic Libp2p2 node is a base64 encoded string of a protobuf containing a DER-encoded buffer. A node buffer is then used to pass the base64 protobuf to the multi hash function for the final PeerId generation. By default, the public key is 2048 bit RSA. As suggested in the security improvements in [7], peerId generation should be an expensive process in order to mitigate the ease of performing Sybil attacks, and although it was expensive compared to the overall effort of the program, this was primarily because of the default usage of RSA. If EC had been used as per CVE-2020-10937 [8], the CPU overhead would have been significantly lower. Table 2 and Fig. 3 illustrate one of the full stack depths with Kad-DHT ancestry.

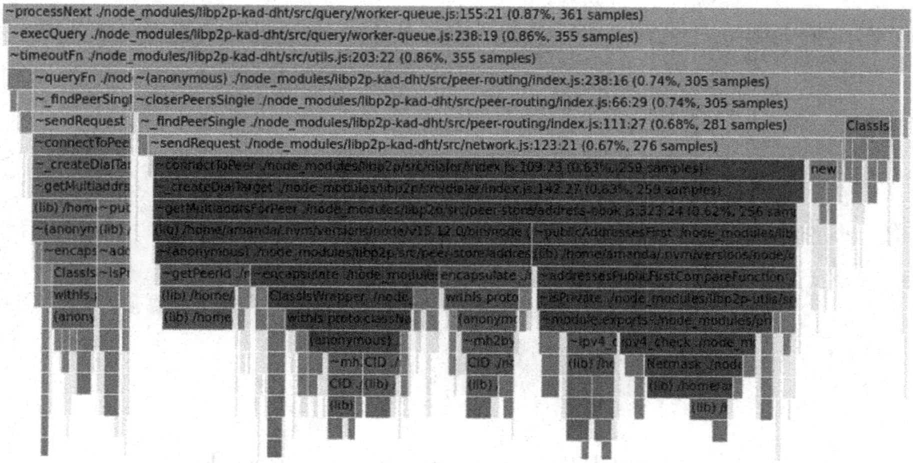


**Fig. 3.** Some of the Kad-DHT specific processes

**Table 2.** CPU time by DHT component based on Fig. 3.

| Package | Function | Percentage |
|---|---|---|
| Network | writeReadMessage | 1.08 |
| Worker-queue | processNext | 0.87 |
| Peer-routing | closerPeersSingle | 0.4 |
| Rrouting | Add | 0.1 |
| Index | nearestPeersToQuery | 0.1 |

Overall the Kad-DHT functions occupied a very low percentage of the CPU time, consistently presenting at less than 3.00%, with the highest usage coming from network functions. The test code being run is a simple start - provide - find - stop sequence, meaning the bulk of the work is being done to configure, connect and route the nodes. It is expected that the longer the program runs, the greater percentage of time the Kad-DHT functions would occupy due to the routing table maintenance functions. During normal operations, the Kad-DHT will force a refresh every 10 min by default. During this, each bucket is gone through - from bucket 0 up until the highest bucket that contains a peer (currently capped at 15). A random address from the address space that could fit in the chosen bucket is then selected, and a lookup is done to find the k closest peers to that random address. This constantly ensures that each bucket is filled with as many peers that will fit. Figure 4 results from timing the original code to run for an one-hour window, enabling multiple routing table refreshes. In the timed run, Kad-DHT functions accounted for 11.58% of CPU usage up from the initial program run of 2.55%, which is a 354% increase in the amount of time spent in functions with Kad-DHT ancestry.

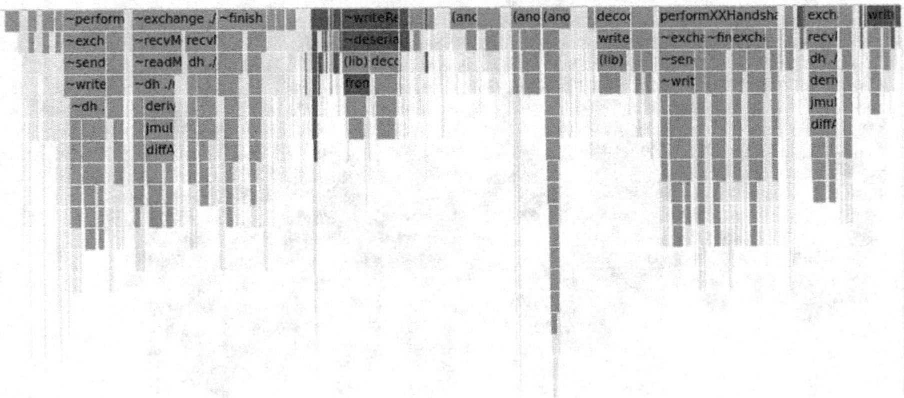


**Fig. 4.** Kad-DHT processes over an one-hour window

## 6 Conclusions

eGovernance presents unique challenges in terms of privacy-preserving and providing secure solutions in eGovernance services. Precisely when the utilized data is derived from industrial control systems and sensors. In this paper, we present GLASS, our decentralized solution, that moves towards that direction by examining the effectiveness and efficiency of distributed cutting-edge technologies and demonstrates the capacity of a public, distributed infrastructure based on the IPFS. Potential challenges on the adoption of a system similar to the proposed one would involve the consensus among the participating entities and the scalability of a decentralized system such as the proposed one.

One practical implementation of the GLASS concept is being done within the aims of the GLASS project, highlighting how the GLASS concept can potentially be integrated into a broad field of use cases. Our proposed GLASS-oriented approach is a decentralized solution that combines the IPFS with Distributed Ledger Technology and Smart Contracts to secure eGovernance services. We show in this paper how our approach can be used to fulfil the needs of the GLASS concept. Finally, and on top of the above, we created a testbed environment to measure the IPFS performance.

**Acknowledgments.** The research leading to these results has been partially funded by the European Union's Horizon 2020 research and innovation programme, through funding of the GLASS project (Grant Agreement No. 959879).

## A Appendices

### A.1 Libp2p Node Initialisation

```
const node = await Libp2p.create({
addresses: {
  listen: ['/ip4/0.0.0.0/tcp/0']
},
modules: {
  transport: [TCP],
  streamMuxer: [Mplex],
  connEncryption: [NOISE],
  dht: KadDHT,
},
config: {
  dht: {
    kBucketSize: 20,
    enabled: true,
    randomWalk: {
      enabled: true,
      interval: 300e3,
      timeout: 10e3
```

```
      }
    }
  }
})
```

**Listing 1.1.** Libp2p node initialisation.

### A.2 Random Walk PeerId Creation

```
const digest = await multihashing(
    crypto.randomBytes(16), 'sha2-256')
const id = new PeerId(digest)
```

**Listing 1.2.** Random walk PeerId creation.

### A.3 Transforming Content to a CID

```
const hash = crypto.createHash('sha256')
    .update('hello world!').digest()
const encoded = multihash.encode(hash, 'sha2-256')
const cid = new CID(multihash.toB58String(encoded))
```

**Listing 1.3.** Transforming content to a CID.

### A.4 A Node Providing Content

```
await node.contentRouting.provide(cid)
```

**Listing 1.4.** A node providing content.

### A.5 Distributing Content to the Closest Peers

```
async provide (key) {
dht._log(`provide: ${key}`)

  /** @type {Error[]} */
  const errors = []

  // Add peer as provider
  console.log('starting to provide')
  await dht.providers.addProvider(key, dht.peerId)
```

```
  const multiaddrs = dht.libp2p ? dht.libp2p.multiaddrs : []
  const msg = new Message(Message.TYPES.ADD_PROVIDER, key.bytes, 0)
  msg.providerPeers = [{
    id: dht.peerId,
    multiaddrs
  }]

  async function mapPeer (peer) {
    dht._log(‘putProvider ${key} to ${peer.toB58String()}‘)
    try {
      await dht.network.sendMessage(peer, msg)
    } catch (err) {
      errors.push(err)
    }
  }

  // Notify closest peers
  await utils.mapParallel(dht.getClosestPeers(key.bytes), mapPeer)

  if (errors.length) {
    throw errcode(new Error(‘Failed to provide to ${errors.length} of ${dht.↪
  kBucketSize} peers‘), ’ERR_SOME_PROVIDES_FAILED’, { errors })
  }
},
```

**Listing 1.5.** Distributing content to the closest peers.

## A.6 Creation of the Datastore

```
const dsKey = [
  makeProviderKey(cid),’/’,
  utils.encodeBase32(peer.id)].join(”)
const key = new Key(dsKey)
const buffer = Uint8Array.from(
  varint.encode(time.getTime()))
store.put(key, buffer)
```

**Listing 1.6.** Creation of the datastore.

## A.7 Calculating the Closest Peers Using the XOR Metric

```
closest (id, n = Infinity) {
ensureInt8('id', id)

if ((!Number.isInteger(n) && n !== Infinity) || n <= 0) {
  throw new TypeError('n is not positive number')
}
let contacts = []

for (let nodes = [this.root],
    bitIndex = 0; nodes.length > 0 && contacts.length < n;) {

  const node = nodes.pop()
  if (node.contacts === null) {
    const detNode = this._determineNode(
        node, id, bitIndex++)
    nodes.push(
        node.left === detNode ? node.right : node.left)
    nodes.push(detNode)
  } else {
    contacts = contacts.concat(node.contacts)
  }
}

return contacts
  .map(a => [this.distance(a.id, id), a])
  .sort((a, b) => a[0] - b[0])
  .slice(0, n)
  .map(a => a[1])
}
```

**Listing 1.7.** Calculating the closest Peers using the XOR metric.

## A.8 Finding Providers

```
await all(nodes[0].contentRouting
    .findProviders(cid))
```

**Listing 1.8.** Finding providers.

## A.9 Result of the "Finding Providers" Query


```
{
 id: PeerId {
   _id: <Buffer 12 20 83 42 f7 0e 33 90 d1 c4 41 d0 80 d7 16 63 be 43 95 20 3c ↩
   b1 79 5e 23 d7 28 12 3e 4a 0f aa d9 d3>,
   _idB58String: 'QmXB3LoMkXQh3HzQo1fy−
     9UEJZZQw2MmJKWRhG4nfbTR7Qe',
   _privKey: undefined,
   _pubKey: undefined
 },
 multiaddrs: []
}
```


**Listing 1.9.** Result of the findProviders query.

# References


1. Ghafur, S., Kristensen, S., Honeyford, K., Martin, G., Darzi, A., Aylin, P.: A retrospective impact analysis of the WannaCry cyberattack on the NHS. NPJ Digit. Med. **2**(1), 1–7 (2019)
2. Analytica, O.: Efforts to curb ransomware crimes face limits. Emerald Expert Briefings (oxan-db) (2021)
3. Maymounkov, P., Mazières, D.: Kademlia: a peer-to-peer information system based on the XOR metric. In: Druschel, P., Kaashoek, F., Rowstron, A. (eds.) IPTPS 2002. LNCS, vol. 2429, pp. 53–65. Springer, Heidelberg (2002). https://doi.org/10.1007/3-540-45748-8_5
4. Rowstron, A., Druschel, P.: Pastry: scalable, decentralized object location, and routing for large-scale peer-to-peer systems. In: Guerraoui, R. (ed.) Middleware 2001. LNCS, vol. 2218, pp. 329–350. Springer, Heidelberg (2001). https://doi.org/10.1007/3-540-45518-3_18
5. Zhao, B.Y., Kubiatowicz, J.D., Joseph, A.D.: Tapestry: an infrastructure for fault-tolerant wide-area location and routing. Technical report No. UCB/CSD-01-1141 (2001). http://people.cs.uchicago.edu/~ravenben/publications/CSD-01-1141.pdf
6. Plaxton, C., Rajaraman, R., Richa, A.: Accessing nearby copies of replicated objects in a distributed environment. Theory Comput. Syst. **32**, 241–280 (1998). https://doi.org/10.1007/s002240000118
7. Baumgart, I., Mies, S.: S/kademlia: a practicable approach towards secure key-based routing, vol. 2, pp. 1–8 (2008)
8. Prünster, B., Marsalek, A., Zefferer, T.: Total eclipse of the heart - disrupting the interplanetary file system (2020)
9. Kothari, R., Jakheliya, B., Sawant, V.: A distributed peer-to-peer storage network. In: International Conference on Smart Systems and Inventive Technology (ICSSIT), November 2019, pp. 576–582
10. Maymounkov, P., Mazières, D.: Kademlia: a peer-to-peer information system based on the XOR metric. In: Druschel, P., Kaashoek, F., Rowstron, A. (eds.) IPTPS 2002. LNCS, vol. 2429, pp. 53–65. Springer, Heidelberg (2002). https://doi.org/10.1007/3-540-45748-8_5

11. Mukne, H., Pai, P., Raut, S., Ambawade, D.: Land record management using hyperledger fabric and IPFS. In: 2019 10th International Conference on Computing, Communication and Networking Technologies (ICCCNT), pp. 1–18 (2019)
12. Andreev, O., Daskalov, H.: A framework for managing student data through blockchain. In: Proceedings of Xth Anniversary International Scientific Conference, pp. 59–66. Academic Press, Sofia (2018)
13. Singh, S.: A blockchain-based decentralized application for user-driven contribution to Open Government Data. Ph.D. thesis (06 2018)
14. Dunphy, P., Petitcolas, F.: A first look at identity management schemes on the blockchain. IEEE Secur. Priv. **16**, 20–29 (2018)
15. Trihinas, D., Pallis, G., Dikaiakos, M.D.: ADMin: adaptive monitoring dissemination for the internet of things. In: IEEE INFOCOM 2017-IEEE conference on computer communications, pp. 1–9. IEEE (2017)
16. Domalis, G., Karacapilidis, N., Tsakalidis, D., Giannaros, A.: A trustable and interoperable decentralized solution for citizen-centric and cross-border eGovernance: a conceptual approach. arXiv preprint arXiv:2103.15458 (2021)
17. Voigt, P., von dem Bussche, A.: The EU General Data Protection Regulation (GDPR): A Practical Guide. Springer, Cham (2017). https://doi.org/10.1007/978-3-319-57959-7
18. Barati, M., Rana, O.: Design and verification of privacy patterns for business process models. In: Patnaik, S., Wang, T.-S., Shen, T., Panigrahi, S.K. (eds.) Blockchain Technology and Innovations in Business Processes. SIST, vol. 219, pp. 125–139. Springer, Singapore (2021). https://doi.org/10.1007/978-981-33-6470-7_8
19. Huang, H., Zhou, S., Lin, J., Zhang, K., Guo, S.: Bridge the trustworthiness gap amongst multiple domains: a practical blockchain-based approach. In: ICC 2020-2020 IEEE International Conference on Communications (ICC), pp. 1–6. IEEE (2020)
20. Papadopoulos, P., Pitropakis, N., Buchanan, W.J., Lo, O., Katsikas, S.: Privacy-preserving passive DNS. Computers **9**(3), 64 (2020)
21. Stamatellis, C., Papadopoulos, P., Pitropakis, N., Katsikas, S., Buchanan, W.J.: A privacy-preserving healthcare framework using hyperledger fabric. Sensors **20**(22), 6587 (2020)
22. Wang, S., Zhang, Y., Zhang, Y.: A blockchain-based framework for data sharing with fine-grained access control in decentralized storage systems. IEEE Access **6**, 38437–38450 (2018)
23. Plank, J.S.: A tutorial on Reed-Solomon coding for fault-tolerance in raid-like systems. Software. Pract. Experience **27**(9), 995–1012 (1997)
24. Huang, H., Lin, J., Zheng, B., Zheng, Z., Bian, J.: When blockchain meets distributed file systems: An overview, challenges, and open issues. IEEE Access **8**, 50574–50586 (2020)
25. Wennergren, O., Vidhall, M., Sörensen, J.: Transparency analysis of distributed file systems: With a focus on interplanetary file system (2018)
26. Shen, J., Li, Y., Zhou, Y., Wang, X.: Understanding I/O performance of IPFS storage: a client's perspective. In: 2019 IEEE/ACM 27th International Symposium on Quality of Service (IWQoS), pp. 1–10 IEEE (2019)
27. Nyaletey, E., Parizi, R.M., Zhang, Q., Choo, K.K.R.: BlockIPFS-blockchain-enabled interplanetary file system for forensic and trusted data traceability. In: 2019 IEEE International Conference on Blockchain (Blockchain), pp. 18–25. IEEE (2019)

28. Norvill, R., Pontiveros, B.B.F., State, R., Cullen, A.: IPFS for reduction of chain size in ethereum. In: 2018 IEEE International Conference on Internet of Things (iThings) and IEEE Green Computing and Communications (GreenCom) and IEEE Cyber, Physical and Social Computing (CPSCom) and IEEE Smart Data (SmartData), pp. 1121–1128. IEEE (2018)
29. Poon, J., Buterin, V.: Plasma: Scalable autonomous smart contracts. White paper, pp. 1–47 (2017)
30. Poon, J., Dryja, T.: The bitcoin lightning network: Scalable off-chain instant payments (2016)
31. Rizzo, L.: Effective erasure codes for reliable computer communication protocols. ACM SIGCOMM Comput. Commun. Rev. **27**(2), 24–36 (1997)
32. Wilkinson, S., Boshevski, T., Brandoff, J., Buterin, V.: Storj a peer-to-peer cloud storage network (2014)
33. Vorick, D., Champine, L.: Sia: Simple decentralized storage (2018). Accessed 8 May 2014
34. Chen, Y., Li, H., Li, K., Zhang, J.: An improved P2P file system scheme based on IPFS and blockchain. In: 2017 IEEE International Conference on Big Data (Big Data), pp. 2652–2657. IEEE (2017)
35. Jia, B., Xu, C., Gotla, R., Peeters, S., Abouelnasr, R., Mach, M.: Opus-decentralized music distribution using interplanetary file systems (IPFS) on the ethereum blockchain V0. 8.3. Opus Foundation 2017 (2016)
36. Tenorio-Fornés, A., Jacynycz, V., Llop-Vila, D., Sánchez-Ruiz, A., Hassan, S.: Towards a decentralized process for scientific publication and peer review using blockchain and IPFS. In: Proceedings of the 52nd Hawaii International Conference on System Sciences (2019)
37. Truong, N., Lee, G.M., Sun, K., Guitton, F., Guo, Y.: A blockchain-based trust system for decentralised applications: When trustless needs trust. Future Gener. Comput. Sys. **124**, 68–79 (2021). ISSN 0167-739X. https://doi.org/10.1016/j.future.2021.05.025
38. Ali, M.: Stacks 2.0 apps and smart contracts for bitcoin (2020)

# Integrated Design Framework for Facilitating Systems-Theoretic Process Analysis

Amna Altaf[1(✉)], Shamal Faily[2], Huseyin Dogan[1], Eylem Thron[3], and Alexios Mylonas[4]

[1] Bournemouth University, Poole, UK
{aaltaf,hdogan}@bournemouth.ac.uk

[2] Robert Gordon University, Aberdeen, UK
s.faily@rgu.ac.uk

[3] CCD Design and Ergonomics Ltd., London, UK
eylem.thron@designbyccd.com

[4] University of Hertfordshire, Hatfield, UK
a.mylonas@herts.ac.uk

**Abstract.** Systems-Theoretic Process Analysis (STPA) helps mitigate identified safety hazards leading to unfortunate situations. Usually, a systematic step-by-step approach is followed by safety experts irrespective of any software based tool-support, but identified hazards should be associated with security risks and human factors issues. In this paper, a design framework using Integrating Requirements and Information Security (IRIS) and open source Computer Aided Integration of Requirements and Information Security (CAIRIS) tool-support is used to facilitate the application of STPA. Our design framework lays the foundation for resolving safety, security and human factors issues for critical infrastructures. We have illustrated this approach with a case study based on real life *Cambrian Coast Line Railway* incident.

**Keywords:** STPA · Safety hazards · Security risks · Human factors · IRIS · CAIRIS · Rail infrastructure

## 1 Introduction

Systems-Theoretic Process Analysis (STPA) is used to identify control actions and causal factors behind accidents to improve system design [21]. The approach revolves around a series of pre-defined steps followed by experts. Using STPA analysis, the identified safety hazards can also mitigate security risks. For example, poor design decisions may lead operators to make human errors or mistakes where rules are un-intentionally disobeyed [19]. Consequently, the system safety and security may be compromised due to human intervention in the form of errors or violations.

Integrating Requirements and Information Security (IRIS) framework has been used to identify security risks leading to safety hazards for identifying human


S. Katsikas et al. (Eds.): ESORICS 2021 Workshops, LNCS 13106, pp. 58–73, 2022.
https://doi.org/10.1007/978-3-030-95484-0_4

factors issues [3]. This is achieved by identifying and modelling assets associations, roles and personas, vulnerabilities, threats, risks, tasks and goals [13]. Based on the IRIS framework and complementary Computer Aided Integration of Requirements and Information Security (CAIRIS) platform, assumptions about security concerns and human factors issues are explicated for critical infrastructures. The framework allows complementary human factors approaches to be used to derive use case specifications based task analysis modelling to determine human failure levels leading to errors or mistakes [4]. These failure levels are used to identify associated safety and security design solutions by identifying potential hazards.

An extended design framework can be formulated by integrating these human factors and security methods for facilitating safety analysis using STPA. By conducting STPA using the IRIS framework and CAIRIS platform. This aims to resolve safety, security and human factors design concerns for critical infrastructures. To demonstrate this approach, we have used the real life incident of *Cambrian Railway*. This case study serves as a guide for human factors, safety and security experts to deal with human factors issues, associated safety hazards and potential security risks.

The rest of the paper is structured as follows. Section 2 describes the related work and Sect. 3 describes our proposed design framework. Our design framework is demonstrated by applying it for case study in Sect. 4. This is followed by discussion and conclusion for future directions of our work in Sect. 5.

## 2 Related Work

### 2.1 Security and Safety Engineering

There are commonalities between safety and security engineering, with both communities now working to bridge their gaps [17]. Safety engineering can be considered from a security mindset [10], and the International Electro-technical Commission (IEC) has suggested a framework TC 65/AHG 1 for coordinating safety and security together [16].

Several existing approaches in safety and security engineering are complementary due to inter-linked concepts. The Defence-in-Depth (DiD) approach, which is also applied in security, was derived from a safety design of nuclear plants [27]. In security, the graphical representation of attacks related to attackers using attack trees was derived from fault trees for safety of systems [30]. A Hazard and Operability Study (HAZOP) is a structured and systematic approach used to identify and evaluate risk problems in safety. The concept has been applied to security because of risk dealing with security properties (confidentiality, integrity, availability) was discovered as a linking factor [36]. Similarly, Failure Mode and Effects Analysis (FMEA) approach from safety has been applied in security as Intrusion Modes and Effects Analysis (IMEA) [7].

**Systems-Theoretic Process Analysis.** A consistent design approach for safety and security can be based on identifying safety hazards using Systems-Theoretic Process Analysis (STPA) [37]. STPA is a safety hazard analysis process model for identifying control actions for possible hazards and accidents in causal scenarios [21]. STPA is derived from Systems-Theoretic Accident Model and Processes (STAMP) process model. STAMP revolves around examining components which operate independently and together by playing their part in a system. The accident causal models are derived by studying patterns and investigating accidents from a safety engineering perspective. The processes and components when interacting with each other give rise to safety and security emergent properties. The control actions and feedback required for controlling these emergent properties based on algorithms leads to recognition of controllers. These control actions and controllers (processes) are subsequently mapped. During design, these activities are considered as high-level functional safety requirements for system. An incorrect process model may lead to an accident, where four types of unsafe control actions may occur; these control actions may occur too soon, too late, incorrect or altogether are missing. This is also known as identification of causal scenarios for unsafe control actions [20].

Safety experts should consider security along with safety as part of STPA [26]; the cyber security considerations in STPA are expanded into the STPA-Sec development method for safety critical systems [25]. Using STPA-Sec, system and component level requirements are dissected to identify safety constraints. These safety constraints help identify hazard scenarios leading to violations. These violations are weaknesses or vulnerabilities in system that allow the loss (accident) to happen [34]. Usually, hazards may also be based on human and system interactions, especially human error [22] which is not acknowledged by STPA-Sec.

The UK's National Cyber Security Centre has introduced the application of STAMP/STPA in various case studies for improving risk framework for cyber security problems. The cyber security risk toolbox have been modified to include STPA approach for enterprise IT infrastructure including automated/ connected products, industrial control systems and critical national infrastructure [5]. These case studies are used to inform about safety and security requirements in a socio-technical environment by considering the human involvement. These requirements further motivate the consideration of human factors for identifying human error source as an impacting factor behind cyber security.

STPA can potentially be used to identify human factors issues as a result of interactions with system, such as human error sources from human behaviour, and the labelling design flaws along with system hazard analysis. The unsafe behaviours behind system automation could be used to connect causal scenarios with hazard analysis. The causal scenarios helps to generate a series of possibilities with cause and effect relationship as a result of human interaction with system. Furthermore, this argument has been supported by applying this approach for case study of Automated Parking Driving System [15].

## 2.2 Safety and Human Factors Engineering

Human safety in critical infrastructures like rail is sometimes compromised due to the occurrence of human error [8,24], so its identification during the design of safety critical systems should be a priority. The rail standard EN 50126-1 emphasises the consideration of human factors during rail system's design process along with Reliability, Availability, Maintainability and Safety (RAMS) [1]. Additionally, the risk assessment for design of safety of systems like transportation industry prescribes the use of a Human Reliability Analysis (HRA)approach [18].

Based on the Swiss Cheese Model of accident causation [29], multiple layers of defence exist within a system or an organisation to protect against emergent errors or mistakes that lead to accidents. The model takes the inspiration from a slice of cheese where the holes represent the human weaknesses and different slices act as the barriers. Some holes are active failures whereas some are latent failures; all holes must be aligned at the same time for the accident to occur. Latent failures originates from active failures and usually have same catastrophic effects on human life [29]. Due to the complexity of consequences of incidents, there is no well-defined methodology for determining the sources of these failures [32]. The *human* is the most important aspect of this model, whose intent and capabilities are typically variable. Therefore, not all possible holes can be generalised before time. Based on Reason's error taxonomy [29] of cognitive, behavioural, personal and organisational factors, the Human Factors Analysis and Classification System (HFACS) framework represents four levels of failures and error sources [35].

**Task Analysis Approach.** Tasks are performed by users to achieve goals. These are assumptions made about the behavioural specifications of users involved and how they are supposed to interact with the system [12]. Task Analysis (TA) determines the set of tasks to be performed by users under observation. The TA is conducted by identifying the task for analysis, determining the associated sub-tasks and writing a step-by-step narrative for sequence of actions to be performed [2]. Previous work has shown how User Experience (UX) techniques can be used to conduct TA, using a combination of Cognitive Task Analysis (CTA) and Hierarchical Task Analysis (HTA) [4]. CTA identifies different types and values of cognitive reactions, which influence human performance during completion of tasks. HTA identifies task dependencies and sequences as a hierarchy, where high-level use cases are refined into low-level use cases. Using the use-case specifications format, different levels of human failures are then identified using tool-support [4].

## 2.3 Human Factors and Security Engineering

The threat to a system in an environment is usually caused by an attacker: the human element responsible for compromising the security [31]. This identifies humans as the biggest source for human error [29]. Similarly, the security engineers now prioritise the human dimension of system during design phases by considering the usability attributes during asset identification, threat scenario, misuse case, task duration, responsibility modelling etc. [14]. Therefore, the concept of effective information security revolves around the idea of Human Computer Interaction - Security (HCI-security) of the system using a user-centered approach [33].

**Integrating Requirements and Information Security.** The Integrating Requirements and Information Security (IRIS) process framework [13] was devised to understand how design concepts associated with security, usability, and software engineering could be aligned. It is complemented by the Computer Aided Integration of Requirements and Information Security (CAIRIS) platform, which acts as an exemplar for tool-support to manage and analyse design data collected when applying an IRIS process.

Using IRIS, vulnerabilities and threats contribute to potential risks, and threats are contingent on attacker's intent [3]. CAIRIS facilitates the creation of personas – narratives of archetypal users that embody their goals and expectations [23] – and the online data analysis that contributes to the specification of their characteristics as argumentation models [14]. Personas narratives are specified based on these characteristics, and supported by the narratives, analysts can identify the tasks and goals using the Knowledge Acquisition in autOmated Specification (KAOS) goal modelling language [11]). Collectively, these help determine human factors issues in the form of human errors (active failures). Personas narrative also contribute towards understanding capability, intent, action and motivation for stakeholder roles, and goal and task models help the security engineers better understand the system threat model on the basis of *obstacles* that obstruct to system goals. CAIRIS also helps to model use-cases and information assets as Data Flow Diagrams (DFDs) where different trust boundaries display various levels of privilege operating within system. Consequently, although not explicitly designed with safety in mind, IRIS and CAIRIS provides a foundation for integrating safety, security and human factors engineering.

## 3 Approach

Our design framework comprises of human factors informed safety analysis and security engineering. The human factors approach draws on the identification of roles, persona building, and the generation of task models and use-case specifications to apply a partial-STPA assessment. The process begins by identifying an accident or loss, where an unplanned situation during performance of tasks by specified roles or use-case actors may lead to catastrophic consequences. The safety engineers work to minimise these occurrences by incorporating safety checks and goals in system design whereas a security engineer focuses on vulnerability and threat recognition for risk analysis. Using CAIRIS, STPA models include a KAOS goal model to show goals and obstacles contributing to the scenario behind the accident.

**Pre-requisite.** Before applying STPA, the stakeholder roles are defined within system. The roles are further used to identify specific personas describing the archetypical behaviour of system actors. Personas are created by following the approach described by [6]. Persona narrative play a significant role in determining the actors intent and capabilities which contribute towards understanding task. Using personas narrative, the concerned tasks within imagined scenarios are elicited based on roles. These elicited tasks form the basis of system and user level goals. Tasks are defined as narrative text, with additional details on their dependencies, consequences, and benefits. The narrative helps to understand the objective of task along with its procedural description, but the persona plays a major role behind the recognition of tasks.

Using CAIRIS, a *Task Participation Form* relates personas with task using usability attributes such as duration, frequency, demands and goal conflict. The usability attributes with different values highlight tasks with different colours during task models. These task models comprise of tasks against specified roles and personas which facilitate the specification for use case actors and use cases for human factors analysis. These models also help relate associated assets, threats and vulnerabilities, which assist experts during security analysis.

With the help of personas narrative and task models, use case specifications are defined. Each use case specification comes with an objective, actor, pre-conditions, steps (task sequence), post-conditions and exceptions. The use-case actors can also be linked with task models, showing relationship between role, persona, task and use-case. These elaborate task models help experts to visualise design of system along with specified environment by conducting TA using use-case specification format [4].

**Step 1: Accident, Hazard and Constraint.** The STPA process begins by defining the accidents (losses) in relation to identified hazards [21]. The system-level constraints are also defined at this stage. During TA, the tasks with *High* level of human failures are analysed for identifying accident (loss) and hazard. Using CAIRIS, the goal and obstacle modelling in KAOS captures accident, hazard and constraints. The *obstacle* with the type "loss" is used to model accident whereas type "hazard" models associated hazard. The constraints are modelled as *goal*. The visual representation of these linked concepts provide more meaning and understanding for further analysis by domain experts.

**Step 2: Model Control Structure.** At this stage, a control structure of the major components and controllers within system, along with the commands used between them is sketched. The commands between components and controllers are usually labelled as control or feedback [21]. An effective way for modelling these control structures within CAIRIS is by using DFD. Using DFDs, the trust boundary may variate between controller, controlled process, sensor or actuator. The processes and data stores are defined using use cases and information assets, and CAIRIS automatically visualises a control structure model as a DFD.

**Step 3: Unsafe Control Action.** The worst case scenarios leading to hazards are recognised by defining unsafe control actions. An unsafe control action is a control action which is either applied too early or too late. The safety constraints are determined for minimising these unsafe control actions [21]. In CAIRIS, an unsafe control action is presented using *obstacle* and the safety constraint is modelled by associating these obstacles with DFDs.

**Step 4: Causal Factor.** The causal factors are identified by analysing the controllers, processes, feedback and control paths [21]. In CAIRIS, the identified tasks during human factors analysis, are linked-up with hazards and system-level constraints using KAOS goal refinement associations. Here, the task model and personas narrative might also contain the detail for an occurrence of event known as causal factor. The model generated is known as the controller process model, which highlights the design-level issues leading to accident scenarios as a result of hazard. By using these models vulnerability, threat and risk analysis can help resolve security, safety and human factors design issues.

**Step 5: Risk Analysis Model.** These identified causal factors are also defined as system vulnerabilities leading to hazards (accidents). The vulnerabilities are also system weaknesses, which, if exploited by attackers as threats, contribute to the realisation of risks. The core IRIS concepts are used for modelling risk elements in the form of attacker, threat and vulnerability. The assets and their associations already defined during STPA are used in this risk analysis. Using risk analysis, the likelihood and severity of an incident is determined based on the ability of an attacker, and the value of assets that need to be protected. Threat scenarios (misuse cases) are also defined to evaluate the rating of each risk. CAIRIS generates visual risk models based on this analysis, which are used as the basis of further security analysis.

## 4 Case Study - Cambrian Incident Investigation

The real life incident of *Cambrian Railway* is used to conduct a case study based on qualitative evaluation of presented design framework[1]. The incident took place in October 2017 on the Cambrian Coast Line in Wales, where a train oversped due to technical failure [9]. The train was following the route of Cambrian Coast Line. During service between Barmouth and Llanaber, the

[1] The final model created, including references to online sources used, is available at GitHub repository: https://github.com/s5121191/CyberICPS_21. This relies on the CAIRIS fork at https://github.com/s5121191/cairis.

train travelled at three times of its normal speed. The over-speeding was timely observed by its train driver, who immediately reported the fault to concerned authority. Following this, manual routing was conducted by the train driver and signaller until the fault was rectified. No accidents occurred and no human was harmed during this incident. A formal investigation was conducted by Rail Accident Investigation Branch (RAIB) and five recommendations were suggested to Network Rail [28].

We chose this incident based on multiple factors like signalling system, service type, form of rail transit, and design implementation. The Cambrian Coast Line implemented the *European Railway Traffic Management System (ERTMS)*. ERTMS is based on European Train Control System (ETCS) as a rail signalling system, which ensures reliability, optimised capability and automation. Achievement of these qualities in ERTMS depends on safe, secure and usable design goals. The service type is *Passenger Train*, which is safety critical, and the goal is to ensure safety and security of human life. The *Light Rail* is preferred as the form of rail transit because of rapid speed, inter-city passenger travel (familiarity of routes) and usable design features.

The Cambrian Incident[2] case study application of the integrated design framework begun with data collection. All open source (online) documentation and literature was collected and surveyed. Moreover, the relevant stakeholders were determined. This included safety expert for STPA process support, security expert for understanding causal factors (including risk analysis) and human factors expert for advise during goal-obstacle modelling, task and personas scenarios. For this project, two environments were identified namely, *peak* and *off-peak hours*. The *Peak Hours* were defined from Monday-Friday 0630–0930 and 1600–1900 hours, whereas the *Off-Peak Hours* were from Monday-Friday at all other times (minus Peak Hours) including all day on Weekends and Bank Holidays.

The Cambrian Incident case study was modelled using KAOS to show a general scenario behind the accident [28]. For this purpose, 6 goals and 4 obstacles were identified and their associations were defined as shown in Fig. 1, where different shades of obstacles were due to varying probability of occurrence; the darker the shade, the higher the probability. The model stated the major goal of *Auto Signalling Computer Restart* being obstructed by obstacle of *No Indication of an Abnormal IT Condition.* This goal was associated with sub-goal of *Temporary Speed Restriction (TSR) Data Uploaded*, where the obstruction was caused due to *Missing Independent Check.* The TSR data was displayed on Driver Machine Interface (DMI) available to train drivers. Therefore, come the sub-goal of *DMI Used for Operational Control Display*, this goal had two sub-goals defined along with an obstacle where *Speed Restriction Not Uploaded* caused a problem during its goal fulfilment. The sub-goal when *Fourth Passenger Train Service Operated* lead to obstacle where normal service delivery was compromised because of *2J03 Passed TSR from 30 km per hour to 80 km per hour.*

[2] This case study is applied for demonstration purpose only and in no way undermines any previous findings or studies.

This fault was timely reported by train driver to the IT technicians. Therefore, the goal of *Reported Fault on Train 2J03 Service* was fulfilled.

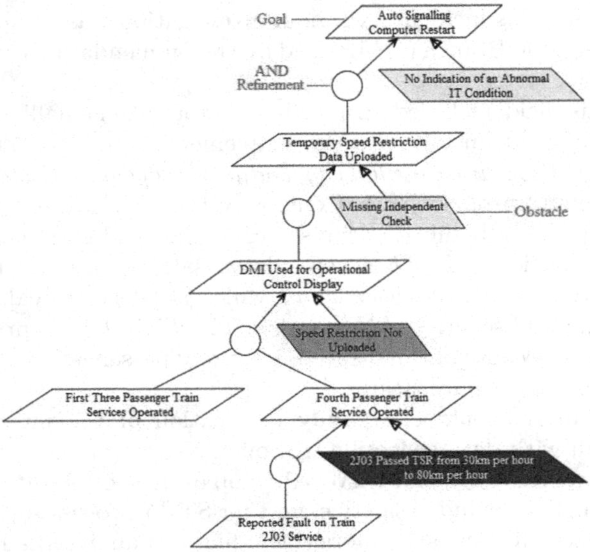


**Fig. 1.** Goal-obstacle model for Cambrian Incident case study

**Pre-requisite.** The train driver and signaller roles were important in this incident. The train driver identified and reported the fault, then reverted to manual routing in order to ensure safety of passengers and normal service delivery. Alongside, the signaller was responsible for doing an independent check of upload of correct TSR. Upon recognition of fault, signaller reported it to technician and co-ordinated routes with train driver for no disruption of service.

Using CAIRIS, a total of 5 roles were identified including *on-board staff, on-board passenger, signaller, train driver* and *train maintainer*. Two personas, *Ray* and *Neil*, were created for the role of train driver and signaller respectively. Ray was based on 22 argumentation models.

Neil's persona was based on 18 argumentation models. These argumentation models were used to understand persona characteristics, which formed the narrative for personas. This narrative and underpinning data analysis contributed to the identification of task models for further analysis.

A total of 19 tasks were created in CAIRIS; 11 were derived from Ray, and 8 from Neil. For example, the task of *Perform ETCS Self-Test Function* was found from persona characteristic of activities for Ray as shown by the bold text in the scenario below.

*Ray as train driver begins his job, by booking on and getting updated information on his laptop. This is based on documentation received about booking depot and preparing train for service.* ***Also, before operating train Ray is going to perform an on-board European Train Control System (ETCS) self-test function for finding faults and failures. He is going to produce a failure report and proceed only if the status of train for service is Safe and Fit.***

With the help of personas narrative and task models, 17 use-case specifications were defined.

**Step 1: Accident, Hazard and Constraint.** During TA, 3 use cases *Combining Workstations, Granting Off-Peak Blockage* and *Conflict Prediction and Resolution* corresponded with *High* levels of human failure. Using these tasks, the accidents were defined using *obstacle* with type loss. In the given scenario 2 accidents were defined as *Collision Between Two or More Trains* and *Train Derailment.* The former was due to loss of operational control data for controlling trains and a cause of concern for road traffic, on-board passengers, staff, train driver and other trains. The latter occurred due to over-speeding where along with on-board passengers, staff, and train driver other concerns included were like movement authority signals, DMI, TSR and driver advisory information.

This was followed by recognition of 4 hazards with respect to these identified accidents, where each hazard was responsible for specified concerns in the form of assets. For example, the hazard of *Train Enters Uncontrolled State* was dependent on occurrence of accident of *Train Derailment.*

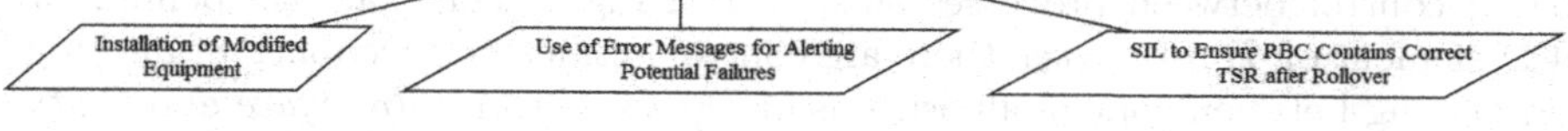

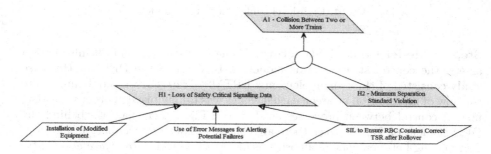


**Fig. 2.** KAOS association between accident, hazard and constraint

At this point the constraints were modelled as goals. There were 8 constraints for preventing these hazards. For example, the hazard of *Loss of Safety Critical Signalling Data* had 3 constraints identified as *Installation of Modified Equipment, Use of Error Messages for Alerting Potential Failures* and *Safety Integrity Level (SIL) to Ensure Radio Block Center (RBC) Contains Correct TSR after Rollover* as shown in Fig. 2.

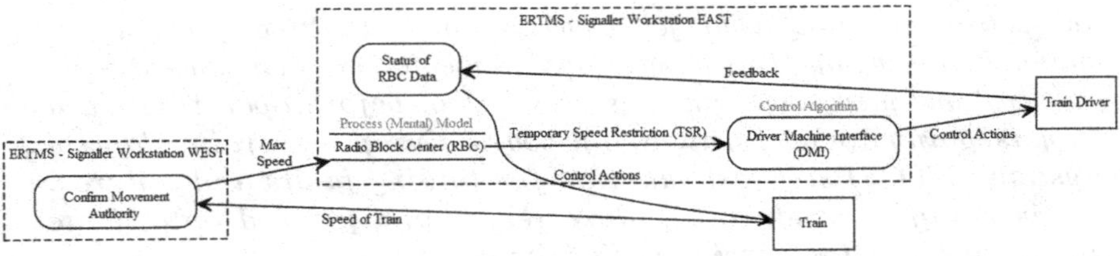


**Fig. 3.** DFD of control structure model using CAIRIS

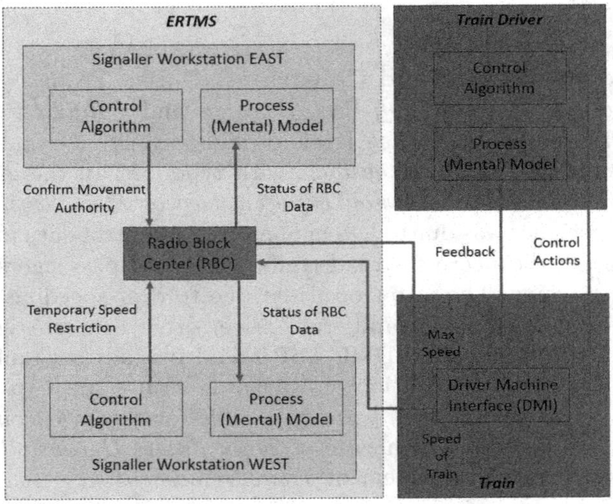


**Fig. 4.** High-level control structure model

**Step 2: Model Control Structure.** Using 17 use-cases and 29 information assets, the control structure was modelled. In CAIRIS the DFD for this case study consisted of three main elements: ERTMS, Train Driver and Train, where the flow of information between each element was taking place in order to display flow of control between processes as shown in Fig. 4. For example, behind the DFD element of *Train Driver* there are control actions and feedback of information flowing between control algorithms of *Driver Machine Interface* and *Status of RBC Data*. The DFD in CAIRIS, shown in Fig. 3, was also used to construct high-level control structure model as shown in Fig. 4.

**Step 3: Unsafe Control Action.** Using UCA keyword, the unsafe control actions were defined in CAIRIS as obstacles. *UCA1 - ETCS Failure* and *UCA2 - Reliance on Procedures to Ensure TSR Application* were defined as *2* UCAs for this incident. UCA1 was related to ERTMS signalling control system and due to safety issues. UCA2 was related to RBC and occurred during RBC rollover. Using KAOS, these UCAs were linked to hazards. Therefore, the hazard of *Train Enters*

*Uncontrolled State* was related to UCA1 and *Minimum Separation Standard Violation* was related to UCA2 (Table 1).

**Table 1.** Unsafe control action corresponding to accident, hazard and constraint

| Accident (Loss) | Hazard | Constraint | Unsafe control action |
|---|---|---|---|
| A1 - Collision Between Two or More Trains | H1 - Loss of Safety Critical Signalling Data | Installation of Modified Equipment | Reliance on Procedures to Ensure TSR Application |
| | | Use of Error Messages for Alerting Potential Failures | |
| | | SIL to Ensure RBC Contains Correct TSR after Rollover | |
| | H2 - Minimum Separation Standard Violation | Implement a Mandatory Safety Assurance Procedure | ETCS Failure |
| A2 - Train Derailment | H3 - Trains Enter Uncontrolled State | Inclusion of defensive Programming (SQL) to Protect Against Unsafe State | ETCS Failure |
| | | Good Safety Management Engineering | |
| | H4 - Operational Planning Violation | Capture and Retention of Data for Investigating Failures | Reliance on Procedures to Ensure TSR Application |
| | | Robust Configuration Management | |

**Step 4: Causal Factor.** At this stage, the identified tasks within human factors analysis were associated with constraints (goals). The model generated was known as the controller process model, where the tasks carry an explanation for unsafe control actions. For example, the constraint defined as *Implement a Mandatory Safety Assurance Procedure* was complemented by a task known as *Send Movement Authority*. The delay or incorrect *Movement Authority* had catastrophic consequences.

**Step 5: Risk Analysis Model.** Using causal factors, risk modelling elements in the form of attacker, threat and vulnerability were also found. An hypothetical attacker was someone defined with capabilities such as knowledge, education and training of software and technology, with a motivation to breach system. 2 vulnerabilities with configuration type and critical severity were identified as *Lack of Safety Integrity Level* and *No Error Messages for Alerting Potential Failures*. Using these vulnerabilities, *2* electronic and malware type of threats were found namely, *Threat of ERTMS Safety Related Failure* and *Threat of Loss of Data Packets*. Each threat was assigned assets and valued for security properties including confidentiality, integrity and availability.

Consequently, these vulnerabilities and threats contributed to 2 risks with misuse cases as *Risk of Loss of Life due to Train Collision or Derailment* and *Risk of Failure of Signalling Network over ERTMS* as shown in Fig. 5. In the risk model, the elements were filled with different colours based on values of security properties, threat and vulnerability type and risk scoring. Like obstacles, the darker the shade, the more likely, severe, and impactful is the threat, vulnerability, and risk respectively.

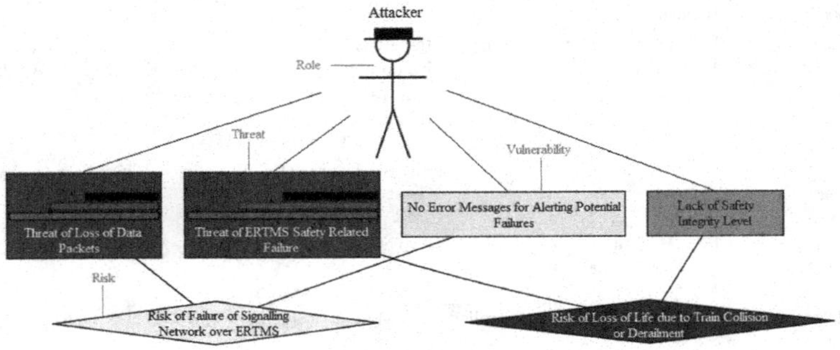


**Fig. 5.** Risk model based on attacker, threat and vulnerability

# 5 Discussion and Conclusion

In this paper, STPA process model was derived using the IRIS framework and CAIRIS platform. As a result, three signification contributions are made. First, we demonstrate how the STPA process model is aligned with IRIS and CAIRIS, providing a single platform for all elements and contributing factors related to hazard analysis. These elements comprise of accident (loss), hazard, system constraint, component (control algorithm), process (mental) model, unsafe control action (obstacle) leading to causal factors. Second, we show how the causal factors including tasks can identify vulnerabilities, threats and risks present within system. This can be visualised using a security risk analysis model in CAIRIS. The risk model enlists tasks related to roles and personas which can be further analysed for use case specifications based task analysis as a combination of CTA and HTA leading to human error sources unlike STPA-Sec. Furthermore, the human error sources has the tendency to contribute towards potential safety hazards. Finally, the approach focused on bringing security and human factors methods support to STPA. Initially, the STPA process model is suggested by keeping in mind the safety where several case study applications suggested the involvement of human element. This human element is considerable in a socio-technical environment, where the system weaknesses (vulnerabilities) are highlighted by recognising human error sources. These human error sources establish grounds for understanding potential hazard scenarios and model better risk analysis. Hence, this research builds the scope of connection and integration between safety, security and human factors.

Using this integrated design framework, safety goals (safety constraints), security risks and human factors concerns (levels of human error) are highlighted.

The STPA process model is derived from human factors approach which contribute towards the identification of potential safety hazards. These safety hazards are then used for identifying control actions and causal factors behind accidents for improving system design. The IRIS framework concepts alignment with STPA lead to better outcome as human perspective (task model and analysis) is understood in more detail. The risk model arising from STPA analysis facilitates security experts as well. Moreover, by using CAIRIS, the effort required by safety, security and human factors experts is minimised by providing automated and efficient design solutions. These efficient design solutions enable experts from different domains to accomplish different tasks by combined and reduced effort.

For demonstration purposes, STPA method is applied using the case study of *Cambrian Incident*. The human factors approach such as identification of roles and personas, task analysis and use-cases are used to understand processes, asset associations and goal-obstacle models. In return, KAOS models and DFDs (processes and datastores) are used to apply STPA, where risk analysis based on recognition of attackers, threats, vulnerabilities, risks and misuse cases are done simultaneously. This helps to evaluate an integration of concepts between safety and security, security and human factors, and human factors and safety. This lays the foundation for overlapping concepts between three domains.

As future work, the application of safe, secure and usable design framework will be done on an industrial live project. For this purpose, safety, security and human factors experts will be consulted for validation of data and process behind approach.

**Acknowledgements.** The work described in this paper was funded by the BU studentship *Integrating Safety, Security, and Human Factors Engineering in Rail Infrastructure Design & Evaluation.*

## References

1. CENELEC - EN 50126–1 - Railway Applications - The Specification and Demonstration of Reliability, Availability, Maintainability and Safety (RAMS) - Part 1: Generic RAMS Process—Engineering360, October 2017. https://standards.globalspec.com/std/10262901/cenelec-en-50126-1
2. Affairs, A.S.F.P.: Task Analysis. /how-to-and-tools/methods/task-analysis.html, September 2013
3. Altaf, A., Faily, S., Dogan, H., Mylonas, A., Thron, E.: Identifying safety and human factors issues in rail using IRIS and CAIRIS. In: Katsikas, S., et al. (eds.) CyberICPS/SECPRE/SPOSE/ADIoT-2019. LNCS, vol. 11980, pp. 98–107. Springer, Cham (2020). https://doi.org/10.1007/978-3-030-42048-2_7
4. Altaf, A., Faily, S., Dogan, H., Mylonas, A., Thron, E.: Use-case informed task analysis for secure and usable design solutions in rail. In: Percia David, D., Mermoud, A., Maillart, T. (eds.) CRITIS 2021. LNCS, vol. 13139, pp. 168–185. Springer, Cham (2021). https://doi.org/10.1007/978-3-030-93200-8_10
5. Anna, G.: Methodological findings from applying STPA in cyber security case studies. In: MIT STAMP Conference. MIT Partnership for Systems Approaches to Safety and Security (PSASS), MIT Campus, Cambridge, USA, March 2019

6. Atzeni, A., Cameroni, C., Faily, S., Lyle, J., Flechais, I.: Here's Johnny: a methodology for developing attacker personas. In: 2011 Sixth International Conference on Availability, Reliability and Security, pp. 722–727. IEEE Vienna, August 2011
7. Babeshko, E., Kharchenko, V., Gorbenko, A.: Applying F(I)MEA-technique for SCADA-based industrial control systems dependability assessment and ensuring. In: 2008 Third International Conference on Dependability of Computer Systems DepCoS-RELCOMEX (2008)
8. Baysari, M.T., McIntosh, A.S., Wilson, J.R.: Understanding the human factors contribution to railway accidents and incidents in Australia. Accid. Anal. Prev. **40**(5), 1750–1757 (2008)
9. BBC: 'Lessons learnt' over train speeding on Cambrian line. BBC News, December 2019
10. Bloomfield, R., Bishop, P., Butler, E., Stroud, R.: Security-informed safety: supporting stakeholders with codes of practice. Computer **51**(8), 60–65 (2018)
11. Dardenne, A., van Lamsweerde, A., Fickas, S.: Goal-directed requirements acquisition. Sci. Comput. Program. **20**(1), 3–50 (1993)
12. Diaper, D., Stanton, N.: The Handbook of Task Analysis for Human-Computer Interaction. CRC Press, Mahwah (2004)
13. Faily, S.: Designing Usable and Secure Software with IRIS and CAIRIS. Springer, Cham (2018). https://doi.org/10.1007/978-3-319-75493-2
14. Faily, S., Fléchais, I.: Barry is not the weakest link: Eliciting Secure System Requirements with Personas, p. 8, September 2010
15. France, M.E.: Engineering for Humans: A New Extension to STPA. Thesis, Massachusetts Institute of Technology (2017)
16. IEC: IEC - TC 65/AHG (2019). https://www.iec.ch
17. Jonsson, E., Olovsson, T.: On the Integration of Security and Dependability in Computer Systems, p. 6 (1998)
18. Kirwan, B.: Validation of human reliability assessment techniques: Part 1—validation issues. Saf. Sci. **27**(1), 25–41 (1997)
19. Lahoz, C.H.N.: Systematic review on STPA A preliminary study, p. 34 (2015)
20. Leveson, N.: Engineering a Safer and More Secure World, p. 72, June 2011
21. Leveson, N.: Systems-Theoretic Process Analysis Handbook, p. 188, March 2018
22. Mindermann, K., Riedel, F., Abdulkhaleq, A., Stach, C., Wagner, S.: Exploratory study of the privacy extension for system theoretic process analysis (STPA-Priv) to elicit privacy risks in eHealth. In: 2017 IEEE 25th International Requirements Engineering Conference Workshops (REW), pp. 90–96. IEEE, Lisbon, September 2017
23. Norman, D.: Emotional Design: Why We Love (or Hate) Everyday Things. Basic Books, New York (2004)
24. O'Hare, D.: The 'Wheel of Misfortune': a taxonomic approach to human factors in accident investigation and analysis in aviation and other complex systems, vol. 43 (2001)
25. Pereira, D., Hirata, C., Pagliares, R., Nadjm-Tehrani, S.: COMBINED SAFETY AND SECURITY CONSTRAINTS ANALYSIS. In: Tonetta, S., Schoitsch, E., Bitsch, F. (eds.) SAFECOMP 2017. LNCS, vol. 10489, pp. 70–80. Springer, Cham (2017). https://doi.org/10.1007/978-3-319-66284-8_7
26. Pereira, D.P., Hirata, C., Nadjm-Tehrani, S.: A STAMP-based ontology approach to support safety and security analyses. J. Inf. Secur. Appl. **47**, 302–319 (2019)
27. Piètre-Cambacédès, L., Bouissou, M.: Cross-fertilization between safety and security engineering. Reliab. Eng. Syst. Saf. **110**, 110–126 (2013)

28. RAIB: Loss of safety critical signalling data on the Cambrian Coast line. https://www.gov.uk/raib-reports/report-17-2019-loss-of-safety-critical-signalling-data-on-the-cambrian-coast-line, December 2019
29. Reason, J.: Human Error by James Reason, October 1990
30. Schneier, B.: Academic: attack trees - Schneier on security by Dr. Dobb's J. (1999). https://www.schneier.com/academic/archives/1999/12/attack_trees.html
31. Schneier, B.: Secrets and Lies: Digital Security in a Networked World. Wiley, New Yok (2000)
32. Shorrock, S.T.: Errors of perception in air traffic control. Saf. Sci. **45**(8), 890–904 (2007)
33. Shostack, A.: Threat Modeling: Designing for Security. Wiley, Indianapolis (2014)
34. Slominski, H.M.: Using STPA and CAST to Design for Serviceability and Diagnostics, p. 106, May 2020
35. Wiegmann, D.A., Shappell, S.A.: A Human Error Approach to Aviation Accident Analysis: The Human Factors Analysis and Classification System, 1st edn. Routledge, Aldershot (2003)
36. Winther, R., Johnsen, O.-A., Gran, B.A.: Security assessments of safety critical systems using HAZOPs. In: Voges, U. (ed.) SAFECOMP 2001. LNCS, vol. 2187, pp. 14–24. Springer, Heidelberg (2001). https://doi.org/10.1007/3-540-45416-0_2
37. Young, W., Leveson, N.G.: An integrated approach to safety and security based on systems theory. Commun. ACM **57**(2), 31–35 (2014)

# Attack Path Analysis and Cost-Efficient Selection of Cybersecurity Controls for Complex Cyberphysical Systems

Georgios Spathoulas, Georgios Kavallieratos, Sokratis Katsikas(✉), and Alessio Baiocco

Department of Information Security and Communications Technology, Norwegian University of Science and Technology, Gjøvik, Norway
{georgios.spathoulas,georgios.kavallieratos,sokratis.katsikas, alessio.baiocco}@ntnu.no

**Abstract.** The increasing integration of information technology with operational technology leads to the formation of Cyber-Physical Systems (CPSs) that intertwine physical and cyber components and connect to each other. This interconnection enables the offering of functionality beyond the combined offering of each individual component, but at the same time increases the cyber risk of the overall system, as such risk propagates between and aggregates at component systems. The complexity of the resulting systems in many cases leads to difficulty in analyzing cyber risk. Additionally, the selection of cybersecurity controls that will effectively and efficiently treat the cyber risk is commonly performed manually, or at best with limited automated decision support. In this paper, we extend our previous work in [1] to analyze attack paths between CPSs on one hand, and we improve the method proposed therein for selecting a set of security controls that minimizes both the residual risk and the cost of implementation. We use the DELTA demand-response management platform for the energy market stakeholders such as Aggregators and Retailers [2] as a use case to illustrate the workings of the proposed approaches. The results are sets of cybersecurity controls applied to those components of the overall system that have been identified to lie in those attack paths that have been identified as most critical among all the identified attack paths.

**Keywords:** Attack paths · Cyber risk aggregation · Cyber security controls · Power grid

## 1 Introduction

The increasing proliferation of cyberphysical systems (CPSs) in critical domains including industrial control systems, energy, transportation and healthcare

This paper has been partially funded by the European Union's Horizon 2020 research and innovation programme under Grant Agreement No 773960 (DELTA project).


S. Katsikas et al. (Eds.): ESORICS 2021 Workshops, LNCS 13106, pp. 74–90, 2022.
https://doi.org/10.1007/978-3-030-95484-0_5

increases automation and facilitates operations. On the other hand, the increased interoperability and interconnectivity of CPSs increase the attack surface, allowing potential adversaries to perform sophisticated cyber attacks by following attack paths that comprise CPSs as stepping-stones [3].

In particular, the realization of the industry 4.0 paradigm in the power industry increases the interconnectivity and complexity of power grids, rendering them prone to cyber attacks. Indeed, several cyber incidents have been reported in the power industry in the past decade [4], and existing system vulnerabilities in power grids have been identified and analyzed [5].

In an infrastructure comprising networked assets, an attack path describes an ordered sequence of assets that can be used as stepping stones by an adversary aiming to attack one or more assets on the path [6]. By analyzing attack paths, the analysis of the risk propagation and the identification of optimal controls are facilitated. Although the analysis of attack paths is well studied in the literature [7,8], most of the approaches focus on the vulnerabilities of the targeted ecosystem; hence, crucial elements of the cyber risk such as impact and likelihood are not considered.

Contemporary CPS-based infrastructures are characterized by complex information and control flows between their constituent CPSs. These flows can be *direct*, where the components cause immediate change in the node transition, or *indirect*, that can directly or indirectly influence the change in the node transition. These information and control flows provide useful insights to the analysis of cyber risk aggregation, risk analysis, and risk treatment between CPSs. By leveraging different security controls cyber risks are retained, minimized, transferred, or avoided. Although several studies have examined the optimal selection of security controls, most are based on empirical analysis, whose results highly depend on the analyst or domain expert and are, therefore, subjective.

In a previous work of ours [1] we proposed an approach for analyzing risk propagation in complex cyber-physical systems comprising other CPSs as components and leveraged the aggregated risk of the overall system to identify the set of security controls for each component by means of a genetic algorithm approach. In this paper, we extend our previous work in [1] to analyze attack paths between CPSs on one hand, and we improve the method proposed therein for selecting a set of security controls that minimizes both the residual risk and the cost. We have used the DELTA demand-response management platform for the energy market stakeholders such as Aggregators and Retailers [2] as a use case to illustrate the workings of the proposed approaches.

The remainder of this paper is structured as follows: In Sect. 2 we review the related work. In Sect. 3 we briefly review our previous work in [1], so as to both ensure the self-sustainability of this work and to facilitate the assessment of its contribution and of its added value over [1]. Section 4 presents our proposal for analyzing attack paths, and Sect. 5 presents our proposed approach to selecting the optimal set of security controls. Section 6 illustrates the workings of the proposed approaches to the DELTA platform [2]. Finally, Sect. 7 summarizes our conclusions and sets out some future research paths.

## 2 Related Work

Several approaches have been proposed in the literature to study attack graphs and the analysis of attack paths within IT infrastructures [9]. The ADversary VIew Security Evaluation (ADVISE) meta modeling approach was used in [10] to facilitate the understating of attack paths within cyber-physical systems. A set of algorithms were proposed in [11] to facilitate the analysis of attack paths and to prioritize them taking into account the system's vulnerabilities. A method for analyzing attack paths in CPSs that takes into account the cyber-risk of the involved components was proposed in [6]. Further, an approach for cyber-physical attack path analysis, based on Common Vulnerabilities and Exposures (CVE), and the Common Vulnerability Scoring System (CVSS), and leveraging a threat modeling technique, was proposed in [12]. The propagation of cyber-attacks in a power grid infrastructure was analyzed in [13], taking on the chronological perspective and considering the interrelationship between the grid side and the information side. The analysis focuses on the survivability aspect.

A quantitative risk assessment model that considers the risk propagation among dependent CPSs was proposed in [14]. The risk propagation and prediction have been studied in [15] using Markov chains. The method utilized prediction graph theory and percolation theory to analyze the risk propagation within cyber physical systems in the power domain. The risk propagation between CPSs is examined in [16] based on logical equations and using attack trees; the examined relationships are between parent and children nodes. The risk propagation within a transport network under various types of attacks was analyzed in [17], using the percolation theory. The risk and threat propagation in Unmanned Aerial Vehicles and in particular the aggregation process of the threats from the cyber to the physical domain were discussed in [18].

Cyberattacks cause both safety- and cybersecurity-related damage to CPSs. Accordingly, failure propagation has been also examined in the literature. Specifically, failure propagation in interdependent supply chain networks was studied in [19]; the focus of the analysis was to study the robustness of the supply chain network. Cascading failures within an interdependent network were examined in [20], using an Erdos-Renyi (ER) model, again to study the robustness of the network. In the power domain, cascading failures in a power grid and communication network were analyzed in [21].

## 3 Background

In [1] we proposed an approach that enables the optimal selection of cybersecurity controls for complex cyberphysical systems, i.e. CPSs that have other CPSs as components. This approach processes the likelihood and impact values for each one of the system's components and, by means of an analysis of how risk propagates through information and control flows components, it calculates the overall, global system risk. It then applies a genetic algorithm workflow that enables the identification of the set of optimal controls for each component.

The identified set minimizes the global system residual risk, and also minimizes the cost of implementation of the controls. The analysis in [1] is conducted on a per-threat basis, for each of the six threats of the STRIDE model. Thus, the approach produces six different control sets, that need to be applied concurrently.

The method assumes a CPS consisting of $N$ interconnected components, each denoted by $c_i$, $i = 1, ...N$. This system can be represented by a directed graph of $N + 1$ nodes, the system itself being one of the nodes, denoted as $c_0$. The edges of the graph represent information and control flows between the nodes. An edge from node $A$ to node $B$ indicates the existence of either an information flow or a control flow, from $A$ to $B$. A consequence of the existence of such an edge is that a cybersecurity event at node $A$ affects node $B$, as well. The *effect coefficient* measures the effect that components may have on each other. Figure 1 depicts a simple graph, where a security event in node A influences node B, while a security event in B influences both nodes A and C. The *total effect coefficient* $eff^T_{AB}$ is computed as a function of $eff^I_{AB}$ and $eff^C_{AB}$ to represent the inverse of the *in degree centrality* measure, as shown in Eq. 1.

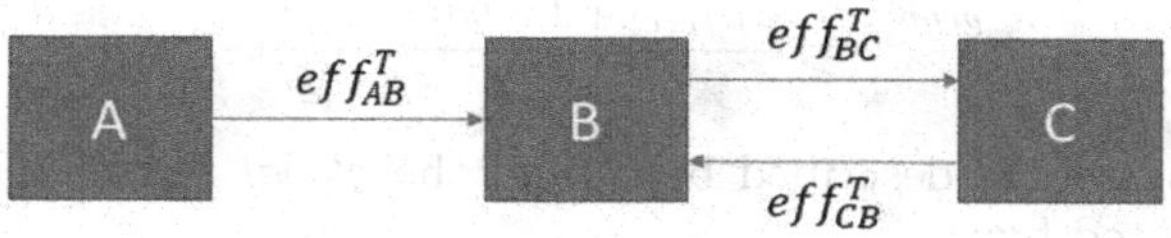


**Fig. 1.** Effect relationship

$$eff^T_{AB} = f(eff^I_{AB}, eff^C_{AB}), \tag{1}$$

where $eff^I_{AB} = \frac{1}{IDC^I_B}$, $eff^C_{AB} = \frac{1}{IDC^C_B}$.

### 3.1 Risk Analysis

The risk value $R$ associated with each STRIDE threat $t \in \{S, T, R, I, D, E\}$ for system $s$ is calculated by using the following formulas [22–24]:

$$Impact^s_t = \frac{Damage + Affectedsystems}{2}, \tag{2}$$

$$Likelihood^s_t = \frac{Reproducibility + Exploitability + Discoverability}{3}, \tag{3}$$

$$Risk^s_t = \frac{(Impact^s_t + Likelihood^s_t)}{2}. \tag{4}$$

$Impact^s_t$ describes the effect of a cyber attack realizing specific threat $t$ upon a component $s$, while $Likelihood^s_t$ describes the probability of the specific threat $t$ being realizing in $s$.

### 3.2 Risk Propagation

The *aggregate* risk $R_t^{agg_{c_j}}$ of component $c_j$ is calculated by using Eq. 5.

$$R_t^{agg_{c_j}} = \max(R_t^{dir_{c_j}}, R_t^{prop_{c_j}}), \tag{5}$$

where *direct* risk $R_t^{dir_{c_j}}$ is the risk of $c_j$ without considering the possible connections with other components and it is estimated using Eqs. (2)–(4), while the *propagated* risk $R_t^{prop_{c_j}}$ is calculated considering the connections to other components that $c_j$ has. The fraction of the impact that an event has on any $c_k$ on any path $p_l$ from $c_i$ to $c_j$ is represented by $eff_{p_l}^T$ and is calculated as

$$eff_{p_l}^T = \prod_{i=1}^{j-1} eff_{c_i c_{i+1}}^T. \tag{6}$$

The risk propagated over path $p_l$, originating at component $c_i$ and terminating at component $c_j$, is calculated by:

$$R_t^{prop_{c_j}^{p_l}} = \frac{eff_{c_i c_j}^{T_{p_l}} * Impact_t^{c_i} + L_t^{c_i}}{2}. \tag{7}$$

The whole system is described by $c_0$ and the *global* risk of threat $t$ for the system is calculated by:

$$R_t^s = R_t^{agg_{c_0}} = \max(R_t^{dir_{c_0}}, R_t^{prop_{c_0}}), \tag{8}$$

where the direct risk for the system is not applicable ($R_t^{dir_{c_0}} = 0$) and the propagated risk for the system is calculated as for any other node ($R_t^{prop_{c_0}} = \max_{p_l} R_t^{prop_{c_0}^{p_l}}$), thus

$$R_t^s = \max_{p_l} R_t^{prop_{c_0}^{p_l}} \tag{9}$$

Further details about the method used and the aforementioned equations are omitted in the interest of saving space and can be found in [1].

## 4 Attack Path Analysis

When the risk of each of a complex CPS components and the propagation of such risk through the interconnection of its components have been analyzed, it is feasible to identify critical attack paths that can potentially induce high risk to the system. Identified critical attack paths can be leveraged by system operators to enhance attack detection measures along the critical paths and to enhance the security of highly interconnected nodes.

The propagation of risk in the system through its components mainly depends on two factors: (a) the structure of the system and (b) the risk to each component. Conceptually, a system can be at high risk because of its components both because it has high risk components and because there exist high correlation paths along the system structure that may propagate such risk to the overall system.

The approach presented herein analyzes both factors, in order to detect critical attack paths. The approach aims at:

- Detecting critical attack paths according to the relationships (correlation) between components, and
- Prioritizing these paths according to the risk to each component in them.

The first step of the approach can be used to assess the risk propagation potential in a complex cyberphysical system, while the second can be used to gain additional insight, giving more information about the components of the system.

Initially the graph of the system is parsed from the system node backwards, to detect and collect paths that are characterized by a high product of the $eff_{c_i c_j}$ values of the nodes on the path (designated as $eff_{path}$) along the path. Algorithm 1 outputs a set of critical attack paths, i.e. attack paths that accumulate an $eff$ value larger than a threshold $eff_{limit}$.

**Algorithm 1:** Identification of critical attack paths

```
Result: Critical attack paths cps
Function process_node(c_j, eff, path):
    foreach edge from c_i to c_j do
        if c_i ∉ path then
            path = path ∪ {c_i};
            eff_path = eff_path * eff_{c_i c_j};
            if eff_path > eff_limit then
                cps = cps ∪ {path};
                process_node(c_i, eff_path, path);
            end
        end
    end
cps = {};
process_node(c_0, 1, {c_0});
```

The second step of the approach, described in Algorithm 2, prioritizes the attack paths that were identified in step 1, by considering the risk of each component in each path.

**Algorithm 2:** Prioritization of critical attack paths

```
Result: Prioritized critical attack paths pri_cps
Function calc_risk(path):
    R = (L_path[0] + I_path[0]) / 2;
    i = 0;
    eff = 1;
    while i < path_length do
        i = i + 1;
        eff = eff * eff_path[i],path[i-1];
        R = max(R, (L_path[i] + I_path[i] * eff) / 2)
    end
    return R;
Function select_paths(cps):
    foreach path in cps do
        R_path = calc_risk(path);
        if R_path > R_path^limit then
            pri_cps = pri_cps ∪ {path};
        end
    end
pri_cps = {};
select_paths();
```

# 5 Optimal Control Set Selection

## 5.1 Cybersecurity Controls

The proposed approach requires a pool of controls that are appropriate for the targeted system. The effectiveness of the controls depends on the effect that each control has per threat and per component $c_i$. The effect influences the values of $Impact_t^{c_i}$ and $Likelihood_t^{c_i}$ and hence the cyber-risk to the components and to the overall system.

An important feature of each control $m$ is the cost $Cost_m$ of its implementation. For a system with $N$ components and a list with $M$ controls with the cost vector $C = [cost_1, cost_2, ..., cost_M]$, the following binary matrix $AC$ compactly depicts the applied controls throughout the system:

$$AC = \begin{bmatrix} ac_{1,1} & ac_{1,2} & ... & ac_{1,N} \\ ac_{2,1} & ac_{2,2} & ... & ac_{2,N} \\ ... & ... & ... & ... \\ ac_{M,1} & ac_{M,2} & ... & ac_{M,N} \end{bmatrix}, \tag{10}$$

where

$$ac_{i,j} = \begin{cases} 0, \textit{if control i is not applied to component j} \\ 1, \textit{if control i is applied to component j} \end{cases}. \tag{11}$$

The total cost $TC_{AC}$ of the applied controls solution $AC$ is $TC_{AC} = AC * C$.

### 5.2 Selection of the Optimal Set

The approach in [1] produced a separate optimal set of controls for each STRIDE threat, and did not take into account that those controls could be possibly combined, to achieve a more efficient, from a global perspective, solution. For example the application of a single control to a specific component could result in reduction of the overall system risk for more than one threats, but this was not taken into account.

To remedy this, the present work proposes a cascading application of the genetic algorithm approach, in which each step (for each different threat) takes as granted that the controls that have been identified in the previous steps are, indeed, implemented. This approach enables the elicitation of controls that are effective for more than one threats. Therefore the selection is more efficient with respect to the global implementation cost. The proposed scheme supports the identification of the set of controls that minimizes the risk over all threats and the implementation cost for the system as a whole.

The concept upon which the approach is based is depicted in Fig. 2. After applying the genetic algorithm for each threat, the resulting controls are fixed in the set of available controls that is used as input for the rest of the threats. After all threats have been analyzed, the resulting controls are being unified as the optimal set of cyber-security controls for the system as a whole.

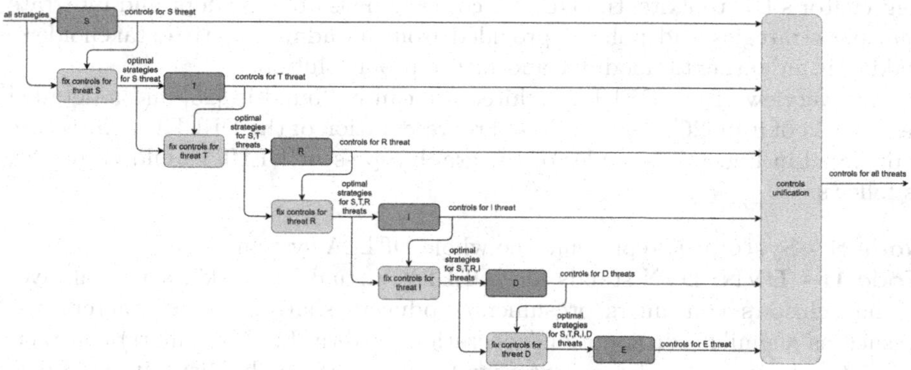


**Fig. 2.** Cascading GA process

The above methodology uses a global $AC^*$ matrix, which has fixed values for the combinations of components/controls that have been defined for all threats. Specifically, the $AC^*$ matrix is an instance of the $AC$ matrix defined in Eq. 10, each element $ac_{i,j}$ of which is related to the application of control $i$ to component $j$ and is:

- either a binary variable whose value can be set according to risk reduction and application cost.

- or a fixed value variable (equal to 1) if control $i$ has been decided to be applied to component $j$ for countering a threat analyzed previously.

This approach fixes the application of controls to components between different threats of the STRIDE model. It will only allow controls to be considered for threat T only if these further reduce the risk for threat $t_i$, given that controls decided for each threat $t_j, i > j$ have already been applied.

The proposed methodology is significantly more efficient in terms of application cost, while it retains residual risk on a similar level as the per threat analysis in [1].

## 6 DELTA System Use Case

### 6.1 The DELTA System

DELTA is the short title of the EU-funded H2020 R&D project "Future tamper-proof Demand rEsponse framework through seLf-configured, self-opTimized and collAborative virtual distributed energy nodes"[1]. DELTA has developed a demand-response management platform that distributes parts of the Aggregator's intelligence into lower layers of its architecture, in order to establish a more easily manageable and computationally efficient Demand-Response (DR) solution. This approach aims to introduce scalability and adaptivity into the Aggregator's DR toolkits; the DELTA core engine is able to adopt and integrate multiple strategies and policies provided from its administrative stakeholders, making it an authentic modular and future-proof solution.

An overview of the DELTA architecture can be found in [25] and a detailed description of it in [26]. A graph-based representation of the DELTA architecture is depicted in Fig. 3. The nodes of the graph represent DELTA building blocks, as follows:

**Node S - System:** it represents the whole DELTA system.

**Node D - DVN:** DVN stands for "DELTA Virtual Network", a virtual layer that clusters consumers/prosumers/producers sharing key characteristics, such as a similar consumption/generation pattern, kind of (smart) contract, existence (or not) of Energy Storage Systems (ESS); the disposition to participate into DR strategies; or their resulting behavior during a DR signal based on the award system, following the guidelines/strategies provided by the Aggregator.

**Node F - FEID:** FEIDs are actual devices which are connected to smart meters to measure energy-related data. Through an intelligent lightweight toolkit they compute real-time flexibility to provide as input to the DVN. FEIDs provide aggregated metering from multiple IoT devices that are connected to customer assets, and they report issuance and interpretation of OpenADR-based DR request signals.

[1] https://www.delta-h2020.eu/.

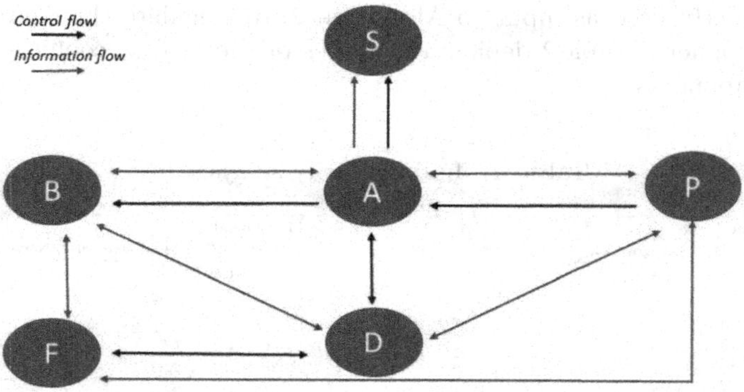


**Fig. 3.** DELTA components

**Node P - P2P Network:** it represents the communications backbone of the entire DELTA framework. The use of the peer-2-peer network guarantees a certain resilience to attacks/malfunctions, and greater modularity in the management of the tasks performed by each of the entities that make up DELTA. DELTA's P2P network allows the use of OpenADR to interface with FEIDS in order to manage DR requests and uses the OpenFIRE as a communication broker, in addition to implementing Access Controls security.

**Node A - Aggregators:** Aggregators are entities, generally TSOs or DSOs, which supply energy to users, but also acquire it from users known as *prosumers*. They balance network loads through DR or other traditional load shedding methods, and they collect data from smart meters for statistical purposes, control and pricing.

**Node B - Blockchain:** it is a block used to ensure the security of the energy information exchange within the DELTA energy network, enabling both energy data traceability and secure access for stakeholders. Technologies employed include certificates, blockchain, smart contracts, and state of the art security and privacy algorithms.

## 6.2 Risk Analysis

In order to apply the proposed approach, a risk analysis of the targeted system is required. To this end, the STRIDE [27] and DREAD [22] methodologies have been used. The *impact* and *likelihood* values for each of the STRIDE threats have been estimated and are depicted in Table 1. Each line of Table 1 represents one of the STRIDE threats, indicated by the corresponding initial (Spoofing, Tampering, Repudiation, Information Disclosure, Denial of Service, Elevation of privileges). Each column of Table 1 represents an individual DELTA component as described in Sect. 6.1. The values in the cells are the corresponding impact and likelihood values per STRIDE threat and per individual component; these have been calculated by means of Eqs. (2) and (3), respectively. These values are subsequently used as input to Algorithm 2, to calculate the aggregate risk of each component. Table 2 depicts the values of the $eff_{c_i c_j}$ coefficients for all pairs of components.

**Table 1.** Initial security analysis

| | System | Impact | | | | | System | Likelihood | | | | |
|---|---|---|---|---|---|---|---|---|---|---|---|---|
| | | FEID | DVN | Aggregator | P2PNetwork | Blockchain | | FEID | DVN | Aggregator | P2PNetwork | Blockchain |
| S | 0 | 1.5 | 2.5 | 2.5 | 2.5 | 1.5 | 0 | 2 | 1.66 | 2 | 1.66 | 1.66 |
| T | 0 | 1.5 | 2 | 2.5 | 2.5 | 1 | 0 | 2 | 1.33 | 1.66 | 2 | 1 |
| R | 0 | 1.5 | 1.5 | 2.5 | 2.5 | 1 | 0 | 2 | 1.33 | 2 | 2 | 1 |
| I | 0 | 1 | 1.5 | 1.5 | 2 | 1 | 0 | 1.66 | 1 | 1.66 | 1.33 | 1.66 |
| D | 0 | 2 | 3 | 1.5 | 3 | 2 | 0 | 2.33 | 1.66 | 2.33 | 3 | 1.66 |
| E | 0 | 1.5 | 2 | 2.5 | 2.5 | 1 | 0 | 1.66 | 1.66 | 2 | 1.66 | 1 |

**Table 2.** Effect coefficients

| | System | FEID | DVN | Aggregator | P2PNetwork | Blockchain |
|---|---|---|---|---|---|---|
| System | 0 | 0 | 0 | 0 | 0 | 0 |
| FEID | 0.3 | 0 | 0.1 | 0 | 0.3 | 0.3 |
| DVN | 0 | 0.2 | 0 | 0.2 | 0.2 | 0.2 |
| Aggregator | 0 | 0 | 0.1 | 0 | 0.2 | 0.2 |
| P2PNetwork | 0.3 | 0.3 | 0.3 | 0.3 | 0 | 0 |
| Blockchain | 0 | 0.3 | 0.3 | 0.3 | 0 | 0 |

### 6.3 Attack Path Analysis

The proposed attack path analysis methodology was subsequently applied to the DELTA system. The results of the first step of the approach (identification) are depicted in Table 3. Each line in Table 3 contains the path ID, the attack path, and the corresponding value of $eff_{path}$, calculated using the values of the effect coefficients in Table 2. The paths that can potentially enable the propagation of high risk to the system (hence they are the most critical) are the ones that are characterized by the highest $eff_{path}$ values; these are the first five paths of Table 3.

The results of the second step of the approach (prioritization) are depicted in Table 4. Each line in Table 4 contains the path ID, the attack path, and the corresponding value of the cyber-risk of the path, taken to be the highest among the risks of the nodes in the path, as in [1].

### 6.4 Selection of the Optimal Security Controls

In order to select the set of optimal controls we applied both the approach in our previous work [1] and the one proposed herein, to validate the claim that the

**Table 3.** List of attack paths

| Path ID | Affected CPSs | $eff_{path}$ |
|---|---|---|
| 1 | FEID → System | **0.3** |
| 2 | P2P Network → System | **0.3** |
| 3 | P2P Network → FEID → System | **0.09** |
| 4 | Blockchain → FEID → System | **0.09** |
| 5 | FEID → P2P Network → System | **0.09** |
| 6 | DVN → FEID → System | 0.06 |
| 7 | DVN → P2P Network → System | 0.06 |
| 8 | Aggregator → P2P Network → System | 0.06 |
| 9 | Blockchain → FEID → P2P Network → System | 0.027 |
| 10 | P2P Network → DVN → FEID → System | 0.018 |
| 11 | Blockchain → DVN → FEID → System | 0.018 |
| 12 | DVN → P2P Network → FEID → System | 0.018 |
| 13 | Aggregator → P2P Network → FEID → System | 0.018 |
| 14 | DVN → Blockchain → FEID → System | 0.018 |
| 15 | Aggregator → Blockchain → FEID → System | 0.018 |

latter is more effective and that it results in a larger ratio of reduction of risk vs control implementation cost. The controls in the NIST guidelines for Industrial Control Systems security [28] have been used as the pool of available controls. As in [1], the effectiveness and the cost of each security control are estimated on the basis of its applicability, the extent to which it reduces the impact or/and the likelihood, and the resources needed to implement it. Table 5 presents the results obtained with the initial method [1], whilst Table 6 presents the results obtained with the improved method proposed herein.

From these results it is obvious that the improved method proposed herein can produce the same effect with respect to residual risk for all threats, whilst it reduces the application cost from 70 to 61. In other words, the improved method increases the risk reduction per application cost ratio by 12.9%. We note that the selected controls differ between the two executions, because of the different approach used, but also because there exist multiple controls that have the same effect, and it is normal for the proposed (randomized search) approach to randomly choose among those in each run.

**Table 4.** Prioritized attack paths per threat and risk level

| | Attack path | Cyber risk |
|---|---|---|
| Path ID | Spoofing | |
| 2 | P2P Network → System | 1.45 |
| 1 | FEID → System | 1.225 |
| 3 | P2P Network → FEID → System | 1.135 |
| 4 | Blockchain → FEID → System | 1.135 |
| Path ID | Tampering | |
| 2 | P2P Network → System | 1.375 |
| 1 | FEID → System | 1.225 |
| 3 | P2P Network → FEID → System | 1.1125 |
| 8 | Aggregator → P2P Network → System | 1.09 |
| Path ID | Repudiation | |
| 2 | P2P Network → System | 1.375 |
| 1 | FEID → System | 1.225 |
| 3 | P2P Network → FEID → System | 1.1125 |
| 8 | Aggregator → P2P Network → System | 1.09 |
| Path ID | Information disclosure | |
| 1 | FEID → System | 1.54 |
| 2 | P2P Network → System | 1.45 |
| 5 | FEID → P2P Network → System | 1.2775 |
| 6 | DVN → FEID → System | 1.24 |
| Path ID | Denial of service | |
| 1 | FEID → System | 1.45 |
| 2 | P2P Network → System | 1.45 |
| 3 | P2P Network → FEID → System | 1.135 |
| 5 | FEID → P2P Network → System | 1.135 |
| Path ID | Elevation of privileges | |
| 2 | P2P Network → System | 1.615 |
| 1 | FEID → System | 1.465 |
| 3 | P2P Network → FEID → System | 1.3 |
| 5 | FEID → P2P Network → System | 1.255 |

**Table 5.** Optimal cybersecurity controls - per threat

| | Initial global risk | Cybersecurity controls | Residual global risk | Overall cost |
|---|---|---|---|---|
| Component | Spoofing | | | |
| Aggregator | 1.3 | Awareness and training | 0.864 | 14 |
| P2P | | Awareness and training | | |
| DVN | | Security assessment and authorization | | |
| BC | | Security assessment and authorization | | |
| FEID | | Configuration management | | |
| Component | Tampering | | | |
| BC | 1.3 | Access control | 0.65 | 17 |
| P2P | | Security assessment and authorization | | |
| Aggregator | | Risk assessment | | |
| FEID | | System and services acquisition | | |
| DVN | | System and communications protection | | |
| Component | Repudiation | | | |
| DVN | 1.3 | Security assessment and authorization | 0.864 | 6 |
| Aggregator | | Security assessment and authorization | | |
| P2P | | Security assessment and authorization | | |
| FEID | | Maintenance | | |
| Component | Information disclosure | | | |
| BC | 1.514 | Privacy controls | 0.65 | 17 |
| FEID | | Security assessment and authorization | | |
| P2P | | Planning | | |
| DVN | | System and services acquisition | | |
| Aggregator | | System and services acquisition | | |
| DVN | | System and information integrity | | |
| Component | Denial of service | | | |
| FEID | 1.3 | Security assessment and authorization | 0.65 | 7 |
| DVN | | Security assessment and authorization | | |
| Aggregator | | Security assessment and authorization | | |
| P2P | | Risk assessment | | |
| BC | | System and communication protection l | | |
| Component | Elevation of privileges | | | |
| P2P | 1.514 | Audit and accountability | 1.079 | 9 |
| BC | | Audit and accountability | | |
| DVN | | Security assessment and Authorization | | |
| Aggregator | | Security assessment and authorization | | |
| FEID | | Risk assessment | | |
| | | | | **Overall cost** |
| | | | | 70 |

**Table 6.** Optimal cybersecurity controls - global

| | Initial global risk | Cybersecurity controls | Residual global risk | Cost per threat |
|---|---|---|---|---|
| Component | Spoofing | | | |
| P2P | 1.3 | Awareness and training | 0.864 | 16 |
| DVN | | Configuration management | | |
| FEID | | Identification and authentication | | |
| BC | | Identification and authentication | | |
| Aggregator | | Incident response | | |
| Component | Tampering | | | |
| P2P | 1.3 | Audit and accountability | 0.65 | 20 |
| DVN | | Security assessment and authorization | | |
| FEID | | Configuration management | | |
| Aggregator | | Identification and authentication | | |
| Aggregator | | Risk assessment | | |
| BC | | System and communications protection | | |
| Component | Repudiation | | | |
| Aggregator | 1.3 | Audit and accountability | 0.864 | 3 |
| P2P | | Audit and accountability | | |
| FEID | | Configuration management | | |
| DVN | | Configuration management | | |
| Component | Information disclosure | | | |
| BC | 1.514 | Access control | 0.65 | 13 |
| Aggregator | | Audit and accountability | | |
| FEID | | Configuration management | | |
| DVN | | Configuration management | | |
| P2P | | Maintenance | | |
| FEID | | Risk assessment | | |
| DVN | | System and services acquisition | | |
| Component | Denial of service | | | |
| P2P | 1.3 | Awareness and training | 0.65 | 3 |
| P2P | | Audit and accountability | | |
| FEID | | Security assessment and authorization | | |
| DVN | | Security assessment and authorization | | |
| FEID | | Configuration management | | |
| DVN | | Configuration management | | |
| Aggregator | | Incident response | | |
| BC | | System and communications protection | | |
| Component | Elevation of privileges | | | |
| P2P | 1.514 | Audit and accountability | 1.079 | 6 |
| BC | | Audit and accountability | | |
| DVN | | Security assessment and authorization | | |
| FEID | | Configuration management | | |
| DVN | | Configuration management | | |
| FEID | | Contingency planning | | |
| Aggregator | | Incident response | | |
| | | | | **Overall cost** |
| | | | | 61 |

## 7 Conclusions

The increasing dependence of critical infrastructures, such as power grids, on interconnected CPSs increases the attack surface and makes them prone to cyberattacks. The analysis of attack paths facilitates the comprehensive understanding of the attack propagation towards the selection of the most appropriate security controls. By leveraging the proposed methods for attack path analysis and optimal control selection, all the elements of cyber risk can be studied, towards defining a security architecture. As future work we intend to develop an automated tool that supports the proposed methods. Additionally, the utilization of the proposed approaches in several instances of the DELTA system will facilitate the development of secure power grids.

## References


1. Kavallieratos, G., Spathoulas, G., Katsikas, S.: Cyber risk propagation and optimal selection of cybersecurity controls for complex cyberphysical systems. Sensors **21**(5), 1691 (2021)
2. Tsolakis, A.C., et al.: A secured and trusted demand response system based on blockchain technologies. In: 2018 Innovations in Intelligent Systems and Applications (INISTA), pp. 1–6 (2018)
3. Stellios, I., Kotzanikolaou, P., Psarakis, M., Alcaraz, C., Lopez, J.: A survey of IoT-enabled cyberattacks: assessing attack paths to critical infrastructures and services. IEEE Commun. Surv. Tutor. **20**(4), 3453–3495 (2018)
4. Macola, I.G.: The five worst cyberattacks against the power industry since 2014 (2020). https://www.power-technology.com/features/the-five-worst-cyberattacks-against-the-power-industry-since2014/. Accessed 20 July 2021
5. Vellaithurai, C., Srivastava, A., Zonouz, S., Berthier, R.: CPIndex: cyber-physical vulnerability assessment for power-grid infrastructures. IEEE Trans. Smart Grid **6**(2), 566–575 (2014)
6. Kavallieratos, G., Katsikas, S.: Attack path analysis for cyber physical systems. In: Katsikas, S., et al. (eds.) CyberICPS/SECPRE/ADIoT 2020. LNCS, vol. 12501, pp. 19–33. Springer, Cham (2020). https://doi.org/10.1007/978-3-030-64330-0_2
7. Xie, A., Cai, Z., Tang, C., Hu, J., Chen, Z.: Evaluating network security with two-layer attack graphs. In: 2009 Annual Computer Security Applications Conference, pp. 127–136. IEEE (2009)
8. Ou, X., Boyer, W.F., McQueen, M.A.: A scalable approach to attack graph generation. In: Proceedings of the 13th ACM Conference on Computer and Communications Security, pp. 336–345 (2006)
9. Lippmann, R.P., Ingols, K.W.: An annotated review of past papers on attack graphs (2005)
10. Cheh, C., Keefe, K., Feddersen, B., Chen, B., Temple, W.G., Sanders, W.H.: Developing models for physical attacks in cyber-physical systems. In: Proceedings of the 2017 Workshop on Cyber-Physical Systems Security and Privacy, pp. 49–55 (2017)
11. Mouratidis, H., Diamantopoulou, V.: A security analysis method for industrial internet of things. IEEE Trans. Industr. Inf. **14**(9), 4093–4100 (2018)
12. Stellios, I., Kotzanikolaou, P., Grigoriadis, C.: Assessing IoT enabled cyber-physical attack paths against critical systems. Comput. Secur. **107**, 102316 (2021)
13. Liang, X., Wu, Y., Ni, M., Li, M.: Survivability index and evaluation framework for cyber physical power systems. In: 2020 12th IEEE PES Asia-Pacific Power and Energy Engineering Conference (APPEEC), pp. 1–5. IEEE (2020)

14. Malik, A.A., Tosh, D.K.: Quantitative risk modeling and analysis for large-scale cyber-physical systems. In: 2020 29th International Conference on Computer Communications and Networks (ICCCN), pp. 1–6. IEEE (2020)
15. Qu, Z., et al.: Power cyber-physical system risk area prediction using dependent Markov chain and improved grey wolf optimization. IEEE Access **8**, 82844–82854 (2020)
16. Potteiger, B., Martins, G., Koutsoukos, X.: Software and attack centric integrated threat modeling for quantitative risk assessment. In: Proceedings of the Symposium and Bootcamp on the Science of Security, pp. 99–108 (2016)
17. Guo, J., Xu, J., He, Z., Liao, W.: Research on risk propagation method of multimodal transport network under uncertainty. Physica A **563**, 125494 (2021)
18. Guo, R., Tian, J., Wang, B., Shang, F.: Cyber-physical attack threats analysis for UAVs from cps perspective. In: 2020 International Conference on Computer Engineering and Application (ICCEA), pp. 259–263. IEEE (2020)
19. Tang, L., Jing, K., He, J., Stanley, H.E.: Complex interdependent supply chain networks: cascading failure and robustness. Physica A **443**, 58–69 (2016)
20. Chattopadhyay, S., Dai, H.: Estimation of robustness of interdependent networks against failure of nodes. In: 2016 IEEE Global Communications Conference (GLOBECOM), pp. 1–6. IEEE (2016)
21. Parandehgheibi, M., Modiano, E.: Robustness of interdependent networks: the case of communication networks and the power grid. In: 2013 IEEE Global Communications Conference (GLOBECOM), pp. 2164–2169. IEEE (2013)
22. Microsoft: Chapter 3 - threat modeling (2010). https://docs.microsoft.com/en-us/previous-versions/msp-n-p/ff648644(v=pandp.10)?redirectedfrom=MSDN
23. Langweg, H., Zinsmaier, S.D., Waldvogel, M.: A practical approach to stakeholder-driven determination of security requirements based on the GDPR and common criteria. In: Proceedings of the 6th International Conference on Information Systems Security and Privacy (ICISSP 2020), pp. 473–480 (2020)
24. Kavallieratos, G., Katsikas, S.: Managing cyber security risks of the cyber-enabled ship. J. Marine Sci. Eng. **8**(10), 768 (2020)
25. Patsonakis, C., Terzi, S., Moschos, I., Ioannidis, D., Votis, K., Tzovaras, D.: Permissioned blockchains and virtual nodes for reinforcing trust between aggregators and prosumers in energy demand response scenarios. In: 2019 IEEE International Conference on Environment and Electrical Engineering and 2019 IEEE Industrial and Commercial Power Systems Europe (EEEIC/I CPS Europe), pp. 1–6 (2019)
26. Psara, K., et al.: DELTA Overall Framework Architecture v2 (2020). https://www.delta-h2020.eu/wp-content/uploads/2020/06/DELTA_D1.6_Final.pdf
27. Shostack, A.: Threat Modeling: Designing for Security. Wiley, New York (2014)
28. Stouffer, K., Pillitteri, V., Marshall, A., Hahn, A.: Guide to industrial control systems (ICS) security. NIST Spec. Publ. **800**(82), 247 (2015)

# Analysis of Cyber Security Features in Industry 4.0 Maturity Models

Antonio João Gonçalves de Azambuja[1,2](✉), Alexander Kern[2](✉), and Reiner Anderl[2](✉)

[1] Technological Institute of Aeronautics - ITA, São José dos Campos, Brazil
azambuja@ita.br

[2] Technische Universität Darmstadt, Otto-Berndt-Straße 2, 64287 Darmstadt, Germany
{kern,anderl}@dik.tu-darmstadt.de

**Abstract.** The increasing digitization and networking of machines and plants has been leading to significant changes in the industrial sector for several years. Particularly in combination with the Internet and other disruptive technologies such as cloud computing, many opportunities and new business models are emerging. This change in industry is subsumed under the term Industry 4.0 and represents an important basis for the future economic success of many companies, especially small and medium-sized manufacturing companies. However, there are also many risks associated with this transformation, particularly with regard to cyber security. Against the backdrop of increasing dependence on networked information technology, the attack surface of companies is increasing. To address the problem, executives need to know the current state of their companies' security maturity. To this end, it is necessary to assess the negative impact on business caused by cyber security attacks in Industry 4.0. So-called maturity models are useful instruments for this purpose. However, it has not yet been thoroughly investigated which maturity models from the literature can be used to assess cyber security in the context of Industrie 4.0 technologies. We have therefore developed a methodology to identify maturity models related to Industrie 4.0 and analyze them with respect to their applicability in the cyber security context. The aim is to use the analysis to identify maturity models most relevant to industry for the cross-sectional topic of cyber security in Industrie 4.0. The results can then be used by companies when integrating security strategies into their own corporate strategy.

**Keywords:** Industry 4.0 · Cyber security · Maturity models

## 1 Introduction

The term Industry 4.0 originated in Germany in 2011 as part of a state strategy to make the country a technology leader and strengthen its global competitiveness. Historically, the 1st Industrial Revolution emerged with the use of water and steam power in production. In the 2nd Industrial Revolution, mass production applications were developed with the use of electric power. The 3rd Industrial Revolution was based on the use of electronic components to automate manufacturing. The 4th Industrial Revolution, called Industry


S. Katsikas et al. (Eds.): ESORICS 2021 Workshops, LNCS 13106, pp. 91–106, 2022.
https://doi.org/10.1007/978-3-030-95484-0_6

4.0, can be characterized by the increasing digitization and interconnection of machines and production systems in industrial manufacturing [1, 2].

Industry 4.0 based on the digitization and interconnection of all production units creates opportunities for competitiveness with efficient, collaborative and sustainable systems in industrial manufacturing. In addition to the opportunities provided by Industry 4.0, many new challenges arise for companies, especially for small and medium-sized enterprises (SMEs) [3]. SMEs are key players in the economy, with a strong capacity to generate jobs and contribute to the gross domestic product [4]. Although Industry 4.0 offers great potential for SMEs, the lack of a methodological framework for these companies to deal with the new concepts of digitization and interconnection of machines is a limitation to exploit this potential.

The complexity of networked digital systems brings with it risks that these companies lack the structure to manage, especially those related to cyber security issues [5, 6]. The digitization of operational processes and business models brings with it greater exposure to possible cyber-attacks [7]. The increasing reliance on information technology interconnected with the use of the Internet is significantly increasing the attack surface [8–10]. Protection against cyber-attacks requires a strategic vision from top management to mitigate security risks and optimize the opportunities of Industry 4.0.

Cyber security is high on the agenda of business leaders, creating the need to assess the maturity of security measures in the company. Proactively addressing cyber security issues is a key factor in strengthening business competitiveness [11]. Cyber-attacks on manufacturing systems lead to productivity losses and have a negative impact on business which can result in loss of competitiveness [12]. Cyber security strategies in a digitized and interconnected environment must be sound, stable, resilient, mature, and must be integrated into the business strategy to ensure security across all links in the manufacturing value chain rather than being limited to individual technologies [13].

For authors Yagiz et al. [14], maturity models related to Industry 4.0 are useful tools to identify specific measures to maximize the benefits of digital transformation. Maturity models enable companies to monitor and assess organizational elements such as weaknesses, strengths and opportunities [15]. In the literature, maturity models for both Industry 4.0 as well as cyber security can be found. Maturity models for Industry 4.0 mostly focus on technologies, processes, knowledge, and sustainability, with a rather holistic view. Examples are presented in the works: Development of an Assessment Model for Industry 4.0 [16], Acatech Study Industrie 4.0 Maturity Index [17], Impuls – Industrie 4.0 Readiness, Industry 4.0 – Digital Operations Self-Assessment, and Industry 4.0 Maturity Model [14].

Cyber security maturity models aim at implementing and managing security practices associated with information technology assets, technology operations, and their operating environment. Some of these models try to incorporate adaptations and modifications for use in industry. Some examples are the Cyber security Capability Maturity Model, the Systems Security Engineering Capability Maturity Model and the Information Security Management Maturity Model [18]. However, it was never assessed to what extend any of these models can be used for the evaluation of the Cyber Security Maturity in an Industry 4.0 environment. With that, in the literature review, a research gap was found, regarding specific maturity models for assessing the current state of cyber security in companies engaged in Industry 4.0.

Given this gap and the relevance of cyber security for Industry 4.0, this paper aims to analyze the maturity models of Industry 4.0 to identify their characteristics that can be used to manage the security of information assets in interconnected manufacturing environments in SMEs. To this end, it is necessary to evaluate the adverse impacts on business arising from cyber-attacks in the context of Industry 4.0. These impacts can reduce competitive advantage, damage the company's image and reputation, and cause financial costs for the recovery of systems affected by cyber-attacks. Therefore, the analysis of cyber security maturity models adapted for industry becomes relevant. The results of the analysis can support companies in assessing the current state of cyber security in the Industry 4.0 environment, for the integration of security strategies into their business strategy.

The article first addresses theoretical background of the concepts to support the research. Next, it discusses the methodological approach of the study. After that, it presents the analysis and discussion of the maturity models of Industry 4.0, the cyber security models, business implications and the related works identified in the literature. Finally, the conclusion closes the article.

## 2 Theoretical Background

This section discusses a number of concepts and requirements specific to SMEs, cyber security, Industry 4.0, and related maturity models.

### 2.1 Small and Medium-Sized Enterprises (SMEs)

SMEs are considered an important part of economic development and job creation. The benefits of these companies are not only limited to economic aspects, but also have positive impacts on society and human well-being [19]. Technological changes enable new opportunities for these companies [4]. Industry 4.0 technologies offer advantages for the sector to increase its competitiveness by transforming traditional factories into smart factories with significant potential.

The shift from the traditional system to Industry 4.0 requires knowledge and action plans to structure their organizational capacity [3]. SMEs need to adopt standardized strategies and approaches with industry-specific solutions. The transfer of knowledge about Industry 4.0 technologies to these companies represents a challenge for the sector, with implications for the entire economy. Despite the potential of Industry 4.0 for SMEs, the lack of methodological frameworks is a limiting factor for its implementation. For SMEs, the question is not whether or not to migrate to Industry 4.0, but how to do it in a structured way to gain competitive advantage [2].

In 2016, the authors Ganzarain and Errasti were the first to discuss the use of maturity models to support the implementation of Industry 4.0 in SMEs [20]. Specific maturity and readiness models for SMEs appeared as early as 2018, published by Wiesner et al. and Jones et al. [21, 22]. Studies related to cyber security for the SMEs present security weakness as a gap that affects the ability of companies to innovate. This fact reinforces the need for an assessment of cyber security maturity for SMEs.

## 2.2 Cyber Security

Technological advancements have brought companies to a point where equipment is connected through computer networks, both internally and externally. Such networks require security to cope with cyber-attacks, which are increasingly present in cyberspace [7]. Cyber security is one of the main challenges for companies as the disruptive concepts of digital transformation applied in Industry 4.0 has become a reality in the industrial environment [23]. Digital manufacturing makes use of the Industrial Internet of Things (IIoT), cloud computing, machine learning, and advanced robotics to improve production competitiveness and optimize financial resources. However, this technological architecture makes the manufacturing sector more vulnerable to cyber-attacks that are aimed to gain access to the system's services, resources, or information of the systems in an attempt to compromise their confidentiality, integrity, or availability [24].

Industrial control systems (ICS), followed by equipment used for IIoT and sensors actuators are considered critical assets in terms of cyber security in Industry 4.0, according to a study conducted by the European Network and Information Security Agency (ENISA) in 2018 [25]. ICS enable industrial automation by controlling and monitoring business processes. IIoT equipment manages multiple technologies using different communication protocols and enables the analysis and control of production data in real time. Sensors provide information of the systems' parameters and perform specific actions on them [26]. Among the possible attacks in the context of digital manufacturing are: i) unauthorized access actions; ii) actions to make the information technology infrastructure unavailable; iii) actions to relay and alter messages between machines and remote control systems; iv) actions to disseminate malicious software in manufacturing systems; and v) actions to manipulate data [7].

In the period from 2010 to 2020 entities such as the European Cyber Security Organization (ECSO) and ENISA have released cyber security standards and guidance documents for Industry 4.0: i) ISA/IEC 62443 (2016); ii) IACS Cyber security Certification Framework (2018); iii) ANSSI Cyber security for Industrial Control System (2014); iv) API Standard 1164 (2016); v) ICS Compendium (2013); vi) Catalog of Control Systems Security (2011); vii) ISC-CERT Assessments (2016); and viii) NIST-800-82 (2015) [12].

## 2.3 Industry 4.0

The incorporation of digital technologies, as well as the integration of physical and digital components, is a defining characteristic of Industry 4.0. This integration allows greater data capture, transport, storage, and analysis. Interconnected products, machines and plants become sources of data and information that support decision making [27]. Industry 4.0 encompasses a set of technologies based on digitization and interconnection that allows to increase production efficiency, productivity, quality, operational flexibility and integration of the production system with customers and the supply chain [28, 29]. New technologies in industrial manufacturing, such as global networks, cloud computing, IIoT, and the 5G networks of the future have driven continuous growth in connectivity, while simultaneously bringing risks to the data and information technology infrastructures. These must be effectively managed to create a reliable industrial environment resilient to cyber-attacks [7].

Major industrialized nations have focused on the development of Industry 4.0 as a strategic industrial policy tool to increase their competitiveness. Several countries have created programs to promote the development and adoption of Industry 4.0 technologies. In Germany, the High-Tech Strategy 2020 program was created with incentives for companies to seek leadership in technological innovation as an integral part of the Industry 4.0 concept. In the United States, the Advanced Manufacturing Partnership program was implemented, in China the Made in China 2025 program, in France the La Nouvelle France Industrielle program and in Brazil the Profuturo - Science, Technology and Innovation Plan (CT&I) for Advanced Manufacturing based on the National Strategy of Science, Technology and Innovation (MCTI) - 2016 to 2022 [1, 31–34].

These initiatives aim to disseminate the concepts and technologies of Industry 4.0 in companies, both in developed and emerging countries. The adoption of advanced technologies by companies in emerging countries that have an industrial base of SMEs, is challenging. The economies of these countries have historically been focused on the extraction and commercialization of commodities. As a result, companies in emerging countries lag behind in terms of technology adoption and investment. Additionally, factors such as the information and communication technology infrastructure, culture, education levels, as well as economic and political instability also influence the perceived value of technology investments [27, 35]. Current literature addresses various opportunities and challenges faced by SMEs, emphasizing the importance of information management for these companies in the manufacturing context [36, 37].

The development of Industry 4.0 opens the way for this new business environment and requires companies' strategies to structure the transition to this ecosystem [38, 39]. The new paradigm enables the development of new innovative business models. Production based on Industry 4.0 technologies creates the conditions to replace the traditional production structure by reconfigurable manufacturing systems and flexible logistics, offering interactive and collaborative decision-making processes [40]. Industry 4.0 seeks to implement efficient and automated manufacturing processes in an industrial environment where customer-specific products are produced in a cost-optimized manner according to mass customization strategies, with cost optimization [41].

According to the Acatech Study Industrie 4.0 Maturity Index - Update 2020, the economic potential of Industry 4.0 lies in accelerating decision making in the corporate context and adapting of processes to increased efficiency in the area of engineering, manufacturing, service, sales and marketing with a focus on business units or business model changes. In this context, digital transformation aims to create a company that is adaptive and agile to continuously adapt to change. Agility is a strategic characteristic that is becoming important and necessary for successful companies [17].

## 2.4 Maturity Models

Maturity models are useful to guide an organization in the development of processes to improve its maturity level in the area the model was developed for [42]. Typically, a maturity model consists of two components. The first one looks for a way to measure and describe the evolution of a domain by showing a hierarchical progress. The second one establishes criteria to measure the processes. These components provide a sequence of maturity levels for a class of domains [43]. Therefore, a maturity model provides a reference for the organization to assess the current level of capability for its domains and practices, and thus to define improvement objectives and priorities [18].

For Mettler (2011), the maturity models focus on assessing people, culture, processes, structures, and technologies. They provide a knowledge base for assessing maturity progress, with metrics organized into categories that are quantified on a performance scale [44]. For an organization to advance to a higher level, it must perform the practices at that level and its predecessor level [45]. The levels of a maturity model can be sequenced in ascending order from initial, repeatable, defined, managed and optimized [15, 46]. In short, maturity models act as a tool that can be used to describe the progression of desired change using ascending levels [47].

Industry 4.0 enables a shift to new business formats with impacts on the value proposition, making top management sponsorship of investment projects essential. It requires a holistic perspective on the company's strategy and operations. In this sense, a maturity model is suitable for companies planning to understand their maturity level in the context of Industry 4.0 [14]. Readiness models are more or less synonymous with maturity models. The difference between the models is explained by the fact that readiness models state whether or not the organization is ready to start the development process. Maturity models, on the other hand, show the current maturity level of the organization for one or more domains. The lack of a structure for companies to assess their ability to implement the new technologies of Industry 4.0, turns out to be a challenge that must be overcome in order to succeed and gain competitiveness [23].

## 3 Methodology

To meet the objective of the article a methodology with four steps was developed to identify the maturity models of Industry 4.0 and cyber security in the literature. The steps are described in the following:

**Step 1 - Data Collection:** The collection sources were the Web of Science and Scopus databases, as they are consolidated databases. The choice of the databases was based on the following aspects: i) the databases allow retrieving a greater diversification of metadata relevant to research; ii) searches can be by topic, title, author, abstract, keywords, year of publication, country, research area, name of publication and publisher; and iii) the databases provide contributions in the production of indicators, by indexing scientific journals. The keywords used in the search were: Industry 4.0, Cyber Security and Maturity Model in the period from 2015 to 2020. Table 1 presents the results of the search.

The total number of publications was 297. Only two of those were concerned with all three topics. These publications are listed in Table 2.

**Step 2 - Applying Filters:** Initially a filter was applied to exclude repeated publications. From a total of 297 publications, 94 repeated publications were identified, leaving a residual of 203 publications. Next, a second filter was applied to identify the publications that contained at least one of the keywords in the title: Industry 4.0, Cyber Security and Maturity Model. With this filter the number of publications decreased to 89. To identify publications related to SMEs, a third filter was applied, resulting in 15 publications. Table 3 lists these publications.

**Table 1.** Search results

| Query | Web of Science | Scopus |
|---|---|---|
| "Industry 4.0" and "Maturity Model" | 95 | 32 |
| "Industry 4.0" and "Cyber Security" | 56 | 13 |
| "Cyber Security" and "Maturity Model" | 16 | 15 |
| "Cyber Security" and "Industry 4.0" | 55 | 13 |
| "Industry 4.0" and "Cyber Security" and "Maturity Model" | 1 | 1 |
| Total | 223 | 74 |

**Table 2.** Query results - "Industry 4.0" and "Cyber Security" and "Maturity Model"

| Article title | Authors/Year |
|---|---|
| Metamodel of indexes and maturity models for Industry 4.0 readiness in enterprises | Basl, Josef and Doucek, Petr (2018) |
| Integration of cyber security frameworks, models and approaches for building design principles for the Internet-of-Things in Industry 4.0 | Radanliev, P.; De Roure, D.; Nurse, J. R. C.; Nicolescu, R.; Huth, M.; Cannady, S. and Montalvo, R. M. (2018) |

**Step 3 - Selected Publications:** In this step, a critical reading of the material identified in the second step was conducted, considering the research gap of specific maturity models to assess the current state of cyber security in companies inserted in Industry 4.0. The reading made it possible to identify Industry 4.0 maturity models that address cyber security issues in their dimensions.

**Step 4 - Analysis and Discussion:** In this step, the models selected in the third step are discussed to analyze the security characteristics for enterprises on their way toward Industry 4.0. Before analyzing the models, the next section discusses the representativeness of the identified publications.

## 4 Validation of the Selected Publications

This section presents the publications related to the research theme and an overview of the representativeness of the keywords used in the papers. To confirm the relevance of the selected publications, an analysis of the representativeness of the keywords used in the publications was performed. Keywords are defined by authors to attract readers, with general, intermediate or specific terms about the research [48]. The analysis of keywords provides information about the merit of the research topic [49]. The larger circle reflects the representativeness of the keywords in a cluster [50]. Figure 1 shows

**Table 3.** Query results - "Industry 4.0" and "Cyber Security" and "Maturity Model"

| No. | Article title | Authors | Year |
|---|---|---|---|
| 1 | The smart SME technology readiness assessment methodology in the context of industry 4.0 | Saad, SM; Bahadori, R; Jafarnejad, H | 2021 |
| 2 | Defining SMEs' 4.0 Readiness Indicators | Chonsawat, N; Sopadang, A | 2020 |
| 3 | Analysis of readiness factors for Industry 4.0 implementation in SMEs using COPRAS | Sriram, RM; Vinodh, S | 2021 |
| 4 | Process model for the successful implementation and demonstration of SME-based industry 4.0 showcases in global production networks | Peukert, S; Trebel, S; Balz, S; Haefner, B; Lanza, G | 2020 |
| 5 | Digital readiness assessment of Italian SMEs: a case-study research | Pirola, F; Cimini, C; Pinto, R | 2020 |
| 6 | A smart manufacturing adoption framework for SMEs | Mittal, S; Khan, MA; Purohit, JK; Menon, K; Romero, D; Wuest, T | 2020 |
| 7 | Evaluation of proceedings for SMEs to conduct I4.0 projects | Schmitt, P; Schmitt, J; Engelmann, B | 2019 |
| 8 | Deriving essential components of lean and industry 4.0 assessment model for manufacturing SMEs | Kolla, S; Minufekr, M; Plapper, P | 2019 |
| 9 | Planning Guideline and Maturity Model for Intra-logistics 4.0 in SME | Krowas, K; Riedel, R | 2019 |
| 10 | A critical review of smart manufacturing & Industry 4.0 maturity models: Implications for small and medium-sized enterprises (SMEs) | Mittal, S; Khan, MA; Romero, D; Wuest, T | 2018 |
| 11 | Change Made in Shop Floor Management to Transform a Conventional Production System into an Industry 4.0 Case studies in SME automotive production manufacturing | Moica, S; Ganzarain, J; Ibarra, D; Ferencz, P | 2018 |
| 12 | Maturity Models for Digitalization in Manufacturing - Applicability for SMEs | Wiesner, S; Gaiardelli, P; Gritti, N; Oberti, G | 2018 |
| 13 | Towards a Smart Manufacturing Maturity Model for SMEs ((SME)-E-3) | Mittal, S; Romero, D; Wuest, T | 2018 |
| 14 | Barnelkar: A Collaborative University-Industry Learning Experience To Boost Diversification Strategy In SMEs | Ganzarain, J; Igartua, JI; Errasti, N | 2016 |
| 15 | Three Stage Maturity Model in SME's towards Industry 4.0 | Ganzarain, J; Errasti, N | 2016 |

the representativeness of the keywords used in the 89 publications selected by applying the second filter in the second step of the methodology.

The keywords "Industry 4.0", "Cyber Security" and "Maturity Model" compose a cluster in green color. Clusters are groups that are formed by affinity or proximity. In the figure below, the connecting lines of the keywords used are thicker, indicating a stronger relationship between these terms compared to the others.

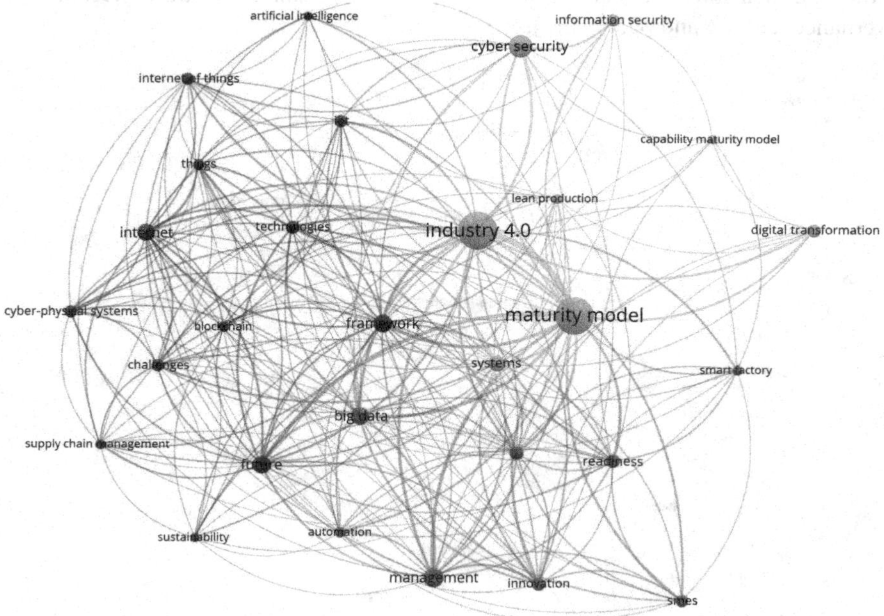


**Fig. 1.** Keywords of the publications identified with the second filter

Figure 2 shows a visualization of the correlation of the keywords of the 15 publications presented in Table 3. The keyword "Maturity Model" is in a separate cluster from the keyword "Industry 4.0", indicating little relation between the terms in these publications. The map analysis did not identify the terms "Cyber Security", "Cyber-Security", or "Cybersecurity" among the 15 publications, which may indicate a gap in the literature regarding cyber security in SMEs.

Transferring knowledge to these companies is a challenge for the industry. Despite the importance of security for companies in the Industry 4.0 ecosystem, the lack of methodological frameworks on cyber security is a limiting factor for SMEs. As already mentioned, the question is not whether or not to migrate to Industry 4.0, but how to do it in a structured way to gain a competitive advantage [2].

Next, this section discusses the publications related to the research topic. First the work of Mittal et al. (2018) was consulted, which critically discusses Industry 4.0 maturity models, analyzes their adaptation to meet the specific requirements of SMEs, and identifies research gaps that need to be considered to support the success of these companies in the context of Industry 4.0 [37]. The work of the authors Yagiz et. al. (2017) emphasizes the importance of top management involvement in defining organizational and operational strategies. For the authors, a maturity model is indicated to structure the transformation planning of business and operations to Industry 4.0 [14]. Schumacher et al. (2016) propose in their paper "A Maturity Model for Assessing Industry 4.0 Readiness and Maturity of Manufacturing Enterprises" a maturity model with the following dimensions: products, customers, operations, technology, strategy, leadership, governance, culture and people [23].

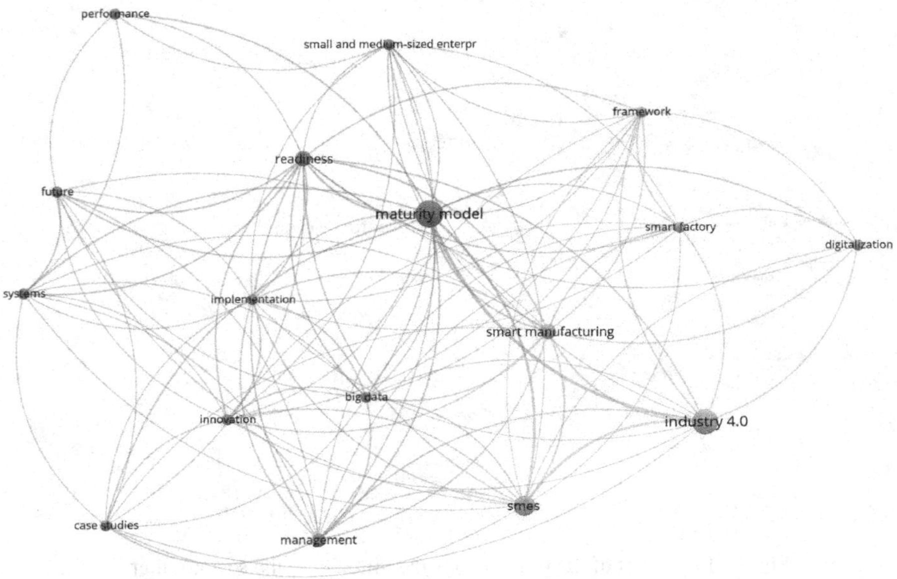


**Fig. 2.** Keywords from SMEs publications

Articles addressing cyber security maturity models focus on assessing adverse impacts of cyber-attacks on business in Industry 4.0. Corallo et al. (2020), perform a cyber security analysis addressing the loss of confidentiality, integrity, and availability of data related to interconnected manufacturing machines. Among the results the work presents a critical asset analysis, business impact analysis, impact matrix definition and business impact level assessment [12]. Radanliev et al. (2018), addresses in the article "Integration of cyber security frameworks, models and approaches for building design principles for the Internet of Things in Industry 4.0" that there is interest from the industry and academia to standardize models and methodologies to structure cyber risk approaches. In the paper, the authors seek to present the integration of governance standards in Industry 4.0 for an assessment of the economic impacts of cyber risks on business [51].

# 5 Analysis

This section presents the analysis of the most relevant maturity models identified, considering the literature review performed using the methodological approach described in Sect. 3 (Methodology).

## 5.1 Industry 4.0 Maturity Model

Schumacher et al. (2016) developed a maturity assessment model with 62 maturity assessment items grouped into nine organizational dimensions: i) strategy, ii) leadership; iii) customers; iv) products; v) operations; vi) culture; vii) people; viii) governance; and ix) technology [23]. This model does not present a specific dimension for cyber security. However, the elements of security assessment items can be analyzed in the governance dimension, following the criteria used in the Cybersecurity Capability Maturity Model (C2M2). This model allows for the combination of cyber security governance standards, structures, programs, and initiatives.

## 5.2 Impuls - VDMA

The self-assessment model of companies' readiness for Industry 4.0 developed by the Foundation for Mechanical Engineering, Plant Engineering, and Information Technology has six dimensions, with 18 areas of interest distributed in the dimensions: i) strategy and organization; ii) smart factories; iii) smart operations; iv) smart products; and v) services derived from collected data; and vi) workforce. The model assesses in the "smart operations" dimension the ability to implement cyber security [14].

## 5.3 The Connected Enterprise Maturity Model

This model has five stages and four technology focused dimensions. The dimensions are: i) information infrastructure, hardware and software; ii) controls and devices; iii) networks; and iv) security policies. The first stage evaluates operational technologies. The second analyzes the ability to provide secure and adaptive connectivity. The third defines how the obtained data will be processed to increase competitiveness. The fourth identifies what information should be available in real time. And finally, the fifth stage implements policies for data sharing [52].

## 5.4 Industry 4.0/Digital Operations Self-assessment

This model is part of the report Industry 4.0: Building the digital enterprise by PWC - 2016, which provides for companies a perspective on Industry 4.0 for companies. The model has four stages and seven dimensions. The stages are: i) digital novice; ii) vertical integrator; iii) horizontal collaborator; and iv) digital champion. The seven dimensions are: i) digital business models and customer access; ii) digitization of product and service offerings; iii) digitization and integration of vertical and horizontal value chains; iv) data and Analytics as core capability; v) agile information technology architecture; vi) compliance, security, legal and tax; and vii) organization, employees and digital culture [14, 53].

## 5.5 Industrie 4.0 Maturity Index

The Industrie 4.0 Maturity Index was developed to provide companies with a guide for introducing and implementing the digital transformation process. Schuh et al. (2017) consider digitization as an enabler for Industrie 4.0. The index establishes six stages of development. The first stage is computerization to strengthen the foundation for digitization. In the second, isolated information technology resources are replaced by inter-connected components, with this connectivity also encompassing the core business processes. The third stage aims to implement holistic data visibility across the enterprise, deploying collaboration platforms to support data-driven decision making. The next stage refers to transparency, making it possible to identify and interpret the data obtained in the third stage. In the fifth stage, the company is able to simulate different future scenarios to develop its predictive capability. Finally, the sixth stage relates to the company's ability to adapt to dynamic business scenarios, including autonomous responses of machines and systems considering their predictive capability [17]. The structural areas, their respective principles and capabilities, are presented in Table 4.

**Table 4.** Structural areas, principles and capabilities

| Structural area | Fundamental principles - Transformation capabilities |
|---|---|
| Resources | Digital capability: providing digital skills; acquire data in an automated way, through sensors and actuators and processing the data, in a decentralized way |
| | Structured communication: carrying out efficient communication and designing intuitive interfaces |
| Information systems | Information processing: automated data analysis; delivering contextualized information; design specific and intuitive interfaces and build a resilient information technology framework |
| | Information systems integration: integrate information systems vertically and horizontally; standardize data interfaces; implement data governance and ensure information technology security |
| Organizational structure | Internal organization with high degree of accountability and qualification: encourage flexible workgroups and implementing agile process management for decision making |
| | Dynamic collaboration along the value chain: focus on customer benefits and cooperate in the value network |
| Organizational culture | Willingness to change: recognize the value of mistakes; be open to innovation; make use of data-driven learning and decision making; continuously develop professional competencies and shaping change |
| | Social collaboration: promoting democratic leadership; making use of open communication and relying on information processes and systems |

### 5.6 Cyber Security Maturity Models

Cyber security maturity models consider security through different areas and dimensions with an understanding of interdependence between them. The dimensions provide practices for cyber capabilities and indicators to assess their maturity. No industry-specific maturity models for cyber security have been identified in the literature. Therefore, security models have been adapted to meet the needs of industry. The C2M2 model has two subdivisions: i) Electricity Subsector Cybersecurity Capability Maturity Model (ES-C2M2); and ii) Oil and Natural Gas Subsector Cybersecurity Capability Maturity Model (NGO-C2M2). The ES-C2M2 serves the electric sector and the ONG-C2M2 is used by gas and fuel utilities [18].

The Systems Security Engineering Capability Maturity Model (SSE-CMM) is a model used as a basis for adaptations for cyber security. It has been used to assess security maturity in the critical infrastructure, electricity, water supply, fuel and transportation sectors [54]. The Community Cyber Security Maturity Model (CSMM) establishes the need for organizations to have metrics and technologies to develop a cyber security program for both large enterprises and SMEs [55].

The analysis of the models confirms the gap in the literature of a maturity model that meets the specific cyber security requirements for SMEs embedded in the Industry 4.0 environment.

## 6 Conclusion

Cyber security is one of the main challenges for companies in general that want exploit the potential of Industry 4.0, in particular for SMEs. While these companies can benefit from the advantages of digitization and interconnectivity that characterize Industry 4.0, the lack of a methodological framework for SMEs to deal with the issues associated with these technologies makes the path to this new scenario more challenging. Cyber security issues are high on the agenda of business leaders, demanding knowledge and assessment of the company's security maturity. Cyber security strategies must be integrated with organizational strategies. This integration requires top management to know their current state of security maturity in order to define security strategies and investments.

Maturity models allow companies to track and assess their organizational elements and are used for concrete measures to maximize the benefits of digital transformation. The Industry 4.0 maturity models, which use structured dimensions to provide a knowledge base for assessing the maturity progress should also be seen in this context. By applying the methodological procedures described in Sect. 3, it was possible to identify the most relevant Industry 4.0 and cyber security maturity models that were the subject of this study.

This paper performed an analysis of these models by identifying their dimensions, stages, structural area, fundamental principles, and transformation capability. In the models analyzed, cyber security characteristics were identified in the following models: Impuls - VDMA, The Connected Enterprise Maturity Model, Industry 4.0/Digital Operations Self-Assessment and Industrie 4.0 Maturity Index. Although the Industry 4.0 Maturity Model does not have a specific dimension for cyber security, the C2M2 can be used to complement this model.

The analysis allowed us to identify a gap in the literature of papers with a specific focus to assess the cyber security maturity of SMEs deploying Industry 4.0. Technological development is reshaping the future of cyber security in the manufacturing sector. In this sense, the development of a maturity model to meet cyber security requirements in SMEs is necessary. The results guide the development of a maturity model to meet the security requirements in SMEs, to help these companies face the challenges inherent in Industry 4.0. Therefore, as future work, it is necessary to use a specific cyber security maturity model for SMEs to identify their current security status, allowing them to define future goals in the context of Industry 4.0.

## References

1. Kagermann, H., Wahlster, W., Helbig, J.: Securing the future of German manufacturing industry: recommendations for implementing the strategic initiative INDUSTRIE 4.0. Final Rep. Ind. 4.0 Work. Gr., 1–84 (2013)
2. Matt, D.T., Modrák, V., Zsifkovits, H. (eds.): Industry 4.0 for SMEs. Springer, Cham (2020). https://doi.org/10.1007/978-3-030-25425-4
3. Sommer, L.: Industrial revolution - Industry 4.0: are German manufacturing SMEs the first victims of this revolution? J. Ind. Eng. Manag. **8**, 1512–1532 (2015). https://doi.org/10.3926/jiem.1470
4. Rotar, L.J., Pamić, R.K., Bojnec, Š: Contributions of small and medium enterprises to employment in the European Union countries. Econ. Res. Istraz. **32**, 3296–3308 (2019). https://doi.org/10.1080/1331677X.2019.1658532
5. Matt, D.T., Modrák, V., Zsifkovits, H.: Industry 4.0 for SMEs: Challenges, Opportunities and Requirements. Springer, Cham (2020). https://doi.org/10.1007/978-3-030-25425-4
6. Ervural, B., Ervural, B.: Overview of cyber security in the Industry 4.0 era. In: Industry 4.0: Managing The Digital Transformation. SSAM, pp. 267–284. Springer, Cham (2018). https://doi.org/10.1007/978-3-319-57870-5_16
7. Wu, D., Ren, A., Zhang, W., Fan, F., Liu, P., Fu, X.: Cybersecurity for digital manufacturing. J. Manuf. Syst. **48**, 3–12 (2018). https://doi.org/10.1016/j.jmsy.2018.03.006
8. Jesus, V., Josephs, M.: Challenges in Cybersecurity for Industry 4.0 (2018)
9. Weber, R.H., Studer, E.: Cybersecurity in the Internet of Things: legal aspects. Comput. Law Secur. Rev. **32**, 715–728 (2016). https://doi.org/10.1016/j.clsr.2016.07.002
10. Benias, N., Markopoulos, A.P.: A review on the readiness level and cyber-security challenges in Industry 4.0. In: South Eastern European Design Automation, Computer Engineering, Computer Networks and Social Media Conference (SEEDA-CECNSM) (2017). https://doi.org/10.23919/SEEDA-CECNSM.2017.8088234
11. Fichtner, L., Pieters, W., Teixeira, A.: Cybersecurity as a Politikum: implications of security discourses for infrastructures. In: Proceedings of the 2016 New Security Paradigms Workshop, pp. 36–48. Association for Computing Machinery (ACM) (2016). https://doi.org/10.1145/3011883.3011887
12. Corallo, A., Lazoi, M., Lezzi, M.: Cybersecurity in the context of industry 4.0: a structured classification of critical assets and business impacts. Comput. Ind. **114**, 103165 (2020). https://doi.org/10.1016/j.compind.2019.103165
13. Waslo, R., Lewis, T., Hajj, R., Carton, R.: Managing risk in an age of connected production. Deloitte Univ. Press. **1**, 1–22 (2017)
14. Yagiz, K., Ustundag, A., Cevikcan, E.: Maturity and Readiness Model for Industry 4.0 Strategy Implementation of Industry 4.0 strategies require wide applications in companies (2017)

15. Proença, D., Borbinha, J.: Maturity models for information systems - a state of the art. Proc. Comput. Sci. **100**, 1042–1049 (2016)
16. Gökalp, E., Şener, U., Eren, P.: Development of an assessment model for Industry 4.0: Industry 4.0-MM. In: Mas, A., Mesquida, A., O'Connor, R.V., Rout, T., Dorling, A. (eds.) SPICE 2017. CCIS, vol. 770, pp. 128–142. Springer, Cham (2017). https://doi.org/10.1007/978-3-319-67383-7_10
17. Schuh, G.G., Anderl, L.R., Gausemeier, J.J., ten Hompel, M.M., Wahlster, W. (eds.): Industrie 4.0 Maturity Index. Managing the Digital Transformation of Companies. Acatech Study, 64 (2020)
18. Rea-Guaman, A.M., Sanchez-Garcia, I.D., Feliu, T.S., Calvo-Manzano, J.A.: Modelos de Madurez en Ciberseguridad: una revisión sistemática. Iber. Conf. Inf. Syst. Technol. Cist. (2017). https://doi.org/10.23919/CISTI.2017.7975865
19. OECD: Enhancing the Contributions of SMEs in a Global and Digitalised Economy. Meet. OECD Counc. Minist. Lev., pp. 7–8 (2017)
20. Ganzarain, J., Errasti, N.: Three stage maturity model in SME's toward industry 4.0. J. Ind. Eng. Manag. **9**, 1119 (2016). https://doi.org/10.3926/jiem.2073
21. Wiesner, S., Gaiardelli, P., Gritti, N., Oberti, G.: Maturity models for digitalization in manufacturing - applicability for SMEs. In: Moon, I., Lee, G.M., Park, J., Kiritsis, D., von Cieminski, G. (eds.) APMS 2018. IAICT, vol. 536, pp. 81–88. Springer, Cham (2018). https://doi.org/10.1007/978-3-319-99707-0_11
22. Jones, M., Zarzycki, L., Murray, G.: Does Industry 4.0 pose a challenge for the SME machine builder? A case study and reflection of readiness for a UK SME. In: Ratchev, S. (ed.) IPAS 2018. IAICT, vol. 530, pp. 183–197. Springer, Cham (2019). https://doi.org/10.1007/978-3-030-05931-6_17
23. Schumacher, A., Erol, S., Sihn, W.: A maturity model for assessing Industry 4.0 readiness and maturity of manufacturing enterprises. Procedia CIRP **52**, 161–166 (2016). https://doi.org/10.1016/j.procir.2016.07.040
24. Jamai, I., Ben Azzouz, L., Saidane, L.A.: Security issues in Industry 4.0. In: 2020 International Wireless Communications and Mobile Computing, IWCMC 2020, pp. 481–488 (2020). https://doi.org/10.1109/IWCMC48107.2020.9148447
25. ENISA: Good Practices for Security of Internet of Things in the context of Smart Manufacturing (2018)
26. Sullivan, D., Luiijf, E., Colbert, E.J.M.: Components of industrial control systems. In: Colbert, E.J.M., Kott, A. (eds.) Cyber-security of SCADA and Other Industrial Control Systems. AIS, vol. 66, pp. 15–28. Springer, Cham (2016). https://doi.org/10.1007/978-3-319-32125-7_2
27. Benitez, G.B., Ayala, N.F., Frank, A.G.: Industry 4.0 innovation ecosystems: an evolutionary perspective on value cocreation. Int. J. Prod. Econ. **228** (2020). https://doi.org/10.1016/j.ijpe.2020.107735
28. Dalenogare, L.S., Benitez, G.B., Ayala, N.F., Frank, A.G.: The expected contribution of Industry 4.0 technologies for industrial performance. Int. J. Prod. Econ. **204**, 383–394 (2018). https://doi.org/10.1016/j.ijpe.2018.08.019
29. Pacchini, A.P.T., Lucato, W.C., Facchini, F., Mummolo, G.: The degree of readiness for the implementation of Industry 4.0. Comput. Ind. **113**, 103125 (2019). https://doi.org/10.1016/j.compind.2019.103125
30. Bosch, G., Ag, R.: 3 Die Projektpartner Autoren des Dokuments (2018)
31. Gayle, F.W.: Accelerating US. Advanced manufacturing. 2015 Erc. (2015)
32. Zhou, J.: Intelligent manufacturing-main direction of "made in China 2025." Zhongguo Jixie Gongcheng/China Mech. Eng. **26**, 2273–2284 (2015). https://doi.org/10.3969/j.issn.1004-132X.2015.17.001
33. Ministère du Redressement productif: LA NouveLLe FrANce INdustrIeLLe, pp. 1–40 (2013)

34. Plano de CT&I para Manufatura Avançada no Brasil: ProFuturo (2017)
35. Science, L., Technology, I., To, R., Subjects, A.: [Quarterly peer reviewed International Journal of Education & Technology]
36. Wuest, T., Thoben, K.-D.: Information management for manufacturing SMEs. In: Frick, J., Laugen, B.T. (eds.) APMS 2011. IAICT, vol. 384, pp. 488–495. Springer, Heidelberg (2012). https://doi.org/10.1007/978-3-642-33980-6_53
37. Mittal, S., Khan, M.A., Romero, D., Wuest, T.: A critical review of smart manufacturing & Industry 4.0 maturity models: implications for small and medium-sized enterprises (SMEs). J. Manuf. Syst. **49**, 194–214 (2018). https://doi.org/10.1016/j.jmsy.2018.10.005
38. Drath, R., Horch, A.: Industrie 4.0: hit or hype? [Industry Forum]. IEEE Ind. Electron. Mag. **8**, 56–58 (2014). https://doi.org/10.1109/MIE.2014.2312079
39. Şener, U., Gökalp, E., Eren, P.E.: Toward a maturity model for Industry 4.0: a systematic literature review and a model proposal. Ind. 4.0 MIS Perspect., 290–302 (2018)
40. Spath, D., Ganschar, O., Gerlach, S., Hämmerle, M., Krause, T., Schlund, S.: Produktionsarbeit der Zukunft. Fraunhofer IAO, pp. 1–150 (2013)
41. Modrak, V., Marton, D., Bednar, S.: Modeling and determining product variety for mass-customized manufacturing. Procedia CIRP **23**, 258–263 (2014). https://doi.org/10.1016/j.procir.2014.10.090
42. Gardiner, T., Weber, C., Curtis, B.: Business process maturity model (BPMM) version 1.0. Bus. Process Trends. 496 (2008)
43. Becker, J., Knackstedt, R., Pöppelbuß, J.: Developing maturity models for IT management. Bus. Inf. Syst. Eng. **1**, 213–222 (2009). https://doi.org/10.1007/s12599-009-0044-5
44. Mettler, T.: Maturity assessment models: a design science research approach. Int. J. Soc. Syst. Sci. **3**, 81 (2011). https://doi.org/10.1504/ijsss.2011.038934
45. Adler, R.M.: A dynamic capability maturity model for improving cyber security. In: 2013 IEEE International Conference on Technologies for Homeland Security HST 2013, pp. 230–235 (2013). https://doi.org/10.1109/THS.2013.6699005
46. Christopher, J.D., et al.: Cybersecurity Capability Maturity Model (C2M2). Department of Homeland Security, pp. 1–76 (2014)
47. Nikkhou, S., Taghizadeh, K., Hajiyakhchali, S.: Designing a portfolio management maturity model (Elena). Procedia - Soc. Behav. Sci. **226**, 318–325 (2016). https://doi.org/10.1016/j.sbspro.2016.06.194
48. Lebrun, J.-L.: Scientific Writing 2.0: a reader and writer's guide (2011)
49. Feng, F., Zhang, L., Du, Y., Wang, W.: Visualization and quantitative study in bibliographic databases: a case in the field of university-industry cooperation. J. Informetr. **9**, 118–134 (2015). https://doi.org/10.1016/j.joi.2014.11.009
50. Chen, C., Ibekwe-Sanjuan, F., Hou, J.: The structure and dynamics of cocitation clusters: a multiple-perspective cocitation analysis. J. Am. Soc. Inf. Sci. Technol. **61**, 1386–1409 (2010). https://doi.org/10.1002/asi.21309
51. Radanliev, P., et al.: Integration of cyber security frameworks, models and approaches for building design principles for the internet-of-Things in industry 4.0. In: IET Conference Publication 2018, pp. 0–7 (2018). https://doi.org/10.1049/cp.2018.0041
52. Rockwell Automation: The connected enterprise maturity model. Ind. Conectada **4**, 1–12 (2014)
53. Forbes, J., Naujok, N., Geissbauer, R., Vedso, J., Schrauf, S.: 2016 Global Industry 4.0 Survey – Industry key findings, 12 (2016)
54. Le, N.T., Hoang, D.B.: Can maturity models support cyber security? In: 2016 IEEE 35th International Performance Computing and Communications Conference, IPCCC 2016 (2017)
55. Curtis, P.D., Mehravari, N.: Evaluating and improving cybersecurity capabilities of the energy critical infrastructure. In: 2015 IEEE International Symposium on Technologies for Homeland Security, HST 2015, pp. 1–6 (2015). https://doi.org/10.1109/THS.2015.7225323

# Cybersafety Analysis of a Natural Language User Interface for a Consumer Robotic System

Antonio Roque[1], Melvin Lin[1], and Suresh Damodaran[2(✉)]

[1] Tufts University, Medford, MA, USA
[2] The MITRE Corporation, Bedford, MA, USA
sdamodaran@mitre.org

**Abstract.** Consumer devices are increasing in sophistication and autonomy, but the security of these devices is often under-studied. Some of these systems provide a Natural Language User Interface (NLUI) in order to better communicate with users. Most of these users are not trained in cyber analysis. Cyber attacks on these devices could have safety ramifications that we refer to as cybersafety. In this paper, we analyze the cybersafety of an off-the shelf robotic vacuum cleaner using an approach based on the System Theoretic Process Analysis (STPA) technique. The analysis includes an explicit modeling of the NLUI and of the threats on it using a control loop. We use a scenario to demonstrate how a sophisticated attack on the NLUI can be emulated, and how an untrained user is able to detect such an attack.

## 1 Introduction

Autonomous systems are increasingly being used in domains from self-driving cars to unmanned aerial vehicles to elder-care systems. However, the security of such systems is often only considered after a high-profile attack, and such security analyses typically focus on larger systems such as industrial *Cyber-Physical Systems* (CPSs). CPSs are software systems that interact with the physical environment [3] such as power grid management systems and dam controllers. But there are a number of smaller systems, frequently consumer-oriented systems that are used in households, which also have security issues worth considering [12]. *Robots* are a type of CPS whose interaction with the physical environment includes the system's movement in physical space [5,26]; automated cars, unmanned airborne vehicles, and robotic vacuum cleaners are examples of consumer-facing robots. Furthermore, such consumer systems are often *Internet of Things* (IoT) systems which are highly interconnected with the aim of creating ubiquitous computing, such as smart fridges and smart speakers [30]. But the users of these consumer systems are usually non-professionals who do not have the skills, ability, or interest to perform sophisticated cyber security analyses.

Implementing a *natural language user interface* (NLUI) to the consumer product is one possible approach to give such users a way to detect and possibly react to cyber-physical attacks on the consumer system. However, the NLUI


S. Katsikas et al. (Eds.): ESORICS 2021 Workshops, LNCS 13106, pp. 107–121, 2022.
https://doi.org/10.1007/978-3-030-95484-0_7

itself is also susceptible to attacks. In a consumer product, attacks may cause cybersafety concerns. Some of the sophisticated cyber effects cause the system beliefs to be inconsistent with the real state of the system, a phenomenon known as *process model inconsistency* (PMI) [10]. PMI is hard to detect because observation of the system state will not reveal anything unusual. In this paper, we perform a *cybersafety analysis*, such as is commonly applied to industrial CPSs [21,28], on a smaller consumer robot: a currently-marketed consumer robot to which we add a NLUI.

Our contributions are: (1) a characterization of a consumer robot, including its NLUI, using a control-loop-based framework, (2) a cybersafety systems analysis (such as is commonly applied to industrial CPSs [21,28]) to a consumer robot, and (3) a demonstration of how NLUIs can be attacked, causing safety problems, and how a user may detect some of these attacks. Section 2 will next describe the approach and its rationale, as well as related works. This includes a description of a System Theoretic Process Analysis (STPA) based cybersafety analysis approach [21,28], as well as the use of control loops in characterizing a system. After that, Sect. 3 will describe the system under analysis, which is a prototype Roomba that is connected to an intelligent NLUI. Then Sect. 4 will describe the details of the analysis using the approach described previously; this includes an emulation of an attack on NLUI, and its detection in Sect. 4.4. Finally, Sect. 5 will discuss limitations and conclusions, including how aspects of the analysis can be used to help non-specialist end users detect (and thus begin to resolve) security incidents in consumer products, focusing on the importance of introspection and interactivity on this process.

## 2 Cybersafety Analysis

Our cybersafety analysis follows a similar approach by Khan and Madnick [21], modified to use a customized control loop framework as described in Sect. 2.1. The approach has the following steps.

First, a *basis for analysis* is defined. This includes defining the primary mission of the system under consideration, identifying unacceptable losses, and identifying the system constraints that prevent system states from leading to losses.

Second, a *functional control structure* is modeled. This represents how the system constraints defined in the previous step are implemented in the system under consideration.

Third, the system's *unsafe control actions* are identified. This includes describing the functions, responsibilities, and control actions for each of the relevant controllers in the functional control structure defined in the previous step. Additionally, a process model is defined for each of the relevant controllers.

Fourth, *loss scenarios* are generated, to identify the situational factors that might lead to the execution of the unsafe control actions that were previously identified. We use one such loss scenario to do our demonstration of threat emulation and detection.

### 2.1 Adversarial System Modeling with Control Loops

As described above, CPSs and robots are defined by their interaction with the physical environment. Besides their interactions with the physical environment, these systems often have interactions with humans. So we can think of CPSs and robots as having both a human-in-the-loop and a physical-process-in-the-loop. Finally, *cybersafety* analysis is to analyze hazards resulting from accidents, attacks, human errors, or some combinations of these. The hazards produced by adversaries can be modeled through adversary loop. All of these loops can be represented with control loops [15] as in Fig. 1.

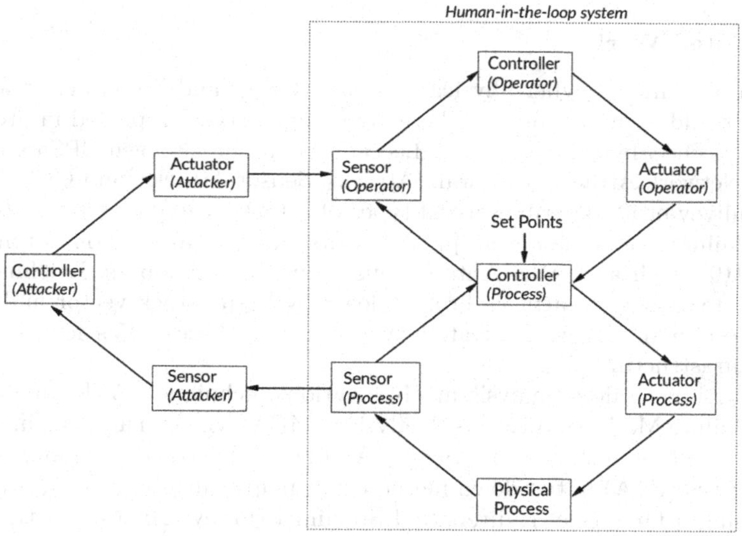


**Fig. 1.** Example control loop diagram of an attack on a human-in-the-loop system

The lower loop involves a Physical Process (such as a machine, or an installation such as a dam, or the natural environment such as with a thermostat) whose state is being tracked by a Process Sensor, and which is being updated by a Process Actuator. A Process Controller determines what commands to send through the Actuator, and tracks the updates from the Sensor. The upper loop involves a human Operator Controller who uses Actuators and Sensors to interact with the Process Controller. Together, these two loops abstract the consumer product for modeling threats.

Since we are also concerned with the actions of attackers, we can think of security as a conflict between users and attackers over control of the system [15,33]. So the attack can also be represented with a control loop as shown in Fig. 1. Figure 1 shows only one possible architecture of the Attacker control loop: the Actuator (Attacker) targeting the Sensor (Operator), and the Sensor

(Attacker) targeting the Sensor (Process). There are, of course, several other possible targets for the Attacker Sensor and Attacker Actuator.

Each of the components in Fig. 1 is given a name, as are the communication channels between them, and the *set points* (initial values) of the Process Controller. This allows us to refer to every part of the system by name, thereby allowing us to be precise while still maintaining a generality across systems. Because in this context, any of the components could be broken down into a subsystem for further analysis. This approach also allows the representation of insider attacks, besides external attacks. It can also represent complex situations where cyber attacks and non-adversarial safety failures act together to contribute to an effect.

### 2.2 Related Work

Robots are a kind of cyber-physical systems (CPS), and therefore, attacks on CPS also could apply to robots. There are several attacks reported in literature surveyed recently by Ding et al. [13]. Leccadito et al. break down CPS exploits in terms of Network Attacks, Firmware Attacks, Sensor Attacks, and GCS Attacks [27]. Alguliyev et al. describe several types of attacks, categorizing the different types of failures [3]. Jahan et al. present a taxonomy of attacks on autonomous systems [19], such as UAVs, Autonomous Vehicles, and robots. Krishna et al. provide a taxonomy of attacks broken down by both attack vector and target focusing on small UAVs, motivated by the use of those UAVs for inspecting critical infrastructure [25].

Conducting a safety analysis involves various techniques. A dominant technique is Failure Modes and Effects Analysis (FMEA) which analyzes fault modes and their effects in a structured way [9]. Another widely used technique is Fault Tree Analysis (FTA), a top-down method that maps subsystem failures to their causes using a fault tree. Ruijters and Stoelinga survey the state of the art in FTA [34]. The potential for safety hazards generated by the lack of cyber security has been a recent active research area. Schmittner et al. explore cybersecurity-safety analysis using FMEA [38]. The automobile industry also has been very interested in cybersafety, and has been developing standards related to cybersecurity and attendant safety implications, as summarized by Macher et al. [29] on ISO/SAE DIS 21434, and described by Kirovskii and Gorelov [24] on ISO PAS 21448.

Cybersecurity and safety co-analysis of CPSs has been an active research area, as surveyed recently by Kavallieratos et al. who identify nine methodologies for such co-analysis [20]. One such methodology is based on the System Theoretic Process Analysis (STPA) technique pioneered by Leveson [28] that uses control loops for safety analyses of CPSs. This approach was developed to increase the *safety* of systems, so its roots are in reaction to accidental or other non-intentional hazards. The STPA approach has been recently adapted for adversarial situations by Young [41] and Torkildson et al. [40]. Giraldo et al. survey the application of control loops for cybersecurity [15]. Khan and Madnick applied STPA to the cybersafety analysis of a chiller plant [21], and in this paper we apply their analysis method to a consumer robot. The comparison of STPA approach with other approaches used for risk analysis has been previously reported [39]. The goal of this paper is not to do a comparative merits analysis between STPA and other approaches, rather just to show how STPA based cybersafety analysis can be applied to NLUI.

Natural language user interfaces (also known by many different names such as natural language interfaces, dialogue interfaces, and voice user interfaces) have been popularized recently by products such as Alexa, Siri, Cortana, and Google Assistant [6]. Researchers investigate use cases such as connecting autonomous vehicles and IoT-connected devices [22] with NLUIs, but with some exceptions, mostly involving speech-based interfaces [8,42], there is little consideration of the security impact of adding such interfaces. Our work is also somewhat similar to recent work in explaining robot failures [11], which is part of a general increased interest in explainability [16], but in our case we focus on failures that are due to cyber attacks.

## 3 Target System

The target of this analysis is a prototype next-generation consumer product: a robotic vacuum cleaner, custom augmented with a natural language user interface (NLUI). The system has several characteristics of a consumer robot or an Internet of Things appliance, and thus could be a stand-in for other possible systems such as automated vehicles or drones.

The platform is shown in Fig. 2. The vacuum cleaner is an iRobot Create-2, which is the developer version of the consumer Roomba 600 series [18]. For cybersafety analysis, attack simulation, and to experiment with the NLUI, the vacuum cleaner is connected to a laptop computer, though in principle the NLUI could run on an on-board chip of the iRobot. Communication between the robot and laptop is through a Bluetooth wireless module that we constructed to plug into the Create-2's serial interface. This interface was built using a SparkFun Bluetooth Mate Gold bluetooth module, a 3A 5V DC-DC Converter Step Down UBEC Module, a 7- or 8-DIN Serial Cable, crimping with 2.54 mm Dupont Connectors, and a bit of soldering. The Bluetooth module communicated with the Linux laptop using the BlueZ bluetooth stack[1] and we used the Java-based RoombaJSSC library[2] to programmatically connect. The NLUI we use is based on the DIARC robotic cognitive architecture, which includes a natural language pipeline: a semantic/syntactic parser, a discourse analyzer, and a goal management system that works with a belief module [37]. We use a text-based "chat" interface, as might be used on a modern cell phone. An important assumption we also make is that the user is not able to see the robot, and can learn about the state of the robot only using this NLUI. This assumption is made to allow the results we describe in this paper to be more widely applicable than just the

[1] http://www.bluez.org/.
[2] https://github.com/maschel/RoombaJSSC.

vacuum cleaner. A control-loop representation of the system is shown in Fig. 3. This representation is further expanded upon in the following sections.

**Fig. 2.** Target system, with natural language user interface.

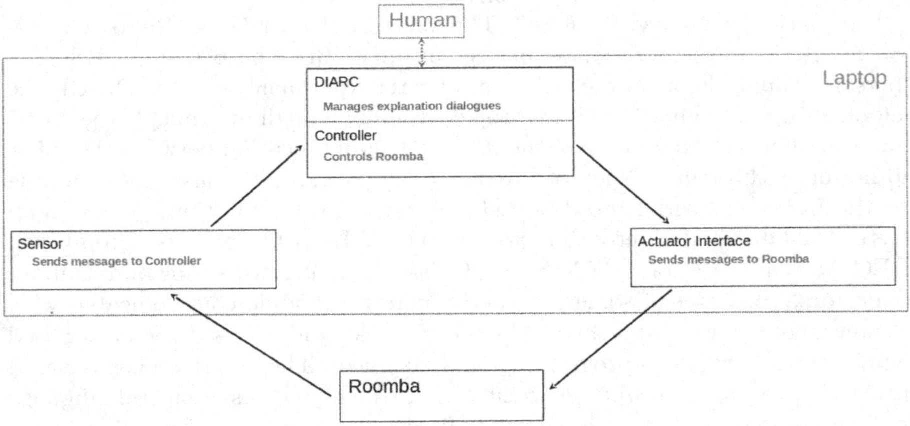


**Fig. 3.** Target system physical control loop.

## 4 Cybersafety Analysis of Target System

This analysis applies the cybersafety methodology described in Sect. 2 to the target system described in Sect. 3.

### 4.1 Basis for Analysis

To perform an analysis, first the primary mission of the system under consideration is determined. In the case of the vacuum cleaner testbed, we can define the following *mission statement*: to keep the floor clean by vacuuming it.

*Unacceptable Losses* include the vacuum cleaner becoming damaged, causing damage to objects in the house, or causing damage to a person (by running into them or tripping them, for example.) We can enumerate these unacceptable losses as follows:

- **L1:** Physical damage to vacuum cleaner
- **L2:** Disabling the vacuum cleaner
- **L3:** Damage to objects in house
- **L4:** Injury to people.

Next we will identify system constraints. As suggested by [21] we will begin by identifying the system-level *Hazards*, associating each with a Loss, and inverting each hazard to identify the system-level *Constraints* as shown in Table 1.

**Table 1.** System constraints

| Hazard | Loss | Constraint |
|---|---|---|
| (H1) vacuum cleaner is damaged by moving into wall or falling down stairs | L1 | Vacuum cleaner must not be moved into unsafe locations |
| (H2) vacuum cleaner is "frozen" and unable to perform its task | L2 | Vacuum cleaner must not be blocked from moving, when there are no problems |
| (H3) vacuum cleaner causes damage to objects in the house | L3 | Vacuum cleaner must not be allowed to crash into fragile objects |
| (H4) person is injured by being hit by vacuum cleaner, or tripping over vacuum cleaner | L4 | vacuum cleaner must maneuver carefully when in the presence of people |

### 4.2 Control Structure

The next step in the cybersafety analysis is to build a model of how the constraints defined in the previous section are enforced in the system. We will use the control-loop representation as was described in Sect. 2.1 to conduct this analysis.

Figure 4 expands upon the fundamental control loop diagram that was shown in Fig. 1. First, the figure shows which the parts of the loop are in the NLUI prototype system, as opposed to in the Vacuum-cleaner robot or in the Human. Second, the NLUI is broken out, showing the communication channels it uses

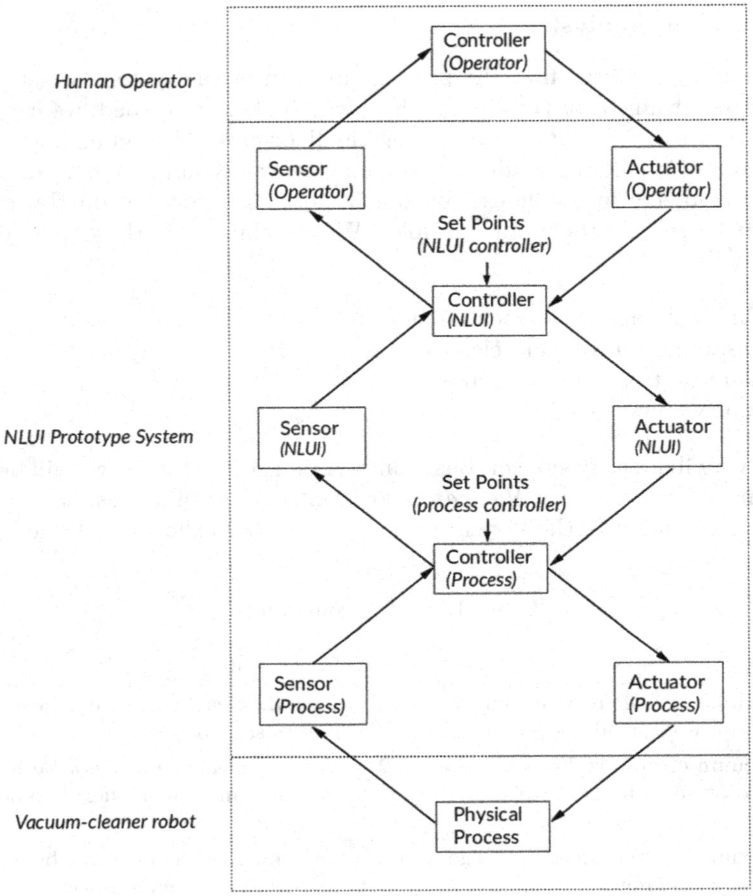


**Fig. 4.** Control-loop representation of NL-enabled vacuum cleaner system

when the human operator interacts with the robotic vacuum cleaner: the Operator Actuator and Operator Sensor are the NLUI text input/output; the NLUI Actuator and the NLUI Sensor are the NLUI's software channels to the Process Controller; the Process Actuator and the Process Sensor are the Bluetooth communication channels between the NLUI and the robotic laptop. This control loop diagram will be further developed below, as we begin to consider what happens when the communication channels are exploited.

### 4.3 Unsafe Control Actions

The next step in the analysis is to identify a list of unsafe control actions. We start by creating a List of Controllers, Functions Performed, Safety Responsibilities, and Control Actions of each of the controllers shown in Fig. 4, and summarizing them in Table 2.

**Table 2.** Controller summaries

| Controller | Function performed | Safety & security responsibilities | Control actions |
|---|---|---|---|
| Controller (Operator) | Provides high-level guidance | Monitor for unusual situation that machine might not detect | Request non-standard activity |
| Controller (NLUI) | Translate between human language and machine state | Identify when it does not understand human or machine update | Transmit command from human to machine |
| Controller (Process) | Decides what low-level actions the vacuum cleaner will do | Sense for possible collisions | Send movement/rotation/stop messages to vacuum-cleaner robot |

At this point there are a number of additional analyses we could perform. For example, we could enumerate all of the process model variables and iterate through those to determine possible problems. Alternately, we could determine the different signals that pass through the communication channels, and iterate through those to determine what problems could occur if signals are missing, or if there are extra signals or if the signals arrive at different times than they are expected. Following [21], we describe unsafe control examples. Table 3 is an example of this, which will be used in the next section to describe a loss scenario.

**Table 3.** Unsafe control actions

| Scenario unsafe control action | |
|---|---|
| *Action by:* | Controller |
| *Control action:* | Move and clean |
| *Not providing causes hazard:* | Vacuum cleaner does not move (H2) |
| *Providing causes hazard:* | Vacuum cleaner is damaged (H1) |
| *Providing at wrong time causes hazard:* | Vacuum cleaner damages items in house (H3), Person is injured by vacuum cleaner (H4) |

However, we are interested in knowing *how* the system is led to create an unsafe control action. One approach to this is to create a *threat model* of known attacks on robots, and determine which ones could possibly be used against the system under analysis. Security researchers have shown how many of the typical attacks against systems can also be directed against robots, including reconaissance [14,23], illicit access [1,12], exploitation [2,31,32,35,36], and actions on objectives [4,7,31]. These can be shown with the control-loop representation shown in Fig. 4. Table 4 maps several channels and their vulnerabilities to known types of attacks. For example we can specify in our Vacuum Cleaner Robot Scenario that an attacker created a false-message attack on the channel between the

Sensor (Process) and the Controller (Process), which is what leads to the unsafe control action "not providing causes hazard" described above. In this way we generally identify potential vulnerabilities, the specifics of which can be further worked out as described in the next Section.

**Table 4.** Example vulnerabilities of control-loop channels

| Channel | Vulnerability |
|---|---|
| Controller (Process) to Actuator (Process) | False message |
| Actuator (Process) to Physical process | Channel overload |
| Physical Process to Sensor (Process) | Man-in-the-middle attack |
| Sensor (Process) to Controller (Process) | False message |

### 4.4 Loss Scenario

The final step in the cybersafety analysis is to create one or more loss scenarios to describe how an unsafe control action might be caused, either by natural hazard or by malicious activity. In our case, we are particularly interested in malicious activity. A narrative of a scenario we created is as follows.

A human user, heading home from the store, uses a cell-phone text interface to turn on their vacuum-cleaner robot at home. They tell the robot, "Clean the floor." The vacuum-cleaner robot starts to clean the floor.

Unknown to the user, the system suffers a software-based denial-of-service attack that falsely tells the robot's controller that its collision-detecting subsystem has detected obstacles on all sides. Suddenly the vacuum-cleaner robot stops, and says: "I cannot clean the floor because to clean the floor I must not see obstacles, and I see obstacles."

The human then says: "try rotating in place." The robot does so successfully, and says, "I am able to rotate in place."

The human then says: "try moving one inch forward even if you see an obstacle." The robot does so successfully, and says, "I am able to move one inch forward even though I see an obstacle."

In our scenario demonstration, we emulate an exploitation of the NLUI prototype system by the attacker. The real attack may have the following attack sequence. First, the attacker remotely accesses the hardware on which the NLUI is running. Next, the attacker escalates privileges and installs a malware program that will launch whenever the NLUI is run. The malware program waits for an execution signal from an external source. When the malware program receives that signal, the malware program sends a "false message" to the NLUI Controller indicating that the system has detected an obstacle. The NLUI Controller updates its beliefs to reflect the fact that it believes it sees an obstacle, and this precludes further movement. This attack can be represented using a control loop as shown in Fig. 5. The control loop does not show a full loop for the attacker, because the attacker's Sensor is irrelevant for the purposes of the scenario (and may indeed be unknown and undetected by the analyst.)

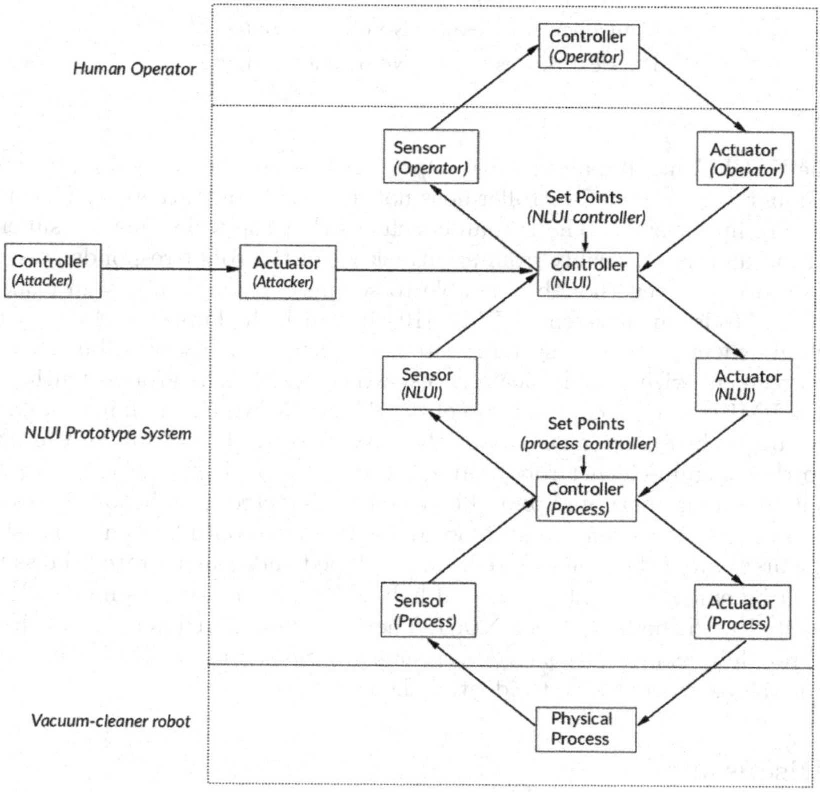


**Fig. 5.** Control loop representation of attack in vacuum cleaner scenario

As indicated in the scenario description, the attack works by falsely updating the state of the NLUI Controller, such that the controller believes that an obstacle has been detected. We emulate this attack by programmatically changing a belief state in the NLUI controller as it executes. This belief is then passed on to the human operator. On the vacuum cleaner itself, the sensor state is closest to the actual reality: it actually detects no obstacles, and this model is passed on to the Process Controller before the Attacker intervenes. Table 5 reflects the process model (intuitive meaning: the beliefs) of the various components.

**Table 5.** Example process model inconsistency after channel attack

| Component | Process model |
|---|---|
| Controller (Operator) | Obstacle detected |
| Controller (NLUI) | Obstacle detected |
| Controller (Attacker) | No obstacle detected |
| Controller (Process) | No obstacle detected |
| Physical process | No obstacle detected |

The NLUI Controller and Human Operator believe that there is an obstacle, even though the Process Controller does not; in other words, their models of the process are inconsistent. The human concludes that the robot may be suffering from a malfunction, possibly from an attack when the robot responds it is able to move forward even though it is able to see an obstacle. This is an example of Process Model Inconsistency (PMI) [10], in which the human and the system are in agreement about the system state that they have observed, but they are in disagreement with the physical process which reflects the ground truth.

This PMI case is in contrast to non-PMI cases in which the human and the system are each in agreement about the system state. For example, the interface to the vacuum-cleaner robot cannot manage excessively-fast data requests without becoming corrupted, but this would be detected with header bytes and checksums, so the problematic state would be known to both human and system.

The first half of the scenario we have developed and demonstrated shows how PMI can be emulated, and the second half of the scenario shows how PMI can be detected with the help of the NLUI. Therefore, this NLUI is able to help the user through its explanations to detect *something is wrong* with the robot, even thought the user is not able to identify the cause.

## 5 Discussion

We performed a cybersafety analysis of a prototypical consumer product robot extended with NLUI. We modeled this system, its NLUI, its human user, and its human or non-human attackers, in a precise enough way to refer to different types of vulnerabilities, while still maintaining some amount of generality. Adding an NLUI resulted in a new control loop, and new types of vulnerabilities. This type of analysis is broadly applicable because every time a new capability is added to a system, the attack surface is increased, and the use of control loop shows precisely how, and how unexpected types of vulnerabilities arise. For example, imagine another situation in which an Internet connectivity is added to an appliance to make it an IoT device. The device's system is attacked to require it to falsely replace its battery, and the appliance is shut down until it arrives; creating a PMI situation.

However, we do like to point out some limitations of the current work, and where additional study is warranted. The ability of the user to detect a potential attack in a consumer robot does not mean that this same approach would work in safety-critical systems [17] that implement a Safety Instrumented System (SIS), an independent control system, that may disallow commands from the user or operator of that system. Therefore, more research is needed to model SIS, and to understand how a user may detect a potential attack in a safety-critical system where an SIS may interfere with such detection.

The technique for detection by the operator of the consumer robot described in this paper required a dialog that took minutes. If the detection time is much lower, say in the milliseconds, then a human may not be able to participate in the detection of inconsistency, and other techniques are needed.

Ultimately, we are interested in enabling the user or operator who is not a cyber analyst to not just detect, but even to respond to an attack. This paper paves the way for future research investigating whether or not the attack could be detected using a combination of introspection and/or interaction, such as through explainable dialogues, and the extent to which this depends on the attack involving PMI.

**Acknowledgment.** The authors are grateful to the reviewers for their helpful comments.

## References

1. Ahmad Yousef, K.M., AlMajali, A., Ghalyon, S.A., Dweik, W., Mohd, B.J.: Analyzing cyber-physical threats on robotic platforms. Sensors **18**(5), 1643 (2018)
2. Alemzadeh, H., Chen, D., Li, X., Kesavadas, T., Kalbarczyk, Z.T., Iyer, R.K.: Targeted attacks on teleoperated surgical robots: dynamic model-based detection and mitigation. In: 2016 46th Annual IEEE/IFIP International Conference on Dependable Systems and Networks (DSN), pp. 395–406. IEEE (2016)
3. Alguliyev, R., Imamverdiyev, Y., Sukhostat, L.: Cyber-physical systems and their security issues. Comput. Ind. **100**, 212–223 (2018)
4. AlMajali, A., Yousef, K.M.A., Mohd, B.J., Dweik, W., Ghalyon, S.A., Hasan, R.: Semi-quantitative security risk assessment of robotic systems. Jordanian J. Comput. Inf. Technol. (JJCIT) **4**(03) (2018)
5. Archibald, C., Schwalm, L., Ball, J.E.: A survey of security in robotic systems: Vulnerabilities, attacks, and solutions. Int. J. Robot. Autom. **32**(2) (2017)
6. Berdasco, A., López, G., Diaz, I., Quesada, L., Guerrero, L.A.: User experience comparison of intelligent personal assistants: Alexa, Google Assistant, Siri and Cortana. In: Proceedings of the 13th International Conference on Ubiquitous Computing and Ambient Intelligence UCAm I 2019, Toledo, Spain, 2–5 December 2019, vol. 31, p. 51 (2019)
7. Bonaci, T., Yan, J., Herron, J., Kohno, T., Chizeck, H.J.: Experimental analysis of denial-of-service attacks on teleoperated robotic systems. In: Proceedings of the ACM/IEEE Sixth International Conference on Cyber-Physical Systems, pp. 11–20 (2015)
8. Carlini, N., et al.: Hidden voice commands. In: 25th USENIX Security Symposium (USENIX Security 2016), pp. 513–530 (2016)

9. International Electrotechnical Commission, et al.: IEC 60812: Analysis techniques for system reliability-procedure for failure mode and effects analysis (FMEA), pp. 1–93. International Electrotechnical Commission, Geneva, Switzerland (2006)
10. Damodaran, S.K., Rowe, P.D.: Limitations on observability of effects in cyber-physical systems. In: Proceedings of the 6th Annual Symposium on Hot Topics in the Science of Security, pp. 1–10 (2019)
11. Das, D., Banerjee, S., Chernova, S.: Explainable AI for robot failures: generating explanations that improve user assistance in fault recovery. In: Proceedings of the 2021 ACM/IEEE International Conference on Human-Robot Interaction (2021)
12. Denning, T., Matuszek, C., Koscher, K., Smith, J.R., Kohno, T.: A spotlight on security and privacy risks with future household robots: attacks and lessons. In: Proceedings of the 11th International Conference on Ubiquitous Computing, pp. 105–114 (2009)
13. Ding, D., Han, Q.L., Xiang, Y., Ge, X., Zhang, X.M.: A survey on security control and attack detection for industrial cyber-physical systems. Neurocomputing **275**, 1674–1683 (2018)
14. Giaretta, A., De Donno, M., Dragoni, N.: Adding salt to pepper: a structured security assessment over a humanoid robot. In: Proceedings of the 13th International Conference on Availability, Reliability and Security, pp. 1–8 (2018)
15. Giraldo, J.: A survey of physics-based attack detection in cyber-physical systems. ACM Comput. Surv. (CSUR) **51**(4), 1–36 (2018)
16. Guidotti, R., Monreale, A., Ruggieri, S., Turini, F., Giannotti, F., Pedreschi, D.: A survey of methods for explaining black box models. ACM Comput. Surv. (CSUR) **51**(5), 1–42 (2018)
17. IEC61511: Functional safety-safety instrumented systems for the process industry sector-part 3, guidance for the determination of the required safety integrity levels. IEC 61511-3 (2003)
18. iRobot: iRobot create 2 open interface (OI) specification based on the iRobot Roomba 600 (2018). https://www.irobotweb.com/-/media/MainSite/Files/About/STEM/Create/2018-07-19_iRobot_Roomba_600_Open_Interface_Spec.pdf
19. Jahan, F., Sun, W., Niyaz, Q., Alam, M.: Security modeling of autonomous systems: a survey. ACM Comput. Surv. (CSUR) **52**(5), 1–34 (2019)
20. Kavallieratos, G., Katsikas, S., Gkioulos, V.: Cybersecurity and safety co-engineering of cyberphysical systems-a comprehensive survey. Future Internet **12**(4), 65 (2020)
21. Khan, S., Madnick, S.: Cybersafety analysis of industrial control systems: chiller systems (revised) (2020)
22. Kim, Y., Oh, H., Kang, S.: Proof of concept of home IoT connected vehicles. Sensors **17**(6), 1289 (2017)
23. Kinzler, M., Miller, J., Wu, Z., Williams, A., Perouli, D.: Cybersecurity vulnerabilities in two artificially intelligent humanoids on the market. In: Workshop on Technology and Consumer Protection (ConPro 2019), held in conjunction with the 40th IEEE Symposium on Security and Privacy (2019)
24. Kirovskii, O., Gorelov, V.: Driver assistance systems: analysis, tests and the safety case. ISO 26262 and ISO PAS 21448. In: IOP Conference Series: Materials Science and Engineering, vol. 534, p. 012019. IOP Publishing (2019)
25. Krishna, C.L., Murphy, R.R.: A review on cybersecurity vulnerabilities for unmanned aerial vehicles. In: 2017 IEEE International Symposium on Safety, Security and Rescue Robotics (SSRR), pp. 194–199. IEEE (2017)
26. Lacava, G., et al.: Current research issues on cyber security in robotics. Technical Report Istituto di Informatica e Telematica, TR-05/2020 (2020)

27. Leccadito, M., Bakker, T., Klenke, R., Elks, C.: A survey on securing UAS cyber physical systems. IEEE Aerosp. Electron. Syst. Mag. **33**(10), 22–32 (2018)
28. Leveson, N.G.: Engineering A Safer World: Systems Thinking Applied to Safety. The MIT Press, Cambridge (2016)
29. Macher, G., Schmittner, C., Veledar, O., Brenner, E.: ISO/SAE DIS 21434 automotive cybersecurity standard - in a nutshell. In: Casimiro, A., Ortmeier, F., Schoitsch, E., Bitsch, F., Ferreira, P. (eds.) SAFECOMP 2020. LNCS, vol. 12235, pp. 123–135. Springer, Cham (2020). https://doi.org/10.1007/978-3-030-55583-2_9
30. Mendez Mena, D., Papapanagiotou, I., Yang, B.: Internet of things: survey on security. Inf. Secur. J. Global Perspect. **27**(3), 162–182 (2018)
31. Pogliani, M., Quarta, D., Polino, M., Vittone, M., Maggi, F., Zanero, S.: Security of controlled manufacturing systems in the connected factory: the case of industrial robots. J. Comput. Virol. Hack. Tech. **15**(3), 161–175 (2019). https://doi.org/10.1007/s11416-019-00329-8
32. Quarta, D., Pogliani, M., Polino, M., Maggi, F., Zanchettin, A.M., Zanero, S.: An experimental security analysis of an industrial robot controller. In: 2017 IEEE Symposium on Security and Privacy (SP), pp. 268–286. IEEE (2017)
33. Roque, A., Bush, K.B., Degni, C.: Security is about control: insights from cybernetics. In: Proceedings of the Symposium and Bootcamp on the Science of Security, pp. 17–24 (2016)
34. Ruijters, E., Stoelinga, M.: Fault tree analysis: a survey of the state-of-the-art in modeling, analysis and tools. Comput. Sci. Rev. **15**, 29–62 (2015)
35. Sabaliauskaite, G., Ng, G.S., Ruths, J., Mathur, A.: Experimental evaluation of stealthy attack detection in a robot. In: 2015 IEEE 21st Pacific Rim International Symposium on Dependable Computing (PRDC), pp. 70–79. IEEE (2015)
36. Sabaliauskaite, G., Ng, G.S., Ruths, J., Mathur, A.: A comprehensive approach, and a case study, for conducting attack detection experiments in cyber-physical systems. Robot. Auton. Syst. **98**, 174–191 (2017)
37. Scheutz, M., Williams, T., Krause, E., Oosterveld, B., Sarathy, V., Frasca, T.: An overview of the distributed integrated cognition affect and reflection DIARC architecture. In: Aldinhas Ferreira, M.I., Silva Sequeira, J., Ventura, R. (eds.) Cognitive Architectures. ISCASE, vol. 94, pp. 165–193. Springer, Cham (2019). https://doi.org/10.1007/978-3-319-97550-4_11
38. Schmittner, C., Gruber, T., Puschner, P., Schoitsch, E.: Security application of failure mode and effect analysis (FMEA). In: Bondavalli, A., Di Giandomenico, F. (eds.) SAFECOMP 2014. LNCS, vol. 8666, pp. 310–325. Springer, Cham (2014). https://doi.org/10.1007/978-3-319-10506-2_21
39. Sulaman, S.M., Beer, A., Felderer, M., Höst, M.: Comparison of the FMEA and STPA safety analysis methods-a case study. Software Qual. J. **27**(1), 349–387 (2019)
40. Torkildson, E.N., Li, J., Johnsen, S.O.: Improving security and safety co-analysis of STPA. In: Proceedings of the 29th European Safety and Reliability Conference (ESREL), Hannover, Germany, 22–26 September 2019. Research Publishing Services (2019)
41. Young, W., Leveson, N.G.: An integrated approach to safety and security based on systems theory. Commun. ACM **57**(2), 31–35 (2014)
42. Zhang, G., Yan, C., Ji, X., Zhang, T., Zhang, T., Xu, W.: DolphinAttack: inaudible voice commands. In: Proceedings of the 2017 ACM SIGSAC Conference on Computer and Communications Security, pp. 103–117 (2017)

# 5th International Workshop on Security and Privacy Requirements Engineering (SECPRE 2021)

# SECPRE 2021 Preface

This part contains revised versions of the papers presented at the Fifth International Workshop on SECurity and Privacy Requirements Engineering (SECPRE 2021) which was co-located with the 26th European Symposium on Research in Computer Security (ESORICS 2021) virtually held in Darmstadt, Germany, on October 8, 2021.

Data protection regulations, the complexity of modern environments (such as IoT, IoE, cloud computing, big data, cyber-physical systems, etc.), and the increased level of user awareness in IT have forced software engineers to identify security and privacy as fundamental design aspects leading to the implementation of more trusted software systems and services. Researchers have addressed the necessity and importance of implementing design methods for security and privacy requirements elicitation, modeling, and implementation in the last decades in various innovative research domains. Today Security by Design (SbD) and Privacy by Design (PbD) are established research areas that focus on these directions. The new General Data Protection Regulation (GDPR) sets even stricter requirements for organizations regarding its applicability. SbD and PbD play a very critical and important role in assisting stakeholders in understanding their needs, complying with the new legal, organizational, and technical requirements, and selecting the appropriate measures for fulfilling these requirements. SECPRE aims to provide researchers and professionals with the opportunity to present novel and cutting-edge research on these topics.

SECPRE 2021 attracted eight high-quality submissions, each of which was assigned to three referees for review; the review process resulted in five papers being selected for presentation and inclusion in these proceedings. The topics covered include privacy by design methods, sociotechnical approaches for privacy, bioprivacy issues, and GDPR issues as well as practical aspects of privacy.

We would like to express our thanks to all those who assisted us in organizing the event and putting together the program. We are very grateful to the members of the Program Committee for their timely and rigorous reviews. Thanks are also due to the Organizing Committee of both the workshop and ESORICS. Last but by no means least, we would like to thank all the authors who submitted their work to the workshop and contributed to an interesting set of proceedings.

November 2021

John Mylopoulos
Christos Kalloniatis
Annie Anton
Stefanos Gritzalis

# SECPRE 2021 Organization

## General Chairs

| | |
|---|---|
| Annie Antón | Georgia Institute of Technology, USA |
| Stefanos Gritzalis | University of Piraeus, Greece |

## Program Committee Chairs

| | |
|---|---|
| John Mylopoulos | University of Ottawa, Canada |
| Christos Kalloniatis | University of the Aegean, Greece |

## Program Committee

| | |
|---|---|
| Frédéric Cuppens | Polytechnique Montréal, Canada |
| Sabrina De Capitani di Vimercati | Università degli Studi di Milano, Italy |
| Vasiliki Diamantopoulou | University of the Aegean, Greece |
| Eric Dubois | Luxembourg Institute of Science and Technology, Luxembourg |
| Carmen Fernandez-Gago | University of Malaga, Spain |
| Eduardo Fernandez-Medina | University of Castilla-La Mancha, Spain |
| Mohamad Gharib | University of Florence, Italy |
| Paolo Giorgini | University of Trento, Italy |
| Jan Juerjens | University of Koblenz-Landau, Germany |
| Maria Karyda | University of the Aegean, Greece |
| Costas Lambrinoudakis | University of Piraeus, Greece |
| Tong Li | Beijing University of Technology, China |
| Javier Lopez | University of Malaga, Spain |
| Aaron Massey | University of Maryland, USA |
| Haralambos Mouratidis | University of Brighton, UK |
| Liliana Pasquale | University College Dublin, Ireland |
| Michalis Pavlidis | University of Brighton, UK |
| David Garcia Rosado | University of Castilla-La Mancha, Spain |
| Pierangela Samarati | Università degli Studi di Milano, Italy |
| Aggeliki Tsohou | Ionian University, Greece |
| Nicola Zannone | Eindhoven University of Technology, The Netherlands |

# Integrating Privacy-By-Design with Business Process Redesign

Vasiliki Diamantopoulou(✉) and Maria Karyda

Department of Information and Communication Systems Engineering, University of the Aegean, Samos, Greece
{vdiamant,mka}@aegean.gr

**Abstract.** Among the numerous challenges that organisations face, information security is undoubtedly an important concern, and as of lately, compliance with personal data regulation (e.g., the General Data Protection Regulation – GDPR in the EU) is a necessity, while requirements for privacy-by-design need also to be met. This paper proposes a comprehensive method to support the identification, modelling, (re)design, implementation, and realisation of privacy aware/compliant business processes, in order to incorporate personal data protection principles into all work practices and business processes in an organisation. More specifically, this method integrates the main steps of a Data Protection Impact Assessment into business process management, to ensure the identification of personal data flow throughout the organisation and support the assessment of privacy-related risks and enhance personal data protection.

**Keywords:** Business process redesign · Data protection impact assessment · Privacy-by-design · Privacy patterns

## 1 Introduction

Information and Communication Technologies (ICT) play a significant role in every-day life, providing users with personalised services that require or collect their personal information. Personal data has become a main asset for modern enterprises and is exchanged on a broad scale (Spiekermann et al. 2015) as it is considered the basis for developing, interacting, and decision making. The necessity of protecting individuals' personal data is of utmost importance, especially when taking under consideration the value that personal data has for the digital economies and the interest that its collection attracts, either for public or private organisations. This necessity has been also imposed by legal and contractual obligations, and since May 2018, is also imposed by the European Union's General Data Protection Regulation (GDPR) (European Parliament 2016). The protection of personal data has seen a major upheaval during the last decades, attracting the attention of politicians, developers, public and private organisations, legislators, authorities, as well as the general public. However, privacy preservation is not a straightforward process, as privacy is a multifaceted concept with various parameters that need to be taken into account, at technical and social level and are often determined by the inner


S. Katsikas et al. (Eds.): ESORICS 2021 Workshops, LNCS 13106, pp. 127–137, 2022.
https://doi.org/10.1007/978-3-030-95484-0_8

and outer context of organisations. Since GDPR came into force, several reports have identified that organisations are still not fully aware of the GDPR's potential impact, e.g., (Reuters 2019) and that they are not fully ready to accommodate GDPR compliance issues. In a recent survey (IAAP-FTI 2020) which was published in 2020 by the International Association of Privacy Professionals, less than half of respondents (47%) answered that they are fully compliant with the GDPR. Reported challenges for GDPR compliance (McKinsey and Company 2019) include the exercising of the rights from the data subjects (GDPR, Articles 12–22), the automation of the records of processing activities (GDPR, Article 30) and the efficiency of the designed business processes during the preparations for the GDPR.

Complying with GDPR is a demanding process for all organisations, requiring various competences from different areas of expertise, including legal and technical, such as the information and communication systems security and privacy requirements engineering domain, as well as in depth knowledge of how different business units' function and, more importantly, the flow of personal information through the organisation. It is therefore important that organisations are supported throughout all tasks involved in fulfilling the GDPR requirements, considering the context, functions and the characteristics of each organisation. The provision of products and systems following privacy-by-design principles (European Data Protection Board 2019), as well as the adoption of business processes that respect data protection principles, can result to several intangible benefits for an organisation, including good reputation, improving trust in customer and business partners relationships (e.g., data processors, third parties, suppliers), by rendering organisations trustworthy and accountable, while these benefits, in a long term can also return tangible benefits, such as increase of profits. Both in the literature (i.e. Langheinrich 2001; Cavoukian 2009) and in accordance with the Article 25 of the GPDR, it is found that privacy-by-design principles should be applied *at the time of the determination of the means for processing and at the time of the processing itself*, to responsibly manage and to effectively protect the personal data processed by an organisation.

In existing approaches (Pullonen et al. 2017; Ahmadian et al. 2018; Tom 2018), it is not easy to follow the flow of information throughout the organisation's business processes, especially when examining it from a privacy perspective, taking personal data within these flows under consideration. Current approaches have mainly relied on the empirical capabilities of the analyst to pinpoint personal data and all related interconnections within business flows. This paper aims to contribute to addressing this challenge by proposing a method that supports personal data protection throughout the entire life cycle of the information within an organisation, focusing on business processes to identify and assess information flows in terms of their privacy impact, so as to ensure the basic requirements of privacy-by-design. The proposed method bridges the gap between business and privacy analysts so as to leverage privacy aware work practices throughout the organisation, improving data protection and raising a privacy aware culture in its members.

The rest of this paper is structured as follows: Sect. 2 presents the background analysis with respect to the components of the proposed method, while Sect. 3 describes the proposed method for integrating business process redesign and Data Protection Impact Assessment (DPIA) in the context of an organisation. In Sect. 4 we further discuss the main pillars of the proposed method as well as the positive impact that its applicability will bring. Finally, in Sect. 5 we conclude the paper by raising issues for further practical research.

## 2 Background Analysis

Conduction of DPIA is a useful tool for the protection of personal data, and also comprises a requirement of the GDPR (GDPR/Article 35). DPIA supports (among others) organisations to gain the public's trust and confidence that privacy has been built into the design of a process, information system or programme. Conducting a DPIA, according to the GDPR, is mandatory when high-risk for the data subjects' rights is introduced by the processing of their data (e.g., when special categories of personal data are processed or when processing involves systematic evaluation of personal aspects or scoring). However, conducting a DPIA also comprises a good practice for data protection, and as the Article 29 Data Protection Working Party (2017) proposes, the organisations that process personal data should conduct DPIA in order to identify and reduce the privacy risks of the activities that process personal data and they are responsible for. Taking into account the high amount of personal data processed by several everyday applications, such as location-based services and fitness/well-being applications, conducting a DPIA emerges as a necessity in most cases of digital services provided to individuals. At the same time, the need for conducting a DPIA is also eminent in cases where extensive personal data collection is imposed by special circumstances, as for instance when the Covid19 lockdown rendered teleworking, telecommunication, and tele-education applications essential for society to continue operating, thus making necessary the extensive use of applications gathering data on the history of user interactions and metadata about their devices. In the same context, several applications have emerged for tracing people's contacts via their location data, found on their cell phone[1], to prevent the spread of the virus.

Taking into consideration the general philosophy of the GDPR, all organisations processing personal data should protect personal data throughout their entire lifecycle, in a holistic and context-aware manner (Henriksen-Bulmer et al. 2020), from their generation/insertion into the organisation till their disposal. This necessity applies not only to data that is preserved and processed via digital infrastructure, but also to personal data kept in hardcopy form. Data protection principles should be followed as a universal requirement for the whole organisation's scope. Privacy-by-design is an approach that requires the integration of key protection parameters by the organisation who is responsible for the processing of individuals' personal data into existing wider project management approaches. GDPR provisions facilitate to this direction by requiring companies, organisations, etc. to ensure that the protection of users' privacy is a basic parameter in the early stages of each project and then throughout its life cycle (Langheinrich 2001; Cavoukian 2009).

However, security and privacy requirements elicitation and the assessment of privacy risk that is imposed by a specific process or information system is not an easy task

[1] https://www.europarl.europa.eu/news/en/press-room/20200512IPR78915/covid-19-tracing-apps-meps-stress-the-need-to-preserve-citizens-privacy.

and security and privacy analysts are not always able to follow the flow of information throughout an organisation's business processes. It is necessary to consider all related business functions, as well as the inner and outer context of an organisation in order to assess the impact of the realisation of a privacy threat at any given point within any business process flow. Conducting a DPIA process, up to now, has mainly relied on the insight of analysts, in order to identify the information flows' interconnections, or it has relied on the repetition of this process for each critical flow. As security and privacy analysis is necessary for organisations that processes personal data, security/privacy requirements methodologies are implemented (indicatively, Kalloniatis et al. 2009; Mellado et al. 2010; Beckers 2012) aiming at evaluating the critical assets of an organisation. These methodologies support security/privacy experts to identify the requirements for the protection of an asset and to analyse the identified threats and vulnerabilities of an organisation.

Available methodologies/tools so far do not support the capturing of the flows of information in conjunction with the corresponding assets and the responsible entity for each process, and there is no connection and association of a system's security and privacy analysis with an organisation's hierarchical roles. The method described in the next section aims at addressing this gap, by integrating the main steps of a DPIA with the business process management, so as to facilitate the identification of personal data flow throughout the organisation, support the assessment of privacy related risks and enhance personal data protection.

The proposed method aims at supporting business processes management and/or (re)design of an organisation to support personal data protection. To achieve this, we draw on the frameworks and tools supporting the (re)design of business processes, i.e. Business Process Management (BPM) (Hammer 2015) disciplines, focusing on the modelling, analysis, and improvement of business processes in terms of efficiency and effectiveness. BPM tools allow analysts to capture the existing business processes within an organisation, including the infrastructure, i.e. the corresponding Information Systems (IS) being used, the involved roles for each process, the documents that each IS uses, produces, stores, etc., the retention period of each document, the origin (source) of each document as well as its final destination. Business process modelling tools can also support the identification of data flows within an organisation. Though the usefulness of BPM tools and methods has been acknowledged by the information security research community in providing comprehensive security for information assets (Kokolakis et al. 2000; Backes et al. 2003; Argyropoulos et al. 2017), such efforts can support the protection of personal information only partially and at a limited level (Diamantopoulou et al. 2017a). Limitations of current approaches also include that the notation of the personal data (and the special categories of personal data, i.e. sensitive data) is not supported, and that the criticality of the IS cannot be prioritised either. For example, in order to prevent data losses in a potential data breach, an organisation must have fortified the IS that stores the personal data rather than e.g., an IS responsible for the daily transaction of an e-commerce web service – that does not process personal data.

## 3 A Method for Integrating DPIA and Business Process Management

Our proposed method supports the identification, modelling, redesign, implementation, and realisation of security and privacy aware/compliant business processes, by identifying security and privacy risks to personal information flows for all business processes, and by employing privacy strategies for realising privacy preserving workflows. Figure 1 presents the steps of the proposed method.

The method follows the logic of a typical BPM approach that allows to capture, analyse, and model, in a systematic way, the organisation's business processes and workflows. Identification and analysis of business processes and information flows provides the basis for conducting a security and privacy requirements analysis, allowing the adoption of a business process perspective, which takes into account all involved roles, internal and external. This process provides an identification of information flows to be evaluated in terms of the basic data protection principles (i.e. data minimisation, accuracy, storage limitation, integrity and confidentiality, lawfulness, fairness and transparency, and purpose limitation) and to assess existing threats and vulnerabilities and identify security and privacy requirements. The proposed method also includes a DPIA process as an optional step. Organisations however are encouraged to conduct DPIA in the activities they perform that process personal data as they can also achieve benefits from the increased trust gained by their clients and collaborators which results from increased data protection.

The output of the analysis provides insights for managing (an, if needed, redesigning) business processes in a more efficient, secure and privacy-aware manner. To (re)design privacy-aware business processes different tools can be used, such as for example privacy process patterns (Diamantopoulou et al. 2017a, b) that will facilitate the analyst to associate privacy requirements with appropriate Privacy Enhancing Technologies (PETs). Privacy patterns can be applied to satisfy the identified privacy requirements, as they allow the capturing and sharing design knowledge (Alexander 1997; Borchers 2000) and encapsulate expert knowledge of PETs implementation at the operational level. Different types of privacy patterns are available (Kalloniatis et al. 2008) including i) administrative tools, ii) information tools, iii) anonymizer products, iv) services and architectures, v) pseudonymizer tools, vi) track and evident erasers, and vii) encryption tools. Each category contains specific technical implementation techniques which can be used as a basis for the designer along with the stakeholders and/or the organisation's developer team to decide and propose the most appropriate ones that will satisfy the identified privacy requirements.

The proposed method includes a repetitive process in accordance with the continuous improvement concept suggested by ISO/IEC 27001:2013 standard (2013) and the GDPR. This repetitive phase is also mandated by the fact that business processes may change within an organisation, and/or new Information Systems may be deployed.

The steps/phases of the proposed method are four. As we mentioned above, conducting a DPIA is not obligatory, however, organisations are encouraged to conduct it for

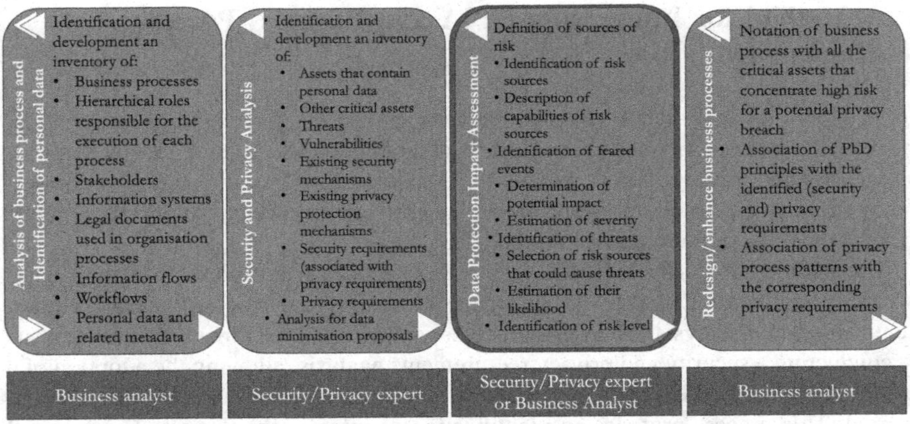


**Fig. 1.** Method for integrating privacy-by-design into business processes/workflows

new projects, products, or services. Below, we explain the main phases of the method, focusing on the main activities:

**Analysis of Business Process and Identification of Personal Data:** Main activities in this step include the capturing, identification, modelling and analysis of the organisation's business processes and workflows, along with the relevant information flows and it will also support the identification of related entities and stakeholders such as the responsible entity for the execution of such processes (internal entities of the organisation or external parties), the IS involved in each processing, the documents requested for each process, the flow of each document, and the responsible hierarchical roles for the execution of business processes. As existing BPM solutions lack characterisation and distinction of "personal data" or "sensitive data" we propose the inclusion of both of these object types in the design process using relevant annotations/metadata. To use the relevant annotations/metadata, analysts will draw on the descriptions and provisions in Article 30 of the GDPR about "records of processing activities".

**Security and Privacy Analysis:** Designing and implementing systems and/or services with respect to security and privacy requires the integration of security and privacy requirements into the typical engineering activities. In this step all critical assets are assessed, as well as the processes and flows of the previous steps, from a security and privacy perspective. More specifically, this step contains the identification of the critical assets of the organisation's business processes that affect the processing of personal data, potential threats that might have an impact on these assets and any vulnerabilities that these assets may have. Additionally, in this step, the interconnections between the corresponding lanes of the under-examination business processes reveal any associations between assets, as well as the impact of threats to all critical assets. By following this method, we are able to capture the impact of threats on any specific asset by examining it throughout its whole lifecycle and flow in the various business information processes. Finally, this step includes the documentation of existing security and privacy mechanisms and the analysis of a security and privacy assessment of all workflows and corresponding assets entailing personal information, considering all security and privacy requirements affecting actors, assets, information, roles, and hierarchies.

**DPIA Process (Optional):** The objective of this step is the assessment of the privacy risk that can be materialised by the data processing activities carried out by the organisation and could have an impact on the privacy of the persons whose personal data is processed. Here, the analyst identifies the processing activities that may be either implemented directly by the organisation who is responsible for the data processing or by the organisation who is directly conducting the processing. The risk of each processing activity is analysed to the severity and the likelihood for a threat to have an impact on the data subject, while mitigation measures are identified in terms of applicable privacy patterns. This step takes as input the outcomes of the first two steps ((i) Analysis of business process and Identification of personal data and (ii) Security and Privacy analysis) and the appropriate (per case) privacy process patterns to guide selection and implementation of mitigation measures.

**Redesign/Enhance Business Processes:** Drawing on BPM concepts, the fourth step aims at the redesign of the business processes of the organisation, taking into account the results of the previous three components and employing privacy preserving patterns. The analyst uses the identified (from the second step) security and privacy requirements in order to construct robust and privacy preserving business processes, thus implementing privacy-by-design principles, impacting all the organisational processes. Analysts implement selected appropriate PETs for satisfying the requested security and privacy requirements. Through the redesign of the business processes and information flows the organisation will be enhancing their activities, leveraging the data protection principles in any node of this system, either systemic or human one.

Concluding, this method supports the aggregation of all the information and modelling analysis of business processes with data protection, supporting the privacy-by-design principles with the identified (security and) privacy requirements and by associating the privacy process patterns with the corresponding privacy requirements (as they have been identified in the second step).

## 4 Discussion

Up to now, and to the best of our knowledge, there is no comprehensive approach supporting organisations to manage the flow of personal information through their business processes that supports the need of organisation to comply with data protection legislation and follow the privacy-by-design principles. The proposed method draws on the concepts of business process management data protection to provide a method to enable organisations model and redesign their business processes in a privacy-aware context, establishing, thus, secure and privacy-aware business processes and delivering secure products/services, following privacy-by-design principles. Our approach allows organisations develop privacy preserving business practices and workflows, resulting in products and services that comply with data protection rules and requirements. In doing so, personal data protection practices and principles are leveraged into all organisational functions. Furthermore, the proposed method guides organisations to perform important tasks with regard to GDPR compliance and provide concrete and detailed work practices and solutions, in the form of privacy patterns. More specifically, the proposed method aims has the following characteristics:

- **Provides comprehensive steps for privacy analysis:** This method supports the modelling, redesign, implementation and realisation of privacy aware/compliant business processes, by a) considering personal and sensitive data in the activity of business process capturing and modelling, b) identifying the responsible roles and associating them with the corresponding business processes, c) analysing business processes from a security and privacy perspective, d) assessing privacy risks to personal information flows of all business processes, and e) employing privacy preserving strategies for realising the respective workflows, utilising existing technologies, frameworks, methods and tools.
- **Supports GDPR compliant services and products:** The proposed method can help redesign an organisation's processes or products/systems they deliver to ensure they are GDPR compliant. This approach supports, from a business process handling perspective, a basic goal of the GDPR, Privacy-by-Design, meaning protecting personal data – from their data entry/acquisition/generation to their disposal. The proposed method also guides the business/privacy analyst in application of the privacy-by-design principles from a technical perspective (by identifying security/privacy requirements and mapping them to privacy patterns) and a business perspective (managing stakeholders involved in each step of the business process). Also, by following our structured approach and documenting each step of the (re)design process, organisations are assisted in demonstrating how they implemented GDPR requirements (accountability requirement of the data controller).
- **Provides Liability:** With the identification of the roles in the recorded business processes, the proposed method facilitates the identification of the key stakeholders involved in the business process steps and the roles involved in the DPIA. As a result, this method provides the analyst with insights to understand which person/role is responsible (or should be consulted) in the context of the analysis and who should be assigned the responsibility for implementation of the proposed changes in the business process (including the implementation of privacy/security measures). This type of guidance enhances the organisations' approach towards compliance, by identifying responsible and accountable entities for the implementation of BPR outcome. It is useful in cases of complex system processes running through different units of the organisation, where stakeholders are unwilling to take ownership for a process, and in cases of complex environments between partners, especially in cases of joint controllership or controller-processor relationships.
- **Utilises privacy patterns:** Privacy patterns assist developers to understand, in a better and more specific way, how to implement the various privacy properties and are considered as a more robust way for bridging the gap between the design and the implementation phase of a system or module of it. Their incorporation within the proposed method facilitates the analyst to associate the privacy requirements with the appropriate PETs.

- **Utilises and extends existing approaches:** The proposed method draws upon existing well-established concepts and approaches, extending them to develop a comprehensive approach that leverages data protection in all business processes and incorporates privacy preserving principles in services, products and projects developed. The familiarisation of the business analysts/security/privacy experts with the basic structure of each component will benefit the design process.
- **Leverages privacy-by-design principles and practices:** With the use of the various different approaches, we are able to redesign the system-based processes as well as the human-based processes. To this end, the organisation is able to demonstrate both the technical and the organisational measures they had apply to protect the personal data they process, satisfying, thus, the GDPR requirement for the accountability as well as for the protection of such data.

## 5 Conclusions

In this paper we have identified the difficulties that organisations face in their attempt to design their business processes so that they are efficient and effective while at the same time, protecting personal data that is being processed, respecting the core requirements imposed by relevant regulations, such as the GDPR, and follow, the privacy-by-design principles. To satisfy these challenges, in this work we propose a method that supports the identification, modelling, redesign, implementation, and realisation of privacy aware/compliant business processes, by identifying privacy risks to personal information flows for all business processes, and by employing privacy strategies for realising privacy preserving workflows. The core idea of the proposed method is that it draws upon existing well-established concepts and approaches, extending them to develop a comprehensive approach that leverages data protection in all business processes and incorporates privacy preserving principles in services, products and projects developed, filling in an important gap in data protection in organisations and assisting them with GDPR compliance.

The proposed method, up to now, has not been validated in a real-life case scenario, but we intend to do so, as part of our future research goals, which also include the following: we aim to extend existing privacy patterns and develop a tool that includes an inventory of privacy patterns that can assist analysts in selecting, developing, managing and implementing them.

Future directions of this work also include the development of a tool that supports the implementation of the proposed method. This tool will provide a combination of BPM modelling functionalities, integrate the privacy patterns inventory, support security and privacy analysis conducting, and DPIA conducting, so that organisations can model and redesign their business processes following a data protection perspective, incorporating privacy-by-design principles, and achieving an end-to-end data protection process within their information flows and their workflows.

Additionally, we intend to provide a validation process to support the proposed method. The validation process will be based on the analysis of a case study approach that will allow us to better examine the steps of each phase of this method.

## References

Ahmadian, A.S., Strüber, D., Riediger, V., Jürjens, J.: Supporting privacy impact assessment by model-based privacy analysis. In: Proceedings of the 33rd Annual ACM Symposium on Applied Computing, pp. 1467–1474 (2018)

Alexander, C.: A Pattern Language: Towns, Buildings, Construction. Oxford University Press, Oxford (1977)

Argyropoulos, N., Mouratidis, H., Fish, A.: Supporting secure business process design via security process patterns. In: Enterprise Business-Process and Information Systems Modeling, pp. 19–33. Springer, Cham (2017)

Article 29 Data Protection Working Party: Guidelines on Data Protection Impact Assessment (DPIA) and determining whether processing is "likely to result in a high risk" for the purposes of Regulation 2016/679 (2017). https://ec.europa.eu/newsroom/document.cfm?doc_id=47711. Accessed 19 Apr 2021

Backes, M., Pfitzmann, B., Waidner, M.: Security in business process engineering. In: van der Aalst, W.M.P., Weske, M. (eds.) BPM 2003. LNCS, vol. 2678, pp. 168–183. Springer, Heidelberg (2003). https://doi.org/10.1007/3-540-44895-0_12

Beckers, K.: Comparing privacy requirements engineering approaches. In: 2012 Seventh International Conference on Availability, Reliability and Security, pp. 574–581. IEEE (2012)

Borchers, J.O.: A pattern approach to interaction design. In: Proceedings of the 3rd Conference on Designing Interactive Systems: Processes, Practices, Methods and Techniques, pp. 369–378. ACM (2000)

Cavoukian, A.: Privacy by Design: The 7 Foundational Principles. Information and Privacy Commissioner of Ontario, Canada 5 (2009)

Diamantopoulou, V., Argyropoulos, N., Kalloniatis, C., Gritzalis, S.: Supporting the design of privacy-aware business processes via privacy process patterns. In: 2017 11th International Conference on Research Challenges in Information Science (RCIS), pp. 187–198. IEEE (2017a)

Diamantopoulou, V., Kalloniatis, C., Gritzalis, S., Mouratidis, H.: Supporting privacy by design using privacy process patterns. In: De Capitani di Vimercati, S., Martinelli, F. (eds.) SEC 2017. IAICT, vol. 502, pp. 491–505. Springer, Cham (2017). https://doi.org/10.1007/978-3-319-58469-0_33

European Data Protection Board: Guidelines 4/2019 on Article 25 Data Protection by Design and by Default (2019). https://edpb.europa.eu/our-work-tools/public-consultations-art-704/2019/guidelines-42019-article-25-data-protection-design_en. Accessed 19 Apr 2021

European Parliament: Regulation (EU) 2016/679 of the European Parliament and of the Council of 27 April 2016 on the protection of natural persons with regard to the processing of personal data and on the free movement of such data, and repealing Directive 95/46/EC (General Data Protection Regulation)

Hammer, M.: What is business process management? In: Handbook on Business Process Management, vol. 1, pp. 3–16. Springer, Berlin (2015)

Henriksen-Bulmer, J., Faily, S., Jeary, S.: DPIA in context: applying dpia to assess privacy risks of cyber physical systems. Fut. Internet **12**(5), 93 (2020)

-FTI 2020: Annual governance report. Technical report (2021) https://iapp.org/media/pdf/resource_center/IAPP_FTIConsulting_2020PrivacyGovernanceReport.pdf. Accessed 19 Apr 2021

ISO 27001:2013 Information Technology – Security Techniques – Information Security Management Systems – Requirements (2013)

Kalloniatis, C., Kavakli, E., Gritzalis, S.: Addressing privacy requirements in system design: the PriS method. Requirem. Eng. **13**(3), 241–255 (2008)

Kalloniatis, C., Kavakli, E., Gritzalis, S.: Methods for designing privacy aware information systems: a review. In: 2009 13th Panhellenic Conference on Informatics, pp. 185–194. IEEE (2009)

Kokolakis, S.A., Demopoulos, A.J., Kiountouzis, E.A.: The use of business process modelling in information systems security analysis and design. Inf. Manag. Comput. Secur. **8**(3), 107–116 (2000)

Langheinrich, M.: Privacy by design — principles of privacy-aware ubiquitous systems. In: Abowd, G.D., Brumitt, B., Shafer, S. (eds.) Ubicomp 2001: Ubiquitous Computing. UbiComp 2001. LNCS, vol. 2201, pp. 273-291. Springer, Berlin (2001). https://doi.org/10.1007/3-540-45427-6_23

McKinsey &Company: GDPR compliance since May 2018: A continuing challenge (2019). https://www.mckinsey.com/business-functions/risk/our-insights/gdpr-compliance-after-may-2018-a-continuing-challenge. Accessed 19 Apr 2021

Mellado, D., Blanco, C., Sánchez, L.E., Fernández-Medina, E.: A systematic review of security requirements engineering. Comput. Stand. Interf. **32**(4), 153–165 (2010)

Pullonen, P., Matulevičius, R., Bogdanov, D.: PE-BPMN: privacy-enhanced business process model and notation. In: International Conference on Business Process Management, pp. 40–56 (2017)

Spiekermann, S., Acquisti, A., Böhme, R., Hui, K.-L.: The challenges of personal data markets and privacy. Electron. Mark. **25**(2), 161–167 (2015). https://doi.org/10.1007/s12525-015-0191-0

Reuters, T.: Study finds organizations are not ready for GDPR compliance issues (2019). https://legal.thomsonreuters.com/en/insights/articles/study-finds-organizations-not-ready-gdpr-compliance-issues. Accessed 19 Apr 2021

Tom, J.: Assessing and improving compliance to privacy regulations in business processes. In: Proceedings of the Doctoral Consortium papers presented at 30th International Conference on Advanced Information Systems Engineering (CAiSE) (2018)

# Disclosing Social and Location Attributes on Social Media: The Impact on Users' Privacy

Katerina Vgena[1](✉), Angeliki Kitsiou[1], Christos Kalloniatis[1], and Dimitris Kavroudakis[2]

[1] Privacy Engineering and Social Informatics Laboratory, Department of Cultural Technology and Communication, University of the Aegean, 81100 Lesvos, GR, Greece
kvgena@aegean.gr

[2] Department of Geography, University of the Aegean, 81100 Lesvos, GR, Greece

**Abstract.** Previous literature summarizes that within social media (SM) more information about users' identity may be disclosed in comparison to their initial intention, imposing various privacy implications. Privacy implications may arise due to the combination of social and location attributes disclosure. The revelation of a substantial amount of users' information can lead to users' identification due to new affiliations created. The main concern of the paper in hand is to discuss the social and location attributes which can play an essential role when implemented in designing privacy-aware information systems in the subject area of SM applications. Privacy requirements are being analyzed as organizational goals during the designing phase, thus, our analysis focuses on the interrelation among privacy requirements and social and location attributes. Interrelations that derive from social and location implications will be further analyzed in a case study, in which a user is presented throughout a potential online routine. The main contribution of this paper is to represent potential privacy implications that derive from both social and location attribute disclosure within SM, when the respective technical privacy requirements are not satisfied.

**Keywords:** Social attributes · Location attributes · Privacy requirements · Social software engineering · Social media

## 1 Introduction

Privacy implications in Social Media (SM) applications may arise due to different reasons [1, 2]. In our analysis, privacy implications will be examined in cases that derive from users' social or location attributes disclosure [3–13]. The combination of those characteristics is powerful enough to provide information about the user's identification [1, 6, 8]. Protecting users' privacy while investigating and implementing privacy requirements from an early stage of designing a system [6, 14, 15] is of primary concern, as it is compatible with previous literature focusing on the designing of traditional systems, the designing of cloud computing systems and the theory of the Social Software Engineering (SSE) [5, 6, 10, 12, 14–17]. Especially, according to the theory of SSE, considering


S. Katsikas et al. (Eds.): ESORICS 2021 Workshops, LNCS 13106, pp. 138–157, 2022.
https://doi.org/10.1007/978-3-030-95484-0_9

social attributes when designing Privacy-aware Information Systems is critical, because designers may tackle privacy issues under a different approach when applying privacy requirements due to the interference of social characteristics.

One of the main challenges that software designers face lays in the protection of users' privacy. As it is underlined by Kalloniatis, meeting users' expected way of handling personal information can be described as their right "to determine when, how and to what extent information about them is communicated to others (p. 3) [17]. Another important issue, raised from previous research, is the need to address privacy issues in the early phases of systems design rather than during the implementation phase of the system [14]. Privacy is perceived as a multidimensional concept, as Kalloniatis underlines, "privacy itself is a multifaceted concept", which should include social aspects in its analysis (p. 1) [14].

This paper focuses on privacy implications imposed by the disclosure of users' social and location attributes, which according to our previous work, provoke privacy issues [18, 19]. The contribution of this paper is that it creates new affiliations among social and location attributes and the respective privacy requirements, which should be combined in better addressing privacy implications originating from social and location attribute disclosure in SM applications.

More specifically, after the introduction, we conduct a short analysis of related work on the most important social aspects in the second section of our paper. After that, we proceed in presenting the privacy requirements which are vital to adequately protect user's privacy in the third section of the paper. Then, we discuss privacy requirements under social aspects in the fourth section of our paper. The fifth section examines the interrelation between privacy requirements and social and location attributes, in which we illustrate how those attributes arise additional implications which should be put under meticulous analysis when designing privacy-aware information systems. In that section of our paper, we also present a case study of a user's online daily routine which combines social and location attributes in a way that creates new affiliations among the aforementioned users' characteristics and privacy requirements.

## 2 The Social Aspects of Privacy

Social aspects should be incorporated when designing privacy-aware information systems [8, 12, 21, 22, 24]. SSE is a relatively new field of study of software engineering, which deals with the investigation and implementation of social aspects and parameters that are concerned from an early stage of designing Privacy-aware Information Systems [6, 15]. SSE applies to a variety of social software applications, as it represents a social activity that focuses on the online community rather than the individual user. It deals with users' capacity of collaborating and forming relationships while engaging in addressing social problems and enabling social inclusion [6, 15]. SSE approach aims to identify how social aspects interact and affect the design of software during the software development cycle, providing an interdisciplinary approach for designing privacy-aware systems. Identity construction and privacy have gradually acquired a digital layer, as Rodota underlines in his work, since users' current identity is also constructed by what Google says about them [20]. Besides that, according to the EU Regulation, GDPR, there are two privacy principles, namely, privacy by design and privacy by default, that also point towards the same direction.

In this respect, we focus on potential privacy implications that arise from social and location attribute disclosure through users' willing choice of representing themselves on SM. The disclosure of a combination of social and location attributes seems to impose additional privacy issues according to our previous work [18, 19]. Face, Frame, Stage, Time and Activity or Performance are the attributes of Social Identity identified as the most compatible to geolocation attributes and privacy implications [1, 2, 5–7], while the Attributes of Location Information, which were examined for conducting the analogy are, namely: Who, What, When and Where [7, 12, 13]. Table 1 presents the interrelation among the Social Labels and Social Domains and Attributes of Location Information on SM. Social labels and location attributes are related to social domains, since the labels reflect parts of users' social domains [6] and therefore when some of these social labels are disclosed, we may have privacy implications. For instance, a user's Face (who the user is) can be determined from a user's name or his or her gender and consequently, the unveiling social labels on Social Media enable users' identification, and they have been marked with an X.

Table 1 is a focal point in our analysis, as it presents the bilateral relationships among Social Labels and Location Information Attributes in a way that is complementary to each other. The Social Labels, included in Table 1, derive from our previous analysis regarding users' self-determination and self-disclosure within social media [33, 34]. The aforementioned interrelations, especially the ones concerning Stage (combination of Frame and Time) may provide supplementary information on users' personal information through online activity traces. More specifically:

Face: It is a notion drawn from Social Identity Theory. Faces are described as social constructs that are perceived as "a kind of social user's manual" (p. 18) [6]. Faces enable users to interact properly under the respective context of communication, i.e., change their expected behavior [1]. Faces are distinct in each context according to non-visibility which retains users' information from one face into another face [1]. Face corresponds to the attribute who of the Location Information Theory [7].

Frame (Space of Action): It is the second notion drawn from Social Identity Theory. Frames refer to the place of action, activity or public performance. In other words, they represent the environment where the social actor (who) performs or "wears" a specific Face [5, 6]. The Frame corresponds to the attribute where of the Location Information Theory [7].

Stage: It is another notion drawn from Social Identity Theory which combines the attributes of where (frame) and when (time) [6, 7]. Stages may function as social settings that incorporate location and time in a way that discloses more information than the disclosure of location or time distinctively. Being present at a certain place at a specific time of the day may arise additional privacy implications. Stage corresponds to the attribute where and when of the Location Information Theory [7].

Activity or Performance: It is the last notion drawn from Social Identity Theory. Activity or Performance represents the occupation of the social actor, and it corresponds to the attribute what of the Location Information Theory [7].

**Table 1.** Labels of social identity on social media, social domains and attributes of location information

| Social labels | Social domains and attributes of location information | | | | |
|---|---|---|---|---|---|
| | Who face | Where frame | Where and when stage | When time | What activity |
| 1. Real name of an individual, name and surname | X | | | | |
| 2. Nicknames, pseudonym, username for SM | X | | | | X |
| 3. Photograph of the user | X | X | X | X | X |
| 4. Gender | X | | | | |
| 5. Civil, marital status | X | | | | |
| 6. Age group or their exact birthdate | | | | X | |
| 7. Permanent, physical address, residence or demographics | X | X | X | | |
| 8. Users' contact information (email) | X | X | X | X | X |
| 9. Users' contact information (phone number) | X | X | X | | |
| 10. Educational degree, Field or Academic classification, their major or their Academic Status | X | X | X | | X |
| 11. Users' Job or occupation | X | X | X | | X |
| 12. User's personal website | X | X | X | X | X |
| 13. Friend network or audience | X | X | X | | X |

(*continued*)

**Table 1.** (*continued*)

| Social labels | Social domains and attributes of location information | | | | |
|---|---|---|---|---|---|
| | Who face | Where frame | Where and when stage | When time | What activity |
| 14. National identity, race, minority | | X | X | | X |
| 15. Religious beliefs | | | | | X |
| 16. Class and Income | | | | | X |
| 17. Users' political orientation or party | | X | | | |
| 18. Groups of interests and hobbies | X | X | X | X | X |

Disclosing attributes that carry both social and location information introduces additional privacy implications that should be met via interdisciplinary approaches while examining reciprocal interrelations between location and identity attributes. The combination of location privacy and identity traits may reveal information unintentionally, without the user opting or realizing it [1, 6]. SM users unveil their true names while interacting in online social encounters. Disclosing one's name by itself may impose privacy implications, which tend to be multiplied when this information is revealed along with geotagging descriptions. Combining both attributes may intensify the need for protecting user's information during the designing phase by incorporating additional privacy requirements, especially due to users' absence of intention in doing so. Privacy implications can be imposed due to the nature of SM applications that engages users in sharing a combination of information in their online profiles. Thus, researchers should aim to provide additional privacy requirements for handling users' information [1, 2, 6, 7].

Users tend to elicit information from their experiences when proceeding in upcoming choices [6]. Users' records of experiences may function as a normativity tracker which can represent their biography. Repetitive patterns might reveal parts of their social identities through their online trajectories. Users' trajectories may provide a potential normativity track that can carry users' past choices while having them defined as biographical subjects [5, 6]. Users' online behavior is tracked as their repetitive online habits leave online traces that enable their past choices to provide inferences and enable third parties to jump to conclusions about their potential future choices. Thus, making predictions about users' activity through having access to their online past records on social status, geographic places, and users' ambitions are facilitated [5, 6]. Online traces may provide clues on users' online behavior, their normativity track through repetitive trajectories, and their identification. Repetitive past trajectories are powerful enough to infer upcoming choices related to their previous normativity tracks. Researchers should further investigate the proper privacy requirements which can be implemented to protect users' privacy.

Examining the social aspects of privacy, we draw on self-determination and self-disclosure. These notions should provide the necessary theoretical background to protect users' privacy from the negative consequences of willing self-revelations on SM applications (type and granularity of information provided). Privacy, self-determination and self-disclosure go hand in hand as SM users represent themselves in all levels of granularity while posting personal information online. Privacy's changing and challenging nature requires constant adaptations to accomplish the optimal level of disclosure in each Stage (Individual Privacy) [21, 22]. Before moving onwards, we will define those concepts in relation to privacy.

### 2.1 Privacy and Self-determination

Online self-revelations were discussed in Westin's "let it all hang out" philosophy (p. 20) [35], since then, the Western World [23] may follow his paradigm. Self-determination is defined as a "moral principle and right" and "a basic positive moral and legal principle of privacy protection" [21] (p. 51). Users tend to correlate self-determination and authenticity, as a simultaneous expression of the so-called "true-self" or "core-self" [21]. Users today tend to disclose their real name [24] along with a repetitive posting attitude of exchanging information between pairs of people, groups, or among individuals and organizations [25]. Self-determination or self-representation refer to how the uploaded information is going to be handled and consumed by other users (impression management).

Westin's definition [23, 26] describes four states of privacy (solitude, intimacy, anonymity, and reserve) which need to be balanced with users' need for social interaction and inclusion [26, 27]. Therefore, privacy is a dynamic, adaptive notion, as well as non-monotonic, including various levels of granularity [23]. Self-determination and privacy warranty the protection of users' Faces from context collapse [21], thus supporting our hypothesis that changing Stages require different Faces.

### 2.2 Privacy and Self-disclosure

Self-disclosure is users' practice of unveiling personal information willingly [21]. Users make themselves known through online messages [27], waffling between privacy implications and SM representation [21, 25, 27, 28]. Self-disclosure is related to the quantity and the quality of the information provided as well as who is going to have access to this information [21, 25]. The notion is vital when referring to the rather vague category of SM "Friends". Users' inability to determine their friendship level more accurately [21, 28] creates a non-realistic estimation of the number of people to whom they disclose personal information. Thus, imposing privacy issues due to incompatibilities between social Stages and users Faces [18, 19, 28].

## 3 Privacy Implications on SM Due to Self-determination and Self-disclosure

Privacy implications may derive from willing disclosures of social attributes on behalf of the user while representing his or her persona online. To choose the requirements which should be put under meticulous analysis, we filter the ones that may not be satisfied through a willing user's disclosure on SM. Users' options point towards the notions of self-determination and self-disclosure, as necessary ones when representing themselves on SM. Users' need of belonging to the online community imposes sharing personal content online in order for them to be engaged in the community while creating and maintaining social relationships.

Towards this, the five core privacy requirements, deriving from PRIS methodology [14] and listed below, are going to be implemented and analyzed as important elements of our interdisciplinary approach, due to their potential non-satisfaction imposed by processes of self-determination and self-disclosure.

**Table 2.** Privacy requirements, self-determination and self-disclosure

| | Self-determination | Self-disclosure |
|---|---|---|
| Privacy requirements | | |
| Anonymity | X | X |
| Pseudonymity | X | X |
| Unlinkability | X | X |
| Undetectability | X | X |
| Unobservability | X | X |

Anonymity, pseudonymity, unlinkability, undetectability and unobservability are related to users' willing uploading of personal information are summarized below as they were defined by [8, 29]. Anonymity protects the user's identity from being accessible and identifiable to unauthorized users or third parties [8, 29]. Pseudonymity protects the identity of a user from a different perspective, i.e., by using pseudonyms. Users utilize alternative fake names to hide their true identities [8, 29]. Unlinkability protects users' relationships and interactions from being disclosed to unauthorized users or third parties [8, 29, 30]. Undetectability and unobservability protect users in a supplementary to each other way, protecting users from being detected by other unauthorized users or third parties. Unobservability can be seen as a combination of anonymity and undetectability [8, 17, 29]. Unobservability is also defined by Kalloniatis as "the undetectability that uninvolved subjects have communication together with anonymity even if items of interest can necessarily be detected by the involved subjects (p. 12) [17].

Table 2 shows that users may encounter privacy implications due to the non-satisfaction of the five core privacy requirements which are strongly associated with self-determination and self-disclosure, as those notions dominate users' choices to establish strong conversational profiles. Users waffle between not revealing and revealing personal information online, however they disclose different types of social information, which can be classified into the five main social domains, namely Face, Frame, Stage, Time, Activity [5, 15, 18, 19]. Users' personal information can be protected by filtering the negative consequences of self-determination and self-disclosure through the five privacy requirements.

Analyzing privacy requirements from a social spectrum within SM, we combine and bridge social notions to technical ones, by using privacy as a common ground among them. Anonymity refers to the unidentifiability of a social actor while online from other social actors. Users can hide their identities while using a service. Despite the opposite practice which is followed on SM applications, anonymity is considered to be an important aspect as it seems to be preferable in certain instances [8, 29]. SM users disclose their actual name in some of the most common SM applications, such as Twitter or Facebook, however, they seem to hide their identity when it comes to writing online reviews on Booking, Google Maps or Airbnb platforms, possibly for plausible deniability purposes. Users are concerned about their identifiability by other users, so they adopt privacy strategies for handling privacy issues. Anonymity can be non-satisfied in cases such as context and time collapse however, pseudonymity could be the answer.

Pseudonymity refers to the use of pseudonyms to preserve unidentifiability in cases that anonymity cannot be effective. It hides and protects a user's identity by reporting unreal or fake names [8, 29]. Pseudonymity is another concept that is important for our analysis as it can also tackle the unidentifiability of a user. Anonymity and pseudonymity are vital aspects in our analysis as, despite users' common practice of sharing their true identity while present in SM, they tend to experience feelings of distress. Those feelings can be identified and analyzed by Marwick's research [31–33]. In her analysis roles, such as employee, academic, daughter, boss and parent are perceived as distinct and separate from one another. Hence, online content disclosure from one specific social role into another distinct role can cause tension or awkwardness due to the disclosure of the user's social attributes in unexpected settings. In this way, Anonymity and Pseudonymity can be read through the social notions of context and time collapse.

According to Marwick's and Beam et al.'s studies context collapse occurs [31, 34] in case "different facets of a person's life, such as friends, family members, and co-workers, are lumped together under the rubric of "friends." (p. 8) [31]. Under those circumstances, information from one role is going to be unveiled in other roles because of certain social media practices of grouping together different social relationships, an example of such a SM application could be Facebook. Different social relationships, such as "Family", "Co-workers" or "Acquaintances" are grouped together under the umbrella social relationship of "Friends" [4, 9, 13, 31]. Context collapse intervenes with the privacy requirements of Anonymity and Pseudonymity.

Time collapse is a term analyzed in Brandtzaeg and Luders' work which incorporates the element of time [35]. Their research describes the blend and easy access to a user's past and present experiences via his/her Facebook timeline as "time collapse". The constantly achieved repository of histories and events of a user's life may cause discomfort when a past aspect of him/herself is unveiled into his/her present moment through instances of absence of proper protection from Anonymity or Pseudonymity. Time collapse seems to trigger potential threats, especially to millennials as they appear to be the first generation whose online self-generated archived content is available from youth to adulthood. Thus, probably creating risks as far as their "right to be forgotten" is concerned because they may experience potential threats from previously posted information through time collapses.

Unlinkability refers to the absence of making connections between the relationships of social actors, their messages, or actions from other social actors (third parties). Any interactions between a sender and a recipient are protected from making further assumptions for a potential relationship between them [8, 29] or the frequency they meet with other users [30]. Social actors and social relationships could experience various unwanted repercussions due to potential leaks of information. The unveiling of social relations between two social actors can lead to awkwardness or even tension among one's social sphere in case it is not protected properly.

Unlinkability is also crucial for our research as SM application usage and the frequency of users' logs and check-ins in different places with different users through their posts provide a considerable amount of information that can potentially point towards assumptions of users' normativity through their trajectories. User's past records of their online activity include information about their location (where) as well as temporal information (when) which can probably lead not only in their re-identification (raising Anonymity and Pseudonymity implications) but also enabling conclusions about users' past, current or future habits [30] through their identification as biographical subjects [6, 15]. Repetitive identification of users' habits and trajectories enables inferences about their online normativity and, thus facilitates predictions about their future choices [6, 11, 15]. Combining users' identities with their place of presence or absence can also raise issues that can be related to the notion of absence privacy and, thus, render users vulnerable to theft issues [30]. An example of a location-based and preference-aware recommendation system is analyzed by Bao et al. [3]. According to their study, the location recommender system receives users' location information, which is available through their location logs history to match them to other users based on their common social opinions. Their example is based on the idea that users who have already been identified as, "sommeliers", for example, will probably enjoy information about potential places of interest relevant to their preference, "wine bars", "distilleries", "wine museums".

Undetectability refers to the ability of a component to remain undetected by other social actors. Third parties are not provided with information, such as the use of a service or any other action that a user may have utilized. Unobservability refers to the undetectability between users in cases where anonymity cannot be effective and thus, the user's identity is accessible to other social actors [8, 29]. Undetectability and unobservability function as supplementary notions to one another [17]. Unobservability, which preceded undetectability as a notion, needed further support for privacy implications that could not be covered by unobservability itself. Thus, undetectability provided the necessary solid background for protecting users' privacy in cases that unobservability could not be effective.

Unobservability is a privacy requirement that can play an essential role in the analysis of users' digital identities. SM representation tends to be completed in two steps while organizing one's social media profile, it includes both a name and surname description and an accompanying image of the user's facial and/or body characteristics. Table 3 draws the analogy.

**Table 3.** Social labels and potential non-satisfaction of privacy requirements on SM

| Privacy requirements | Social labels | | | | | | | | | | | | | | | | | |
|---|---|---|---|---|---|---|---|---|---|---|---|---|---|---|---|---|---|---|
| | 1 | 2 | 3 | 4 | 5 | 6 | 7 | 8 | 9 | 10 | 11 | 12 | 13 | 14 | 15 | 16 | 17 | 18 |
| Anonymity | X | X | X | | | | | X | | | | X | | | | | | |
| Pseudonymity | | X | X | X | X | | | X | | | | | | | | | X | X |
| Unlinkability | | | X | X | X | | X | X | X | X | X | | X | X | X | X | X | X |
| Undetectability | X | X | X | X | X | X | X | X | X | X | X | X | X | X | X | X | X | X |
| Unobservability | X | X | X | X | X | X | X | X | X | X | X | X | X | X | X | X | X | X |

Before moving to our case study, it is crucial to underline that the majority of privacy requirements may not be satisfied due to social and location attribute disclosure. The main point in our analysis is that privacy requirements cannot be satisfied either due to the direct disclosure of users' information when choosing to unveil part of their identity or due to potential indirect disclosure of information as well. In the first case, the user will be aware of the information uploaded on his account, while on the other hand, the information provided may exceed the intention of the user because of the combination of social and location information which can lead to the potential identification of the user. That is the reason why our case study aims to identify the combination of social and location attributes that contribute to information disclosure on behalf of a user through a case study scenario.

# 4 Case Study

## 4.1 Preparing the Case Study

After focusing on the privacy requirements and the possible implications, we turned towards designing case study scenarios. We draw on simultaneous disclosures of social and location attributes to investigate privacy implications or privacy leaks, as the European white book suggests [36]. This book categorizes both SM networks and geolocation information as cases in which potential leaks are falling under the category that requests "either a tacit or informed consent of the user" (p. 114) [36].

Tacit consent on behalf of the users can potentially lead to an unveiling of information that they did not intend to disclose in the first place. Those privacy leaks can happen through social and location privacy implications that remain present despite the implementation of the existing privacy requirements. To address this need, our analysis focuses on social and location attributes as long as the interrelated affiliations between them, based on our previous work [18, 19]. This interrelation can also be illustrated in Fig. 1.

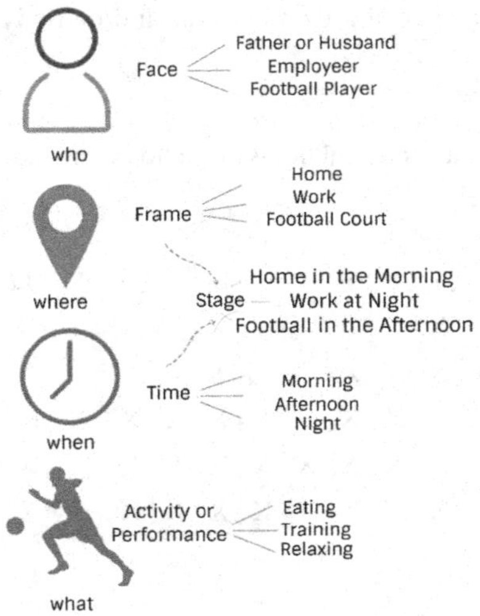


**Fig. 1.** Interrelations between social and location attributes

Users combine social and location attributes to represent themselves online, depending on the level of granularity users may choose when unveiling attributes for their representation, they can be targeted to a different level of precision. The more precise the level of granularity and the amount of information provided, the easier it becomes to target a user's actual identity through matching faces. Thus, tracing their habits and trajectories for a present or future reference. Users may encounter a wide variety of potential malware implications due to the revelation of either social or location attributes or the revelation of their combination, as was examined in our previous work [18]. These new affiliations were powerful enough to exacerbate the unveiling of users' personal information when combined.

Consequently, it seems that there are additional privacy implications that should be incorporated in our analysis towards designing privacy-aware information systems. Except for the attributes of location privacy, which are namely, who, what, when, and where, we can proceed in an analogy with the Social Identity Theory, namely face, frame, stage, time, and activity or performance. Therefore, the perseverance of threats and concerns can raise multiple questions about the presence of additional characteristics or attributes which should be taken into consideration when designing privacy-aware information systems.

### 4.2 Setting the Case Study

To address this need, we design an example that could serve as a way to illustrate how a typical user changes his or her face in multiple contexts around the clock. The devices that the user would probably use are also thought to play an important role in his or her routine, so they are chosen for users' main uses, more specifically, "Mobile phone for entertainment purposes" and "PC for working purposes".

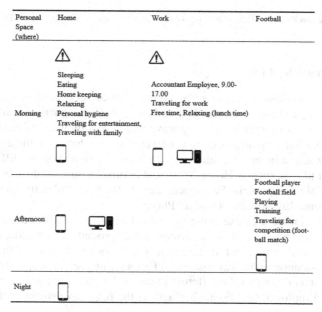

| Personal Space (where) | Home | Work | Football |
|---|---|---|---|
| Morning | Sleeping<br>Eating<br>Home keeping<br>Relaxing<br>Personal hygiene<br>Traveling for entertainment,<br>Traveling with family | Accountant Employee, 9.00-17.00<br>Traveling for work<br>Free time, Relaxing (lunch time) | |
| Afternoon | | | Football player<br>Football field<br>Playing<br>Training<br>Traveling for competition (foot-ball match) |
| Night | | | |

**Fig. 2.** An example of personal space and time

To proceed with the analysis of the case study, we set three different personal spaces, such as "Home", "Work" and "Football", which serve as settings. Those settings are activated when the user enters the respective place around the clock. The time of the activation of the action is described as "Morning", "Afternoon" and "Night".

Figure 2 represents an example of the combination of a user's personal space and time. In the table below, we tried to incorporate the interplay of the characteristic of complexity according to the social identity theory which plays an important role in the representation of user's identity. Complexity, multiplicity, and permeability are the core characteristics of social identity [5].

Those three characteristics play an important role as they trigger the interplay of social faces in different contexts and around the clock. Complexity, according to the characteristics of Social Identity Theory, occurs when different social faces are intertwined, in cases when different social norms are expected on behalf of the user. Some instances that complexity may be present on a SM application is when a user updates his or her SM account while being late for work in the morning or posting about personal interests or football during his presence at work.

Every time that a user unveils an otherwise hidden part of his or her social identity that corresponds to a different social face from the one that he or she is supposed to use while conducting regular or usual activities during a specific period of time at a specific place, awkwardness may arise. Therefore, we tried to be as descriptive as possible to include both expected and unexpected users' activities during the respective time of the day. The instances in which users may change their predictable ways of behavior and probably create awkward effects are represented by a hazard symbol in the respective cells.

### 4.3 The Normativity Line

To address the multi-dimensional privacy issues due to social and location attribute disclosure, we expand our understanding of how system designers should satisfy the privacy requirements in interdisciplinary ways which will include the reconsideration of social and location attributes as carriers of users' social identity in the digital sphere. Figure 3 illustrates another case study in which a user is present in different social backgrounds or places, such as Home, Work and Football Court, while at the same time he changes social roles or social Faces, according to the Social Identity Theory, such as Father or Husband, Employee or Football Player.

We focus on a male user executing everyday tasks in his daily routine. We follow the user in the most anticipated social places or backgrounds in the vertical axis, such as his house, his occupation and his free time activity or sport, while at the same time paying special attention to the way that social Faces are utilized or dropped accordingly. The horizontal axis illustrates the different Faces of the user, such as being a Father or a Husband, an Employee or a Football Player at the respective social backgrounds or places.

One of the most important findings is the revelation of the normativity line. The geolocation example helps in formulating the dashed line which joints all the expected instances of the combination of social backgrounds along with proper social Faces. Therefore, the presence of a normativity line can include all the anticipated activities while being present at a specific place wearing a specific social Face. In the current study case, we identified three such instances. The first one includes activities such as eating, home keeping, using social media, relaxing, training for work or football or sleeping at Home while wearing the Face of the Father or Husband. The second category includes the anticipated activities when the user is being present at Work while wearing the Face of the Employee. Then, he was supposed to carry out activities, such as working, training for work, or having some spare time to eat, socialize or use social media for entertainment purposes during his break. The last group of anticipated activities was while he is being present at the Football Court while wearing the Football Player Face. In this case, the user could train, have fun, socialize, or travel as an example of expected activities according to his enabled Face and Place of presence.

Any activity performed above or under the normativity line can trigger awkwardness either due to wearing an unexpected social Face or being present at an unexpected place. Thus, additional privacy implications except for the already existing ones in all instances along the normativity line can be identified.

### 4.4 Outside the Normativity Line

While analyzing the aforementioned case of indicative usage of SM applications in time and space, we should also include the example of traveling. The instance of traveling raised questions as far as location is concerned. The initial reference to a place caught

| | | *Places* | | |
|---|---|---|---|---|
| | | **Home** | **Work** | **Football** |
| *Roles or Social Faces* | **Father or Husband** | • Eating<br>• Home keeping<br>• Social media<br>• Relaxing<br>• Training for work or football<br>• Sleeping | • Communicating<br>• Using social media | • Communicating<br>• Physical presence of a relative |
| | **Employee** | • Working at home<br>• Communicating<br>• Training | • Working<br>• Training for work<br>• Relaxing during his free time (eating, socializing, using social media) | • Communicating (answering phone calls, emails) |
| | **Football Player** | • Using social media<br>• Educating himself<br>• Training<br>• Talking about eating habits | • Using social media<br>• Talking about eating habits<br>• Educating himself (about health and nutrition) | • Training<br>• Having fun<br>• Socializing<br>• Traveling |

**Fig. 3.** A User changing among different social backgrounds and social faces

our attention. For example, a city, such as "Thessaloniki", did not necessarily presuppose wearing a specific social Hat or Face on behalf of the user.

Figure 4 represents a user being at the location of a city, while at the same time utilizing different Faces or Places of presence in the same city. The same user may be wearing the face of the Father for entertainment purposes, thus visiting a museum, a restaurant or relaxing at a hotel, the Face of an Employee at a Convention Center, or a hotel, while visiting the city for working purposes or even wearing the Face of the Football player, visiting the city for a soccer match in a football field or relaxing at a hotel before or after the football match. We also observed that the only common environment which was shared in all Faces of our example is the Hotel. The reason for that overlapping is that the Hotel is used to signify a temporary hosting environment provided that the user is presupposed to travel in a different place from his or her permanent residence.

Traveling is one of the most important cases in which social and location attribute disclosure may exacerbate privacy implications because traveling is placed outside of the normativity line of the user. The user changes Faces (who), Time descriptions (when) and Performances (what) while at the same time remains at a very specific, common place (where). The direct or indirect disclosure of user's online information can lead to privacy requirements non-satisfaction and subsequent privacy implications.

The privacy implications may derive as Place is always revealed through various ways of communicating information on SM, such as posting photographs, hashtagging

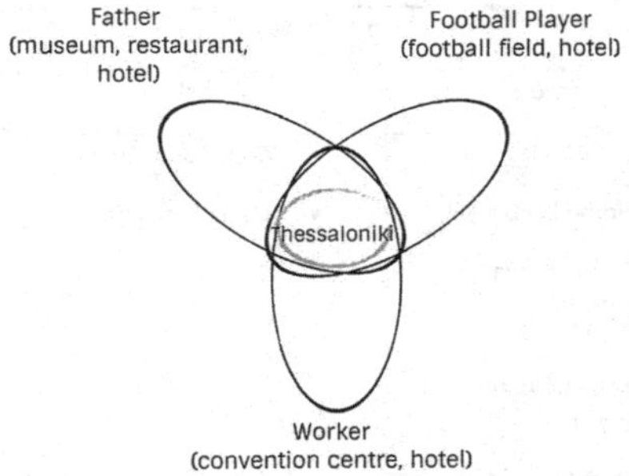


**Fig. 4.** The example of traveling

places, referring to specific landmarks or disclosing exact spatial information (x, y). If Place is revealed, Time can be easily accessed through the time description of SM posts or check-ins, making the other two remaining social and location attributes of who and what more easily identifiable through a potential combination of social and location attributes. If where and when are available, who and what can be easily presumed, leading to unveiling all four social and location attributes (who, where, when, what), targeting the true identity of the user. User's identity (who) along with the place of his presence (where) and the Time description (when) unveiled from a potential SM post (photograph or hashtag) will make the assumption of his Activity (what) easier to be made due to the combination of his social and location attributes.

In that case, Anonymity and Pseudonymity will not be satisfied, as the user's identity can be accessed due to the "context collapse" of his information to an improper audience or due to the "time collapse" of information during an improper period of time. Unlinkability can also be non-satisfied as the user's check-ins can disclose information on both his Place of presence and the simultaneous presence of other users who may also be there. In that way, unobservability and undetectability will be not satisfied as the user's photographs can reveal both his and his friends' true identity while making their real names available. Real names and photographs of oneself are frequently displayed on SM accounts for identification purposes.

### 4.5 Privacy Requirements, Social and Location Attributes

Having discussed the social aspects and the respective privacy requirements for addressing SM privacy implications, we turned towards examining the aforementioned case study. An indicative example could provide an initial practical analysis of the privacy requirements which can be either satisfied or not.

To proceed in checking if the aforementioned privacy requirements could be applied in our case study scenario, we examined all privacy issues which may appear either along the normativity line or outside of it. On the one hand, the implications that lie along the normativity line refer to the privacy issues which may be encountered when executing activities inside the expected social norms, i.e., wearing a proper social face for conducting the respective social activity in a presupposed context and time. For instance, a user may face privacy implications even while he is performing the activity of Relaxing at Home, wearing the face of Father of Husband, while he is Working, wearing the face of an Employee at this Work or while he is Training, wearing the face of a Football Player at the Football Court.

On the other hand, we expect that the privacy issues imposed outside the normativity line will be more in numbers and complexity in comparison to the privacy issues along the normativity line for the respective Social Faces of the user. In both cases, privacy implications may appear due to the violation of anonymity and pseudonymity, in cases when the identity of the user cannot be protected from a leak. SM applications frequently interfere with users' need for sharing information in practice, encouraging the unveiling of one's identity. Additional information leaking from photographs or hashtags may lead to detectability and observability non-satisfaction.

Context and time collapse can also pose privacy implications as the requirements of Anonymity and Pseudonymity are not satisfied. Users' identity can be violated through a potential leak of information either to the wrong audience or during an improper, upcoming moment when it may cause discomfort to the user.

Unlinkability cannot be reassured along the normativity line, as SM application usage and the frequency that users tend to log in to an SM application and/or check-in at a specific place may arise privacy implications in relation to other users' trajectories. For example, the presence of the user at a specific place where other users are also present can imply that he has friendly encounters with them or the least that he is familiar with those people. Tagging can also be a considerable way of conveying information and potentially threaten the user. The user may be tagged by his friends even without his consent in a way that will expose his presence at a place at night (bar or restaurant) to his working or athletic community, raising additional privacy implications.

Unobservability and undetectability may also be not satisfied when the user's identity is accessible to other social actors, especially due to users' common practice of sharing both their name and an actual photograph of their facial and/or body characteristics to their accounts.

Table 4 represents the potential non-satisfaction of privacy requirements due to social and location attribute disclosure. In the horizontal axis, we list social and location attributes with all potential labels taken from our case study. The vertical axis represents all privacy requirements that have already been chosen, based on the analysis of privacy requirements that are compatible with SM applications. We have marked with a cross checkmark (X) all the instances of potential privacy implications in which privacy requirements may fail to protect the user because of intentional or unintentional information disclosure on behalf of the user through social and location attribute disclosure.

According to our case study, the user is expected to behave in certain ways because of the social face and the location or time connotations imposed by his social sphere. In this scenario, if the user discloses information about himself while online, he will conform to the socially expected way of behavior, wearing the proper Face for conducting a specific Activity during the expected Time in an anticipated Place. For example, the user will perform as a Football Player, playing a sport during the Afternoon at the Football Court. In this example, the user performs alongside his normativity line.

**Table 4.** Privacy requirements non-satisfaction based on social and location attribute disclosure within SM applications

| Social and Location Attributes | Face (who) | | | Frame (where) | | | Time (when) | | | Stage (when and where) | | | Activity or Performance (what) | | |
|---|---|---|---|---|---|---|---|---|---|---|---|---|---|---|---|
| Privacy Requirements | Father | Worker | Football Player | Home | Work | Football Court | Morning | Afternoon | Night | Home in the morning | Football in the afternoon | Work at night | Relaxing | Training | Working |
| Anonymity | | | | X | | | | | | X | X | X | | | |
| Pseudonymity | | | | X | | | | | | X | X | X | | | |
| Unlinkability | | | | X | X | X | | | | X | X | X | | | X |
| Undetectability | X | X | X | X | X | X | X | X | X | X | X | X | X | X | X |
| Unobservability | X | X | X | X | X | X | X | X | X | X | X | X | X | X | X |

On the contrary, the user discloses the same information about his free time activity of playing football at a different Stage (combination of when and where). That example would impose very important privacy implications which are not present along his normativity line. Users' normativity lines provide information on both users' habits and the expected way of their behavior in accordance with the social norms which are presupposed for each user. If the user posted the same information during his Office Hours at Work, this action would carry different connotations and perhaps consequences for the user (his boss could complain about his carelessness). Here, the user performs an Activity outside of his normativity line.

Privacy requirements are vital because the user's content should be revised in a concrete and immediate way to restore the awkwardness that he experiences due to the revelation of a Football post during his Working hours or during his presence at Home while taking care of his new-born child. Access to that information should be restricted as they represent actions performed outside of his normativity line, imposing serious privacy implications. In particular, if the user of our case study posted something about his free time activity of playing football during his working hours (when) at Work (where), it would be considered inappropriate.

Social and Location attributes seem not to presuppose the non-satisfaction of certain privacy requirements when they are disclosed separately. The situation changes when attributes are combined, then, they can carry various privacy implications. Implications arise due to SM nature which triggers the combination of attributes by boosting users' confidence in doing so. Users' Face is one of the most frequently disclosed on SM, therefore, conclusions may easily be made either by malicious attackers or other SM users.

Interestingly, Stage, the combination of Time and Place, provides a powerful attribute that can enable additional implications because of the conclusions drawn. In particular, making predictions about the user is facilitated when Time and Place are provided, making his Face or Activity easily tracked. To illustrate it, we represented a potentially complete non-satisfaction of all privacy requirements based on Stage disclosure by marking those privacy implications with bold checkmarks.

That type of disclosure may impose severe privacy implications, especially when performing outside of the normativity line. That is because, despite the already existing privacy implications which may occur along the normativity line, we should add the ones that lie outside of it. In cases of a combination of social and location attributes and unintentional unveiling of attributes, additional awkward instances may cause sentiments of discomfort based on our case study.

## 5 Conclusion

The main purpose of this paper is to focus on the social and location attributes that may provoke the non-satisfaction of certain privacy requirements and to start a new dialogue when designing privacy-aware information systems. Our analysis incorporated privacy implications that are imposed due to potential social and location attributes disclosure through SM applications. The aforementioned privacy requirements were examined through a different way of analysis extending our understanding to investigate how they can be satisfied or non-satisfied within SM environments, as parts of the cloud computing environments. In addition, we investigated the privacy requirements which were compatible with our analysis on social and location aspects, providing the necessary affiliations between them.

Bridging technical privacy requirements, social and location theories, is the main contribution of the paper, as well as the case study scenarios. There, users were presented to utilize SM accounts in plausible everyday situations. Performing potential online posting routines, we identified two possible activity functions, either along or outside users' normativity line. The importance of protecting the respective privacy requirements during the designing phase of a system is underlined by the principles of SSE and supported by our case studies. Privacy requirements non-satisfaction can impose more serious privacy implications when users perform outside of their normativity line because of privacy's multidimensionality, which requires both a technical and a social analysis [14]. SSE can provide the necessary background in our case study scenarios on SM as it focuses on the online community and the social relationships among users.

Besides that, we should also include the limitations of the paper. Sociological notions such as the one of Face can prove to be multidimensional as well as complex to identify, especially because of the different naming devices used by different authors to be analyzed. In addition, examining users' faces both around the clock and in different settings is a multifaceted task that needs further exemplification through additional case studies. The interdisciplinary approach of our research should further expand our understanding of both technical and social aspects through the careful implementation of additional case studies or experiments with volunteers. Another important aspect that we aim to incorporate in our future research is a qualitative tool for conducting a validating and testing process.

Future research on this topic will focus on interdisciplinary approaches combining social and location attributes with technical aspects of privacy requirements, proposing a solid background towards addressing users' concerns and designing privacy-aware information systems [1, 2, 6, 7, 18, 19]. Supplementary case study scenarios can extend our research in various types of services. Developing new techniques and processes will contribute to formulating measurement scales for further understanding users' privacy within SM, so as to improve the existing privacy requirements based on a more social and spatially aware designing procedure. In that way, social media app developers could build apps that empower users to make informed decisions related to their normativity line.

## References


1. Lenberg, P., Feldt, R., Wallgren, L.G.: Behavioral software engineering: a definition and systematic literature review. J. Syst. Softw. **107**, 15–37 (2015)
2. Storey, M.-A., Treude, C., van Deursen, A., Cheng, L.-T.: The impact of social media on software engineering practices and tools. In: Proceedings of the FSE/SDP Workshop on Future of Software Engineering Research. pp. 359–364. ACM (2010)
3. Bao, J., Zheng, Y., Mokbel, M.F.: Location-based and preference-aware recommendation using sparse geo-social networking data. In: Proceedings of the 20th International Conference on Advances in Geographic Information Systems - SIGSPATIAL 2012, p. 199. ACM Press, Redondo Beach (2012)
4. Consolvo, S., Smith, I.E., Matthews, T., LaMarca, A., Tabert, J., Powledge, P.: Location disclosure to social relations: why, when, & what people want to share. In: Proceedings of the SIGCHI Conference on Human Factors in Computing Systems, pp. 81–90. ACM (2005)
5. Jenkins, R.: Social Identity. Routledge, London (2008)
6. Lahlou, S.: Identity, social status, privacy and face-keeping in digital society. Soc. Sci. Inf. **47**(3), 299–330 (2008)
7. Liu, B., Zhou, W., Zhu, T., Gao, L., Xiang, Y.: Location privacy and its applications: a systematic study. IEEE Access. **6**, 17606–17624 (2018)
8. Liu, L., Yu, E., Mylopoulos, J.: Security and privacy requirements analysis within a social setting. In: Proceedings of the 11th IEEE International Requirements Engineering Conference, 2003. pp. 151–161 (2003)
9. Mascetti, S., Freni, D., Bettini, C., Wang, X.S., Jajodia, S.: Privacy in geo-social networks: proximity notification with untrusted service providers and curious buddies. arXiv:10070408 (2010)
10. Nario-Redmond, M.R., Biernat, M., Eidelman, S., Palenske, D.J.: The social and personal identities scale: a measure of the differential importance ascribed to social and personal self-categorizations. Self Identity. **3**(2), 143–175 (2004)
11. Puttaswamy, K.P.N., Wang, S., Steinbauer, T., Agrawal, D., Abbadi, A.E., Kruegel, C., et al.: Preserving location privacy in geosocial applications. IEEE Trans. Mob. Comput. **13**(1), 159–173 (2014)
12. Schwartz, R., Halegoua, G.R.: The spatial self: Location-based identity performance on social media. New Media Soc. **17**(10), 1643–1660 (2015)
13. Snekkenes, E.: Concepts for personal location privacy policies. In: Proceedings of the 3rd ACM Conference on Electronic Commerce, pp. 48–57. ACM, New York (2001)
14. Kalloniatis, C., Kavakli, E., Gritzalis, S.: Addressing privacy requirements in system design: the PriS method. Req. Eng. **13**(3), 241–255 (2008)
15. Miguel, C., Medina, P.: The Transformation of identity and privacy through online social networks (The CouchSurfing case). (2011)

16. Kalloniatis, C.: Incorporating privacy in the design of cloud-based systems: a conceptual meta-model. Info Comput. Secur. **25**(5), 614–633 (2017)
17. Kalloniatis, C.: Increasing internet users trust in the cloud computing era: the role of privacy. J. Mass Commun. Journal. **06**(03) (2016)
18. Vgena, K., Kitsiou, A., Kalloniatis, C., Kavroudakis, D.: Do identity and location data interrelate? New affiliations and privacy concerns in social-driven sharing. In: Gritzalis, S., Weippl, E.R., Katsikas, S.K., Anderst-Kotsis, G., Tjoa, A.M., Khalil, I. (eds.) Trust, Privacy and Security in Digital Business, pp. 3–16. Springer International Publishing, Cham (2019). https://doi.org/10.1007/978-3-030-86586-3
19. Vgena, K., Kalloniatis, K., Gritzalis, K.: Toward addressing location privacy issues: new affiliations with social and location attributes. Fut. Internet **11**(11), 234 (2019)
20. Rodotà, S.: Privacy, freedom, and dignity. Presented at the Conclusive Remarks at the 26th International Conference on Privacy and Personal Data Protection (2004)
21. Trepte, S., Reinecke, L (eds): Privacy Online. Springer, Berlin (2011). https://doi.org/10.1007/978-3-642-21521-6
22. Westin, A.F.: Social and political dimensions of privacy. J. Soc. Issu. **59**(2), 431–453 (2003)
23. Margulis, S.T.: On the status and contribution of Westin's and Altman's theories of privacy. J Soc. Issu. **59**(2), 411–429 (2003)
24. Hogan, B.: Pseudonyms and the rise of the real-name web. In: Hartley, J., Burgess, J., Bruns, A.A. (eds.) Companion to New Media Dynamics, pp. 290–307. Wiley-Blackwell, Oxford (2013)
25. Joinson, A.N., Paine, C.B.: Self-disclosure, privacy and the internet. In: Joinson, A.N., McKenna, K.Y.A., Postmes, T., Reips, U.-D. (eds.) Oxford Handbook of Internet Psychology Oxford University Press, Oxford (2012)
26. Austin, L.M.: Re-reading Westin. Theor. Inqu. Law **20**(1), 53–81 (2019)
27. Taddicken, M.: The 'Privacy Paradox' in the social web: the impact of privacy concerns, individual characteristics, and the perceived social relevance on different forms of self-disclosure. J. Comput-Mediat. Comm. **19**(2), 248–273 (2014)
28. Bazarova, N.N., Choi, Y.H.: Self-disclosure in social media: extending the functional approach to disclosure motivations and characteristics on social network sites. J. Commun. **64**(4), 635–657 (2014)
29. Mavroeidi, A.-G., Kitsiou, A., Kalloniatis, C., Gritzalis, S.: Gamification vs. privacy: identifying and analysing the major concerns. Fut. Internet **11**(3), 67 (2019)
30. Ruiz Vicente, C., Freni, D., Bettini, C., Jensen, C.S.: Location-related privacy in geo-social networks. IEEE Internet Comput. **15**(3), 20–27 (2011)
31. Marwick, A.: The public domain: surveillance in everyday life. https://www.researchgate.net/publication/279673507_The_Public_Domain_Surveillance_in_Everyday_Life
32. Marwick, A.E.: boyd danah. I tweet honestly, I tweet passionately: Twitter users, context collapse, and the imagined audience. New Media Soc. **13**(1), 114–133 (2011)
33. Marwick, A.E.: boyd danah. Networked privacy: how teenagers negotiate context in social media. New Media Soc. **16**(7), 1051–1067 (2014)
34. Beam, M.A., Child, J.T., Hutchens, M.J., Hmielowski, J.D.: Context collapse and privacy management: diversity in Facebook friends increases online news reading and sharing. New Media Soc. **20**(7), 2296–2314 (2018)
35. Brandtzaeg, P.B., Lüders, M.: Time collapse in social media: extending the context collapse. Soc. Media Soc. **4**(1), 205630511876334 (2018)
36. Inria: Scientific reviews and challenges in cybersecurity. https://www.inria.fr/en/news/news-from-inria/inria-publishes-its-white-book-on-cybersecurity

# BioPrivacy: Development of a Keystroke Dynamics Continuous Authentication System

Ioannis Stylios(✉), Andreas Skalkos, Spyros Kokolakis, and Maria Karyda

University of the Aegean, Mytilene, Greece
{istylios,ask,sak,mka}@aegean.gr

**Abstract.** Session authentication schemes establish the identity of the user only at the beginning of the session, so they are vulnerable to attacks that tamper with communications after the establishment of the authenticated session. Moreover, smartphones themselves are used as authentication means, especially in two-factor authentication schemes, which are often required by several services. Whether the smartphone is in the hands of the legitimate user constitutes a great concern, and correspondingly whether the legitimate user is the one who uses the services. In response to these concerns, Behavioral Biometrics (BB) Continuous Authentication (CA) technologies have been proposed on a large corpus of literature. This paper presents a research on the development and validation of a BBCA system (named BioPrivacy), that is based on the user's keystroke dynamics, using a Multi-Layer Perceptron (MLP). Also, we introduce a new behavioral biometrics collection tool, and we propose a methodology for the selection of an appropriate set of behavioral biometrics. Our system achieved 97.18% Accuracy, 0.02% Equal Error Rate (EER), 97.2% True Acceptance Rate (TAR) and 0.02% False Acceptance Rate (FAR).

**Keywords:** Machine learning · Behavioral biometrics · Continuous authentication · Mobile devices · Multi-layer perceptron (MLP)

## 1 Introduction

User authentication technology plays a critical role in securing access to online services. Authentication systems identify users only when the session is initiated (entry point authentication model), thus leaving them exposed to attacks that take place after the initial authentication process [1, 7–10, 39, 41]. These systems defend themselves against such attacks by performing an additional authentication step at critical points in the session but are not popular with users due to the inconvenience caused by repetitive authentications. Also, smartphones are used as authentication means, especially in two-factor authentication schemes, which are often required by several electronic services. Whether the smartphone is in the hands of the legitimate user constitutes a great concern, and correspondingly whether the legitimate user is the one who uses the services. In addition, mobile devices are vulnerable to smudge attacks [40], i.e., the mark of the fingerprints left by our finger on the screen, as it is easy to reveal the touch pattern or


S. Katsikas et al. (Eds.): ESORICS 2021 Workshops, LNCS 13106, pp. 158–170, 2022.
https://doi.org/10.1007/978-3-030-95484-0_10

the PIN of the device. Thus, stealing a device carries the risk of granting full access to personal data and crucial applications. Moreover, smartphone users are unaware of privacy and security threats and keep large amounts of private information including PINs, credit card numbers, etc., stored in their mobile devices [1].

For the above reasons, Behavioral Biometrics (BBs) and Continuous Authentication (CA) are employed by a new method of user authentication which is also based on the "something that the user is" paradigm [2–7, 9]. The technological advancement of mobile devices has led to the efficient capture of user behavior via their incorporated sensors, thus enabling the authentication of users based on their behavioral biometrics [11–15]. The incorporated sensors of mobile devices are used to enroll BB templates [7, 14, 16]. The BBs that may be employed are walking gait, touch gestures, keystroke dynamics, hand waving, user profile, and power consumption. The advantage of BBs is that they use some characteristic feature of a single individual and provide continuous authentication [7]. Alongside the initial login process CA technology represents an extra security mechanism since it monitors user behavior and re-authenticates continuously the user's identity throughout a session [5, 17–20]. Finally, the work of [10, 22, 23] showed the eagerness of users to adopt biometric authentication methods in order to protect their privacy.

This paper presents a research on the development and validation of a keystroke dynamics Continuous Authentication System, named BioPrivacy. We aim at building a system that will continuously authenticate the user of a smartphone. We start with an experimental biometric data collection process via mobile smartphones. The main objective is to propose a methodology and a data collection tool (BioPrivacy Collection Tool) for the selection of an appropriate set of behavioral biometrics. In this experiment, we recorded users' keystroke dynamics. Also, the present research aims to designing and evaluating new approaches to Continuous Authentication (CA) by developing and using a Multi-Layer Perceptron (MLP).

## 2 Background

In this section, we present an overview of the keystroke dynamics, the Multi-Layer perceptron (MLP) and the evaluation metrics.

### 2.1 Keystroke Dynamics

The procedure of recording the typing keyboard inputs of an individual on a mobile device and the effort to identify him via an analysis based on his tapping habits is called keystroke dynamics [7]. Some researchers on keystroke dynamics collect data from predefined texts, for example during the typing of a text message, or during the log-in session when entering passwords. Others conduct their research by collecting data not restricted on predefined sentences or passwords. In both cases the results are of high accuracy [7].

## 2.2 Multi-layer Perceptron (MLP)

Artificial Neural Networks (ANNs) are structures inspired by human brains' function. These networks can estimate model functions and handle linear/nonlinear functions by learning from data associations and generalizing to previously unknown scenarios. Multi-Layered perceptron (MLP) is a widely used Artificial Neural Network approach (ANNs) [46]. Specifically, a feedforward artificial neural network called a Multi-Layer Perceptron (MLP) is a type of Feedforward Artificial Neural Network (FANN). Each unit in an MLP neural network performs a biased weighted sum of its inputs and then passes this activation level through a transfer function to generate output.

MLP networks typically include three layers: input, hidden, and output. The number of neurons in the input layer is equal to the number of parameters affecting the problem. Almost all problems can be solved with just one hidden layer. The number of neurons in the hidden layer or layers should be arbitrarily chosen [47]. This is a powerful modeling tool that employs a supervised training procedure with data examples with known outputs. Training for the MLP approach is accomplished in two steps. In the first step, the training data set is fed by a randomly picked input vector. The activated neurons output is subsequently propagated from hidden layer(s) to the output layer. The back propagation step, begins by calculating the gradient descent error and then propagates it backwards to each neuron in the output layer, followed by the hidden layer. The neural network's weights and biases are recomputed at the end of the second step. These two steps are repeated until the network's total error is less than a predetermined rate or the maximum number of epochs is reached [47]. Although, MLP network is a widely-used ANN approach, the MLP network still has certain limitations, such as time-consuming issues in reaching a solution [48].

## 2.3 Evaluation Metrics

The basic metrics applied to evaluate an authentication system depend on the error rates. Following, we discuss some basic metrics used to calculate authentication errors [7, 31–33]:

- True Acceptance Rate (TAR) is the conditional probability of a pattern to be classified in the class "Genuine" given that it belongs to it. TAR is given by the formula:

$$\mathrm{TAR} = \mathrm{TA}/(\mathrm{TA} + \mathrm{FR}) \tag{1}$$

- False Acceptance Rate (FAR) is the conditional probability a pattern to be classified in the class "Genuine" given that it does not belong to it. FAR is given by the formula:

$$\mathrm{FAR} = \mathrm{FA}/(\mathrm{FA} + \mathrm{TR}). \tag{2}$$

- False Reject Rate (FRR) is the conditional probability a pattern not to be classified in the class "Genuine" given that it belongs to it. FRR is given by the formula:

$$\mathrm{FRR} = \mathrm{FR}/(\mathrm{FR} + \mathrm{TA}) \tag{3}$$

- Accuracy is defined as the probability of correct classification of a pattern. Accuracy is given by the formula:

$$\text{Accuracy} = (\text{TA} + \text{TR})/(\text{TA} + \text{TR} + \text{FA} + \text{FR}). \tag{4}$$

- Equal Error Rate (EER) is the error rate that is achieved by tuning the detection threshold of the system such that FAR and FRR are equal [28].

## 3 Related Work

In this section we present a recent state-of-the-art literature review focusing on keystroke dynamics. The majority of keystroke dynamics methods are restricted to using a specific context with a prearranged text. In the work of Clark and Furnell [24], the authors employed the typing patterns of users when entering telephone numbers and text messages, to authenticate them. They used Multi-Layer Perceptron (MLP), Radial Basis Functions (RBF), and General Regression Neural Network (GRNN) classifiers. The best results achieved were 12.8% average EER with the Multi-Layer Perceptron (MLP) classifier.

In the work of Draffin et al. [4], the authors conducted a real-world study and collected 86000 keystrokes from 13 participants in three weeks. Keystrokes were not restricted to the use of prearranged text or passwords. They used Feed Forward Neural Network for classification and achieved 86% accuracy after 15 keypresses with 2.2% FRR, and 14% FAR.

In the work of Darren and Inguanez [25], they collected typing data while users were entering 15 prearranged text sentences during four different scenarios, namely, One-Handed stationery, Two-handed stationery, One-Handed moving, and Two-handed moving. The participants were free to choose one of the four scenarios, while the smartphone owner had to complete all 4 activities. The authors used a Least Squares SVM classifier with RBF kernel and the one-handed scenario achieved the best results, namely, 0.44% EER, 100% accuracy, 0% FAR, and 1% FRR, while all their results achieved around 1% EER.

In the work of Krishnamoorthy [26], the classification of users was based on keystroke dynamics, by applying concepts of machine learning. The participants of this study were asked to type a specific password and their typing characteristics were recorded. Krishnamoorthy effectively identified each one of the 94 users and achieved 98.44% identification accuracy with the Random Forest classifier.

In Table 1, we present the performance of machine learning models on keystroke dynamics. For each system, there is at least one of the five basic metrics, namely FAR, TAR, FRR, EER, and Accuracy.

As we can see in Table 1, RF and SVM classifiers have achieved very good results while the performance of the MLP and the FFNN is relatively low. We believe that further research is necessary to see if FFNN and MLP can have better performance. By applying a new design approach to MLP, using the BioPrivacy collection tool dataset, we will see if we have an improvement in the performance. In case a high performance is achieved, we will apply MLP in our system.

**Table 1.** A literature review

| Method | Works | Platform | Classification | Performance | | | | |
|---|---|---|---|---|---|---|---|---|
| | | | | FAR | TAR | Accuracy | FRR | EER |
| Keystroke dynamics | [24] in 2006 | Smartphone | MLP | | | | | 12.8 |
| | [4] in 2013 | Smartphone | FFNN | 14 | | 86.0 | | 22 |
| | [4] in 2013 | Smartphone | SVM | 0 | | 100 | 1 | 0.44 |
| | [25] in 2018 | Smartphone | Random forest | | | 98.44 | | 2.2 |

## 4 Experimental Setup

In this part we present the BioPrivacy System Architecture. Specifically, we present the biometrics collection architecture by which we can collect the biometric data of the users, and the data preparation for introduction to machine learning algorithms.

### 4.1 Bioprivacy's Collection Tool

Bioprivacy's collection tool is an Android application for collecting cell phone keystroke dynamics values [7, 34]. The BioPrivacy Application sends the data to an API endpoint that stores the data in an online MySQL database. This API is an online application running continuously. It is built to retrieve data from the application and store it in the online database. Each operation is performed on different files so that if one file has an error it will not affect the other. Each of the files receives different input parameters. The online database is designed to allow multiple users to store their sensor data at any time. Thus, there is no concern about data separation and synchronization. The application also handles any probable communication malfunctions. A software system must be sustainable and scalable. For this reason, the structure of the application follows an architecture that accommodates possible software modifications and expansions. The application was developed in Android Studio.

When a user types on the BioPrivacy's keyboard, the inputs are recorded and analyzed in order to identify him based on his tapping habits [7, 34]. The BioPrivacy application extracts the duration and latency of the pressure on keys and the location points of fingers as described [7, 29, 35–37]:

- *Duration*: is the time period between pressing and releasing a key.
- *Latency*: is the time period between releasing a pressed key until pressing the next key.
- *Pressure*: is the pressure on a key.
- *Location*: are the location points (xi, yi) of the finger on the screen.

In Fig. 1 we see the keystroke recording interface.

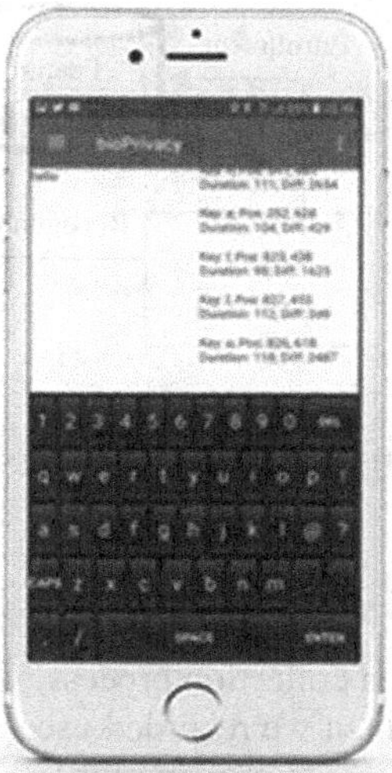

**Fig. 1.** Bioprivacy's keystroke interface

### 4.2 BioPrivacy System Architecture

The registration process, which is the first step of the BioPrivacy system, involves collecting the biometric sample, processing the biometric data to extract the reference sample, and storing it for further use (see Fig. 2). The efficiency and accuracy of a biometric system are directly dependent on the registration process. During the life cycle of a biometric, it is sometimes necessary to re-record, taking into account the normal as well as the unexpected change or evolution of biometric characteristics. There is a set of basic modules included in the BioPrivacy system which are as follows [7, 38]:

1. *Data acquisition:* Sample acquisition: To acquire biometric data we must use the appropriate sensor.
2. *Feature extraction:* The raw data must be preprocessed before extracting the distinctive features. More specifically, we must identify and extract outliers and improve the quality of data, especially in cases where data are collected in uncontrolled environments from uncooperative users. The set of discriminative features are extracted once the data is cleaned and processed.
3. *Feature templates:* This is a repository database containing a concatenation of the extracted feature vectors for a particular user (i.e., the device owner). It is created during the enrollment phase and used during the recognition phase to be compared with the captured feature sample and verify the claimed identity.
4. *Decision-making:* This is used only during the recognition process. This step compares the template that is currently being extracted with the saved template to generate a matching score and make a decision. The decision validates the claimed identity to see if it is done by the legitimate user (genuine) or an impostor.

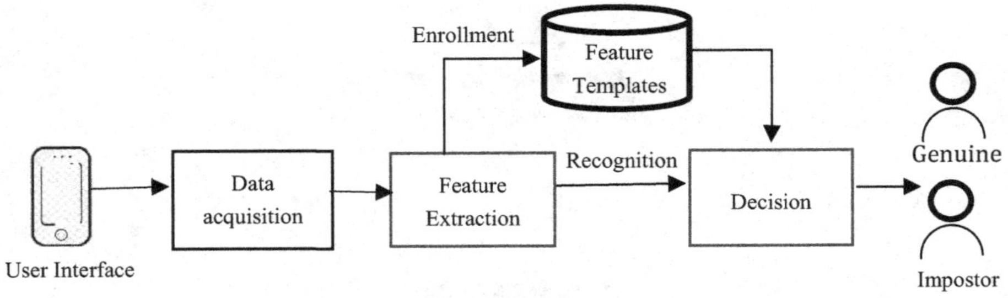


**Fig. 2.** BioPrivacy system architecture.

## 5 Methodology

In this section, we present the data collection process, via mobile smartphones and the BioPrivacy collection tool, by which we recorded users keystrokes. We have a sample of 39 individuals. All the participants are smartphone owners and familiar with the experimental part of the process. The data collection process consists of 16 sessions in total and each session lasts 2 min approximately. During the sessions, a predefined sentence or a sequence of numbers were displayed on the screen and participants had to either memorize and input them or input them immediately after they were displayed. In this way, we have two kinds of inputs, one that the participants must read, memorize, and then write and another that the participants must read and then immediately write. We select one individual from the 39 participants of our sample as Genuine user and the rest 38 as impostors. Finally, we will evaluate our system which is based on a Multi-Layer Perceptron (MLP).

## 6 Results

In this section we present the results of our research. Firstly, we present the results from the bioprivacy's collection tool. In Table 2 we see records in the database regarding keystroke dynamics. The features are duration, latency, the pressure on keys, and the location points (x, y) of the finger. The data received from the database were in accordance and consistent with the theoretical framework presented in Sect. 4.1.

**Table 2.** Keystroke dynamics data

| Sensor | Key | Duration | Latency | Pressure | X_value | Y_value |
|---|---|---|---|---|---|---|
| TouchScreen (Keyboard) | p | 134 | 189 | 1.0 | 943.0 | 404.0 |
| | u | 96 | 176 | 1.0 | 637.0 | 417.0 |
| | f | 57 | 358 | 0.50 | 339.0 | 243.0 |

From the data collected with the bioprivacy collection tool, we created a dataset that consists of 39 individuals and 1488 Instances. We separated the users into 2 classes

(Genuine–impostor), one individual as a Genuine user and the rest 38 individuals as impostors. We also inserted a data preprocessing step by applying Normalize with scale 1.0.

We applied the MLP classifier with the following configurations: L 0.3 -M 0.2 -N 500 -H 3. The learning rate (L) is set to 0.3, the Momentum to 0.2, the training time (N) to 500, and we used 3 hidden layers (H). Our system achieved 97.18% Accuracy and 0.02% Equal Error Rate. In Table 3, we summarize the accuracy and EER.

**Table 3.** Accuracy and EER

| Accuracy | Equal error rate |
|---|---|
| 97.18% | 0.02% |

In Table 4, we present the detailed results by class. In the class Impostor, we achieved 94.5% True Acceptance Rate (TAR) while we have 0% False Acceptance Rate (FAR). In the class Genuine, we achieved 100% True Acceptance Rate (TAR) while the False Acceptance Rate (FAR) is 0.05%. Finally, in the Weighted Average, we have 97.2% TAR and 0.02% FAR.

**Table 4.** Detailed results by class

| Classifier | TA rate | FA rate | Class |
|---|---|---|---|
| MLP | 94.5% | 0% | Impostor |
| | 100% | 0.05% | Genuine |
| Weighted Avg. | 97.2% | 0.02% | |

## 7 Discussion

This paper presents our research on the development and validation of a BBCA system (BioPrivacy) that is based on the user's keystroke dynamics using Multi-Layer Perceptron (MLP). Also, we introduce a new biometrics collection tool of the BioPrivacy system. We applied an experimental procedure of biometrics data collection where 39 individuals participated and completed the process. We received positive feedback on the application and users stated that they enjoyed the procedure. The data received from the database were in accordance and consistent with the analysis presented in the Sect. 4.1 of the present paper.

Regarding the challenges of the keystroke dynamics collection methodology, they are based on something that the user must recall from his/her memory, like a password, and something that the user sees and types, like a captcha. In this way, we have two kinds of inputs, one that the participants must read, memorize, and then write and another that the participants must read and then immediately write. We created a dataset that consists of 39 individuals and 1488 Instances and 2 classes (Genuine–impostor). One individual as a Genuine user and the rest 38 individuals as impostors.

By applying a new design approach of the MLP and the BioPrivacy dataset we achieved an improved performance in relation to the literature. In [4] the performance of the FFNN is relatively low achieving FAR 14%, Accuracy 86% and EER 22%. In [24] the MLP achieved 12.8% EER. Our approach achieved Accuracy 97.18%, EER 0.02%, TAR 97.2% and FAR 0.02%.

### 7.1 Contribution

The principal contributions of this paper are as follows:

- **A new behavioral biometrics collection tool.** We develop a new BB collection tool, named BioPrivacy Collection Tool, by which we can collect behavioral biometrics of users on mobile devices.
- **We propose a methodology for the selection of an appropriate set of behavioral biometrics.** We present a methodology for the collection of behavioral biometrics.
- **We developed a BBCA System.** We present the development of a BBCA system based on MLP.

### 7.2 Limitations

As suggested by Stylios et al. [7], CA systems need to be evaluated under the high effort approaches to see the actual performance of machine learning and deep learning models under the spectrum of today's possible threats. Therefore, our system should be evaluated against the Frog-Boiling attack [27], the Algorithmic attack [42], the Mimic attacks [43, 44], and the Snoop-forge-replay attack [45]. Finally, our system was tested in a sample of 39 individuals and we plan to evaluate it in a larger sample of users.

## 8 Conclusions and Further Research

Smartphones are used as a mean to authenticate individuals, particularly in two-factor authentication schemes, which are often obligatory by several electronic services. Whether the legitimate user possesses the smartphone constitutes a great concern, and correspondingly whether the services are used by the legitimate user. In this paper, we presented our research on the development and validation of a keystroke dynamics Continuous Authentication System, named BioPrivacy. In our paper, we present a new behavioral biometrics collection tool, named BioPrivacy Collection Tool and we propose a methodology for the selection of an appropriate set of behavioral biometrics. We applied an experimental test to examine the consistency of the collected data with the theoretical framework presented in Sect. 4.1. Our results showed that the collected data are consistent and in accordance with the theoretical framework. In the present research we developed a BBCA system based on MLP. Our system achieved Accuracy 97.18%, EER 0.02%, TAR 97.2% and FAR 0.02%.

Our future research focuses on the extension of the BioPrivacy Collection Tool to include more behavioral modalities. Also, we will collect data from a larger population to create a dataset that will be publicly available. Finally, we will evaluate our model against possible attacks vectors and highlight relevant countermeasures.

**Acknowledgments.** This research is co-financed by Greece and the European Union (European Social Fund-ESF) through the Operational Programme «Human Resources Development, Education and Lifelong Learning 2014–2020» in the context of the project "BioPrivacy: Development and validation of a Behavioral Biometrics Continuous Authentication System" (MIS 5052062).

## References

1. Stylios, I., Kokolakis, S., Thanou, O., Chatzis, S.: Users' attitudes on mobile devices: can users' practices protect their sensitive data? In: 10th Mediterranean Conference on Information Systems, MCIS 2016 (2016)
2. Corcoran, P., Costache, C.: Biometric technology and smartphones: a consideration of the practicalities of a broad adoption of biometrics and the likely impacts. IEEE Consum. Electron. Mag. **5**(2), 70–78 (2016). https://doi.org/10.1109/MCE.2016.2521937
3. Cherifi, F., Hemery, B., Giot, R., Pasquet, M., Rosenberger, C.: Performance evaluation of behavioral biometric systems. In: Behavioral Biometrics for Human Identification: Intelligent Applications, pp. 57–74. IGI Global (2010)
4. Draffin, B., Zhu, J., Zhang, J.: KeySens: passive user authentication through micro-behavior modeling of soft keyboard interaction. In: Memmi, G., Blanke, U. (eds.) MobiCASE 2013. LNICSSITE, vol. 130, pp. 184–201. Springer, Cham (2014). https://doi.org/10.1007/978-3-319-05452-0_14
5. Biometric authentication: the how and why. https://about-fraud.com/biometric-authentication. Accessed 21 Feb 2019
6. Dorizzi, B.: Biometrics at the frontiers, assessing the impact on society technical impact of biometrics, background paper for the institute of prospective technological studies, DG JRC-Sevilla, European Commission (2005)
7. Stylios, I., Kokolakis, S., Thanou, O., Chatzis, S.: Behavioral biometrics and continuous user authentication on mobile devices: a survey. Inf. Fusion 66, 76–99. ISSN 1566-2535 (2021). https://doi.org/10.1016/j.inffus.2020.08.021
8. Frank, M., Biedert, R., Ma, E., Martinovic, I., Song, D.: Touchalytics: on the applicability of touchscreen input as a behavioral biometric for continuous authentication. IEEE Trans. Inf. Forensics Secur. **8**(1), 136–148 (2013). https://doi.org/10.1109/TIFS.2012.2225048
9. Stylios, I.C., Thanou, O., Androulidakis, I., Zaitseva, E.: A review of continuous authentication using behavioral biometrics. In: Conference: ACM SEEDACECNSM, At Kastoria, Greece (2016). https://doi.org/10.1145/2984393.2984403
10. Clarke, N.L., Furnell, S.M.: Authentication of users on mobile telephones–a survey of attitudes and practices. Comput. Secur. **24**, 519–527 (2005)
11. Shi, W., Yang, J., Jiang, Y., Yang, F., Feng, T., Xiong, Y.: SenGuard: passive user identification on smartphones using multiple sensors. In: International Conference on Wireless and Mobile Computing, Networking and Communications, pp. 141–148 (2011). https://doi.org/10.1109/WiMOB.2011.6085412

12. Lane, N.D., Miluzzo, E., Lu, H., Peebles, D., Choudhury, T., Campbell, A.T.: A survey of mobile phone sensing. IEEE Commun. Mag. Arch. **48**(9), 140–150 (2010)
13. Patel, V.M., Chellappa, R., Chandra, D., Barbello, B.: Continuous user authentication on mobile devices: recent progress and remaining challenges. IEEE Sig. Process Mag. **33**(4), 49–61 (2016)
14. Murmuria, R., Stavrou, A., Barbará, D., Fleck, D.: Continuous authentication on mobile devices using power consumption, touch gestures and physical movement of users. In: Bos, H., Monrose, F., Blanc, G. (eds.) RAID 2015. LNCS, vol. 9404, pp. 405–424. Springer, Cham (2015). https://doi.org/10.1007/978-3-319-26362-5_19
15. Introduction to android: sensors overview, android developers. https://goo.gl/MGWQy8. Accessed 21 Feb 2020
16. Jain, K., Chen, Y., Demirkus, M.: Pores and ridges: fingerprint matching using level 3 features. In: Proceedings International Conference Pattern Recognition, vol. 4, pp. 477–480, (2006)
17. Crouse, D., Han, H., Chandra, D., Barbello, B., Jain, A.K.: Continuous authentication of mobile user: fusion of face image and inertial measurement unit data. In: International Conference Biometrics, pp. 135–142 (2015)
18. Abdulaziz, A., Kalita, J.K.: Authentication of smartphone users using behavioral biometrics. IEEE Commun. Surv. Tutor. **18**, 1998–2026 (2016)
19. Ahmed, E.A., Traor´e, I.: Continuous authentication using biometrics: data, models, and metrics. IGI Global, Hershey (2011)
20. Wu, Z., Chen, Z.: An implicit identity authentication system considering changes of gesture based on keystroke behaviors. Int. J. Distrib. Sens. Netw. **2015**, 110–130 (2015)
21. Pons, P., Polak, P.: Understanding user perspectives on biometric technology. Commun. ACM **51**(9), 115–118 (2008)
22. Clarke, N.L., Furnell, S.M., Rodwell, P.M., Reynolds, P.L.: Acceptance of subscriber authentication methods for mobile telephony devices. Comput. Secur. **21**(3), 220–228 (2002)
23. Karatzouni, S., Furnell, S.M., Clarke, N.L., Botha, R.A.: Perceptions of user authentication on mobile devices. In: Proceedings of the 6th Annual ISOneWorld Conference, 11–13 April 2007, Las Vegas, NV (2007)
24. Clarke, N.L., Furnell, S.M.: Authenticating mobile phone users using keystroke analysis. Int. J. Inf. Secur. **6**(1), 1–14 (2007)
25. Darren, C., Inguanez, F.: Multi-model authentication using keystroke dynamics for smartphones. In: IEEE 8th International Conference on Consumer Electronics, Berlin (ICCE-Berlin) (2018)
26. Krishnamoorthy, S.: Identification of user behavioural biometrics for authentication using keystroke dynamics and machine learning, Electron. Theses Dissertations, vol. 7440 (2018)
27. Wang, Z., Serwadda, A., Balagani, K.S., Phoha, V.V.: Transforming animals in a cyber-behavioral biometric menagerie with Frog-Boiling attacks. In: IEEE Fifth International Conference on Biometrics: Theory, Applications and Systems (BTAS), Arlington, VA, pp. 289–296 (2012)
28. Samarin, N.: A Key to Your Heart: Biometric Authentication Based on ECG Signals. 4th Year Project Report Computer Science, School of Informatics, University of Edinburgh (2018)
29. Lamiche, I., Bin, G., Jing, Y., Yu, Z., Hadid, A.: A continuous smartphone authentication method based on gait patterns and keystroke dynamics. J. Ambient. Intell. Humaniz. Comput. **10**(11), 4417–4430 (2018). https://doi.org/10.1007/s12652-018-1123-6
30. Cherifi, F., Hemery, B., Giot, R., Pasquet, M., Rosenberger, C.: Performance evaluation of behavioral biometric systems. In: Behavioral Biometrics for Human Identification: Intelligent Applications, pp. 57–74. IGI Global (2010)

31. Lykas, A.: Computational Intelligence. University Printing Press, University of Ioannina, Ioannina (1999)
32. Eberz, S., Rasmussen, K.B., Lenders, V., Martinovic, I.: Evaluating behavioral biometrics for continuous authentication: challenges and metrics. In: Proceedings of the 2017 ACM on Asia Conference on Computer and Communications Security (ASIA CCS 2017). Association for Computing Machinery, New York, pp. 386–399 (2017). https://doi.org/10.1145/3052973.3053032
33. Dash, R., Dash, P.: MDHS–LPNN: A Hybrid FOREX Predictor Model Using a Legendre Polynomial Neural Network with a Modified Differential Harmony Search Technique. Chapter 25 (2017). https://doi.org/10.1016/b978-0-12-811318-9.00025-9
34. Chang, T.-Y., Tsai, C.J., Tsai, W.J., Peng, C.C., Wu, H.S.: A changeable personal identification number-based keystroke dynamics authentication system on smartphones. In: Security and Communications Networks 2016, vol. 9, pp. 2674–2685. Wiley Online Library (wileyonlinelibrary.com) (2016)
35. Alves, D.D., Cruz, G., Vinhal, C.: Authentication system using behavioral biometrics through keystroke dynamics. In: Proceedings of the IEEE Symposium on Computational Intelligence in Biometrics and Identity Management (CIBIM 2014), pp. 181–184. IEEE (2014)
36. Zhang, H., Yan, C., Zhao, P., Wang, M.: Model construction and authentication algorithm of virtual keystroke dynamics for smart phone users. In: IEEE International Conference on Systems, Man, and Cybernetics (SMC), Budapest, pp. 000171–000175 (2016)
37. Stylios, I., Kokolakis, S., Skalkos, A., Chatzis, S.: BioGames: A New Paradigm and a Behavioral Biometrics Collection Tool for Research Purposes. Information and Computer Security, Emerald Publishing, Bingley (2021)
38. Mahfouz, A., Mahmoud, T.M., Eldin, A.S.: A survey on behavioral biometric authentication on smartphones. J. Inf. Secur. Appl. **37**, 28–37 (2017)
39. Androulidakis, I., Christou, V., Bardis, N.G., Stilios, I.: Surveying users' practices regarding mobile phones' security features. In: Proceedings of the 3rd International Conference on European Computing Conference (ECC 2009). Tbilisi, Georgia, pp. 25–30 (2009)
40. Aviv, A.J., Gibson, K., Mossop, E., Blaze, M., Smith, J.M.: Smudge attacks on smartphone touch screens. In: Proceedings of the 4th USENIX Conference on Offensive Technologies, p. 1 {7. USENIX Association} (2010)
41. Shila, D.M., Eyisi, E.: Adversarial gait detection on mobile devices using recurrent neural networks. In: 17th IEEE International Conference on Trust, Security and Privacy in Computing and Communications/12th IEEE International Conference on Big Data Science and Engineering (TrustCom/BigDataSE), pp. 316–321 (2018). https://doi.org/10.1109/TrustCom/BigDataSE.2018.00055
42. Serwadda, A., Phoha, V.V.: Examining a large keystroke biometrics dataset for statistical-attack openings. ACM Trans. Inf. Syst. Secur. **16**(2), 1–30 (2013)
43. Negi, P., Sharma, P., Jain, V.S., Bahmani, B.: K-means++ vs. behavioral biometrics: one loop to rule them all. In: Network and Distributed Systems Security (NDSS) Symposium 2018, San Diego, CA, USA. ISBN 1-1891562-49-5 (2018)
44. Meng, T.C., Gupta, P., Gao, D.: I can be you: questioning the use of keystroke dynamics as biometrics. In: Proceedings NDSS, pp. 1–16 (2013)
45. Rahman, K.A., Balagani, K.S., Phoha, V.V.: Snoop-Forge-Replay attacks on continuous verification with keystrokes. IEEE Trans. Inf. Forensics Secur. **8**(3), 528–541 (2013)
46. Taud, H., Mas, J.F.: Multilayer perceptron (MLP). In: Camacho Olmedo, M.T., Paegelow, M., Mas, J.-F., Escobar, F. (eds.) Geomatic Approaches for Modeling Land Change Scenarios. LNGC, pp. 451–455. Springer, Cham (2018). https://doi.org/10.1007/978-3-319-60801-3_27

47. Oral, M., Laptalı Oral, E., Aydın, A.: Supervised vs. unsupervised learning for construction crew productivity prediction. Autom. Constr. **22**, 271–276 (2012). https://doi.org/10.1016/j.autcon.2011.09.002
48. Arslan, O., Kurt, O., Konak, H.: Yapay sinir ağlarının jeodezide uygulamaları üzerine öneriler [Suggestions on geodesy applications of artificial neural networks], in 11.Türkiye Harita Bilimsel ve Teknik Kurultayı, 2–6 April 2007, Ankara, Turkey (2007)

# Privacy and Informational Self-determination Through Informed Consent: The Way Forward

Mohamad Gharib[1,2](✉)

[1] University of Tartu, Tartu, Estonia
mohamad.gharib@ut.ee, mohamad.gharib@unifi.it
[2] University of Florence, Florence, Italy

**Abstract.** *"I have read and agree to the Privacy Policy"*. This can be described as one of the biggest lies in the current times, and that is all what a service provider needs to acquire what can be called "informed consent", which allows it to do as it pleases with your Personal Information (PI). Although many developed countries have enacted privacy laws and regulations to govern the collection and use of PI as a response to the increased misuse of PI, these laws and regulations rely heavily on the concept of informational self-determination through the "notice" and "consent/choice" model, which as we will see is deeply flawed. Accordingly, the full potential of these privacy laws and regulations cannot be achieved without tackling these flaws and empowering individuals to take an active role in the protection of their PI. In this paper, we argue that to advance informational self-determination, a new direction should be considered. In particular, we propose a model for informed consent and we introduce a proposed architecture that aims at tackling existing limitations in current approaches.

**Keywords:** Privacy · GDPR · Personal information · Informed consent · Notice and choice · Privacy policy

## 1 Introduction

Nowadays, most service providers (including online retailers) try to collect information concerning the behavior of their potential users/customers (called Behavioral data [41]), and use such information to increase their sales by delivering personalized service offerings, or even influencing the behavioral marketing of such individuals [48]. That is why information can be described as the new gold in the 21st century since it is fueling the success of many enterprises [29]. This trend has led to what can be called "Privacy Merchants" that shadow Internet users to create very detailed profiles concerning their online behavior and activities (e.g., what they view, read, purchase, etc.). Then, sell these profiles to whoever pays the demanded price [19]. In principle, this can benefit both sides since individuals can enjoy access to a variety of online services, news


S. Katsikas et al. (Eds.): ESORICS 2021 Workshops, LNCS 13106, pp. 171–184, 2022.
https://doi.org/10.1007/978-3-030-95484-0_11

sites, email, social networking, videos, music, etc. without explicitly paying with money [8,27]. However, many individuals may not even know that they are paying with their PI as their behavior is being tracked and their PI is being collected and used [8,15], just because they blindly accepted the privacy policies or terms of services offered by these websites. This leads us to the biggest lie on the internet *I have read and agree to the terms and conditions* [35].

In response to the excessive collection, use, and potential misuse of PI, many governments around the world have enacted laws and regulations for privacy protection [24]. However, these laws and regulations rely heavily on the concept of informational self-determination that is, usually, implemented through the notice and consent/choice model [53], where a *notice* (e.g., privacy policy, terms of use agreement) is supposed to inform a data subject about how her PI will be processed and shared, and *consent/choice* is supposed to acquire a signifying acceptance at the data subject's side concerning the notice [15,49].

Although notifying data subjects about organization's data practices is supposed to enable them to make informed privacy decisions, current mechanisms for presenting the notice and obtaining the consent are deeply flawed as indicated by many researchers because they are neither useful nor usable [8,15,32,35,45,48,50,56]. More specifically, most notices are long and complex [3]; hard to be understood by ordinary people [8,35], do not enable a data subject to make an informed decision [3], do not help much in predicting potential future use of PI nor assessing the consequences and risks related to such potential use [15], and do not, usually, offer data subjects with a choice that reflects their preferences [48]. Moreover, it is neither feasible nor practical to read notices as one study [32] estimated that reading privacy policies carries costs in time of approximately 201 h a year, which is worth about $3,534 annually per American Internet user.

Additionally, the notice and consent model is, usually, neutral concerning whether certain forms of collecting, using, or disclosing PI are good or bad [50]. Instead, it focuses on whether data subjects consent to privacy practices, which means "As long as a company provides notice of its privacy practices, and people have some kind of choice about whether to provide the data or not, privacy is sufficiently protected" [48]. This shifted the main purpose of the notice and consent model from protecting the best interest of data subjects to indemnify companies that collect or use their PI. Several newly developed regulations (e.g., the General Data Protection Regulation (GDPR) [38] that replaced the EU Data Protection Directive 95/46/EC [20]) forbid the collection of certain sensitive data (e.g., race or ethnic origin, political opinions, etc.) and define legal bases for the collection and processing of PI (e.g., comply with the vital interest of the individual, the public interest, the legal obligations, etc.). However, most of the problems associated with the notice and consent model still hold, which has been highlighted by several recent studies [6,16–18,35].

By now, we can understand why most data subjects blindly accept the privacy policies or terms of services, not because they do not value their privacy, but because of the flawed mechanism of the notice and consent model. To this end, we strongly believe that if data subjects are offered a useful and usable means to appropriately manage their privacy preferences, most likely, they will.

The rest of the paper is structured as follows, we start by discussing informational self-determination through the notice and consent model in Sect. 2, and the problem statement and research questions are presented in Sect. 3. In Sect. 4, we develop a model for informed consent, followed by a proposed architecture that aims at tackling existing limitations in current approaches and empowering data subjects to take an active role in the protection of their PI in Sect. 5. Section 6 concludes the paper and discusses future work.

## 2 Informational Self-determination Through Notice and Consent: Origins and Criticism

Although various definitions of privacy exist, the ones that define privacy as a type of "control" over when and by whom our PI can be collected and used by others gained significant attention [40]. The notion of privacy as control has been reflected in the 1973 U.S. Department of Health, Education, and Welfare (HEW) Fair Information Practices ("FIPs") [13], which is also commonly referred to as the Fair Information Practice Principles (FIPPs) [21]. FIPPs have been developed to address concerns about the increasing digitization of data by demanding notice of data collection and use as well as providing data subjects with the right to control the use of their data for purposes beyond which it was collected. In particular, FIPPs offer several principles to achieve that, including 1-transparency of systems managing PI, 2-the right to notice about what information was being collected about individuals, (3) the right to prevent PI from being used for purposes without consent, or other purposes that are not specified in the consent, (4) the right to correct/amend PI, and (5) lay responsibilities on the holders of PI to prevent its misuse [13,21,50].

These principles have influenced privacy laws and practices in several countries around the world (e.g., U.S., the European Union (EU), Canada, etc.) [35], and also helped to shape the OECD Privacy Guidelines[1] as well as the Asia Pacific Economic Cooperation (APEC) Privacy Framework[2] [50]. In Europe, privacy laws are based closely on the OECD Guidelines. While in the U.S., the OECD principles were selectively adopted, i.e., a more market-driven approach to privacy protection that is mainly based on self-regulatory was followed. More specifically, these principles were considerably simplified and reduced into the concept of "notice and choice" [13]. In other words, only the third principle listed above survives in the "notice and choice" approach, and the fourth - often referred to as the purpose-specification principle - is recast as "choice" [48]. Despite the fact that the U.S. Federal Trade Commission (FTC), in its report to Congress in 2000, endorsed the industry's simplified view of privacy that eliminates the collection and use limitation principles, FTC criticized the shortcomings of the privacy notice and consent model by 2010, and it even starts questioning the efficiency of the market-driven notice and consent model to protect privacy [13].

[1] https://www.oecd.org/.

[2] https://www.apec.org/publications/2005/12/apec-privacy-framework.

According to Solove [50], almost all instantiations of the FIPPs fail to specify what data may be collected or how it may be used. Instead, most forms of data collection, usage, and disclosure are permissible under the FIPPs, if individuals were notified and provide consent. This has led, in recent years, to worldwide efforts to create or update privacy laws and regulations (e.g., the EU GDPR [38], and the California Consumer Privacy Act (CCPA) [10], which went into effect on May 25, 2018, and January 1, 2020, respectively) to address these challenges by increasing transparency requirements for companies' data collection practices and strengthening individuals' rights regarding their PI. However, most of these laws and regulations uphold the concept of informational self-determination through the notice and consent model [53].

The underlying notion of the notice and consent model is that data subjects make conscious, rational and autonomous choices about the processing of their PI. But whether data subjects are always capable of making these choices and willing to do so in practice is questionable [47]. That is why most privacy laws and regulations (especially the GDPR) have brought to light the concept of "informed consent" [31], stating that consent cannot be valid if it is not informed [15], i.e., the data subject who is asked for consent should be properly informed of what exactly she is consenting to and (made) aware to some extent of the consequences such consent may have [14].

Despite this, models for informed consent fail to offer adequate protection for data subjects and have received considerable criticism. For example, Solove [50] discussed the main reasons why such models fail to offer adequate protection for people, as they have too many hurdles:

1-People do not read privacy policies [15,32], as most of them find reading long and complex privacy policies does not worth their time [3];
2-If people do read privacy policies, they do not understand them [8,35]. Several studies (e.g., [4,13,32]) showed that privacy policies require a college reading level and an ability to decode legalistic phrases to understand;
3-If people read and understand them, they often lack enough background knowledge (cognitive competence) to make an informed decision [3]. It can be extremely difficult for a data subject to predict potential future use of her PI [15], and assess the consequences and risks of such use [15]. Accordingly, data subjects may unwittingly consent to types of data processing that they do not want [47]; and
4-If people read them, understand them and can make an informed decision, they are not always offered the choice that reflects their preferences. More specifically, data subjects are, usually, left with a take-it-or-leave-it choice, i.e., give your PI or go elsewhere [48].

Although the idea of informational self-determination through notice and consent model is deeply flawed to defend privacy [8,15,32,35,45,48,50,56], policymakers still heavily depend on it [8,35]. Most likely, because they see no need to seek an alternative [49]. In this paper, we argue that in order to advance informational self-determination, a new direction should be considered.

## 3 Problem Statement and Research Questions

According to the GDPR (Article 4(11)) [38], a valid consent should be: 1-freely given (Rec. 43, Art. 7(4)), it provides data subjects with real choice to consent or not with the absence of coercion by others, i.e., refusing to consent is a viable option [47]; 2-specific (Rec. 42), the consent should be requested about specific data; 3-informed (Rec. 42, Art. 7(3), and Art. 13 that describe what kind of information should be provided to a data subject), the consent should include elements that are crucial for making the data subject understand what she is consenting for and make a choice; and 4-unambiguous (Rec. 32), which indicate the data subject's wishes by which they, by a statement or by clear affirmative action, signify agreement to the processing of their PI, i.e., there must be no uncertainty about the intent of the data subject [15].

There is almost a general agreement on what freely given, specific and unambiguous consent is, yet it is arguable what is considered informed consent. As discussed earlier, if a data subject did not read the privacy policies, or she read them but did not understand, or she read and understand them, but lack the cognitive competence to make an informed decision, such consent cannot be informed [37], accordingly, it is not valid [14,15]. This leads us to the first Research Question *RQ1: What constitutes informed consent?*

As previously discussed, most agree that ignoring privacy policies and terms of service is both a reality and a problem [35]. Why people do not engage in informational self-determination? Several reasons lead to this behavior as consent requests (e.g., privacy policies, terms and conditions) are still ready-made static descriptions [32], long [3,13,32,36], vague and ambiguous [37], full of legal jargon [13,32], complex/complicated [3,13,32], hard to be understood/comprehend by ordinary people [4,33,35,36], change frequently [13], do not, usually, precisely specify potential future use of PI nor assessing the consequences and risks related to such use [15,50], and do not offer data subjects with a much choice [48].

Moreover, the volume of privacy notices, especially for internet users, is overwhelming that cause fatigue to data subjects [53]. Therefore, data subjects, usually, blindly accept such notices [47]. According to Degeling et al. [16], privacy notices have increased by more than 50% in 6,579 popular websites in Europe after the adoption of the GDPR in May 2018. All of this means that privacy notices are not designed with the needs of data subjects in mind [43], which was confirmed by the work of Waldman [54], who reported that the review of 191 privacy policies proven that they were not designed with readability, comprehension, and end-users in mind.

The challenges of providing usable privacy notice have been recognized by regulators and researchers [45], and suggestions to improve the informed consent process are scattered over the literature. For example, one of the most suggested improvements is simplifying the consent process by reducing information overload in the notice [6,15,25,44], i.e., instead of presenting a long text to the data subject, a summary of information or useful headings can be used, or some text can be replaced by privacy icons, colors, etc. [25,32]. However, several studies (e.g., [33,42]) showed that translating an entire privacy policy into a grid that conveyed information by icons and colors did not improve comprehension much. Moreover, it is not always easy to determine whether the notice can be considered informed after the simplification as some essential information might be lost in the process [15]. Additionally, Solove [50] stated that privacy is quite complicated, and simplifying privacy notices neglect a fundamental dilemma: making a notice simple and easy to understand conflicts with fully informing data subjects about the consequences of consenting.

A different approach for reducing acts on the data subject side is by allowing them to manage their privacy globally [15,50]. In such approach, a data subject specifies her acceptable or unacceptable forms of PI usage/collection, where such pattern can be used when being asked for consent for different services. A similar approach is using *informational norms* that restrict the collection and use of PI concerning already defined privacy preferences [49]. However, such approaches have been criticized as it is difficult to find a uniform set of privacy options that fit all potential types of usage [50].

Due to the cognitive and structural problems with informational self-determination, ideas for mixing consent with some sort of paternalism was suggested [50], where a legal body can restrict the usage and collection of PI as some data subjects may consent to the collection and use of their PI even when it is not in their self-interest. Yet, such approaches neglect the main principle of informational self-determination. Finally, ideas for representing a data subject's privacy preferences as a privacy profile that can be matched against privacy policies have been suggested by Broenink et al. [9], yet their implementation of this idea suffered from several limitations.

In summary, most existing approaches present interesting ideas and useful techniques that focus on tackling some specific problems of informational self-determination but fail short in proposing a solution that tackles the essence of the overall problem. This leads us to the second Research Question *RQ2: How can we make informational self-determination usable?*, i.e., how can we empower data subjects to take an active role in the protection of their PI under informational self-determination? In the following sections, we will propose a model for informed consent, followed by a proposed architecture that aims at simplifying the informed consent transaction without reducing its effectiveness.

## 4 A Model for Informed Consent

According to Drozd and Kirrane [17], the attributes of informed consent should include: (i) the type of PI collected from/about the data subject; (ii) the processing performed on such PI; (iii) the purpose(s) such PI are processed for; (iv) where PI is stored and for what duration; and (v) if the PI is shared, who are the recipients. Barocas and Nissenbaum [5], on the other hand, argued that to make informed consent, data subjects must understand: (i) which actors have access to her PI; (ii) what PI they have access to; (iii) what they do or may do with such PI; (iv) whether the PI is directly or indirectly shared with third parties; and (v) what privacy policies apply to the publisher as compared to the all the third parties (if any). The previously mentioned attributes can be found in almost every definition of informed consent, yet most researchers and practitioners argue that these attributes are only a subset of what a data subject might need to know to be meaningfully informed.

In this paper, we advocate that a data subject can make an informed consent if she is well-informed (*personal informedness*) concerning what she is consenting to, which means having sufficient knowledge about any given choice and the desire motivating it[3]. More specifically, being well-informedness concerning a privacy consent requires having:

1-***Procedural awareness*** refers to the *knowing-how* to perform a specific task, i.e., it is the knowledge exercised in the performance of some task [11,12]. *Procedural awareness* aims at enabling a data subject to have procedural know-how competency concerning the technical means involved in the consent transaction. In particular, a consent can be active or passive[4], it might be requested through various techniques (e.g., paper-based, online, pop-up message, etc.), it might have a different types (e.g., (i) no consent, (ii) specific consent, (iii) broad consent, and (iv) blanket consent) [52], and it might involve several confirmation actions, etc. Therefore, the data subject should be made familiar with the technical means for granting, modifying, or withdrawing her consent, and she should be made aware of the possible results of her actions during the consent transaction. This guarantees that the data subject has the knowing-how competence required for making an informed consent.

2-***Situational context awareness,*** privacy is contextual in nature, thus, PI that may be sensitive in one context, might not be sensitive in another [56]. More specifically, the sensitivity of PI can be determined by when and where such information has been collected/generated, by whom and for what purposes, i.e., the context related to such PI [22]. To this end, *situational context awareness* aims at enabling a data subject to evaluate the situational context of the collection/usage of her PI, i.e., what PI is collected/used, by whom, how, and for what purpose(s) [15,46]. That is why it is a prerequisite for making informed privacy decisions.

3-***Cognitive competence,*** the cognitive limitation of data subjects in terms of understanding what exactly they consented to and its consequences is an open research challenge [8,15,18]. *Cognitive competence* centers around the rational capacities of the individual [30], and it refers to the acquisition of new knowledge, critical thinking, problem-solving skills, and their application for analyzing and reflecting on an individual's own actions [28]. More specifically, cognitive competence enables a data subject to make informed, rational and

[3] In [55], well-informedness is defined as "having a **complete** knowledge concerning any given choice", which we believe is not possible when dealing with a complex concept such as privacy.

[4] In passive consent (called also opt-out), a consent is being the default that can be explicitly withdrawn [34] as in the CCPA [10]. While in active consent (called also opt-in), a non-consent being the default [26,34] as in the GDPR [38].

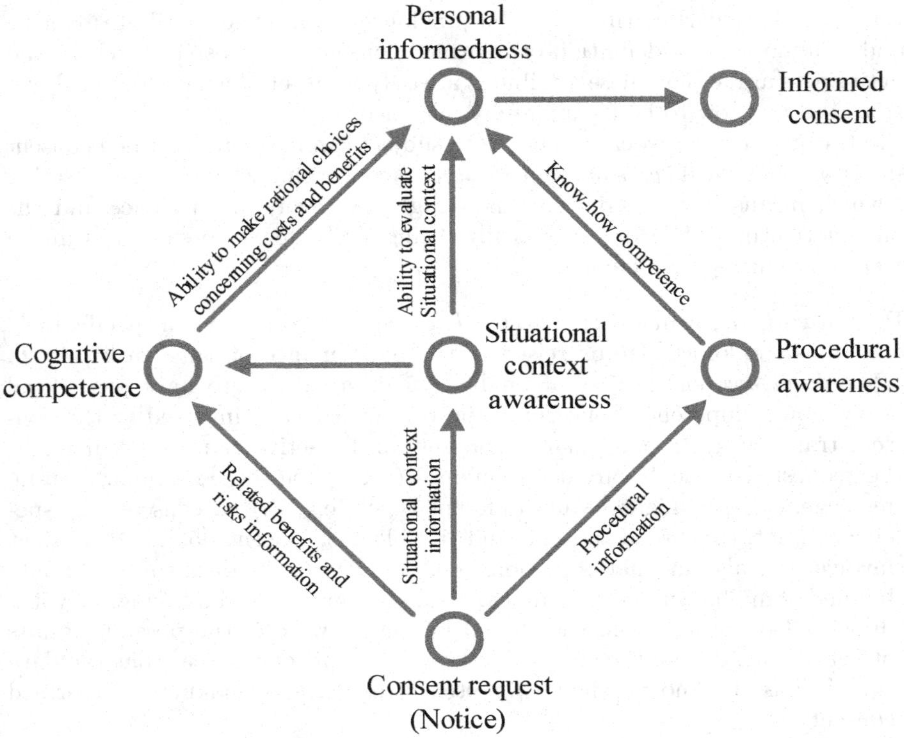


**Fig. 1.** A simplified model of the preconditions for informed consent

moral choices concerning the benefits and costs of their consent [15,47,50], where *Benefits* are the value that data subjects receive from consenting and *Costs* is a combination of data subject's privacy concern, as well as potential risks that may result as consequences of consenting [39][5]. The *cognitive competence* is influenced by the *situational context awareness* as what PI is collected/used, by whom, how, and for what purpose(s) is essential for constructing the *cognitive competence* and, in turn, assessing related benefits and costs.

To conclude, in order to get informed consent, adequate notice should deliver sufficient information concerning 1-the consent procedural means; 2-the consent situational context; and 3-the benefits and risks of consenting. Figure 1 shows a model of the preconditions for informed consent and their interrelations.

[5] Karwatzki et al. [27] identified seven types of risks (e.g., costs, negative consequences) that a data subject might be subject to, namely physical, social, resource-related, psychological, prosecution-related, career-related, and freedom-related risks.

## 5 A Proposed Architecture for Usable Informational Self-determination

The main aim of the proposed architecture is to simplify the informed consent transaction without reducing its effectiveness by decreasing the overwhelming volume of privacy notices, minimizing the time cost and the number of actions at the data subject side while providing them with the required information for making informed decisions concerning the protection of their PI. This will empower data subjects to take an active role in the protection of their PI. A simplified representation of the proposed architecture is shown in Fig. 2.

As people interact with an increasing number of technologies during their daily lives such as websites, cellphone apps, wearable devices, or any other gadgets that collect or use PI, the volume of privacy notices became overwhelming. However, it is unlikely that our privacy preferences change that frequently to answer each of these notices separately. A way forward to deal with this problem is allowing data subjects to define their own privacy policies [9,15,37], which we refer to by *Personal Privacy Profile (PPP)*. The PPP will contain policies defined by the data subject, which clearly specify the category of PI of concern, the purpose(s) for which PI is collected/used, allowed types of usage, retention period, and whether such PI can be shared with others, as follows:

**1-Category of PI:** PI can be specialized into (i) Personally Identifiable Information (PII), any information that can be used, on its own, to distinguish, trace and/or identify an individual's identity; and (ii) Non-PII, any personal information that cannot be used, on its own, to distinguish, trace and/or identify an individual's identity. Moreover, PI can be Sensitive Personal Information (SPI) and Non-SPI, depending on information type (e.g., private, intimate) as well as when, where, and for which purposes such information has been collected [23]. For each type of these categories, a data subject might have different requirements. Accordingly, different policies might be defined for each of them.

**2-Type of use:** describes the type of operations (e.g., read, collect, aggregate) that can be performed on the PI.

**3-Purpose of use:** describes the purpose(s) for which PI can be used for. Based on [7], the purpose of use can be categories under *1-Service purposes* concerning the provision of services to individuals. *2-Legal purposes* related to complying with court orders, or any other legal reasons. *3-Communication purposes* related to contacting individuals about products, services, or other related purposes. *4-Protection purposes* related to information protection, fraud detection, potential misuse, etc. *5-Merger purposes* related to mergers, transfer of company/entity that is managing the PI. *6-Other*, purposes that are not covered by the previous purposes.

**4-Retention period,** a consent should have a temporal aspect, after which it became invalid. As for some providers consenting once implies consent "forever" [14].

**5-Sharing option,** specifies whether PI can be shared with third parties.

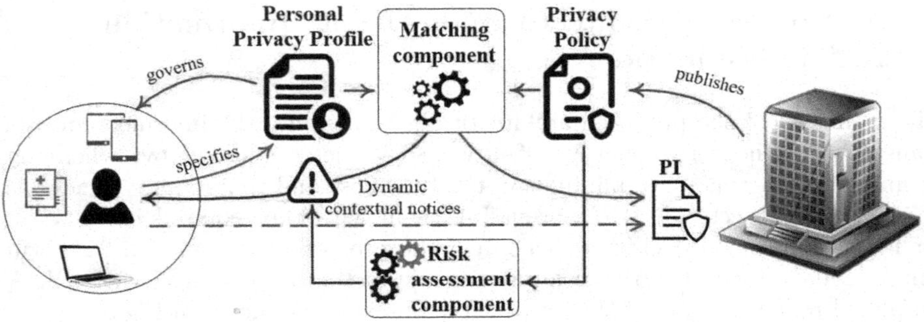


**Fig. 2.** An architecture for usable informational self-determination

Although the public privacy awareness has increased, especially since the introduction of the new privacy regulations (e.g., GDPR) [6,51], some data subjects may still need help from experts or peers to set up their PPP.

On the other hand, each service provider needs to provide/publish a formalized privacy policy that specifies their privacy practices. Such policies should reduce the knowledge gap between data subjects and service providers [2], as the latter know with a high degree of specificity what PI they want to collect and how it will be used, whereas data subjects tend to have very little to no idea about what PI they share with the service providers or other third parties [1]. Privacy policies should include clear details concerning the type and purpose of PI usage, sharing with third parties options as well as the retention period, which facilitates the automated matching between such policies and policies defined in the PPP by the *Matching component*. In particular, when a data subject wants/needs a service that collects or uses PI, the *Matching component* checks whether the privacy policy of the service provider matches a policy in the PPP. If there is a match, consent is provided automatically without the intervention of the data subject.

If the policies do not match, the *Matching component* provides the data subject with a *dynamic contextual notice*, which is a type of notices constructed based on the idea of layered and contextualized notices [46], and it provides a short description indicating where the policies differ. Such notice is further enriched by risks/consequences of consenting provided by the *risk assessment component* that should be administrated by a neutral third party (not the service provider) to increase the trust in the provided information concerning the potential risk of consenting[6]. After the data subject is presented with *dynamic contextual notice*, she should be able to analyze and adequately assess the consequences of consenting. Accordingly, she can make a conscious, rational and informed decision concerning the consent request.

[6] Note that the *dynamic contextual notice* should include sufficient consent procedural information to assure informed consent as discussed in Sect. 4.

## 6 Conclusions and Future Work

In this paper, we worked toward solving some of the prominent problems of informational self-determination since existing approaches are deeply flawed. In particular, we proposed a model for informed consent as well as introducing a proposed architecture that aims at tackling existing limitations in current approaches. The main objective of this architecture is to simplify the informed consent process without reducing its effectiveness, which will empower data subjects to take an active role in the protection of their PI.

This is still a research-in-progress, which provides opportunities for future research. We aim at implementing the proposed architecture relying on semantic web technologies (Resource Description Framework (RDF), Web Ontology Language (OWL), and Simple Protocol and RDF Query Language (SPARQL)), which have been proven to be very efficient for modeling, visualizing, verifying compliance, etc. for privacy/consent related aspects [24,31][7]. Moreover, we plan to develop an ontology for risks (e.g., costs, negative consequences) related to various PI usage, which most existing frameworks do not offer [37]. Finally, we are planning to investigate the influence of trust on the consent transaction.

## References

1. Acquisti, A., et al.: Nudges for privacy and security: understanding and assisting users' choices online. ACM Comput. Surve. **50**(3), 1–41 (2017). https://doi.org/10.1145/3054926
2. Acquisti, A., Brandimarte, L., Loewenstein, G.: Privacy and human behavior in the age of information. Science **347**(6221), 509–514 (2015). https://doi.org/10.1126/science.aaa1465
3. Acquisti, A., Grossklags, J.: Privacy and rationality in individual decision making. IEEE Secur. Priv. **3**(1), 26–33 (2005). https://doi.org/10.1109/MSP.2005.22
4. Anton, A.I., Earp, J.B., He, Q., Stufflebeam, W., Bolchini, D., Jensen, C.: Financial privacy policies and the need for standardization. IEEE Secur. Priv. **2**(2), 36–45 (2004). https://doi.org/10.1109/MSECP.2004.1281243
5. Barocas, S., Nissenbaum, H.: On notice: the trouble with notice and consent. In: Proceedings of the Engaging Data Forum: The First International Forum on the Application and Management of Personal Electronic Information, pp. 1–6 (2009)
6. Bergram, K., Maingot, P., Gjerlufsen, T., Holzer, A.: Digital nudges for privacy awareness: from consent to informed consent? In: Proceedings of the 28th European Conference on Information Systems (ECIS), pp. 15–17, June 2020
7. Bhatia, J., Breaux, T.D.: A data purpose case study of privacy policies. In: Proceedings - 2017 IEEE 25th International Requirements Engineering Conference, RE 2017, pp. 394–399 (2017). https://doi.org/10.1109/RE.2017.56
8. Borgesius, F.Z.: Informed consent: we can do better to defend privacy. IEEE Secur. Priv. **13**(2), 103–107 (2015). https://doi.org/10.1109/MSP.2015.34
9. Broenink, G., Hoepman, J.H., Hof, C.V.T., van Kranenburg, R., Smits, D., Wisman, T.: The Privacy Coach: Supporting customer privacy in the Internet of Things. Technical report, January 2010. http://arxiv.org/abs/1001.4459

[7] Please refer to [31] for an extensive overview of existing semantic solutions for dealing with privacy consent.

10. Bukaty, P.: The California Consumer Privacy Act (CCPA). The California Consumer Privacy Act (CCPA), June 2019. https://doi.org/10.2307/j.ctvjghvnn
11. Carl, W.: The first-person point of view. Walter de Gruyter GmbH, January 2014. https://doi.org/10.1515/9783110362855/HTML
12. Corbett, A.T., Anderson, J.R.: Knowledge tracing: modeling the acquisition of procedural knowledge. User Model. User-Adap. Interact. **4**(4), 253–278 (1994). https://doi.org/10.1007/BF01099821
13. Cranor, L.: Necessary but not sufficient: standardized mechanisms for privacy notice and choice. J. Tele High Technol. Law **10**, 273–307 (2012)
14. Custers, B.: Click here to consent forever: expiry dates for informed consent. Big Data Soc. **3**(1), 2053951715624935 (2016). https://doi.org/10.1177/2053951715624935
15. Custers, B., Dechesne, F., Pieters, W., Schermer, B., van der Hof, S.: Consent and privacy. Technical report (2018). https://doi.org/10.4324/9781351028264-23
16. Degeling, M., Utz, C., Lentzsch, C., Hosseini, H., Schaub, F., Holz, T.: We Value Your Privacy ... Now Take Some Cookies: Measuring the GDPR's Impact on Web Privacy. Technical report (2019). https://doi.org/10.14722/ndss.2019.23378
17. Drozd, O., Kirrane, S.: I agree: customize your personal data processing with the CoRe user interface. In: Gritzalis, S., Weippl, E.R., Katsikas, S.K., Anderst-Kotsis, G., Tjoa, A.M., Khalil, I. (eds.) TrustBus 2019. LNCS, vol. 11711, pp. 17–32. Springer, Cham (2019). https://doi.org/10.1007/978-3-030-27813-7_2
18. Drozd, O., Kirrane, S.: Privacy CURE: consent comprehension made easy. In: Hölbl, M., Rannenberg, K., Welzer, T. (eds.) SEC 2020. IAICT, vol. 580, pp. 124–139. Springer, Cham (2020). https://doi.org/10.1007/978-3-030-58201-2_9
19. Etzioni, A.: The privacy merchants: what is to be done? Uni. PA. J. Const. Law **14**, 929 (2011). https://doi.org/10.2139/ssrn.2146201
20. European Parliament: Directive 95/46/EC of the European Parliament and of the Council of 24 October 1995 on the protection of individuals with regard to the processing of personal data and on the free movement of such data. Official Journal of the European Union 23(L281/31), pp. 31–50 (1995). ISSN 0378–6978
21. Gellman, R.: Fair information practices: a basic history. Soc. Sci. Res. Netw. Electron. J. **2415020**, 1–52 (2014). https://doi.org/10.2139/ssrn.2415020
22. Gharib, M., Giorgini, P., Mylopoulos, J.: An ontology for privacy requirements via a systematic literature review. J. Data Seman. **9**(4), 123–149 (2021). https://doi.org/10.1007/s13740-020-00116-5
23. Gharib, M., Giorgini, P., Mylopoulos, J.: COPri v.2 - a core ontology for privacy requirements. Data and Knowl. Eng. **133**, 101888 (2021). https://doi.org/10.1016/j.datak.2021.101888
24. Gharib, M., Mylopoulos, J., Giorgini, P.: COPri - a core ontology for privacy requirements engineering. In: Dalpiaz, F., Zdravkovic, J., Loucopoulos, P. (eds.) RCIS 2020. LNBIP, vol. 385, pp. 472–489. Springer, Cham (2020). https://doi.org/10.1007/978-3-030-50316-1_28
25. Holtz, L.E., Zwingelberg, H., Hansen, M.: Privacy policy icons. In: Camenisch, J., Fischer-Hübner, S., Rannenberg, K. (eds.) Privacy and Identity Management for Life, pp. 279–285. Springer, Heidelberg (2011). https://doi.org/10.1007/978-3-642-20317-6_15
26. Johnson, E.J., Bellman, S., Lohse, G.L.: Defaults, framing and privacy: why opting in-opting out. Mark. Lett. **13**(1), 5–15 (2002). https://doi.org/10.1023/A:1015044207315

27. Karwatzki, S., Trenz, M., Veit, D.: Yes, firms have my data but what does it matter? Measuring privacy risks. In: 26th European Conference on Information Systems: Beyond Digitization - Facets of Socio-Technical Change, ECIS 2018, vol. 184, pp. 1–16 (2018)
28. Kassymova, G.K., Kenzhaliyev, O.B., Kosherbayeva, A.N., Triyono, M.B., Ilmaliyev, Z.B.: E-learning, dilemma and cognitive competence. Int. Res. Assoc. Talent Dev. Excell. **12**(2), 3689–3704 (2020)
29. Kirrane, S., et al.: A scalable consent, transparency and compliance architecture. In: Gangemi, A., Gangemi, A., et al. (eds.) ESWC 2018. LNCS, vol. 11155, pp. 131–136. Springer, Cham (2018). https://doi.org/10.1007/978-3-319-98192-5_25
30. Kluge, E.H.W.: Competence, capacity, and informed consent: beyond the cognitive-competence model. Can. J. Aging/La Revue canadienne du vieillissement **24**(3), 295–304 (2005). https://doi.org/10.1353/cja.2005.0077
31. Kurteva, A., Chhetri, T., Pandit, H.J., Fensel, A.: Consent Through the Lens of Semantics: State of the Art Survey and Best Practices (2020). semantic-web-journal.net, https://dblp.uni-trier.de
32. Mcdonald, A.M., Cranor, L.F.: The cost of reading privacy policies. J. Law Policy Inf. Soc. **4**, 543 (2008)
33. McDonald, A.M., Reeder, R.W., Kelley, P.G., Cranor, L.F.: A comparative study of online privacy policies and formats. In: Goldberg, I., Atallah, M.J. (eds.) PETS 2009. LNCS, vol. 5672, pp. 37–55. Springer, Heidelberg (2009). https://doi.org/10.1007/978-3-642-03168-7_3
34. Noain-Sánchez, A.: "Privacy by default" and active "informed consent" by layers: Essential measures to protect ICT users' privacy. J. Inf. Commun. Ethics Soc. **14**(2), 124–138 (2016). https://doi.org/10.1108/JICES-10-2014-0040
35. Obar, J.A., Oeldorf-Hirsch, A.: The biggest lie on the Internet: ignoring the privacy policies and terms of service policies of social networking services. Inf. Commun. Soc. **23**(1), 128–147 (2020). https://doi.org/10.1080/1369118X.2018.1486870
36. Oltramari, A., et al.: PrivOnto: a semantic framework for the analysis of privacy policies. Seman. Web **9**(2), 185–203 (2018). https://doi.org/10.3233/SW-170283
37. Pardo, R., Le Métayer, D.: Analysis of privacy policies to enhance informed consent. In: Foley, S.N. (ed.) DBSec 2019. LNCS, vol. 11559, pp. 177–198. Springer, Cham (2019). https://doi.org/10.1007/978-3-030-22479-0_10
38. Parliament, E.: Regulation (EU) 2016/679 of the European Parliament and of the Council of 27 April 2016 on the protection of natural persons with regard to the processing of personal data and on the free movement of such data, and repealing Directive 95/46/EC. Off. J. Eur. Communities **59**, 1–88 (2016)
39. Pötzsch, S.: Privacy awareness: a means to solve the privacy paradox? In: Matyáš, V., Fischer-Hübner, S., Cvrček, D., Švenda, P. (eds.) Privacy and Identity 2008. IAICT, vol. 298, pp. 226–236. Springer, Heidelberg (2009). https://doi.org/10.1007/978-3-642-03315-5_17
40. Prosser, W.L.: Privacy. Calif. Law Rev. **48**, 383 (1960)
41. Raschke, P., Küpper, A., Drozd, O., Kirrane, S.: Designing a GDPR-compliant and usable privacy dashboard. In: Hansen, M., Kosta, E., Nai-Fovino, I., Fischer-Hübner, S. (eds.) Privacy and Identity 2017. IAICT, vol. 526, pp. 221–236. Springer, Cham (2018). https://doi.org/10.1007/978-3-319-92925-5_14
42. Reeder, R.W., Kelley, P.G., McDonald, A.M., Cranor, L.F.: A user study of the expandable grid applied to P3P privacy policy visualization. In: Proceedings of the ACM Conference on Computer and Communications Security, pp. 45–54 (2008). https://doi.org/10.1145/1456403.1456413

43. Renaud, K., Shepherd, L.A.: How to make privacy policies both GDPR-compliant and usable. In: International Conference on Cyber Situational Awareness, Data Analytics and Assessment, CyberSA, pp. 1–8 (2018). https://doi.org/10.1109/CyberSA.2018.8551442
44. Ryan Calo, M.: Against notice skepticism in privacy (and elsewhere). Notre Dame Law Rev. **87**(3), 1027–1072 (2012)
45. Schaub, F., Balebako, R., Durity, A.L., Cranor, L.F.: A design space for effective privacy notices. In: SOUPS 2015 - Proceedings of the 11th Symposium on Usable Privacy and Security, pp. 1–17 (2019). https://doi.org/10.1017/9781316831960.021
46. Schaub, F., Könings, B., Weber, M.: Context-adaptive privacy: leveraging context awareness to support privacy decision making. IEEE Pervasive Comput. **14**(1), 34–43 (2015). https://doi.org/10.1109/MPRV.2015.5
47. Schermer, B.W., Custers, B., van der Hof, S.: The crisis of consent: how stronger legal protection may lead to weaker consent in data protection. Ethics Inf. Technol. **16**(2), 171–182 (2014). https://doi.org/10.1007/s10676-014-9343-8
48. Schwartz, P.M., Solove, D.: Notice and choice. In: The Second NPLAN/BMSG Meeting on Digital Media and Marketing to Children, pp. 1–7 (2009)
49. Sloan, R.H., Warner, R.: Beyond notice and choice: privacy, norms, and consent. J. High Technol. Law **14**, 370 (2014). https://doi.org/10.2139/ssrn.2239099
50. Solove, D.J.: Introduction: privacy self-management and the consent dilemma. Harv. Law Rev. **126**(7), 1880–1903 (2013)
51. Stabauer, M.: The effects of privacy awareness and content sensitivity on user engagement. In: Nah, F.F.-H., Siau, K. (eds.) HCII 2019, Part II. LNCS, vol. 11589, pp. 242–255. Springer, Cham (2019). https://doi.org/10.1007/978-3-030-22338-0_20
52. Steinsbekk, K.S., Kare Myskja, B., Solberg, B.: Broad consent versus dynamic consent in biobank research: is passive participation an ethical problem. Eur. J. Hum. Genet. **21**(9), 897–902 (2013). https://doi.org/10.1038/ejhg.2012.282
53. Utz, C., Degeling, M., Fahl, S., Schaub, F., Holz, T.: (Un)informed consent: studying gdpr consent notices in the field. In: Proceedings of the ACM Conference on Computer and Communications Security, pp. 973–990. ACM, November 2019. https://doi.org/10.1145/3319535.3354212
54. Waldman, A.E.: Privacy, notice, and design. Stanf. Technol. Law Rev. **21**, 74 (2018)
55. Wiśniewski, J.B.: Well-informedness and rationality: a philosophical overview. Q. J. Austrian Econ. **12**(3), 43–56 (2009)
56. Wu, P.F., Vitak, J., Zimmer, M.T.: A contextual approach to information privacy research. J. Assoc. Inf. Sci. Technol. **71**(4), 485–490 (2020). https://doi.org/10.1002/asi.24232

# Building a Privacy Testbed: Use Cases and Design Considerations

Joseph Gardiner[1], Partha Das Chowdhury[1(✉)], Jacob Halsey[1], Mohammad Tahaei[1], Tariq Elahi[2], and Awais Rashid[1]

[1] University of Bristol, Bristol, UK
{joe.gardiner,partha.daschowdhury,vw18148, mohammad.tahaei,awais.rashid}@bristol.ac.uk
[2] University of Edinburgh, Edinburgh, UK
t.elahi@ed.ac.uk

**Abstract.** Mobile application (app) developers are often ill-equipped to understand the privacy implications of their products and services, especially with the common practice of using third-party libraries to provide critical functionality. To add to the complexity, most mobile applications interact with the "cloud"—not only the platform provider's ecosystem (such as Apple or Google) but also with third-party servers (as a consequence of library use). This presents a hazy view of the privacy impact for a particular app. Therefore, we take a significant step to address this challenge and propose a testbed with the ability to systematically evaluate and understand the privacy behavior of client server applications in a network environment across a large number of hosts. We reflect on our experiences of successfully deploying two mass market applications on the initial versions of our proposed testbed. Standardization across cloud implementations and exposed end points of closed source binaries are key for transparent evaluation of privacy features.

**Keywords:** Privacy-enhancing technologies · Testbed · Usable privacy · Privacy professionals

## 1 Introduction

For developers privacy is often not the explicit goal [5,22]. The benefits of making use of fine-grained personal information are immediate, but the consequences of this insecure behavior is delayed and difficult to comprehend [3]. Furthermore, the software collecting and processing personal information encapsulates complex mathematics, tools, and a diverse understanding of privacy. The complexity is increased when Privacy Enhancing Technologies (PETs) are integrated into apps as a mitigation against unwanted data leaks.

Solove et al. argue that privacy is far too complex to be left in the hands of average consumers (including developers); the solution lies in regulating the infrastructure that collects, stores, and transfers information [21]. However, it


S. Katsikas et al. (Eds.): ESORICS 2021 Workshops, LNCS 13106, pp. 185–193, 2022.
https://doi.org/10.1007/978-3-030-95484-0_12

is currently not possible to gain insights into these infrastructures due to an absence of a mechanism to ascertain the flow of information in practice. This absence impedes developers, regulators, and users to verify the claims made by applications about their data practices and the PETs they employ.

In this paper, we address this gap by proposing a privacy testbed. We sketch use-cases, discuss design considerations, and reflect on the initial implementations of our proposed **automated testbed** to verify the privacy features/claims of mass market client server applications that use PETs. This forms the basis of the testbed proposed by the National Research Centre on Privacy, Harm Reduction and Adversarial Influence Online (REPHRAIN) announced by UK Research and Innovation in October 2020. While testbeds have been proposed in other settings, e.g., security of control systems and IoT [11,14,18], to our knowledge, this paper is the first to propose a privacy testbed.

## 2 Use Cases

Our proposed testbed can assist software developers, system administrators, and privacy professionals, to run large scale analysis without the need to deploy any infrastructure or have access to several (potentially costly) target devices. They will be able to instantiate multiple virtual devices with various versions of operating systems to facilitate executing privacy-related analyses. Regulators can use our testbed as well for certification and verification purposes. We outline three sample use cases for exposition.

### 2.1 Contact Tracing Applications

A developer of a contact tracing app uses the Google Apple exposure notification (GAEN) framework [13]. The application uses exposure notification framework to detect individuals who might be exposed to other individuals with a virus. The cryptographic operations are handled by GAEN. The app developers are required to use the *ExposureNotificationClient* class to implement functions allowing users to start/stop tracing, handle exposure related notifications, medical information and receive broadcasts. There is a ephemeral key which is generated at regular intervals and upon infection the history of the keys over a fixed period of time are sent to the authorities for alerting potential contacts within that period. Applications should not reveal any personal sensitive information either during the exchange, broadcasts or while data is at rest. Recent research suggests the security and privacy of contact tracing applications are fraught with imperfections [24].

Our testbed would allow the users to run multiple tests on both the server and the client side using multiple virtual instances. For example, at the client side potential concerns like *can a user de-anonymize infected contacts or other contacts using the app?* can be tested using our testbed. The *enormity and scale of server side data* can be independently explained to regulators, developers and/or end users. Furthermore the data can be interfaced with privacy evaluation frameworks like (Privacy by Design [16] and LINDDUN [9]) to preempt a repeat of CARE data scandals [19]. The ability to refute through practical manifestations of the threat will lead to effective and privacy enhancing application development. This would be useful in authentication situations (e.g., Kerberos deployments) where privacy is not a requirement but the remote entity is untrustworthy.

### 2.2 Privacy Preserving Peer to Peer (P2P) File Sharing Systems

Participants in P2P systems also run the infrastructure [25] and rely on the honesty and competence of other participants. One way to disrupt the system is to infiltrate the membership of the network through favored pawns and gain control [4]. Wang et al. describe possible horizontal and vertical attacks to put enough traffic in the hands of the attacker to identify participants in the network [23]. Some solutions suggest the presence of a strong central authority to prevent hostile takeover of the network [10], which leads to a single point of failure. The threat of partitioning by insiders also applies to cryptographic ways of stamping digital documents [15], decentralized property [8], and programmable replicated state machines based upon the Byzantine General's problem [17].

Our testbed can replicate large number of independent instances through virtualization. This gives the ability to deploy a large number varied independent instances with similar diversity of real world infrastructure. Attacks can then be simulated by turning a subset of the virtual machines malicious. These simulations would enable systems to observe attacks as they happen and depending on the specific attack scenario, the testbed can measure the impact on application performance whilst under attack, measure if a subset of compromised nodes can deanoymize users, and other security, privacy, and performance metrics.

### 2.3 Privacy Preserving Browsers Using Privacy Preserving Networks

The *Tor browser*, *Brave* and other *Onion* browsers use the Tor anonymity network [1] to prevent traceability of communicating parties. They are available for both the *Android* and *iOS* platforms. For *iOS* devices the browsers use the *WebKit* framework, which can override some anonymity features, leaving *iOS* users potentially vulnerable. The *DuckDuckGo* browser promises privacy yet they also have a search engine, which may lead to privacy leaks.

The testbed we propose in this paper can be used to do a comparative study of the browsers on anonymous networks. For example the leakages that might or might not happen due to compulsive use of *WebKit* framework. The economic incentives of *DuckDuckGo* browser against their claims of privacy and how that translates in the network traffic can be tested using our testbed. Our ability to deploy multiple hosts and instances can enable tests to be carried out on the effectiveness of *Tor* against push notifications.

## 3 Design

The testbed stems from the acknowledgment of the power yet the limit of theoretical models [12]. The requirements of the testbed are captured in Fig. 1:

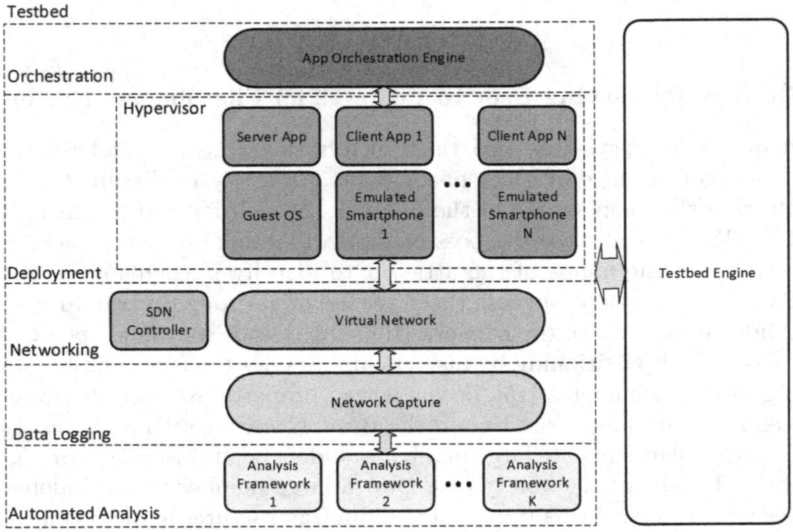


**Fig. 1.** High-level design of the testbed

*Deployment.* The testbed needs to support the easy deployment of potentially thousands of hosts and services (i.e. the back-end) as well as individual hosts representing users. As well as deploying simple virtual machines, the ability to deploy more modern types of host, such as emulated smartphone environments, is also required. The testbed should provide the functionality to configure machines automatically, including setting machine properties such as hostnames, installing applications to be tested and configuring individual application deployment specific variables such as usernames.

*Networking.* A realistic virtual network should be deployed for virtual hosts. Complex topologies resembling a real-world deployment can thus be produced. In a real-world setting there may be hundreds of routers and switches involved in the routing of traffic. Each of these, if compromised, becomes a potential point for information leakage to occur and so emulating this environment can provide richer analysis. For greater flexibility and finer control, software-defined networking is used which allows for the easy deployment of network applications.

*Orchestration.* Users should be able to automate application functions in order to test at scale without manual intervention. For example, for the contact tracing use cases, users should be able to simulate the broadcast and receive functions required by the application, as well as simulate the interaction between the virtual hosts. This will be done for diverse platforms as well as for diverse users. Our testbed would include automated navigation within smartphone applications, replaying of network traffic from previous captures or simulated users.

*Data Logging.* The purpose of the testbed is credible data collection. The diversity of platforms and hosts would mean that the testbed is agnostic and should be able to support data capture from these devices and platforms. The obvious data type to capture is network traffic. As an example, when testing a contact tracing application a tester should be able to send an infection report and the packets containing that report should be captured, which can then be analyzed for privacy violations. As well as network traffic, this can also include data such as live memory captures from virtual hosts and automated screen captures of administrator and user screens.

*Automated Analysis.* Whilst some users of the testbed will want to perform manual analysis of data captured, for a developer not familiar with privacy analysis frameworks, the testbed should be able to automatically apply such frameworks. For example, by interfacing the data logs with the LINDDUN framework a user will be able to understand the privacy implications resulting out of the trust relationship on the remote entity. The framework includes *hard* and *soft* privacy properties like *unlinkability, undetectability, plausible deniability* and *user content awareness* respectively [9].

## 4 Prototype Implementation

In order to demonstrate the intended operation of the testbed, we have implemented a prototype. The prototype consists primarily of a command line utility called `kvm-compose`, written in Rust and modeled after the `docker-compose` utility used to manage Docker containers. The `kvm-compose` utility reads a configuration YAML file which specifies which virtual machines should be launched, as well as the network topology to be deployed. Once the configuration file is written, then the testbed can be brought up using a simple `kvm-compose up` command, and shut down using `kvm-compose down`. The utility also allows the user to bring up or tear down specific virtual machines without affecting the rest of the testbed environment.

**Listing 1.1.** Example machine configuration

```
- name: example1                       # VM Name
  memory_mb: 4096                      # Optional: default 512MiB
  cpus: 4                              # Optional: default 1
  disk:                                # Two variants: cloud_image
    cloud_image:                       #   or existing_disk
      name: ubuntu_18_04
      expand_gigabytes: 25             # Optional
  interfaces:                          # Connected network interfaces
    - bridge: br0                      #
  run_script: ./script.sh              # Optional: path to a script
  context: ./file.txt                  # Optional: path to a file or folder
  environment:                         # Dictionary of arbitrary environment variables
    key: value                         # Use /etc/nocloud/env.sh *key* to query
```

If disk image supports *cloud-init* at first boot the following will happen:

- The machine `name` (with project prefix) is used as the hostname.
- The SSH public key is injected into the instance.
- File(s) specified in `context` are copied into the `/etc/nocloud/context` directory.
- The `run_script` is executed, with its output log saved into `/etc/nocloud/`.

*Virtualization.* Virtualization is provided by Kernel-based Virtual Machine (KVM), which is a kernel module for the Linux operating system that allows it to function as a hypervisor. In order to assist in automated machine deployment, `cloud-init` [7] is used, which allows virtual machines to receive a list of data sources (such as URLs or files) with machine deployment information (such as locale, hostname and SSH keys) to be used for that instance.

*Networking.* Networking is provided using OpenVSwitch (OVS) virtual switches. OVS is used due to its support of software-defined networking (SDN), which allows fine-grained control over the network. The Floodlight SDN controller is used to provide control.

*Network Capture.* When a test environment has been built (using the `kvm-compose up` command), network traffic can then be collected using the `ovs-tcpdump` utility of OVS [2]. This creates a temporary mirror port on the specified bridge, with traffic from specified ports being mirrored.

## 5 Reflection and Evaluation with Example Deployments

We used a messaging application *Signal* and a contact tracing application Decentralized Privacy-Preserving Proximity Tracing (DP3T) [6] to test the design considerations of our testbed. The *DP3T* project provides an SDK (Software Development Kit) for both *Android* and *Apple iOS* which is used to communicate with the backend server. It is this library which is used in the official implementations such as *SwissCovid*. *Signal* is a messaging service built using its own custom end-to-end encryption protocol (the *Signal Protocol*), available for a number of platforms on mobile and desktop, designed with a focus on privacy [20].

We have been able to successfully deploy instances of *DP3T* and *Signal* where the virtual machines communicated with external networks to download their dependencies. The SDN controller can be attached to multiple bridges and used to deploy more complex networks. Our testbed successfully captured network traffic from the example projects. A potential improvement could be to integrate the packet capture commands as part of the *kvm-compose* utility to produce a more streamlined experience for the user.

The *DP3T* example demonstrates the use of multiple hosts namely a desktop computer and a mobile phone (*Anbox* and *Android Emulator*). These implementations do not support *Bluetooth* and that can be a limitation for closed binaries (without exposed end-points) where inputs cannot be simulated. However, in our *DP3T* tests, this has not been an impediment as we could simulate inputs. The UK's NHS COVID-19 contact tracing app implementation is highly coupled to Amazon Web Services (AWS), and as such it is difficult to run within the testbed. *Cloud-native* applications do need standardization for transparent evaluation.

The *kvm-compose* used with *cloud-init* utility makes the testbed easy to deploy and replicate such as the servers for the *DP3T* and *Signal* examples. The level of automation for mobile apps requires further work. While in the *DP3T* example the emulators are installed automatically, it still requires the app to be launched and driven by a user using a window manager. Furthermore, the progress and status (success or failure) during the virtual machine `run_script` phase are not easily accessible, which also impedes extensive automation.

**Future Work:** We will further develop this testbed to allow for greater orchestration of applications and implement the relevant mapping to be able to apply privacy frameworks for automated analysis.

## 6 Conclusion

The testbed is relevant for developers of systems used by traditional as well as modern hosts in the modern digital economy based on capturing, utilizing and monetizing large-scale information flows. We address at the heart of the information asymmetry that has been characteristic to this eco-system. An entity producing the technologies has more information than the user; the user has no way to verify the claims made by the producer. Our work is a stepping stone towards empowering developers and users.

## References

1. https://www.torproject.org. Accessed June 2021
2. https://docs.openvswitch.org/en/latest/ref/ovs-tcpdump.8/. Accessed June 2021
3. Acquisti, A., Brandimarte, L., Loewenstein, G.: Secrets and likes: the drive for privacy and the difficulty of achieving it in the digital age. J. Consum. Psychol. **30**(4), 736–758 (2021)

4. Baqer, K., Anderson, R.: Do you believe in tinker bell? The social externalities of trust. In: Christianson, B., Švenda, P., Matyáš, V., Malcolm, J., Stajano, F., Anderson, J. (eds.) Security Protocols 2015. LNCS, vol. 9379, pp. 224–236. Springer, Cham (2015). https://doi.org/10.1007/978-3-319-26096-9_23
5. Braz, L., Fregnan, E., Çalikli, G., Bacchelli, A.: Why don't developers detect improper input validation? DROP TABLE papers. In: 2021 IEEE/ACM 43rd International Conference on Software Engineering (ICSE), pp. 499–511 (2021). https://doi.org/10.1109/icse43902.2021.00054
6. Busvine, D.: Rift opens over European coronavirus contact tracing APPs, April 2020. https://www.reuters.com/article/uk-health-coronavirus-europe-tech-idUKKBN2221U6?edition-redirect=uk
7. Canonical: cloud-init - The standard for customising cloud instances. https://cloud-init.io/
8. Crispo, B., Lomas, M.: A certification scheme for electronic commerce. In: Lomas, M. (ed.) Security Protocols 1996. LNCS, vol. 1189, pp. 19–32. Springer, Heidelberg (1997). https://doi.org/10.1007/3-540-62494-5_2
9. Deng, M., Wuyts, K., Scandariato, R., Preneel, B., Joosen, W.: A privacy threat analysis framework: supporting the elicitation and fulfillment of privacy requirements. Requir. Eng. **16**(1), 3–32 (2011)
10. Druschel, P., Kaashoek, F., Rowstron, A. (eds.): IPTPS 2002. LNCS, vol. 2429. Springer, Heidelberg (2002). https://doi.org/10.1007/3-540-45748-8
11. Gardiner, J., Craggs, B., Green, B., Rashid, A.: Oops I did it again: further adventures in the land of ICS security testbeds. In: Proceedings of the ACM Workshop on Cyber-Physical Systems Security and Privacy, CPS-SPC 2019, pp. 75–86. Association for Computing Machinery, New York (2019). https://doi.org/10.1145/3338499.3357355
12. Golomb, S.: Mathematical models-Uses and limitations. Astronaut. Aeronaut. **6**(1), 57 (1968). Amer Inst Aeronaut Astronaut 1801 Alexander Bell Drive, Ste 500, Reston, Va
13. Google, Apple. Exposure notifications: Helping fight COVID-19. https://www.google.com/covid19/exposurenotifications/. Accessed June 2021
14. Green, B., Lee, A., Antrobus, R., Roedig, U., Hutchison, D., Rashid, A.: Pains, gains and PLCs: Ten lessons from building an industrial control systems testbed for security research. In: 10th USENIX Workshop on Cyber Security Experimentation and Test (CSET 17). USENIX Association, Vancouver, August 2017. https://www.usenix.org/conference/cset17/workshop-program/presentation/green
15. Haber, S., Stornetta, W.S.: How to time-stamp a digital document. J. Cryptol. **3**(2), 99–111 (1991). https://doi.org/10.1007/BF00196791
16. Hoepman, J.H.: Privacy Design Strategies (The Little Blue Book). Radbound University (2019)
17. Lamport, L., Shostak, R., Pease, M.: The Byzantine Generals Problem, pp. 203–226. Association for Computing Machinery, New York (2019). https://doi.org/10.1145/3335772.3335936
18. Mathur, A.P., Tippenhauer, N.O.: SWaT: a water treatment testbed for research and training on ICS security. In: 2016 International Workshop on Cyber-Physical Systems for Smart Water Networks (CySWater), pp. 31–36 (2016). https://doi.org/10.1109/CySWater.2016.7469060
19. Triggle, N.: Care.data: how did it go so wrong? https://www.bbc.co.uk/news/health-26259101. Accessed June 2021
20. Signal Foundation: Speak freely. https://signal.org/en/. Accessed June 2021

21. Solove, D.J.: The myth of the privacy paradox. George Washington Law Rev. **89**, 1 (2021)
22. Tahaei, M., Frik, A., Vaniea, K.: Privacy champions in software teams: understanding their motivations, strategies, and challenges. In: Proceedings of the 2021 CHI Conference on Human Factors in Computing Systems, CHI 2021, pp. pp. 1–15. Association for Computing Machinery, New York (2021). https://doi.org/10.1145/3411764.3445768
23. Wang, L., Kangasharju, J.: Real-world sybil attacks in Bittorrent mainline DHT. In: 2012 IEEE Global Communications Conference (GLOBECOM), pp. 826–832 (2012). https://doi.org/10.1109/GLOCOM.2012.6503215
24. Wen, H., Zhao, Q., Lin, Z., Xuan, D., Shroff, N.: A study of the privacy of COVID-19 contact tracing apps. In: Park, N., Sun, K., Foresti, S., Butler, K., Saxena, N. (eds.) SecureComm 2020, Part I. LNICST, vol. 335, pp. 297–317. Springer, Cham (2020). https://doi.org/10.1007/978-3-030-63086-7_17
25. Yeh, L.Y., Lu, P.J., Huang, S.H., Huang, J.L.: SOChain: a privacy-preserving DDoS data exchange service over SOC consortium blockchain. IEEE Trans. Eng. Manage. **67**(4), 1487–1500 (2020). https://doi.org/10.1109/TEM.2020.2976113

# 4th International Workshop on Attacks and Defenses for Internet-of-Things (ADIoT 2021)

# ADIoT 2021 Preface

The 4th International Workshop on Attacks and Defenses for Internet-of-Things (ADIoT 2021) was held on October 4, 2021, in conjunction with ESORICS 2021 in Darmstadt, Germany. Due to the COVID-19 situation, it was held online.

Internet of Things (IoT) technology has been widely adopted by the vast majority of businesses and is impacting every aspect of the world. However, the nature of the Internet, communication, embedded OS, and backend recourses make IoT objects vulnerable to cyber attacks. In addition, most standard security solutions designed for enterprise systems are not applicable to IoT devices. As a result, we are facing a big IoT security and protection challenge, and there is an urgent need to analyze IoT-specific cyber attacks to design novel and efficient security mechanisms. This workshop focuses on IoT attacks and defenses, and seeks original submissions that discuss either practical or theoretical solutions to identify IoT vulnerabilities and IoT security mechanisms.

This year, ADIoT received 15 submissions, and each submission was reviewed by at least three reviewers. According to the novelty and quality, six regular papers were accepted along with one short paper, resulting in an acceptance rate of 40%.

For the success of ADIoT 2021, we would like to first thank the authors of all submissions and all the Program Committee members for their great efforts in reviewing the papers. We also thank all the external reviewers for assisting in the reviewing process.

November 2021

Weizhi Meng
Steven Furnell

# ADIoT 2021 Organization

## General Chairs

| | |
|---|---|
| Anthony T. S. Ho | University of Surrey, UK |
| Kuan-Ching Li | Providence University, China |

## Program Committee Chairs

| | |
|---|---|
| Weizhi Meng | Technical University of Denmark, Denmark |
| Steven Furnell | University of Nottingham, UK |

## Program Committee

| | |
|---|---|
| Claudio Ardagna | Universita' degli Studi di Milano, Italy |
| Ali Ismail Awad | Lulea University of Technology, Sweden |
| Chao Chen | Swinburne University of Technology, Australia |
| Jianming Fu | Wuhan University, China |
| Georgios Kambourakis | University of the Aegean, Greece |
| Wenjia Li | New York Institute of Technology, USA |
| Wenjuan Li | Hong Kong Polytechnic University, China |
| Jiqiang Lu | Beihang University, China |
| Xiaobo Ma | Xi'an Jiaotong University, China |
| Reza Malekian | Malmo University, Sweden |
| Jianbing Ni | Queen's University, Canada |
| Jun Shao | Zhejiang Gongshang University, China |
| Meng Shen | Beijing Institute of Technology, China |
| Kar-Ann Toh | Yonsei University, South Korea |
| Lei Wang | Shanghai Jiao Tong University, China |
| Bin Xiao | Hong Kong Polytechnic University, China |
| Lam Kwok Yan | Nanyang Technological University, Singapore |
| Xuyun Zhang | Macquarie University, Australia |
| Peng Zhou | Shanghai University, China |

## Additional Reviewer

Efstratios Chatzoglou

# Assessing Vulnerabilities and IoT-Enabled Attacks on Smart Lighting Systems

Ioannis Stellios(✉), Kostas Mokos, and Panayiotis Kotzanikolaou

SecLab, Department of Informatics, University of Piraeus, 85 Karaoli & Dimitriou, 18534 Piraeus, Greece
jstellios@unipi.gr

**Abstract.** The rapid evolution of the Internet-of-Things (IoT) introduces innovative services that span across various application domains. As a result, smart automation systems primarily designed for non-critical environments may also be installed in premises of critical sectors, without proper risk assessment. In this paper we focus on IoT-enabled attacks, that utilize components of the smart lighting ecosystem in popular installation domains. In particular, we present a holistic security evaluation on a popular smart lighting device (The specific model is not referred in this paper, since we are currently in the process of a responsible disclosure procedure with the vendor.), that is focused on vulnerabilities and misconfigurations found on hardware, embedded software, cloud services and mobile applications. In addition, we construct a Common Vulnerability Scoring System (CVSS) like vector for each attack scenario, in order to define the required capabilities and potential impact of these attack scenarios and examine their potential exploitability and impact.

**Keywords:** Internet of Things · Smart lights · Vulnerability analysis · Reverse engineering · IoT-enabled attacks

## 1 Introduction

Within the last decade, the combination of innovative technologies such as Machine-to-Machine communications and Artificial Intelligence, fuse physical and digital worlds via the introduction of interconnected, cyber-physical devices, known as 'smart things'. These IoT technologies enable the development and operation of autonomous, self-aware systems with remote control and interoperability capabilities. Smart things are usually equipped with wireless interfaces, sensing and processing capabilities, and can be remotely managed via cloud-based, Internet-facing services. Due to their low cost and easy deployment, various IoT devices are incorporated into critical sectors such as healthcare, transportation, supply chain, agriculture, industry, energy production/distribution

This research has been co-financed by the European Union and Greek national funds through the Operational Program Competitiveness, Entrepreneurship and Innovation, under the call RESEARCH - CREATE - INNOVATE (project code: T1EDK-01958).


S. Katsikas et al. (Eds.): ESORICS 2021 Workshops, LNCS 13106, pp. 199–217, 2022.
https://doi.org/10.1007/978-3-030-95484-0_13

and urban environments. Adversaries, can then utilize the above characteristics to launch remote, stealthy, cyber-physical attacks in ways that cannot be easily identified and assessed [36].

Smart lighting systems combine the state-of-the-art lighting technology including Light Emitting Diode (LED) and/or Organic LED (OLED) with sensors (e.g. ambient light, acoustic, ultrasonic, infrared, location), wireless network interfaces, (e.g. Ethernet, WiFi, Z-Wave, ZigBee Light Link - ZLL), vendor-specific application software, as well as cloud services (e.g. If-This-Then-That – IFTTT) [24], in order to enable remote control, interoperability and autonomous operation. Via these features they achieve optimization of energy consumption, visual comfort, safety, remote control and adaptability in various environments. Their vast adoption has lead to a significant production cost reduction which, in turn, resulted in making them one of the most wide-spread smart IoT technologies. Smart lighting systems can be remotely managed via smartphone applications that utilize local and/or remote connectivity through cloud services. Popular smart lighting systems utilize Apple's HomeKit (Siri), Amazon's Echo (Alexa) and Google Home, in order to enable remote control via voice commands. Near-future advanced intelligent lighting technologies may include, real-time luminosity and spectrum self-adjustment capabilities.

*Smart Lighting Systems and Critical Infrastructures: Risk Dependencies.* Attacking critical cyber-physical systems by exploiting a vulnerable IoT device or service, has been an alarmingly increasing trend in recent years [36]. The interconnectivity, interoperability and proximity of legacy Information and Communication Technology (ICT) systems with IoT devices, acts as an enabler for a plethora of new types of interactions on both cyber and physical level. Depending on the installation site, the attacks on smart lighting systems can attract diverse types of attackers, ranging from security enthusiasts up to highly skilled and motivated adversaries such as nation-state and organized cybercrime. An adversary can take advantage of existing vulnerabilities and characteristics of an IoT-enabled automation system such as smart lights to abuse and/or extend its functionality (e.g. sensing capabilities, network connectivity, wireless adaptor's operating frequency and available luminosity levels) and launch a variety of cyber-physical attacks against nearby critical systems or even people [28,29].

The potential impact of IoT-enabled attacks is usually overlooked and can be tricky to estimate since it depends heavily on the organization under study, the systems being exploited and the type of the attack. For example, an organization can sustain heavy damage from a Distributed Denial-of-Service (DDoS) attack scenario that involves a plethora of seemingly non-critical, internet-connected compromised home IoT devices and its Internet-facing ICT infrastructure [3]. Similarly, a network infiltration attack enabled by existing vulnerabilities in smart lighting systems (e.g. CVE-2020-6007), may have a significant impact on organizations such as banks or pharmaceutical companies. IoT-enabled attack scenarios that involve vulnerable smart lighting systems in various environments, may also result in data exfiltration, ransomware campaigns, disruption of organizations business' processes, harm individuals by inducing epileptic seizures in a hospital's environment [29] or trigger car accidents by manipulating the public traffic lighting system [4,28]. In Fig. 1 we present a list of applicable attacks on smart lighting ecosystem and the potential bussineswise impact for a variety of installation domains.

*Motivation.* Although several security vulnerabilities for smart lighting devices have been identified in the recent literature (e.g. [21,37]), still various systems and components have not been tested. In addition, the related work is focused on individual components of each smart lighting device or service rather than follow a holistic approach and assess vulnerabilities found on hardware, embedded software, radio networks, applications and cloud services. Moreover, although risks that derive from IoT devices against legacy ICT/industrial systems have been studied in the recent past [2,36,38] there hasn't been a research that focuses on the individual characteristics of smart lighting systems.

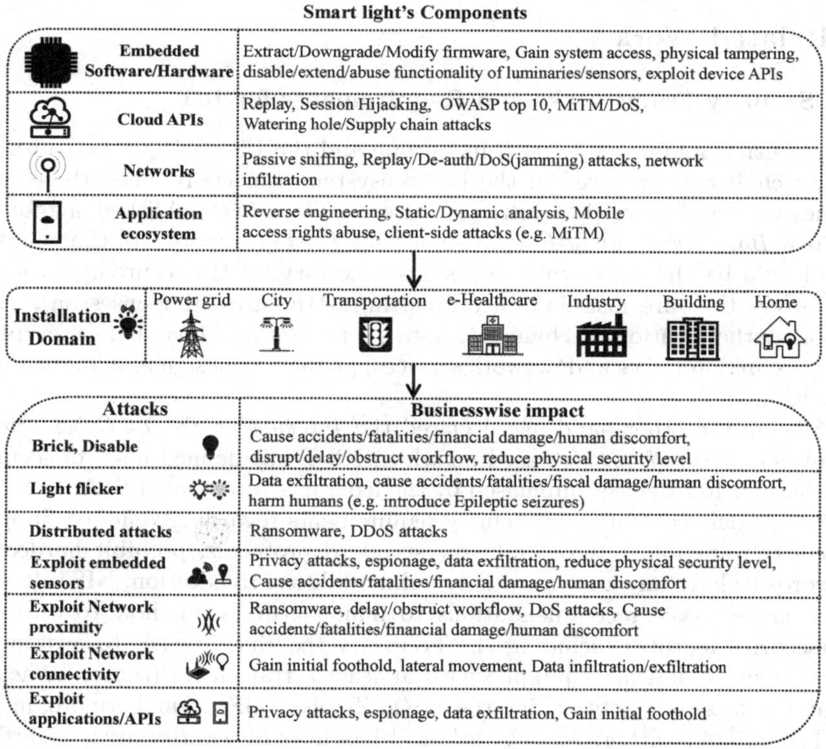


**Fig. 1.** Potential impact of attacks on smart lighting systems for critical domains

*Contribution.* In this paper, we conduct a holistic hands-on security analysis on a popular IoT smart lighting device. In addition, we analyze applicable attack vectors enabled by vulnerable smart lighting systems and examine their potential impact in various sectors. In Sect. 3 we present an overview of our vulnerability assessment methodology, as well as our findings on hardware, embedded software, smart lighting cloud servers and mobile application. In addition, we conduct security tests on ZLL as well as 802.11.x wireless interfaces and their corresponding network services. The assessment takes into consideration previous work on similar devices. In Sect. 4, we utilize our assessment findings, in order to construct CVSS-like vectors, namely $IntCVSS$ as defined in [35], which model the required capabilities (exploitability metrics) and impact characteristics of each attack scenario. This information may be useful by organizations when conducting risk assessment in order to identify potential adversaries and risks originating from IoT-enabled attacks scenarios that involve vulnerable smart lighting systems. Finally, Sect. 5 concludes this paper.

## 2 Related Work

### 2.1 Security Frameworks and Requirements for IoT

Cybersecurity organizations both in Europe and the US begin to recognize the security challenges involved in the IoT ecosystem, especially when these technologies are used in critical infrastructures. ENISA has published a tool[1] as well as a *Baseline Security Recommendations for IoT* report [10] that aims in presenting a baseline of security measures necessary for the secure operation of IoT devices that are installed on critical infrastructures. It focuses on authorization/authentication mechanisms, data protection and compliance, cryptography, secure interfaces and network services, privacy by design and Third-Party relationships.

USA, on the other hand has declared the *Internet of Things Cybersecurity Improvement Act of 2017*[2], based on which NIST has defined a set of security guidelines for IoT devices purchased by the federal government [13]. Among others, the act defined minimum security requirements regarding vendors: Support of security patching, rely on industry standard protocols, prohibit hardcoded passwords or have any known security vulnerabilities. In addition, NISTIR 8259 [11] describes basic recommendations to manufacturers, on how to establish cybersecurity features including the necessary security services to customers, for IoT devices that are equipped with at least a transducer (sensor or actuator) and at least one network interface (e.g. Zigbee, WiFi). Furthermore, in [12] (NISTIR 8259A) authors specify technical baselines in security areas regarding *Device Identification*, *Device Configuration*, *Software Update*, *Data Protection*, *Logical Access to Interfaces* and *Cybersecurity State Awareness*.

---

[1] https://www.enisa.europa.eu/topics/iot-and-smart-infrastructures/iot/good-practices-for-iot-and-smart-infrastructures-tool/.

[2] https://www.congress.gov/bill/115th-congress/senate-bill/1691.

## 2.2 Attacks on Lighting Systems

Several works can be found in the literature that examine practical attacks against smart lighting systems, as summarized below.

**Privacy/Side Channel Attacks on Light Emitting Devices.** Xu et al. [40] demonstrated an attack that exploits the emanations of changes in light so as to reveal the actual television programs. The researchers were able to identify the content being watched among a reference library of tens of thousands of videos within several seconds. In [31,32] the authors demonstrated that it is possible to determine what the user is currently watching on TV, just by exploiting the ambient light sensor of a user's smartphone/smartwatch whereas Ferrigno et al. [15] were able to retrieve AES keys by capturing the light (photons) emitted from a micro-controller (picosecond imaging circuit analysis). In [22,23] the feasibility of privacy attacks was examined on audio-visualizing and video-visualizing systems as well as the exfiltration of potentially sensitive information by exploiting infrared light sensors/actuators.

**Covert Channels/Remote Control.** Covert channels can occur when sources of electromagnetic, acoustic, thermal and/or optical wavelength are used as transmitters to create communication channels [42]. Ronen and Shamir [29] demonstrated how the exfiltration of potentially sensitive data from air-gaped systems is possible by creating a covert channel via the extension of the functionality features of a smart lighting system. Zhou et al. [42] demonstrated that is possible to create a covert channel via infrared module of an air-gaped system. Guri et al. [18] manage to exfiltrate data via invisible to human eye, low contrast and/or fast flickering images whereas in [17] researchers achieved similar results by exploiting security cameras with infrared modules. Similarly in [6], abusing the functionality of normal/Infrared LEDs can lead to hard-to-identify optical covert channels and/or even disable visual equipment via Denial-of-Service (DoS) and jamming attacks. In another approach Ronen et al. [28] proved that is possible to take over a large number of smart lighting systems by remotely infecting just one smart lamp and a self-propagation infection process whereas researchers investigated the possibility of triggering events in a smart home environment by manipulating a smart lighting system presence sensors [34].

**Smart Lighting Ecosystem Vulnerabilities.** Vulnerability analysis of smart lighting systems have been studied in [7,25]. Quang Do et al. [8] analyze the threats for three types of adversaries, forensic passive/active and real-time active for smart lighting systems. In particular, they analyzed security vulnerabilities of both LIFX 1000 series as well as Belkin WeMo switch for all three predefined type of attackers. The researchers examined specific capabilities such as passive/active eavesdropping (intercept/selective forwarding) and replay control messages (transmit and modify). In [1] the researchers examined popular IoT devices, including a WeMo switch, for leaking sensitive data to outsiders such as

Internet Service Providers (ISPs). Via Domain Name Service (DNS) queries and relative network data streams they managed to identify the actual type and/or state of an IoT device. Another study for privacy risks in smart household appliances [26] revealed that WeMo motion sensor and switch kit do not implement encryption and authentication schemes for network communications as well as easy-to-discover communication ports thus making them prone to Man-in-The-Middle (MiTM) and replay attacks. Researchers in [21] analyzed vulnerabilities found in the WeMo smartphone application and communication protocols and simulated cross-site scripting based phishing attack scenario.They managed to recover WiFi password as well as exposing personal information by introducing a 'fake' emulated device.

# 3 Security Analysis on a Smart Lighting System

The examined smart lighting system comprises of a smart light controller and a light bulb with the former to have the following features and specifications:

- A Software restore push button, a region specific AC plug and a LED to indicate power and Wi-Fi status.
- An internal IEEE 802.11 b/g/n WiFi radio 2.4 GHz antenna for communicating with the local network and the Internet.
- An internal IEEE 802.14.5x b/g/n ZigBee radio 2.4 GHz antenna Home Automation 1.2 Certified for communicating with the light bulb.
- One Spatial stream.
- Works with *If-This-Then-That* web platform that is used to connect to other web applications.

## 3.1 Methodology Overview

A holistic approach is followed to identify the vulnerabilities and security misconfigurations of the smart lighting system. In particular, hardware characteristics and embedded software, radio interfaces and network services as well as the corresponding mobile application and cloud Application Programming Interfaces (APIs) are examined.

**Hardware Components.** Disassembling the smart light controller enabled us to access its main circuit board. In particular, we managed to locate: the flash memory chip (*winbond 25Q128FVSG 1603*) with 16 MB serial NOR flash memory that communicates over a Serial Peripheral Interface (SPI); the *winbond W9825G6KH-61 1513P 643803400ZU* chip that contains the Electrically Erasable Programmable Read-Only Memory (EEPROM) of the device; the *Ralink RT5350F TP4KW33609 1601STA1* WiFi controller; the *EM357 1536A00MB8 TM ARM (e3)* 802.15.4x/ZigBee controller; and finally a Universal Asynchronous Receiver/Transmitter (UART) debugging interface, which enables communication with any device equipped with a universal bus interface such as *Bus Pirate*, accessible via a three pin layout.

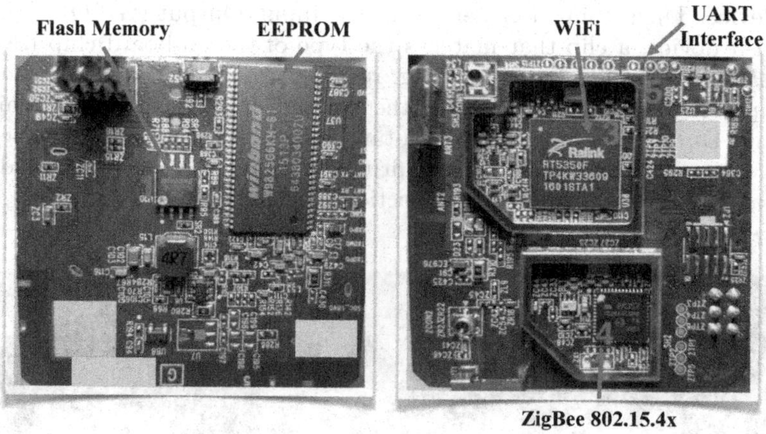


**Fig. 2.** Printed circuit of the tested control device and its main components.

**Smart Lighting System Mobile Application and Cloud Services.** The mobile application is available for both Android and IOS platforms. It is used for setting up, remote control and firmware update of the smart light controller and light bulb(s). During our research we conducted both dynamic as well as static analysis of the application. Via static analysis, hardcoded information such as domain names, emails, passwords and encryption/verification keys were retrieved. Via dynamic analysis, the interaction of the application with the devices and/or the cloud servers can further be examined.

**Radio Communications.** By utilizing open source tools and a HackRF radio antenna, we analyzed the network traffic between the mobile application, the cloud servers and the control device. In particular, we examined both 802.15.4.x (ZLL) and 802.11.b/g/n, 2.4 GHz, network interfaces that the control device utilizes to communicate with the smart light bulbs and the mobile application/cloud services respectively.

**Risk Analysis of the Security Findings.** Based on the vulnerabilities and misconfigurations found, we defined all the corresponding exploitability and impact metrics of each predefined attack. In particular, we adopt the risk assessment methodology of [35] to assess the individual required exploitability and impact characteristics of each attack scenario.

### 3.2 Security Analysis of the Smart Lighting Control Device

**Firmware Extraction and Analysis.** After disassembling the control device the main board was accessible (see Fig. 2). Each chip of the main board was identified in order to locate the on-board chip that contains the embedded software of the device. Then, using a General-Purpose Input/Output (GPIO) of a *Raspberry PI 3* device, a clip that matches the type of the on-board chip (SOIC8), and *flashrom*[3], a utility for identifying, reading, writing, verifying and erasing flash chips, enabled us to extract all of the contents of the flash memory chip to a binary file. During this process, no anti-tampering mechanisms or other security countermeasure(s) that could prevent firmware extraction were identified (e.g., encrypted filesystems, read/write protection mechanisms [9]) (Fig. 3).

**Fig. 3.** Lab setup for firmware extraction

In order to access the extracted filesystems from the binary file, the *binwalk* software tool[4] was utilized. After an analysis of the dumped files we identified that the extracted file systems and the boot-loader are stored on the same memory chip. This is considered a bad security practise, since the bootloader should always be stored in a write-protected chip to ensure the integrity and validity of the operating system during the boot process. As the bootloader is contained within the same re-writable flash memory chip with the main filesystem, this makes possible to modify the bootloader in order bypass security mechanisms (e.g. [37]). An analysis of the extracted filesystems revealed the following:

- The file named *wireless* in *etc./config* directory indicates that the initial values of WiFi with 'encryption' option set to 'none' and also contains the initial

[3] https://flashrom.org/Flashrom.
[4] https://github.com/ReFirmLabs/binwalk.

'passkey' for a given Service Set Identifier (SSID). This in turn means that during the device initialization process, an adversary may connect to the network and intercept sensitive information (e.g. the new WiFi key).
- The file `root/.gnupg` contains the public key in .asc format (`XXXPubKey.asc`) that is used for verification of the downloaded signed firmware file during the update process.
- The *passwd* file of *etc.* folder contains only the root user. This actually means that all system and network services are being run with root privileges. An adversary could utilize this information and target *any* network service available, since, compromising the network service via an existing remote code execution vulnerability (e.g. CVE-2019-12780) would result in accessing the device with administrator rights.
- Many of the recovered script files included several informative comments regarding the functionality of the code, similar to the ones that can be found in the source code of development stage of an application. This in turn, can assist an adversary to further understand and reverse engineer the functionality of a program in order to bypass any security countermeasures. For example, by reading the comments and relative code of the file `sbin/firmware_update.sh`, we manage to understand that during an Over-The-Air (OTA) update process the script does not ensure that the downloaded firmware is a newer version from the already installed version. Although we did not perform such an attack, this can be used as an indicator that a firmware downgrade attack is feasible.

**Mobile Application and Cloud Servers Security Analysis.** Android mobile applications can be easily decompiled and, depending on the obfuscation level, reverse engineered. Via *apktool* we manage to decompile the application and access the configuration (*AndroidManifest.xml*) as well as *smali* files of the smart lighting system application. Further analysis of the *AndroidManifest.xml* file revealed that the application supports Android version 6.0 (referred as Software Development Kit - SDK version 23) which by default allows user added certificates. This was a clear indication that MiTM attacks are possible for this version of the application without any modification of the application. By using open-source tools such as jadx[5], we reversed the application code to its `.class` files. Applying some minor modifications of the configuration file *res/xml/network_security_config.xml* enable us to make the application to trust our user added certificate in order to perform MiTM attacks between the mobile application and the control device/cloud services. In particular:

```
.....
<xml version="1.0" encoding="utf-8"?>
<network-security-config>
 <base-config cleartextTrafficPermitted="true">
  <trust-anchors>
```

[5] https://github.com/skylot/jadx.

```
   <certificates src="user" />
  </trust-anchors>
 </base-config>
</network-security-config>
.....
```

After recompiling the modified application into an *apk* file and installing it to a smartphone, we proceeded in launching the MiTM attacks. We utilized the application's firmware update functionality to intercept the network communications. During the authentication process with the cloud servers, the application crafts two new packets with the location of the firmware file(s) and post them to the server. Then, each firmware file is forwarded to the device's location in order to trigger the firmware update task. Static analysis of the application's decompiled code revealed several *Https* links of cloud APIs. Although we were able to validate their existence, we considered them out of scope, since, they did not play any part in our vulnerability assessment scenario.

A closer look to the network packet containing the firmware update link, revealed a publicly available Internet location containing a plethora (aprox. 1400) of firmware update files of several types: Build Verification Testing (BVT), Design Validation Test (DVT), Engineering Validation Test (EVT) and Production Validation Test (PVT). We also managed to map the firmware update files to a number of types of smart IoT devices that included smart light bulbs, light switches, control-link, air purifiers, dimmers, relays and coffee maker machines. In addition, for each device there were available firmware update versions since 2016. To further evaluate the available firmware files we first extracted the majority of the filesystems from gpg images using the already obtained public key (`XXXPubKey.asc`) and the *binwalk* tool. Then, via custom scripts to automate the process, we analyzed the extracted filesystems. The operating system discovered, was an obsolete version (10.03), dating back to 2010 (latest release 21.02.0-rc4[6]), of the Open Wireless router (OpenWrt) Linux distribution, that is mainly used for devices like routers and IoT devices. Furthermore, the analysis revealed that, in most cases, the root was the only user of the system and that all the available root passwords were limited to just four, for the majority of the update firmware files. This, in turn, amplifies significantly the impact for a plethora of Internet-facing IoT devices in case where these passwords are reversed/cracked (e.g. via brute force/dictionary techniques) since they are in danger of being fully compromised.

Non-intrusive, enumeration checks of web servers and API services (e.g. via banner-grabber techniques) revealed that they run on obsolete and/or vulnerable software including an Apache Tomcat 8.5.38 (latest stable version 8.5.65) with several vulnerabilities including a potential Remote Code Execution (RCE) vulnerability (CVE-2019-0232) and an obsolete Apache 2.2.31 (latest version 2.4.46) that runs over `Http`. Interestingly enough, the latter operates also in `Https` mode but only for Secure Sockets Layer (SSL) version 3 and Transport

[6] https://downloads.openwrt.org/releases/.

Layer Security (TLS) version 1.0 protocols, both of which are considered as depreciated. Even though SSL/TLS is not utilized during the update process, it might be used in other vendor legacy products. The SSL 3.0 and TLS 1.0 are susceptible to several high-severity vulnerabilities such as POODLE (CVE-2014-3566), SWEET32 (CVE-2016-2183, CVE-2016-6329) and BEAST (CVE-2011-3389, CVE-2013-2566, CVE-2015-2808). During our tests we have also discovered that the secure client-initiated renegotiation process is susceptible to DoS attacks[7] and that both sites were prone to Cross Site Scripting (XSS) and data injection attacks. In addition, several other Internet-facing directories with publicly available, update firmware files of other IoT devices were discovered, but they were considered as out-of-scope and were not further assessed.

**Fig. 4.** The intercepted packets during the authentication process of the mobile application with the cloud servers

During the authentication process the mobile application sends a `POST` request to the cloud server containing the `refresh-token`, the `Client-secret`, the `XXX-Client-type-id` and the `Client-id`. Via static analysis we were able to locate in unencrypted form both the `Client-secret` and the `Client-id` hardcoded in the mobile application. This is a bad security practice as it can significantly increase the possibility of compromising the authentication process, since all but one of the variables of the `POST` request are already known. Furthermore, it can lead to a session hijacking in the case where the authentication token (access-token) is intercepted (see Fig. 4). During the authentication process the authentication cookie was intercepted and confirmed as a JavaScript Object Notation (JSON) web token[8]. Even thought the token is signed and the modification of its contents is not possible, some information can be inferred: From the header we can deduce that the encryption algorithm in use is the

[7] https://owasp.org/www-pdf-archive/OWASP_-TLS_Renegotiation-_Vulnerability.pdf.

[8] https://jwt.io/.

Hash-based Message Authentication Code (HMAC) SHA-256 (`'alg': HS256`). Moreover, from the creation and the expiration time we can infer that the validity time period of the token is set to 3 days. The latter is considered as a bad security practise, since it is very hard to revoke an authentication token once it is delivered to a recipient. This is the main reason why expiration time should not exceed a short period of minutes/hours. Finally, during the password reset process, the new password was included in the POST request both in encrypted as well as plain-text form. Although the communication was via `Https`, this leave the password exposed in MiTM attacks if the SSL/TLS encryption is compromised (Fig. 5).

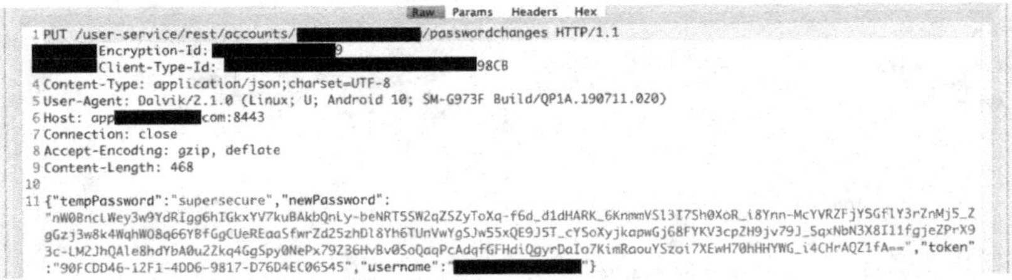

```
Raw Params Headers Hex
PUT /user-service/rest/accounts/[redacted]/passwordchanges HTTP/1.1
[redacted]Encryption-Id: [redacted]9
[redacted]Client-Type-Id: [redacted]98CB
Content-Type: application/json;charset=UTF-8
User-Agent: Dalvik/2.1.0 (Linux; U; Android 10; SM-G973F Build/QP1A.190711.020)
Host: app[redacted]com:8443
Connection: close
Accept-Encoding: gzip, deflate
Content-Length: 468

{"tempPassword":"supersecure","newPassword":
"nW0BncLWey3w9YdRIgg6hIGkxYV7kuBAkbQnLy-beNRT5SW2qZ5ZyToXq-f6d_d1dHARK_6KnmmVS13I7Sh0XoR_i8Ynn-McYVRZFjYSGflY3rZnMj5_Z
gGzj3w8k4WqhW08q66YBfGgCUeREaaSfwrZd25zhDl8Yh6TUnVwYgSJw55xQE9J5T_cYSoXyjkapwGj68FYKV3cpZH9jv79J_5qxNbN3X8I11fgjeZPrX9
3c-LM2JhQAle8hdYbA0u2Zkq4GgSpy0NePx79Z36HvBv0SoQaqPcAdqfGFHdiQgyrDaIo7KimRaouYSzoi7XEwH70hHHYWG_i4CHrAQZ1fA==","token"
:"90FCDD46-12F1-4DD6-9817-D76D4EC06545","username":"[redacted]"}
```

**Fig. 5.** The intercepted POST request during the password reset process. The password is sent both in plain-text (temmPassword) and encrypted (newPassword) form

## Network Communications Analysis

*ZigBee Light Link Network Protocol Vulnerabilities.* ZLL network protocol is utilized by the control device to administer the smart light bulbs. In ZLL a master network key is used each time a new device is registered in the network. Unfortunately, the ZLL master key was leaked thus compromising the light bulb pairing process [5]. An adversary can send a control signal forcing the light bulb out of the network. Then, the network key can be retrieved by intercepting the network pairing process. Other types of attacks include signal interference (jamming), unauthorized network commissioning as well as Distributed DoS (DDoS) and replay attacks.

In order to validate the vulnerabilities of ZLL network protocol, two python scripts were created utilizing the Open Source Mobile Communications (OSMOCOM)[9] drivers and a HackRF device as a ZigBee jammer/receiver/transmitter. In addition, the *Wireshark* network protocol analyzer was paired with gnu-radio companion with IEEE 802.15.4x libraries such as Foo[10] and RFtap[11] (Fig. 6).

[9] https://osmocom.org/.
[10] https://github.com/bastibl/gr-foo.
[11] https://rftap.github.io/.

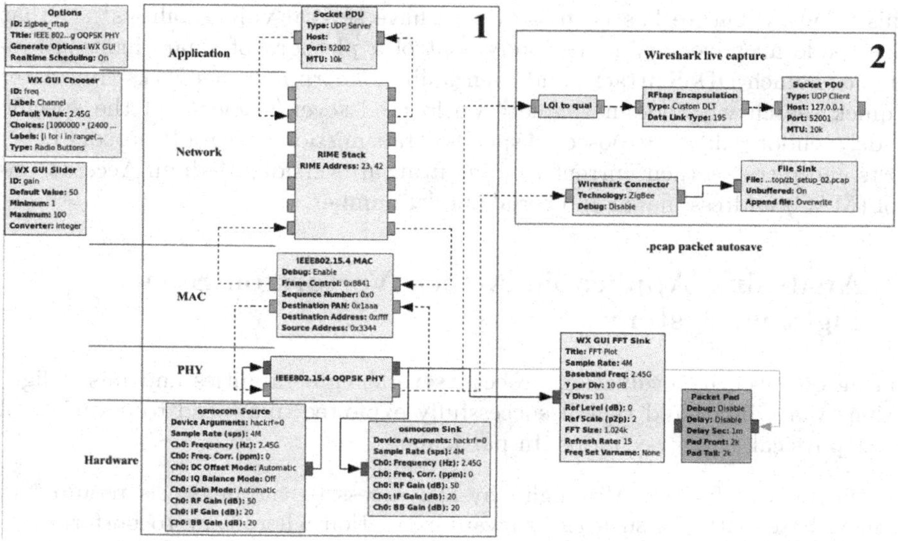


**Fig. 6.** Flowgraph of ZigBee network protocol (1) and Wireshark connectors with live capture (2) and pcap autosave

We first simulate a real case scenario of a jamming attack and were able to significantly expand the time-frame window of the pairing process thus enabling us to capture the network key. In particular, we observed that an injection of a 5 s signal noise from the HackRF antenna towards the ZigBee network resulted in a total loss of the communication of the control device with the smart light bulbs for a period ranging between two up to five minutes. This in turn, allowed us to capture the network key during the re-pairing process –by utilizing the leaked global trust center link key– thus decrypting the whole network traffic. In a similar attack scenario, an adversary would be able to launch both passive and active network attacks (sniffing/replay attacks) and even infiltrate a corporate network[12]. In addition, due to its characteristics, the jamming process could be utilized in a low-profile, stealthy DoS attack scenarios (e.g. via war flying/driving techniques) in diverse installation domains.

*Wi-Fi Network Protocol Vulnerabilities.* As described in previous work [21], the WiFi passphrase could be reconstructed just by retrieving the Media Access Control (MAC) address and serial number of a switch device. During the initial setup of the device we managed to validate the findings of the firmware analysis (open access WiFi during setup process). We discovered that in order for the device to communicate with cloud servers, Universal Plug and Play (UPnP) network service is enabled by default. Via UPnP a request is made to the local router to forward a port without any authentication requirements and user intervention.

[12] https://research.checkpoint.com/2020/dont-be-silly-its-only-a-lightbulb/.

This network feature has been known to have several vulnerabilities[13,14] that can enable an adversary to remotely control a plethora of smart lighting systems to launch DDoS attacks and even infiltrate corporate networks [19]. After a quick search via Shodan engine[15] we located several devices of the specific model/vendor publicly exposed on specific Transmission Control Protocol (TCP) ports and retrieve, their current running firmware version, Medium Access Control (MAC) address, name and serial/model number.

## 4 Analyzing Applicable Attack Vectors on Smart Lighting Systems

During our security evaluation process, several vulnerabilities and misconfigurations were discovered that if successfully exploited, may lead to a variety of cyber-physical attack scenarios. In particular:

- Embedded software: Although physical access to the device is required in most cases, attacks such as firmware extraction where easy to perform due to the lack of anti-tampering mechanisms. In addition, modification attacks can be considered plausible since the U-Boot partition resides on the same memory chip without any write protection mechanisms. Furthermore, gaining system access is possible via the Joint Test Action Group (JTAG) connectors. Finally, downgrade attacks could potentially be performed via local network and/or the Internet, since the communication with the servers is via plain *Http*, while the main system update script does not check for the version number.
- Mobile application: Some obfuscation in the source code prohibited us from discovering the full functionality of the device's mobile application but there were no anti-tampering (integrity protection) mechanisms to prevent from reversing and modifying the code. Forcing the application to trust our certificates enabled us to perform MiTM attacks. In addition, the hardcoded IDs may be used to potentially compromise the authentication process with the cloud servers. Moreover, misconfigurations such as the extended (3-day) validity period of the authentication cookie, can be exploited in various attack vectors.
- Cloud APIs: Cloud servers proved to be poorly protected against leaking of sensitive information directly to the Internet, such as multiple (aprox. 1400) unencrypted update firmware files of several types of IoT devices. The majority of the firmware files were using an obsolete version (10.03) of OpenWrt linux distribution dating back to 2010, were signed with the same key that was extracted from the control device and utilized just the root user with common root passwords across different types of IoT devices (4 different

[13] https://www.checkpoint.com/defense/advisories/public/2020/cpai-2019-1605.html/.

[14] https://nvd.nist.gov/vuln/detail/CVE-2020-12695.

[15] https://www.shodan.io/.

passphrases for the majority of approximate 1400 firmware files). Furthermore, the installed versions of web application software as well as network protocols were outdated and/or susceptible to attacks due to high-severity vulnerabilities with publicly available exploits[16]. These vulnerabilities can allow an adversary to launch potentially high-impact attacks with minimum effort (e.g. supply chain/waterhole atatcks).
- Networks: Most (if not all) of wireless network types suffer from de-auth attacks which was true for both ZLL and WiFi network interfaces of the device. In addition, the device's WiFi initial setup proved to be insecure during the initiation/pairing process. Via HackRF and open source software we managed to effectively jam both ZLL as well as WiFi signals which resulted in an extensive period of unresponsiveness among the control device and smart light bulbs and/or the connection in the local WiFi. Furthermore, we easily managed to gain access in both networks and perform passive sniffing and Deauth attacks. Finally via the Shodan search engine we managed to discover several IoT devices of this type that utilize UPnP protocol to be accessible from the Internet, leaking sensitive information such as MAC address and firmware version.

Following the approach described in [35], we utilize the above information to construct the relevant $IntCVSS$ vectors, as presented in Table 1. These vectors follow the CVSS structure, but in contrast to CVSS which describes the characteristics of a vulnerability, $IntCVSS$ is used to represent the minimum capabilities required by an attacker in order to successfully trigger an attack against an interacting device. The exploitability characteristics of $IntCVSS$ are used to determine the type(s) of the applicable threat actor(s) for each organization under assessment. For example, if physical access to the device is required (AV:P), then only adversaries with physical access are capable to trigger an attack. In the same way, $IntCVSS$ vectors characterized with `High` attack complexity (AC:H) can only be triggered by highly skilled attackers. In addition, the impact characteristics of $IntCVSS$ are utilized to ascertain the level of the sustained damage to the target device. In particular, individual C/I/A metrics are used in order to determine whether an attack can result in a full or partial compromisation of an IoT device, thus allowing an adversary to propagate to the actual target. The status field in Table 1 has the following meaning: *Confirmed* indicates that the corresponding vulnerability was actually exploited whereas *plausible* implies that there were strong indicators that a vulnerability is exploitable.

Using Table 1 we can infer that attacks like firmware extraction/modification require physical access to the device, with the exception of firmware downgrade, for which there were strong indicators that it is plausible via network. Attacks against Cloud APIs required only Internet access whereas session hijacking and API exhaustion attacks were feasible only via local network. For network related attack vectors we confirmed that both ZLL and WiFi are susceptible to passive sniffing, replay, DoS and network infiltration attacks. The various attack vectors

[16] https://www.exploit-db.com/exploits/47073.

**Table 1.** *IntCVSS* vectors representing the required capabilities and impact metrics for all applicable attack scenarios

| | Attack type | Status | *IntCVSS* | | | | | | | |
|---|---|---|---|---|---|---|---|---|---|---|
| | | | AV | AC | PR | UI | S | C | I | A |
| IoT control device | Firmware extraction | Confirmed | P | L | N | N | C | H | N | N |
| | Firmware downgrade | Plausible | N | L | N | N | C | L-H | L-H | L-H |
| | Firmware modification | Plausible | P | H | N | N | C | H | H | H |
| | Device system access | Plausible | P | L | N | N | C | H | H | H |
| Cloud API servers | Access sensitive information | Confirmed | N | L | N | N | C | H | N | N |
| | Waterhole attack | Plausible | N | H | N | N | C | H | H | N |
| | API manipulation | Plausible | A | ND | N | N | C | L | L | L |
| | session hijacking | Confirmed | A | L | N | N | C | L-H | L-H | L-H |
| | API exchaustion | Confirmed | N | L-H | N | N | C | N | N | L-H |
| | XSS/SQL injection etc. | Plausible | N | L-H | N | N | C | L-H | L-H | L-H |
| | Server-side Man-in-The-Middle attacks | Plausible | N | L-H | N | N | C | L-H | L-H | N |
| Device's ZigBee network | De-Auth attacks | Confirmed | A | L | N | N | C | N | N | H |
| | Passive sniffing | Confirmed | A | L | N | N | C | L-H | N | N |
| | Replay attacks | Confirmed | A | L | N | N | C | L-H | L-H | N-H |
| | DoS attacks | Confirmed | A | L | N | N | C | N | L | L |
| | Gain network access | Confirmed | A | L | N | N | C | L | N | N |
| Device's WiFi network | De-Auth attacks | Plausible | A | L | N | N | C | N | N | H |
| | Passive sniffing | Confirmed | A | L | N | N | C | L | N | N |
| | Replay attacks | Plausible | A | L-H | N | N | C | L-H | L-H | N-H |
| | DoS attacks | Confirmed | A | L | N | N | C | N | L | L |
| | Gain network access | Confirmed | N | L | N | N | C | L | N | N |
| Device's mobile application | Reverse engineering | Confirmed | N | L | N | N | C | L-H | L-H | N |
| | Dynamic analysis | Confirmed | N | L | N | N | C | L-H | L-H | N |
| | Application rights abusal | Plausible | L | L-H | L | N | C | L-H | L-H | N-H |
| | Application modification | Confirmed | N | L | N | N | U | L-H | L-H | N-H |
| | Client-side Man-in-The-Middle attacks | Confirmed | A | L | N | N | U | L-H | L-H | N |

AV: P = Physical, L = Logical access, A = Adjacent/Proximity, N = Remote network access
AC/PR/UI/S/CIA: N = None, L = Low, H = High, ND = Not Defined

when combined with Low *Attack Complexity* metric and the fact that there is no *privilege requirements*, favor the diversity of applicable threat agents with varied motives ranging from e.g. activists who just want to protest and seek to harm the reputation of a government's organization[17], to nation-state adversaries who may target against other nations' critical infrastructures [16,20]. As smart lighting systems may be installed in a variety of critical sectors, they may act as attack enablers or attack amplifiers against nearby critical targets [36].

## 5 Conclusions

Although vulnerabilities of smart lighting systems have been studied in recent years, risks that derive from these systems have been mostly overlooked. As a step towards covering this gap, in this paper we presented a thorough security evaluation of a popular smart lighting IoT device. In particular, we examined potential attack vectors for hardware, embedded software, mobile application,

[17] https://www.bbc.com/news/technology-12110892.

wireless networks and cloud services. During our research we combined known vulnerabilities with new ones found in embedded software, mobile application and cloud APIs. In addition, we analysed potential attack scenarios regarding smart lighting systems for various installation domains, including critical ones.

Although the direct impact of attacks against smart lighting systems is usually considered as limited, it may be very high if vulnerable smart lighting systems are part of IoT-enabled attacks against critical systems. Depending on the installation environment, the impact may vary significantly including service disruption, pivoting to other systems, data exfilteration or even affect patients' health [36]. Therefore, operators and security administrators should realize that installing off-the-shelf IoT devices in direct/indirect connectivity and/or proximity with critical cyber-physical systems can increase significantly the risk level since it can create new, subliminal attack scenarios that can have an adverse impact on organizations [36]. Adopting security best practices as described in ENISA and NIST [10–13] can help set a security baseline for vendors when manufacturing IoT devices. In addition, state-of-the-art solutions which may improve IoT security in the near future include, including among others, the use of blockchain, artificial intelligence and machine learning techniques [14,27,39], improved IoT authentication schemes [33], securing the update process [41] and IoT related security frameworks [30].

## References


1. Apthorpe, N., Reisman, D., Feamster, N.: A smart home is no castle: Privacy vulnerabilities of encrypted iot traffic. arXiv preprint arXiv:1705.06805 (2017)
2. Bakhshi, Z., Balador, A., Mustafa, J.: Industrial IoT security threats and concerns by considering cisco and microsoft IoT reference models. In: 2018 IEEE Wireless Communications and Networking Conference Workshops (WCNCW), pp. 173–178. IEEE (2018)
3. Herzberg, B., Igal Zeifman, D.B.: Breaking down Mirai: an IoT DDoS botnet analysis. https://www.imperva.com/blog/malware-analysis-mirai-ddos-botnet/
4. Cerrudo, C.: An emerging us (and world) threat: cities wide open to cyber attacks. Secur. Smart Cities **17**, 137–151 (2015)
5. Colin, O.: A lightbulb worm? Details of the Philips Hue smart lighting design (Black Hat USA 2016 White Paper) (2016)
6. Costin, A.: Security of CCTV and video surveillance systems: threats. vulnerabilities, attacks, and mitigations. In: TrustED, vol. 16, pp. 45–54
7. Dhanjani, N.: Hacking lightbulbs: security evaluation of the Philips hue personal wireless lighting system. In: Internet of Things Security Evaluation Series (2013)
8. Do, Q., Martini, B., Choo, K.K.R.: Cyber-physical systems information gathering: a smart home case study. Comput. Netw. **138**, 1–12 (2018)
9. Dubrova, E.: Anti-tamper Techniques. KTH Royal Institute of Technology, Sweden (2018)
10. ENISA: Baseline security recommendations for IoT in the context of critical information infrastructures, November 2017
11. Fagan, M., Fagan, M., Megas, K.N., Scarfone, K., Smith, M.: Foundational cybersecurity activities for IoT device manufacturers. US Department of Commerce, National Institute of Standards and Technology (2020)

12. Fagan, M., Fagan, M., Megas, K.N., Scarfone, K., Smith, M.: IoT Device Cybersecurity Capability Core Baseline. US Department of Commerce, National Institute of Standards and Technology (2020)
13. Fagan, M., Marron, J., Brady, K., Cuthill, B., Megas, K., Herold, R.: IoT device cybersecurity guidance for the federal government: Establishing IoT device cybersecurity requirements. Technical report, National Institute of Standards and Technology (2020)
14. Fakhri, D., Mutijarsa, K.: Secure IoT communication using blockchain technology. In: 2018 International Symposium on Electronics and Smart Devices (ISESD), pp. 1–6. IEEE (2018)
15. Ferrigno, J., Hlaváč, M.: When AES blinks: introducing optical side channel. IET Inf. Secur. **2**(3), 94–98 (2008)
16. Goodin, D.: Hackers trigger yet another power outage in Ukraine (2017). https://arstechnica.com/security/2017/01/the-new-normal-yet-another-hacker-caused-power-outage-hits-ukraine/
17. Guri, M., Bykhovsky, D.: aIR-jumper: covert air-gap exfiltration/infiltration via security cameras & infrared (IR). Comput. Secur. **82**, 15–29 (2019)
18. Guri, M., Hasson, O., Kedma, G., Elovici, Y.: An optical covert-channel to leak data through an air-gap. In: 2016 14th Annual Conference on Privacy, Security and Trust (PST), pp. 642–649. IEEE (2016)
19. Kayas, G., Hossain, M., Payton, J., Islam, S.R.: An overview of UPnP-based IoT security: threats, vulnerabilities, and prospective solutions. In: 2020 11th IEEE Annual Information Technology, Electronics and Mobile Communication Conference (IEMCON), pp. 0452–0460. IEEE (2020)
20. Lee, R.M., Assante, M.J., Conway, T.: Analysis of the cyber attack on the Ukrainian power grid. SANS Industrial Control Systems (2016)
21. Liu, H., Spink, T., Patras, P.: Uncovering security vulnerabilities in the Belkin Wemo home automation ecosystem. In: 2019 IEEE International Conference on Pervasive Computing and Communications Workshops (PerCom Workshops), pp. 894–899. IEEE (2019)
22. Maiti, A., Jadliwala, M.: Light ears: information leakage via smart lights. Proc. ACM Interact. Mob. Wearable Ubiquit. Technol. **3**(3), 1–27 (2019)
23. Maiti, A., Jadliwala, M.: Smart light-based information leakage attacks. GetMobile Mob. Comput. Commun. **24**(1), 28–32 (2020)
24. Mi, X., Qian, F., Zhang, Y., Wang, X.: An empirical characterization of IFTTT: ecosystem, usage, and performance. In: Proceedings of the 2017 Internet Measurement Conference, pp. 398–404 (2017)
25. Morgner, P., Mattejat, S., Benenson, Z.: All your bulbs are belong to us: Investigating the current state of security in connected lighting systems. arXiv preprint arXiv:1608.03732 (2016)
26. Notra, S., Siddiqi, M., Gharakheili, H.H., Sivaraman, V., Boreli, R.: An experimental study of security and privacy risks with emerging household appliances. In: 2014 IEEE Conference On Communications and Network Security, pp. 79–84. IEEE (2014)
27. Rathee, G., Balasaraswathi, M., Chandran, K.P., Gupta, S.D., Boopathi, C.: A secure IoT sensors communication in industry 4.0 using blockchain technology. J. Ambient Intell. Humaniz. Comput. **12**(1), 533–545 (2021)
28. Ronen, E., O'Flynn, C., Shamir, A., Weingarten, A.O.: IoT goes nuclear: Creating a ZigBee chain reaction. IACR Cryptology ePrint Archive **2016**, 1047 (2016)

29. Ronen, E., Shamir, A.: Extended functionality attacks on IoT devices: the case of smart lights. In: 2016 IEEE European Symposium on Security and Privacy (EuroS&P), pp. 3–12. IEEE (2016)
30. Samaila, M.G., Sequeiros, J.B., Simões, T., Freire, M.M., Inácio, P.R.: IoT-HarPSecA: a framework and roadmap for secure design and development of devices and applications in the IoT space. IEEE Access **8**, 16462–16494 (2020)
31. Schwittmann, L., Boelmann, C., Matkovic, V., Wander, M., Weis, T.: Identifying tv channels and on-demand videos using ambient light sensors. Pervasive Mob. Comput. **38**, 363–380 (2017)
32. Schwittmann, L., Matkovic, V., Weis, T., et al.: Video recognition using ambient light sensors. In: 2016 IEEE International Conference on Pervasive Computing and Communications (PerCom), pp. 1–9. IEEE (2016)
33. Shah, T., Venkatesan, S.: A method to secure IoT devices against botnet attacks. In: Issarny, V., Palanisamy, B., Zhang, L.-J. (eds.) ICIOT 2019. LNCS, vol. 11519, pp. 28–42. Springer, Cham (2019). https://doi.org/10.1007/978-3-030-23357-0_3
34. Sikder, A.K., Babun, L., Aksu, H., Uluagac, A.S.: Aegis: a context-aware security framework for smart home systems. In: Proceedings of the 35th Annual Computer Security Applications Conference, pp. 28–41 (2019)
35. Stellios, I., Kotzanikolaou, P., Grigoriadis, C.: Assessing IoT enabled cyber-physical attack paths against critical systems. Comput. Secur. **107**, 102316 (2021)
36. Stellios, I., Kotzanikolaou, P., Psarakis, M., Alcaraz, C., Lopez, J.: A survey of IoT-enabled cyberattacks: assessing attack paths to critical infrastructures and services. IEEE Commun. Surv. Tutor. **20**(4), 3453–3495 (2018)
37. Tanen, J.: Breaking bhad: Getting local root on the Belkin Wemo switch (2016)
38. Tsiknas, K., Taketzis, D., Demertzis, K., Skianis, C.: Cyber threats to industrial IoT: a survey on attacks and countermeasures. IoT **2**(1), 163–188 (2021)
39. Xiao, L., Wan, X., Lu, X., Zhang, Y., Wu, D.: IoT security techniques based on machine learning: how do IoT devices use AI to enhance security? IEEE Signal Process. Mag. **35**(5), 41–49 (2018)
40. Xu, Y., Frahm, J.M., Monrose, F.: Watching the watchers: automatically inferring tv content from outdoor light effusions. In: Proceedings of the 2014 ACM SIGSAC Conference on Computer and Communications Security, pp. 418–428 (2014)
41. Zandberg, K., Schleiser, K., Acosta, F., Tschofenig, H., Baccelli, E.: Secure firmware updates for constrained IoT devices using open standards: a reality check. IEEE Access **7**, 71907–71920 (2019)
42. Zhou, Z., Zhang, W., Yu, N.: IREXF: data exfiltration from air-gapped networks by infrared remote control signals. arXiv preprint arXiv:1801.03218 (2018)

# TAESim: A Testbed for IoT Security Analysis of Trigger-Action Environment

Xinbo Ban[1,2](✉), Ming Ding[3], Shigang Liu[1], Chao Chen[4], Jun Zhang[1], and Yang Xiang[1]

[1] Swinburne University of Technology, Melbourne 3122, Australia
{XBan,ShigangLiu,JunZhang,YXiang}@swin.edu.au
[2] Data61, CSIRO, Sydney 2015, Australia
Xinbo.Ban@data61.csiro.au
[3] Information Security and Privacy Group, Data61, CSIRO, Sydney 2015, Australia
Ming.Ding@data61.csiro.au
[4] James Cook University, Townsville 4811, Australia
Chao.Chen@jcu.edu.au

**Abstract.** The Internet of Things (IoT) networks promote significant convenience in every aspect of our life, including smart vehicles, smart cities, smart homes, etc. With the advancement of IoT technologies, the IoT platforms bring many new features to the IoT devices so that these devices can not only passively monitor the environment (e.g. conventional sensors), but also interact with the physical surroundings (e.g. actuators). In this light, new problems of safety and security arise due to the new features. For instance, the unexpected and undesirable physical interactions might occur among devices, which is known as inter-rule vulnerability. A few work have investigated the inter-rule vulnerability from both cyberspace and physical channels. Unfortunately, only few research papers take advantage of run-time simulation techniques to properly model trigger action environments. Moreover, no simulation platform is capable of modeling primary physical channels and studies the impacts of physical interactions on IoT safety and security. In this paper, we introduce TAESim, a simulation testbed to support reusable simulations in the research of IoT safety and security, especially for the IoT activities in home automation that could involve possibly unexpected interactions. TAESim operates over MATLAB/Simulink and constructs a digital twin for modeling the nature of the trigger-action environment using simulations. It is an open-access platform and can be used by the research community, government, and industry who work toward preventing the safety and security consequences in the IoT ecosystem. In order to evaluate the effectiveness and efficiency of the testbed, we conduct some experiments and the results show that the simulations are completed in a few seconds. We also present two case studies that can report unexpected consequences.

**Keywords:** Iot security · SmartThings · Inter-rule vulnerability · Simulation


S. Katsikas et al. (Eds.): ESORICS 2021 Workshops, LNCS 13106, pp. 218–237, 2022.
https://doi.org/10.1007/978-3-030-95484-0_14

## 1 Introduction

Internet of Things (IoT) greatly revolutionizes home automation due to the exponential growth of IoT devices. It is expected to have over 50 billion IoT devices connected to the Internet by the end of 2020 [20]. Although the IoT technologies can offer a lot of convenience, new concerns have been raised about the safety and security of the smart home environment [2,7]. For instance, Mirai malware launched a large-scale Distributed Denial of Service (DDoS) attack through controlling over 600,000 vulnerable IoT devices [31]. The adversary can break into the home network by exploiting the flaw in firmware [44]. More specifically, a worm could self-replicate and spread throughout ZigBee among smart bulbs [42]. Moreover, design flaws have been recently found in the SmartThings platform and vulnerable third-party applications could compromise the platform [22]. Some work investigate the possibility of launching attacks by leveraging the physical capabilities of IoT devices. For example, a smart bulb could eavesdrop the sensitive traffic and expose it by flashing the light stealthily [41].

The recent research has improved the IoT safety and security by working at addressing the traditional issues of IoT security including design flaws [22,24,29,50], malware [22,44], protocol vulnerabilities [27,33,40] and firmware vulnerabilities [26,44]. Different from these work, we focus on a new type of safety and security issue caused by the inter-rule vulnerability. Due to the increasing complexity of smart home configuration, IoT apps are co-employed in an environment and they can interact with each other via a common device. Besides, some IoT devices can not only communicate via network but also have the functionalities of sensing and affecting the physical environment. These interactions may lead to undesired and unexpected consequences. The attack can be launched to leave the user in a risky state. For example, the door is unlocked when there is no person at home or the heater is turned off to create the 'unpleasant' state when it is winter. In order to alleviate the security problem caused by the interactions of IoT devices and apps, some research recently shed light on the discovery of the risky interactions [8,10,14,17,36].

According to [19], there are two types of the interactions given an IoT environment with IoT apps and devices co-employed:

- *Cyberspace interaction.* The network enables the interaction of apps via the channels in cyberspace such as time, and home mode. For instance, given two apps, a light is turned on when the sunsets and a door is unlocked when this light is on [10]. The event *light.on* is shared in the same device in cyberspace. The term 'cyberspace interaction' represents IoT app interaction when IoT apps operate on the same device.
- *Physical interaction* IoT has a unique feature that devices can interact with each other via physical channels such as temperature, illuminance, and humidity [4,17]. For example, an app turns on a heater and another app opens a window when the temperature is higher than a threshold. The heater and the temperature sensor are connected through a temperature channel then a physical interaction is generated.

Cyberspace interactions consist of one or multiple IoT apps and they can leave users in an unexpected state. Some research such as Soteria [8] and IoTSan [36] utilized a collection of safety policies to assess the safety and security of an IoT ecosystem. More specifically, they discovered the cyberspace interactions that violate the designed safety policies through model checking. For example, conflicts usually happen when several IoT apps control a common IoT device.

Physical interactions can also lead to insecure situations, in which the adversaries can exploit the vulnerability. For instance, an app can control the window when the temperature rises above a threshold and it exposes a potential break-in vulnerability if a burglar manipulates the temperature. IoTMon [17] leveraged static analysis techniques to discover all potentially vulnerable physical interactions. Differently, IoTGuard [10] and IoTSafe [19] are dynamic solutions to enforce the safety policy at run-time. IoTGuard mainly focuses on cyberspace interactions in an IoT ecosystem and IoTSafe aims to capture real physical interactions.

Different from cyberspace interaction, physical interaction faces more challenges for analysis. Firstly, static analysis techniques poorly explore the possible paths for physical interaction since it highly depends on the real-world environment. For example, a program executed on a computer has the same behavior wherever the computer is. However, an IoT app operates variously if the physical channels differ. Secondly, dynamic analysis techniques rely on the development of program simulation. For instance, the fuzzing technique runs the program and mutates the input cases until a crash occurs. However, applying similar techniques for IoT apps cannot resolve this situation because physical interactions affect the operation of IoT apps in a different environment. IoTSafe successfully modeled the physical channels depending on the employment of real devices and sensors. However, the input cases have poor scalability, which means that they cannot represent diverse scenarios. Moreover, recent work depend on the SmartThings simulator, which requires the instrumentation in early-stage and limits the variety of IoT devices. In order to fill this gap, we propose a testbed to simulate the vast number of possible cyberspace and physical interactions among multiple IoT devices and apps.

In this paper, we present a proof of concept of a simulation testbed, TAESim, for IoT security of trigger-action platform, which is not included in previous studies. Our method addresses the main challenges of the IoT trigger action security analysis and makes the IoT environment simulation possible. By taking advantage of MATLAB/Simulink, we implement a testbed with the capacity for expansion, and it can properly model the behavior of the channels and devices. In the proposed testbed, multiple IoT apps can be executed simultaneously, and joint behavior on channels from multiple devices can be represented as well. We implement several devices, two cyberspace channels (i.e., time and home state) and seven physical channels (i.e., temperature, humidity, smoke, motion, illumination, ultraviolet, and water). It is worth noting that more devices and channels can be added to the simulation testbed. Moreover, the testbed is allowed to randomly adopt unexpected factors such as human interaction, sudden shutdown, etc. Furthermore, the proposed testbed supports several research directions. For example, simulating the IoT system before installing devices and apps at home, or creating the corresponding digital twin to predict future behavior for the inter-rule vulnerability. We also verify the effectiveness and efficiency of the testbed. The simulation results demonstrate that our testbed can properly model the interactions between devices and the joint effects on the physical channels. Although some other testbeds have been proposed in previous work, there is widely adopted testbed for researching safety and security of trigger-action environment. Han et al. [28] proposed a simulation toolkit, DPWSim, for supporting the development of IoT application that used Devices Profile for Web Services. Lee et al. [32] proposed CyPhySim that leveraged the state machine, continuous-time solver, and discrete-event simulation engine to simulate an cyber-physical system. FIT loT-LAB, presented by Adjih et al. [1] composed thousands of wireless nodes to accelerate the IoT development. Comparatively, our proposed testbed investigates the practical interaction modeling and has substantial scalability and superior performance.

The rest of the paper is organized as follows. Section 2 presents the related work and motivation of this paper. In order to establish this testbed for IoT security research, we discuss the main challenges in modeling the IoT trigger-action environment and assessing its safety and security. Section 4 introduces the details of the components in the implementation of the TAESim. We evaluate the efficiency of the testbed and present the representative case studies in Sect. 5. Finally, Sect. 6 concludes this paper.

## 2 Related Work and Motivation

This paper aims at modeling the trigger-action environment that can be helpful at steps in the assessment of security, safety, and privacy of IoT automation systems. We first reviewed the recent work and present the motivation of our proposed testbed.

### 2.1 Related Work

Previous work have proved that static techniques can identify and improve IoT safety and security. Without executing programs, it provides scalability especially when the large-scale study is performed. Fernandes et al. [22] analyzed the SmartApps obtained from the official store in 2016 and identified that over 55% of them were vulnerable to the over-privileged attacks. Besides, they reported that no sufficient protection was provided from SmartThings for the sensitive data, which leaded to exploitable vulnerabilities such as event spoofing and leakage. SAINT [7] detected the sensitive data flow by tracking the sensitive sources to the external sinks in the information flows. SOTERIA [8] leveraged model checking to discover the violations based on the user-defined security and safety properties. Similarly, IotSan [36] verified the security and safety properties using model checking especially focusing on the interactions between devices and apps. However, both SOTERIA and IotSan only consider cyberspace interactions in the proposed approaches. IoTMon [17] first discovered all potential physical interaction chains from the IoT apps and reported security and safety risks. Nevertheless, it cannot find the violations for run-time policy violations in real-world IoT deployments as well.

On the other hand, the results from the static analysis on IoT apps can provide rich information to guide run-time enforcement. SmartAuth [48] used the static analysis model obtained from the descriptions of IoT apps to keep the run-time behaviors of IoT apps consistent. It alleviated the security threats of over-privileged IoT apps. FlowFence [23] addressed the data leakage and permission abuse issues through leveraging the information flow resulting in blocking undefined ones. HoMonit [51] analyzed the source code of IoT apps and defined a normal traffic behavior model to detect the risky behaviors at run-time. IoTGuard [10] enforced the policies in multi-app environments to detect the violations by means of chaining rules and analyzing their reachability. IoTSafe [19] practically inspected physical interactions in a IoT environment and dynamically assessed the safety and security of it.

### 2.2 Motivation

An IoT device can not only be triggered by the cyberspace event and the physical channels but also exert influence on the physical environment (e.g. temperature, humidity, brightness). The attacker can exploit an IoT environment via an insecure and unsafe interaction leading the users to be in an unexpected state [17]. For example, if a robot vacuum is tampered with, the window could be opened via the physical motion interaction. Given three apps, a home mode app, a window app, and a robot app, a potentially unsafe interaction might exist in this smart home. The first app assigns the home mode 'Occupied' when the motion sensor detects a movement.

The window app controls the window to be opened if the temperature rises above a threshold and the home mode is 'Occupied'. The robot app sets a timer to trigger a vacuum operation. In this example, the temperature near the thermometer sensor could be raised above 85F to trigger a window opening action, which may leave home in a potentially unsafe situation, such as burglar break-in.

This type of vulnerability is called inter-rule vulnerability and it is very difficult to be identified by a manual process. Different from the software and hardware vulnerability, inter-rule vulnerability potentially exists in the interactions between devices. It is an unexpected consequence after the devices interact with each other. On the other hand, it is similar to the traditional vulnerability because it directly leaves the user in an unsafe state or can be exploited by adversaries. There are a few factors that might lead to inter-rule vulnerability including malicious apps, broken devices, user's vulnerable configurations, etc. Meanwhile, many research work aim at eliminating the real-world risks through dynamically discovering the vulnerabilities in run-time before the users set up the devices in an IoT ecosystem. The authors deploy the apps on the SmartThings simulator to capture the run-time information including the device status and user's configurations but there are some limitations. Firstly, although it provides a collection of the devices for selection, new products are often not available in the simulator. Secondly, SmartThings simulator is running on the online server maintained by Samsung. Previous work leveraged a collection of SmartThings commands from its documentation for information collection in run-time. So, it is necessary to instrument the target apps before dynamic analysis starts. Moreover, if the SmartThing server does not allow the data exchange for security consideration, it will be impossible to utilize the SmartThing simulator for security analysis. So, we are motivated to propose a dynamic analysis simulator that is capable of modeling IoT environments including channels, devices, and apps.

## 3 Challenges in Testbed Simulation

Compared to traditional computing platform, IoT reveals several unique functional characteristics while it poses unusual challenges in terms of code analysis for security. In order to properly model the IoT environment and propose the testbed, we focus on the trigger action environment and discuss the challenges that a simulation testbed faces. In this section, we present five challenges from different aspects, including physical channels modeling, IoT apps modeling, automated test-case generation, multiple apps analysis, and interactions between IoT devices and apps.

**Physical Channels Modeling:** A vulnerability can potentially lead the program to crash, thus the system is at risk. IoT devices that execute the program in firmware are in the same danger as well. Differently, the physical channels are interacted into cyberspace connectivity by IoT devices. It can achieve unexpected consequences that the IoT apps deviate from the device functionality caused by the misuse of physical channels. For example, the temperature can be increased through maliciously turning on a heater by an adversary. Once it exceeds a threshold, the window will be opened. The heater-temperature-window interaction leads the room to be insecure and unsafe. Therefore, a burglar can break into the house by controlling the indoor temperature.

Besides, the physical channels and the joint influence of physical channels are different from the consequence of a single device when multiple IoT devices and apps operate together. For instance, the temperature is rising quickly when a heater and an AC operate together. So the safety and security of apps of trigger action platforms not only affect the stability of the program but also raise the concerns on the physical environment.

**IoT Apps Modeling:** Most of the IoT devices usually constitute a complex system, and it is hard to conduct a security assessment on them. In other words, these systems cannot be executed and analyzed directly in a short time, which requires appropriate simulation to accurately execute and analyze these kinds of IoT systems. Importantly, the state and computational logic among these devices should be able to be gathered during the simulation process on the heterogeneous IoT system [30]. In addition, it is worth noting that simulating the physical channels is difficult, including temperature, humidity, illuminance, etc. Similar to cyber-physical system simulation, it must involve the evolution of IoT system state over time. So those requirements prompt to develop a simulator that can execute the IoT apps by means of a discrete-event simulation engine through continuous-time solvers and state machine-based modeling [32]. Many research explored the demands of IoT system modeling and simulation [1,16,28,32]. For example, IoTify provides the virtual device simulation on the cloud for IoT app development [30]. However, existing simulators mainly focus on the development of IoT device functionalities and often adopt the SmartThings web-based IoT simulator. These simulators insufficiently support the diverse IoT devices and apps, which limits the various functionality simulation for IoT apps.

**Automated Test-Case Generation:** A requirement of the dynamic analysis deployment is the input data for program execution. Generally, inputs are the entry points of a program. For IoT apps, the event triggers of IoT apps can be considered as the inputs. Since input generation needs to be scalable, systematic, and automated, it introduces the difficulties of input generation for IoT apps, which manage multiple devices with different states. For instance, the thermostat has an integer value attribute that introduces a large space for input generation and a large number of test cases.

Fuzzing and symbolic execution are usually utilized for input generation and code coverage increase. Fuzzing feeds the randomly generated inputs to an executed app, while symbolic execution explores the paths using symbolic inputs [5]. For example, IoTFuzzer [11] identified contents of IoT apps through dynamic analysis and discovered the memory corrupted vulnerabilities based on the mutation. Meanwhile, many work leveraged heuristics that intelligently explored the code paths via input generation guidance to avoid redundants [6,15,34,39,49]. Yet, to our knowledge, tools that automate test input data and event generation to execute IoT apps are non-existent. This motivates us to improve test-case generation techniques as applied to IoT in the future.

**Multiple Apps Analysis:** Individual app analysis always focuses on the single app in isolation while multiple apps analysis investigates the joint behavior of several apps. In an IoT environment, apps can interact via the devices or events in two ways: (1) when a device attribute is changed by an event handler and this behavior triggers another event of a device. For instance, when the smoke is detected, a light is turned, then the window is closed because the light is turned on; (2) multiple apps operate on the same device. For example, the water valve is closed when the leak is detected meanwhile it should be opened when the sprinkler is activated by a smoke detector;

Although all individual apps are verified that each of them is secure and safe, the interactions still can cause security and safety issues [9,13,18,37]. To avoid the unexpected consequence through interactions, identifying the interactions is essential for securing the IoT environment with multiple apps employed. It motivates us to develop the dynamic approach for checking that the IoT apps conform to safety properties when interacting with each other.

**Interactions Between IoT Devices and Apps:** The services from trigger-action platforms can be connected and employed simultaneously, including IFTTT, Zapier, and Apiant. This platform provides a collection of APIs that allow users to authorize services. For instance, a user with a SmartThings IoT platform account can authorize the SmartThings service through the OAuth protocol to communicate with their SmartThings account. REST APIs support the service communication based on HTTP protocol [25]. So users are capable to create their personally customized automation through using rules, which connect the trigger event and the action event. When the event happens as the trigger in service, the action of the rule is automatically operated in another service.

The interactions between IoT apps from different trigger action platform can make the IoT environment insecure and unsafe [3,10,46]. The analysis of interactions between IoT apps requires Natural Language Processing for the key information extraction. Specifically, rules called IoT apps, automated the device behavior via either cyberspace interaction or physical interaction. So, it is necessary to figure out the types of devices, channels, and events in the rules. No matter what platforms the IoT system uses, determining the key information from the description of rules can be accomplished using advanced natural language processing techniques.

## 4 TAPSim: A Simulation Testbed

### 4.1 Overview

To model the trigger-action environment and address the challenges for the IoT scenario simulation, we propose TAPSim to simulate the behaviors of the IoT devices, apps, and interaction channels. We use MATLAB/Simulink as the simulation engine because it fits the requirements of the proper discrete-event simulation.

MATLAB is a programming and numeric computing platform for data analysis, algorithms development, and model creation. It integrates Simulink that is a block diagram environment for multi-domain simulation and Model-Based Design, enabling the algorithms incorporation and result analysis. Simulink provides a graphical editor, customizable block libraries, and solvers for modeling/simulating dynamic systems. We find that MATLAB/Simulink is proper for the simulation of an interactive IoT system. We create the complex digital twin of smart home through system componentization and reuse components throughout the model with subsystems and model references. The detailed components will be discussed in the following sections.

### 4.2 Devices

In this section, we present the way to model the IoT devices in this testbed. Simulink provides a block, Data Store Memory, to store a global variable during

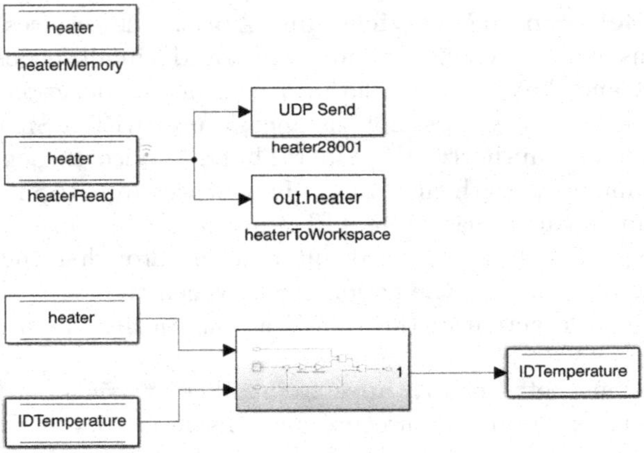


**Fig. 1.** An IoT device (heater) modeled in Simulink

the simulation. It meets the demands of the modeling status of the device (e.g. on and off). For example, in Fig. 1, we create a Data Store Memory block for storing the device state.

Initially, the default value is set up with 0 and can be randomly specified for test case generation. In the properties page of each Data Memory block, it allows to visually input a default value from the Signal Attributes tab. Value 0 or 1 for each Data Store Memory block represents on or off for status of the relevant device. We also create a value output module for saving and sending the device state with the time series. It consists of three blocks: Data Store Read, UDP Send, and To Workplace.

Data Store Read block outputs the value of the corresponding device state at every sampling time. We connect this block to the other two blocks for data saving and sending. The upper one, the UDP Sender block could send its received value to a particular IP address based on UDP communication for data storage. We create this block for further research if users need to communicate with the analysis engine. Besides, the To Workspace block saves the input signal to a workspace during simulation. When the simulation is paused or completed, the data written in the workspace can be retrieved or viewed visually.

Our testbed considers smart plugs as the particular smart devices that plug connect to. For instance, a plug is viewed as a bulb when a smart plug connect to a bulb The plug is modeled as an integral part of its connected device because these kinds of devices have limited functions like turning on and off.

A device can affect one or multiple physical channels. So we need to identify the physical channels and interactions between them. Many research discovered the potential physical interactions among IoT devices [9,14,18,37]. They statically analyzed the IoT apps to construct a Dependency Graph and discover the possible physical channels and corresponding interactions. The physical interactions between devices are context-sensitive in a real-world IoT system. To capture the real physical channels, Ding et al. [19] dynamically identified the real and context-sensitive physical interactions using the practical devices. The results are shown in Table 1.

In this study, we model the physical interactions between the heater channel and the temperature channel. We adopted the heater simulation from Simulink [43] and the model of the heating influence can be described as follows:

$$\frac{dQ}{dt} = (T_{heater} - T_{room}) \cdot Mdot \cdot c \tag{1}$$

where $\frac{dQ}{dt}$ represents heat flow from the heater into the room. $c$ is the heat capacity of air at constant pressure. $Mdot$ is the air mass flow rate through the heater (kg/min). $T_{heater}$ is the temperature of hot air from the heater and $T_{room}$ is the indoor temperature at the same time. These parameters are pre-defined before the simulation starts. For different devices, adjusting relevant parameters deals with the various situations. If the device cannot be easily modeled based on this equation, it allows the function to directly change the value of the physical channel by a minute. Once the state of the heater is on, the room gains heat and temperature changes over time.

**Table 1.** Summary of interactions of 16 IoT devices. ✓ represents the physical interaction is identified which means that the IoT device has the influence on the physical channel.

| Device | Temperature | Humidity | Smoke | Motion | Illuminance | Ultraviolet | Water |
|---|---|---|---|---|---|---|---|
| AC | ✓ | ✓ | | | | | |
| Heater | ✓ | ✓ | | | | | |
| Vent | ✓ | ✓ | | | | | |
| Fan | ✓ | | | | | | |
| Window | ✓ | ✓ | | ✓ | | ✓ | |
| Radiator | ✓ | ✓ | | | | | |
| Humidifier | | ✓ | | | | | |
| Coffee machine | | ✓ | | | | | |
| Robot | | | | ✓ | | | |
| Stove | ✓ | ✓ | | | | | |
| PC | ✓ | | | | | | |
| TV | | | | | ✓ | | |
| Air fryer | ✓ | | ✓ | | | | |
| Light | | | | | ✓ | | |
| Shade | ✓ | | | | ✓ | ✓ | |
| Valve | | | | | | | ✓ |

### 4.3 Channels

In an IoT environment, the automation is achieved by producing interactions via channels. More specifically, the devices can communicate and act under a certain condition via network, such as Wi-Fi, Zigbee. Moreover, the physical environment can enable the device to activate the automation including temperature, illuminance, etc. Thus, there are two kinds of channels including cyberspace channels and physical channels. In this section, we introduce how to model the both types of channels.

**Cyberspace Channels:** In order to model the interaction in cyberspace, we create a time channel measured in minutes. The IoT apps are always executed with one or two minutes' delay [35]. In the TAESim, we assume that channels and devices update their states every minute, since the time in simulation is different from it in the real world. To simulate a dynamic system, we compute its states at successive time steps over a specified time span. Time steps are time intervals when the computation happens. The size of this time interval is called step size. The process of computing the states of a model in this manner is known as solving the model. Besides, we need a solver that applies a numerical method to solve the set of ordinary differential equations that represent the model. Through this computation, it determines the time of the next simulation step. In the process of solving this initial value problem, the solver also can satisfy the accuracy requirements. We use the Fixed-step solver and set the time step as one, which means that the stop time represents the minutes that the simulation executes.

Time is an important factor to simulate the smart home environment. In order to fit several IoT apps that require time as the condition, we create a time channel through a time block in Simulink. Moreover, we use a Function block to convert minutes to hours and days for data analysis. Similar to modeling devices, the Data Store Memory block stores the value and can be outputted to trigger devices. Importantly, none of the devices can change the time channel.

Besides, many IoT apps complete the automation tasks based on a specified condition. For example, an official SmartThing app usually uses the scheduled-mode-change.groovy to change mode at a specific time of day. To properly capture the cyberspace interactions, we create another channel that is the home mode. According to the practical usage of smart home, we design that there are three home modes including Home, Occupied, and Sleep. The home mode can be a condition in an IoT app and changing of home mode can be either trigger or action. The home mode channel is editable to the IoT apps (Home is 0; Sleep is 1; Occupied is 2). Similarly, it also can be read by a Data Store Read block.

**Physical Channels:** Simulating the physical channels at run-time can properly capture the interactions between devices. The physical modeling process is often difficult to replicate because many complex factors are necessary to be considered such as the house geometry, materials of the house, outdoor weather [12,21,38,45,47]. These factors collaboratively influence physical channels including temperature, humidity, illuminance, smoke and so on. To address the physical channel modeling challenges, we first identify the physical channels and interactions in an IoT system. Table 1 shows the summary of implicit and explicit physical interactions [19]. In order to simulate both implicit and explicit interactions, we use the Function and Subsystem block in Simulink's library to model the states and changes of physical channels.

We create seven physical channels in this simulation testbed including temperature, humidity, smoke, motion, illuminance, ultraviolet, and water. For each channel, a Data Store Memory block stores the value that represents the corresponding unit on the specific scale. For example, the Data Store Memory of indoor temperature channel stores the degree Celsius that measures the temperature on the Celsius scale. It can be affected by many factors such as the outdoor temperature, heater, fan, etc. We provide a function that defines the daily change of the temperature based on the changes in outdoor temperature. The way device affects the temperature channel is similar.

The model process is adapted from the example officially provided by Simulink [43]. In this model, we present how to model the indoor heat losses and then give detailed parameters.

$$\left(\frac{dQ}{dt}\right)_{losses} = \frac{T_{in} - T_{out}}{R_{eq}} \tag{2}$$

$$\frac{dT_{room}}{dt} = \frac{1}{M_{air} \cdot c} \cdot \left(-\frac{fQ_{losses}}{dt}\right) \tag{3}$$

where $\left(\frac{dQ}{dt}\right)_{losses}$ is the heat loss in the room. $T_{in}$ and $T_{out}$ are the temperature for indoor and outdoor, respectively. $Req$ is the equivalent thermal resistance of the room, which can be calculated by pre-defined parameters including room geometry (size of room; size and number of window) and thermal properties and resistance of the room. $\frac{dT_{room}}{dt}$ is the temperature time derivative. $M_{air}$ represents the mass of air indoor and $c$ is the heat capacity of air at constant pressure. To simulate the environment, we use the default values as the initial set for a few characters of room and outdoor temperature.

The humidifiers are set to vary within the range 0% to 100% since most humidifiers sense and report the relative humidity. The relative humidity is the proportion of water vapor in the air relative to the maximum water vapor that can be held in the air at a given temperature, and thus a temperature-dependent measure. The parameter for modeling humidity is different from the temperature changes. We leave the humidity channel modeling for future work because it is hard to model the humidity. To simplify the problem, if a device has either an implicit or explicit effect on humidity, a function can rise the value to the Data Store Memory of humidity.

In addition, the other physical channels have been set to the default value in advance and we leave the modeling process for future work. To quickly set up a simulation in a very basic configuration, the default value is specified before the simulation starts to fit the modeling requirements.

### 4.4 Apps

Home automation rules, called IoT apps, are the core of the smart home to automatically trigger the devices to act. Generally, the IoT apps have three elements: trigger event, condition, and action event. The trigger event is either a specific action of a device such as turning on/off or reaching a threshold in a physical channel such as temperature. The condition is optional in IoT apps and can be either from cyberspace or physical space. Many IoT apps have only trigger events and action events to compose automation. SmartThings supports multiple conditions while IFTTT allows users to specify one condition for one applet. The action event is the capability of the device. Importantly, in an IoT ecosystem, an action event is possibly another app's trigger event composing a rule chain. Thus it is difficult to figure out the real rule chain by statically analyzing the IoT apps. With the help of Simulink, we attempt to model the behaviors of an IoT app using several blocks from the native library.

Figure 2 shows an app named 'Turn off light if motion detected'. It is an official SmartApp from the SmartThings community written in the Groovy programming language. The testbed needs the description of every IoT app because the necessary elements for setting simulation are trigger and action events. The description of this app is 'Turns off a device if there is motion' and it indicates at least two devices exist in this IoT ecosystem: a user-specified device and a motion sensor. In Fig. 2, an area contains all blocks and the apps' name is shown on the top. The block named 'motionSensor' is a 'Data Store Read' block, that outputs the state of the motion sensor to an 'if' block. There are basically two ways that could happen. Firstly, if the motion sensor is activated by the movement, the signal from the 'Data Store Read' block is '1' and the 'if' block is executed, which means the 'constant' block sends the signal '0' to the device block. Otherwise, it reaches the 'terminator' block which is used to terminate output signals. Since we create the single model file for reuse, none of the 'Data Store Memory' blocks is added in this file and 'Data Store Read' blocks are missing in the corresponding data store. It leads such 'Data Store Read' blocks to be highlighted as warnings. Once the app is integrated into a complete digital twin of the IoT ecosystem in the testbed with all relevant 'Data Store Memory' blocks, the warnings disappear. In this example, we model the light as the simulated device. Finally, the Data Store Write receive the constant and refresh the state of light.

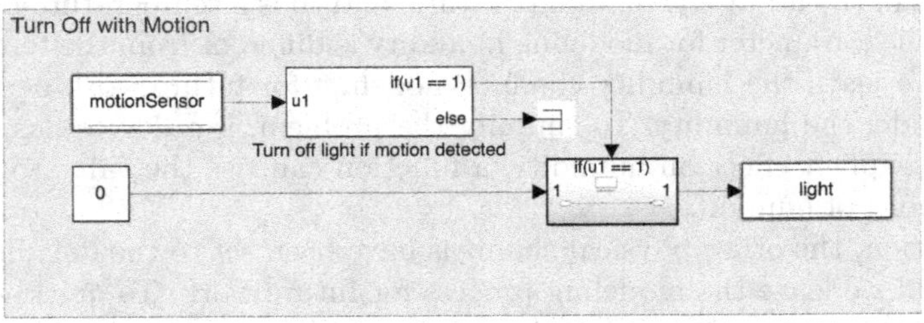


**Fig. 2.** An SmartApps 'Turn off light if motion detected' from official SmartThings repository

## 4.5 Unexpected Factors

In order to explore all possible situations and discover potential risky interactions in the real world, we deem the unexpected factors as those events that occasionally occur and lead to an unknown consequence. There are two factors we adopt in the testbed: Human interaction and broken devices.

**Human Interactions:** We mainly consider interactions between devices and direct users' interactions in the environment. It needs the dynamic analysis, which may be disturbed by human activities like moving. This actively demonstrates that human activities results in a false-positive interaction in the analysis. The testbed is expected to randomly imitate human behaviors, that may affect the device automation. We consider this as future work.

**Broken Devices:** Previous research investigates the inter-rule vulnerability under a perfect situation that all devices work appropriately. However, a part or whole home may have no power. During the simulation, the device state changes under the situation of apps usage. We design a random modular to turn off some devices to simulate the broken device.

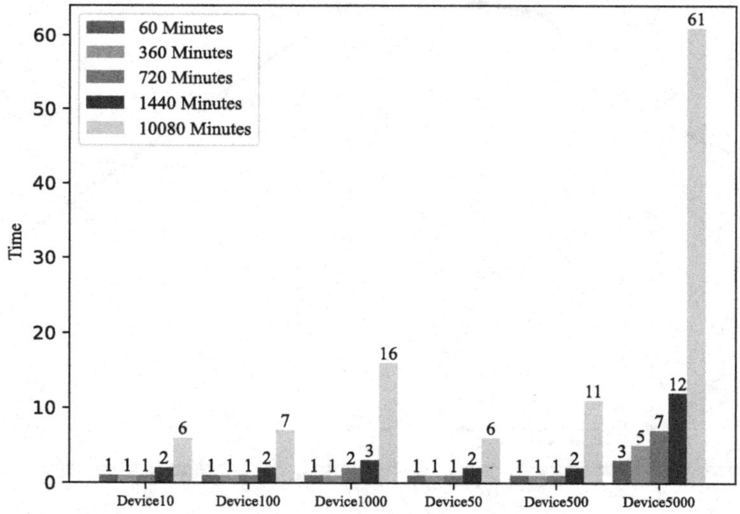


**Fig. 3.** The overhead of testbed on large scale simulation.

# 5 Evaluation and Case Study

## 5.1 Evaluation

For evaluating the overhead of the testbed simulation, we tested the average simulation time of different Stop Time settings in groups of devices. The results are output from the Simulation Manager in Simulink. We performed the experiments on a desktop computer with a 2.1 Ghz 2-core Intel Xeon Silver processor and 64 GB RAM, using MATLAB 2018b version with one active worker. We ran each test 10 times in each group and reported the average result. For each group, the marked number of devices were modeled in a single file and we simulated with different Stop Time settings including 60, 360, 720, 1440, 10080. The Stop Time is viewed as the minutes in the simulation. So we designed the simulation with a large number of devices that continually ran from minutes to days. For example, the simulation with 5000 devices and 10080 min represent that devices are running for 7 days. We selected 10 modeled devices and repeatedly add them into the simulation. As is shown in Fig. 3, the time consumption of Stop Time 60, 360, 720 for the four groups (Device 10, Device100, Device50, Device500) is 1 s in real-world and the time consumption of Stop Time 1440 for them is 2 s. For simulation of 10080 min, four groups (Device 10, Device100, Device50, Device500) cost 6 to 11 ss, which is roughly 5 times the result of 1440 min. The last group with 5000 devices consume 3, 5, 7, 12, 61 ss for each Stop Time setting, respectively.

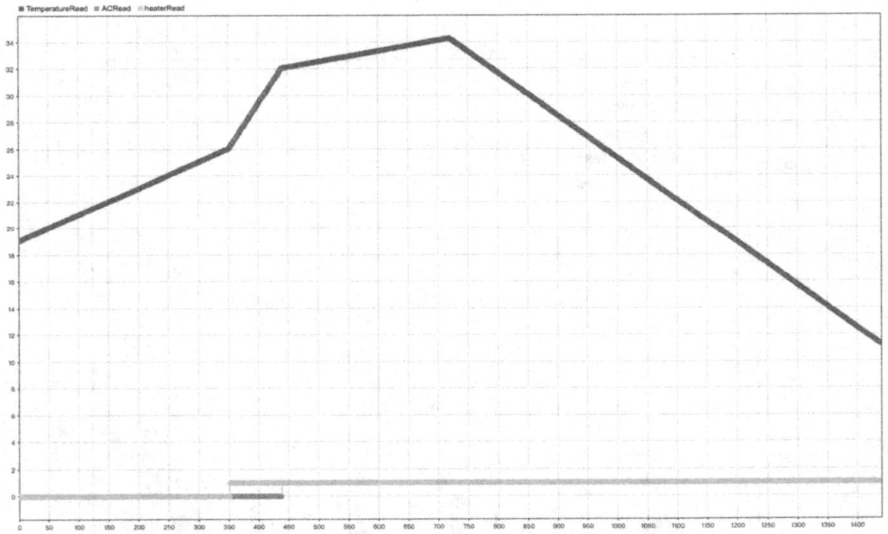


**Fig. 4.** The results of simulation with two devices, a heater and an AC. Value 1 indicates the state on for device and the value 0 means the device is in off state. A physical channel is modeled to represents the indoor temperature and its change over time.

### 5.2 Case Study

In this section, we demonstrate a few case studies to show the effectiveness and usability of our testbed. The first study case models a smart home described in [10]. In this simple scenario, a misconfiguration causes a policy violation where the AC and heater run at the same time when the temperature thresholds of heating and cooling are not configured properly. Thus these errors depend on the user's configuration of apps' attributes at the installation time. Specifically, we use the same IoT apps obtained from the official SmartThings community and simulate two apps: the first one indicates that if the room temperature is

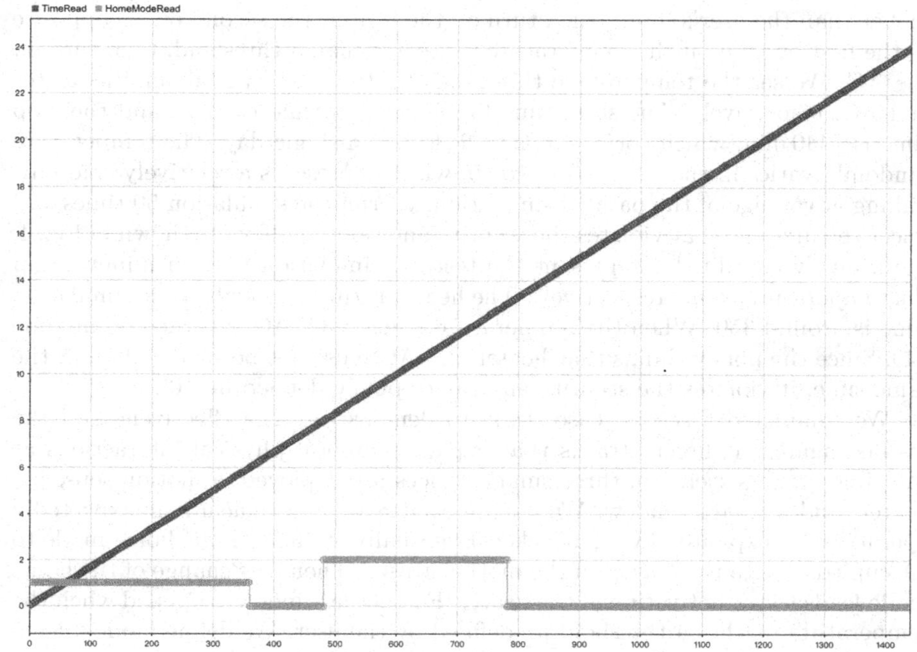


(a)

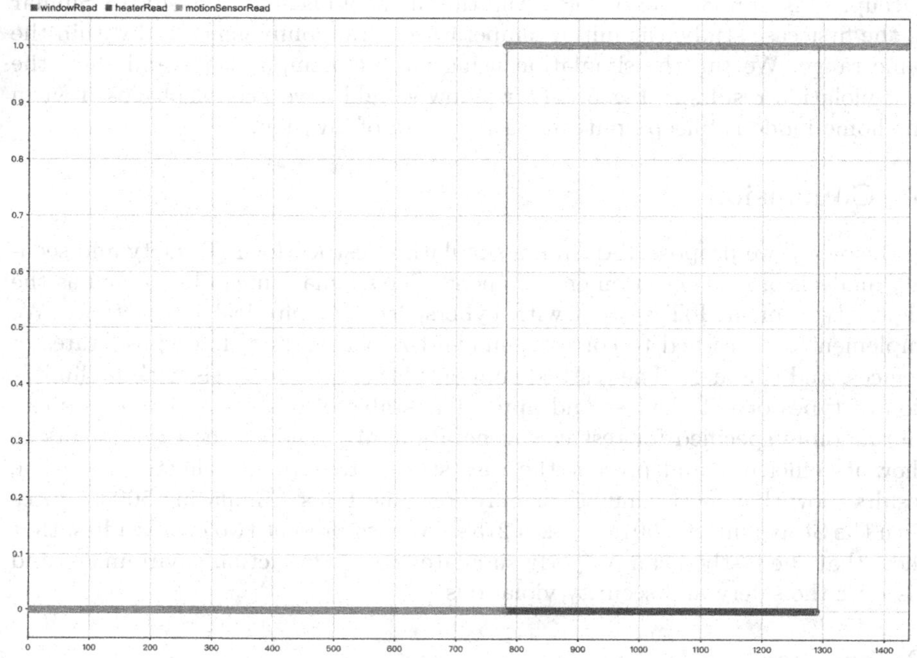


(b)

**Fig. 5.** In (a), time changed in a single day is illustrated and three home mode (Home; Sleep; Occupied) changed over time is represented. In (b), three devices are simulated including a window, a heater, and a motion sensor.

higher than the user's input, then turn on the heater; the second one is opposite to the first one, i.e., if the temperature is greater than a threshold, then turn on the AC. We set the temperature thresholds to 27 °C and 32 °C for the heater and AC, respectively. The start time for simulation time is 0 min and the stop time is 1440 min, which corresponds to 24 h, i.e., a single day. The temperature randomly varies in the range of 10 to 20, which represents a relatively cold day. Taking advantage of the parallel simulation, we run the simulation 50 times and select the first one that violates the security and safety policy. As shown in Fig. 4, the x and y coordinates represent the testbed simulation time in minutes and the temperature value, respectively. The heater is turned on when the simulation time is around 350. When the temperature reaches 32, AC is turned on at time 440. Since the policy claims that heater and AC must not be switched on at the same time, it violates the security and safety policy defined in [10].

We conducted a second case study to demonstrate the effectiveness of the testbed against indirect attacks that exploit temporal physical interactions at run-time. In this scenario, three smart devices are deployed: a motion sensor, a heater, and a smart window. We assume that a vacuum machine unexpectedly operates or is exploited by an attacker. Eventually, it changes the home mode to 'Occupied' due to the trigger of the motion sensor. Then, the change of the home mode leads to the activation of the heater. Further, a window is opened when the temperature reaches a threshold predefined by the user. We define mode 'Sleep' is from 0 to 6 o'clock; 'Home' is from 6 to 8 o'clock and from 18 to 24 o'clock; and 'Occupied' is from 8 to 18 o'clock. And the threshold is defined as 40 °C. Similar to the first case study, the initial temperature is randomly generated within the same range. We run the simulation using parallel computations and show the first violation results in Fig. 5. The window should have been kept closed when the home mode is 'Sleep', putting users at risk of invasion.

## 6 Conclusion

In this work, we propose TAESim, a simulation testbed for IoT safety and security analysis of trigger-action environment. The simulation can be viewed as the digital twin of an IoT system with cyberspace and physical interactions. We implement this testbed to correctly model the behaviors of IoT apps, states of devices, and channels. The testbed supports large-scale analysis with no limitation of types of IoT devices and apps. The states of devices and channels can be randomly specified for test case generation. We conduct the experiments to show its efficiency and present the case studies to show its effectiveness. The results show that most simulations only consume 1–3 s. Simulating 5000 devices with the Stop Time 43200 min takes 275 s. We also present two case studies, that show that the testbed can properly simulate the trigger action environment and discover the safety and security violations.

## References

1. Adjih, C., et al.: Fit IoT-lab: a large scale open experimental IoT testbed. In: 2015 IEEE 2nd World Forum on Internet of Things (WF-IoT), pp. 459–464. IEEE (2015)

2. AlrAlrawi, O., Lever, C., Antonakakis, M., Monrose, F.: SoK: security evaluation of home-based IoT deployments. In: 2019 IEEE Symposium on Security and Privacy (SP), pp. 1362–1380. IEEE (2019)
3. Bastys, I., Balliu, M., Sabelfeld, A.: If this then what? Controlling flows in IoT apps. In: Proceedings of the 2018 ACM SIGSAC Conference on Computer and Communications Security, pp. 1102–1119 (2018)
4. Birnbach, S., Eberz, S.: Peeves: physical event verification in smart homes (2019)
5. Cadar, C., et al.: Symbolic execution for software testing in practice: preliminary assessment. In: 2011 33rd International Conference on Software Engineering (ICSE), pp. 1066–1071. IEEE (2011)
6. Carter, P., Mulliner, C., Lindorfer, M., Robertson, W., Kirda, E.: CuriousDroid: automated user interface interaction for android application analysis sandboxes. In: Grossklags, J., Preneel, B. (eds.) FC 2016. LNCS, vol. 9603, pp. 231–249. Springer, Heidelberg (2017). https://doi.org/10.1007/978-3-662-54970-4_13
7. Celik, Z.B., et al.: Sensitive information tracking in commodity IoT. In: 27th {USENIX} Security Symposium ({USENIX} Security 18), pp. 1687–1704 (2018)
8. Celik, Z.B., McDaniel, P., Tan, G.: Soteria: automated IoT safety and security analysis. In: 2018 USENIX Annual Technical Conference (USENIX ATC 18), pp. 147–158. USENIX Association, Boston, July 2018. https://www.usenix.org/conference/atc18/presentation/celik
9. Celik, Z.B., McDaniel, P., Tan, G.: Soteria: automated IoT safety and security analysis. In: 2018 {USENIX} Annual Technical Conference ({USENIX}{ATC} 18), pp. 147–158 (2018)
10. Celik, Z.B., Tan, G., McDaniel, P.D.: IotGuard: dynamic enforcement of security and safety policy in commodity IoT. In: NDSS (2019)
11. Chen, J., et al.: IOTFUZZER: discovering memory corruptions in IoT through app-based fuzzing. In: NDSS (2018)
12. Cheng, Z., Shein, W.W., Tan, Y., Lim, A.O.: Energy efficient thermal comfort control for cyber-physical home system. In: 2013 IEEE International Conference on Smart Grid Communications (SmartGridComm), pp. 797–802. IEEE (2013)
13. Chi, H., Zeng, Q., Du, X., Yu, J.: Cross-app threats in smart homes: Categorization, detection and handling. arXiv preprint arXiv:1808.02125 (2018)
14. Chi, H., Zeng, Q., Du, X., Yu, J.: Cross-app interference threats in smart homes: categorization, detection and handling. In: 2020 50th Annual IEEE/IFIP International Conference on Dependable Systems and Networks (DSN), pp. 411–423. IEEE (2020)
15. Choudhary, S.R., Gorla, A., Orso, A.: Automated test input generation for android: are we there yet?(e). In: 2015 30th IEEE/ACM International Conference on Automated Software Engineering (ASE), pp. 429–440. IEEE (2015)
16. D'Angelo, G., Ferretti, S., Ghini, V.: Simulation of the internet of things. In: 2016 International Conference on High Performance Computing and Simulation (HPCS), pp. 1–8. IEEE (2016)
17. Ding, W., Hu, H.: On the safety of iot device physical interaction control. In: Lie, D., Mannan, M., Backes, M., Wang, X. (eds.) Proceedings of the 2018 ACM SIGSAC Conference on Computer and Communications Security, CCS 2018, Toronto, ON, Canada, 2018 October 15–19, pp. 832–846. ACM (2018). https://doi.org/10.1145/3243734.3243865
18. Ding, W., Hu, H.: On the safety of IoT device physical interaction control. In: Proceedings of the 2018 ACM SIGSAC Conference on Computer and Communications Security, pp. 832–846 (2018)

19. Ding, W., Hu, H., Cheng, L.: IOTSAFE: Enforcing safety and security policy with real IoT physical interaction discovery (2021)
20. Egham: Gartner says 8.4 billion connected "things" will be in use in 2017, up 31 percent from 2016 (2017). https://www.gartner.com/en/newsroom/press-releases/2017-02-07-gartner-says-8-billion-connected-things-will-be-in-use-in-2017-up-31-percent-from-2016
21. En, O.S., Yoshiki, M., Lim, Y., Tan, Y.: Predictive thermal comfort control for cyber-physical home systems. In: 2018 13th Annual Conference on System of Systems Engineering (SoSE), pp. 444–451. IEEE (2018)
22. Fernandes, E., Jung, J., Prakash, A.: Security analysis of emerging smart home applications. In: IEEE Symposium on Security and Privacy, SP 2016, San Jose, CA, USA, 22–26 May 2016, pp. 636–654. IEEE Computer Society (2016). https://doi.org/10.1109/SP.2016.44
23. Fernandes, E., Paupore, J., Rahmati, A., Simionato, D., Conti, M., Prakash, A.: FlowFence: practical data protection for emerging IoT application frameworks. In: 25th {USENIX} security symposium ({USENIX} Security 16), pp. 531–548 (2016)
24. Fernandes, E., Rahmati, A., Jung, J., Prakash, A.: Decoupled-IFTTT: Constraining privilege in trigger-action platforms for the internet of things. arXiv preprint arXiv:1707.00405 (2017)
25. Fernandes, E., Rahmati, A., Jung, J., Prakash, A.: Decentralized action integrity for trigger-action IoT platforms. In: Proceedings 2018 Network and Distributed System Security Symposium (2018)
26. Fisher, D.: Pair of bugs open Honeywell home controllers up to easy hacks (2015)
27. Fouladi, B., Ghanoun, S.: Honey, i'm home!!, hacking Z-wave home automation systems. In: Black Hat, USA (2013)
28. Han, S.N., et al.: DPWSim: a simulation toolkit for IoT applications using devices profile for web services. In: 2014 IEEE World Forum on Internet of Things (WF-IoT), pp. 544–547. IEEE (2014)
29. Jia, Y.J., et al.: ContexIoT: towards providing contextual integrity to applied IoT platforms. In: NDSS (2017)
30. Kecskemeti, G., Casale, G., Jha, D.N., Lyon, J., Ranjan, R.: Modelling and simulation challenges in internet of things. IEEE Cloud Comput. **4**(1), 62–69 (2017)
31. Kolias, C., Kambourakis, G., Stavrou, A., Voas, J.M.: DDos in the IoT: Mirai and other botnets. IEEE Comput. **50**(7), 80–84 (2017). https://doi.org/10.1109/MC.2017.201
32. Lee, E.A., Niknami, M., Nouidui, T.S., Wetter, M.: Modeling and simulating cyber-physical systems using CyPhySim. In: 2015 International Conference on Embedded Software (EMSOFT), pp. 115–124. IEEE (2015)
33. Lomas, N.: Critical flaw identified in ZigBee smart home devices (2015)
34. Mao, K., Harman, M., Jia, Y.: Sapienz: multi-objective automated testing for android applications. In: Proceedings of the 25th International Symposium on Software Testing and Analysis, pp. 94–105 (2016)
35. Mi, X., Qian, F., Zhang, Y., Wang, X.: An empirical characterization of IFTTT: ecosystem, usage, and performance. In: Proceedings of the 2017 Internet Measurement Conference, pp. 398–404 (2017)
36. Nguyen, D.T., Song, C., Qian, Z., Krishnamurthy, S.V., Colbert, E.J.M., McDaniel, P.D.: Iotsan: fortifying the safety of IoT systems. In: Dimitropoulos, X.A., Dainotti, A., Vanbever, L., Benson, T. (eds.) Proceedings of the 14th International Conference on emerging Networking EXperiments and Technologies, CoNEXT 2018, Heraklion, Greece, 04–07 December 2018, pp. 191–203. ACM (2018). https://doi.org/10.1145/3281411.3281440

37. Nguyen, D.T., Song, C., Qian, Z., Krishnamurthy, S.V., Colbert, E.J., McDaniel, P.: IoTSan: fortifying the safety of IoT systems. In: Proceedings of the 14th International Conference on emerging Networking EXperiments and Technologies, pp. 191–203 (2018)
38. Ott, W.R.: Mathematical models for predicting indoor air quality from smoking activity. Environ. Health Perspect. **107**(suppl 2), 375–381 (1999)
39. Rastogi, V., Chen, Y., Enck, W.: AppsPlayground: automatic security analysis of smartphone applications. In: Proceedings of the Third ACM Conference on Data and Application Security and Privacy, pp. 209–220 (2013)
40. Ronen, E., Shamir, A., Weingarten, A., O'Flynn, C.: IoT goes nuclear: creating a ZigBee chain reaction. IEEE Secur. Priv. **16**(1), 54–62 (2018)
41. Ronen, E., Shamir, A.: Extended functionality attacks on IoT devices: the case of smart lights. In: 2016 IEEE European Symposium on Security and Privacy (EuroS&P), pp. 3–12. IEEE (2016)
42. Ronen, E., Shamir, A., Weingarten, A.O., O'Flynn, C.: IoT goes nuclear: creating a ZigBee chain reaction. In: 2017 IEEE Symposium on Security and Privacy (SP), pp. 195–212. IEEE (2017)
43. Simulink, M.: Thermal model of a house. https://www.mathworks.com/help/simuli-nk/examples/thermal-model-of-a-house.html
44. Sivaraman, V., Chan, D., Earl, D., Boreli, R.: Smart-phones attacking smart-homes. In: Proceedings of the 9th ACM Conference on Security and Privacy in Wireless and Mobile Networks, pp. 195–200 (2016)
45. Son, N.H., Tan, Y.: Simulation-based short-term model predictive control for HVAC systems of residential houses. VNU J. Sci. Comput. Sci. Commun. Eng. **35**(1), 11–22 (2019)
46. Surbatovich, M., Aljuraidan, J., Bauer, L., Das, A., Jia, L.: Some recipes can do more than spoil your appetite: analyzing the security and privacy risks of IFTTT recipes. In: Proceedings of the 26th International Conference on World Wide Web, pp. 1501–1510 (2017)
47. TenWolde, A., Pilon, C.L.: The effect of indoor humidity on water vapor release in homes (2007)
48. Tian, Y., et al.: Smartauth: user-centered authorization for the internet of things. In: 26th {USENIX} Security Symposium ({USENIX} Security 17), pp. 361–378 (2017)
49. Vidas, T., Tan, J., Nahata, J., Tan, C.L., Christin, N., Tague, P.: A5: automated analysis of adversarial android applications. In: Proceedings of the 4th ACM Workshop on Security and Privacy in Smartphones and Mobile Devices, pp. 39–50 (2014)
50. Yu, T., Sekar, V., Seshan, S., Agarwal, Y., Xu, C.: Handling a trillion (unfixable) flaws on a billion devices: rethinking network security for the internet-of-things. In: Proceedings of the 14th ACM Workshop on Hot Topics in Networks, pp. 1–7 (2015)
51. Zhang, W., Meng, Y., Liu, Y., Zhang, X., Zhang, Y., Zhu, H.: HoMonit: monitoring smart home apps from encrypted traffic. In: Proceedings of the 2018 ACM SIGSAC Conference on Computer and Communications Security, pp. 1074–1088 (2018)

# Adversarial Command Detection Using Parallel Speech Recognition Systems

Peng Cheng[1,2], M. S. Arun Sankar[3(✉)], Ibrahim Ethem Bagci[4], and Utz Roedig[3]

[1] School of Cyber Science and Technology, Zhejiang University, Hangzhou, China
peng_cheng@zju.edu.cn
[2] Key Laboratory of Blockchain and Cyberspace Governance of Zhejiang Province, Hangzhou, China
[3] School of Computer Science and Information Technology, University College Cork, Cork, Ireland
a.sankar@cs.ucc.ie, u.roedig@ucc.ie
[4] VMware Inc., London, UK
bagcie@vmware.com

**Abstract.** Personal Voice Assistants (PVAs) such as Apple's Siri, Amazon's Alexa and Google Home are now commonplace. PVAs are susceptible to adversarial commands; an attacker is able to modify an audio signal such that humans do not notice this modification but the Speech Recognition (SR) will recognise a command of the attacker's choice. In this paper we describe a defence method against such adversarial commands. By using a second SR in parallel to the main SR of the PVA it is possible to detect adversarial commands. It is difficult for an attacker to craft an adversarial command that is able to force two different SR into recognising the adversarial command while ensuring inaudibility. We demonstrate the feasibility of this defence mechanism for practical setups. For instance, our evaluation shows that such system can be tuned to detect 50% of adversarial commands while not impacting on normal PVA use.

## 1 Introduction

Personal Voice Assistants (PVAs) such as Apple's Siri, Amazon's Alexa and Google Home are now commonplace. A PVA can be integrated as functionality in other devices such as smart phones or TVs or may be implemented as dedicated device referred to as smart speaker. We use PVAs to interact with infrastructures such as our smart home and services such as e-mails and news.

There are a number of PVA security and privacy concerns and research has investigated a large variety of attacks on these systems. One prominent attack example is the so called *hidden command injection*. The aim of such attack is to supply a specially crafted voice signal, referred to as adversarial command, to the PVA which is interpreted differently by the PVA than it is by humans. For example, the supplied adversarial command may be interpreted by humans


S. Katsikas et al. (Eds.): ESORICS 2021 Workshops, LNCS 13106, pp. 238–255, 2022.
https://doi.org/10.1007/978-3-030-95484-0_15

as *'Alexa, tell me what the weather is like'* while the SR of the PVA interprets this signal as *'Alexa, open the front door'*. An adversarial command is created by adding small perturbations to an audio recording until the PVA's SR recognises the intended command of the attacker instead of the command contained in the original audio recording. If the perturbations are small and added carefully, a human will not notice the modification of the audio signal while the SR algorithms recognise different words. How to create adversarial commands has been studied in detail [4,12]. However, less effort has been put into devising defence methods against this serious attack form.

In this paper we describe a low complex defence method against adversarial attacks based on the weak transferability of adversarial commands. The generation of an adversarial command that can successfully target multiple SR systems is still an open question [16]. Our method makes use of a second SR, we call it the *protection SR*, within a PVA which analyses the supplied voice sample in parallel to the *main SR*. The speech transcription output of the protection SR is compared with the transcription output of the main SR and only if both outputs are a close enough match the transcription output is accepted and the command is executed. The protection SR may use different training data or even an entire different SR architecture compared to the main SR.

The protection SR does not have to produce the same transcription quality as the main SR. Voice recognition of this component must only be sufficiently accurate to provide protection, transcription accuracy is delivered by the main SR. Thus, the protection SR can be simpler and can also be based on much smaller training data. It is possible to implement the protection SR without much resource requirements and it is possible to use frequent re-training. Frequent re-training adds additional complexity for a potential attacker that may try to craft an adversarial command targeting main and protection SR jointly. It is assumed to be infeasible for an attacker to add unnoticeable perturbations to the original audio such that two entirely different SR are tricked into producing the same transcriptions. The main contributions of this paper are:

- *Adversarial Command Detection (ACD):* We describe a novel protection mechanism against adversarial commands using parallel SR systems.
- *Demonstration of ACD:* We demonstrate the effectiveness of ACD using 20 adversarial commands and show that our ACD using Pocketsphinx [7] and Kaldi can detect all adversarial commands. We also show that the ACD does not prevent normal PVA operations due to false positives.
- *ACD Complexity:* We show that the protection SR can be significantly less complex than the main SR in terms of architecture and training data. Thus, frequent retraining of the protection SR is feasible, providing a ACD as moving target defence.

The remaining paper is structured as follows. Section 2 provides a very brief introduction to Automatic Speech Recognition (ASR) and describes adversarial command generation. Section 7 discusses related work and Sect. 3 introduces our novel Adversarial Command Detection (ACD) method. In Sect. 4, Sect. 5 and

Sect. 6 we describe our evaluation setup, experimental results and discussion. Section 8 concludes the paper.

# 2 Preliminaries

In this section we give a brief definition of a PVA as considered in this work. We also provide a definition of adversarial commands and provide a description on how these are crafted.

## 2.1 Personal Voice Assistant (PVA)

A PVA is a service which understands voice commands and is able to take corresponding actions. A PVA may reuse hardware of existing devices such as mobile phones or TVs or may use dedicated hardware such as a smart speaker.

The acoustic signal (i.e. human voice) is captured by microphones. Usually, the signal is processed locally to identify a wake word (e.g., 'Alexa' or 'Hey Google'). For wake word recognition a simple SR system is sufficient. After the wake word is recognised the following audio recording is transported to a back-end where a more sophisticated SR system analyses the audio sample to extract the command. After command extraction the back end system initiates the required action (interact with a system or query a service). User feedback in form of audio may be generated and transported to the local device where it is played back via speakers.

In this work we assume one local SR component is used to implement a PVA and we do not distinguish wake word recognition SR and back-end SR. However, our work can be applied to systems that distribute SR.

## 2.2 Hidden Commands

Hidden voice command injection aims to inject voice commands into a PVA without users noticing this injection. The injected command is 'hidden' from users present in the vicinity of the PVA. In order to conceal this interaction existing work has looked at various techniques ensuring that a person is unable to hear the submitted command while the PVA's ASR is able to understand it. While these techniques are the essential component to enable hidden voice commands it is also often necessary for an attacker to modify other elements of PVA interaction. After submitting a command, the PVA usually responds with a confirmation via it's speakers. For example, the voice command for a home automation system 'Alexa, open the front door' would result in a response 'Front door opened' which an attacker would need to suppress too in order to achieve a fully hidden interaction. However, it has to be noted that not all services provide a user with feedback and in some cases a user may simply ignore unexpected feedback.

Three types of hidden commands have to be distinguished: *Hardware Non-Linearity*, *Obfuscated Commands* and *Adversarial Commands*.

Work in the first category targets the analogue signal processing path of a PVA and makes use of the fact that humans are unable to hear in the high frequency range (typically above 18 kHz). The voice command is submitted in the frequency space unnoticeable to users while non-linear behaviours of the analogue signal processing path ensures that the signal is processed by SR.

The second class of work aims at submission of an audio signal which humans perceive as noise, the command is understood by PVAs but not by humans. For this purpose, the attacker starts with the target command and this audio signal is gradually changed until it becomes unintelligible for a human but the PVA still decodes the command. The resulting audio signal is called the obfuscated command.

The third class is similar to the second. The original audio signal (original command) is gradually modified until the PVA recognises the target command while a human still hears the original command. The resulting audio signal is called the adversarial command.

In this paper we focus on methods for hidden command detection of the third type: adversarial commands. We focus on this specific type as it is considered the most effective attack and consequently attracts currently most research effort. However, our proposed defence method may also protect against the other two types but we have not verified this in our experimentation.

### 2.3 Obfuscated and Adversarial Commands

The purpose of ASR is to transcribe speech to corresponding text. This process can be defined as:

$$y = \arg\max_{\widetilde{y}} p(\widetilde{y}|x) \tag{1}$$

$x$ here is the audio input, and $\tilde{y}$ are all possible transcription candidates. The ASR aims to find the most likely transcription $y$ given the audio input $x$. Once the ASR has been trained it's function is $y = f(x)$.

A human listening to the audio signal $x$ also interprets the signal and normally would conclude that the same transcription $y$ recognised by the ASR is the meaning of the command. This process can be described as $y = f_H(x)$ with $f_H$ describing the human's processing capability.

An adversary can modify an input signal $x$ by adding perturbation $\delta$, resulting in $x' = x + \delta$. The following situation may arise when an ASR decodes $x'$:

$$y = f(x') \quad \text{and} \quad \emptyset = f_H(x') \tag{2}$$

$y$ here is the obfuscated command transcription which remains the same as the one decoded from unperturbed input $x$. However, a human may not perceive the same transcription $y$ this time from the audio signal $x'$ (it is perceived as noise; $f_H(x') = \emptyset$ which means the human transcription is empty). In this case, the audio input $x'$ is called the *obfuscated command*.

There is as well the other situation where $y = f_H(x')$ and $\emptyset = f(x')$ which means the ASR is unable to transcribe the input while a human is understanding the command well. There is work in this direction (such as work by Abdullah et al. [3]) which aims to prevent machines listening into conversations.

$$\emptyset = f(x') \quad \text{and} \quad y = f_H(x') \tag{3}$$

The situation of interest in this paper is where $y = f_H(x')$ and $y' = f(x')$ which means the ASR transcription and human transcription are different. In this case $x'$ is called an *adversarial command*:

$$y' = f(x') \quad \text{and} \quad y = f_H(x') \tag{4}$$

In case of the adversarial command, even with the added perturbation, a human still perceives the adversarial audio input $x'$ as original benign command transcription $y$, while an ASR recognises the audio input $x'$ as the adversarial command transcription $y'$.

We distinguish so called *targeted* and *non-targeted* adversarial commands. In case of a *targeted* adversarial command the attacker is interested in one specific command transcription $T$ which is carefully selected ($y' = T$). In case of a *non-targeted* adversarial command the attacker does not care about what specific command would be decoded by the ASR; the attacker only wants to ensure that human and machine transcription are not the same.

### 2.4 Adversarial Command Generation

To create an adversarial command it is helpful for the attacker to have access to the internal workings of the ASR. An attack relying on such internal knowledge (e.g. such as the trained Deep Neural Network (DNN) model) is referred to as a *white-box* attack. If the attacker is not able to access the internals and is only able to obtain ASR decoding results the attack is classified as a *black-box* attack. Generally, attacks assuming the ASR as a black-box are more difficult to execute and have a lower attack performance (i.e. successfully generating adversarial examples providing the desired transcription). It has to be noted that we generally have to assume that an attacker has access to the ASR and a white-box attack is likely. As in any other area of computer security we cannot provide security by obscurity and assume that the ASR remains hidden.

The exact process of generating adversarial commands may vary depending on the ASR model, black-box/white-box assumption and perturbation target such as feature vectors or raw audio input. Recent work focuses on adding perturbations directly to the audio input rather than the result of the preprocessing (e.g., FBANK) as this approach reduces the perceptible noise in adversarial examples [4].

We use the generation of adversarial commands for a Deep Neural Network - Hidden Markov Model (DNN-HMM) ASR as example. Adversarial commands are generated through an iterative process. In each iteration, the output of the DNN (the acoustic model) is compared with the target using a loss function. Then the gradient of the loss function with respect to the corresponding input is calculated through back-propagation. By finding the perturbed input resulting in the local/global minimum it is ensured that the input is transcribed as the target command. In addition, the perturbation value is constrained by a threshold, ensuring that people cannot perceive the difference between the new signal and the original audio input. There are variations in different studies in regard to techniques on where to add the perturbations. For example, they can be added to the feature vectors such as Mel-Frequency Cepstrum Coefficient (MFCC) or directly to the raw audio input.

## 3 Adversarial Command Detection (ACD)

### 3.1 Threat Model

The attacker may have access to a PVA's SR when crafting adversarial commands. In addition, an attacker may also have access to the protection SR which we propose as defence method.

*A1: General Attacks:* We assume the attacker is only able to inject commands via the audio channel. There is no way for the attacker to bypass the SR entirely; i.e. by a conventional hack of the PVA.

*A2: Adversarial Command:* We assume that the attacker is only able to supply a rogue command as a hidden command constructed as adversarial command. We assume that the attacker must submit a command within an audio sample such that a present user is not aware of this embedded threat. We do not consider direct non-authorised interaction with the PVA or submission of hidden commands using different techniques.

*A3: Main SR Access:* We assume that the attacker has access to the main ASR; i.e. we consider a white-box attack. The attacker has full access to the main ASR when crafting the attack signal. This is a reasonable assumption as it is not feasible to keep an ASR used for millions of devices a secret.

*A4: Protection SR Access:* We assume that the attacker does not have access to the protection ASR; i.e. we assume a black-box attack by considering the protection ASR as a moving target. As we will show, it is possible to frequently retrain the protection ASR which ensures that an attacker is not able to obtain a copy of the used protection ASR. It has to be noted that there is currently no study showing that it is feasible to construct an adversarial command targeting multiple ASR in parallel under either white or black-box assumption. However, making the assumption that the protection ASR is black-box will make this problem significantly harder as the attacker would need to craft an adversarial command working with all possible ASR configurations at the same time.

### 3.2 ACD Approach

The ACD approach is shown in Fig. 1. The *main ASR* of the PVA is accompanied by a *protection ASR* and both process the incoming audio signal. Both ASR may

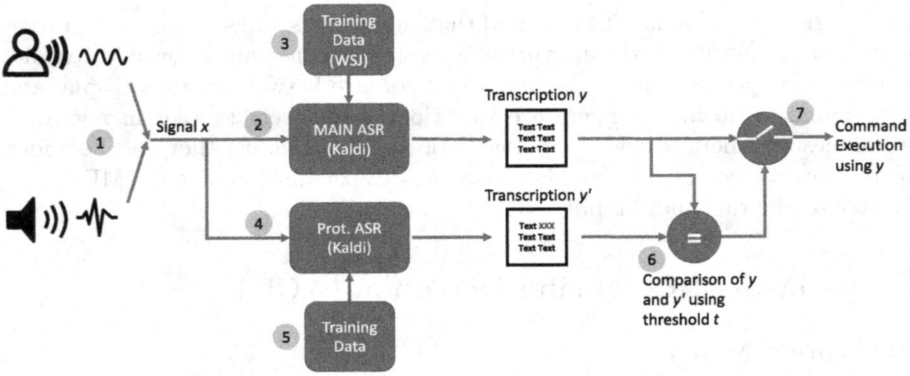


**Fig. 1.** Adversarial Command Detection (ACD) - The audio signal is analysed by the main ASR and the protection ASR in parallel. If both transcriptions differ significantly, defined by a threshold, the command is rejected.

share the same front-end (Microphone, filters, gain control, ...) and both ASR produce a transcription of voice. The main ASR transcription is only passed on to the PVA command execution if a comparison of both transcriptions determines that no adversarial command is present.

1. An input signal $x$ is provided. Either the audio input signal is provided by a human speaker or it may be supplied by an attacker via a loudspeaker. In case of an attacker the supplied signal is the adversarial command.
2. The voice audio signal $x$ is fed to the main ASR used to transcribe the voice signal into text $y$.
3. The main ASR is a sophisticated ASR, using a complex structure and trained with a large corpus to provide an accurate transcription $y$ for a diverse set of speakers. The transcription process is described as: $y = f_M(x)$.
4. A copy of the audio signal is also fed to a protection ASR which creates it's own text transcription $y'$.
5. The protection ASR is far less sophisticated than the main ASR and is also trained with a much smaller data set. The transcription is less accurate than that of the main ASR. The protection ASR produces the following transcription output: $y' = f_P(x)$.
6. The output of both ASRs $y'$ and $y$ is compared using the metric Word Error Rates (WER) (WER is introduced in Sect. 4) against an error threshold $t$. The WER difference between $y'$ and $y$ should not be greater than $t$. If the input is a legitimate voice command from a user, the difference between the two transcription is assumed to not be greater than the threshold. The threshold can be selected according to goals of the overall system.
7. Only if the recognition difference is below threshold $t$ the transcribed command is considered valid and transcription $y$ is passed to the PVA command execution.

### 3.3 ACD and Protection ASR Properties

To create an adversarial command the attacker executes an iterative process in which the signal is modified by adding inaudible perturbations such that the ASR recognizes the desired command. The signal is adapted taking into account the ASR's model which is defined by (i) ASR architecture and (ii) ASR training data. We assume that if the protection ASR model differs from the main ASR it is infeasible for an attacker to modify iterative the input signal such that two entirely different ASR are forced to produce the same transcription while ensuring that signal modifications remain inaudible.

*Different Architectures.* Different ASR architectures may use different types of features and may also extract different internal features. The adversarial example generation is an iterative process which aims to find the optima for the loss function with respect to the input by adding perturbation. It will be difficult for an attacker to add perturbations with the aim of changing features important for one architecture and also the other.

*Different Training Data.* The details of the model parameters used by the ASRs depend on the used training data. The parameter values keep being modified to improve prediction results during the training process. Thus, when generating an adversarial command the attacker needs to take into account not only the ASR architecture but also the specific trained model. An adversarial command generated for an ASR is only likely to work when the same trained model is used.

## 4 Evaluation Setup

The ACD is evaluated using a number of different ASRs in the role of a protection ASR. A number of benign and adversarial commands are used to evaluate ACD detection capabilities and normal operation scenarios.

### 4.1 ASR Selection

Our selection of ASRs used for evaluation is summarised in Table 1. Each ASR model (comprising architecture and model) is given a label which we use in the remaining document for reference.

*MASR1.* As main ASR (Label *MASR1*) we use an nnet2 Kaldi model which is a DNN-HMM structure using the Wall Street Journal (WSJ) corpus [9] as training data. Note that the latest Kaldi is an nnet3 chain model. However, we use a nnet2 Kaldi as the main ASR as we use adversarial command generation based on work by Schönherr et al. [11] which relies on this ASR variant.

The nnet2 Kaldi used by Schönherr makes use of some modifications. The feature extraction and the DNN acoustic model are combined. This integration

**Table 1.** Kaldi using an nnet2 model is used as main ASR (MASR1). Three different ASR are used as protection ASRs, labeled PASR1, PASR2, PASR3 and PASR4. The protection ASRs are Pocketsphinx and different Kaldi variations.

| ASR label | ASR variant | ASR architecture | Training data |
|---|---|---|---|
| MASR1 | Kaldi nnet2 | DNN-HMM | WSJ |
| PASR1 | Pocketsphinx | GMM-HMM | Unknown1 |
| PASR2 | Kaldi nnet3 | DNN-HMM | Unknown2 |
| PASR3 | Kaldi GMM | GMM-HMM | WSJ |
| PASR4 | Kaldi GMM | GMM-HMM | 50% of WSJ |

is for the convenience of adding perturbation directly to the input rather than the intermediate features when generating adversarial commands. According to Schönherr, this design modification does not affect the accuracy of the ASR system. We treat this modified nnet2 Kaldi model and the standard one as equivalent in this work. When evaluating adversarial commands we use this modified nnet2 Kaldi ASR; when evaluating benign commands we use the standard nnet2 Kaldi ASR.

*PASR1.* The first candidate of a protection ASR (Label *PASR1*) is the Pocketsphinx for a standard Raspberry Pi 3 Model B+. Pocketsphinx is using a Gaussian Mixture Model - Hidden Markov Model (GMM-HMM) model, while the main ASR MASR1 is using DNN-HMM model. These two models have completely different acoustic model architectures. Although it is not clear what corpus is used to train Pocketsphinx, it is safe to assume Pocketsphinx is trained with different training corpus than the main ASR (Pocketsphinx is provided with the already trained model and a clear description of the used training data is not provided). GMM-HMM training requires less resources and is considered to be an older fashion of ASR compared to DNN-HMM model. However, as the protection component can handle a lower transcription accuracy for the benefit of less complexity Pocketsphinx is a suitable choice.

*PASR2.* The second candidate (Label *PASR2*) is from an open-source project called Zamia Speech [2] which provides pre-built Kaldi ASR packages for Raspbian (A commonly used Operating System (OS) for Raspberry Pi) complete with pre-trained models for English. It uses Kaldi nnet3 chain audio models. nnet3 and nnet2 are both DNN, but nnet3 supports more general networks. Therefore, we treat nnet3 as a variation of the Kaldi DNN. Specifically, we use $kaldi - generic - en - tdnn\_f$ which is a pre-trained nnet3 chain model trained on 1200 h of audio. We treat it as an ASR with different architecture and trained with different training dataset compared to the main ASR.

*PASR3.* The third candidate (Label *PASR3*) is the standard GMM-HMM model from Kaldi trained using the Wall Street Journal (WSJ) Corpus. Note that although the principal architecture of this ASR is the same as for Pocketsphinx, but the specific parameters are different. Note this candidate is trained using the same dataset as the main one, but it has a completely different architecture.

*PASR4.* The fourth candidate (Label *PASR4*) is identical to PASR3 except the used training data. Only 50% of the Wall Street Journal (WSJ) Corpus are used for training the ASR.

In summary, MASR1 uses a DNN-HMM architecture using the WSJ corpus as training data. PASR1 uses a different architecture and different training data compared to MASR1. PASR2 shares the architecture with MASR1 but uses different training data. PASR3 shares the training data with MASR1 but uses a different architecture. PASR4 uses a less complex training data set compared to PASR3.

### 4.2 Adversarial and Benign Command Generation

*Adversarial Commands.* We used the adversarial commands based on work by Schönherr et al. [11] and provided by them. The 20 adversarial commands are hidden in 20 music segments as provided on the GitHub repository [1].

*Benign Commands.* To show how the main ASR and the defence ASRs perform in a normal setting we also generate benign commands. We generate 20 benign commands based on the transcriptions of the 20 adversarial commands using the Google online Text-to-Speech (TTS).

### 4.3 Experiment Setup

We conduct three sets of experiments. For each set we used the main ASR MASR1 and one of the three protection ASRs PASR1 to PASR3. In each experimental set we evaluate how the 20 adversarial commands and the 20 benign commands are classified by the ACD. The audio commands are directly fed into the main ASR and the protection ASR candidates.

For each adversarial and benign command, we compare the decoding results between the main ASR and the protection ASR using the WER metric. The ACD decision in dependency of WER threshold $t$ is recorded. Based on the ground truth we record if this was a true positive ($TP$), false positive ($FP$), true negative ($TN$) or false negative ($FN$) decision.

True positive means that we decide the command is an adversarial one and the decision is correct; false positive means we decide the command is an adversarial one and it turns out the command is benign; true negative means we decide the command is a benign one and this decision is correct; false negative means we decide the command is a benign one but actually it turns out to be adversarial.

### 4.4 Evaluation Metrics

*Word Error Rates (WER)* WER is defined as

$$WER = ((N_{sub} + N_{ins} + N_{del}))/N_{ref} \tag{5}$$

where $N_{sub}$ is the number of words which are incorrectly transcribed, $N_{ins}$ is the number of words which appear in the current transcription but are not present in the reference, and $N_{del}$ is the number of words in the reference that do not appear in the transcription. Note that WER can be greater than 100% as the transcription can be longer than the reference.

*Receiver Operating Characteristic (ROC).* We draw ROC curves for the ACD with the False Positive Rate (FPR) as the x-axis and the True Positive Rate (TPR) as the y-axis. Each ROC curves shows FPR versus TPR for all possible ACD decision thresholds $t$. TPR is defined as:

$$TPR(t) = TP(t)/(TP(t) + FN(t)) \tag{6}$$

FPR is defined as:

$$FPR(t) = FP(t)/(FP(t) + TN(t)) \tag{7}$$

For each ROC curve, the area under the curve (AUC) is calculated and the ACD has a better prediction skill the greater the AUC value is. An ACD with no skill has an AUC of 0.5 and a useful ACD mut provide an AUC value above 0.5.

## 5 Evaluation Results

We first present a performance evaluation of the five different ASR used (MASR1, PASR1, PASR2, PASR3, PASR4 as shown in Table 1). Each of the ASR are used to decode 20 benign and 20 adversarial commands. Then we evaluate the ACD performance where different combinations of main ASR and protection ASR are used.

### 5.1 Decoding Results of Normal Speech

The 20 benign commands are fed to the different ASR; the results are shown in Table 2 and there exists always a certain amount of WER. From a speech recognition perspective, the WER has to be minimized and there exists various methods for doing it. This include the following Natural Language Processing (NLP) component to analyse intents and semantics of the ASR transcription which can mitigate some errors generated in the ASR decoding step. Since our goal is not to optimize parameters of ASR to achieve high performance but to verify the proposed defence method, the main concern is in the relative variation

**Table 2.** The effect of the 20 benign TTS and 20 adversarial commands on variations of ASR systems. The benign commands are best recognised by MASR1 which is based on kaldi nnet2 model. The adversarial commands are only effective on MASR1, the ASR for which the commands were generated. For all other ASR the WER is high, indicating an unsuccessful transcription.

| ASR | ASR variants | ASR architecture | WER benign | WER adversarial |
|---|---|---|---|---|
| MASR1 | Kaldi nnet2 | DNN-HMM | 39.73% | 12.33% |
| PASR1 | Pocketsphinx | GMM-HMM | 63.01% | 139.73% |
| PASR2 | Kaldi nnet3 | DNN-HMM | 73.28% | 98.63% |
| PASR3 | Kaldi GMM | GMM-HMM | 44.52% | 97.26% |
| PASR4 | Kaldi GMM | GMM-HMM | 47.94% | 100% |

of WER with benign and adversarial commands. Also the reasons for the performance variations for the ASR models are analysed in Sect. 6. MASR1 based on the advanced DNN-HMM architecture shows the best transcription results for benign TTS commands. Even with same architecture used in PASR3 and PASR4, the transcription performance of PASR4 is lower than PASR3 as it uses only half the training data. The worst performance in decoding commands is shown by PASR2 followed by PASR1 that uses different corpus from WSJ which is used for training the rest of ASRs.

*MASR1.* First we use the nnet2 Kaldi (main ASR). Using this ASR results in WER of 39.73% with 31 insertions, 17 deletions and 87 substitutions.

*PASR1.* The Pocketsphinx decoding results of these 20 human spoken commands result in a WER of 63.01% with 48 insertions, 12 deletions and 62 substitutions.

*PASR2.* The decoding results from Kaldi nnet3 compared to the ground truth transcription result in a WER of 73.28% with 3 insertions, 50 deletions and 41 substitutions.

*PASR3.* Feeding these commands to the Kaldi GMM-HMM model results in WER of 44.52% with 11 insertions, 11 deletions and 55 substitutions.

*PASR4.* The decoding results for the 20 human spoken commands are 47.94% with 20 insertions, 8 deletions and 5 substitutions.

### 5.2 Decoding Results of Adversarial Commands

The 20 adversarial commands are fed to the different ASR. As shown in Table 2, it is clear that the crafted adversarial commands are only effective against the ASR used in the adversarial command generation. Any other ASR, differing in architecture, training data or both does not transcribe the commands usefully. The detailed results are as follows:

*MASR1.* The adversarial commands are successful resulting in the best overall WER of 12.33%. Specifically, 2 word insertions, 9 word deletions and 7 word substitutions are recorded when comparing the transcription with the reference. The accuracy is 35% which means 7 sentences out of 20 are exactly the same as the target transcription (all words in the sentence are correct). This proves the white-box attack is successful as expected. The adversarial commands are crafted specifically for MASR1.

*PASR1.* The decoding results from Pocketsphinx is far from the target, resulting in WER of 139.73% when compared with the reference text. Specifically, 64 word insertions, 11 word deletions and 129 word substitutions.

*PASR2.* When feeding the adversarial commands to the Kaldi nnet3 chain model running on a raspberry Pi, none of the target sentences are correctly transcribed. Specifically, WER is 98.63% with 0 insertion, 129 deletions and 15 substitutions.

*PASR3.* None of the target sentences are correctly transcribed. Specifically, WER is 97.26% with 3 insertions, 101 deletions and 38 substitutions.

*PASR4.* The results are similar to PASR3 with a reduced training data. Specifically, WER is 100% with 1 insertion, 118 deletions and 27 substitutions.

### 5.3 Adversarial Command Detection (ACD)

We evaluate the ACD ASR combinations. The benign commands and adversarial commands are fed to the system. For each combination, we evaluate the WER threshold and draw the ROC curve (Fig. 2).

A good ACD should produce a ROC curve passing close to the top left corner (i.e. from (0, 0) via point (0, 1) to (1, 1)). A curve following a diagonal (i.e. from (0, 0) to (1, 1) would represent a bad ACD that cannot discriminate and represents a random guess. A good ACD would have an AUC value close to 1 while a bad ACD would have an AUC value close to 0.5.

As shown in Fig. 2, the four pairs of ASR do not differ significantly in terms of detection performance. However, the ACD using PASR1 (Pocketsphinx) provides the best ROC curve. The AUC value for PASR1 is $AUC_{PASR1} = 0.898$ which is the highest among the four ($AUC_{PASR2} = 0.833$, $AUC_{PASR3} = 0.889$, and $AUC_{PASR4} = 0.773$).

*PASR1.* We see that Pocketsphinx (PASR1) tends to transcribe our 20 music based adversarial commands to longer sentences than the original command transcription, which results in WER values above 100%. This makes it easier to select a threshold with higher TPR and lower FPR.

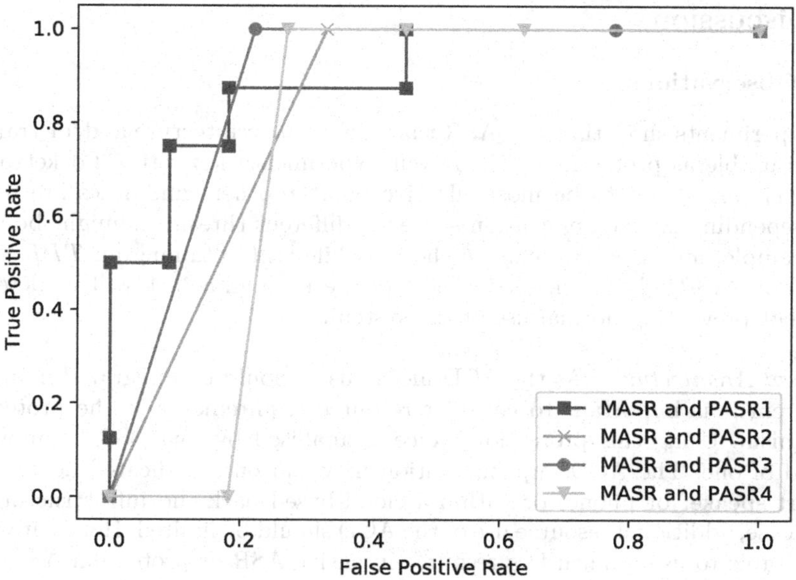


**Fig. 2.** ROC curves for all protection ASR options. Pocketsphinx (PASR1) provides the best option for the ACD with an AUC value of $AUC_{PASR1} = 0.898$.

*PASR2.* The Kaldi nnet3 (PASR2) model often only transcribes a few words or even nothing when fed with our 20 adversarial commands. This results in a WER value of 98.63% which is greater than the WER in recognizing the normal TTS generated commands by a value of only 25.35. This smaller WER difference is due to the worst decoding performance shown by Kaldi nnet3 in recognising spoken commands which makes it not an optimal choice when coupled with the main ASR here in our setup.

*PASR3 and PASR4.* The Kaldi GMM-HMM (PASR4) uses half the training data than the Kaldi GMM-HMM (PASR3). These two models have similar performances in decoding the 20 adversarial commands. The decoding results for most samples are either shorter than the target transcriptions or nothing can be decoded. There are only two WER results beyond 100% for both PASR3 and PASR4. Overall, the WERs for both PASR3 and PASR4 decoding 20 adversarial commands are high and around 100%, so the true positive value for both of these reach 100% easily. When decoding TTS generated benign commands, the performance of PASR3 is slightly better than PASR4 as shown in Table 2. There are more high WER values for PASR4 than PASR3, so as the threshold varies, the false positive rate of PASR4 is greater than that of PASR3, which is presented in Fig. 2.

# 6 Discussion

## 6.1 Observations

The experiments show that any ASR that differs in architecture and/or training data is usable as protection ASR. In our experimentation setup, Pocketsphinx (PASR1) turned out to be most effective but the other candidates are usable too. Depending on the application scenario, different thresholds might be used. For example, an $FPR = 0$ can be chosen while still obtaining an $TPR = 0.5$ in case of PASR1. For such setting 50% of the time an attack will be detected while not preventing normal use of the system.

*Different Architectures.* As the ACD mechanism should be integrated in a PVA ecosystem it is important to consider resource requirements of the protection mechanism. Using this protection, voice is analysed by two ASR components instead of one. The ACD implementation may run on a dedicated device (e.g. a smart speaker or phone) or within a cloud-based back-end infrastructure. In either case, additional resource use of the ACD should be limited. Hence, it would be desirable to use a much less resource intensive ASR as protection ASR. The experiments show that this approach is feasible. For example, Pocketsphinx is an ASR designed for systems with limited resources and is less complex than Kaldi which we used as main ASR.

*Different Training Data.* In order to increase difficulty for an attacker to bypass the ACD it should not be possible for the attacker to obtain knowledge on the internal workings of the protection ASR. This can be achieved by frequently changing the configuration of the ASR by using a different training data set. Thus, the protection ASR becomes a moving target. However, frequent re-training requires resources and such effort should be limited. The effort can be limited by reducing the training effort by reduction of the used training data. PASR4 uses half the training data compared to PASR3 producing comparable ACD protection results. In our setup this 50% reduction in training data led to a training time reduction of 22%.

## 6.2 Limitations

While our work shows the principle feasibility of ACD there are limitations which we would like to address in future work: *Adversarial Commands:* The adversarial commands are generated based on adding perturbations to music rather than normal speech. *Benign Commands:* We used the Google online TTS service to generate the 20 benign commands. We would like to use human speakers for further evaluation. *Sample Size:* The number of used samples was relatively small.

# 7 Related Work

Recent work has thoroughly investigated the construction and efficiency of adversarial examples. Among the earlier works, adversarial attacks are generated using tuned MFCC features [12] and inverse feature extraction [5] in the form of obfuscated commands that are not intelligible to human listeners. By exploiting the temporal and frequency masking property of the psychoacoustic model, the voice commands are embedded in speech or music which is perceived by listeners as speech or music but recognized by ASR as commands [6,11,15]. In this work, we used the method proposed by Schönherr et al. [11] that hides voice commands in audio locations which minimizes perceptual distortion.

Only a few works investigating the construction of adversarial examples for ASR have also analysed in detail if the examples are transferable. CommanderSong [15] that targets Kaldi ASR has found to be unsuccessful on DeepSpeech but an improvement for this is obtained in [4] by generating a few adversarial examples that targets DeepSpeech using the adversarial commands for Kaldi ASRs. Similarly, the adversarial examples that are successful on DeepSpeech2 with little perceptual distortion generate invalid transcription for Google Voice [6]. Abdullah et al. [3] obtained a reasonably good transferability for an *evasion* attack. A systematic approach for the generation of transferable adversarial commands is not yet achieved.

Some existing work has proposed defence mechanisms against adversarial examples. This includes a neural network-based classifier for detection of hidden commands [5] and the use of audio pre-processing methods (addition of noise, down sampling, audio compression, band-pass filtering, audio panning) in individual or in combination to render adversarial examples ineffective [10,15]. The temporal consistency of speech signal is exploited in [14] for developing the countermeasure due to the limited robustness shown by signal processing methods towards adversarial attacks [13]. The narrow-band vocoder G.729 along with Pulse-code Modulation (PCM) is used to eliminate the perturbations due to adversarial commands [8]. The ASR outputs of this filtered audio signal and the raw input signal are compared to detect adversarial commands when the difference is greater than a threshold.

Closest to our work is work by Zeng et al. [16] which proposes a multiversion programming inspired approach to detect audio adversarial examples. This work also uses additional ASRs to detect adversarial examples. The proposed detection mechanism consists of one main ASR system based on DeepSpeech and three auxiliary ASR systems that comprise DeepSpeech, Long Short-Term Memory (LSTM) based Google Cloud Speech, and Amazon Transcribe with unknown internal architecture. The detection accuracy of this approach is very high but it drops with the similarity between the commands and transcribes. In addition to the internal architecture, the type and volume of training data is also a significant factor that makes any ASR system unique. However, our work differs as we aim to minimise complexity of the defence mechanism. Reduced complexity is essential to support implementation on resource constraint PVAs or to facilitate deployment on scale when used in a cloud infrastructure. Our work also differs as we investigate not only the effectiveness of different ASR architectures but also the impact of using a reduced training data sets.

## 8 Conclusion

We increasingly rely on PVA to interact with smart environments and services. It is essential that security of these systems can be ensured. Adversarial commands are a serious threat to PVAs. While it is well understood how adversarial commands can be generated and used little work has been carried out to devise defence methods.

In this paper we have shown that it is possible to use a parallel ASR (a protection ASR) to defend against adversarial commands. In our experiments it is shown that a less capable protection ASR is sufficient to achieve protection. It is possible to implement the protection ASR without much resource requirements and it is possible to use frequent re-training. Thus, an attacker needs to adapt to an ever changing target.

The efficacy of our proposed protection mechanism has been shown for the evaluated scenarios. However, it would be desirable to provide a formal proof that it is impossible for an attacker to construct a hidden command that can target two different ASR systems.

**Acknowledgement.** This publication has emanated from research conducted with the financial support of Science Foundation Ireland under Grant number 19/FFP/6775. For the purpose of Open Access, the author has applied a CC BY public copyright licence to any Author Accepted Manuscript version arising from this submission.

## References

1. Adversarial Attacks. https://github.com/rub-ksv/adversarialattacks. Accessed 26 July 2020
2. Zamia Speech. https://github.com/gooofy/zamia-speech#asr-models. Accessed 26 July 2020
3. Abdullah, H., et al.: Hear “No Evil”, see “Kenansville”: efficient and transferable black-box attacks on speech recognition and voice identification systems. arXiv preprint arXiv:1910.05262 (2019)
4. Carlini, N., Wagner, D.: Audio adversarial examples: targeted attacks on speech-to-text. In: 2018 IEEE Security and Privacy Workshops (SPW), pp. 1–7, May 2018. https://doi.org/10.1109/SPW.2018.00009
5. Carlini, N., et al.: Hidden voice commands. In: Proceedings of the 25th USENIX Security Symposium (USENIX Security 2016), pp. 513–530. USENIX Association, Austin, August 2016. https://www.usenix.org/conference/usenixsecurity16/technical-sessions/presentation/carlini
6. Cisse, M., Adi, Y., Neverova, N., Keshet, J.: Houdini: fooling deep structured prediction models (2017)
7. Huggins-Daines, D., Kumar, M., Chan, A., Black, A.W., Ravishankar, M., Rudnicky, A.I.: Pocketsphinx: a free, real-time continuous speech recognition system for hand-held devices. In: ICASSP 2006 Proceedings. 2006 IEEE International Conference on Acoustics, Speech and Signal Processing, vol. 1, p. I. IEEE (2006)

8. Jiajie, Z., Zhang, B., Zhang, B.: Defending adversarial attacks on cloud-aided automatic speech recognition systems, pp. 23–31, July 2019. https://doi.org/10.1145/3327962.3331456
9. Paul, D., Baker, J.: The design for the Wall Street Journal-based CSR corpus. In: HLT (1992)
10. Rajaratnam, K., Shah, K., Kalita, J.: Isolated and ensemble audio preprocessing methods for detecting adversarial examples against automatic speech recognition. In: Proceedings of the 30th Conference on Computational Linguistics and Speech Processing (ROCLING 2018), pp. 16–30. The Association for Computational Linguistics and Chinese Language Processing (ACLCLP), Hsinchu, October 2018. https://www.aclweb.org/anthology/O18-1002
11. Schönherr, L., Kohls, K., Zeiler, S., Holz, T., Kolossa, D.: Adversarial attacks against automatic speech recognition systems via psychoacoustic hiding. In: Proceedings of the 2019 Network and Distributed System Security Symposium (NDSS 2019) (2019)
12. Vaidya, T., Zhang, Y., Sherr, M., Shields, C.: Cocaine noodles: exploiting the gap between human and machine speech recognition. In: Proceedings of the 9th USENIX Workshop on Offensive Technologies (WOOT 2015). USENIX Association, Washington, D.C., August 2015. https://www.usenix.org/conference/woot15/workshop-program/presentation/vaidya
13. Yang, Z., Li, B., Chen, P., Song, D.: Characterizing audio adversarial examples using temporal dependency. CoRR abs/1809.10875 (2018). http://arxiv.org/abs/1809.10875
14. Yang, Z., Li, B., Chen, P.Y., Song, D.: Towards mitigating audio adversarial perturbations (2018). https://openreview.net/forum?id=SyZ2nKJDz
15. Yuan, X., et al.: CommanderSong: a systematic approach for practical adversarial voice recognition. In: Proceedings of the 27th USENIX Security Symposium (USENIX Security 2018), pp. 49–64. USENIX Association, Baltimore, August 2018. https://www.usenix.org/conference/usenixsecurity18/presentation/yuan-xuejing
16. Zeng, Q., et al.: A multiversion programming inspired approach to detecting audio adversarial examples. In: 2019 49th Annual IEEE/IFIP International Conference on Dependable Systems and Networks (DSN), pp. 39–51 (2019). https://doi.org/10.1109/DSN.2019.00019

# Security Measuring System for IoT Devices

Elena Doynikova(✉), Evgenia Novikova, Ivan Murenin, Maxim Kolomeec, Diana Gaifulina, Olga Tushkanova, Dmitry Levshun, Alexey Meleshko, and Igor Kotenko

St. Petersburg Federal Research Center of the Russian Academy of Sciences (SPC RAS), St. Petersburg Institute for Informatics and Automation of the Russian Academy of Sciences, 14-th Liniya, 39, St. Petersburg 199178, Russia
{doynikova,novikova,kolomeec,gaifulina,tushkanova,levshun, meleshko,ivkote}@comsec.spb.ru

**Abstract.** Wide application of IoT devices together with the growth of cyber attacks against them creates a need for a simple and clear system of security metrics for the end users and producers that will allow them to understand how secure their IoT devices are and to compare these devices with each other, as well as to enhance the security of the devices. The paper proposes a security measuring system that is based on the hierarchy of metrics representing different security properties and integrates these security metrics in one clear and reasonable score depending on available data. The algorithms used for metrics calculation are briefly described with the main focus on the algorithms for integral scores. To demonstrate the operation of the proposed security measuring system, the case study describing metrics calculation for the IoT device is given.

**Keywords:** Security measuring · IoT devices · Metrics · Integral scores · Data analysis · Confidentiality · Integrity · Availability · Privacy · Anomalies

## 1 Introduction

The market of IoT devices nowadays is extremely heterogeneous. At the same time the number of cyber attacks using such devices increases. Thus, it is important to provide a simple and clear system of security metrics for the end users and producers that will allow them to understand how secure their IoT devices are and to compare these devices with each other, as well as to enhance the security of the devices.

Currently, there are checklists of security requirements for the IoT devices and corresponding metrics, for example, IoT Security Compliance Framework 2.0 (IoT Security Foundation) [9].

Besides, there are researches that propose the approaches and techniques for calculation of different IoT security metrics, such as Confidentiality, Integrity,


S. Katsikas et al. (Eds.): ESORICS 2021 Workshops, LNCS 13106, pp. 256–275, 2022.
https://doi.org/10.1007/978-3-030-95484-0_16

Availability (CIA) [8,10], Authenticity [15], Privacy [12–14], Transparency, Readability [11], Trustworthiness [18], and others.

At the same time there is no comprehensive framework that incorporates interconnected security and privacy metrics for different security properties of the IoT devices and algorithms for their calculation, and integrates these security metrics in one clear and reasonable score, as well as there is no security measuring system that implements calculation of such comprehensive set of metrics including the integral security metric. Thus, there is a gap between a need for comprehensive security measuring system for IoT devices and current solutions that implement a limited set of security measurements.

**Contribution.** The main contribution of the research paper consists in the elimination of the gap mentioned above via the development of the comprehensive security measuring system for IoT devices. The proposed system automatically calculates a set of security metrics representing different security and privacy device characteristics considering available data and integrates them into the common integral security & privacy score. Namely:

- The authors propose the hierarchy of the security and privacy metrics for the IoT devices incorporating metrics that are calculated on the basis of static and dynamic data describing device specification and behavior. The security metrics determined based on the static data are as follows: static CIA score (calculated based on the internal criticality of the device by confidentiality, integrity and availability properties, exploitability, and confidentiality, integrity and availability impact considering device criticality); privacy policy based score (defined based on the readability score and ontology-based representation of privacy policy); APK (Android Package) based score (calculated based on the application description-based score and APK permission-based score), as well as integral static score. The security metrics determined based on the dynamic data are as follows: dynamic privacy score (calculated based on the APK based score and dynamic information on the privacy relating anomalies detected in device and system logs); dynamic CIA score (computed based on the dynamic exploitability, and static CIA score); as well as integral dynamic score.
- The authors introduce the algorithms for the metrics calculation including novel algorithms for static CIA score, ontology-based privacy score, APK based score, dynamic privacy and CIA score.
- The authors introduce the set of novel algorithms for the calculation of the integral security metrics.
- The authors develop an architecture of the security measuring system that implements the proposed algorithms.
- The authors demonstrate the operation of the developed system on the case study.

**Novelty.** The novelty of the proposed solution consists in the introduced hierarchy of the security metrics for the IoT devices, novel algorithms for separate metrics calculation, and novel algorithms for the integral metrics calculation depending on the available input data.

The paper is organized as follows. Section 2 analyzes the related research in the area. Section 3 introduces the proposed security measuring system and its components, the hierarchy of security metrics, the algorithms for their calculation and the algorithms for the calculation of the integral scores. Section 4 describes the implementation of the proposed security measuring system and a case study demonstrating its operation. Section 5 contains the discussion and conclusion.

## 2 Related Research

A lot of research has been done in IoT security measuring. There are security guidelines that specify main security principles that should be satisfied for IoT devices, for example, Cyber Assessment Framework (CAF) [16] and IoT Security Compliance framework [17]. Such guidelines represent what security requirements should be satisfied and measured but do not describe how.

The study of these documents and of the security standards allowed us to outline and specify the main security metrics that should be calculated for the IoT devices, including Confidentiality, Integrity, Availability, Authenticity, Privacy, Trustworthiness, and others. Researchers proposed various approaches for the calculation of these metrics. Thus, confidentiality, integrity, and availability for a device can be calculated based on available information on device vulnerabilities. Known vulnerabilities and their Common Vulnerability Scoring System (CVSS) scores [8] representing a likelihood of their exploitation and impact from their exploitation for CIA can be found in publicly available databases such as National Vulnerability Database (NVD). These scores can be used by themselves or in the scope of more complicated approaches considering connections between the devices and vulnerabilities that can lead to higher damage for device security [10]. Another approach that can be used for confidentiality measuring as well as for privacy measuring is the analysis of permissions granted to the device software and hardware. There are also approaches that calculate privacy and transparency based on the policy text analysis. There are rule-based approaches [12], ontology-based approaches [13,20–23], and machine learning approach [14]. For readability calculation, different algorithms that assess text complexity can be used [11]. Besides, to calculate CIA and authenticity machine learning based approaches can be used [15].

Though a lot of research has been done in the field of IoT devices' security and privacy there is no comprehensive framework that incorporates interconnected security and privacy metrics for different security properties of the IoT devices and algorithms and algorithms for their calculation, and integrates these security metrics in one clear and reasonable score, as well as there is no security measuring system that implements calculation of such comprehensive set of metrics including the integral security & privacy metric.

## 3 Security Measuring System

We propose a security measuring system that aims to provide security tags (i.e. grades or scores) for the IoT devices to compare them in security terms. It is based on a hierarchy of security and privacy metrics that are calculated on the basis of various attributes and characteristics of the device. The system takes the following information as input: software installed on the device, description of the software, corresponding privacy policies; names of the .apk installed on the devices; NVD data on products (Common Platform Enumeration, CPE) and known vulnerabilities (Common Vulnerabilities and Exposures, CVE), log describing normal device's behavior, their specification, and outputs a set of metrics. The metrics could be divided into two groups - static and dynamic depending on the type of input data. The hierarchy of proposed static metrics is shown in Fig. 1. The static metrics serve as initial values for corresponding dynamic scores recalculated on the basis of streaming logs of the device (Fig. 2).

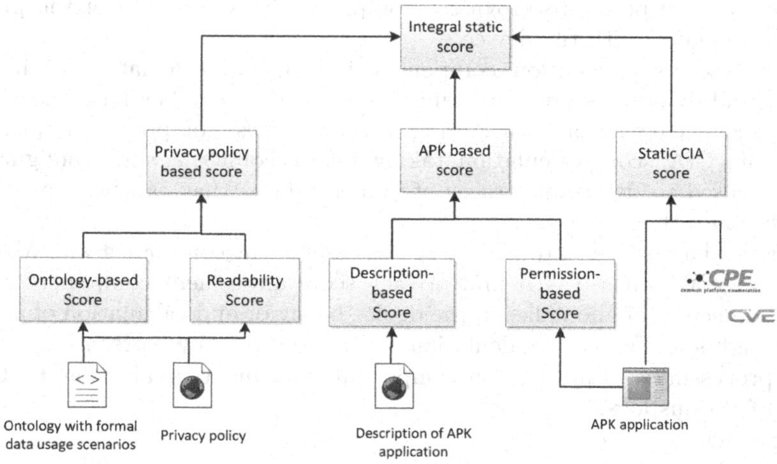


**Fig. 1.** Hierarchy of static security and privacy metrics.

The calculation of the metrics is implemented by the corresponding components of the security measuring system that are described in detail below:

1. Static CIA score calculation component implements CIA score calculation on the basis of CVSS scores of known vulnerabilities of the devices.
2. APK based score calculation component implements privacy calculation for the device considering requested and required permissions of the installed applications based on its description.
3. Ontology based privacy score calculation component implements risk calculation for the device considering its privacy policy.

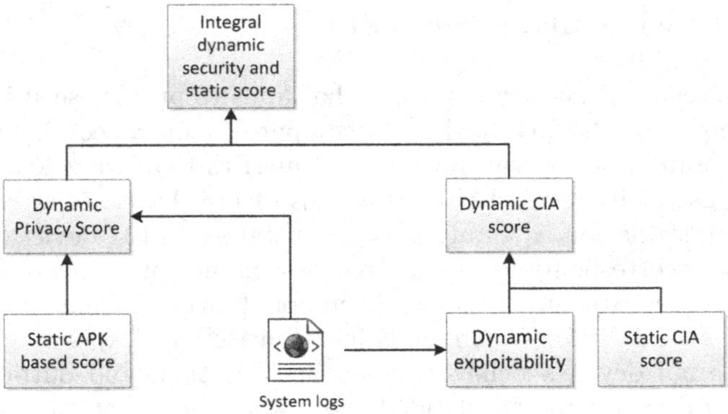


**Fig. 2.** Hierarchy of dynamic security and privacy metrics.

4. Readability score calculation component calculates the readability score of the device privacy policy to provide a comprehensive evaluation of the privacy risks associated with the device.
5. Integral scores calculation component implements calculation of integral static and dynamic scores, including integral privacy policy based score.
6. CIA score calculation considering attack traces component implements dynamic CIA score calculation taking into account network configuration that is used to determine traces of vulnerabilities that can be exploited to compromise the device.
7. Statistics based CIA and privacy scores assessment component and Machine Learning (ML) based CIA and privacy score assessment component implement detection of anomalies in the device behavior and calculation of anomalies weights for further recalculation of CIA and privacy scores in dynamics.
8. Log processing and integration component implements analysis and integration of various logs.
9. Measuring database.

The common scheme of the proposed system is given in Fig. 3.

**Static CIA Score Calculation Component.** The static CIA score calculation is based on the analysis of known vulnerabilities of the device software and firmware. The risk assessment procedure includes the following basic steps: (1) find vulnerabilities of the specific device; (2) get environmental CVSS scores for vulnerabilities found; (3) calculate CIA score as maximum environmental CVSS score across all found vulnerabilities.

The information about devices' vulnerabilities could be found either in open databases, such as NVD, or obtained from the penetration testing team. NVD contains information about vulnerabilities in CVE format linked to CPE that is a formal description of software and hardware. To find vulnerabilities, it is necessary to form the list of hardware, applications or operational systems that

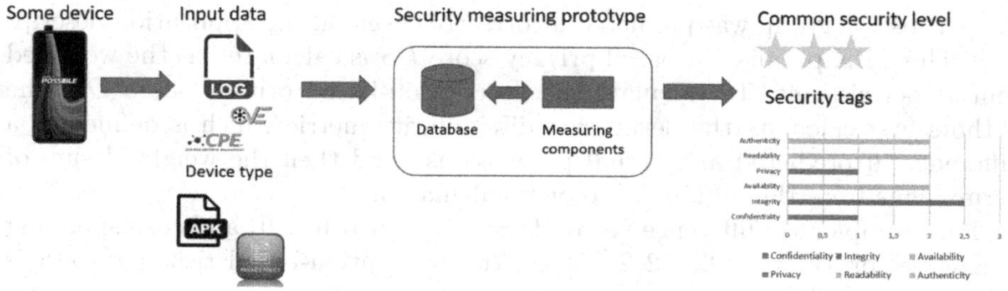


**Fig. 3.** Common scheme of the proposed security measuring system.

needs to be analysed, to search the CPEs (for each element from the list), to search the CVEs by CPE.

Each CVE entry has a CVSS score that captures the principal technical characteristics of vulnerabilities. This score incorporates information both on the impact on CIA in case of the vulnerability exploit and ease of its exploitation. In the static CIA score calculation component the modified environmental CVSS score is used. It allows considering the criticality of the device under analysis.

**APK Based Score Calculation Component.** This component implements privacy calculation for the Android device considering the requested and required permissions of the installed applications. The idea is to assess permissions of the application in context with its description available in mobile application store (Google Play Store, Huawei App Gallery, etc.). The application description is used to predict a set of permissions that the user expects from the app. For example, the user does not expect the flashlight application to have access to the contacts list but expects it for the social network application. The difference between predicted and actual permissions may serve as a basis for risk calculation. Thus, the authors outline the following types of permission-based risks:

1. APK description-based privacy score with the range in $[0, 1.0]$;
2. APK permission-based privacy score with the range in $[0, 1.0]$;
3. APK based score that lies in the range $[0, 10]$ and could be transformed to nominal risk value, i.e. High, Medium, Low.

Permissions could be grouped by the data type they may be associated with. We outlined eight groups. Each group is assigned a weight $w$ that reflects criticality of the permissions in the context of GDPR personal data types [25], for example, the "Health" permission group includes {BODY_SENSORS} permission with $w = 4$ as it corresponds to "Special" GDPR personal data type. The predictions could be transformed into an 8-element binary vector, where each element corresponds to the permission group. For actual permissions, the vector is filled with 0, and the element is set to 1 if any permission from the permission group is present in permissions of the APK application. For predicted permissions, the vector is filled with 1 and the element is set to 0 if any permission from the permission group was predicted incorrectly based on the application description. The APK permission-based privacy score $PS$ is calculated as the weighted sum of permissions. To calculate the description-based privacy score $DS$, the authors first calculate the permission dissimilarity metric which is defined as a difference in predicted and actual permissions. And then the weighted sum of permissions from the obtained vector is calculated.

For example, for difference vector $\boldsymbol{D} = (0, 0, 1, 0, 0, 0, 0, 0)$ and corresponding weight vector $\boldsymbol{W} = (4, 2, 2, 2, 2, 2, 1, 0)$, the description-based risk score $DS$ is calculated as follows:

$$DS = \frac{0*4+0*2+1*2+0*2+0*2+0*2+0*1+0*0}{4+2+2+2+2+2+1+0} = 0.13.$$

The integral APK based score is calculated using the Algorithm 1.

**Algorithm 1**

```
log_base = round(10 * PS)
if log_base < e then
    ipps = PS * ln(1 + ln(1 + DS))
else
    ipps = PS * log_{log_base}(1 + ln(1 + DS))
end if
if ipps > 1 then
    ipps = 1
end if
return ipps * 10
```

In the provided algorithm $PS$ – permission-based score in range [0.0; 1.0], $DS$ – description based score (risk) in range [0.0; 1.0]; $ipps$ – the output integral permissions based risk score in range [0.0; 10].

The underlying idea of the algorithm is as follows. The permission-based score $PS$ reflects risks associated with permissions requested by the application. Description-based score $DS$ reflects the risks that are calculated according to the conformance between permissions requested by the application and its description, therefore it can be considered as conformance between requested data and purposes they are collected. Thus if purposes are unclear and the corresponding score is high, we need to increase the integral score, however, if the purposes are clear, the integral score is defined by permission-based score, as risks associated with usage of personal data are still present.

**Ontology Based Privacy Score Calculation Component.** The basis of the privacy risk assessment implemented by this component is an ontology that provides a formal representation of personal data processing scenarios. The proposed system uses ontology and privacy risk calculation algorithm described in [6]. It provides a formal description of three basic personal usage scenarios - first party collection and usage, third party sharing, and data retention.

Each personal data usage scenario is described by a set of linked concepts that correspond to different attributes of a given usage scenario, for example, type of personal data being collected or shared, the purpose of data processing, retention time, etc.

However, the key concept is Data and its sub-classes such as Sensitive data, User Account Info, Tracking Data, App & Dev Info, User Financial Data, etc., that define the risk score base. Other concepts of usage scenario could either increase it or decrease. Thus, the generic scheme for scenario risk calculation is defined as follows:

$$PDDataUsageScenarioRisk = PDRiskScoreBase * riskCoeff,$$

where $PDDataUsageScenarioRisk$ is a privacy risk score for the particular usage scenario, e.g. data retention, $PDRiskScoreBase$ is a risk base calculated on the basis of personal data types used in the usage scenario and their criticality. $riskCoeff$ is a risk coefficient that is defined on the basis of other usage scenario concepts, i.e. purpose, and legal basis, opt-in/opt-out choices. To calculate risk coefficient $riskCoeff$, it is necessary to determine concepts relating to a given usage scenario except for the Data concept. Each concept has subclasses or categories, for example, the Retention Time concept has 4 categories (sub-classes): Not Defined, Stated, Indefinite and Other. For each category, it is possible to determine their criticality level in a manner similar to the criticality defined for categories of Data concept. Then $riskCoeff$ is calculated on the basis of categories of the related concepts with highest criticality [6].

Currently, the final ontology based score is calculated as a mean sum of privacy risk scores calculated for each usage scenario detected in the privacy policy.

**Readability Score Calculation Component.** The readability metric relates to the group of privacy aware metrics and reflects an indicator of the ease or difficulty of reading any text and, as a consequence, the difficulty of understanding it [14]. If, for example, the text of a product privacy policy is difficult to read, then there is a risk of misunderstanding how user data is used. Therefore, the readability relating risks are also needed to be addressed.

The security measuring system uses the Flesch-Kincaid Grade Level readability (FKGLR) to assess readability risks. This is a fairly well-known formula that is used to test the difficulty of written texts.

The conclusion about the readability indicator of a specific text is made based on the resulting FKGLR number, namely, based on the following intervals:

- $FKGLR = [0, 6]$ - low level of readability risk, the text is very easy to read;
- $FKGLR = (6, 10]$ - low level of readability risk, the text is simple for the average reader;
- $FKGLR = (10, 12]$ - average level of readability risk, the text is somewhat more complicated for the average reader;

- $FKGLR = (12, \infty]$ - high level of readability risk, complex text, loyal to an experienced reader who is ready to read scientific texts.

**CIA Score Calculation Considering Attack Traces Component.** This component considers that device vulnerability depends on relations between the vulnerabilities detected for the device and the network configuration, i.e. on the attack traces. An attack trace is a sequence of atomic attack actions where each action corresponds to the vulnerability exploitation. For example, some vulnerability $v1$ of the device has a low risk because it requires user privileges for exploitation. But if there is another vulnerability $v2$ that allows obtaining the required privileges we get the attack trace that increases the risks: $v2- > v1$.

The component takes logs from the device as input and implements the following steps:

1. Extract networks, namely the devices that are connected to the same Gateway.
2. Extract devices within each network (their types and roles) to determine their vulnerabilities.
3. Determine CVEs of vulnerabilities of the devices.
4. Classify CVEs. To generate attack traces it is necessary to determine pre and post conditions of the vulnerabilities exploitation on the basis of the CVSS of version 3 (CVSSv3) metrics: Attack Vector (AV), Required Privileges, and Obtained Privileges. The authors outline 5 groups of vulnerabilities based on their characteristics, they are shown in Table 1.
5. Generate CVE-based trees. In this step, CVE-based attack traces are generated considering relations between 5 outlined groups in Fig. 4.
6. Calculate the CIA score considering attack traces for the device. The CIA score is calculated on the basis of CVSSv3 scores as in the static case. Confidentiality, integrity, and availability impact for the trace are calculated as the maximum impact of its vulnerabilities. Total exploitability for the attack trace is calculated as the product of the maximum AV score of the vulnerabilities in the trace, Access Complexity for all vulnerabilities in the trace, and Privileges Required and User Interaction scores (depending on their values). The CIA score for the trace is calculated based on the modified impacts and exploitability. Finally, the CIA score considering attack traces for the device is calculated as the maximum of CIA scores from all traces of the device.

The component outputs the attack traces based CIA score in the range $[0; 10]$ that could be further transformed to the qualitative CIA score in range $\{low, medium, high\}$.

**Dynamic CIA and Privacy Score Calculation Components.** This component updates security and privacy scores in dynamics based on the detected anomalies. The confidentiality, integrity, availability, and privacy anomalies are outlined. To detect anomalies statistics based and ML based methods are used, which results are integrated. Depending on the number of the detected anomalies

**Table 1.** Vulnerability groups

| Group \characteristic | AV | Required privileges | Obtained privileges |
|---|---|---|---|
| V0 | Network OR local | None | None |
| V1 | Network OR local | None | !None |
| V2 | Any | Equal to obtained privileges of V1 | Any |
| V3 | Adjacent network | None | Any |
| V4 | Any | Equal to obtained privileges of V3 | Any |

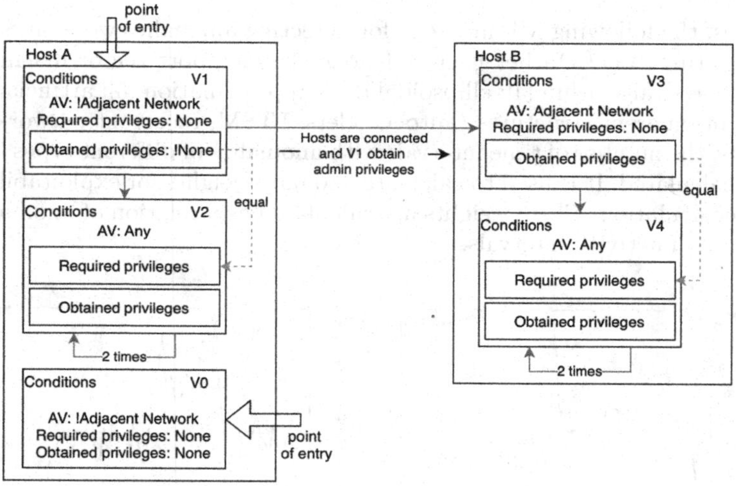


**Fig. 4.** The connections between the vulnerabilities of different groups

the weight coefficients are calculated for privacy score and exploitability score. Exploitability score is a dynamic part of the CIA score and should be changed to recalculate dynamic CIA.

For a given device or user the component builds feature vectors based on timescale log aggregation first. Then it computes the normal range for different feature values for all devices or users and checks user or device activity searching for significant deviations known as anomalies.

The selected features are constructed based on a time-aggregated count of messages considering values of specific attributes of source logs (e.g. errors). For assessment of device activity based on computed features, the time interval of 60 s was selected. The experiments showed that such interval is enough to track some minor changes in device activity and at the same time gives the ability to generalize the device activity patterns. An example of overall device activity on a certain time period and activity pattern for the device for 60 s is shown in Fig. 5.

To determine the device's normal behavior the range of normal values for each feature is calculated. We used sequentially the following methods: Interquartile range (iqr), Grubbs test, ESD-test, and Exponential smoothing.

Normal feature values and device features are used as input for anomaly detection. To detect time intervals with anomalies the component: (1) compares the feature values for each device with ranges of normal values to detect anomalous activity for devices and calculates an anomaly intensity defined as the relation of the distance between feature value and closest bound of the range to feature value, (2) uses Local Outlier Factor ML method [2] to detect anomalous activity for devices, (3) integrates the results taking into account the anomaly intensity.

Besides, the following ML methods for detecting anomalies were investigated before selecting Local Outlier Factor [1]: one class support vector machines [3]; Isolation Forest algorithm [4]; ellipsoidal data approximation [5]; artificial neural networks of different structures (autoencoders, LTSM, recurrent networks).

Finally, the number of time intervals with anomalies of different types for each device is calculated. It is used to calculate anomaly weights for exploitability and privacy recalculation. These weights are calculated as a relation of anomaly time intervals to all activity intervals.

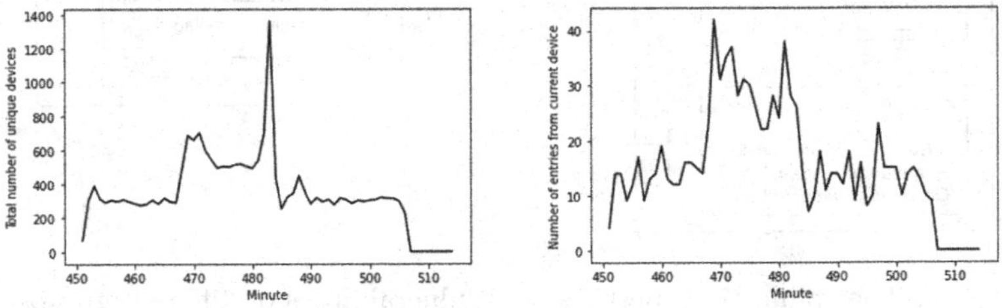


**Fig. 5.** Device activity plot time interval = 60 s.

**Integral Security and Privacy Scores Calculation Component.** Integral security and privacy scores calculation component implements calculation of integral scores. There are several approaches for calculating integral security metrics: expert (or table-based) approach; min-max approach; weighted sum function.

The most common approach is a table-based approach that is used mostly for nominal parameters. The first row and column of such table contain possible values of input metrics, while the inner cells of the table contain values of an integral score. For example, this approach is used facilitated risk analysis and assessment process (FRAAP) proposed in [7]. An obvious benefit of such an approach is the transparency of the calculation procedure, however, creating tables for more than three metrics is a quite complicated process. The min-max approach is usually used in the context of security measures selection and supposes minimization of such parameters as attack probability, attack impact, response costs, while maximization of such parameters as benefit from security measures implementation [19]. The approach based on weighted sum is also widely used, for example, it is adopted for calculating CVSS scores [8]. Application of the weighted sum requires setting ranks or weights for the metrics. In some cases, the definition of metrics weights is a quite natural process. For example, when calculating integral static privacy score based on privacy policy, it is necessary to consider two metrics - readability score and ontology-based score. The readability score characterizes the transparency of privacy policy, while information about the usage of personal data is incorporated in the ontology-based score. Thus, its priority is higher than the priority of readability score, and this difference in metrics priority could be easily reflected by weight coefficients. Currently, we suggest using the following values of weight coefficients: weight coefficient for ontology-based score $w_o = 0.9$; weight coefficient for readability score $w_r = 0.1$.

It should be also noted that the readability score lies in range $[0, \infty]$, and it needs to be re-scaled to the range $[0, \infty]$, this could be done as follows:

1. If $(rs > rescaling\_threshold)$ then $rs = rescaling\_threshold$.
2. $Rescaled\_rs = rs * 10/rescaling\_threshold$.

The $rescaling\_threshold$ artificially defines the possible maximum value of readability score, it is set to 16 because the average range of readability score intervals that define the different level of text difficulty is 4, and the lower border of the interval that corresponds to the highest difficulty level of text is 12. Let $os$ be ontology based score in range $[0, 10]$, and $rs$ - readability score in range $[0, +\infty]$ then the integral policy-based privacy score calculation algorithm includes the following steps:

1. Rescale readability score $rs$ to range $[0; 10]$.
2. Calculate integral static privacy policy based score as $pps = w_o * os + w_r * rs$.

The algorithm outputs the integral score $pps$ in the range $[0, 10]$. The following small example illustrates the calculation procedure of integral privacy score based on analysis of privacy policy. Let ontology-based score $os = 5.6$, readability score $rs = 12$, then privacy policy based score $pps = w_o * os + w_r * RESCALE(rs) = 0.9 * 5.6 + 0.1 * 7.5 = 5.8$

The weighted sum function could be used also for calculating integral privacy and security static and dynamic scores, but in many cases it is not possible to define what metric has a higher priority. To solve this problem, the authors suggest the following algorithm for the case when all input metrics are considered equally meaningful. The metric with the highest risk score serves as a basis, then the values of other metrics are added, but firstly the logarithm dependent on their values and maximum values is calculated to scale the value nonlinear. Authors introduce non-linearity to avoid the fast growth of integral metric value. Let $SCORES$ be a list of metrics with values in the range [0, 10], then the generic algorithm for integral privacy and security calculation consists of the following steps:

1. If all metrics in $SCORES$ are not defined (or null), return not defined (or null)
2. Set $max\_score$ as a maximum element of $SCORES$
3. Remove $max\_score$ from $SCORES$
4. Calculate $integral\_score = max\_score + log(1 + sum(SCORES),$ $10 * length(SCORES))$
5. If $integral\_score > 10$ set $integral\_score$ as 10.
6. Return $integral\_score$.

The algorithm outputs the integral score $integral\_score$ in the range $[0, 10]$. The following small example illustrates the calculation procedure of integral static privacy & security score. Let static CIA score be 4.6, APK-based score be 3.0, and integral privacy policy based score is 4.5. The maximum score is static CIA score, and it serves as the basis of the integral score. Then the final static privacy & security score is calculated as follows: $integral\_score = 4.6 + log(1 + (3.0 + 4.5), 10 * 2) = 5.2$.

To analyze the difference between the proposed algorithm and the weighted sum, the authors implemented the following experiment. We considered the case when three metrics are used to calculate integral score - static CIA score, APK-based score, and privacy-policy based score. All these metrics are equally meaningful and that is why corresponding weights were set equal to each other. Then we evenly changed the values of two metrics (static CIA score, APK-based score) from 0.0 till 10.0 while the value of privacy policy based score was fixed to 5.0, and analyzed how the values of integral score changed. Figure 6 and Fig. 7 show the difference in values of integral security & privacy metric when it is calculated using the weighted sum and proposed algorithm. When the weighted sum was used, the integral score changed linearly in the range from 1.7 to 8.3. The score of 1.7 corresponds to the case when static CIA score and APK-based score were set to 0, and the privacy policy based score was equal to 5. The score of 8.3 corresponds to the case when two metrics have the highest scores. Thus, the algorithm based on weighted sum reduces the values of the integral score when one metric has either high or small score relatively other metrics, because for the case when all metrics are equally important it simply averages the values. The proposed algorithm does not reduce the highest value of the metric, as it is selected as a base for the integral score, and this base is increased proportionally to the values of the rest metrics. Figure 7 shows that integral score grows slowly when the Static CIA and APK-based score are either small or comparable with privacy policy based risk, but when these two metrics became greater than privacy policy based risk (more than 6), the integral score starts growing faster reaching the highest score when Static CIA and APK-based score equal to 8.6. So it could be concluded that the proposed algorithm produces cumulative scores.

## 4 Implementation and Test Case

Common architecture of the developed system is provided in Fig. 8. The proposed system is implemented using Python. We use the PostgreSQL database

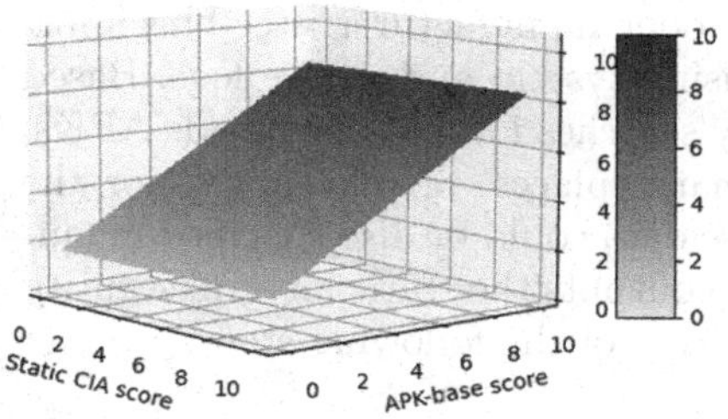


Fig. 6. The values of integral security & privacy metric when they are calculated with the weighted sum algorithm, all weights are equal to each other.

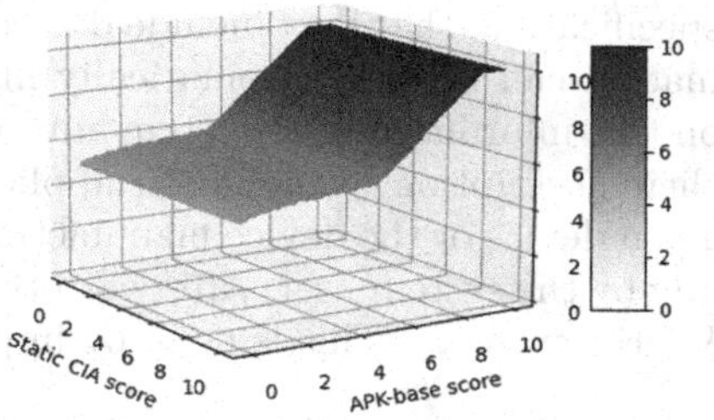


Fig. 7. The values of integral security & privacy metric values when they are calculated with the proposed algorithm.

to store information about the devices under analysis, values of metrics, normal profiles of the devices, and intermediate data about detected anomalies in device functioning. This database also contains data about known vulnerabilities in IoT devices. This information is updated every 6 h automatically or each time the NVD update script is launched manually.

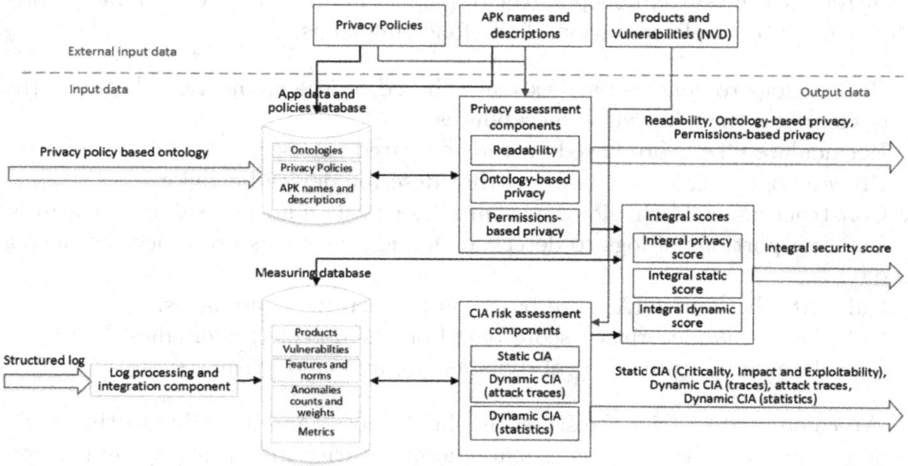


Fig. 8. Common architecture of the proposed security measuring system.

The suggested workflow with the security measuring system is as follows. Initially, the system updates information about known vulnerabilities and takes a description of privacy policy ontology as input data. Then user fills in a device specification, that may include device type, model, manufacturer, etc. This information can be also automatically filled in using system and device logs. Based on this information the system automatically searches for and downloads APKs, their description available on application marketplaces, privacy policy for the given device or the device manufacture. These data could be also specified manually by the system user. Afterward the system outputs the static integral security & privacy score. This is done by implementation of the following steps:

1. Calculate readability score for the device/manufacture privacy policy.
2. Construct P2Onto ontology based on given template and calculate ontology-based privacy score.
3. Calculate integral privacy policy based score.
4. Calculate static CIA score based on vulnerabilities associated with downloaded APKs.
5. Calculate description-based scores and permission-based scores for the APKs.
6. Calculate integral APK based score.
7. Calculate and output integral static security and privacy score.

To produce dynamic scores it is required to provide security measuring system access to device and system logs. The system extracts from logs the following information: information about the connections between the devices; information about the devices, such as device internal characteristics, device state information, time of login/logout; and information about the errors.

Afterward the system outputs the dynamic integral security & privacy score. This is done by implementation of the following steps:

1. Process logs to generate attack traces based on the connections between the devices and their known vulnerabilities.
2. Recalculate CIA score based on the generated traces.
3. Process logs to calculate features that describe device behavior.
4. Construct normal behavior device profiles based on normal values of features.
5. Use new portions of logs to detect anomalies. New logs are processed once a day.
6. Calculate dynamic CIA score based on the detected anomalies.
7. Calculate dynamic privacy score based on the detected anomalies.
8. Calculate and output integral dynamic security and privacy score.

All calculated metrics are stored in the database and available to the user.

Let us consider the following example of security measuring system operation. The analyzed device is a smart lock produced by August company [24]. This company produces devices for the smart home environment, such as smart locks, doorbell cameras, and other accessories. Their smart lock allows implementing a variety of convenient functions such as remote locking and unlocking the door, logging exit/entrance activity of smart lock owners as well as their guests, supporting identification, and voice assistant. To obtain the static integral security and privacy score, the system uploaded the following data:

- the application August Home 11.5.1 for Android that manages the activity of smart devices including smart lock and its description from APKPure market place;
- privacy policy for website and products from manufacture's site [24].

The obtained readability score was defined as 13.0, that corresponds to the text with high difficulty.

The analysis of privacy policy using its ontology representation revealed some interesting scenarios such as a collection of personal data from guests who visit the owner of a smart lock. Figure 9 shows the collection of financial data by the first party. This type of data is collected in order to provide Internet payment services and legal authorization. The calculated ontology based score is equal to 8.37, that is quite high, but could be explained by a variety of data types - user account data, application and device data, tracking and financial information - being collected and shared.

Thus, the integral privacy policy based score is 8.34.

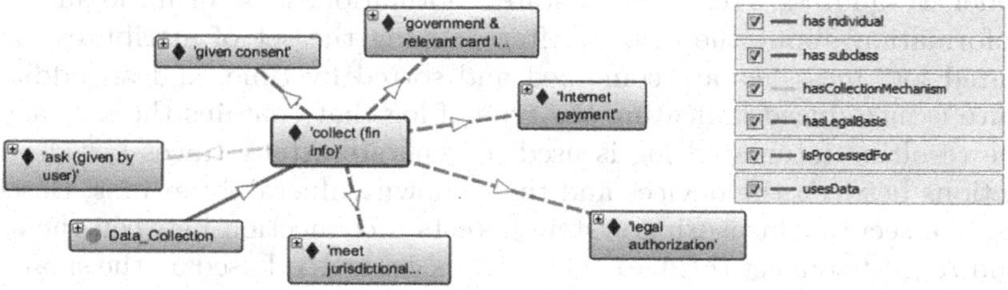


**Fig. 9.** First party collection of financial data presenting using P2Onto ontology.

The analysis of APK permissions and description showed that the actual permissions set for the "August Home" app is {READ_CONTACTS, ACCESS_FINE_LOCATION, ACCESS_COARSE_LOCATION, READ_EXTERNA-L_STORAGE, READ_PHONE_STATE, CAMERA, RECORD_AUDIO}, while a set of predicted permissions - {ACCESS_FINE_LOCATION, READ_EXTERN-AL_STORAGE, READ_PHONE_STATE, RECORD_AUDIO}. Thus, permissions READ_CONTACTS, ACCESS_COARSE_LOCATION', CAMERA were not predicted. This resulted in the following values for permission and description based scores:

- permission-based risk score $DS = 0.6$;
- description-based risk score $PS = 0.4$.

Thus, APK based score equals 7.1.

For the given APK security measuring system detected the following CPE entry in NVD database: cpe:2.3:a:august:august_home:-:*:*:*:*:android:*:*, and the corresponding CVE: CVE-2019-17098 (Fig. 10). Thus, the static CIA score is 6.5 considering the CVSS score of CVE-2019-17098 and device criticality.

| part | vendor | product | version | cve_id |
|---|---|---|---|---|
| a | august | august_home | - | CVE-2019-17098 |

**Fig. 10.** Detected CVEs for smart lock APK.

Integrating scores of static CIA score, APK based score, and integral privacy policy based score we obtain integral static security & privacy score equal to 9.2 when calculating using proposed non-linear algorithm and 7.4 when calculating using the weighted sum function.

The next part of the case study is related to dynamic assessments. The log processing and integration component of the security measuring system processes the logs first. Input logs are represented as series of csv files, partitioned by different days of activity. The component aggregates and normalizes the heterogeneous data in logs of various types. The resulting integrated log contains attributes representing the time of message registration in the log, the connections between the devices, information about the devices (such as device ID, its model, IP-address, etc.), device state information, time of its login/logout, and information about the errors. After defining the set of attributes for the integrated log, messages are combined and sorted by time, and an additional attribute is introduced indicating the type of log that contains the message.

The resulting integrated log is used to generate attack traces based on the connections between the devices and their known vulnerabilities first. Based on this log the security measuring system detects a connection between the smart lock and August connect (bridge). The trace is generated based on the smart lock APK vulnerability (CVE-2019-17098) and August connect vulnerability (CVE-2018-20100). The dynamic CIA score based on the attack traces calculation component classified CVE-2019-17098 as V3 and CVE-2018-20100 as V1 according to Fig. 4. As soon as CVE-2018-20100 helps to obtain admin privileges, there is a following trace between the devices: CVE-2018-20100 -> CVE-2019-17098. It increases the exploitability of CVE-2019-17098 considering traces from 2.84 to 2.99. CIA score changes from 6.5 to 6.59, that doesn't influence on integral static security & privacy score. High integral static security & privacy score values grows rather slowly with growth of the CIA score (the CIA score should increase on 1.9 to affect the integral score).

On the next step the security measuring system processes the logs to calculate features that describe device behavior and constructs normal behavior device profiles based on normal values of features. Further new logs are processed once a day to detect anomalies in the device behavior. If anomalies are detected then dynamic CIA score or dynamic privacy score is recalculated depending on the type of the detected anomaly that, in its turn, changes the integral dynamic security and privacy score. The authors used the generated logs with anomalies to test the dynamic scores calculation. Detected anomalies affect the CIA score and privacy score (depending on anomaly type). Thus, 10% of CIA anomalies detected in log resulted in changing the CIA score from 6.59 to 6.7. But, as it is said above the CIA score should increase on 1.9 to affect the integral static security & privacy score and it stays 9.2.

## 5 Discussion and Conclusion

The paper described the developed security measuring system for IoT devices. The introduced system is based on the novel hierarchy of the security and privacy metrics, algorithms for their calculation, and integral scores calculation algorithms. The developed system automates all stages of data gathering, processing and analysis for calculation of the selected metrics and their recalculation when new data arrives. The difference of the proposed measuring system from the other analogical frameworks consists in consideration of different security and privacy aspects for comparison of the security level of different IoT devices and integration of these aspects in one integral security and privacy score. The underlying approach supposes calculating the base static score for the device using its internal characteristics and its further recalculation in dynamics considering new obtained data, such as data on device connections and behavior. It is implemented via the following steps: calculate readability score for the device/manufacture privacy policy; construct P2Onto ontology based on given template and calculate ontology-based privacy score; calculate integral privacy policy based score; calculate static CIA score based on vulnerabilities associated with downloaded APKs; calculate description-based scores and permission-based scores for the APKs; calculate integral APK based score; calculate and output integral static security and privacy score; get and process new portion of logs; construct normal device behavior profile; get and process new portion of logs every specified time interval; recalculate CIA score considering connections between the devices in logs and constructing possible attack traces; check for anomalies in normal device behavior; recalculate scores if there are anomalies. The whole process is demonstrated on the case study for the IoT device.

While novel algorithms were proposed for separate metrics the main contribution consists in the algorithms for the integral security and privacy scores calculation. There are different approaches to integral scores calculation, including the expert (or table-based) approach [7], the min-max approach [19] and the approach based on weighted sum [8]. We selected the weighted sum approach but modified it as soon as all input metrics are considered equally meaningful. If we would set corresponding weights equal to each other the algorithm would reduce the values of integral security and privacy score because it simply averages the values. The authors consider it unacceptable in the case of the security and privacy scores. Thus, in the proposed algorithm the metric with the highest score serves as a basis, while the values of other metrics are added to it, but firstly the logarithm dependent on their values and maximum values is calculated to scale the value nonlinear. The authors introduced non-linearity to avoid the fast growth of integral metric value. The experiments showed that the proposed algorithm does not reduce the highest value of the metric, as it is selected as a base for the integral score, and this base is increased proportionally to the values of the rest metrics.

There are some features of the proposed system that can and should be improved in future work. New metrics, such as authenticity and transparency can be added. Currently, device criticalities that are used to calculate static CIA score are set depending on the device type. In the future calculation of the criticalities can be automated considering the device's role in the system. Automated searching for CPEs and CVEs should be improved as soon as because of lack of unification and errors sometimes they are missed. The anomaly detection process can be enhanced by introducing new complex features. Besides, anomaly detection by device type profile should be added. Integration with intrusion detection systems can enhance the solution as well. And in the future work the authors plan to add the security recommendations that will allow improving the calculated metrics.

And finally, the main challenge consists in the verification of the proposed security measuring system. While separate algorithms were tested on the experiments and applicability of the proposed system was shown on the use case, the only usage of the device and statistics on real successful incidents can demonstrate if the calculated security and privacy scores were correct. In future work the authors plan to research and overcome this challenge by developing the test stand for scoring and compromising the IoT devices.

## References


1. Ahmed, M., Mahmood, A.N., Hu, J.: A survey of network anomaly detection techniques. J. Netw. Comput. Appl. **60**, 19–31 (2016)
2. Local Outlier Factor. https://en.wikipedia.org/wiki/Local_outlier_factor
3. Schölkopf, B., Platt, J.C., Shawe-Taylor, J., Smola, A.J., Williamson, R.C.: Estimating the support of a high-dimensional distribution. Neural Comput. **13**(7), 1443–1471 (2001). https://doi.org/10.1162/089976601750264965
4. Liu, F.T., Ting, K.M., Zhou, Z.-H.: Isolation-based anomaly detection. ACM Trans. Knowl. Discov. Data **6**(1), 1–39 (2012). https://doi.org/10.1145/2133360.2133363
5. Rousseeuw, P.J., Van Driessen, K.: A fast algorithm for the minimum covariance determinant estimator. Technometrics **41**(3), 212 (1999)
6. Novikova, E., Doynikova, E., Kotenko, I.: P2Onto: making privacy policies transparent. In: Katsikas, S., et al. (eds.) CyberICPS/SECPRE/ADIoT -2020. LNCS, vol. 12501, pp. 235–252. Springer, Cham (2020). https://doi.org/10.1007/978-3-030-64330-0_15
7. Peltier, T.R.: Information Security Risk Analysis, 3d edn., p. 456. CRC Press, Boca Raton (2010)
8. Common Vulnerability Scoring System v3.1: Specification Document. https://www.first.org/cvss/specification-document. Accessed 29 Dec 2019
9. IoT Security Foundation. https://www.iotsecurityfoundation.org/best-practice-guidelines. Accessed 30 July 2021
10. Doynikova, E., Chechulin, A., Kotenko, I.: Analytical attack modeling and security assessment based on the common vulnerability scoring system. In: Proceedings of the XXth Conference of Open Innovations Association FRUCT, pp. 53–61 (2017). https://doi.org/10.23919/FRUCT.2017.8071292

11. Kincaid, J.P., Fishburne, R.P., Rogers, R.L., Chissom, B.S.: Derivation of new readability formulas (automated readability index, fog count, and flesch reading ease formula) for Navy enlisted personnel. Research branch report 8–75. Chief of Naval Technical Training: Naval Air Station Memphis (1975)
12. Ardagna, C.A., De Capitani di Vimercati, S., Samarati, P.: Enhancing user privacy through data handling policies. In: Damiani, E., Liu, P. (eds.) DBSec 2006. LNCS, vol. 4127, pp. 224–236. Springer, Heidelberg (2006). https://doi.org/10.1007/11805588_16
13. Pardo, R., Le Métayer, D.: Analysis of privacy policies to enhance informed consent. In: Foley, S.N. (ed.) DBSec 2019. LNCS, vol. 11559, pp. 177–198. Springer, Cham (2019). https://doi.org/10.1007/978-3-030-22479-0_10
14. Tesfay, W.B., Hofmann, P., Nakamura, T., Kiyomoto, S., Serna, J.: PrivacyGuide: towards an implementation of the EU GDPR on internet privacy policy evaluation. In: Proceedings of the Fourth ACM International Workshop on Security and Privacy Analytics (IWSPA 2018), pp. 15–21. Association for Computing Machinery, New York (2018). https://doi.org/10.1145/3180445.3180447
15. Wei, R., Cai, L., Yu, A., Meng, D.: AGE: authentication graph embedding for detecting anomalous login activities (2020). https://doi.org/10.1007/978-3-030-41579-2_20
16. National Cyber Security Center. NCSC CAF guidance. https://www.ncsc.gov.uk/collection/caf/cyber-assessment-framework. Accessed 30 July 2021
17. IoT Security Foundation, IoT Security Compliance Framework, Release 2, December 2018. https://www.iotsecurityfoundation.org/wp-content/uploads/2018/12/IoTSF-IoT-Security-Compliance-Framework-Release-2.0-December-2018.pdf. Accessed 30 July 2021
18. Najib, W., Sulistyo, S., Widyawan: Survey on trust calculation methods in Internet of Things. Procedia Comput. Sci. **161**, 1300–1307 (2019). https://doi.org/10.1016/j.procs.2019.11.245
19. Khouzani, M.H.R., Liu, Z., Malacaria, P.: Scalable min-max multi-objective optimization over probabilistic attack graphs. Eur. J. Oper. Res. **278**(3), 894–903 (2019)
20. De, S.J., Le Metayer, D.: Privacy risk analysis to enable informed privacy settings. In: 2018 IEEE European Symposium on Security and Privacy Workshops (EuroS&PW), London, pp. 95–102 (2018)
21. Bar-Sinai, M., Sweeney, L., Crosas, M.: DataTags, data handling policy spaces and the tags language. In: 2016 IEEE Security and Privacy Workshops (SPW), San Jose, CA, pp. 1–8 (2016)
22. Métayer, D.: A formal privacy management framework. In: Degano, P., Guttman, J., Martinelli, F. (eds.) FAST 2008. LNCS, vol. 5491, pp. 162–176. Springer, Heidelberg (2009). https://doi.org/10.1007/978-3-642-01465-9_11
23. Pandit, H.J., Fatema, K., O'Sullivan, D., Lewis, D.: GDPRtEXT - GDPR as a linked data resource. In: Gangemi, A., et al. (eds.) ESWC 2018. LNCS, vol. 10843, pp. 481–495. Springer, Cham (2018). https://doi.org/10.1007/978-3-319-93417-4_31
24. August Device and Service Privacy Policy. https://august.com/pages/privacy-policy. Accessed 30 Mar 2021
25. General Data Protection Regulation (GDPR). https://gdpr-info.eu/. Accessed 31 July 2021

# Battery Depletion Attacks on NB-IoT Devices Using Interference

Vlad Ionescu(✉) and Utz Roedig

School of Computer Science and Information Technology, University College Cork, Cork, Ireland
{v.ionescu,u.roedig}@cs.ucc.ie

**Abstract.** Narrowband-Internet of Things (NB-IoT) is a relatively new Low PowerWide Area Network (LPWAN) technology used to implement large-scale IoT applications. The economic viability of most applications depends on a long battery life of deployed devices ($\tilde{1}0$ years). In this paper, we document two interference attacks on the NB-IoT communication link that lead to a battery depletion in devices. These attacks can be carried out without disruption of data delivery and are therefore hard to detect. We describe a Matlab based simulation environment that can be used to investigate interference on NB-IoT communication, and we then use this environment to study the two attacks. For example, we show that battery lifetime can be reduced from 17 years to as low as four months.

## 1 Introduction

NB-Io is a relatively new LPWAN technology developed by 3rd Generation Partnership Project (3GPP). NB-IoT aims to provide low-cost devices with long battery life and supports a high connection density. NB-IoT makes use of a subset of the Long-Term Evolution (LTE) standard, limiting the bandwidth to a single narrow-band of 200 kHz. As the technology uses the existing LTE infrastructure, deployment of devices is simplified as the existing base station infrastructure can be used. NB-IoT devices are increasingly used to implement Internet of Things (IoT) applications such as smart cities, industrial automation and smart grids. To be commercially viable, these applications require a very long device lifetime. Frequent battery changes in devices are not feasible as this would increase maintenance costs to a point where the application is not viable. Therefore, a device battery lifetime of many years (10 years in most commercial settings) is required.

The energy consumption of an IoT device is in most cases dominated by communication. By choosing a low communication duty cycle, it is possible to achieve the required ten year lifetime of a device. In this case, a duty cycle is chosen where a node wakes once a day to report sensed information via the LTE base station infrastructure to a back-end.


S. Katsikas et al. (Eds.): ESORICS 2021 Workshops, LNCS 13106, pp. 276–295, 2022.
https://doi.org/10.1007/978-3-030-95484-0_17

The communication link between the NB-IoT device and the base station is dynamically adjusted to the communication environment. This is done to balance communication reliability and energy consumption. For example, transmission power and the number of transmission repetitions are dynamically adjusted to compensate for link quality fluctuations. As the communication protocol allows for dynamic adjustments, it provides an angle of attack for an adversary. An attacker can interfere with the communication link such that (i) communication is still possible and (ii) the energy consumption of a device is maximised. An interferer can execute a *battery depletion attack*.

To the best of our knowledge, this work is the first study of energy depletion attacks via an interferer on NB-IoT devices. We present two different methods an attacker can employ to interfere with the communication, increasing device energy consumption. We use a customised Matlab simulation environment to investigate communication between NB-IoT devices and base-station. We show that such attacks can reduce device lifetime significantly. Thus, such attacks can be used to render an IoT deployment commercially infeasible. At the same time, such attacks are hard to detect as data communication from the NB-IoT device is not prevented, and the attacker is not continuously jamming as these activities are carefully timed.

The main contributions of our work are:

- *NB-IoT Battery Depletion Attacks:* We describe in detail two possible attacks on NB-IoT communication via interference that result in energy depletion.
- *NB-IoT Simulation:* We describe our extension to the Matlab simulation environment that can be used to evaluate NB-IoT communication and interference of an attacker with it.
- *NB-IoT Battery Depletion Attack Analysis:* We provide a thorough analysis of the impact of the NB-IoT battery depletion attacks. We show that a device lifetime reduction from 17 years to around four months is feasible.

In the next section, we describe related work. In Sect. 3 we give a brief overview of NB-IoT, describe the attacker (threat model), and we describe in detail the identified NB-IoT battery depletion attacks. Section 4 describes the evaluation scenario, metrics used for assessment and the simulation environment that was developed. In Sect. 5 we describe our obtained results and also discuss possible countermeasures. Section 6 concludes the paper.

## 2 Related Work

Battery depletion attacks on wireless devices is a well-known class of attack that has received a lot of research attention over recent years.

Energy depletion attacks, in general, aim at tricking a device into spending unnecessary effort on tasks that lead to energy depletion. For example, a device can be forced to spend additional computational effort [24] or prevented from entering into an idle or sleep state [22], also known as a sleep deprivation attack. Another common approach is to force a device to perform unnecessary communication as the additional transmissions and receptions require additional energy [7]. Such an attack is particularly effective on small embedded devices (IoT devices, sensor nodes) where the communication transceiver dominates energy consumption.

Forcing a device into unnecessary communication can be achieved in different ways. An attacker may target an individual device or the network as a whole. To attack an individual device, the attacker may send messages to the device which response, for example, to state that such message is incorrect (see Vasserman et al. [26], and Krejčú et al. [12] for examples). Of course, such an attack is only possible if the protocol allows for such a situation to occur. The attacker may also target the behaviour of the entire network. A popular approach here is to target the routing protocol (see Buttyán et al. [6], and Pu et al. [23] for examples). The attacker may be able to insert a node in the network which modifies routing behaviour such that messages have to travel unnecessary long paths or are frequently dropped, requiring retransmissions. Again here, the used protocols must enable such attack.

The approach investigated in this paper is to use interference as a form of attack leading to battery depletion. An attacker may use an interference signal such that a node is spending additional effort in communication. For example, a node may use increased transmission power or additional transmissions to compensate for the perceived communication channel degradation. If a node does not limit this adaptation, it can lead to significant battery drain. To the best of our knowledge, such interference-based attacks on NB-IoT nodes have not yet been explored.

Hossein et al. [21] review existing jamming attacks and anti-jamming approaches in Wireless Local Area Networks (WLAN) including but not limited to cellular networks, ZigBee networks, LoRa networks, Bluetooth networks, vehicular networks and others. The article presents an in-depth analysis of jamming and anti-jamming techniques, as well as an insight into the design of jamming-resilient wireless networks.

Chiara et al. [20] emphasise the vulnerability of IoT networks with battery-powered nodes against jamming. Moreover, the authors state that an attacker can reduce the lifetime of energy-constrained User Equipment (UE)s by disrupting packet delivery. By considering a scenario as a multistage game, the article determines optimal strategies for both sides and evaluates their impact on network performance. Furthermore, they highlight the compromise between battery lifetime and the reliability of communication and the impact a jamming device has on both.

Andres et al. [4] propose an NB-IoT energy consumption model and validate it in an experimental setup used to measure the energy consumption of UE connected to a base station emulator. The article analyses the latency and battery lifetime needed for the control plane procedure. The energy expenditure estimation resulted in a maximum relative error of 21% between the proposed model and the measurement setup. Furthermore, the authors conclude that the

NB-IoT lifespan target of ten years is feasible as long the traffic profile has a large assumed interarrival time or the radio resources' configuration does not demand an extensive number of repetitions.

## 3 NB-IoT Battery Depletion Attacks

### 3.1 NB-IoT

NB-IoT is a LPWAN technology introduced by 3GPP for data gathering designed for low-data-rate applications [8]. For example, common usage of the protocol might be found in smart metering or intelligent environment monitoring devices [2].

For communication purposes, NB-IoT can be deployed as standalone, in-band or guard-band as depicted in Fig. 1. For in-band and guard-band, the protocol occupies one Physical Resource Block (PRB) of 180 kHz for the downlink and uplink in the LTE spectrum. By "reframing" the GSM spectrum, the standalone deployment inhabits a 200 kHz bandwidth [13,17]. Furthermore, to support the massive deployment target of 1 million connected devices for every square kilometre, tones (frequency domain) with different time allocations are assigned to the User Equipment (UE). This allows the network to allocate one Resource Unit (RU) to multiple UE, contrary to LTE, where every UE is assigned one RU [27]. One tone can occupy 3.75 kHz or 15 kHz bandwidth for uplink using the Single-Carrier Frequency-Division Multiple Access scheme (SC-FDMA) scheme and 15 kHz bandwidth based on the Orthogonal Frequency Division Multiplexing (OFDM) scheme similar to LTE. While on 15 kHz spacing, either single-tone (8 ms) or multi-tone 12, 6 and 3 tones with a span of 1 ms, 2 ms or 4 ms can be used for various UEs, on the 3.75 kHz spacing, only single-tone allocation is supported to several UEs with the duration of 32 ms [3,5,17].

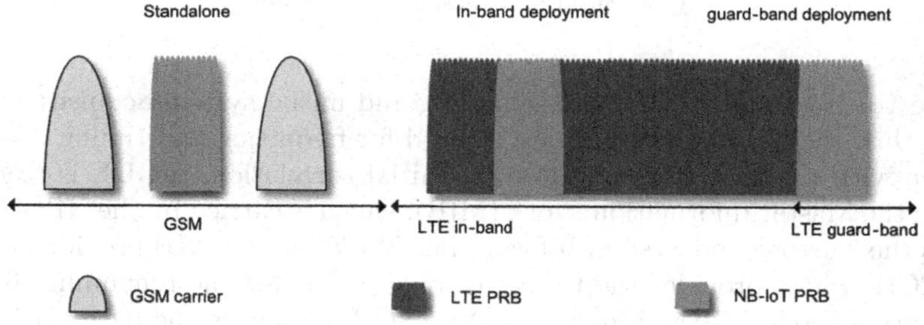


**Fig. 1.** NB-IoT deployment modes

The NB-IoT utilises the frame structure of LTE with 1024 hyper frames. One hyper frame contains 1024 frames, and each frame consists of 10 subframes with two slots of 0.5 ms. In the frequency domain, 12 subcarriers with seven OFDM symbols are mapped to every slot. Furthermore, when the 3.75 kHz spacing is used for the uplink, 48 subcarriers are allocated with a slot span of 2 ms.

Several channels and signals are used for both downlink and uplink to facilitate the communication between the base station and the UE.

**Downlink.** The following are used for the downlink communication, and their allocation is shown in Fig. 2.

- Narrowband Reference Signal (NRS).
- Narrowband Primary Synchronization Signal (NPSS).
- Narrowband Secondary Synchronization Signal (NSSS).
- Narrowband Physical Broadcast Channel (NPBCH).
- Narrowband Physical Downlink Shared Channel (NPDSCH).
- Narrowband Physical Downlink Control Channel (NPDCCH).

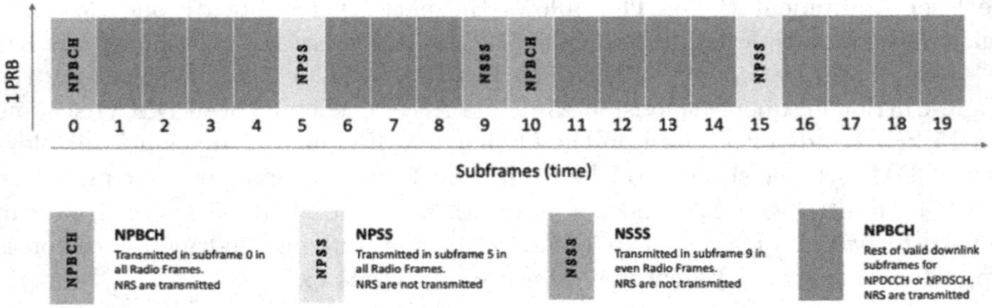


**Fig. 2.** Subframe channel assignments

The UE uses the NRS for cell searching and initial system acquisition. Following this, the NPSS and NSSS are utilised for frequency and timing synchronisation with the base station. After the initial correlation, the UE is ready to acquire the Master Information Block (MIB), which is carried by the NPBCH, as well as the Narrowband System Information Block 1 (SIB1-NB) provided by the NPDCCH, which provides the timing configurations for the remaining System Information Block (SIB)s. Finally, the NPDSCH is used by the base station for transmitting the data packets [13].

**Uplink.** For the uplink, the following channels and signals are used for communication

- Narrowband Physical Random Access Channel (NPRACH).
- Narrowband Physical Uplink Shared Channel (NPUSCH).
- Demodulation Reference Signal (DMRS).

The UE utilises the NPRACH to conduct the initial access to the network and request the transmission resources or reconnect in case of a link failure. NPUSCH is used to send the uplink data packets, while DMRS is used to estimate the channel accuracy [17].

One advantage of the NB-IoT protocol is its capability to enhance the coverage area for rural and deep indoor applications. Furthermore, by delivering an extra 20 dB compared to LTE, NB-IoT can operate at 164, NB-IoT can operate at 164 Maximum Coupling Loss (MCL) with up to 128 retransmission for uplink and 2048 for downlink, therefore making the protocol suitable for latency insensitive applications with up to ten seconds of transmission delay.

### 3.2 Threat Model

We assume two scenarios: *simple jammer* and *intelligent jammer.*

**Simple Jammer.** A simple jammer is a device that can output a continuous interference signal. The signal power can be adjusted, but the attacker is not able to analyse communication and adjust the jamming behaviour.

A malicious entity can use a simple jammer to force both the Evolved Node B (eNodeB) and NB-IoT devices to allocate more resources in order to communicate. To deploy such an attack, the entity will need to use an "all in one frequency jammer" that is able to jam all signals and be immune to frequency hopping [18,25]. Furthermore, the device needs to have configurable transmission power to degrade the signal's quality and not just block communication entirely. In order to perform the attack, a constant power supply is needed as a limited one would not be feasible for an energy depletion attack.

**Intelligent Jammer.** An intelligent jammer is outputting an interference signal at precise times. The device can follow the communication on the channel that it is attacking. Depending on observations, jamming times and signal power can be adjusted. However, they cannot decrypt observed communication; only unencrypted data and aspects such as slot occupancy and transmission times are available to the attacker.

The attacker will use an intelligent jammer that transmits noise in a burst-like pattern. It only uses energy when it needs to, thus functioning as a duty-cycled device. The intelligent jammer has some understanding of the upper-layer protocols. It can also understand some communication parameters by decoding the unencrypted data elements. The malicious device must be capable of eavesdropping on the downlink channel while reacting on the uplink channel and the other way around. Because of the nature of the NB-IoT protocol described in Sect. 3.1, data such as NRS, NPSS, NSSS, MIB, SIB1-NB, Narrowband System Information Block 2 (SIB2-NB), and others are sent unencrypted in order to perform synchronization, and authentication [13], thus making the end device vulnerable to energy depletion attacks. An intelligent jammer can use such exposure to gain more information about the communication and pressure the legitimate devices to increase their transmission power and the number of repetitions while remaining hidden.

### 3.3 Degradation of Quality of Signal (DQS) Attack

The LTE specification provides a set of data and parameters to estimate the channel between an eNodeB and a UE [2]. In order to properly evaluate the QoS in an NB-IoT network, we have to look at both the downlink radio channel as well as the uplink one. The downlink radio channel is estimated with the help of the Narrowband Reference Signal (NRS), while on the uplink side, the estimation is done using the Single-Carrier Frequency-Division Multiple Access scheme (SC-FDMA) within a resource grid that is configured to use either a 15 kHz or a 3.75 kHz.

**Downlink Radio Channel Quality of Signal (QoS) Estimation.** In the downlink channel, the NRS can be found in the last two OFDM symbols of each slots [16]. In Fig. 2, an adaptation from [11], a graphical representation depicts the subframes by index from zero to 19 within one PRB. It is worth noting that NPSS, NSSS and NPBCH have set channel assignments according to the NB-IoT standard and that the NRS can be transmitted in all subframes except NPSS and NSSS.

Furthermore, multiple parameters and their relationships have to be described in order to properly assess the impact of decreasing the in order to properly assess the by adding noise to the transmission.

- Reference Signal Received Power (RSRP), according to the 3GPP definition, is the linear average over the power in Watts of the resource elements that carry NRS [2]. Due to the fact that NB-IoT downlink is an OFDM transmission with 15 kHz carrier spacing, the RSRP will become the power of a single 15 kHz NRS.
- Received Signal Strength Indicator (RSSI) is the linear average of the total power received by a device in Watts only from the configured OFDM symbol and in the measurement bandwidth over N number of resource blocks, by the UE from a multitude of sources, including co-channel, adjacent channel interference, thermal noise and others. Because the downlink is deployed with a 15 kHz spacing and always uses 12 subcarriers, the evaluated bandwidth is equal to

$$15\,\text{kHz} * 12 = 180\,\text{kHz} \tag{1}$$

  or exactly one PRB. Moreover, depending on the cell load, the RSSI varies according to the allocated subcarriers [16].

- Reference Signal Received Quality (RSRQ) is defined as the ratio RSRP and RSSI, with the constraint that both the numerator and denominator shall be measured in the same set of resource blocks.

$$\text{RSRQ} = \frac{\text{RSSI}[W]}{\text{RSRP}[W]} \tag{2}$$

- The Signal-to-Interference and Noise Ratio (SINR) is the ratio between a received signal level and the Interference amount (PI) from other sources, along with the Effective Noise Floor ($P_{N,eff}$).

$$\text{SINR} = \frac{\text{RSRP}[W]}{P_{I,15\,\text{kHz}} + P_{N,eff,15\,\text{kHz}}} = \frac{\text{RSSI}[W]}{P_{I,180\,\text{kHz}} + P_{N,eff,180\,\text{kHz}}} \tag{3}$$

Matz et al. [16] validated the correlation between SINR and RSRQ via the subcarrier activity factor x as the ratio occupied by the Resource Element (RE) in a Resource Block (RB): x = RE/RB, thus proving the relation derived in [19].

$$\text{SINR} = \frac{12}{\frac{1}{\text{RSRQ}} - \text{RE}} = \frac{12}{\frac{1}{\text{RSRQ}} - 12 * x} \tag{4}$$

**Uplink Radio Channel QoS Estimation.** MCL is a parameter calculated by substrating the Receiver Sensitivity ($P_{RX,min}$) from the Power Level at the Antenna Connector ($P_{TX}$):

$$MCL = P_{TX} - P_{RX,min} \tag{5}$$

MCL is a key metric to estimate the radio coverage, and in the case of NB-IoT, it is used to set up the number of repetitions and the $P_{TX}$. Furthermore, in the case of uplink for up to two repetitions, the UE adjust the $P_{TX}$ based on multiple cell variables, including coupling loss. In case of more than two repetitions are needed, a maximum cell-specific $P_{TX}$ is used. The receiver sensitivity $P_{PRXmin}$ represents the smallest input energy level at the receiver antenna compared to a QoS threshold. To further understand the MCL complexity, the following notions have to be explained. NB-IoT has the capability to dynamically adjust the Modulation and Coding Scheme (MCS) depending on the radio conditions. The MCS is defined as how many useful bits can be carried per RE, resulting in the MCS being directly correlated with the radio link quality and error probability. In other words, MCS is periodically adjusted in order to keep the connection within a Block Error Rate (BLER) threshold, typically 10% for the NPUSCH) and NPDSCH NB-IoT channels [13]. NB-IoT can further extend its range by increasing the number of symbol repetitions NRep. Consequently, the BLER becomes dependent on the MCS and the Nrep used for any given Signal-to-Noise Power Ratio (SNR). The Minimum Signal-to-Noise Power Ratio ($SNR_{min}$) needed for the aforementioned BLER has to take into consideration firstly the thermal noise as defined below:

$$P_N = 10 * log(kTB/1\,\mathrm{mW}) \tag{6}$$

where k = Boltzmann constant, T = temperature, B = bandwidth. According [16] and [13] the $P_{N,eff}$ is defined as the Noise Figure (NF) of the receiver front-end in addition to the Thermal Noise ($P_N$). Taking the previous definitions into account the $P_{RX,min}$ can be defined as:

$$P_{RX,min} = P_N + NF + SNR_{min} = P_{N,eff} + SNR_{min}. \tag{7}$$

By understanding the full involvement of the MCL in the NB-IoT capability to adjust the number of repetitions and the power transmission, a malicious entity could exploit it by adding noise to the subframes carrying the NRS on the downlink channel and to the NPUSCH. By doing so, the attack will trick both the base station and the UE into higher coverage levels, increasing power consumption drastically. An example of such noise is the Additive White Gaussian Noise (AWGN). AWGN is a theoretical term for noise that can occur in many natural processes. For example, if we consider the is NPDSCH transmitted at $P_{TX} = 35$ dBm and a scenario at room temperature, T = 290 K, for a bandwidth of 180 kHz with a noise figure equal to 7 dB, the effective noise power would be calculated as:

$$P_{N,eff} = 10 * log(k * 290 * 180) + 7\,\mathrm{dB} = -104.4\,\mathrm{dB} \tag{8}$$

Furthermore by considering a $SNR_{min}$ at a medium coverage level at −14 dB, we could finally calculate the MCL as:

$$\mathrm{MCL} = P_{TX} - PRX_{min} \approx 154\,\mathrm{dB} \tag{9}$$

In order to maximise the efficiency of such an attack, an intelligent jamming device can be used. Roger et al. [10] describe a low-power intelligent jamming device that is capable of targeting specific control channels. Another effect of such intrusion would force the carrier to allocate more resources in the form of subcarriers, thus reducing the bandwidth. Because this type of attack does not aim to interrupt the communication immediately, it is harder to detect than full jamming. Additionally, the MCL increase could emerge naturally from the ever-changing environmental conditions, reducing suspicion.

To summarise, in order to effectively perform a Degradation of Quality of Signal (DQS) attack, the malicious device has to estimate the MCL class of the UE and adapt its transmission power to force base station and UE to allocate more resources in terms of the number of repetitions and the energy consumption.

### 3.4 Random Access Procedure (RAP) Attack

In NB-IoT, the RAP is done with the help of the Narrowband Physical Random Access Channel, also known as NPRACH.

Comparing to the LTE Physical Random Access Control Channel (PRACH), the NPRACH has been completely redesigned [14]. In contrast to the LTE

PRACH, which occupies a bandwidth bigger than the entire NB-IoT carrier up to 1.05 MHz, NPRACH is based on a Single-Tone configuration with frequency hopping and uses 3.75 kHz subcarrier spacing. Furthermore, it supports different cell sizes by providing two cyclic prefix lengths, thus utilising from 45 kHz to 180 kHz depending on the number of subcarriers [15]. In order to enhance the coverage, the transmissions can be repeated up to 128 times.

For the random access procedure to start, the UE needs to receive the SIB2-NB. In Fig. 3 a complete procedure is illustrated, including the steps needed before and after.

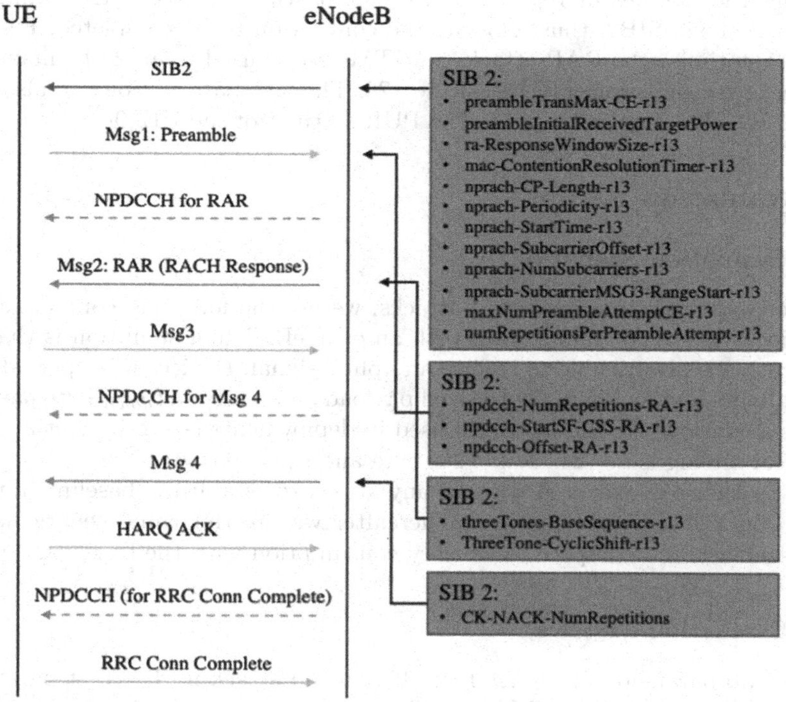


**Fig. 3.** Random access procedure and the related messages.

Because of the coverage enhancement feature, which allows transmissions to be repeated up to 128 times, the random access procedure can be vulnerable to energy depletion attacks. A smart jamming device, similar to the one described in Sect. 3.3 can listen for the preamble message transmitted by the UE and jam the Random Access Response onto the NPDCCH. Another way of taking advantage of the RAP is to deploy a Man in The Middle Attack by using a fake base station and alter the SIB2-NB in order to maximise the energy consumption used by the UE. It is worth mentioning that with 3GPP release 16 [1] the UE can have preconfigured resources, where up to two users can send NPUSCH simultaneously in the specific case when the latency is greater or equal to 64 ms for 12-tone allocation. In case the UE is making use of the Preconfigured Uplink Resources (PUR), it can bypass both the Random Access Preamble Transmission (Msg1) and the Random Access Response (Msg2), thus reducing the power consumption and also reducing the efficiency of the aforementioned attacks [9].

In summary, a malicious entity can deploy a Random Access Procedure (RAP) attack by listening on the downlink channel and jam the Msg1 while counting the number of repetitions so that it will not exceed the configured number sent via SIB2, thus allowing the connection to be completed. Furthermore, to optimise the RAP attack, a MITM can be used to alter the maximum number of transmissions of Msg1 up to 128. The fake base station can also alter the cell ID, therefore invalidating the PUR settings of the UE [9].

## 4 Evaluation Setup

### 4.1 Evaluation Scenario

In order to analyse the impact of attacks, we use the following communication scenario: UEs are communicating with an eNodeB. The assumption is that the base station is always able to receive an uplink signal. Devices wake periodically every $t$ hours and send a $b_{up}$ byte-sized payload and receive a $b_{down}$ byte payload. This is a common NB-IoT scenario used in deployments (see Liberg et al. [13]). A typical setting is $t = 2\,\text{h}$, $b_{up} = 200\,\text{byte}$ and $b_{up} = 60\,\text{byte}$.

The scenario is executed without any attack to establish a baseline in terms of the nodes energy consumption. Thereafter we run the same scenario with a present attack and compare the energy consumption with the baseline.

### 4.2 Evaluation Metrics

We use two parameters to judge how effective an attack is. The first parameter is Energy Depletion Rate (EDR) which describes how much an attack depletes a device battery compared to the baseline scenario without attack. The second parameter is Jammer Duty Cycle (JDC) which captures the percentage of time that the jamming device has to be active.

**Energy Depletion Rate (EDR).** The EDR is defined as:

$$EDR = 1 - \frac{E_{baseline}}{E_{attack}} \tag{10}$$

Here $E_{baseline}$ is the energy consumed by the UE during normal operation while $E_{attack}$ is the energy consumption under a specific attack scenario. EDR produces a value between 0 and 1; the attack is not effective for values close to 0, while values close to 1 indicate an effective attack. We use this metric also separately for transmission and reception of the UE in order to see if an attack has more impact on upstream or downstream channels.

**Jammer Duty Cycle (JDC).** The JDC is defined as:

$$JDC = \frac{T_{active}}{T_{total}} \tag{11}$$

Here $T_{active}$ is the time the jamming device is transmitting a jamming signal while $T_{total}$ is the experiment duration. JDC is a measure for the effort the attacker has to undertake to achieve their goal. It also describes how active an attacker is and how easy it might be spotted.

### 4.3 Simulation Environment

In order to simulate the battery consumption of NB-IoT devices, we used Matlab together with the LTE-Toolbox as our simulation environment. It is worth mentioning that the LTE-Toolbox implementation of the NB-IoT protocol is not a full end-to-end reactive simulation, thus focusing more on generating modulating, demodulating coding and decoding the appropriate waveform. For this reason, some of the parameters in our environment have to be set prior to executing the simulator (e.g. SIB2-NB maxPreambleTrans). In Fig. 4 we can see a simulated waveform with the allocated subframes over the number of subcarriers.

For our scenario, we have chosen the three coupling loss specifications of NB-IoT as outlined by Liberg et al. [13]. These settings were used as the basis for defining the performance requirements and power consumption of the UE. By analysing the latest NB-IoT devices technical specifications, including the Sara N3-NB-IoT from U-Blox, 212 LTE IoT Modem from Qualcomm and averaging their power consumption, the following values were used: maximum $TX_{max}$ = 330 mA, and maximum $RX_{max}$ = 30 mA, *idle* = 3 mA and *deepsleep* = 0.003 mA. Furthermore, to simulate the environment as close to real-life as possible, we have chosen a 1000 mAh lithium polymer battery (LiPo) perfect battery at a nominal 3.7 V. The reason for choosing this battery is that it is one of the most popular, standard type LiPo batteries available on the market. However, the actual battery will likely be less reliable as we do not model the battery degradation and external factors such as temperature.

### 4.4 Jammer

We simulate 4 different jamming attacks:

- The simple jammer for decreasing the quality of the signal: simple Degradation of Quality of Signal Attack (sDQS)

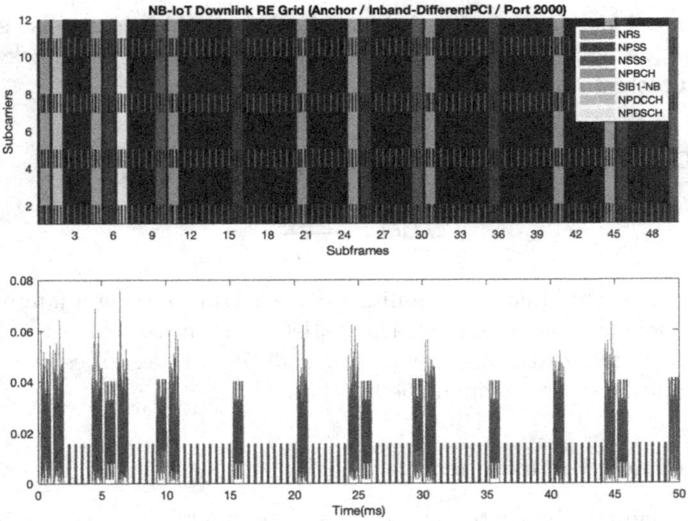


**Fig. 4.** NB-IoT waveform generated by the Matlab simulation environment. The upper representation displays the channels and signal assign to each subframe. The lower figure display the allocation of the same signals and channels in a time-frequency domain.

- The intelligent jammer for decreasing the quality of the signal: intelligent Degradation of Quality of Signal Attack (iDQS)
- The intelligent jammer targeting the random access procedure: Random Access Procedure (RAP)
- The intelligent jammer for decreasing the quality of the signal and targeting the random access procedure: (iDQS + RAP)

Both the sDQS and the iDQS attack were modelled in Matlab by adapting our base environment to maximise the resources needed to complete the communication. More specifically, setting the number of repetitions for both the downlink and uplink in accordance to the 164 MCL as described in Sect. 3.1 and the transmission power as specified in Sect. 4.3. Thus, on the one hand, the sDQS uses a simple AWGN function that adds noise to the legitimate signal depending on the transmission power. On the other hand, the iDQS comprises multiple steps, including but not limited to synchronisation, demodulation, decoding, MIB parsing, and BLER calculation and lastly, adding the AWGN to the signal. Furthermore, we assumed that the intelligent jammer has learned the communication pattern of the UE and that it is able to time the attack.

For the RAP vulnerability described in Sect. 3.4, we use our baseline environment as a starting point and then model only the access procedure. More specifically, on the downlink channel, the jammer has to receive and correlate the NPSS and NSSS in order to be able to receive the MIB, which in turn is used for acquiring the other SIBs, especially SIB1-NB and SIB2-NB. After decoding and retrieving the information from SIB2-NB, the malicious device will start jamming on the uplink channel the Random Access Preamble Transmission (Msg1) in order to maximise the number of retransmissions according to the information obtained before. In Matlab, we simulated this by increasing the number of repetitions in the simulated RAP to 120 from the maximum of 128 and calculate the depletion rate and the duty cycle for sending the Msg1 but also for receiving the System Information Block 2 (SIB2).

# 5 Evaluation Results

## 5.1 Baseline

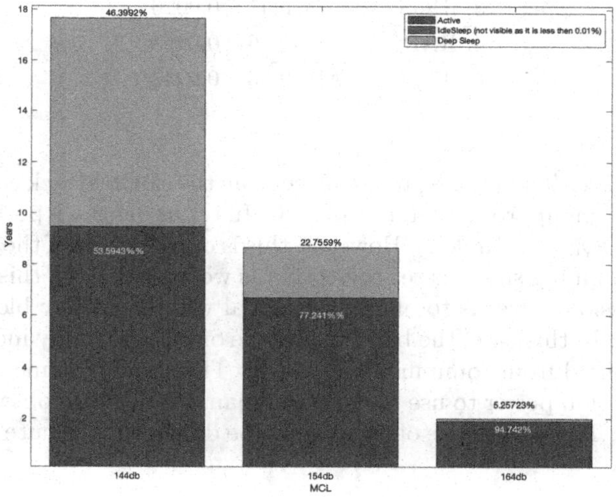


**Fig. 5.** Achievable battery lifetime of an NB-IoT node in our baseline scenario using communication parameter settings of $t = 2\,\text{h}$, $b_{up} = 200\,\text{byte}$ and $b_{up} = 60\,\text{byte}$ under different MCL scenarios. No jamming attack is present (Baseline Scenario).

The energy efficiency of NB-IoT devices varies a lot depending on the selected MCL. For our scenario presented in Sect. 4, Fig. 5 depicts the years of battery life achieved and the percentage of energy spent in each communication state (Active (TX/RX), IdleSleep and DeepSleep). For this experiment the communication parameters in our scenario are set to $t = 2\,\text{h}$, $b_{up} = 200\,\text{byte}$ and $b_{up} = 60\,\text{byte}$.

The simulation results for our baseline environment are in line with other results reported in literature [13]. We observe that only the MCL = 144 db setting achieves the 3GPP standard requirements in terms of lifetime [2]. It is worth noting that the reporting interval of $t = 2\,\text{h}$ might be considered aggressive, but many real-life applications are requiring such a schedule.

### 5.2 Jamming

Table 1 summarises the results of our evaluation assessing EDR and JDC for the different attack types considered (sDQS, iDQS, RAP and iDQS + RAP). Communication parameter settings of $t = 2\,\text{h}$, $b_{up} = 200\,\text{byte}$ and $b_{down} = 200\,\text{byte}$ are used here.

**Table 1.** EDR and JDC for the different attack types considered (sDQS, iDQS, RAP and iDQS + RAP).

| Type | EDR | JDC |
|---|---|---|
| 1. Baseline | 0 | 0.0003 |
| 2. sDQS | 0.41 | 1 |
| 3. iDQS | 0.41 | 0.0026 |
| 4. RAP | 0.76 | 0.0223 |
| 5. iDQS + RAP | 0.85 | 0.0246 |

**Simple Jammer.** The simple jammer executing the sDQS attack is, as expected, the most inefficient approach in terms of JDC. In terms of attack performance it is equivalent to iDQS (see Table 1). However, this is only the case if the transmission power of the jamming signal is set correctly (as we have done in this simulation). If the transmission power is too high, the signal will be entirely blocked instead of degrading it. In this case, the battery lifetime of a UE actually increases as the device is prevented from communicating at all. The simple jammer cannot learn which transmission power to use to effectively jam as it cannot observe the effect of its jamming. Thus, this type of attack may be difficult to execute in practice.

**Intelligent Jammer.** The effectiveness of the intelligent jammer is dependant on the type of attack considered (iDQS, RAP and iDQS + RAP). As expected, the efficiency in terms of JDC is much greater than in the case of a simple jammer (see Table 1). The RAP attack is more efficient from the attackers perspective than iDQS (achieving an EDR of 0.76 compared to an EDR of 0.41). However, the RAP attack is significantly more energy costly (JDC of 0.0223 compared to a JDC of 0.0026). The combination of both attack types requires a JDC combining the effort for both attacks, which leads to the highest attack success with an EDR of 0.85. Next, we evaluate the effectiveness of the intelligent jammer in more detail, considering variable payload sizes for up and downlink ($b_{up}$ and $b_{up}$). Figure 6 shows the resulting EDR separately for uplink and downlink (TX/RX). Figure 7 shows the combined EDR together with the JDC.

In Fig. 6, we can see the different types of depletion rates based on the chosen attack over the payload size for sending and receiving. The chart is based on multiple simulations with different payload sizes, ranging from 0 to 300 bytes (for $b_{up}$ and $b_{up}$). The EDR varies from zero to one, where zero represents the baseline with no interference present while 1 expresses an attack with a 100% impact on the battery. On the left side, coloured in blue, we can see the receiving depletion rate for the iDQS, RAP and iDQS+RAP attacks, while at the same time, on the right side, coloured in orange, we show the sending depletion rate. While the iDQS has the smallest impact compared to other attacks, we can observe that its impact is nonlinear, and it increases with payload size. Contrary to iDQS, the RAP attack has a constant impact as it targets only the random access procedure. However, upon further analysing, we can see that the RAP+iDQS attack depletes the most energy for sending and receiving data. As expected, the energy depletion rates have less impact on the receiving side, ranging from zero to approximately 0.55 compared to the sending side, which varies from zero to roughly 0.9. This difference is caused mainly by the fact that the UE spends more energy while transmitting data than receiving.

In Fig. 7, we see the combined EDR coloured in blue together with JDC coloured in orange. The iDQS attack though not the most effective in terms of EDR has the most significant difference between the JDC and EDR (A high impact is achieved for little effort). The latter increases significantly over the payload size, thus expanding the gap even further. Identically to the chart presented in Fig. 6, the RAP attack has a linear impact on both JDC and EDR, as the payload size does not influence the random access procedures. On the other hand, we can observe that when we combine iDQS+RAP in the same attack, the impact converse compared with only iDQS. The EDR in this case increases slightly with the payload size while the JDC has a steeper ascending trajectory.

### 5.3 Evaluation Discussions

The simple jammer is easy to construct. However, it requires a constant battery supply, and it will be easy to spot as it is continuously active. Furthermore, as this jammer cannot observe the communication channel, it cannot adjust the power of the interference signal. Thus, it might be challenging to execute this attack efficiently in practice, and by interfering too much, the entire communication may be blocked. In this case, the intended battery depletion attack results in a communication denial of service attack.

The intelligent jammer is much more challenging to construct. The communication must be observed, and jamming is executed at specific times. Thus, it is very difficult to spot the attacker as the attacker is only active in very brief time periods. Furthermore, as activity is only briefly necessary, it is possible to deploy the jammer as a battery-powered device. This further enables the attacker to hide their malicious activity. For example, when executing the iDQS attack, the most efficient attack in terms of JDC using $t = 2\,\mathrm{h}$, $b_{up} = 200\,\mathrm{byte}$ and $b_{down} = 200\,\mathrm{byte}$ requires a = JDC of only 0.0026. If the jammer uses the same construction as the NB-IoT device (In terms of transceiver power consumption and battery), a jammer lifetime of two years is possible.

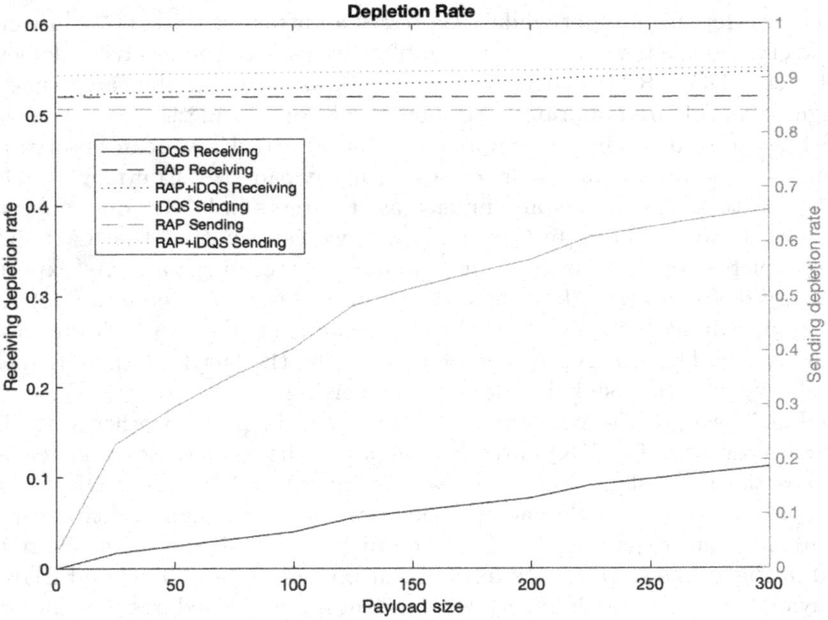


**Fig. 6.** EDR, separately shown for reception and transmission channel, for the different attack types considered (iDQS, RAP and iDQS + RAP). Communication parameter settings are $t = 2\,\text{h}$, $0 < b_{up} = 300\,\text{byte}$ and $0 < b_{down} < 300\,\text{byte}$.

The intelligent jammer can significantly reduce battery life. The baseline scenario shown in Fig. 5 supporting over 17 years of operation is only able to support around two years under an iDQS attack, six months under an RAP attack and as little as four months when both attacks are combined.

### 5.4 Countermeasure

One effective countermeasure that would prevent the intelligent jammer from learning the communication schedule of an NB-IoT device is to become active to transmit and receive data at random times rather than a fixed schedule (i.e. every two hours). This would force the intelligent jammer to consume more resources in synchronising with the communication. One such example where the UE is required to transmit every two hours would be to keep an average of 12 transmissions per day but randomly select the time slots within an interval.

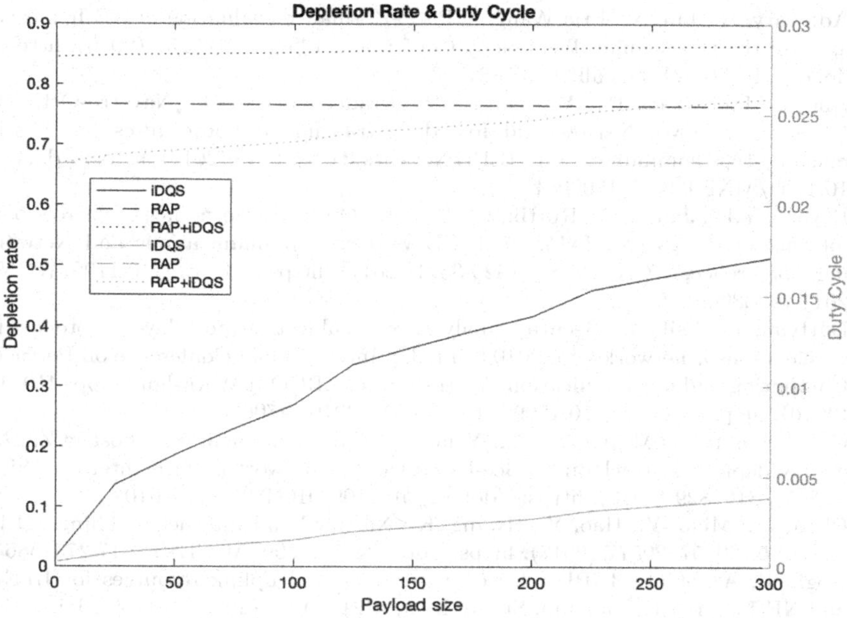


**Fig. 7.** EDR and JDC for the different attack types considered (iDQS, RAP and iDQS + RAP). Communication parameter settings are $t = 2\,\mathrm{h}$, $0 < b_{up} = 300\,\mathrm{byte}$ and $0 < b_{down} < 300\,\mathrm{byte}$.

# 6 Conclusion

We have shown by simulating the NB-IoT communication that different types of jamming attacks can significantly impact the lifespan of the UE with over 90% energy depletion, resulting in a decrease of device lifetime from over 17 years to around four months. Clearly, a jamming device using the attacks described in this work can be used to render any NB-IoT deployment commercially infeasible. Therefore, more consideration to jamming attacks should be given before rolling out NB-IoT installations on a large scale. Our next steps are to improve the simulation environment to perform a more comprehensive analysis and devise appropriate countermeasures as briefly outlined in the previous section.

**Acknowledgement.** This publication has emanated from research conducted with the financial support of Science Foundation Ireland under Grant number 18/CRT/6222.

# References

1. 3GPP: 3GPP release 16. http://www.3gpp.org/release-16
2. 3GPP: Evolved universal terrestrial radio access (E-UTRA); physical layer; measurements. https://portal.3gpp.org/desktopmodules/Specifications/SpecificationDetails.aspx?specificationId=2428

3. Adhikary, A., Lin, X., Eric Wang, Y.P.: Performance evaluation of NB-IoT coverage. In: IEEE Vehicular Technology Conference. ISSN 1550-2252 (2016). https://doi.org/10.1109/VTCFall.2016.7881160
4. Andres-Maldonado, P., Ameigeiras, P., Prados-Garzon, J., Navarro-Ortiz, J., Lopez-Soler, J.M.: Narrowband IoT data transmission procedures for massive machine-type communications. IEEE Network **31**(6), 8–15 (2017). https://doi.org/10.1109/MNET.2017.1700081
5. Beyene, Y.D., Jantti, R., Ruttik, K., Iraji, S.: On the performance of narrow-band internet of things (NB-IoT). In: IEEE Wireless Communications and Networking Conference, WCNC. ISSN 1525-3511 (2017). https://doi.org/10.1109/WCNC.2017.7925809
6. Buttyán, L., Csik, L.: Security analysis of reliable transport layer protocols for wireless sensor networks. In: 2010 8th IEEE International Conference on Pervasive Computing and Communications Workshops (PERCOM Workshops), pp. 419–424 (2010). https://doi.org/10.1109/PERCOMW.2010.5470633
7. Cao, X., Shila, D.M., Cheng, Y., Yang, Z., Zhou, Y., Chen, J.: Ghost-in-ZigBee: energy depletion attack on ZigBee-based wireless networks. IEEE Internet Things J. **3**(5), 816–829 (2016). https://doi.org/10.1109/JIOT.2016.2516102
8. Chen, M., Miao, Y., Hao, Y., Hwang, K.: Narrow band Internet of Things. IEEE Access **5**, 20557–20577 (2017). https://doi.org/10.1109/ACCESS.2017.2751586
9. Hoglund, A., et al.: 3GPP release-16 preconfigured uplink resources for LTE-M and NB-IoT. IEEE Commun. Stand. Mag. **4**(2), 50–56 (2020). https://doi.org/10.1109/MCOMSTD.001.2000003
10. Jover, R.P., Lackey, J., Raghavan, A.: Enhancing the security of LTE networks against jamming attacks. EURASIP J. Inf. Secur. **2014**(1), 7 (2014). https://doi.org/10.1186/1687-417X-2014-7
11. Keysight: Downlink channel parameters (NB-IoT). http://rfmw.em.keysight.com/wireless/helpfiles/89600B/WebHelp/Subsystems/nbiot/Content/nbiot_dlcontrolchannelproperties.htm
12. Krejčí, R., Hujňák, O., Švepeš, M.: Security survey of the IoT wireless protocols. In: 2017 25th Telecommunication Forum (TELFOR). pp. 1–4 (2017). https://doi.org/10.1109/TELFOR.2017.8249286
13. Liberg, O., Sundberg, M., Wang, Y.P.E., Bergman, J., Sachs, J., Wikström, G.: Cellular Internet of Things: From Massive Deployments to Critical 5G Applications. Academic Press, Cambridge (2020)
14. Lin, X., Adhikary, A., Eric Wang, Y.P.: Random access preamble design and detection for 3GPP narrowband IoT systems. IEEE Wirel. Commun. Lett. **5**(6), 640–643 (2016). https://doi.org/10.1109/LWC.2016.2609914, http://ieeexplore.ieee.org/document/7569029/
15. Martiradonna, S., Piro, G., Boggia, G.: On the evaluation of the NB-IoT random access procedure in monitoring infrastructures. Sensors **19**(14), 3237 (2019). https://doi.org/10.3390/s19143237, https://www.mdpi.com/1424-8220/19/14/3237
16. Matz, A.P., Fernandez-Prieto, J.A., Cañada-Bago, J., Birkel, U.: A systematic analysis of narrowband IoT quality of service. Sensors **20**(6), 1636 (2020). https://doi.org/10.3390/s20061636, https://www.mdpi.com/1424-8220/20/6/1636
17. Mwakwata, C.B., Malik, H., Alam, M.M., Moullec, Y.L., Parand, S., Mumtaz, S.: Narrowband Internet of Things (NB-IoT): from physical (PHY) and media access control (MAC) layers perspectives. Sensors **19**(11), 2613 (2019). https://doi.org/10.3390/s19112613

18. Navda, V., Bohra, A., Ganguly, S., Rubenstein, D.: Using channel hopping to increase 802.11 resilience to jamming attacks, pp. 2526–2530 (2007). https://doi.org/10.1109/INFCOM.2007.314
19. Nokia: Nokia siemens network. RF measurements quantities and optimization. https://www.academia.edu/8902974/Soc_Classification_level_1_Nokia_Siemens_Networks_Presentation_Author_Date_RF_measurements_quantities_and_optimization_Soc_Classification_level_2_Nokia_Siemens_Networks_Presentation_Author_Date_Content?auto=download
20. Pielli, C., Chiariotti, F., Laurenti, N., Zanella, A., Zorzi, M.: A game-theoretic analysis of energy-depleting jamming attacks. In: 2017 International Conference on Computing, Networking and Communications (ICNC), pp. 100–104 (2017). https://doi.org/10.1109/ICCNC.2017.7876109
21. Pirayesh, H., Zeng, H.: Jamming attacks and anti-jamming strategies in wireless networks: A comprehensive survey (2021)
22. Pirretti, M., Zhu, S., Vijaykrishnan, N., McDaniel, P., Kandemir, M., Brooks, R.: The sleep deprivation attack in sensor networks: analysis and methods of defense. Int. J. Distrib. Sens. Networks **2**(3), 267–287 (2006)
23. Pu, C.: Energy depletion attack against routing protocol in the Internet of Things. In: 2019 16th IEEE Annual Consumer Communications Networking Conference (CCNC), pp. 1–4 (2019). https://doi.org/10.1109/CCNC.2019.8651771
24. Shakhov, V.: On a new type of attack in wireless sensor networks: depletion of battery. In: 2016 11th International Forum on Strategic Technology (IFOST), pp. 491–494 (2016). https://doi.org/10.1109/IFOST.2016.7884162
25. Torrieri, D.: Frequency hopping with multiple frequency-shift keying and hard decisions. IEEE Trans. Commun. **32**, 574–582 (1984). https://doi.org/10.1109/TCOM.1984.1096105
26. Vasserman, E.Y., Hopper, N.: Vampire attacks: draining life from wireless ad hoc sensor networks. IEEE Trans. Mob. Comput. **12**(2), 318–332 (2013). https://doi.org/10.1109/TMC.2011.274
27. Xu, J., Yao, J., Wang, L., Ming, Z., Wu, K., Chen, L.: Narrowband internet of things: evolutions, technologies, and open issues. IEEE Internet Things J. **5**(3), 1449–1462 (2018). https://doi.org/10.1109/JIOT.2017.2783374

# Security- and Privacy-Aware IoT Application Placement and User Assignment

Zoltán Ádám Mann(✉)

University of Amsterdam, Amsterdam, The Netherlands

**Abstract.** Applications for the Internet of Things (IoT) may use, beyond the IoT devices themselves, also edge and cloud resources. Thus, the modules of an application can be placed on a variety of nodes with different capabilities in terms of security, trustworthiness, and capacity. Application modules may exist in multiple instances. This makes it possible to assign users to the most appropriate module instances, taking into account requirements on security, privacy, and latency. There is a non-trivial interplay between application placement decisions and user assignment decisions. For example, if a certain user is assigned to a module, then that module may not be allowed to be placed on nodes not trusted by the user. However, most existing research neglects this interplay and its implications on security and privacy. In this paper, we address the joint problem of application placement and user assignment. Beside capacity and latency constraints, we consider several types of security and privacy constraints: (i) module-level location constraints, (ii) user-level location constraints, (iii) co-location constraints, and (iv) $k$-anonymity constraints. We formalize the problem and develop an algorithm to solve it using quadratically constrained mixed integer programming. We demonstrate the applicability of the proposed approach by applying it to an IoT system in the smart home domain. Controlled experiments on problem instances of increasing size show that the algorithm can solve even large problem instances in acceptable time.

**Keywords:** Internet of Things · IoT · Fog computing · Edge computing · Application placement · Security · Privacy

## 1 Introduction

Modern computing infrastructures offer a continuum of computational resources, from cloud data centers through fog and edge nodes to end devices in the Internet of Things [4]. Network connections among the different compute nodes make it possible to place the modules of an application on different nodes. Taking into account the different capacity of the nodes and the network latency between nodes, optimal decisions on application placement can be made [5]. However, it is also important to take into account the heterogeneity of the nodes in terms of


S. Katsikas et al. (Eds.): ESORICS 2021 Workshops, LNCS 13106, pp. 296–316, 2022.
https://doi.org/10.1007/978-3-030-95484-0_18

security and privacy protection: for example, cloud data centers may offer better security than fog nodes, whereas processing data from end devices in nearby fog nodes may be more advantageous from a privacy point of view than offloading to the cloud [2,3,22].

To optimally serve users, a distributed application may contain multiple instances of the same module. This is beneficial for example for a geographically dispersed user base: the different instances of a module can be placed in such a way that all users can access a nearby instance with low latency. Beside the latency implication, the assignment of users to module instances is also important from a data protection point of view. For example, a module may have to have at least $k$ users assigned to guarantee $k$-anonymity [15,24].

Decisions on application placement (i.e., which application module to place on which infrastructure node) and decisions on user assignment (i.e., which user to assign to which module instance) may mutually impact each other. For example, for data protection reasons it may not be allowed to process the data of certain users in certain locations. Hence, if such a user is assigned to a module, then that module is not allowed to be placed on nodes that are in the forbidden locations. Moreover, if many users are assigned to a module, this may lead to an increase in the computational needs of the module, thus requiring a node with high computational capacity.

Despite this interplay between application placement and user assignment, most existing work in this domain targets either application placement [6] or user assignment [10], but not both. Furthermore, most related work either completely ignores security and privacy requirements, or handle them in a rudimentary way.

To the best of our knowledge, this is the first paper to address the joint problem of application placement and user assignment with a focus on security and privacy requirements. Beside capacity and latency constraints, we investigate four types of constraints that result from security and privacy requirements:

- Module-level location constraints, which prohibit the placement of certain critical application modules on certain insecure infrastructure nodes
- User-level location constraints, which prohibit the placement of modules processing the data of certain users on infrastructure nodes not trusted by those users
- Co-location constraints, which prohibit the placement of certain pairs of application modules on the same infrastructure node (e.g., because such co-location could lead to side-channel attacks)
- $k$-anonymity constraints, which ensure that the data pertaining to at least $k$ users is processed together

We formalize the resulting problem, which combines application placement and user assignment, also taking into account the mentioned types of security and privacy constraints. We devise a quadratically constrained mixed integer formulation, which can be solved by an appropriate solver. The resulting algorithm is guaranteed to always find a placement of the application modules and an assignment of the users that satisfy all constraints, whenever this is possible. The practical applicability of the proposed approach is shown by applying it to

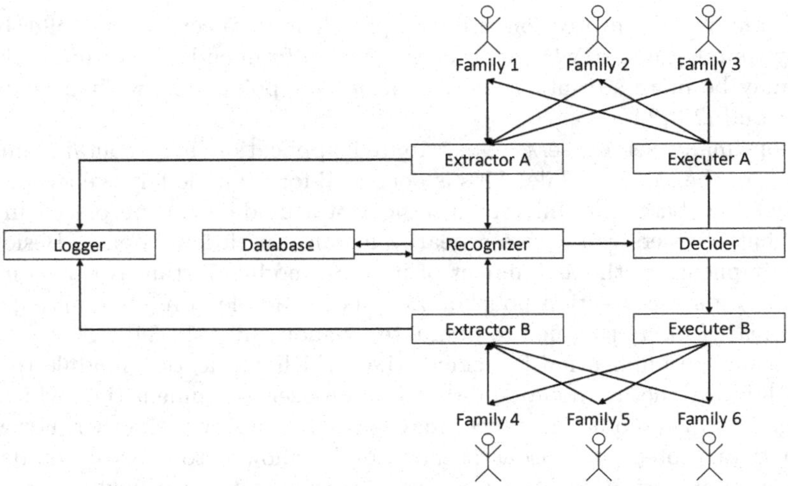


(a) Software application

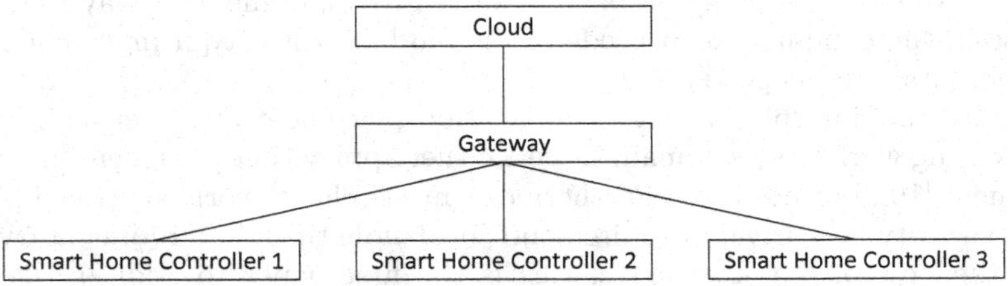


(b) Infrastructure

**Fig. 1.** The Smart Bell example

a fog computing case study from the smart home domain. Moreover, we perform controlled experiments on problem instances of increasing size to assess the scalability of the approach. The results show that the algorithm can solve even quite large problem instances in acceptable time on a commodity computer.

## 2 A Motivating Example

We consider an example IoT system from the smart home domain, based on the Smart Bell system presented in [28]. The aim of Smart Bell is to recognize visitors of a set of smart homes and react intelligently. For this purpose, cameras capture images of visitors. The captured images are compared to images stored in a database. This way, the system can recognize inhabitants, their friends, neighbors, and neighbors' friends. On this basis, the system can automatically open the door, notify the inhabitants of the home, or activate an alarm.

The Smart Bell system serves a block of smart homes that are connected via a network. The Smart Bell software application is shown in Fig. 1(a). The rectangles in the figure are the modules of the application, the arrows represent data flows. Extractor modules are used to extract faces from pictures taken by the cameras. The Recognizer compares the extracted face with the faces in the Database in order to recognize known faces. Based on the result of the Recognizer, the Decider decides how to react, and the reaction is carried out by the Executer. The Logger logs the visits in an anonymized form.

The stick figures represent users together with their end devices. In our case, a family, together with the smart end devices in their home (camera, door control, alarm) is represented by a stick figure, and is referred to as a user in the following.

To serve several users, some modules may exist in multiple instances. In the example of Fig. 1(a), there are two instances of the Extractor and Executer modules. Thus, users (in this case, the families whose homes are to be served) can be assigned to one of two alternative *data processing paths*:

1. User → Extractor **A** → Recognizer → Database → Recognizer → Decider → Executer **A** → User
2. User → Extractor **B** → Recognizer → Database → Recognizer → Decider → Executer **B** → User

In the shown example, Families 1–3 are assigned to the first, and Families 4–6 to the second data processing path. However, this assignment is not predefined; also other assignments would be possible.

The infrastructure available for the Smart Bell system is shown in Fig. 1(b), consisting of nodes and links. Different nodes may have different computational capacity: the capacity of the Smart Home Controllers is very limited, while the Gateway offers higher capacity, and the capacity of the Cloud is practically unlimited. On the other hand, the link between the Cloud and the Gateway is characterized by a much higher latency than the links between the Gateway and the Smart Home Controllers. Each module of the application has to be placed onto one of the infrastructure nodes. It has to be ensured for each infrastructure node that its computational capacity is not exceeded by the total computational load of the modules that the node should host.

An application processing private or otherwise sensitive data may have to satisfy different types of security and privacy requirements. In our case, for reasons of privacy protection, the Database is not allowed to be placed in the Cloud (module-level location constraint), since the Database contains sensitive personal information and placing it in the Cloud would potentially enable unauthorized parties to gain access to that sensitive information. Smart Home Controller 1 is mounted in the home of Family 1, and Family 2 does not trust Family 1, so that modules processing data of Family 2 must not be placed on Smart Home Controller 1 (user-level location constraint). Executer A and B must not be placed on the same node, so that at least one of them works even in the case of the failure of a node and can provide backup for the other instance (co-location constraint). Both Extractor A and B must be assigned at least three users each so that the required level of anonymity can be guaranteed ($k$-anonymity constraint).

## 3 Problem Formulation

In this section, we formalize the combined problem of application placement and user assignment, also taking into account security and privacy constraints. For this purpose, we describe the inputs of the problem, the output that needs to be computed, and the constraints that the output must fulfill. The used notation is summarized in Table 1.

### 3.1 Inputs

The inputs to the addressed problem comprise the description of the infrastructure, of the applications to deploy, and of the users to serve, as well as further information needed for formulating the security and privacy requirements.

**Infrastructure.** The set of infrastructure nodes (servers, data centers etc.) is denoted by $N$. Each node $n \in N$ is characterized by its computational capacity $C_n \in \mathbb{R}_{\geq 0}$. For each pair of nodes $n_1, n_2 \in N$, the network connection between them is characterized by a latency value $\ell_{n_1,n_2} \in \mathbb{R}_{\geq 0}$.

**Applications.** The set of applications to deploy is denoted by $A$. Each application $a \in A$ consists of a set of modules $M_a$. The set of all modules of all applications is $M = \bigcup\{M_a : a \in A\}$. For a module $m \in M$, its size (i.e., the computational capacity required by the module) is given by

$$S_m(w_m) = \alpha_m + \beta_m \cdot w_m,$$

where $\alpha_m \in \mathbb{R}_{\geq 0}$ and $\beta_m \in \mathbb{R}_{\geq 0}$ are given constants and $w_m \in \mathbb{N}$ is the number of users served by module $m$. Note that only $\alpha_m$ and $\beta_m$ are part of the input, $w_m$ is not; hence, the input defines the function $S_m(\cdot)$.

In an application $a \in A$, a data processing path $P$ is a sequence $(m_1, m_2, \ldots, m_{\kappa_P})$, where $m_i \in M_a \cup \{*\}$ for all $1 \leq i \leq \kappa_P$. Here, $*$ is a symbol representing a user. An element of the sequence (either a module or the symbol $*$) can appear multiple times in a data processing path. We write $m \in P$ if module $m$ appears at least once in the sequence of the data processing path $P$. For each application $a \in A$, a set of data processing paths $\mathcal{P}_a$ is given. Moreover, each $P \in \mathcal{P}_a$ is associated with a maximum allowed latency, denoted as $L_P$. The set of all data processing paths of all applications is $\mathcal{P} = \bigcup\{\mathcal{P}_a : a \in A\}$. For a module $m \in M$, the set of data processing paths containing $m$ is $\mathcal{P}(m) = \{P \in \mathcal{P} : m \in P\}$.

**Users.** A finite set $U$ of users is given. For each user $u \in U$, the location of the user in the network is given as $n_u \in N$. Moreover, for each user $u \in U$, the application that $u$ wants to use is given as $a_u \in A$.

**Information for Security and Privacy Requirements.** For formulating the security and privacy requirements, some further notation is necessary. For a module $m \in M$, $I_m \subset N$ denotes the set of illegal nodes for $m$, i.e., the nodes that are not allowed to host $m$. In addition, for a user $u \in U$ and a module $m \in M_{a_u}$, $I_{m,u} \subset N$ denotes the set of illegal nodes for the pair $(m, u)$, i.e., the nodes that are not allowed to host $m$ if $m$ processes data of user $u$.

**Table 1.** Notation overview

| Notation | Description |
|---|---|
| *Inputs* | |
| $N$ | Set of all infrastructure nodes |
| $C_n$ | Computational capacity of node $n$ |
| $\ell_{n_1,n_2}$ | Latency between nodes $n_1$ and $n_2$ |
| $A$ | Set of applications to deploy |
| $M_a$ | Set of modules of application $a$ |
| $M$ | Set of modules of all applications |
| $\alpha_m, \beta_m$ | Parameters in the function $S_m(\cdot)$ |
| $\mathcal{P}_a$ | Set of data processing paths in application $a$ |
| $\mathcal{P}$ | Set of all data processing paths of all applications |
| $\mathcal{P}(m)$ | Set of data processing paths containing module $m$ |
| $\kappa_P$ | Length of data processing path $P$ |
| $*$ | Symbol representing a user in a data processing path |
| $L_P$ | Maximum allowed latency of data processing path $P$ |
| $U$ | Set of users |
| $n_u$ | Location (i.e., node) of user $u$ |
| $a_u$ | Application that user $u$ wants to use |
| $I_m$ | Set of illegal nodes for module $m$ |
| $I_{m,u}$ | Set of illegal nodes for module $m$ with data of user $u$ |
| $\mathcal{I}$ | Set of pairs of modules that must not be colocated |
| $k_m$ | Minimum number of users for module $m$ |
| *Outputs* | |
| $f(m)$ | Node on which module $m$ is placed |
| $f^{-1}(n)$ | Set of modules placed on node $n$ |
| $g(u)$ | Data processing path to which user $u$ is assigned |
| $g^{-1}(P)$ | Set of users assigned to data processing path $P$ |
| *Other* | |
| $w_m$ | Number of users served by module $m$ |
| $S_m(w_m)$ | Computational capacity required by module $m$ |
| $L(u)$ | Latency perceived by user $u$ |

The set $\mathcal{I}$ consists of pairs of modules that must not be colocated. If $(m_1, m_2) \in \mathcal{I}$, then the modules $m_1$ and $m_2$ must not be placed on the same node.

For a module $m \in M$, $k_m \in \mathbb{N}$ denotes the minimum number of users that must be assigned to $m$ to achieve a sufficient level of anonymity. ($k_m = 0$ means that there is no such limitation for the given module.)

### 3.2 Outputs

Our aim is to determine two mappings: the placement of the applications and the assignment of the users.

The placement of the applications is a function $f : M \to N$. For a module $m \in M$, $f(m)$ is the node in $N$ on which $m$ is placed. The inverse function of $f$ is denoted by $f^{-1}$; for a node $n \in N$, $f^{-1}(n)$ is the set of modules placed on $n$.

The assignment of the users is a function $g : U \to \mathcal{P}$. For a user $u \in U$, $g(u)$ is the data processing path in $\mathcal{P}$ to which user $u$ is assigned. The inverse function of $g$ is denoted by $g^{-1}$; for a data processing path $P \in \mathcal{P}$, $g^{-1}(P)$ is the set of users assigned to $P$.

The output that we need to determine thus consists of the functions $f$ and $g$. Based on the function $g$, we can compute the number of users served by a module $m \in M$ as follows:

$$w_m = \sum_{P \in \mathcal{P}(m)} |g^{-1}(P)|. \tag{1}$$

To see the correctness of (1), it should be noted that each user is assigned to exactly one data processing path, and hence is contained in exactly one of the $g^{-1}(P)$ sets. Therefore, each user served by module $m$ is counted exactly once in (1). Moreover, it should be noted that $w_m$ is not an output, but an auxiliary number depending on the function $g$ and playing a role in formulating the constraints (see below).

### 3.3 Constraints

To build a valid solution, a number of constraints have to be satisfied. For the validity of the function $g$, it is necessary that each user is assigned to a data processing path of the application that the user wants to use, i.e.:

$$\forall u \in U : \quad g(u) \in \mathcal{P}_{a_u}. \tag{2}$$

The following capacity constraint ensures that the total size of the modules that are placed on a node $n$ does not exceed the capacity of $n$:

$$\forall n \in N : \quad \sum_{m \in f^{-1}(n)} S_m(w_m) \leq C_n. \tag{3}$$

To formulate the latency constraints, we first compute the latency perceived by a user $u$, depending on the $f$ and $g$ functions. For this purpose, let $P = (m_1, m_2, \ldots, m_{\kappa_P})$ be a data processing path, where $m_i \in M \cup \{*\}$ for all $1 \leq i \leq \kappa_P$, and let $g(u) = P$, i.e., user $u$ is assigned to data processing path $P$. The latency between $m_i$ and $m_{i+1}$ (where $1 \leq i \leq \kappa_P - 1$), perceived by user $u$, is given by

$$\lambda_{P,i,u} = \begin{cases} \ell_{f(m_i),f(m_{i+1})} & \text{if } m_i, m_{i+1} \in M \\ \ell_{f(m_i),n_u} & \text{if } m_i \in M \text{ and } m_{i+1} = * \\ \ell_{n_u,f(m_{i+1})} & \text{if } m_i = * \text{ and } m_{i+1} \in M \\ 0 & \text{if } m_i = m_{i+1} = * \end{cases}$$

With this notation, the latency perceived by user $u$ can be computed as

$$L(u) = \sum_{i=1}^{\kappa_P - 1} \lambda_{P,i,u},$$

and the latency constraint can be formulated as follows:

$$\forall u \in U: \quad L(u) \leq L_P, \text{ where } P = g(u). \tag{4}$$

Now we formulate the constraints stemming from security and privacy requirements. The module-level location constraints ensure that modules are not placed on illegal nodes:

$$\forall m \in M: \quad f(m) \notin I_m. \tag{5}$$

User-level location constraints enforce that modules processing data of a given user are not placed on the disallowed nodes:

$$\forall u \in U, \forall m \in M_{a_u}: \quad m \in g(u) \Rightarrow f(m) \notin I_{m,u}. \tag{6}$$

(Note that $m \in g(u)$ means that module $m$ processes data of user $u$.)

Colocation constraints stipulate that given pairs of modules are not allowed to be placed on the same node:

$$\forall (m_1, m_2) \in \mathcal{I}: \quad f(m_1) \neq f(m_2). \tag{7}$$

$k$-anonymity constraints ensure that a sufficient number of users are assigned to modules that require this to achieve the predefined level of anonymity:

$$\forall m \in M: \quad w_m \geq k_m. \tag{8}$$

Thus, our aim is to find functions $f$ and $g$ such that constraints (2)–(8) are satisfied. It should be noted that while some constraints only relate to the application placement $f$ (e.g., (7)) or only to the user assignment $g$ (e.g., (2)), several constraints express the interdependence of $f$ and $g$ (e.g., (6)). This underlines the importance of jointly handling application placement and user assignment.

### 3.4 Discussion

We would like to emphasize that our problem formulation is an abstraction. Applying our formulation in practice will raise some questions. In particular, obtaining the input data (e.g., the set of disallowed nodes for a module) may be challenging and may require complex manual or automated processes (e.g., in the field of risk management), which are out of the scope of this paper. Also, in a specific system, possibly only a subset of the types of security and privacy requirements considered in this paper is relevant.

Another aspect is what happens if the problem defined here is not solvable. In this case, either the design of the system needs to be changed, or the requirements may have to be re-negotiated.

**Table 2.** Variables

| Variable | Index set | Range |
|---|---|---|
| $x_{m,n}$ | $m \in M, n \in N$ | $\{0,1\}$ |
| $y_{u,P}$ | $u \in U, P \in \mathcal{P}$ | $\{0,1\}$ |
| $w_m$ | $m \in M$ | $\mathbb{N}$ |
| $\lambda_{P,i,u}$ | $P \in \mathcal{P}, i \in \{1,\ldots,\kappa_P - 1\}, u \in U$ | $\mathbb{R}_{\geq 0}$ |

# 4 Algorithm Using Mixed Integer Programming

To solve the problem defined in Sect. 3, we devise an algorithm, which reads the inputs and transforms them to a quadratically constrained mixed integer programming formulation. This mixed integer program is solved using an appropriate external solver. Finally, our algorithm transforms the output of the solver back to create the output of the problem as defined in Sect. 3.

To create the mixed integer program, we first define appropriate variables, which are summarized in Table 2. The function $f$ is encoded using a set of binary variables. For a module $m \in M$ and a node $n \in N$:

$$x_{m,n} = \begin{cases} 1 & \text{if } f(m) = n \\ 0 & \text{otherwise} \end{cases}$$

The function $g$ is encoded using another set of binary variables. For a user $u \in U$ and a data processing path $P \in \mathcal{P}$:

$$y_{u,P} = \begin{cases} 1 & \text{if } g(u) = P \\ 0 & \text{otherwise} \end{cases}$$

The following equation ensures that each module is placed on exactly one node:

$$\forall m \in M : \sum_{n \in N} x_{m,n} = 1 \tag{9}$$

The following pair of equations ensure that each user is assigned to exactly one of the data processing paths of the application that the user wants to use, and to no data processing path of any other application:

$$\forall u \in U : \sum_{P \in \mathcal{P}_{a_u}} y_{u,P} = 1 \tag{10}$$

$$\forall u \in U,\ \forall P \notin \mathcal{P}_{a_u} : \ y_{u,P} = 0 \tag{11}$$

In addition, a set of integer variables is used to reflect the number of users served by each module, corresponding to the quantity $w_m$ in Sect. 3. By a slight abuse of notation, we use $w_m$ here as a variable: for a module $m \in M$, the number of users served by $m$ is captured by variable $w_m$. The value of $w_m$ is determined by the values of the $y$ variables as follows:

$$w_m = \sum_{P \in \mathcal{P}(m)} \sum_{u \in U} y_{u,P} \tag{12}$$

To see the correctness of (12), it should be noted that the value of the inner sum is the number of users assigned to data processing path $P$. In addition, the equations (10)–(11) ensure that for each user $u$, $y_{u,P}$ will be 1 for exactly one data processing path, so that no user is counted twice in (12).

Using the $w_m$ variables, the capacity constraint can be formulated as follows:

$$\forall n \in N: \sum_{m \in M} x_{m,n} \cdot (\alpha_m + \beta_m \cdot w_m) \leq C_n \tag{13}$$

To calculate latencies, we consider a data processing path $P = (m_1, m_2, \ldots, m_{\kappa_P})$, where $m_i \in M \cup \{*\}$ for all $1 \leq i \leq \kappa_P$. Again by a slight abuse of notation, we use $\lambda_{P,i,u}$ to denote the real-valued variable that captures the latency between $m_i$ and $m_{i+1}$ for user $u$. The value of $\lambda_{P,i,u}$ can be computed from the $x$ variables as follows:

$$\lambda_{P,i,u} = \begin{cases} \sum_{n \in N} \sum_{n' \in N} \ell_{n,n'} \cdot x_{m_i,n} \cdot x_{m_{i+1},n'} & \text{if } m_i, m_{i+1} \in M \\ \sum_{n \in N} \ell_{n,n_u} \cdot x_{m_i,n} & \text{if } m_i \in M,\ m_{i+1} = * \\ \sum_{n \in N} \ell_{n_u,n} \cdot x_{m_{i+1},n} & \text{if } m_i = *,\ m_{i+1} \in M \\ 0 & \text{if } m_i = m_{i+1} = * \end{cases} \tag{14}$$

To see the correctness of (14), it should be noted that, because of (9), exactly one term will be non-zero in each sum.

Using the $\lambda_{P,i,u}$ variables, the latency constraint can be formulated as follows:

$$\forall u \in U: \sum_{P \in \mathcal{P}_{a_u}} y_{u,P} \cdot \left( \sum_{i=1}^{\kappa_P - 1} \lambda_{P,i,u} \right) \leq \sum_{P \in \mathcal{P}_{a_u}} y_{u,P} \cdot L_P \tag{15}$$

To see the correctness of (15), it should be noted that, because of (10)–(11), $y_{u,P}$ will be non-zero for exactly one $P$.

Module-level location constraints can be easily formulated using the $x$ variables as follows:

$$\forall m \in M,\ \forall n \in I_m: \ x_{m,n} = 0. \tag{16}$$

User-level location constraints depend on both the $x$ and $y$ variables and can be formulated as follows:

$$\forall u \in U,\ \forall m \in M_{a_u},\ \forall n \in I_{m,u}: x_{m,n} \leq 1 - \sum_{P \in \mathcal{P}(m)} y_{u,P} \tag{17}$$

To see the correctness of (17), it should be noted that the sum on the right-hand side is 1 if module $m$ processes data of user $u$ and 0 otherwise. In the former case, (17) ensures that $x_{m,n} = 0$, while in the latter case, (17) imposes no constraint.

**Table 3.** Settings used in the experiments

| Setting | Values |
|---|---|
| Size | Each module: $30 + 5 \cdot w_m$ |
| Capacity | Smart Home Controllers: 100<br>Gateway: 200<br>Cloud: $\infty$ |
| Latency | Users – Smart Home Controllers: 0<br>Smart Home Controllers – Gateway: 10<br>Gateway – Cloud: 100<br>Maximum allowed latency for the data paths: 300 |

Colocation constraints can be formulated using the $x$ variables as follows:

$$\forall (m_1, m_2) \in \mathcal{I},\ \forall n \in N: \quad x_{m_1,n} + x_{m_2,n} \le 1. \tag{18}$$

Finally, $k$-anonymity constraints can be directly formulated using the $w$ variables as follows:

$$\forall m \in M: \quad w_m \ge k_m. \tag{19}$$

As can be easily seen, Eqs. (9)–(19) describe exactly the constraints that a solution to the problem of Sect. 3 has to satisfy. Hence, the mixed integer program is solvable if and only if the original problem was solvable. It should also be noted that the constraints are either linear (e.g., (9)), or quadratic (e.g., (15)) in the variables.

A solution to the mixed integer program can be transferred back to a solution to the problem of Sect. 3 by using the following rules:

- For a module $m \in M$, $f(m)$ is the single node $n \in N$ for which $x_{m,n} = 1$.
- For a user $u \in U$, $g(u)$ is the single data processing path $P \in \mathcal{P}$ for which $y_{u,P} = 1$.

# 5 Evaluation

We implemented our approach in the form of a Java program, which uses the Gurobi Optimizer[1] version 9.0.1 to solve mixed integer programs. To foster reproducibility, we made our implementation available online[2].

## 5.1 Example Application

To validate the applicability of our approach, we first apply it to the example of Sect. 2. The values that are used for the parameters of the infrastructure and the application are given in Table 3.

[1] https://www.gurobi.com.
[2] https://sourceforge.net/p/vm-alloc/sec-place-usr-asgn.

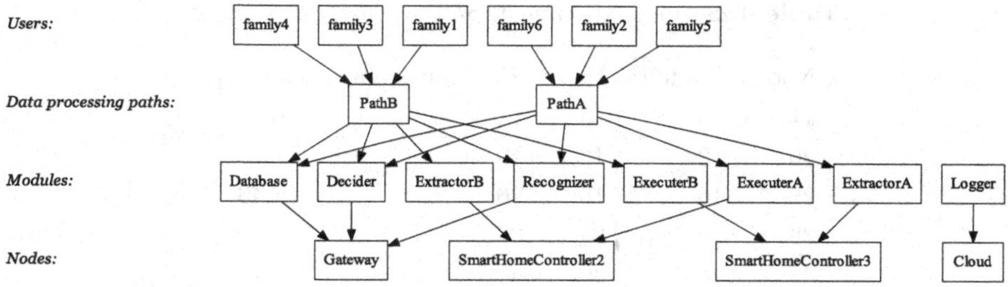


**Fig. 2.** Result of applying the proposed algorithm to the example of Sect. 2

The result of applying our approach is shown in Fig. 2. The arrows between users and data processing paths show the $g$ function (i.e., the assignment of users) computed by our approach. The arrows between data processing paths and modules show which modules each data processing path consists of, which is given as part of the input. The arrows between modules and nodes show the $f$ function (i.e., the placement of application modules) computed by our approach.

It can be verified that all constraints described in Sect. 2 are satisfied in the computed solution. In particular, the Database is not in the Cloud, modules processing data of Family 2 are not placed on Smart Home Controller 1, Executer A and Executer B are on different nodes, and Extractor A and B are assigned at least three users, as stipulated by the security and privacy requirements.

The experiment also shows that finding an application placement and user assignment satisfying all constraints is quite complicated and challenging even for problem instances of moderate size. Manually solving the problem is hard and may take a long time. Our algorithm, however, solves the problem in a fraction of a second.

### 5.2 Scalability

In the next set of experiments, we investigated the scalability of the proposed approach. This is important because our method is based on quadratically constrained mixed integer programming, which has exponential worst-case complexity. Hence it is interesting to evaluate how big problem instances can be solved in acceptable time.

To investigate the effects of increasing problem instance size, we scale the Smart Bell system of Sect. 2 to an increasing number of homes. We simultaneously increase the number of nodes (adding new Smart Home Controller nodes), the number of modules (adding new Extractor and Executer instances) and corresponding data processing paths, as well as the number of users (one more family with each new home). As a result, also the number of constraints stemming from security and privacy requirements increases. Table 4 summarizes the parameters of the considered problem instances.

Figure 3 shows the execution time of our algorithm for increasing problem size. The execution time includes the time to create the mixed integer program,

**Table 4.** Scaling experiment. S&P: security & privacy

| Nodes | Modules | Users | S&P constraints | Time [s] |
|---|---|---|---|---|
| 11 | 8 | 6 | 12 | 0.16 |
| 20 | 12 | 12 | 19 | 0.75 |
| 29 | 16 | 18 | 26 | 1.43 |
| 38 | 20 | 24 | 33 | 3.99 |
| 47 | 24 | 30 | 40 | 8.76 |
| 56 | 28 | 36 | 47 | 16.25 |
| 65 | 32 | 42 | 54 | 28.86 |
| 74 | 36 | 48 | 61 | 45.56 |
| 83 | 40 | 54 | 68 | 74.38 |
| 92 | 44 | 60 | 75 | 109.61 |

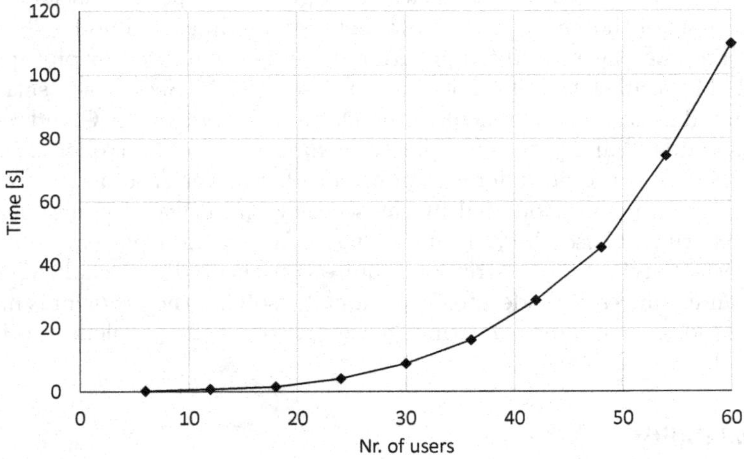


**Fig. 3.** Scaling behavior of the algorithm's execution time

solve it with the external solver, and retrieve the application placement and user assignment from the results. The experiments were carried out on a Lenovo ThinkPad X1 laptop with Intel Core i5-4210U CPU @ 1.70 GHz and 8 GB RAM. Note that, although the horizontal axis in Fig. 3 only shows the number of users (which equals the number of smart homes considered), the problem instances also grow at the same time in the other dimensions as shown in Table 4.

From Fig. 3 it is clear that the execution time indeed exhibits rapid growth. Nevertheless, even the largest problem instance, which comprises the joint optimization of module placement and user assignment for 60 smart homes, takes less than 2 min. Thus we can conclude that our approach can solve even quite

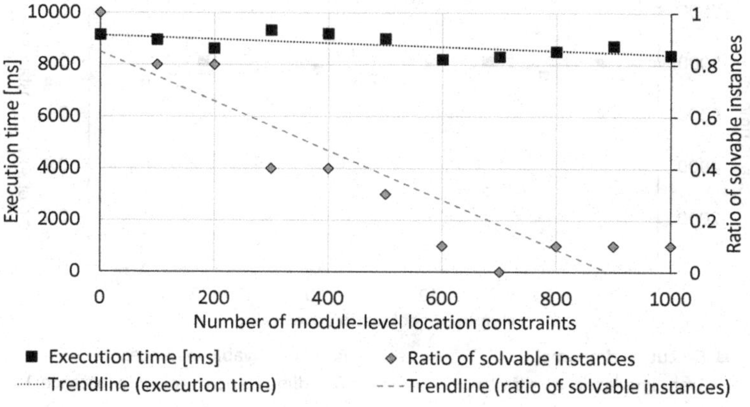


**Fig. 4.** Impact of the number of *module-level location constraints*

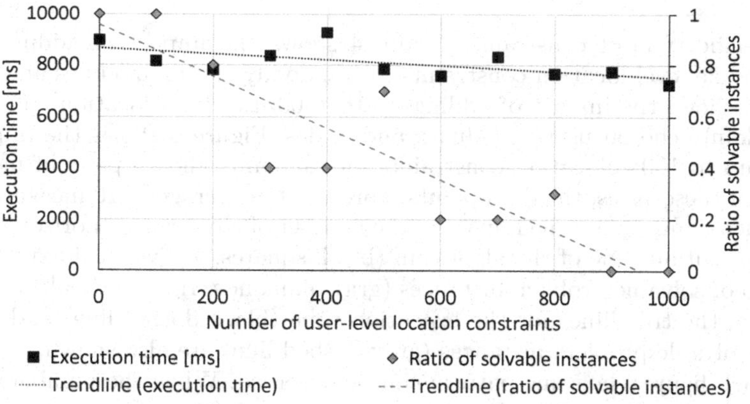


**Fig. 5.** Impact of the number of *user-level location constraints*

complex problem instances (which would be an overwhelming challenge for humans) with acceptable execution time, using a commodity computer.

### 5.3 Impact of Security and Privacy Constraints

We also investigate how an increasing number of security and privacy constraints impacts the solvability of the problem instances and the execution time of our algorithm.

Figures 4, 5 and 6 show the impact of location and colocation constraints. In these experiments, we started from the instance of the previous scaling experiment (see Table 4) with 30 homes, which includes 47 nodes, 24 modules, and 30 users. Unlike in the previous scaling experiment, we now started with an empty set of security and privacy constraints, and then added an increasing number

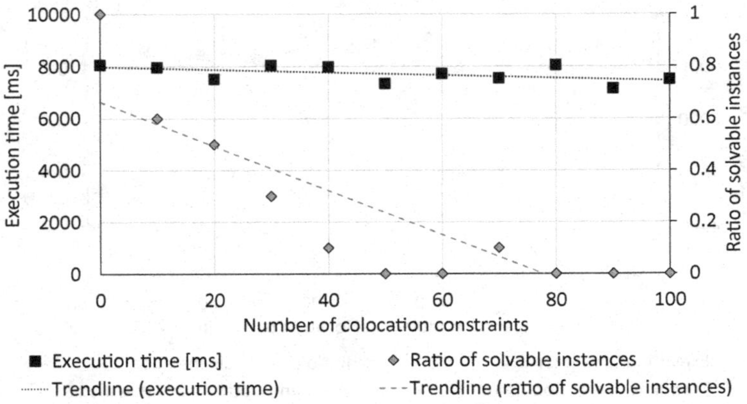


**Fig. 6.** Impact of the number of *colocation constraints*

of a specific type of constraint. Figure 4 shows the impact of adding up to 1000 module-level location constraints for randomly chosen modules and nodes. Figure 5 shows the impact of adding up to 1000 user-level location constraints for randomly chosen users, modules, and nodes. Figure 6 shows the impact of adding up to 100 colocation constraints for randomly chosen pairs of modules. In each of these cases, the data points represent the average of 10 measurements each. Each figure shows the impact of the number of constraints (horizontal axis) on the execution time of the algorithm (black squares, left vertical axis) and on the ratio of solvable problem instances (gray diamonds, right vertical axis). Furthermore, the trendlines for the execution time (black dotted line) and for the ratio of solvable problem instances (gray dashed line) are also shown.

In each figure, the same pattern can be observed. When the number of constraints is low, most problem instances are solvable. As the number of constraints increases, the ratio of solvable problem instances decreases. With the highest number of constraints, most problem instances are not solvable anymore. Hence, security and privacy constraints have a large impact on whether a solution that satisfies all constraints can be found. On the other hand, the impact of security and privacy constraints on the algorithm's execution time is very limited. The algorithm's execution time seems to have a small peak roughly at the point where the ratio of solvable instances drops. This is in line with previous experience on other combinatorial problems: when there are few constraints, it is relatively easy to find a solution and when there are many constraints, it is relatively easy to come to a contradiction, but deciding solvability in-between is more difficult [16]. Overall, there is a slight negative correlation between the number of constraints and the algorithm's execution time, as demonstrated by the negative slope of the trendlines. This may be attributed to the fact that a higher number of constraints enables the solver to more effectively prune the parts of the search space that certainly do not contain any solutions.

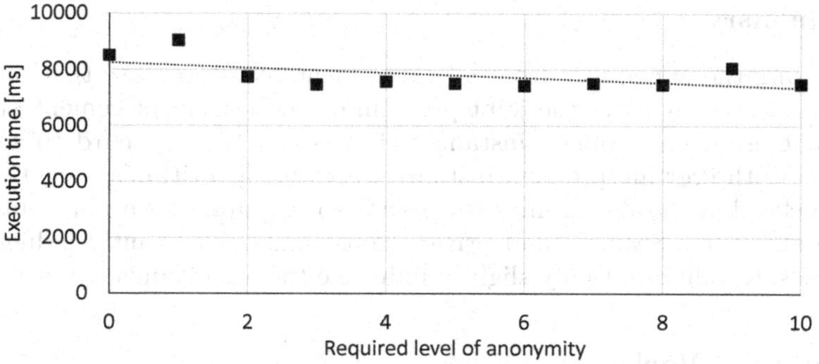


(a) Impact of the required level of anonymity

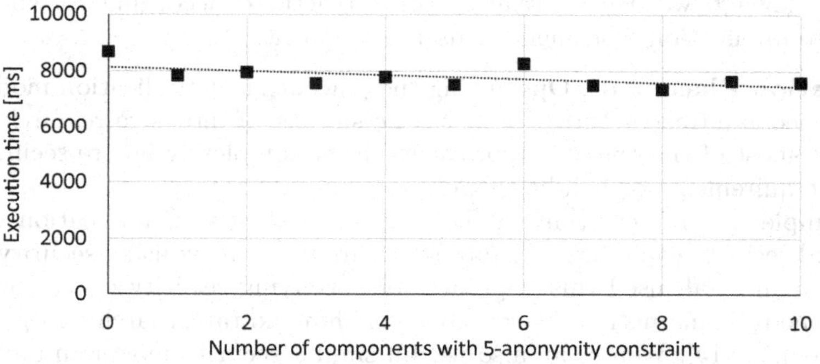


(b) Impact of the number of components with 5-anonymity constraints

**Fig. 7.** Impact of the $k$-anonymity constraints

Regarding the $k$-anonymity constraints, two different parameters can be varied, as shown in Fig. 7. We start from the same setup as in the previous experiment, i.e., with 30 homes, which includes 47 nodes, 24 modules, 30 users, and no security or privacy constraints. In the experiment whose result is shown in Fig. 7(a), all 10 Extractor components are associated with a $k$-anonymity constraint, and we vary $k$ from 0 to 10. The figure shows the impact on the algorithm's execution time. For $k \leq 3$, the problem is solvable, for $k \geq 4$, the problem is not solvable. In the experiment whose result is shown in Fig. 7(b), we apply 5-anonymity constraints to a varying number of the 10 Extractor components. The figure shows the impact on the algorithm's execution time. For at most 6 components with 5-anonymity constraints, the problem is solvable, for 7 or more components with 5-anonymity constraints, the problem is not solvable. Altogether, Fig. 7 supports the same conclusions that we could draw from Figs. 4, 5 and 6: the number and tightness of security and privacy constraints has only a minor impact on the algorithm's execution time, and more or tighter constraints tend to slightly decrease the algorithm's execution time.

### 5.4 Summary

Summarizing the experience from all experiments, we can state that our algorithm can effectively solve the joint problem of application placement and user assignment, even for problem instances that would be very hard to solve for a human. With growing problem instances, also the algorithm's execution time grows quickly, but the algorithm is still able to solve quite large problem instances in acceptable time. Security and privacy constraints significantly influence the problem's solvability, but only slightly influence the algorithm's execution time.

## 6 Related Work

In the following, we discuss related work structured according to whether it applies to application placement or user assignment.

**Application Placement.** Optimizing the placement of application modules in heterogeneous infrastructures has been the subject of intensive research [6,17]. However, most of the existing approaches either completely ignore security and privacy requirements or handle them in a rudimentary way.

A simple way of representing security requirements of application components and security capabilities of infrastructure nodes is by using security levels. Goettelmann et al. used this approach for specifying security constraints, and then applied a combination of a greedy algorithm and tabu search for optimizing the placement [14]. Wen et al. also used a similar security model and a custom heuristic algorithm for placement optimization [26,27]. Mezni et al. also adopted a similar security model and used particle swarm optimization to find a good placement [20]. In contrast to these approaches, we use a rich set of rigorous security and privacy constraints. In addition, we apply an exact algorithm that guarantees the fulfillment of all stipulated constraints.

Instead of security levels, a more precise way of capturing security constraints is by defining the specific security controls required by the different application modules, respectively offered by the different infrastructure nodes. Massonet et al. used this approach for specifying security constraints [19]. They proposed a method based on constraint programming that finds an optimized placement respecting the given security requirements. Forti et al. also used a similar approach, extended with probabilities and trust relations among stakeholders [13]. Our approach also allows to capture security constraints stemming from the security controls required by application modules and offered by infrastructure nodes, in the form of location constraints, but also many other types of constraints – including co-location and $k$-anonymity constraints – not supported by the mentioned previous works.

Co-location constraints have been taken into account by some previous approaches. Fdhila et al. considered such constraints when partitioning and placing composite applications on federated clouds [12]. Agarwal and Duong also focused on the risks of co-location in public infrastructure clouds [1]. In our earlier work, we devised custom heuristics for handling co-location constraints during application placement, also taking into account the availability of secure hardware enclaves [18]. The approach of the present paper also takes into account co-location constraints, but in combination with several other types of security and privacy requirements.

Workflow scheduling was considered in conjunction with data protection concerns by Wen et al. [25]. However, in that work, data protection constraints are limited to the specification of the allowed set of data centers for a task. Also for the placement of applications on a fog infrastructure, several approaches take security and privacy concerns into account by means of constraining the placement of certain application modules to trusted hosts [7,21,28]. While our approach also supports such location constraints, it can take into account various other types of security and privacy constraints as well.

Yuchi and Shetty define simple metrics to quantify the vulnerability of virtual machines containing application modules and the survivability of physical infrastructure nodes [30]. They use these pieces of information to place the application modules on the nodes with the aim of minimizing the overall risks. They propose a heuristic algorithm for this purpose. In contrast, our approach can guarantee the fulfillment of strict security and privacy requirements.

**User Assignment.** The assignment of users to different modules has also been investigated in different contexts.

Deng et al. address the problem of assigning requests of users to fog devices and cloud servers, with the goal of balancing latency and energy consumption objectives [10]. A similar problem is addressed by Shah-Mansouri and Wong, aiming to allocate fog and cloud resources to users with the objective of serving as many users as possible with as low latency as possible [23]. Xiao and Krunz also consider the assignment of users' workload to fog nodes, with the aim of improving quality of experience for the users [29]. Chen et al. address the allocation of user requests to a heterogeneous set of network resources in a mobile-edge cloud computing scenario, with the objective of minimizing the overhead observed by users [9]. Dräxler et al. assign users to instances of network services, with the objective of minimizing the number of violations of capacity constraints [11].

Our approach also takes into account the key objectives of these works, including low latency and good utilization of the available capacity of the nodes. On the other hand, none of the above works consider security and privacy requirements, despite the huge importance of such requirements in modern computing systems. Our approach significantly advances the state of the art by adding security and privacy constraints.

## 7 Conclusions and Future Work

In this paper, we have addressed the joint problem of application module placement and user assignment in the context of heterogeneous applications, heterogeneous infrastructure, and different types of security and privacy constraints, in addition to the more traditional constraints on capacity and latency.

Beside formally defining the problem, we devised an algorithm to solve the problem by means of quadratically constrained mixed integer programming. The algorithm is guaranteed to find a placement of the application modules and assignment of the users satisfying all constraints, whenever this is possible.

We demonstrated the applicability of the proposed approach by applying it to an IoT system from the smart home domain. In addition, we assessed the scalability of the algorithm by applying it to problem instances of increasing size. We also investigated the impact of the number of security and privacy constraints. The experiments showed that the proposed algorithm can solve even quite large problem instances in acceptable time using a commodity computer.

Several interesting paths for future research can be identified. One promising direction is to consider an online variant of the module placement and user assignment problem, in which the aim is to react to changes (e.g., the appearance of new users) by adapting the module placement and/or the user assignment so that the continued satisfaction of the requirements is guaranteed. Another interesting possibility is the parallelization of the proposed algorithm using multiple nodes, so as to reduce the execution time of the algorithm. (For distributed solving of integer programs, see [8] and references therein.)

**Acknowledgments.** This work was partially supported by the European Union's Horizon 2020 research and innovation programme under grant 871525 (FogProtect).

## References

1. Agarwal, A., Duong, T.N.B.: Secure virtual machine placement in cloud data centers. Fut. Gene. Comput. Syst. **100**, 210–222 (2019)
2. Alrawais, A., Alhothaily, A., Hu, C., Cheng, X.: Fog computing for the Internet of Things: security and privacy issues. IEEE Internet Comput. **21**(2), 34–42 (2017)
3. Ayed, D., Jaho, E., Lachner, C., Mann, Z.Á., Seidl, R., Surridge, M.: FogProtect: protecting sensitive data in the computing continuum. In: Zirpins, C., et al. (eds.) ESOCC 2020. CCIS, vol. 1360, pp. 179–184. Springer, Cham (2021). https://doi.org/10.1007/978-3-030-71906-7_17
4. Baresi, L., Mendonça, D.F., Garriga, M., Guinea, S., Quattrocchi, G.: A unified model for the mobile-edge-cloud continuum. ACM Trans. Internet Technol. **19**(2), 29 (2019)
5. Bellendorf, J., Mann, Z.Á.: Classification of optimization problems in fog computing. Fut. Gene. Comput. Syst. **107**, 158–176 (2020)
6. Brogi, A., Forti, S., Guerrero, C., Lera, I.: How to place your apps in the fog: state of the art and open challenges. Softw. Pract. Exp. **50**(5), 719–740 (2020)
7. Brogi, A., Forti, S., Ibrahim, A.: Predictive analysis to support fog application deployment. In: Fog and Edge Computing: Principles and Paradigms, pp. 191–222 (2019)
8. Chamanbaz, M., Notarstefano, G., Sasso, F., Bouffanais, R.: Randomized constraints consensus for distributed robust mixed-integer programming. IEEE Transa. Control Netw. Syst. **8**(1), 295–306 (2021)
9. Chen, X., Jiao, L., Li, W., Fu, X.: Efficient multi-user computation offloading for mobile-edge cloud computing. IEEE/ACM Trans. Netw. **24**(5), 2795–2808 (2015)

10. Deng, R., Lu, R., Lai, C., Luan, T.H., Liang, H.: Optimal workload allocation in fog-cloud computing toward balanced delay and power consumption. IEEE Internet of Things J. **3**(6), 1171–1181 (2016)
11. Dräxler, S., Karl, H., Mann, Z.Á.: JASPER: Joint optimization of scaling, placement, and routing of virtual network services. IEEE Trans. Netw. Serv. Manag. **15**(3), 946–960 (2018)
12. Fdhila, W., Dumas, M., Godart, C., García-Bañuelos, L.: Heuristics for composite web service decentralization. Softw. Syst. Model. **13**(2), 599–619 (2014)
13. Forti, S., Ferrari, G.L., Brogi, A.: Secure cloud-edge deployments, with trust. Fut. Gene. Comput. Syst. **102**, 775–788 (2020)
14. Goettelmann, E., Fdhila, W., Godart, C.: Partitioning and cloud deployment of composite web services under security constraints. In: IEEE International Conference on Cloud Engineering (IC2E), pp. 193–200. IEEE (2013)
15. Jiang, W., Clifton, C.: Privacy-preserving distributed *k*-anonymity. In: Jajodia, S., Wijesekera, D. (eds.) DBSec 2005. LNCS, vol. 3654, pp. 166–177. Springer, Heidelberg (2005). https://doi.org/10.1007/11535706_13
16. Mann, Z.Á.: Optimization in Computer Engineering-Theory and Applications. Scientific Research Publishing, Inc. USA (2011)
17. Mann, Z.Á.: Secure software placement and configuration. Fut. Gen. Comput. Syst. **110**, 243–253 (2020)
18. Mann, Z.Á., Metzger, A.: Optimized cloud deployment of multi-tenant software considering data protection concerns. In: 17th IEEE/ACM International Symposium on Cluster, Cloud and Grid Computing (CCGrid), pp. 609–618. IEEE (2017)
19. Massonet, P., Luna, J., Pannetrat, A., Trapero, R.: Idea: Optimising multi-cloud deployments with security controls as constraints. In: International Symposium on Engineering Secure Software and Systems. pp. 102–110. Springer (2015). https://doi.org/10.1007/978-3-319-62105-0
20. Mezni, H., Sellami, M., Kouki, J.: Security-aware SaaS placement using swarm intelligence. J. Softw. Evol. Process **30**(8), e1932 (2018)
21. Nardelli, M., Cardellini, V., Grassi, V., Presti, F.L.: Efficient operator placement for distributed data stream processing applications. IEEE Trans. Parall. Distrib. Syst. **30**(8), 1753–1767 (2019)
22. Roman, R., Lopez, J., Mambo, M.: Mobile edge computing, fog et al.: a survey and analysis of security threats and challenges. Fut. Gen. Comput. Syst. **78,** 680–698 (2018)
23. Shah-Mansouri, H., Wong, V.W.: Hierarchical fog-cloud computing for IoT systems: a computation offloading game. IEEE Internet of Things J. **5**(4), 3246–3257 (2018)
24. Sweeney, L.: k-anonymity: a model for protecting privacy. Int. J. Uncert. Fuzziness Knowl.-Based Syst. **10**(05), 557–570 (2002)
25. Wen, Y., Liu, J., Dou, W., Xu, X., Cao, B., Chen, J.: Scheduling workflows with privacy protection constraints for big data applications on cloud. Fut. Gen. Comput. Syst. **108**, 1084–1091 (2020)
26. Wen, Z., Cala, J., Watson, P.: A scalable method for partitioning workflows with security requirements over federated clouds. In: IEEE 6th International Conference on Cloud Computing Technology and Science (CloudCom), pp. 122–129 (2014)
27. Wen, Z., Cala, J., Watson, P., Romanovsky, A.: Cost effective, reliable and secure workflow deployment over federated clouds. IEEE Trans. Serv. Comput. **10**(6), 929–941 (2017)

28. Xia, Y., Etchevers, X., Letondeur, L., Coupaye, T., Desprez, F.: Combining hardware nodes and software components ordering-based heuristics for optimizing the placement of distributed IoT applications in the fog. In: Proceedings of the 33rd Annual ACM Symposium on Applied Computing (SAC), pp. 751–760 (2018)
29. Xiao, Y., Krunz, M.: QoE and power efficiency tradeoff for fog computing networks with fog node cooperation. In: INFOCOM - IEEE Conference on Computer Communications (2017)
30. Yuchi, X., Shetty, S.: Enabling security-aware virtual machine placement in IaaS clouds. In: IEEE Military Communications Conference (MILCOM), pp. 1554–1559 (2015)

# Room Identification with Personal Voice Assistants (Extended Abstract)

Mohammadreza Azimi(✉) and Utz Roedig

School of Computer Science and Information Technology, University College Cork, Cork, Ireland
{m.azimi,u.roedig}@cs.ucc.ie

**Abstract.** Personal Voice Assistants (PVAs) are used to interact with digital environments and computer systems using speech. In this work we describe how to identify the room in which the speaker is located. Only the audio signal is used for identification without using any other sensor input. We use the output of existing trained models for speaker identification in combination with a Support Vector Machine (SVM) to perform room identification. This method allows us to re-use existing elements of PVA eco-systems and an intensive training phase is not required. In our evaluation rooms can be identified with almost 90% accuracy. Room identification might be used as additional security mechanism and the work shows that speech signals recorded by PVAs can also leak additional information.

## 1 Introduction

PVAs such as Amazon Alexa or Google Home are now commonplace. We use these systems to interact with our environment and computer systems. A PVA records a user's voice and converts speech to text using Automated Speech Recognition (ASR). The obtained transcript is then interpreted by the system and actions are carried out. The system may then generate an audio response which is played back to the user via the PVA's integrated speakers.

A PVA may also use other techniques in addition to ASR to analyse recorded speech samples. For example, speaker identification may be carried out. In this case the speech signal is analysed in order to identify who the speaker is that is supplying a voice command. Such method may be useful in order to tailor a PVA action to the interacting user. For example, if a user requests to play their favourite music it is necessary for the system to identify the correct user. Also, such feature can be used to improve security and is used to implement user specific PVA access control. Other features that can be extracted from speech signals are the user's gender [9], emotional state [14] or health condition [2].

In this work we investigate how to extract features from audio samples captured by a PVA that allow us to determine the room in which the sample has been recorded. Such *room identification* feature is useful to further tailor PVA usage to the user environment. For example, if the user requests to play their


S. Katsikas et al. (Eds.): ESORICS 2021 Workshops, LNCS 13106, pp. 317–327, 2022.
https://doi.org/10.1007/978-3-030-95484-0_19

favourite music the system can recognise in which room the command was issued and play music via the correct speaker system. We assume here that either the PVA is mobile (a mobile Phone) or that it is a smart speaker that can be easily carried into another room. Room identification is also important from a security perspective. Room identification can be used as additional security feature. A PVA could be configured to only accept commands that are placed in specific rooms. For example, a doctor may only interact with patient data via a PVA in specific environments such as the consultation room but not the hospital's cafeteria. It has also to be noted that audio based room identification represents a privacy issue. Users that interact with a PVA do not necessarily want to sacrifice location privacy.

Existing work has shown that a Deep Neural Network (DNN) can be trained to identify the room in which a sound was recorded. However, a large data set is required and training of the DNN takes considerable effort. Also, this new capability requires additional processing capabilities. To overcome these issues we investigate in this work a different approach. We propose to use existing trained models used for speaker recognition to perform the additional task of room identification. Specifically we evaluate this approach using two trained speaker recognition systems that we call *thinResnet* [13] and *VGGVox* [8]. We use the output vectors of the speaker recognition system as input for an SVM which we then use for room identification. The SVM can be configured using a relatively small number of sound samples and complex training of a specialised DNN is not necessary. In a PVA eco-system sophisticated trained models for ASR and speaker recognition are available and the effort to implement room identification can be reduced.

The specific contributions of this work are:

- *Room Identification via Trained Models*: We describe a method for room identification using existing trained models; specifically trained speaker recognition models.
- *Evaluation of Room Identification*: We evaluate the proposed method using the two well known speaker recognition systems that we call *thinResnet* [13] and *VGGVox* [8]. We use a public available data set from the Acoustic Characterisation of Environments (ACE) challenge. We show that rooms are identified with 89% accuracy.

In the next section we discuss related work. Section 3 describes on a system level how room identification is used in a PVA context. Section 4 describes our method for room identification using existing speaker recognition models. In Sect. 5 we detail our evaluation; evaluation setup, data sets and results are described. Section 6 concludes the paper.

## 2 Related Work

A number of techniques are available to characterise a room. Some of techniques have been used to perform room characterization and/or room identification.

Here we detail work closest to ours and highlight differences. The main difference to existing work is that i) we use unprocessed original audio files recorded in different rooms and ii) we use preexisting NN-based models trained for a different purpose than room identification or verification.

Peters et al. [11] introduced in 2012 a system for room identification by analysing audio in a video clip. Mel-Frequency Cepstral Coefficient (MFCC) features are used for analysis. An accuracy of 61% for music and 85% for voice signals is achieved with no shared data between training testing phase. The term "Room Identification" was first coined by the authors [12]. Our work differs as we re-use existing speaker identification models.

Moore et al. [5,6] proposed in 2013 the use of Gaussian Naive Bayes Classifier (GNBC) using Frequency Dependent Reverberation Times (FDRTs) features for room identification. A database consisting of 484 Room Impulse Responses (RIRs) for 22 rooms, with volumes ranging from 29 to 9500 cubic meters, were used. The FDRTs was used as input feature to the classifier. According to the obtained results, in the best case scenario an Equal Error Rate (EER) of 3.9% can be achieved. Special equipment is required to measure the FDRTs. In our work we use recorded speech directly for room identification instead of dedicated acoustic measurements.

Murgai et al. [4] conducted research to see if blind estimation of the reverberation fingerprint of an unknown room could be performed by monitoring recorded speech signals. Despite the fact that the cited paper's main research goal was room volume classification, the obtained reverberation fingerprints can also be used for room identification. In this work we look at how to extract characteristics from audio samples to specifically identify a room using existing speech identification models.

In 2018 Moore et al. [7] proposed a new method for room identification using sub-band negative-side variance features. A GNBC is used to classify the features. The evaluation used recording samples taken from the evaluation dataset of the ACE challenge [3]. Voice recordings in five rooms were used. For the best-case scenario where the training data includes utterances spoken from the same position as the test data, a 90.5% accuracy is obtained. While our work uses the same dataset for evaluation we use a different analysis method. We use existing trained speaker identification models and their output as features to identify rooms using an SVM.

Papayiannis et al. [10] explored room identification based on the influence of reverberation on speech. The authors propose Convolutional Recurrent Neural Networks (CRNNs) to identify the room. For evaluation, Acoustic Impulse Responses (AIRs) are used from the ACE challenge dataset, measured in 7 rooms. The AIRs are used to artificially add reverbaration to speech samples; then these artificial samples are used to identify the rooms. According to the achieved results, the classification accuracy of the CRNN is 78%. In our work we do not use generated samples and we use existing trained speaker identification models to identify rooms.

## 3 System Overview

A PVA is a system comprised of two major components: the front end and the back end (see Fig. 1). The front end is either implemented as a dedicated device, often called a *smart speaker*, or realised as an app on the user's smartphone or other system such as a TV.

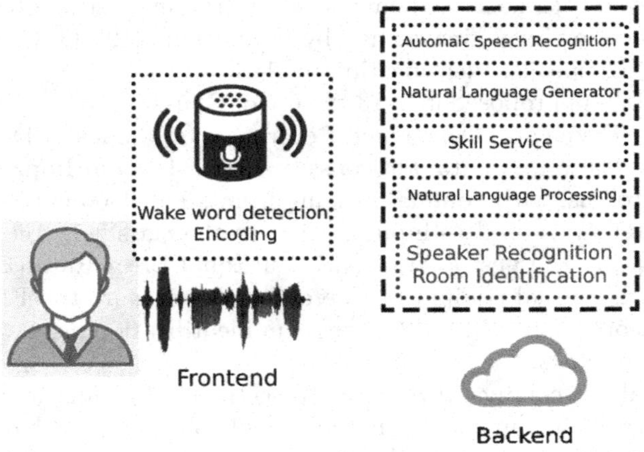


**Fig. 1.** PVA system overview comprising front end and back end infrastructure.

The front is able to record and play audio. It also comprises a wake word detection; once a wake word such as *Alexa* is recognised the following speech signal is recorded and transmitted to the back end.

The following are the key components usually found in the back end: ASR module, Natural Language Processing (NLP) module, skills management module (skill service) and natural language generator module (text to speech generator).

The process of turning the recorded speech into text is implemented by the ASR. This process is carried out using acoustic and language models. An NLP module is needed for intent recognition. The meaning of the speech and the user's expectations are expressed by the *intent* which results in a structured codified user request. The natural language generator module may be used to generate a speech response message played to the user by the front end.

A speaker recognition module may also be used in the back in order to identify the speaker. The obtained user identification might be used to prevent execution of a command. For example, when a specific user is deemed not to be allowed to issue a specific command.

To implement room identification it would be possible to include an additional module specifically for this purpose in the back end. This module would be supplied with the recorded voice, similar to the Speech Recognition (SR) to perform the task of room identification. As discussed in the related work, models are existing that could be used for this purpose.

However, this approach introduces two challenges. Firstly, the additional back end module would require resources to execute; all currently processed speech samples submitted by front ends require this additional resource. Thus, the back end infrastructure would need to be scaled up which is costly and also not energy efficient (Energy consumption is a significant cost factor of data centers). Secondly, the additional back end module would require to be trained which requires effort. Significant amount of data from user homes would need to be available. While it is possible to do to it is an additional overhead.

To overcome these challenges we propose therefore another approach. We propose to use the output (the feature vectors after processing) of the existing speaker recognition module to perform room identification. The output of the speech recognition module is used within a simple SVM to classify the rooms.

## 4 Room Identification

For speaker identification a neural network can be used. These take an acoustic signal (the speech signal) as input and then classify the speaker based on the features extracted from the input signal. Here we make use of a trained neural network for speaker identification, however, we take the output feature vector of the neural network to feed an Support Vector Machine (SVM) which is then used to classify the different rooms.

We take a number of acoustic signals collected in the rooms of interest and feed these to the trained neural network for speaker recognition. Then we use the resulting feature vectors to train an SVM. The training of the SVM can be performed with relatively few samples from rooms and training to classify rooms is much simpler than training a full end-to-end DNN for this purpose.

The SVM input data is mapped to a higher dimensional feature space via a kernel function. The feature space is derived using the kernel function, instead of being strictly defined. In this way, the selection of the kernel is the key to determine the feature space. We chose the Gaussian Radial Basis Function (RBF) for our SVM. We use in our system two well known speaker recognition systems that we call *thinResnet* [13] and *VGGVox* [8].

*thinResNet (512 Dimensional Feature Vector):* In this case we use the 'thinResNet' [13] trunk architecture with a dictionary-based NetVLAD layer for aggregating extracted features across time. This neural network model was trained end-to-end. It is also worth mentioning that here, voice activity detection (or automatic silence removal) is not applied. The output of the fully connected layer is used here as the extracted feature vector of 512 elements that is used as input for our SVM.

*VGGVox (1024 Dimensional Feature Vector):* VGGVox was proposed by Nagrani et al. [8] and this architecture is based on the VGG-M [1] Convolutional Neural Network (CNN), which is noted for its great efficiency and image classification ability. Using the 1024 dimension FC7 vectors, feature vectors from the classification network can be obtained. Here, we use the extracted feature vectors for training our SVM classifier.

# 5 Evaluation

In this study, the evaluation of acoustical characteristics is utilized to determine the room in which an audio recording was acquired. The suggested room recognition systems are based on an SVM-based system that extracts auditory characteristics using two pretrained neural network feature extractors.

Previously, reverberant and noisy speech samples were created artificially by convolving anechoic speech samples with a room impulse response (then adding it to a noisy signal). The numerical experiments were subsequently conducted using the intentionally produced samples. The ACE challenge database was utilized to create a database of original babbling noise samples for this work.

## 5.1 Dataset

The ACE Challenge database is used. The ACE Challenge was set up to encourage research on blind estimation of acoustic parameters from noisy speech using newly collected reverberant speech samples under different conditions [3]. The database contains so called *babble noise* recorded in seven different rooms (Two offices, two lecture rooms, two meeting rooms and lobby).

The babel noise is created by four to seven persons sitting in close proximity and chat constantly for the duration of the audio recording. The files were recorded on two separate occasions using the same microphones, with the microphones moved to the new position between the two occasions. For each of the rooms, two babble noise samples were obtained (for two different microphone positions).

We have seperated the babble noise samples into 2.5 s length audio samples. This way we obtained 1352 samples in total distributed across the 7 rooms as follows: No. 1. First Living Room (FLRoom) 200 samples, No. 2. First Meeting Room (FMRoom) 167 samples, No. 3. First Office (FOffice) 153 samples, No. 4. Second Living Room (SLRoom) 243 samples, No. 5. Second Meeting Room(SMRoom) 178 samples, No. 6. Second Office (SOffice) 205 samples, and No. 7. Lobby (Lobby) 206 samples. Here, the samples for the training and test data sets were picked at random.

## 5.2 ThinResNet

In order to train our SVM we used 502 voice samples, with 850 samples being used to test the chosen model. The training and test data-set samples were chosen randomly. Table 1 shows the summary of results obtained. Figure 2 shows the obtained confusion matrix.

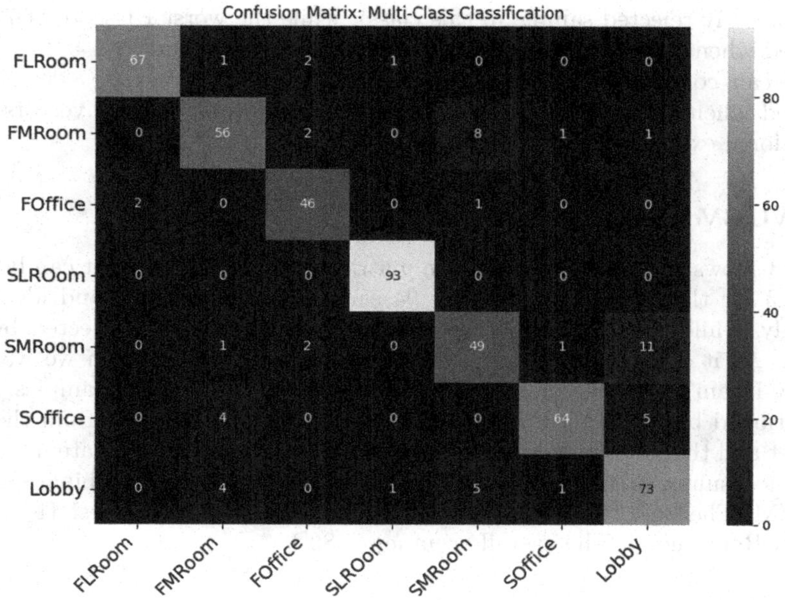


**Fig. 2.** thinResnet: The obtained confusion matrix using 850 voice samples.

**Table 1.** SVM classification results-thinResnet

| Type of rooms | Precision | Recall | F1-score | Support |
|---|---|---|---|---|
| FLRoom | 0.97 | 0.94 | 0.96 | 71 |
| FMRoom | 0.85 | 0.82 | 0.84 | 68 |
| FOffice | 0.88 | 0.94 | 0.91 | 49 |
| SLRoom | 0.98 | 1.00 | 0.99 | 93 |
| SMRoom | 0.78 | 0.77 | 0.77 | 64 |
| SOffice | 0.96 | 0.88 | 0.91 | 73 |
| Lobby | 0.81 | 0.87 | 0.84 | 84 |
| Accuracy | | | 0.89 | 502 |

As seen in Fig. 2, the multiclass-classifier accurately identified all samples as belonging to the first office, with the exception of three that were wrongly identified as samples being recorded in the first living room (two samples) and the second meeting room (one sample). It can be illustrated in the same figure that, for the second meeting room, the number of mistakenly rejected samples was zero and the false negative rate is zero.

According to Table 1, the best F1-score of 99% is achieved for the second living room (there were only two incorrectly classified samples and there was no incorrectly rejected sample in this class), while the worst F1-score of 77% is achieved when we want to recognize the second meeting room.

We can conclude from Table 1 that, the overall accuracy of 89% can be obtained when we train our model using the thinResnet feature vectors (512 dimensional extracted feature vectors).

### 5.3 VGGVox

Figure 3 shows the resulting confusion matrix using VGGVox. As it can be seen in Fig. 3 for the second living room, 94 samples were classified and identified correctly, while two samples were mistakenly and incorrectly rejected by the system. As it is shown in Fig. 3, the worst case scenario is when we want to identify Room no. 2 (the first meeting room) using the obtained samples. As it is mentioned before, the training data set is completely separate from the test data-set and the samples were randomly chosen for these two separate data sets.

Table 2 summarises the results obtained using VGGVox in combination with the SVM. The best f1-score is 98% for Room no. 4 and the lowest f1-score is 67% for Room no. 2. The overall accuracy is 86%.

**Table 2.** SVM classification results-VGGVox

| Type of rooms | Precision | Recall | F1-score | support |
|---|---|---|---|---|
| FLRoom | 0.79 | 0.89 | 0.84 | 66 |
| FMRoom | 0.74 | 0.61 | 0.67 | 51 |
| FOffice | 0.87 | 0.93 | 0.90 | 56 |
| SLRoom | 0.98 | 0.98 | 0.98 | 96 |
| SMRoom | 0.87 | 0.78 | 0.82 | 76 |
| SOffice | 0.74 | 0.82 | 0.80 | 71 |
| Lobby | 0.92 | 0.93 | 0.92 | 82 |
| Accuracy | | | 0.86 | 498 |

In case of training a binary classifier instead of the explained seven-class classifiers, we should choose different pairs of the rooms.

We have seven rooms and due to the rule of symmetry we have 21 different cases. To have a better and more comprehensive understanding of the achieved results we have also presented the results of binary classifiers for best and worst case scenarios.

For the collection of the ACE challenge database, there were two different recording sessions for each of the rooms. Hence, for each seven rooms, we have two babble noise files (two different sessions with two different microphone positions).

In this part, for preparation of training and test data-sets we didn't use the random picking engine anymore and instead, we used the samples were being

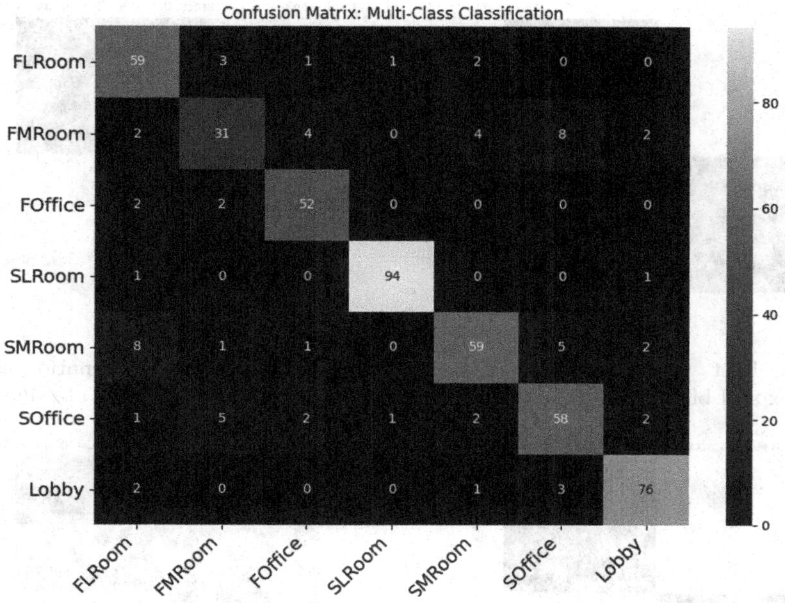


**Fig. 3.** VGGVox: The obtained confusion matrix using 850 voice samples.

recorded during the first session (with microphone in position A) for training data-set and the samples were being recorded during the second session (with microphone in position B) for test data-set. In other words, the results presented in the first two figures and tables are not exactly reproducible, as we utilized a random picking engine but the next figures can be obtained again exactly by repeating the experiment.

Figure 4 and Fig. 5 were obtained after achieving VGGVox vectors. These figures show the confusion matrix of SVM with kernel "Gaussian" (C = 40 and, gamma = 1) for the best and worst case scenarios, respectively. As it can be illustrated in Fig. 4, the overall accuracy is 100% and the classifier can recognize the rooms perfectly (Second Living Room vs. Second Meeting Room). As it is shown in Fig. 5, the overall accuracy will decrease to 74% when the classifiers want to discriminate between the samples of First Living Room and Second Meeting Room. The same set of results for thinResnet vectors are presented in Fig. 6 and Fig. 7. As it is depicted in Fig. 7, In First Living Room vs. Second Meeting Room scenario the overall accuracy is 72%.

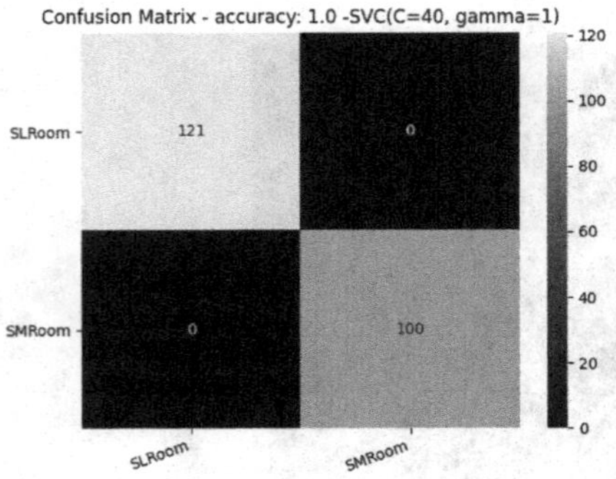


**Fig. 4.** Best case scenario using VVGvox and binary SVM classifier

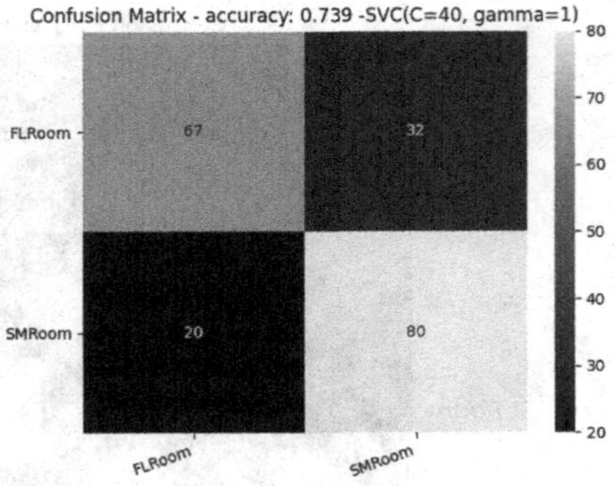


**Fig. 5.** Worst case scenario using VVGvox and binary SVM classifier

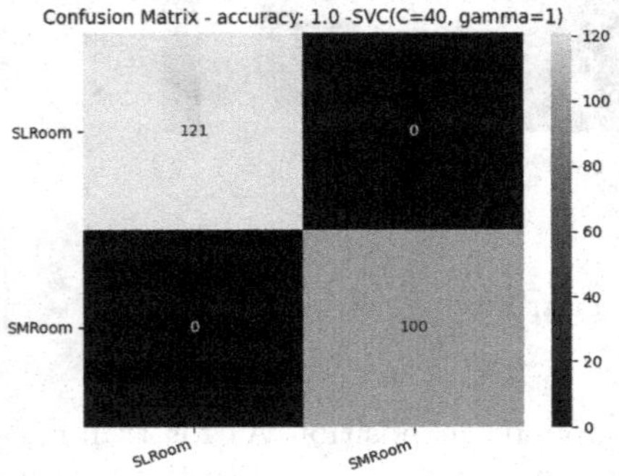


**Fig. 6.** Best-case scenario using thin-Resnet and a binary SVM classifier

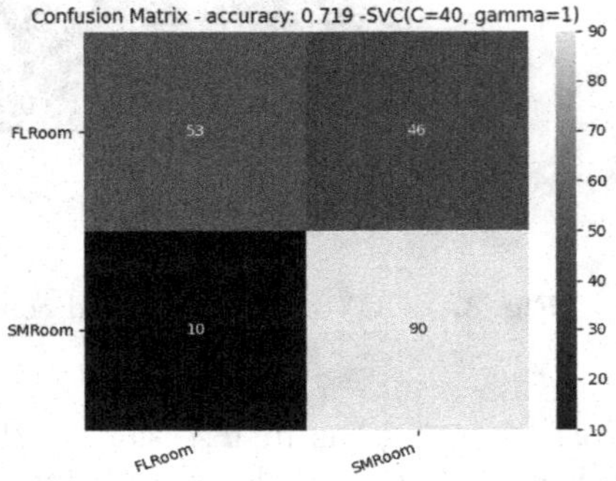


**Fig. 7.** Worst-case scenario using thin-Resnet and a binary SVM classifier

## 6 Conclusion

This work has shown that room identification based on voice samples are feasible and that existing neural networks used for other tasks such as speaker identification can be re-purposed for this task. By doing so it can be avoided to train complex networks just for this task and existing elements of a PVA infrastructure can be re-used.

In this work we used the public available dataset collected by the Acoustic Characterisation of Environments (ACE) Challenge. This data was not specifically collected for a PVA context. Thus, in our next steps we plan to collect our own data set issuing voice commands to a PVA. We will then repeat the experiments detailed in this paper using this more specific dataset.

**Acknowlegement.** This publication has emanated from research conducted with the financial support of Science Foundation Ireland under Grant number 19/FFP/6775. For the purpose of Open Access, the author has applied a CC BY public copyright license to any Author Accepted Manuscript version arising from this submission.

## References

1. Chatfield, K., Simonyan, K., Vedaldi, A., Zisserman, A.: Return of the devil in the details: delving deep into convolutional nets (2014)
2. Deb, S., Dandapat, S., Krajewski, J.: Analysis and classification of cold speech using variational mode decomposition. IEEE Trans. Affect. Comput. **11**(2), 296–307 (2020). https://doi.org/10.1109/TAFFC.2017.2761750
3. Eaton, J., Gaubitch, N.D., Moore, A.H., Naylor, P.A.: Estimation of room acoustic parameters: the ace challenge. IEEE/ACM Trans. Audio Speech Lang. Process. **24**(10), 1681–1693 (2016). https://doi.org/10.1109/TASLP.2016.2577502
4. Murgai, M.P., Rau, J.: Blind estimation of the reverberation fingerprint of unknown acoustic environments. J. Audio Eng. Soc. **143** (2017)
5. Moore, A.H., Brookes, M., Naylor, P.A.: Room geometry estimation from a single channel acoustic impulse response. In: 21st European Signal Processing Conference (EUSIPCO 2013), pp. 1–5 (2013)
6. Moore, A.H., Brookes, M., Naylor, P.A.: Room identification using room prints. J. Audio Eng. Soc. **54** (2014)
7. Moore, A.H., Naylor, P.A., Brookes, M.: Room identification using frequency dependence of spectral decay statistics. In: 2018 IEEE International Conference on Acoustics, Speech and Signal Processing (ICASSP), pp. 6902–6906 (2018). https://doi.org/10.1109/ICASSP.2018.8462008
8. Nagrani, A., Chung, J.S., Zisserman, A.: VoxCeleb: a large-scale speaker identification dataset. In: Interspeech 2017, August 2017. https://doi.org/10.21437/interspeech.2017-95
9. Nediyanchath, A., Paramasivam, P., Yenigalla, P.: Multi-head attention for speech emotion recognition with auxiliary learning of gender recognition. In: ICASSP 2020-2020 IEEE International Conference on Acoustics, Speech and Signal Processing (ICASSP), pp. 7179–7183 (2020). https://doi.org/10.1109/ICASSP40776.2020.9054073
10. Papayiannis, C., Evers, C., Naylor, P.A.: End-to-end classification of reverberant rooms using DNNs. IEEE/ACM Trans. Audio Speech Lang. Process. **28**, 3010–3017 (2020). https://doi.org/10.1109/TASLP.2020.3033628
11. Peters, N., Lei, H., Friedland, G.: Name that room: room identification using acoustic features in a recording. In: Proceedings of the 20th ACM International Conference on Multimedia. MM 2012, pp. 841–844. Association for Computing Machinery, New York (2012). https://doi.org/10.1145/2393347.2396326
12. Peters, N., Lei, H., Friedland, G.: Room identification using acoustic features in a recording. US patent US 9,449,613 B2, 20 September 2016
13. Xie, W., Nagrani, A., Chung, J.S., Zisserman, A.: Utterance-level aggregation for speaker recognition in the wild. In: ICASSP 2019-2019 IEEE International Conference on Acoustics, Speech and Signal Processing (ICASSP), pp. 5791–5795 (2019). https://doi.org/10.1109/ICASSP.2019.8683120
14. Yeh, S.L., Lin, Y.S., Lee, C.C.: A dialogical emotion decoder for speech emotion recognition in spoken dialog. In: ICASSP 2020-2020 IEEE International Conference on Acoustics, Speech and Signal Processing (ICASSP), pp. 6479–6483 (2020). https://doi.org/10.1109/ICASSP40776.2020.9053561

# 3rd Workshop on Security, Privacy, Organizations, and Systems Engineering (SPOSE 2021)

# SPOSE 2021 Preface

Over the past decades, a multitude of security- and privacy-enhancing technologies has been developed and brought to considerable maturity. However, the design and engineering of such technologies often ignores the organizational context that respective technologies are to be applied in. A large and hierarchical organization, for example, calls for significantly different security and privacy practices and respective technologies than an agile, small startup. Similarly, whenever employees' behavior plays a significant role for the ultimate level of security and privacy provided, their individual interests and incentives as well as typical behavioral patterns must be taken into account and materialized in concrete technical solutions and practices. Even though research on security- and privacy-related technologies increasingly considers questions of practical applicability in realistic scenarios, implementation decisions are still mostly technology-driven, and existing technical limitations and notions of "this is how we've always done it" hamper innovation.

On the other hand, a substantial body of organization-related security and privacy research already exists, incorporating aspects like decision and governance structures, individual interests and incentives of employees, organizational roles and procedures, organizational as well as national culture, or business models and organizational goals. However, there is still a large gap between the generation of respective insights and their actual incorporation in concrete technical mechanisms, frameworks, and systems.

This disconnect between technical and organization-focused security and privacy research leaves ample room for improving the fit between organizational practices and the engineering of concrete technical solutions. Achieving a better "fit" through security and privacy technologies that incorporate organizational and behavioral theories and practices promises substantial benefits for organizations and staff, engineers, data protection officers, policy makers, regulators, and society as a whole.

The aim of the third Workshop on Security, Privacy, Organizations, and Systems Engineering (SPOSE 2021), therefore, was to discuss, exchange, and develop ideas and questions regarding the design and engineering of technical security and privacy mechanisms in organizational contexts. We invited researchers and practitioners working in security- and privacy-related systems engineering as well as in the field of organizational science to submit their contributions. Besides regular and short papers, we also invited practical demonstrations, intermediate reports, and mini-tutorials on respective technologies currently under development to stimulate forward-looking discussions.

The papers included on the following pages demonstrate the possible spectrum for fruitful research at the intersection of security, privacy, organizational science, and systems engineering:

Uta Menges, Jonas Hielscher, Annalina Buckmann, Martina Angela Sasse, Annette Kluge, and Imogen Verret argue that the old-school command-and-control approach to designing security technology and enforcing security policies has created dysfunctional relationships between employees and IT security staff, indicated by the dominance of guilt and blaming in their communication. They introduce their Therapy Framework, combining approaches from the OLaF framework on organisational learning from mistakes and individual and group therapy, to identify and analyze dysfunctional relationships and mend them to develop empathy, trust, and cooperation in organizational settings.

Matthias Fassl, Michaela Neumayr, Oliver Schedler, and Katharina Krombholz report from a field study and an online survey that shed light on how users transfer their understanding and behavior regarding updates from smartphones to smart consumer devices and how this might fail. Based on their assessment of why common transfer strategies are difficult to apply to smart consumer devices, such as evaluation by expected changes, they provide design implications for such devices, for instance to distinguish clearly between important and unimportant updates and treat them differently through the user interface.

Tania Wallis, Greig Paul, and James Irvine provide a thorough investigation of the cybersecurity situation for the energy sector. They discuss and recommend methods and approaches for improving resilience in the supply chain and across interdependent actors, such as the need for defining and agreeing on cybersecurity expectations and requirements appropriate to each actor, clear responsibilities for assurance and effective coordination across stakeholders, and resilience measures for each actor that contribute to whole system resilience.

Mattia Mossano, Benjamin Berens, Philip Heller, Christopher Beckmann, Lukas Aldag, Peter Mayer, and Melanie Volkamer address users' difficulties in identifying malicious and obfuscated URLs in phishing emails. They propose an approach that provides relevant information to users to distinguish between legitimate and phishing emails by replacing links in emails, including image-based links, with easy-to-read versions they call SMILE-strings. These strings only provide the minimum information required to decide on a URL's legitimacy, such as the domain and the TLD or an IP address, which also prevents conflicts or overlaps with existing tools in this field.

In their short paper, Salatiel Ezennaya-Gomez, Claus Vielhauer, and Jana Dittmann introduce a semantic model based on Helen Nissenbaum's concept of privacy as contextual integrity to help system designers during the modeling and design process in identifying and analyzing privacy implications of design decisions. They highlight the model's present primary aim of being an educational tool, which therefore does not yet help to identify mitigations to be employed to reduce privacy risks, but aim for future extension in this direction.

Finally, Michael Friedewald, Ina Schiering, Nicholas Martin, and Dara Hallinan report on empirical results and experiences from tests of a methodology and process operationalization for data protection impact assessments in workshops with stakeholders from private companies and public institutions. They outline major learnings from their empirical work, such as the tendency of participants to consider risks for internal data subjects as of lower priority, the challenges posed by the vagueness of the concept of privacy or the use of terms with negative connotations such as "attacker", or their common desire for checklists and risk catalogues, and how they have been used for the refinement of the operationalization.

Altogether, these papers, complemented by an open-minded, keen-to-debate, and constructively thinking audience made the third iteration of the workshop another success, even given the special conditions under which ESORICS 2021 had to take place. We would thus like to thank everybody who contributed – authors, presenters, participants, reviewers, and, of course, the whole organizing team of ESORICS 2021. Special thanks go to the Forum Privatheit – funded by the German Federal Ministry for Education and Research – for sponsoring Open Access fees for all accepted SPOSE papers included herein and for thereby fostering their broad recognition.

We are definitely looking forward to the next – and hopefully face-to-face – iteration of SPOSE.

November 2021

Frank Pallas
Jörg Pohle
Angela Sasse

# SPOSE 2021 Organization

## Program Committee Chairs

| | |
|---|---|
| Frank Pallas | TU Berlin, Germany |
| Jörg Pohle | Humboldt Institute for Internet and Society, Germany |
| Angela Sasse | Ruhr-University Bochum, Germany |

## Program Committee

| | |
|---|---|
| Athena Bourka | ENISA, Athens, Greece |
| Adrian Dabrowski | University of California, Irvine, US |
| Matthias Fassl | CISPA, Saarbrücken, Germany |
| Lea Gröber | CISPA, Saarbrücken, Germany |
| Seda Gürses | TU Delft, The Netherlands |
| Marit Hansen | ULD, Kiel, Germany |
| Heleen Janssen | University of Cambridge, UK |
| Gabriele Lenzini | University of Luxembourg, Luxembourg |
| Sebastian Pape | Goethe University Frankfurt, Germany |
| Simon Parkin | TU Delft, The Netherlands |
| Katharina Pfeffer | SBA Research, Austria |
| Karen Renaud | University of Strathclyde, UK |
| Burkhard Schäfer | University of Edinburgh, UK |
| Andrew Simpson | University of Oxford, UK |
| Jatinder Singh | University of Cambridge, UK |
| Max-R. Ulbricht | TU Berlin, Germany |
| Tobias Urban | if(is) and secunet, Germany |
| Melanie Volkamer | KIT, Germany |

# Why IT Security Needs Therapy

Uta Menges[1](✉), Jonas Hielscher[2], Annalina Buckmann[2], Annette Kluge[1], M. Angela Sasse[2], and Imogen Verret[2]

[1] Faculty of Psychology, Ruhr-University Bochum, Bochum, Germany
{uta.menges,annette.kluge}@ruhr-uni-bochum.de

[2] Horst-Görtz-Institute of IT-Security, Ruhr-University Bochum, Bochum, Germany
{jonas.hielscher,annalina.buckmann,m.sasse}@ruhr-uni-bochum.de, hcs-studies@rub.de

**Abstract.** Over the past decade, researchers investigating IT security from a socio-technical perspective have identified the importance of trust and collaboration between different stakeholders in an organisation as the basis for successful defence. Yet, when employees do not follow security rules, many security practitioners attribute this to them being "weak" or "careless"; many employees in turn hide current practices or planned development because they see security as "killjoys" who "come and kill our baby". Negative language and blaming others for problems are indicators of dysfunctional relationships. We collected a small set of statements from security experts' about employees to gauge how widespread this blaming is. To understand how employees view IT security staff, we performed a prolific survey with 100 employees ($n = 92$) from the US & UK, asking them about their perceptions of, and emotions towards, IT security staff. Our findings indicate that security relationships are indeed often dysfunctional. Psychology offers frameworks for identifying relationship and communication flows that are dysfunctional, and a range of interventions for transforming them into functional ones. We present common examples of dysfunctionality, show how organisations can apply those interventions to rebuild trust and collaboration, and establish a positive approach to security in organisations that seizes human potential instead of blaming the human element. We propose Transactional Analysis (TA) and the OLaF questionnaire as measurement tools to assess how organisations deal with error, blame and guilt. We continue to consider possible interventions inspired by therapy such as conditions from individual and group therapy which can be implemented, for example, in security dialogues or the use of humour and clowns.

**Keywords:** Human factors in IT security · IT security awareness · Dysfunctional relationship · Socio-technical systems · Interpersonal communication · Transactional analysis · Joint optimisation

## 1 Introduction

Awareness that the "human element" is an important factor in IT security (ITS) has been growing steadily over the past decades. But to this day, the discourse


S. Katsikas et al. (Eds.): ESORICS 2021 Workshops, LNCS 13106, pp. 335–356, 2022.
https://doi.org/10.1007/978-3-030-95484-0_20

is dominated by the "weakest link" narrative, originally coined in 2000 by leading security practitioner Bruce Schneier (see Sect. 2.1), which implicitly blames humans as the reason for security problems. As we shall see in Sects. 5, this view shapes academic and industry discourse on human behaviour in security, and means that most solutions aim to somehow "fix" defective humans. The assumption that this is the way to improve security is ingrained into ITS practice in organisations, who run awareness campaigns reminding employees of organisational policies, and attacking employees through simulated phishing campaigns in the name of training. On the other hand, there is a growing recognition for the need to reconfigure ITS in a positive manner, as the root cause lies in security solutions that are impossible to follow, or conflict with other demands people face – such as productivity [8,29]. Research has repeatedly shown that most people *do* care about security, and are willing and able to use security measures that cater for those needs [13]. Research has also shown that most people are willing to contribute to a broader organisational and societal security effort beyond their own needs if their stance towards those entities are mostly positive [10,21]. The conclusion from socio-technical research very firmly is that

**"Trust and collaboration [...] are necessary for effective cybersecurity."** [16]

Beyond security benefits, recent research has shown that in productive and innovative organisation there are three essential factors: employees feel safe, connected to members of the organisation, and believe they have a shared future [17]. Currently, many ITS practices work in exactly the opposite direction – in anti-phishing training, for instance, employees experience being attacked by their own company (or an agent acting for the company), and subsequently don't feel safe. When they recognise that an anti-phishing campaign is being run, they are told not to inform their colleagues since this would "undermine the effectiveness of the campaign" – and creating the impression that security is something everyone has to do alone, rather than something to be tackled collectively. Finally, "failing" security tests or non-compliance are associated with the threat of sanctions and dismissal – not creating the impression of a long-term future. Relationships between different stakeholders are a long way from trust and collaboration when it comes to security: security experts see employees as stupid and lazy, and feel entitled to demand time and attention from employees "because security is important". As Herley puts it: "security practitioners treat users' time as an unlimited resource" [22] and "think we [the security practitioners] can convince people to spend more time on security" [23]. Many organisational leaders don't engage with how to manage security because they see security as "technical" and leave most decisions to experts; even when they do engage, their focus is often on complying with regulatory requirements, not whether security arrangements are working in practice. Developers hide their ideas for innovations from security staff, because they think their "default setting is NO" and fear "they will come and kill our baby" [4]. Security practitioners are forced to accept security training packages they know to be out-of-date and ineffective by procurement officers who insist they take the cheapest offer. In modern organisations, dysfunctional relationships are everywhere when it comes to security. In this paper, we present a roadmap for organisations looking to work their way back from that brink, and towards a trusting and collaborative culture. We present knowledge and tools for detecting dysfunctional relationships, and interventions for transforming them into working ones. Our approach is an interdisciplinary one, bringing together knowledge and tools from clinical psychology (psychology therapy), organisational psychology, social and cultural anthropology and human centred security.

The remainder of this paper is structured as follows: In Sect. 2 we introduce the different ITS relationships in organisational ITS, the narrative of users as "the weakest link" and indicators of dysfunctional relationships. In Sect. 3 we explain our research method and present our results of in Sect. 4. In Sect. 5 we analyse our data in terms of dysfunctional relationships before introducing our Therapy Framework in Sect. 6 to address the problem of dysfunctional relationships. In Sect. 7 we discuss limitations and conclude.

## 2 Background

### 2.1 ITS Relationships in Organisations

Organisations are socio-technical systems, and the effectiveness of ITS measures organisations chose ultimately depends on the behaviour of employees, which in turn is shaped by the interaction of different Communities of Practice (CoP) [48]. CoPs in their various positions and departments, having their own work tasks and needs towards IT and security accordingly. Currently, interactions between communities are unfortunately dominated by value conflicts, distrust, lack of cooperation and hierarchy, or circuits of power [15,26]. Over the past decades, responsibility for security has increasingly been shifted on the shoulders of employees, often creating value conflicts between their primary working and secondary security tasks – primarily productivity [8,29]. Policies forbid some behaviours and mandate others, and are "supported" by security awareness and training measures that aim to change employees' attitudes and behaviour, in other words: "fixing the human".[1] Most of these are either developed by security specialists, built on their professional knowledge, or by security awareness providers copying what they consider "best practice", i.e. what publicly available guidance documents by government or regulators recommend. Most of it is not tested for feasibility or effectiveness – and the resulting experience of not being able to follow what they are told haunted by the deficit construction of users [30] – and are often experienced by employees as fear-inducing [6], overly technical and as putting responsibility and blame on them [10,44].

[1] We are not saying that employees don't have to learn about security – there are new threats they need to be aware of, and security behaviours that are effective. But currently, security awareness wrongly seen as a "Cure-all" – it cannot "fix" security that is ineffective, security tasks that exceed human capabilities, or conflict with productivity targets organisations expect employees to meet.

IT security professionals have their own CoP whose main, primary task is the security of the organisation.

While their work is mostly seen as technical, it is worth noting that the basis for most of those rules is not scientific, but promotes and copies "best practice" – which should more actually called "common practice" since their effectiveness has rarely been evaluated [24]. ITS research until late 90s was almost exclusive technical – but always contains human elements, as security is played out in socio-technical systems. Today, most security specialists are not trained in dealing with human factors – something Ashenden & Lawrence tried to address with Security Dialogues [4]. Further, this often leads to restrictive security measurements that create value conflicts for other employees, who, in turn, revert to workarounds or practice "shadow security" [29] to be able to pursue their primary goals.

Management sits at the top of organisations, which increasingly rely on digital technologies. With reports about data breaches and attacks, there is growing awareness about the importance of security among this CoP. Due to the nature of their work, management tends to focus on numbers, and sees security as a product you can buy, rather than as a collective process that builds on practices of maintenance and care [32]. This misconception of ITS and the work it entails can lead to miscommunication between management and ITS [5] and the devaluation of security practices, resulting in overworked staff within understaffed departments, which, in turn, negatively affects the security of the organisation. Additionally, management often relies on external security specialists, such as national security agencies, consulting firms and security vendors that often have little to no inside into specific work requirements of the other COPs.

### 2.2 The Curse of the "Weakest Link"

With increasing user numbers of IT systems, the realisation that human capabilities and limitations need to be considered to keep them functioning gave birth to the disciplines of human-computer interaction (HCI) in the 1980s. HCI provides knowledge and methods for designing technology to "fit" the capabilities and limitations of a specific user population, the tasks they perform with the technology in pursuit of their goals, and the context in which that interaction takes place. Technology that doesn't fit reduces productivity in organisations, and puts of consumers spending their own money – so by the end of the century, HCI had become firmly embedded in computer science teaching and most development practice. Except computer security, where the idea was that people should do as they are told, because security is important. In 1999, two seminal papers highlighted the consequences of unusable security "Users are not the enemy" [1] and "Why Johnny can't encrypt" [51]. In 2000, Bruce Schneier introduced the narrative of "the user as weakest link" [47]. This implicitly blames people – a perspective that even most usable security researchers subscribe to: when they can't or won't follow expert prescriptions, it is because they are "unmotivated" [51] or "lazy" [45]. Klimburg-Witjes [30] recount how this perspective is pervasive in both academic and practioner events today, and so deeply ingrained that some employees believe it themselves [14]. Whilst initially the focus was on "educating" people ignorant of the threats, increasing technology is used to monitor people and enforce "secure" behaviour, using scare tactics and bullying [46]. There is little reflection that there might be something wrong with the security approach, and the tasks it sets for users, or the experts themselves. Assigning the blame to people works its magic every time we tell it to each other, creating ingroups and outgroups hostile to each other – a situation [1] described and diagnosed as a fatal: the enemy is not the legitimate user, but the attacker out there.

### 2.3 Indicators of Dysfunctional Relationships

Our aim is to identify and transform dysfunctional relationships between ITS professionals and employees in organisations. Based on research on dysfunctional family relationships, the indicators are outlined in Fig. 1 and backed up by psychological theories and empirical studies ITS in practice from [1,2,7,14,19,20,33,37,40,43,49,50,52]. We propose that security needs therapy in order to cultivate cultures of security that build on collaboration and trust.

## 3 Method

To find indicators of the dysfunctionality of ITS relationships, we chose a two-fold approach for data gathering: ITS practitioner statements and an employee survey.

*ITS Practitioner Statements.* We collected indicators on the security professionals' view on "the human element" by analysing public statements of security awareness vendors, security conferences, security consultant vendors, security news portals and newspapers. We searched for articles, statements, reports and whitepapers that contain one of the following keywords: "Employee", "Human", "User", "Weakest", "Error" or "Insider". Selection of the conferences, consultant vendors and newspapers is based on a loose collection of what we see as leading in their respective areas, and the twelve leading security awareness vendors (according to [28]) were chosen. We limited our search to statements not older than 5 years. We aimed to find statements that point towards negative relationships.

*Employee Survey.* To find out the perspective of employees, we conducted an online survey with open questions. We only accepted pre-screened participants that have English as their first language, are US or UK residents, are currently employed and do not have a student status. Participants answered 12 open questions in total regarding negative and positive attributes and experiences of the relationship with the ITS staff in the organisations of the participants (see Appendix A for the full questionnaire). In a first step, the answers were coded deductively based on the survey questions (e.g. "positive experience", "negative

**Indicators of Dysfunctional Relationships**

**1. High level of conflict between parties**

- Mutual misunderstanding, annoyance and incomprehension with regard to the work of the other party (Adams & Sasse 1999)
- Overburdened employees are more prone to make dangerous compromises in ITS measures (Posey, Roberts, Lowry & Hightower 2014)
- Criticizing the work of another person can cause lasting damage to the relationship and can lead to further conflicts (Tracy & Eisenberg 1990)

**2. Negativity in communication**

- Poor communication leads to negative feelings among employees in an organisation (Proctor & Doukakis 2003)
- Communication activities go far beyond merely exchanging explicit information with one another (Octavia, van den Hoven & De Mondt 2007)
- To support what has been said and to prevent ambiguity, people use non-verbal signals and cues (Barrett 2002)
- Lack of non-verbal forms of communication (via email) can have serious consequences (Barrett 2002)

**3. Negative feelings towards each other**

- Enduring and recurring negative feelings and a relatively stable pattern of dislike for the other person (Labianca & Brass 2006)
- Negative feelings might lead to the intention of negatively influencing the disliked person's outcomes (Labianca & Brass 2006)
- Jealousy and envy can be described as stress-related reactions (Dogan & Vecchio 2001)
- Jealousy and envy can have a negative effect on the quality of the work, since cooperation is no longer possible due to the stress caused by the negative feelings (Dogan & Vecchio 2001)

**4. Imbalance of power**

- Power imbalance in the relationship between ITS professionals and other employees on different levels
- ITS department often is on a higher level within the organisational hierarchy than others
- ITS have special responsibility due to their role, knowledge, special expertise in the field of ensuring security in practice and in dealing with digital technologies in a secure manner (Albrechtsen & Hovden 2009)
- Employees can find themselves in a position of dependency of the ITS professionals in regard to their working tasks, as well as personal and potential sensitive information

**5. Emotional disengagement**

- Interpersonal communication requires that all persons involved attach relevance to the relationship (Galvin & Wilkinson 2006)
- Distance describes impersonal ties that exist when functional relationships are not merged with more personal communication (Galvin & Wilkinson 2006)
- Development of trust and closeness is the basic requirement for impersonal relationships to develop into personal relationships (Galvin & Wilkinson 2006)
- Uniqueness, replaceability, interdependence, self-revalation and intrinsic rewards are named dimensions to distinguish between interpersonal and personal communication (Zhu, Nel & Bhat 2006)

**6. Blaming others**

- Employees have various options to deal with mistakes, for example holding others responsible for their own behaviour (Tjosvold, Yu & Hui 2004)
- In the course of the person approach, it is assumed that if something does not work, individuals are responsible for it (Reason 2000)

**Fig. 1.** We summarise six indicators for dysfunctional relationships.

experience"). In a second step, the answers were coded inductively to categorise emerging themes and patterns.

With this, we got a deeper understanding of the relationship between ITS staff and employees from the employees' point of view, which is so far rather absent from the discourse.

*Relationship Analysis and Therapy Framework.* We analysed the data for indicators of dysfunctional relationships, to further identify topics and patterns that indicate the presence of obstacles to the functioning of relationships.

## 4 Results

### 4.1 Security Vendor Statements

The URI-sources for all quotations can be found in the Appendix B.

Two industry surveys among security experts performed in 2019 suggest that "IT and security professionals think normal people are just the worst". From 5,856 experts, 54% believe that the one single most dangerous threat to ITS are employees' mistakes [39]. In the other survey with 500 experts, 91% are afraid of insider threats and 62% believe that "the biggest security threat comes from well-meaning but negligent end users" [12]. In 2016 Ponemon institute found that 66% of 601 security experts "admit employees are the weakest link in their efforts to create a strong security posture" [27].

Among security consulting companies, blaming employees is common, e.g. in this statement from EY *"Insider threats can originate from lack of awareness. For example, employees creating workarounds to technology challenges."* that makes employees responsible for problems raised by non-working technological solutions. It is well established in research that many employees won't let non-working security measures stop them from performing their primary task [29]. At KPMG an author is directly speaking to security end users in Australia: *"YOU are the weakest link: where are we going wrong with cyber security in Australia?"*. Such weakest link statements can be found in whitepaper from PwC, Deloitte and Accenture as well. IBM on the other side does identify a relationship problem in teams: *"Your employees might not trust you - many times, the relationship between the manager and the workers causes the threats to go undetected."*

As expected, security awareness vendors actively use an image of employees as a defect or risk to security that needs to be fixed with the help of their awareness raising and measuring products. 9 out of 12 analysed vendors use the term "users[/ employees] are the weakest link" as a key term to introduce the problem "human error" in their product description or their case studies and whitepapers. The market leader Know4Be for example states: *"More than ever, your users are the weak link in your network security. They need to be trained by an expert like Kevin Mitnick, and after the training stay on their toes, keeping security top of mind."* Some vendors are promoting the idea that organisations should see and handle employees as an active danger, as you can see in Kaspersky's statement: *"The Human Factor in ITS: How Employees are Making Businesses Vulnerable from Within"*

The leading ITS conference for ITS practitioners, RSA, has dedicated a complete program to "the human element" in 2020, underlining the importance of employees for a successful security strategy besides any technological solution. A search in the conference library and the webcast offer a diverse image: While employees are sometimes still seen as the weakest link, others tackle this idea and try to convince their readers and listeners that employees are only a threat if other parts of the ITS infrastructure fail. Also the highly technical conference Black Hat has a tradition of employee blaming: *"What is the weakest link in today's enterprise IT defences? End users who violate security policy and are too easily fooled by social engineering attack."* The different ITS and cybercrime magazines and journalistic platforms are all over with articles about "weakest link incidents", human errors and employee blaming. This view is often provided by journalists in reports, but also by comments from experts. Furthermore, ITS journalists are partially pushing the negative image of humans proactively. Namely in the *Ask the CISO podcast* the interviewers regularly ask suggestive question like *"[...] you know people are the weakest link in the security chain. You can have all the wonderful technologies and layers of Technology security protections in place but ultimately it comes down to the person, right?"*.

### 4.2 Employee Survey Results

Prolific offered us 20,874 eligible participants. We paid £1.35 per participant (£8.1/h), which is slightly more than the prolific average of £7.50/h. From initially 100 participants, 8 were excluded from analysis as they proofed not eligible due to stating to not have any experience with ITS staff, resulting in a sample size of **n = 92**. Prolific provided us with demographic data. 67 participants were female, 25 male. 86 participants were UK citizens, 6 US citizens. Respondents' age varied from 19 to 73 years, with an average of 36 years. 64 were employed full-time and 28 part-time. Participants came from diverse fields such as Sales, Transportation, Social Services, Finances, Administration, Health Care, Human Resources, Finances, Education and IT. Due to the different natures of their work, the frequency and kinds of interaction with the ITS department differed widely. We offer a glimpse into our preliminary analysis carried out by one researcher that is still indefinite as we plan to further analyse and contrast our findings. Nonetheless, we present insights into the obstacles and facilitators of the (dys-)functioning of the relationships between ITS staff and other employees.

*Helpfulness.* The experience of helpfulness of ITS staff can be split into four categories: **helpful** (to varied degrees) (71), **not helpful** (18), **not able to say due to lack of contact** (4) and referring to the overall **importance for the organisation** (10). The vast majority (71 participants) found ITS staff to be helpful or very helpful, referring to them being knowledgeable and able to protect – employees, their data, systems and the organisation as a whole: *"Everything feels secure and safe"* (P44). However, many in this group also mentioned their helpfulness was limited by their lack of time to solve issues, not being approachable: *"[They are] helpful when I can actually get a hold of them!"* (P60) as well as capability to offer explanations, as they use *"complicate explanations instead of in lay man's terms"* (P52).

*ITS: Tasks and Working Style.* Asked what participants thought about the job and tasks of ITS staff, most of them referred to their responsibility to monitor the organisation's systems, handle *"IT Queries"* and offer protection to the employees and company: *"[they] keep the employees computers safe so we can effectively carry out our work"* (P24). Many also considered it their job to provide help, giving advice and educating people: *"to provide advice and guidance on how to securely handle data, and educate when things go wrong"* (P23). Overall, there was an appreciation of the ITS's job to be complex and demanding, dealing with lots of different issues, technical as well as human.

*Experiences with ITS Staff.* Roughly 2/3 of our participants (62) stated to never have had a negative experience with ITS staff. The remaining 31 who did report on negative experiences mostly referred to long waiting times, issues in communication and security measures as obstacles to their workflows: *"9/10 attempts to get issues sorted have results in having to call back or sort the problem myself, or it has taken a long time on a call to them to get it fixed. Usually they don't understand the issue to begin with."* (P63).

*Communication.* The question how understandable communication with ITS staff was experienced yielded a variety of answers, ranging from **"not at all"** to **"very understandable"**. Most noticeably, there was a differentiation on the **media of communication** (e.g. face-to-face, on the phone, via e-mail or fixed templates/digital platforms) impacting the understandability of communication. However, the most important factor was ITS staff's ability to offer explanations and a shared language. Those who found the communication to be "very understandable" usually also stated that their ITS staff is very good at explaining, refrain from using overly technical language, and offer step-by-step guides and good examples. On the other hand, those who found communication hard to understand complained about using lots of jargon: *"they speak in technical details which nobody understands and they don't try to explain anything"* (P61). All in all, 26 participants specifically referred to *"IT speak"* (P51) as being an obstacle to communication, even when they think of themselves as *"IT literate"*: *"I'd consider myself pretty IT literate as a millennial but I often don't understand what they mean and neither do my older colleagues."* (P10). This is amplified by the unwillingness of ITS staff to offer explanations: *"They do send out communication but it is very IT heavy jargon and is quite difficult to understand. They don't tend to tone down this type of language even if asked"* (P15). Some participants further elaborated on the tone of communication, that they experienced as being talked down to, as e.g. by P51: *"I think they see themselves as supportive, but the way they talk to staff, they think that staff are simpletons,* *because they don't understand how IT systems work. And we're talking about doctors and nurses being talked down to here!"*

*Relationship Between ITS Staff and Employees.* We asked several questions regarding the relationship between ITS staff and other employees. First, they should describe their view of the relationship, and then how ITS staff might see it. Further, we asked to elaborate on the positive and negative aspects of that relationship (see Appendix C). Finally, we asked for indicators of how ITS staff might feel about them. We categorised 6 answers as describing a **poor** or **bad** relationship. P51 complained about them as *"talking in IT-speak"*, so they had to *"sort it out"* for their team members who were *"not very computer literate"*. P61 described the relationship as *"poor"*, as *"they don't know/care who I am."* P57 referred to a *"constant power struggle between the business needs and that of IT security"* and P82 criticised hierarchy: *"I feel like I am their servant. That everything I do must be reviewed as if they're my managers"*. The two other participants started to avoid them if they could and instead tried to fix the issues themselves (P63, P91). Overall, most participants described their relationship as **good** (39), **professional** (6), **friendly** (12) and **helpful** (14). However, only 5 participants stated to have regular contact. 33 participants described the relationship as being **distant** to **non-existent**. Out of all participants, 11 described their interaction as being **focused on issues and problems**, which is underscored by the overall high focus on *"helpfulness"* which runs throughout the answers in our survey. 10 participants thought they would describe the relationship in negative terms, such as being **not IT literate** (4), **frustrating** (4), and **demanding** (1). P6 felt ITS staff would think that *"Likely they have to deal with idiots on a daily basis."* and P87 *"That we are a pain in the bum."*

## 5 Data Analysis – Dysfunctional Relationship

Having presented a short overview of our data, we now analyse them using the aforementioned indicators for dysfunctional relationships. All results and statements presented in this section are a drawn from qualitative text questions, rather than from multiple-choice questions.

*High Level of Conflict.* Our participants named several sources of conflict in their relationship with ITS staff. The most obvious are in frequent misunderstandings and obstacles in communication due to a lack of shared language. This is highly influenced by ITS staff's ability to explain the concepts they use to others, as well as by the IT literacy of employees. Another source of conflict are the differing expectations of ITS staff's tasks as well as a lack of knowledge about employees' work requirements. Some of the answers indicated that employees feel it is ITS staff's job to help, assist and support as well as educate on *"IT issues"*, which is something (most) ITS specialists are not trained to do. Further, it only represents a minor part of their actual workload. On the other hand, lack of knowledge about the working requirements of employees could lead to frustration. Also, this can cause security measurements that negatively affect employees' workflows. This leads to the next source of conflicts: ITS as an obstacle. While most participants were conscious about its necessity and acknowledged that ITS staff had to adhere to rules and regulations themselves, some of them also experienced ITS as negatively affecting their productivity. One major source of conflict was ITS staff's (lack of) time and approachability.

*Negativity in Communication.* Negativity in communication exceeds the difficulty of understanding *"IT language"*: most participants described the communication as friendly and helpful, still the majority of answers indicate that all communication and interaction between ITS staff centred around problems or issues that needed to be solved, giving a negative touch as baseline to their entire communication. Further, answers signalled that in many cases there was no face-to-face communication at all, and usually focused on the transmission of factual information. This lack of non-verbal cues and forms of expression can negatively affect the relationship itself, as well as employees' ability to express their issues and concerns, especially when they lack the "proper language" to explain them.

*Negative Feelings Towards Each Other.* The high potential for conflicts, the problem-centred communication and an overall sense of complexity of ITS that permeates participants' responses can induce negative feelings towards ITS in general, despite all the displayed friendliness and helpfulness of ITS staff. Some of our participants explicitly described feelings of fear and worry in regards to ITS, as induced by Security training or of accidentally doing something wrong.

ITS practitioner reported negative feelings, too: they seem disappointed of employees not able to follow the rules or use the tools, they are afraid of employees open up holes in security or even of getting betrayed by insider threats. While the practitioners do not report about the feelings of single individuals the overall tone of the reports does transport these feelings.

*Power Imbalance.* Few participants explicitly described their relationship to ITS staff as hierarchical. Still, the overall appreciation of knowledge and expertise that runs through their answers also indicates a power imbalance in terms of knowledge and skills, which is amplified by employees' dependency on ITS staff's help and support. Some answers described ITS (staff) as obscure, working in the background, an *"invisible force"*. Others explicitly described the demeanour of ITS staff as arrogant, being talked down to and not respected for their fields of expertise, or being embarrassed. This power imbalance decreases trust and cooperation, and can cause disengagement between the employee groups.

*Emotional Disengagement.* One topic that ran through the answers was "distance" as well as an impersonal relationship. While this might be due to the nature of working interaction those employee groups have, others felt ITS staff to not be "people-persons", that like to keep to themselves and "seem to dislike having to deal with colleagues". On the employees' side, we found some participants who actively avoided interaction with ITS themselves, rather trying to fix the issues themselves due to the negativity of their experiences with them. This disengagement is further fostered by practices of blaming the other. Blame users as "weakest link" on the practitioner side is a clear sign for disengagement. The practitioner are in their own circles they don't care about how employees might feel about their measures, training and evaluations.

*Blaming Others.* Blaming of employees for security problems is a core theme that runs through practitioner statements and reports. Even reports that state that employees "need to be empowered" talk about employees making mistakes. The experience of being blamed is echoed in some of our survey participants' statements. Some participants referred to ITS as acting *"as if their colleagues are the problem, rather than external forces"* (P6), others seem to have internalised this notion, referring to themselves as *"trouble"* (P72) and making them feel bad (P82). P66 framed it more positively, acknowledging their role and responsibility for security, and hoping to be perceived as *"respectful IT users"*. However, we also found participants blaming ITS staff as "useless", putting obstacles in their way, causing delays in their work, not prioritising their issues, being too strict and not willing to communicate in an understandable manner.

## 6 Therapy Framework

We found a significant number of indicators of dysfunctional relationships between the different CoPs. The most common signs are guilt and blaming, which run along and amplify all the aforementioned indicators of dysfunctional relationships. How can an organisation looking to build trust and collaboration between the different groups do transform those relationships? We suggest starting with Transactional Analysis (TA) and the OLaF questionnaire as measurement tools to assess how the organisation deals with error, blame and guilt, before looking at possible interventions inspired by therapy. Our complete Therapy Framework is shown in Fig. 2.

*Learning from Errors: OLaF.* We know from the HCI and Human Factors literature that good design can minimise the likelihood of human error on commonly executed tasks.[2] While this is true for employees as well as ITS, current ITS approaches tend to centre employee errors and put blame on them. To foster functional relationships between the CoPs, it is essential to stop the "scaring and bullying" [46] of any CoP and rather cultivate a culture of resilience and learning from errors. For this, we need to develop an understanding of how individuals as well as organisations deal with and learn from errors.

[2] This is because not all situations that employees encounter can be foreseen at the design stage. For cost reasons, even not all foreseeable ones are designed and tested for usability – safety-critical systems, where the cost of the consequences of error can be extremely high, being an exception.

The behaviour of supervisors and colleagues, work processes, task structures as well as principles and values of an organisation with regard to the handling of errors influence the effectiveness of the successive learning stages [42] and therefore need to be incorporated. To assess the organisational climate for learning from mistakes, we propose **OLaF** (German: *Organisationales Lernen aus Fehlern/organisational learning from mistakes*) [41], a questionnaire designed to measure the organisational climate with regard to how mistakes are dealt with. Its strength is that it includes the perspectives of employees as well managers. The results help to generate ideas from different viewpoints on how human error can serve as avenue for individual and organisational learning processes. Complementary to OLaF, Knapp's scale [31] can be used to assess the organisational climate in dealing with guilt to identify leverage points for joint optimisation.

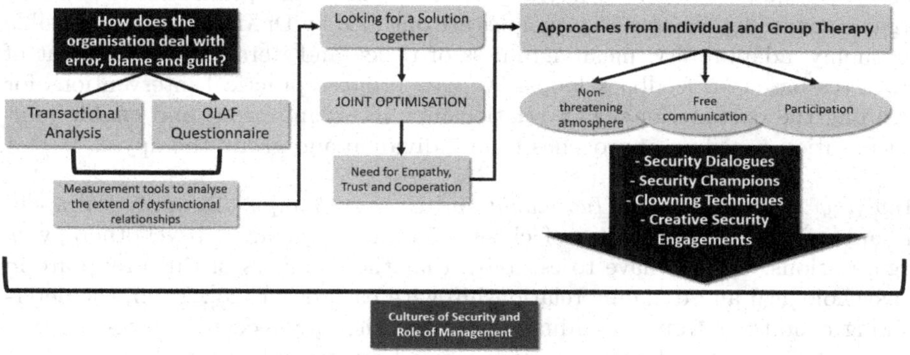


**Fig. 2.** Our proposed therapy framework.

*Evaluating Communication: Transactional Analysis (TA).* As we have seen, fraught communication is one of the major hindrances to the functioning of the different relationships. Therefore it needs to be targeted specifically. Here, TA [11] known as "a communication theory which allows for the systematic analysis of a communication transaction between individuals" [36] can help. Individuals and organisational units have life positions or self-concepts – about themselves and others. In the position "I am o.k. - You are o.k.", the individual or organisational unit accepts both themselves and others without judgement. The position "I am o.k. - You are not o.k." is self-accepting and blaming others. The third position, "I am not o.k. - You are o.k." is characterised by self-rejection and -belittling. Lastly, a negative attitude to oneself and others is reflected in the position "I am not o.k. - You are not o.k." [36]. The ideal position is that both sides perceive each other as "o.k". When people make errors, behaviour should be considered separately from the person - factors contributing to the error identified, and the interaction re-designed to stop triggering the error. Especially in the long-term cooperation with other people, these life positions are useful to understand the patterns and to derive appropriate interventions to get into the "o.k." positions.

These insights provide a path to transform the dysfunctional relationships between the different CoPs. Current approaches to "improving" ITS in organisations start from the "I am o.k. - You are not o.k."-mindset of ITS, as evidenced in the deficit construction of users, and futile attempts to "fix the human". To some extent this view is also held by employees, who blame ITS as "baby-killers", or less dramatically for creating obstacles to task completion, or not being not approachable. To foster collaboration and trust between these CoPs, both need to gain empathy for each other and their specific situations.

For this, everyone needs to stop looking for a culprit – someone to blame – and start cooperatively looking for solutions in **joint optimisation** [3], shifting from blame-centring to solution-centring. In socio-technical systems, it is essential that the requirements of different parties are met for optimal functioning of organisations [38]. Some core principles are outlined by Di Maio [18]: Responsible autonomy, adaptability, meaningfulness of tasks, and iterative development of processes based on feedback loops. We now propose practical interventions for mending the dysfunctional ITS relationships in organisations and enable joint optimisation based on approaches from individual and group therapy.

*Applying Approaches from Individual and Group Therapy.* To apply therapeutic approaches and principles of client-orientated individual psychotherapy in organisations, we first have to establish that the members of this group are in a psychological and dynamic relationship with each other [25]. Then, the determining conditions from individual and group therapy need to be created by a group-related leader. These conditions have been formulated by Hobbs [25] as follows: (1) Members of a group need to feel that they are given the opportunity to participate in matters that concern them directly, (2) All members of a group must be able to communicate freely with one another, (3) A non-threatening atmosphere needs to be created.

*Developing Empathy, Trust and Cooperation.* One major hindrance for functioning relationships between the different groups is lack of interpersonal contact and share language. To counter this, organisations should implement opportunities for employees to engage with each other as well as with security issues in a non-threatening manner. This has successfully been done e.g. in the form of security dialogues [4]; this is more likely to be successful after releasing tension and hostility through humour, and getting everyone to see the problem from everyone's else side – Coles-Kemp et al. [34], for instance used clowns. Communication can be made more effective, and mutual understanding built, by recruiting security champions to act as a conduit – they can explain security to their fellow employees, help them master new behaviours, and report security that isn't working back to the ITS CoP [9] that can serve as intermediaries between the different CoPs and facilitate communication and cooperation. Doing so helps decrease the experienced social distance, gives "a face to security" and further cultivates a sense of ITS as a shared activity and goal, fostering cooperation. Further, having an intermediary person to talk to will decrease the workload of ITS personnel and increase self-efficacy of CoPs in dealing with ITS issues. This will further decrease the negativity in communication as well as the imbalance of power between the CoPs. These attempts can be furthered by deploying Creative Security Engagements [35], an approach in which different stakeholders can address and reflect on their security needs in a participatory manner, bypassing the complexity of ITS terms by using creative methods.

*Management Support.* The relationships between management and ITS also needs attention, but diagnosis and suggestions of intervention are beyond the scope of this paper. However, beyond attending to their own relationships, management needs to lead, enable and resource the changes we have outlined for transforming the relationship between ITS and employees. They need to initiate the rebuilding process, and foster mutual empathy, trust and cooperation between the different CoPs within the organisation. Only then it is possible to cultivate flourishing cultures of security that build on mutual trust and cooperation, seizing human potential instead of demonising it, and framing ITS in a positive and productive manner. For this, it is of major importance that management and leadership actually take *care* of ITS, implementing information security strategies that are tailored to (1.) the specific CoPs and context, (2.) create a shared language between CoPs in terms of ITS, (3.) induce skill-building by communal and apprenticeship-learning and (4.) foster a sense of cooperation between CoPs in the pursuit of the shared goal of ITS of the organisation.

## 7 Discussion and Conclusions

*Limitations.* Our search for practitioner statements is not representative – we set out to find examples of those terms. We primarily chose vendors, conferences and magazines that have their origins in the US and UK. During our search we also found multiple statements that stress that security practitioners should not blame employees but rather the systems they are using – a leading example being the UK NCSC "People are the strongest link"[3] campaign, created by staff in its socio-technical team. But the fact remains that negative characterisation and language that blame employees is out there and dominates. Taken together with the studies of security in organisations [4,8,29], they provide evidence that dysfunctional relationship exist around ITS in a multitude of organisations. Furthermore, did we not link the practitioner statements with the survey results but left both parts for themselves. We might compare both sides more directly in future studies.

*Concluding Remarks.* The relationships between employees and ITS professionals can have a major impact on the well-being, work performance, job satisfaction and, in particular, on the handling of ITS in the everyday work of the persons

[3] https://www.ncsc.gov.uk/speech/people--the-strongest-link, accessed July 29th 2021.

concerned and are therefore of high relevance for organisations. Our study provides insights into the feelings of employees towards ITS professionals and shows that security relationships are often - despite various efforts - still dysfunctional.

We therefore introduced our Therapy Framework to analyse and identify dysfunctional relationships and gave suggestions how they could be mended. We argue that approaches from therapy can help improve relationships and can help bridging the distance between employees and ITS professionals. Organisations may profit from this framework by applying it to identify the problem and take action.

**Acknowledgements.** We would like to thank Simon Parkin for his valuable feedback. We would like to thank the anonymous reviewers for their constructive and fair review. The work was (partially) supported by the PhD School "SecHuman - Security for Humans in Cyberspace" by the federal state of NRW, Germany and also by the Deutsche Forschungsgemeinschaft (DFG, German Research Foundation) under Germany's Excellence Strategy - EXC 2092 CASA - 390781972.

# A Prolific Survey Questions

The following questions were asked in our prolific survey.

*Your Experience with IT Security*

1. What are the first keywords that come into your mind when you think about the IT security personnel in your organisation?
2. How helpful do you consider the IT security personnel?
3. How would you describe the job of IT security personnel that you are in contact with?
4. Have you had any negative experience with IT security personnel?
5. Do you ever feel that you can't follow organisational IT security rules? [All the time, Quite often, About half the time, Sometimes, Never]
6. How would you describe your relationship to the IT security personnel in your organisation?
7. How do you think the IT security personnel would describe this relationship?
8. How much do you think the IT security personnel in your organisation knows about you and your everyday work requirements?
9. What are negative attributes about your relationship with the IT security personnel in your organisation?
10. What are positive attributes about your relationship with the IT security personnel in your organisation?
11. How understandable do you find the communication from the IT security personnel?

12. What indicators of how the IT security personnel feel about you have you noticed?
13. How often do you have contact to IT security personnel? [Every day, Every week, Every month, One or few times a year, Lesser]
14. Which of the following attributes best describe your relationship with the ITS personnel? [Productive, On eye-level, Functional, Respectful, Friendly, Empathetic, Cooperative, Supportive, Open minded, Collegial, Capable of Criticism, Unbiased, Trustful, Balanced, Dysfunctional, Arrogant, Incomprehensible, Top-down/Hierarchical, Uncooperative, Distant, Unsupportive, Patronising, Unapproachable, None of the above]

*Demographic Questions*

1. How would you describe your current employment status? [Employed without management responsibility, Employed with management responsibility, Self-employed, A student, Other]
2. Does your organisation have IT security personnel or even a IT-Security department?
3. Do you currently work in an organisation that requires you to follow certain IT security rules (e.g. password policies, browsing restrictions, data protection policies) or use IT-Security tools (e.g. VPN, Password Managers, encrypted flash drives)?
4. Do you have contact with the IT-Security personnel (e.g. in IT security trainings, when they send you security advice via mail, or when they help you after an security incident or data breach)?
5. Do you work as a IT security specialist and/or was IT security part of your education?
6. In which sector are you employed? [Private Sector, Public Sector, University or Research Institute, Other]
7. In what type of field or department do you work (e.g. sales, human resources, IT, compliance, maintenance)?

## B Security Vendor Statements with Sources

- *"Insider threats can originate from lack of awareness. For example, employees creating workarounds to technology challenges."*[4]
- *"YOU are the weakest link: where are we going wrong with cyber security in Australia?".*[5]

[4] https://tinyurl.com/ey-insider-1.
[5] https://newsroom.kpmg.com.au/weakest-link-going-wrong-cyber-security-australia/ accessed July 12th 2021.

- *"Your employees might not trust you- many times, the relationship between the manager and the workers causes the threats to go undetected."*[6]
- *"More than ever, your users are the weak link in your network security. They need to be trained by an expert like Kevin Mitnick, and after the training stay on their toes, keeping security top of mind."*[7]
- *"The Human Factor in ITS: How Employees are Making Businesses Vulnerable from Within"*[8]
- *"What is the weakest link in today's enterprise IT defenses? End users who violate security policy and are too easily fooled by social engineering attack."*[9]
- *"[...] you know people are the weakest link in the security chain. You can have all the wonderful technologies and layers of Technology security protections in place but ultimately it comes down to the person, right?"*[10]

## C Statement Clouds

See Figs. 3, 4 and 5.

**Fig. 3.** The participants used 93 keywords at least 2 times to describe the IT security staff.

---

[6] https://www.ibm.com/downloads/cas/GRQQYQBJ accessed July 12th 2021.

[7] https://www.knowbe4.com/products/kevin-mitnick-security-awareness-training/ accessed July 07th 2021.

[8] https://www.kaspersky.com/blog/the-human-factor-in-it-security/ accessed July 07th 2021.

[9] https://www.blackhat.com/docs/us-18/black-hat-intel-where-cybersecurity-stands.pdf accessed July 12th.

[10] https://www.youtube.com/watch?v=fFFpj71G6sY accessed July 08th 2021.

**Fig. 4.** 33 positive attributes were mentioned at least 5 times.

**Fig. 5.** Overall, there were 81 negative attributes that were mentioned at least 3 times.

## References

1. Adams, A., Sasse, M.A.: Users are not the enemy. Commun. ACM **42**(12), 40–46 (1999)
2. Albrechtsen, E., Hovden, J.: The information security digital divide between information security managers and users. Comput. Secur. **28**(6), 476–490 (2009)
3. Appelbaum, S.H.: Socio-technical systems theory: an intervention strategy for organizational development. Manag. Decis. **35**(6), 452–463 (1997)
4. Ashenden, D., Lawrence, D.: Security dialogues: building better relationships between security and business. IEEE Secur. Priv. **14**, 82–87 (2016)

5. Ashenden, D., Sasse, A.: CISOs and organisational culture: their own worst enemy? Comput. Secur. **39**, 396–405 (2013)
6. Bada, M., Sasse, A.M., Nurse, J.R.C.: Cyber Security Awareness Campaigns: why do they fail to change behaviour? In: Satapathy, S.C., Joshi, A., Modi, N., Pathak, N. (eds.) Proceedings of International Conference on ICT for Sustainable Development. AISC. Springer, Singapore (2016)
7. Barrett, S.: Overcoming transactional distance as a barrier to effective communication over the Internet. Int. Educ. J. **3**, 34–42 (2002)
8. Beautement, A., Sasse, M.A., Wonham, M.: The compliance budget: managing security behaviour in organisations. In: Keromytis, A., Somayaji, A., Probst, C.W., Bishop, M. (eds.) Proceedings of the 2008 Workshop on New Security Paradigms, p. 47. Association for Computing Machinery, New York (2008)
9. Becker, I., Parkin, S., Sasse, M.A.: Finding security champions in blends of organisational culture. In: Acar, Y., Fahl, S. (eds.) Proceedings 2nd European Workshop on Usable Security. Internet Society, Reston (2017)
10. Beris, O., Beautement, A., Sasse, M.A.: Employee rule breakers, excuse makers and security champions: mapping the risk perceptions and emotions that drive security behaviors. In: Proceedings of the 2015 New Security Paradigms Workshop, NSPW 2015, pp. 73–84. Association for Computing Machinery, New York (2015)
11. Berne, E.: Spiele der Erwachsenen: Psychologie der menschlichen Beziehungen, rororo, vol. 61350: rororo-Sachbuch. Rowohlt-Taschenbuch-Verl., Reinbek bei Hamburg, neuaufl. edn. (2002)
12. BetterCloud: State of Insider Threats in the Digital Workplace (2019)
13. Burdon, M., Coles-Kemp, L.: The significance of securing as a critical component of information security: an Australian narrative. Comput. Secur. **87**, 101601 (2019)
14. Posey, C., Roberts, T.L., Lowry, P.B., Hightower, R.T.: Bridging the divide: a qualitative comparison of information security thought patterns between information security professionals and ordinary organizational insiders. Inf. Manag. **51**(5), 551–567 (2014)
15. Clegg, S.: Frameworks of Power. Sage Publication, London (1989)
16. Coles-Kemp, L., Ashenden, D., O'Hara, K.: Why should i? Cybersecurity, the security of the state and the insecurity of the citizen. Politics Gov. **6**(2), 41–48 (2018)
17. Coyle, D.: The Culture Code: The Secrets of Highly Successful Groups, 11th edn. Bantam Books, New York (2018)
18. Di Maio, P.: Towards a metamodel to support the joint optimization of socio technical systems. Systems **2**(3), 273–296 (2014)
19. Dogan, K., Vecchio, R.P.: Managing envy and jealousy in the workplace. Compens. Benefits Rev. **33**(2), 57–64 (2001)
20. Galvin, K.M., Wilkinson, C.A.: The communication process: Impersonal and interpersonal (2006). Accessed 1 May 2011
21. Heath, C.P., Hall, P.A., Coles-Kemp, L.: Holding on to dissensus: participatory interactions in security design. Strateg. Des. Res. J. **11**(2), 65–78 (2018)
22. Herley, C.: So Long, and no thanks for the externalities: the rational rejection of security advice by users. In: Proceedings of the 2009 Workshop on New Security Paradigms Workshop, NSPW 2009, pp. 133–144. Association for Computing Machinery, New York (2009)
23. Herley, C.: More is not the answer. IEEE Secur. Priv. **12**(1), 14–19 (2014)
24. Herley, C., van Oorschot, P.C.: SoK: science, security and the elusive goal of security as a scientific pursuit. In: 2017 IEEE Symposium on Security and Privacy (SP), pp. 99–120 (2017)

25. Hobbs, N.: Gruppen-bezogene Psychotherapie. In: Rogers, C.R. (ed.) Die klientenzentrierte Gesprächspsychotherapie. Client-Centered Therapy. FISCHER Taschenbuch (2021)
26. Inglesant, P., Sasse, M.A.: Information security as organizational power: a framework for re-thinking security policies. In: 2011 1st Workshop on Socio-Technical Aspects in Security and Trust (STAST), pp. 9–16 (2011)
27. Ponemon Institute: Managing Insider Risk Whitepaper (2016)
28. Budge, J., O'Malley, C., Blankenship, J., Flug, M., Nagel, B.: The Forrester Wave$^{TM}$: Security Awareness and Training Solutions, Q1 2020 (2020)
29. Kirlappos, I., Parkin, S., Sasse, M.A.: Learning from "Shadow Security": why understanding non-compliant behaviors provides the basis for effective security. In: Smith, M., Wagner, D. (eds.) Proceedings 2014 Workshop on Usable Security. Internet Society, Reston, 23 February 2014
30. Klimburg-Witjes, N., Wentland, A.: Hacking humans? Social engineering and the construction of the "deficient user" in cybersecurity discourses. Sci. Technol. Hum. Values **46**(6), 1316–1339 (2021)
31. Knapp, L.: Zum Umgang mit Schuld in Organisationen. Entwicklung und erste Validierung einer Skala zur Erfassung eines Klimas der Schuldzuweisungen. Master thesis, Ruhr University Bochum, Chair for Organisational Psychology (2016)
32. Kocksch, L., Korn, M., Poller, A., Wagenknecht, S.: Caring for IT security: accountabilities, moralities, and oscillations in IT security practices. Proc. ACM Hum.-Comput. Interact. **2**(CSCW), 1–20 (2018)
33. Labianca, G., Brass, D.J.: Exploring the social ledger: negative relationships and negative asymmetry in social networks in organizations. Acad. Manag. Rev. **31**(3), 596–614 (2006)
34. Coles-Kemp, L., Stang, F.: Making digital technology research human: learning from clowning as a social research intervention. Rivista Italiana di Studi sull'Umorismo (RISU) **2**(1), 35–45 (2019)
35. Coles-Kemp, L., Hall, P.: TREsPASS Book 3: Creative Engagements. Royal Holloway (2016)
36. Lukenbill, W.B.: The OK reference department-using transactional analysis in evaluating organizational climates. RQ **15**(4), 317–322 (1976). http://www.jstor.org/stable/41354348
37. Octavia, J.R., van den Hoven, E., de Mondt, H.: Overcoming the distance between friends. In: Electronic Workshops in Computing, BCS Learning & Development (2007)
38. Pasmore, W., Francis, C., Haldeman, J., Shani, A.: Sociotechnical systems: a North American reflection on empirical studies of the seventies. Hum. Relat. **35**(12), 1179–1204 (1982)
39. Ponemon Institute: Global Encryption Trends Study (2019)
40. Proctor, T., Doukakis, I.: Change management: the role of internal communication and employee development. Corp. Commun. Int. J. **8**(4), 268–277 (2003)
41. Putz, D., Schilling, J., Kluge, A., Stangenberg, C.: OlaF. Fragebogen zur Erfassung des organisationalen Klimas für Lernen aus Fehlern. In: Sarges, W. (ed.) Organisationspsychologische Instrumente: Handbuch wirtschaftspsychologischer Testverfahren; 2, pp. 251–258. Pabst, Lengerich [u.a.] (2010)
42. Putz, D., Schilling, J., Kluge, A., Stangenberg, C.: Measuring organizational learning from errors: development and validation of an integrated model and questionnaire. Manag. Learn. **44**(5), 511–536 (2013)
43. Reason, J.: Human error: models and management. BMJ (Clinical Research Ed.) **320**(7237), 768–770 (2000)

44. Renaud, K., Searle, R., Dupui, M.: Shame in cyber security: effective behavior modification tool or counterproductive foil? In: Proceedings of the 2021 New Security Paradigms Workshop, NSPW 2021. Association for Computing Machinery, New York (2021, To appear)
45. Wilson, S.H.: Combating the Lazy User: An Examination of Various Password Policies and Guidelines (2002)
46. Sasse, A.: Scaring and bullying people into security won't work. IEEE Secur. Priv. **13**(3), 80–83 (2015)
47. Schneier, B.: Secrets and Lies: Digital Security in a Networked World. Wiley, New York (2000)
48. Susan, S., Shade, M.: People, the weak link in cyber-security: can ethnography bridge the gap? In: Ethnographic Praxis in Industry Conference Proceedings, vol. 2015, no. 1, pp. 47–57 (2015)
49. Tjosvold, D., Yu, Z.Y., Hui, C.: Team learning from mistakes: the contribution of cooperative goals and problem-solving*. J. Manag. Stud. **41**(7), 1223–1245 (2004)
50. Tracy, K., Eisenberg, E.: Giving criticism: a multiple goals case study. Res. Lang. Soc. Interact. **24**(1–4), 37–70 (1990)
51. Whitten, A., Tygar, J.D.: Why Johnny can't encrypt: a usability evaluation of PGP 5.0. In: Proceedings of the 8th Conference on USENIX Security Symposium, SSYM 1999, vol. 8, p. 14. USENIX Association (1999)
52. Zhu, Y., Nel, P., Bhat, R.: A cross cultural study of communication strategies for building business relationships. Int. J. Cross Cult. Manag. **6**(3), 319–341 (2006)

# Transferring Update Behavior from Smartphones to Smart Consumer Devices

Matthias Fassl[1,2(✉)], Michaela Neumayr[1], Oliver Schedler[1], and Katharina Krombholz[1]

[1] CISPA Helmholtz Center for Information Security, Saarbrücken, Germany
{matthias.fassl,neumayr,oliver.schedler,krombholz}@cispa.de
[2] Saarland University, Saarbrücken, Germany

**Abstract.** Automatic updates are becoming increasingly common, which minimizes the amount of update decisions that users have to make. Rapidly deployed important updates have a major impact on security. However, automatic updates also reduce the users' opportunities to build useful mental models which makes decision-making harder on other consumer devices without automatic updates. Users generally transfer their understanding from domains that they know well (i.e. smartphones) to others. We investigate how well this transfer process works with respect to updates and if users with automatic updates fare worse than those with manual updates.

We conducted a formative field study ($N = 52$) to observe users' update settings on smartphones and examine reasons for their (de-)activation. Based on the results, we conducted an online survey ($N = 91$) to compare how users perceive update notifications for smartphones and smart consumer devices. One of our main findings is that update decisions based on *expected changes* do not apply well to these devices since participants do not expect meaningful and visual changes. We suggest naming updates for such devices 'maintenance' to move users' expectations from 'new features' to 'ensuring future functionality'.

## 1 Introduction

Keeping systems and software up to date is the most common expert advice for securing devices [11,20]. Consequently, prior work extensively studied update attitudes and behavior [12,13,23,24,26,27]. Vendors introduced partially or fully automatic updates since users often delay or skip updates. Windows 10 introduced intervention-less automatic update downloads and installation, Android and iOS introduced automatic updates, and Google Chrome started using silent automatic updates over ten years ago. Automatic updates improve the rate and speed of update deployment [3]. However, automatic updates create two potential pitfalls: (1) Users feel betrayed as soon as automated systems make choices that defy their expectations [4] and these incidents will impact all future update decisions [26]; (2) Automated updates reduce users' understanding of what is happening on their computers [27]. These pitfalls diminish users' ability to make informed decisions when updates cannot be fully automated.


S. Katsikas et al. (Eds.): ESORICS 2021 Workshops, LNCS 13106, pp. 357–383, 2022.
https://doi.org/10.1007/978-3-030-95484-0_21

Update behaviors and attitudes on desktops and smartphones are well studied [3–5,7,12–15,23–27]. However, smart consumer devices with minimalistic user interfaces (UIs) and inconspicuous computing power became common after the Internet-of-Things emerged. Gartner predicted 20.8 billion IoT devices for 2020, thereof 13.5 billion consumer devices [16]. In contrast to communication and entertainment heavy smartphones, IoT devices control day-to-day life. Some smart consumer devices, e.g., dishwashers, have very minimal UIs, impacting how users perceive and handle updates. However, there is still little research on how users transfer update behavior to other application areas beyond smartphones and desktops. Automatic updates alleviate some update issues. However, sometimes they are neither practical nor safe, and maybe not even possible for devices with limited UIs – making questions on user understanding and engagement even more pressing [1,21]. Since traditional computing devices move towards automatic updates, awareness of updates' effects and importance decreases. However, users may have to decide on updates again when handling smart consumer devices. It remains unclear how users make their update decisions on these devices and how they transfer their update-knowledge from traditional computing devices.

The aim of this work is (1) to study users' reasons for (de-)activating automatic updates, (2) to understand how users handle manual update decisions on smartphones, and (3) to evaluate if their update reasoning is transferable to smart consumer devices found in the IoT. We conducted an exploratory field study ($N = 52$) on users' reasons for deactivating automatic updates. We used a mixed-methods online survey ($N = 91$) to explore how automatic updates affect users' manual update decisions and how users transfer their update behavior smart consumer devices (in our study: dishwasher, self-lacing shoes, and a modern car). Our main contributions are: (1) we **observed an increased rate of automatic updates** for smartphone apps (compared to Tian et al. [23]) and provide **ranked lists of reasons for (de)activating automatic updates**; (2) we **describe the differences between users that activated automatic updates and those who did not** (3) we discuss how **transferring users' update behavior to smart consumer devices might fail** since two main strategies (evaluation by expected changes and evaluation by notification) are difficult to apply to smart consumer devices; (4) we provide **design implications** for smart consumer device updates.

## 2 Methodology

Guided by the following research questions, we study how automatic updates affect users' remaining update decisions on smartphones and how well these decisions transfer to smart consumer devices.

RQ1: How common is deactivation of automatic updates and what are the users' reasons for it?

RQ2: How do users' update attitudes (information demand, perceived importance, and expected effects) transfer from smartphones to smart consumer devices?

Our *formative field study* establishes the share of users who (do not) use automatic updates and their (de)activation reasons. Based on these results, we designed an *online survey* which compares how participants make update decisions on smartphones and smart consumer devices. We explained the purpose, the procedure, and the type of questions to all study participants. We did not collect identifying information and instructed participants to provide screenshots without identifiers.

All participants gave us their informed consent. We compensated participants for their time, based on the minimum wage. Our university's ethical review board approved this study.

### 2.1 Formative Field Study

In the formative field study ($N = 52$), we collected the participants' OS version, the OS update settings (if applicable), and update settings for installed apps. We asked open-ended questions to understand their reasons for changing settings. Afterwards we used a questionnaire to collect demographic data. Section B presents the entire questionnaire. We conducted a pre-study with 8 participants. For three days, we recruited participants with Android or Apple phones in front of our university's dining hall during lunch time. Table 3 in the Appendix presents the demographics.

We analyzed the observed frequencies of smartphone OS settings. We used *open coding* to evaluate qualitative free-response data. Two researchers independently coded the responses and constructed two independent codebooks, then constructed a common codebook (see Sect. C) and resolved all disagreements.

### 2.2 Online Survey

The formative field study showed that participants like to maintain control over installed software. They preferred to update apps they considered important and influence the installation time to avoid bugs and data-loss, confirming previous work [5,15,25,26].

*Questionnaire.* We used those results to construct an online survey on Amazon MTurk ($N = 91$) which exposed participants to five different update scenarios, two for mobile phones (system and app update) and three concerning smart consumer devices (dishwasher, shoes, car). Appendix E shows the notifications that we used in the survey. We chose update scenarios that (1) concern devices with a low barrier to use – so most participants could imagine a use-case for them, and (2) includes an update decision that participants will not have faced before. Similarily, Fagan et al. [5] used fictional update notifications to understand users' update behaviors and attitudes. For each update notification, we asked participants to explain the update's importance, what kind of changes they expect, when they would prefer to install it, and how they would redesign the notification.

To evaluate users' responses in context we also asked for their update settings (phone OS version, screenshots of OS and app update settings), their potential update avoidance behavior (connected to WiFi and charging habits), and their 5-point Likert evaluation of (de)activation reasons. Since prior work [9] suggests that update behavior depends on technology-savyness, sense of autonomy, and personality, we added appropriate psychometric scales (Affinity for Technology Interaction (ATI) [8], Reactance to Autonomy [10], and Big Five Inventory (BFI-K) [18]). We asked for general demographic information such as gender, occupation, educational background, and household income and added three attention check questions throughout the survey. Section D in the Appendix presents the full questionnaire (translated into English).

*Evaluation.* We used a repeated-measures ANOVA to find significant differences between perceived importance of the five notifications. We evaluated the open-ended responses to the five notifications with thematic analysis [2]. Two researchers used *open coding* to independently assign initial codes to their part of the data. They used the other's initial codebook to independently code the remaining data, resulting in an inter-coder reliability (ICA) of Brennan and Prediger's $\kappa = 0.63$. In an iterative approach, the two researchers discussed the categories with the most mismatches, renamed or merged codes, and revised the segments in questions, resulting in an inter-coder reliability (ICA) of Brennan and Prediger's $\kappa = 0.83$. During the last session they used *axial coding* to restructured the entire codebook and identify themes. Section F in the Appendix contains the final codebook (containing 8 categories with a total of 70 codes).

To understand how well update decisions transfer to smart consumer devices, we qualitatively compare users responses according to their update preferences (automatic vs. manual) and the type of notification they responded to (smartphone vs. smart consumer device). We report differences between those groups if: (1) codes are not included in both groups, (2) the most frequently assigned codes are different, or (3) if a code was assigned three times more often in one group.

*Recruitment and Participants.* After conducting a pilot study ($N = 3$), we recruited Amazon MTurk workers from Germany with an approval rate of 99.0% and compensated them with USD 5.60. We excluded five of 96 participants, either because the GeoIP results showed that they were not in Germany or two researchers independently agreed that their provided answers did not answer the open questions. Table 6 in the Appendix presents the demographics.

## 3 Results

We report the prevalence of automatic updates that we observed in our formative field study and our online survey in Sect. 3.1. Using that information we evaluate (in Subsect. 3.2) how activated automatic updates influence the participants' responses to the shown update notifications. In Subsect. 3.3 we describe how participants decide if and when they would like to install updates and how well this decision-process transfers from smartphones to smart consumer devices. During the evaluation we found several contradicting user requirements which we present in Subsect. 3.4.

### 3.1 Automatic Update Settings and Reasons for (De)activation

Most of the participants in the formative field study did not change default update settings. Almost all Android users had operating system updates enabled and used the "WiFi only" option for application updates (the default). Most iOS users had activated OS updates, but more than a third of them deactivated automatic application updates. Table 4 in the Appendix shows a summary of the observed update settings. Table 5 compares update settings of users with high (≥4) and low (<4) self-efficacy scores. Participants most commonly mentioned three types of security-relevant practices that they did on a regular basis: *authentication*, *privacy settings*, and *abstention* from potentially useful products or features. Even though our study procedure primed all participants on updates, only four participants mentioned that they regularly apply updates to keep their mobile secure. In the online survey 63 (69%) participants had an Android phone, whereas 28 (31%) had an iPhone. By default, Android enables automatic OS updates, and iOS will ask during the initial setup. 52 participants (57%) had automatic OS updates enabled, 17 (19%) had them disabled, and 22 (24%) did not submit a suitable screenshot. By default, both Android and iOS enable automatic app updates. 79 participants (87%) had enabled automatic app updates, 10 (11%) disabled them, and 2 (2%) did not submit a suitable screenshot.

In the formative field study, the two most common reasons for deactivating updates were the wish to maintain control over installed software or concerns about data usage. Two aspects of maintaining control came up: (1) participants only wanted increased agency over updates for apps they perceived as important enough, and (2) they would like to decide when to install an update since they know from experience that new updates may have bugs and could lead to data-loss. In the formative field study the two most common reasons for participants to activate automatic updates were convenience and the general desire to be up to date. The online survey asked participants to rate these reasons for (de)activation of automatic updates on a 7-point Likert scale (see Table 7 in the Appendix).

### 3.2 Automatic Updates and Their Effect on Update Decisions

We assumed activated automatic updates would influence users in two ways: (1) that some of the users that are unhappy with automatic updates would try to avoid triggering the installation criteria for them (thereby delaying or skipping updates). This would increase participants' agency in deciding the installation time without deactivating automatic updates. (2) that users that are happy with automatic updates would slowly lose the ability to make update decisions over time and factor in fewer potential problems before deciding. In order to find evidence for these assumptions we added two sections to our online survey.

*Avoidance Behavior.* On Android and iOS, automatic updates are performed by default when the phone charges and is connected to a WiFi network. For 80% of the participants the time of day that they most often charge their phone coincides with a time of day that they are usually connected to WiFi. That means that most participants are able to receive their automatic updates during the course of 24 h and do not show signs of update avoidance. Table 8 in the Appendix presents the participants' complete responses.

*Effects of Automatic Update Settings.* We compared the qualitative answers of participants that activated automatic updates with the answers of participants who favored manual updates. We found no qualitative differences between these groups regarding their preferred installation time and their suggested changes to the update notification. Participants who activated automatic updates mainly mentioned three concepts: (1) updates are necessary for maintenance, (2) updates are necessary for security, and (3) updates can be important without having visible effects. Only participants that favored manual updates stated that they would like to wait for experience reports from other users.

### 3.3 Transferring Update Behavior to Smart Consumer Devices

In an effort to understand how well the users' update behavior transfers to smart consumer or IoT devices, we start by reporting general results on the responses to update notifications shown in the online study. We present our results according to three of the six update stages discovered by Vaniea et al. [25]: deciding, preparation, and deployment. Afterwards, we elaborate on the participants' different attitudes to smartphone and smart consumer device update notifications.

*Deciding.* Our formative field study indicated that the participants' perception of a manual update's importance influences their decision to install them. Therefore, we asked participants to rate the importance of the presented manual update notifications on a 5-point Likert scale and provide a qualitative explanation. We present the participants' ranking of importance before going into more detail with the qualitative evaluation of the response.

Participants considered system updates the most important type of update ($m = 3.69$, $sd = 1.09$), followed by updates for cars ($m = 3.1$, $sd = 1.20$), phone apps ($m = 2.41$, $sd = 1.1$), and dishwashers ($m = 2.29$, $sd = 1.28$). Updates for shoes were considered least important ($m = 1.9$, $sd = 1.03$) of all five update notifications. Figure 1 provides an overview of the resulting scores and which group comparisons revealed significant differences. We used a one-way repeated measures ANOVA to compare the mean importance scores of the update notifications. Shapiro-Wilk's test indicated that we cannot assume a normal distribution. However, a repeated-measures ANOVA is robust against such a violation. Mauchly's test indicated that the assumption of sphericity had been violated, therefore we report Greenhouse-Geisser corrected tests. Mean scores for the perceived importance of the update situation were statistically different ($F(3.39, 331.94) = 44.25$, $p < .001$, $\eta^2 = .33$). Table 1 shows notification comparisons with differences according to the post-hoc tests. The resulting ranking of importance indicates that participants might view smart consumer devices (that are not evidently safety-critical) to be less important than other kind of updates.

The evaluation of the open-ended questions for each update notification resulted in different themes covering the *decision* stage. Many participants reported possible positive or negative effects that they considered before updating. Amongst others, participants named new features, performance, stability, and usability improvements as potentially positive effects. Almost all of the reported negative effects were based on personal experience: participants reported that some updates removed features, introduced bugs, led to loss of personal data, and that they took too much time.

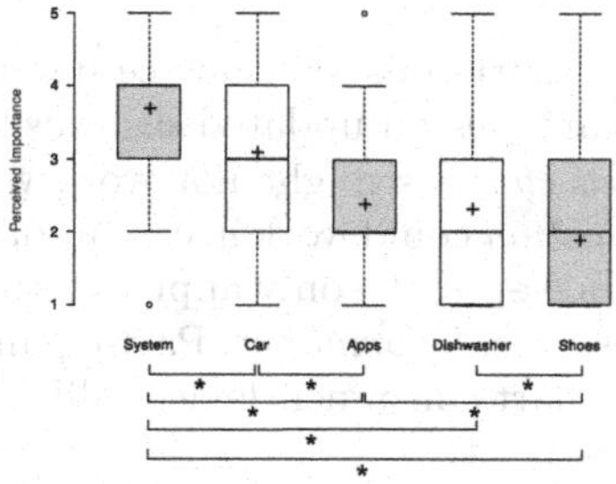


**Fig. 1.** Ranking of updates according to perceived importance (*) marks pairwise significant differences

**Table 1.** Significant differences in importance between update notifications

| Comparison | Mean Diff. | Sign. | |
|---|---|---|---|
| System & Apps | 1.29 | <.001 | *** |
| System & Dishwasher | 1.41 | <.001 | *** |
| System & Shoes | 1.79 | <.001 | *** |
| System & Car | 0.59 | <.001 | *** |
| Apps & Shoes | 0.51 | .02 | * |
| Apps & Car | −0.69 | <.001 | *** |
| Dishwasher & Car | −0.81 | <.001 | *** |
| Shoes & Car | −1.20 | <.001 | *** |

*Sign. codes:* 0 '***' 0.001 '**' 0.01 '*' 0.05 '.' 0.1 ' ' 1

Amongst participants with negative experience were also some who did not have any expectations from updates, but were happy if they did not impede the functionality: "if it still works afterwards, then it's fine" (P96). In the qualitative data we found three different strategies that participants used to evaluate the importance of updates:

1. *By expected changes.* Expected changes can increase or decrease an update's perceived importance. Device maintenance, new features, and security increased the perceived importance, except in cases of minor bug fixes: "probably just some bug fixes" (P74).
2. *By the presentation and content of the update notification.* Some participants scrutinized update notifications to understand the updates' importance. Participants concluded that notifications without information are not important: "the green color is a sign that it [the update] is not important" (P20) or "it did not appear to be important" (P80).

**Table 2.** Participants' preferred update timing.

| | At notification | Later | Never | No opinion |
|---|---|---|---|---|
| Phone (System) | 35 (38.%5) | 52 (57.1%) | 4 (4.4%) | – |
| Car (System) | 40 (44.0%) | 47 (51.6%) | 4 (4.4%) | – |
| Phone (App) | 32 (35.2%) | 49 (53.8%) | 10 (11.0%) | – |
| Dishwasher (System) | 39 (42.8%) | 24 (26.4%) | 19 (20.9%) | 9 (9.9%) |
| Shoe (System) | – | – | 37 (40.7%) | 54 (59.3%) |

3. *By principle.* Often, participants used a general principle such as "software updates are always important" (P66) to guide their update-decisions. However, participants sometimes based their principles on the type of device, e.g., smart consumer device updates were not important, and smartphone system updates were important.

Many participants could not imagine what a smart consumer device update would change, e.g., "I can not imagine what advantages an updated dishwasher could offer" (P35). Hence, evaluating *by expected changes* might not work well with smart consumer devices. *Evaluating by notification* could work in case update notifications provide the necessary information. However, the only approach that transfers well to smart consumer devices is the last one, *by principle.* Participants applied this approach to smartphones and other smart consumer devices alike.

*Preparation.* Answers from the *Preparation* stage mainly concerned the update procedures' timing: delay updates in general, inconvenient update time, waiting for specific resources (power or WiFi access), or create backups before update. Participants commonly waited until bed time to install updates: "I prefer updating just before bedtime. Since I don't need a smartphone during that time." (P23).

*Deployment.* For the *Deployment* stage, participants wanted to decide the updates' installation time and demanded detailed information in notifications. As P62 put it: "I like having the option to decide for myself when something will be installed". More users preferred to postpone smartphone and car updates, although between 35% and 44% would update right away. The majority of participants would perform dishwasher updates right away, even though they did not regard it as especially important (ranked fourth in Fig. 1). Participants either had no opinion on the preferred time of installation or would like to skip installing the self-lacing shoes update altogether, suggesting that users do not see any benefit of updating self-lacing shoes. Table 2 shows the preferred time to perform updates.

In some cases participants did not care about small and unimportant changes and wanted to install them automatically, while still keeping the agency for important updates. In contrast, other participants preferred automatic installation of important updates: "Special updates should be installed automatically" (P65).

*Comparing Update Behavior for Smartphones and Smart Consumer Devices.* While participants focused on security benefits of smartphone updates (by principle), participants did not consider smart consumer device updates important by principle, probably because they did not see the point of them. Compared to smartphone updates, they focused more on safety aspects and maintenance, e.g., "Ensures that the system runs correctly" (P69 regarding car software updates). Participants focused on potential security benefits and privacy-infringements with smartphone updates, which was not a concern with smart consumer device. Most participants did not expect any visible changes to smart consumer devices after updates. Commonly, participants preferred to install smartphones updates "Instantly if WiFi is available and the battery is sufficiently charged" (P5). Additionally, some participants install smartphone updates because they are curious about potential changes, which they did not do with smart consumer devices. Participants suspected that they could not use smart consumer devices during the update process, which is why they preferred to delay updates. Participants demanded similar changes to update notification for smartphone and smart consumer device updates. However, more participants did not have design suggestions for smart consumer device update notifications, probably because they did not deem updates necessary for these types of devices.

### 3.4 Contradicting User Requirements

During the evaluation, we uncovered the following five different contradictions of user requirements:

**CR1: Installation Time.** Some participants thought updates that take a long time to install are important because they change a lot. Other participants delay these updates because they fear disrupting their regular activities. Resulting in a small conundrum: small, quickly installed, security patches may reduce the perceived importance to users – while bundling them in large updates keeps users vulnerable who defer them. This contradicting requirement is a problem for systems in immediate use such as cars or even self-lacing basketball shoes, while it is not an issue for asynchronously used smart consumer devices, e.g., dishwashers.

**CR2: Amount of Information.** Some participants demanded detailed update notifications that explain its purpose and affected software parts. They carefully vet updates to avoid specific negative consequences. Others did not care about information, preferred influencing the installation time, or did not want any agency. Systems may accommodate all these user types by asking them about their policy preference and adapting to their update behavior. Detailed information in update notifications is crucial for smart consumer devices since participants had difficulties understanding their purpose and effect.

**CR3: UI and Changes.** A few participants disliked updates that changed UIs, they claimed that older UI versions worked better and did not confuse them. Others enthusiastically looked forward to using new UIs. Hence, everyone demands information about UI changes, even though users' reaction can vary. This contradicting requirement only applies to smart devices with malleable user interaction, such as car's touchscreens or voice interfaces. It does not apply to smart consumer devices with fixed interaction, such as the basketball shoes (only two buttons) or dishwashers.

**CR4: Time of Notification.** Participants could not agree on appropriate times for update notifications. Several factors influenced the appropriate installation time: (1) necessary resources (remaining battery life or internet access), (2) necessary preparations (reading the installation notes or creating a backup), and (3) when they are planning on using the device. While smartphones consider the first point, the second and third are highly context-dependent or specific to the users' update attitudes. Smart consumer device users are concerned with (3) since they want to immediately use their device (such as the basketball shoes or the car) – for these devices notification should arrive at the end of a usage session or offer to delay the installation accordingly.

**CR5: Automating Updates.** For several participants it was important to control updates for applications they considered important, but would even welcome automatic updates for all other applications. Other participants' approach was exactly opposite, they wanted to automatically install important updates, because they felt their decision was not necessary or beneficial in those cases. While still maintaining control for update decisions that were not critical. This contradicting user requirement applies to all IoT devices and smartphones. This issue warrants closer inspection in future work to see if those are actually opposite requirements or if participants thought about different levels of importance. Different levels of importance would result in three categories: (1) critical: automatic updates, (2) important for personal use: manual update decisions, and (3) others: automatic updates.

Interestingly, participants reported being annoyed by manual and automatic updates. Some said that update notifications requiring their decision annoyed them, which they resolved by enabling automatic updates. Others felt that updates slowed down the system or reduced the available download speed, which they resolved by disabling them. Some of those contradictions result from a fixed security policy and could be remedied by dynamic policies that are adaptable to the individual user, as suggested by Edwards et al. [4].

## 4 Discussion

Like all other study designs, this work and its results come with limitations. The results from our formative field study have an age bias (Table 3), our online survey' participants felt more comfortable with technology than the average population (Table 6), and both datasets have a gender bias to men. However, Amazon MTurk is more representative of the U.S. than the census-representative panel responses [19]. In the foreseeable future, the average (target) users of smart consumer and IoT devices will be older than today. Hence, more research on the security of smart consumer devices with an older population will be necessary.

Given the nature of an online survey, we collected self-reported data about update notifications that participants did not experience on their own devices.

However, we were primarily interested in the participants' update thought-process, which we could not have researched without self-reported data, even if participants experienced a real update situation.

### 4.1 Automatic Update Settings

The push for automatic updates by default has been effective at increasing the amount of users that keep automatic updates enabled. Previous work by Tian et al. [23] concluded that 47.7% updated their apps automatically, which has increased to 86.8% according to our results. We observed that iOS users more commonly deactivated automatic updates than Android users: 33% of them disabled automatic system updates (compared to 18% of Android users) and 16% of them disabled automatic app updates (compared to 14% of Android users). We assume that the reason for this difference is grounded in the UI: on iOS, the options to deactivate updates are in the general settings menu, whereas they are harder to find on Android. Prior to our work, we assumed that users change their update settings at most once. However, four (7.6%) participants of the formative field study stated that they had changed their update settings multiple times, indicating that the available options do not fit the participants' needs. For those users a more dynamic, context-sensitive security policy might be important [4].

We analyzed the participants' answers according to their update settings to find possible effects of those settings on the remaining manual update decisions. Participants with automatic update settings more commonly referenced concepts such as maintenance, security, and the invisibility of software-changes. We assume the reason for this difference is that users who think of the necessary but invisible changes included in updates are generally more comfortable with the idea of automatic updates. Additionally, we found that only users with manual updates wait for experience reports from other users before updating themselves. A possible explanation for this difference is that users with negative update experiences in the past are more risk-averse when installing updates. This would also explain why they deactivate automatic updates in the first place.

### 4.2 Transferring Update Behavior

Not all IoT device updates are automatable and some of them have minimalistic UIs, so we have to know how users will handle update decisions. Prior work [25] and our formative field study identify an update's perceived importance as a decision factor. Participants ranked the importance of the five update notifications as follows: operating system updates, car, apps, dishwasher, shoes. Indicating that users might think IoT device updates are less important than other kinds of updates, except for safety-relevant IoT devices.

In our qualitative data, we found three different approaches to evaluate the importance of updates: by the expected changes, by the presentation or content of the update notification, or by principle. We discovered that participants in our study could often not imagine what kind of changes updates for IoT devices might entail. However, some users judge the importance of an update by evaluating the expected changes, impacting their install decision.

One of the root causes for this could be the analogical transfer of update behavior based on the term 'update'. An 'update' often implies new and improved software, which either scares or excites users. In recent years, we saw how major updates with invisible changes are bundled with minor visible changes, such as dark mode[1], or a new set of emojis, to communicate the update's importance. Analogical transfer of update decisions from smartphones to IoT devices may cause similar expectations. Son et al. [22] discussed how words influence the analogical transfer of concepts. Renaming 'updates' for IoT devices may avoid expectations of visible changes. Participants often mentioned 'maintenance', e.g. P43 "So that I can use the device without problems". We suggest this term for IoT updates that (1) do not contain visible changes and (2) cannot lead to loss of data. We do not recommend a name change for other updates to avoid undermining users' trust. Separating the terms "updates" and "maintenance" could eliminate unwarranted expectations of visible changes and reduce the fear of unexpected functionality or user interface changes.

More than half of the participants would have delayed the updates for the smartphone or the car which is in stark contrast to the update for the dishwasher or shoes. We think that this is a sign of risk-aversion, since the participants heavily rely on the functionality of those devices. While this study focused on smart consumer devices used by individuals, there is also communal use of smart consumer and IoT devices. While we expect increased risk-aversion in these cases, future research would be valuable to get a more complete picture of users' update preferences. The most popular option for the dishwasher update was to install it at the time of the notification, presumably as the distraction from the main task was perceived as less severe and participants had no issues with postponing an unattended task. Regarding the updates for shoes, participants either had no opinion about their preferred time of installation or did not want to install them at all. We interpret this as a sign that participants did not see the point of self-lacing shoes in general and did not want to maintain them in a working condition.

Comparing participants' perspective on updating smartphones and IoT devices also warrants a discussion about differences between devices and applications: (1) if the device has a fixed user interface or a reconfigurable one, (2) if the device is for a single purpose or for multiple purposes, (3) the type and amount of available resources such as Internet connection and power supply, and (4) how frequently people use them in everyday life. Comparing along these categories suggests that smartphones and IoT devices have different usage patterns - an exception being multi-purpose IoT devices with a malleable user interface such as voice assistants. If we instead compare specific IoT and smartphone applications it makes sense to classify according to user-centered themes from the qualitative analysis: urgency of use, importance of continued functionality, importance of

[1] Dark mode changes the UI to a darker color palette to reduce strain on the eyes in low ambient light.

specific feature-set, and importance of personal data associated with application. Especially the first two themes are important factors for smartphones as well as IoT devices and they will shape users' update decisions. However, we should not overestimate the usage patterns specific to applications or devices, since decisions for new devices or applications are often based on prior experience with other applications [26].

User interaction design is a tool for communication between users and the underlying technology. It should take the users' mental models into account and translate them as well as possible to corresponding mechanisms. Our findings can serve as a basis to understand user-specific constraints on update procedures. This gives several design indications which we will present in the next section. The technical goal of broadly deployed updates for security and maintenance purposes does not seem far-fetched and does not necessarily contradict users' values.

### 4.3 Implications for Design

Users consider several types of information before installing updates: how important they perceive the update, if they update interferes with their current primary task, and if they can live with the expected changes. How users perceive those factors can be influenced to some degree by design mechanisms. In the following, we provide a series of design implications based on the open-ended questions in our online survey to lay foundations for future work. In future work, we plan to expand and validate these recommendations.

**ID1: Store information about users' software or IoT device usage and use this data to adapt update procedures to them.** A common sentiment among participants was that they only consider apps that they frequently use as important and worthy of updates. This allows auto-updating IoT devices (if possible) or smartphones apps that user do not consider important without infringing on their sense of control.

**ID2: Reduce the amount of update notifications as much as possible.** Participants considered frequently occurring updates as not interesting and unimportant. In contrast, they perceive rare updates as special and probably important enough to warrant their attention. This applies to IoT devices and smartphones equally.

**ID3: Important updates should take longer to install than unimportant ones.** Participants perceived large updates that take longer to install as more important than quickly installed updates. Hence, the duration of the installation should reflect the update's importance. In most cases, developers should consider an update important if it reflects the users' values of important updates (this requires some feedback from individual users). However, systems should be able to (if possible) install critical updates that do not impact user experience without user-interaction. This applies equally to IoT devices and smartphones. However, immediate use is important for some types of IoT devices (e.g., the car, shoes, TVs, ...) the timing of these longer updates is critical.

**ID4: Restrict install options for important updates to convey importance.** The interface options available in the update notification also communicate how important an update is. As one participant phrased it: "Since I can delay the update, it is apparently not an important update" (P53). This type of modifications has even more effect on IoT devices with immediate use requirements, since an update has to be very important to force active waiting until the update is finished. Other devices, such as a dishwasher or apps that are not used often, will not be as affected as much by such a design change.

**ID5: Clearly communicate possible consequences of an update.** The fear of data loss made our participants delay an update until they create a backup of their data. Informing users if their personal data will be affected by the update and creating automatic backups could reduce the users' fear of updating. Participants were worried that an update could take longer than expected and prevent them from completing their primary task. Therefore, it is important that the update notification conveys these aspects ahead of time. This is important for software and devices that users depend on for regular activities that cannot be arbitrarily delayed: software required for work related tasks, and mobility devices (cars, shoes).

**ID6: Provide context-dependent options to delay installation time.** One of the major suggestions of improvement for update notifications was that users want more agency to select the time of installation. Some participants proposed a "later" button, some wanted to select a certain time, and one suggested an option "install after current task". We suggest decoupling the decision time from installation time in a context-sensitive way to provide a user-centered installation time. All software and devices that users immediately require and that are task-centered would benefit from such an option. Distinguishing tasks might be easier for IoT devices even (as in all our presented IoT devices), since they are often only used for a single purpose.

**ID7: Changes of the User Interface should remain optional wherever possible.** Updated user interfaces were considered unimportant by most participants. Some considered UI changes a burden, others thought they had the potential to make them feel as if they had gotten a new device. Since UI updates could be a barrier to updating, those should be separated from the rest and remain optional for users. This design would probably not affect IoT devices as much, because many of them do not have a malleable user interface in the first place. However, this could be a necessary option for devices that are controlled by a touch screen or voice.

**ID8: Let users decide if software that they consider important should update automatically.** Some participants were annoyed by the amount of updates that they considered unimportant: they wanted to have these automated but still manually update apps they consider important. Other participants thought it did not make sense for them to be able to decline important updates, instead they were willing to decide upon less important updates. Especially for smartphones a choice like this could severely improve the amount of update notifications that users see, while increasing the relevance of these notifications.

This distinctions is less important for IoT devices, because they receive a smaller amount of updates in general.

## 5 Related Work

*Reasons for (Not) Updating.* Vaniea et al. [25] found that participants who always installed updates or believed in an update's importance readily installed updates, whereas participants who were satisfied with current versions delayed updates. Satisfaction with the current software version, undesired UI changes, the perceived lack of purpose of software updates, and negative prior update experiences hinder participants from updating [26]. Mathur et al. [15] found that 40.5% of participants thought about the costs of updating, 29.2% considered the necessity of updates before installing, and 7.5% were concerned about the potential risk of updating. We extend Mathur et al.'s work with a focus on smartphones and smart consumer devices.

Users' main source of information about updates is the notification that they see. Users often misunderstand how updates change their system, which frustrates them and about 16% of them refuse to apply updates [5]. Tian et al. [23] found that 42.6% participants regretted updating a smartphone app in the past because of bugs, "bad" UIs, and privacy-invasive practices. Since participants relied on reviews for their update-decisions, the authors introduced a review-based support system. Mathur et al.'s [14] formative study found that users want know about an update's purpose and that trust in vendors, expected compatibility issues, user interface changes, social influences, and installation time affected update decisions. They built a prototype of a corresponding OS update process which satisfied half of the participants because it decreased interruptions.

*Effects of Automating Updates.* According to Marthur et al. [13], users are comfortable with auto-updating apps if they consider them important; trustworthy, or if they are satisfied with them. Previous negative experience with updates reduces users' comfort with auto-updating. Edwards et al. [4] finds that removing users from security choices creates a problem when automation fails: users are ill-equipped to understand and cope with security decisions. Wash et al. [27] found that users misunderstand their own update behavior, which is bad since future update decisions are based on wrong assumption, which improved education cannot fix. They argue that removing users from most decisions makes it difficult for them to intelligently make the remaining decisions. Worryingly, there is some indications that users transfer their expectations from one system to another, e.g., Ponticello et al. [17] found participants who transfer their authentication expectations. The same could hold true for users' update expectations and decision strategies. Forget et al. [7] found that users with misaligned estimated and actual security expertise might make rational decisions that lead to ineffective security. Hence, user engagement which might lead to risky decisions in these cases.

*Updating IoT Devices.* Fernandes et al. [6] found that over 55% of existing SmartApps on SmartThings are over-privileged and have inadequate security controls. Zeng et al. [28] used an exploratory design study to understand users' requirements for access control in multi-user smart home designs. In 2006, Bellissimo et al. [1] found that secure updates for IoT devices face challenges such as untrusted infrastructure, sporadic network connectivity, or limited local resources. Simpson et al. [21] discuss usability challenges of applying updates on IoT devices, specifically update notification and predicting convenient update times.

## 6 Conclusion and Future Work

Among other things, we found that the prevalence of automatic updates for applications on mobile phones has increased to 86.8% (in comparison to 47.7% [23]) and that 18.7% of participants deactivated automatic system updates. Our results suggest that iOS users deactivate automatic updates more often than Android users. We hypothesize that easy access to the relevant option in the UI explains most of that difference (see Sect. A). Users explained their deactivated automatic updates with a fear that updates might introduce flaws and agency in update decisions, fear of compatibility issues, and a limited or expensive data plan. The most important reasons to activate automatic updates were staying up to date, convenience, and security. We expected to find evidence of avoidance behavior amongst participants (i.e., avoiding charging their phone while connected to WiFi), but our results do not support this. Participants who enabled automatic updates approached update decisions similar to those with manual updates. However, three concepts were more important to them: the idea that updates are necessary for maintenance, for security, and that updates could be important even if they do not have any visible effects. Additionally, participants who favored automatic updates were not interested in other users' experience reports.

Prior work [25] and our formative field study provide evidence that the perceived importance of an update is a decisive factor for installing it. Our results indicate that users perceive updates for smart consumer devices as less important than regular updates, except for safety-relevant devices. Our contribution includes a classification of how users evaluate the importance of updates: by expected changes, by the presentation and content of the notification, and by principle. Participants in our study could not imagine meaningful changes for smart consumer devices; the corresponding notification lacked information. Therefore, the evaluation by principle is the only method that led participants to conclude that updates for these devices are important and that they would install them soon or immediately after receiving the notification. Prior work [22] indicates that a concept's name promotes analogical transfer: An 'update' might imply new features or at least focus on visible changes. However, in the case of IoT device updates, participants mentioned the concept of 'maintenance' more often. We hypothesize that using the word 'maintenance' to describe updates without visible changes might increase users' willingness to install them. We provide a list of areas of tension based on conflicting motivations and themes from our data. These open up new directions for designing update solutions that work well for everyone.

At the workshop, participants discussed areas of future research with us. The first idea was identifying and developing a fine-granular terminology to describe the exact nature of updates. Using such terminology, developers could easily communicate updates' effects to end users – simplifying their update decision. The second idea concerned how the companies who create software updates manage this process. Understanding the rationale for changing user interfaces, deprecating features, packaging update bundles, and automating update decisions may help in improving end users' update experiences.

## A Instructions on Finding Update Settings

### A.1 Android

*Operating System Updates*: (1) Check if developer options are activated - until version 8.x they are found at the bottom of the main settings menu. From version 9 they are found in the system settings menu; (2) If developer options are activated and the corresponding menu exists: check if "Automatic System updates" are activated (default) or not.

*Application Updates:* (1) Open your Google Play Store Application; (2) Tap the hamburger-menu in the upper-left corner to open the Play Store menu; (3) Scroll down to the settings option; (4) Tap on the option "automatic updates".

### A.2 iOS

*Operating System Update:* (1) Open the iOS settings; (2) Scroll down to the option "General" and tap it; (3) In this menu the entry "Software update" should be in the second place; (4) Wait for the listing to load, the option for automatic updates should be at the bottom of display.

*Application Updates:* (1) Open the iOS settings; (2) Scroll down and choose the option "iTunes & App Store"; (3) Below the heading "Automatic Downloads" there is an option for applications; (4) A green button shows that automatic downloads are enabled, and a grey button shows that they are not.

## B Formative Field Study: Questionnaire

- **Update Settings:**
  (1) Which operating system and which version is currently installed on your phone? (2) What is your current setting for automatic operating system updates? (3) Why did you choose this setting? (4) What is your current setting for automatic application updates? (5) Why did you choose this setting?

- **Demographic data:**
(6) What is your gender (female, male, diverse, I prefer not to answer)? (7) How old are you? (8) What is your major (for students) or what is your occupation (for non-students)? (9) Please tell us how well the following statements apply to you (1 = Not at all ... 7 = Very much): (a) It is difficult for me to convince computers to do what I want. (b) Concerning computers, I don't think I am very competent. (c) I think I am a skilled computer user. (d) I can help others with their computer problems. (e) I find it difficult to learn new computer software. (f) I am able to learn a programming language. (10) Provide three things that you regularly do in order to keep your smartphone or your personal data secure.

**Table 3.** Participants' demographics in the formative field study

| | # | m | sd |
|---|---|---|---|
| N | 52 | | |
| Age | | 23.62 | 3.71 |
| Self-Efficacy (all) | | 5.21 | 1.26 |
| Self-Efficacy (w/out students) | | 4.88 | 1.27 |
| Gender | | | |
| Women | 13 | | |
| Men | 37 | | |
| Preferred not to say | 2 | | |
| Students | 45 | | |
| Computer Science | 13 | | |
| Business | 8 | | |
| Teaching | 7 | | |
| Law | 6 | | |
| Psychology | 4 | | |
| Other | 7 | | |
| Non-students | 7 | | |

# C Formative Field Study: Demographics, Codebooks, and Update Settings

- **Reasons for OS update settings:**
Do not remember (18); Maintain control over installed software (2); General desire to be up to date (2); Installed OS does not provide automatic update option (2); Practicality (1); Compatibility problems (1); Data cap on their mobile contract (1); Security (1)

- **Reasons for application update settings:**
  Did not change it (15); Maintain control over installed software (8); Data cap on their mobile contract (7); Practicality (4); Annoyance (4); Do not remember (4); General desire to be up to date (2); Installed OS does not provide automatic update option (2); Not enough storage space (1); Security (1)
- **Security-relevant day-to-day behavior:**
  Authentication (23); Self-Denial of potentially useful products or features (18); Check data protection specific settings (16); Password management (10); Secure network access (10); Backup (7); Use common sense (7); Protection software (6); Encryption (4); Physical access control (4); Updates (4); Others (4)

**Table 4.** Distribution of OS and application updates for Android and Apple users.

| | OS updates | | Application updates | |
|---|---|---|---|---|
| Apple | On: | **17** | On: | **15** |
| | Off: | **6** | Off: | **10** |
| Android | DO on/Updates on: | **3** | Always: | **1** |
| | DO off/Updates off: | **1** | WiFi only: | **21** |
| | DO off/Updates on: | **16** | Never: | **3** |
| **Total** | | **43** | | **50** |

*Annotations.* Number of participants that chose the possible option. DO = Developer options.

**Table 5.** Distribution of OS and application updates regarding self-efficacy.

| OS version | Self-efficacy ≥ 4 | | | | Self-efficacy < 4 | | | |
|---|---|---|---|---|---|---|---|---|
| | OS updates | | App updates | | OS updates | | Application updates | |
| Apple | On: | 4 | On: | 14 | On: | **1** | On: | **1** |
| | Off: | **16** | Off: | 8 | Off: | **2** | Off: | **2** |
| Android | DO on/Updates on: | **3** | Always: | 1 | DO on/ Updates on: | **0** | Always: | **0** |
| | DO off/Updates off: | 1 | WiFi only: | **13** | DO on/Updates off: | **0** | WiFi only: | **8** |
| | DO off/Updates on: | **11** | Never: | 3 | DO off/Updates on: | **5** | Never: | **0** |

*Annotations.* Number of participants that chose the possible option. DO = Developer options.

# D Online Survey: Questionnaire, Demographics, Reasons for (De)activation, and Update Avoidance Behavior

1. **Update settings on your smartphone:**
(a) Which OS do you use on your smartphone? [Android, iOS, other]; (2) Which exact version of the chosen OS do you use?; (3) Take a screenshot of your OS update settings and upload it; (4) Have you changed those settings in the past?; (5) Why did you choose this setting? (6) Take a screenshot of your app update settings and upload it; (7) Have you changed those settings in the past?; (8) Why did you choose this setting?
2. **Personal expectations about updates:**
*For all update notifications shown in Sect.* E*:* (1) You are just about to use (insert device here) and the following update notification pops up; (2) How important do you think is this update? [5-point Likert scale]; (3) State your reasons for the last answer; (4) What kind of changes would you expect from such an update?; (5) When would you update? [Now, Later, Never]; (6) State your reasons for the last answer; (7) How would you change the update notification?
*Afterwards:* (1) How large do you think is the share of app updates that are relevant for security? (2) How large do you think is the share of OS updates that are relevant for security? (3) How should an update be presented so that you perceive it as security-relevant?
3. **Reasons for (de)activation of automatic updates:**
(1) Other people gave the following reasons for their activation of automatic updates. Please state how much you agree with them [5-point Likert scale]: I want to keep up with the current version, It is convenient to have them done automatically, Installing updates is good for security, I am annoyed by notifications in case of manual update installation, other; (2) Other people gave the following reasons for their deactivation of automatic updates. Please state how much you agree with them [5-point Likert scale]: I want to control which software and which version is installed on my phone, I fear compatibility problems with other software, my phone contract includes a low amount of data, I am annoyed by automatic updates, My phone does not have enough free storage for updates, others.
4. **Update avoidance behavior:**
(1) At what time of day do you charge your phone battery?; (2) At which location do you usually charge your phone battery?; (3) At which locations is your phone usually connected to a WiFi network?; (4) At which times of the day is your phone connected to the WiFi, so that automatic updates could be installed?
5. **Personality:**
(1) Psychological Reactance Scale [Hong et al. 1996]; (2) Affinity to Technology scale; (3) Big Five Inventory scale [Agreeableness and Conscientiousness]
6. **Demographic data:**
(1) Gender; (2) Age; (3) How would you rate your knowledge of German?;

(4) Type of occupation; (5) Field of occupation; (6) Highest completed educational level; (7) Available household-income per month

7. **Comments:**
   (1) Did you experience technical problems during this questionnaire?; (2) Please describe your problems; (3) General comments

# E Online Survey: Update Notifications

We showed participants five update notifications: (1) Figure 2 shows a system update, (2) Figure 3 shows several available application updates, (3) Figure 4 shows an open dishwasher that displays a notification of an ongoing update, (4) Figure 5 shoes an available update for self-lacing basketball shoes, and (5) Figure 6 shows an available update in a car.

# F Online Survey: Codebook

- **Curiosity (11)**
- **Update Preparation** after relevance check (11), Update as soon as electricity and/or internet available (84), use own WiFi (6), Prevention of data loss [after Backup (15), Threat of data loss intimidating (9)]

**Table 6.** Participants' demographics in the online survey

| | # | m | sd |
|---|---|---|---|
| N | 91 | | |
| Age | | 29.13 | 8.39 |
| Affinity for technology interaction scale | | 4.56 | 0.95 |
| Reactance to autononmy scale | | 2.85 | 0.59 |
| Big five inventory scale | | | |
| *Extraversion* | | 2.90 | 0.36 |
| *Agreeableness* | | 3.52[a] | 0.57 |
| *Conscientiousness* | | 3.51[a] | 0.49 |
| *Neuroticism* | | 3.15 | 0.39 |
| *Openness to experience* | | 2.69 | 0.55 |
| Gender | | | |
| *Women* | 16 | | |
| *Men* | 73 | | |
| *Preferred not to say* | 2 | | |

[a]The above average scores for conscientiousness and agreeableness are noteworthy, since they correlate with increased security awareness [9].

**Table 7.** Ranked reasons for (de)activing automatic updates

| Reasons for deactivation | m | sd |
|---|---|---|
| *I want to control which software (version) will be installed* | 4.45 | 1.82 |
| *My phone contract has a limited data cap* | 4.09 | 2.11 |
| *I am concerned about potential compatibility problems* | 3.47 | 1.74 |
| *I am annoyed by automatic updates* | 3.46 | 2.01 |
| *My phone has insufficient storage space for updates* | 2.97 | 1.9 |
| Reasons for activation | | |
| *Security reasons* | 5.49 | 1.41 |
| *"Stay up to date"* | 5.19 | 1.54 |
| *Convenience* | 5.14 | 1.68 |
| *Annoying update notification* | 4.62 | 1.79 |

**Table 8.** Participants who avoid charging their battery and connecting to WiFi at the same time might demonstrate update avoidance behavior

| | Morning | Before noon | Noon | Afternoon | Dinnertime | Night | Whenever necessary |
|---|---|---|---|---|---|---|---|
| Charge battery | 5 | 4 | 0 | 3 | 8 | 68 | 4 |
| WiFI[a] | 40 | 36 | 27 | 0 | 55 | 75 | |

[a]Multiple choice response

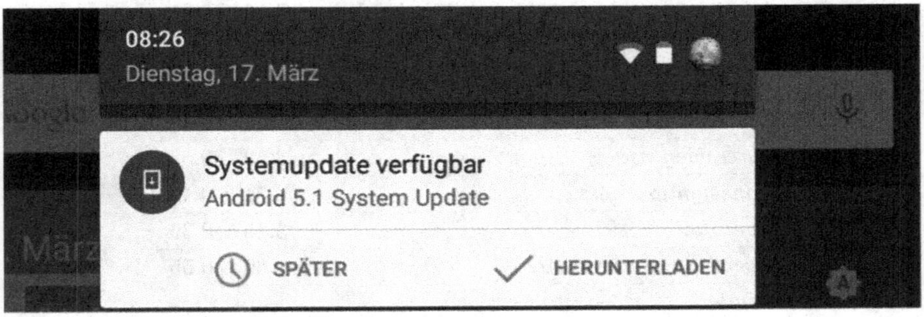


**Fig. 2.** Android system

**Fig. 3.** Android app

- **Scheduling** Time for Update [Immediately (61), At next opportunity (116), Point in time of no importance (11), No time for Updates (22)], Update prevents use (150), not while out and about (25), Not leave pending/remove notification (42), no counter-argument apparent (9), No disruption because in background/finished quickly (40), App Updates do not disrupt use (15)
- **Scepticism** IoT incomprehension (99), Incomprehension (40), no demand/unimportant (95), New devices error-prone (3),
- **Principles of importance** Update size implies importance [Small changes are unimportant (7), Update important if finished quickly (2), Bigger Update → later, smaller → sooner (3), Important because of long installation duration (1), System Updates take longer (7)], Rare Updates important (16), Updates are important (113), System updates are important (79), Update only important for used apps (63), Apps differ in importance (2), important → sooner (20), Updates unimportant for IoT devices (133)
- **Expected changes** User Interface [UI Changes (75), Device in mint condition through update (3), Updates important for UX change (2), Improved Usability (27)], No noticeable changes (244), Maintenance (185), Bug-fixing (290), New features (252), Improvements (114), Performance (198), Changes anticipated by users (4), Safety (59), Privacy (8), Security (338), (only) devices attached to network need be up-to-date (3)

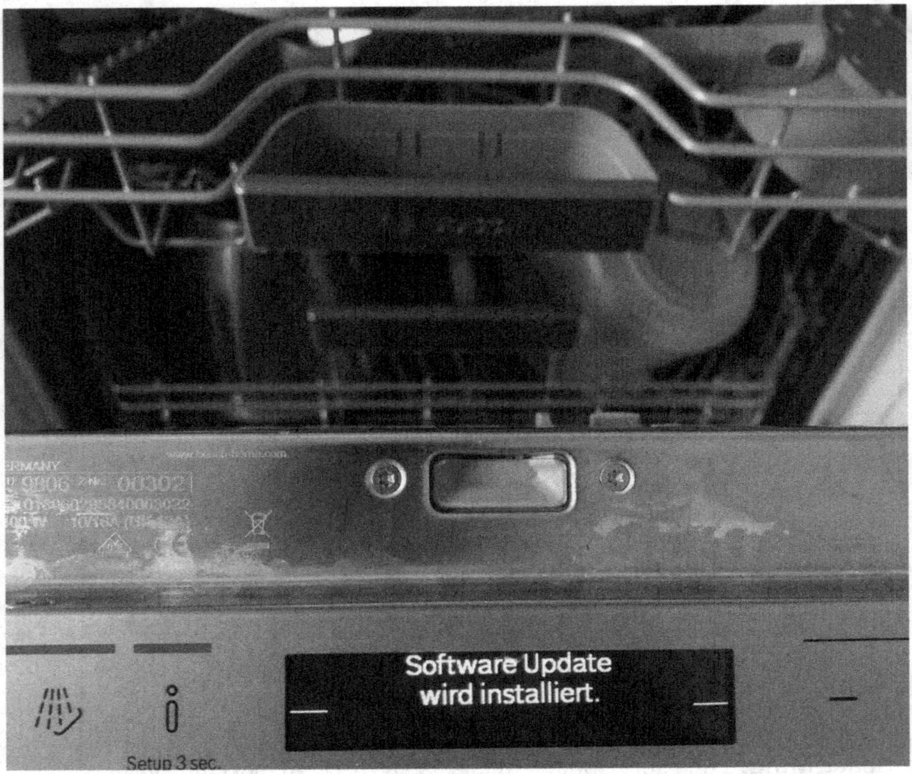


**Fig. 4.** Dishwasher

- **Negative Experiences** Never change a running System (51), Wait for field reports (11), Updates can cause errors (17), No update because of space lacking (2), Negative experience long duration (2), Negative experience as reason without explanation (7)
- **Update Deployment** Right to a say [Choice to delay makes update unimportant (4), Right to a say desired (49), Choice when to install update (25)], Information through notification [Notification no boost to confidence (10), Improved update notification (58), visual information within notification (32), More information within notification (349), Notification emphasizes importance (2), Notification as source of information (16), Less information within notification (49), Notify through phone (4)], Automatic updates [Automatic updates preferred (48), Unimportant updates should happen unsupervised (6), Critical updates automatically (22)], Timing of notification disruptive (14), Timing of notification convenient (1), Download vs. installation of update (4), No suggestion (529).

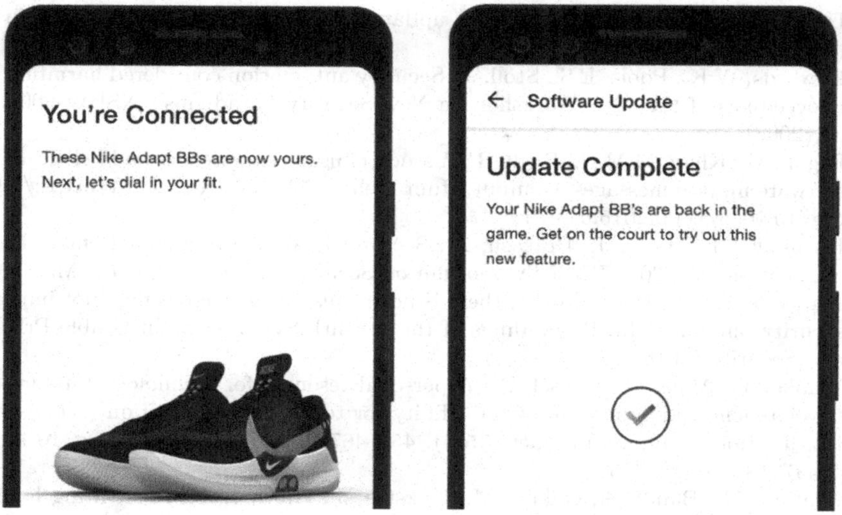


**Fig. 5.** Basketball shoes

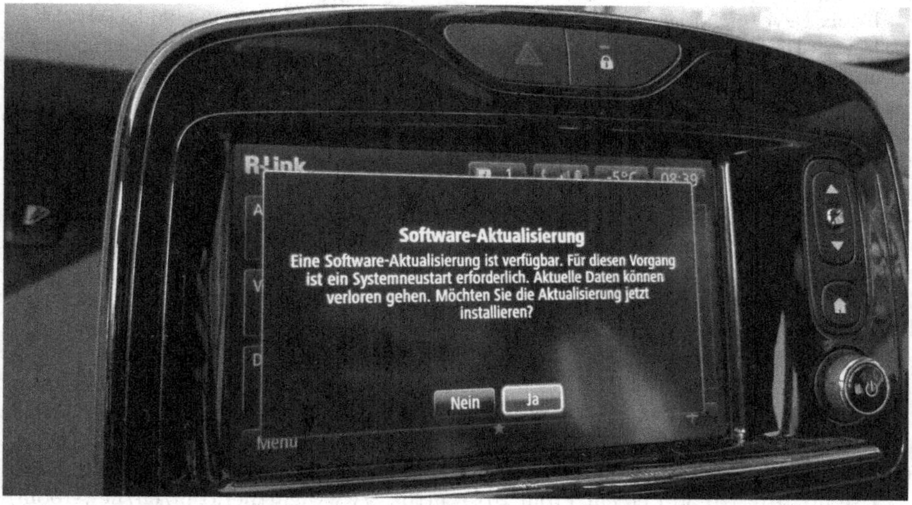


**Fig. 6.** Car system

## References


1. Bellissimo, A., Burgess, J., Fu, K.: Secure software updates: disappointments and new challenges. In: 1st USENIX Workshop on Hot Topics in Security, pp. 37–43 (2006)
2. Braun, V., Clarke, V.: Using thematic analysis in psychology. Qual. Res. Psychol. **3**(2), 77–101 (2006)

3. Duebendorfer, T., Frei, S.: Why silent updates boost security. TIK 302, ETH Zürich (2009)
4. Edwards, W.K., Poole, E.S., Stoll, J.: Security automation considered harmful? In: Proceedings of the 2007 Workshop on New Security Paradigms - NSPW 2007, p. 33 (2008)
5. Fagan, M., Khan, M.M.H., Buck, R.: A study of users' experiences and beliefs about software update messages. Comput. Hum. Behav. **51**, 504–519 (2015). https://doi.org/10.1016/j.chb.2015.04.075
6. Fernandes, E., Jung, J., Prakash, A.: Security analysis of emerging smart home applications. In: 2016 IEEE Symposium on Security and Privacy (SP), May 2016
7. Forget, A., et al.: Do or do not, there is no try: user engagement may not improve security outcomes. In: Proceedings of the Twelfth Symposium on Usable Privacy and Security (2016)
8. Franke, T., Attig, C., Wessel, D.: A personal resource for technology interaction: development and validation of the affinity for technology interaction (ATI) scale. Int. J. Hum.-Comput. Interact. **35**(6), 456–467 (2019). https://doi.org/10.1080/10447318.2018.1456150
9. Gratian, M., Bandi, S., Cukier, M., Dykstra, J., Ginther, A.: Correlating human traits and cyber security behavior intentions. Comput. Secur. **73**, 345–358 (2018). https://doi.org/10.1016/j.cose.2017.11.015
10. Hong, S.M., Faedda, S.: Refinement of the Hong psychological reactance scale. Educ. Psychol. Measur. (1996). https://doi.org/10.1177/0013164496056001014
11. Ion, I., Reeder, R., Consolvo, S.: "... No one can hack my mind": comparing expert and non-expert security practices. In: Proceedings of the Eleventh Symposium on Usable Privacy and Security (2015)
12. Li, F., Rogers, L., Mathur, A., Malkin, N., Chetty, M.: Keepers of the machines: examining how system administrators manage software updates. In: Proceedings of the Fifteenth Symposium on Usable Privacy and Security (2019)
13. Mathur, A., Chetty, M.: Impact of user characteristics on attitudes towards automatic mobile application updates. In: Proceedings of the Thirteenth Symposium on Usable Privacy and Security (2017)
14. Mathur, A., Engel, J., Sobti, S., Chang, V., Chetty, M.: "They keep coming back like Zombies": improving software updating interfaces. In: Proceedings of the Twelfth Symposium on Usable Privacy and Security (2016)
15. Mathur, A., Malkin, N., Harbach, M., Peer, E., Egelman, S.: Quantifying users' beliefs about software updates. arXiv (2018). https://doi.org/10.14722/usec.2018.23036
16. van der Meulen, R.: Gartner Says 6.4 Billion Connected "Things" Will Be in Use in 2016, Up 30 Percent From 2015. https://www.gartner.com/en/newsroom/press-releases/2015-11-10-gartner-says-6-billion-connected-things-will-be-in-use-in-2016-up-30-percent-from-2015
17. Ponticello, A., Fassl, M., Krombholz, K.: Exploring authentication for security-sensitive tasks on smart home voice assistants. In: Proceedings of the Seventeenth Symposium on Usable Privacy and Security (2021)
18. Rammstedt, B., John, O.P.: Kurzversion des big five inventory (BFI-K): Diagnostica **51**(4), 195–206 (2005). https://doi.org/10.1026/0012-1924.51.4.195
19. Redmiles, E.M., Kross, S., Mazurek, M.L.: How well do my results generalize? Comparing security and privacy survey results from MTurk, web, and telephone samples. In: 2019 IEEE Symposium on Security and Privacy (SP) (2019)

20. Reeder, R.W., Ion, I., Consolvo, S.: 152 simple steps to stay safe online: security advice for non-tech-savvy users. IEEE Secur. Priv. **15**(5), 55–64 (2017). https://doi.org/10.1109/msp.2017.3681050
21. Simpson, A.K., Roesner, F., Kohno, T.: Securing vulnerable home IoT devices with an in-hub security manager. In: 2017 IEEE International Conference on Pervasive Computing and Communications Workshops (2017)
22. Son, J.Y., Doumas, L.A.A., Goldstone, R.L.: When do words promote analogical transfer? J. Probl. Solving **3**(1) (2010). https://doi.org/10.7771/1932-6246.1079
23. Tian, Y., Liu, B., Dai, W., Ur, B., Tague, P., Cranor, L.F.: Supporting privacy-conscious app update decisions with user reviews. In: Proceedings of the 5th Annual ACM CCS Workshop on Security and Privacy in Smartphones and Mobile Devices (2015)
24. Tiefenau, C., Häring, M., Krombholz, K.: Security, availability, and multiple information sources: exploring update behavior of system administrators. In: Proceedings of the Sixteenth Symposium on Usable Privacy and Security (2020)
25. Vaniea, K., Rashidi, Y.: Tales of Software Updates: the process of updating software. In: Proceedings of the 2016 CHI Conference on Human Factors in Computing Systems (2016)
26. Vaniea, K.E., Rader, E., Wash, R.: Betrayed by updates: how negative experiences affect future security. In: Proceedings of the SIGCHI Conference on Human Factors in Computing Systems (2014)
27. Wash, R., Rader, E., Vaniea, K., Rizor, M.: Out of the loop: how automated software updates cause unintended security consequences. In: Symposium on Usable Privacy and Security, pp. 89–104 (2014)
28. Zeng, E., Rösner, F.: Understanding and improving security and privacy in multi-user smart homes: a design exploration and in-home user study. In: Proceedings of the 28th USENIX Security Symposium (2019)

# Organisational Contexts of Energy Cybersecurity

Tania Wallis(✉), Greig Paul, and James Irvine

University of Strathclyde, Glasgow, UK
Tania.wallis@strath.ac.uk

**Abstract.** The energy system is going through huge transformation to integrate distributed renewable generation and to achieve the goals of net-zero carbon emissions. This involves a significant adjustment to how the system is controlled and managed, with increasing digitalisation of technology and growing complexities across interconnected systems. Traditionally electricity networks adjusted their supply of energy in response to changes in demand. The future energy system will require more flexible demand to be able to use or store energy when renewables are generating. This change is exacerbated by additional demand for electricity for heat and transport uses.

Utility organisations hold responsibility for securing their networks and assuring the supply of electricity. This paper describes a full investigation of cybersecurity issues and concerns for utilities. This industry review was carried out to create a clear organisational context for the ongoing design of cybersecurity improvements. The assessment of potential impact and consequences of cyber-attack is recommended to direct necessary preparations towards protecting essential functions and processes. Improving resilience across interdependent actors is discussed and resilience measures suggested to guide the contributions of different actors towards whole system resilience.

**Keyword:** Cybersecurity · Critical infrastructure · Organisational resilience

## 1 Introduction

Energy distribution networks are undergoing significant change. Traditionally based on a relatively smaller number of central generation sites with simple control and stability through overprovisioning, generation is becoming increasingly distributed with the introduction of renewables such as solar and wind. The network is becoming a 'smart grid' with enhanced control and demand management to improve efficiencies and reduce overprovisioning, and the net zero agenda is increasing demand on the electricity network through the electrification of heat and transport. This has significant cyber security implications. Electrical distribution networks will have to interact more with sources of supply and demand, and more sophisticated control is more vulnerable to attack.

The University of Strathclyde's Power Network Demonstration Centre (PNDC) brings together academics, industry organisations and technologists for pre-commercial


S. Katsikas et al. (Eds.): ESORICS 2021 Workshops, LNCS 13106, pp. 384–402, 2022.
https://doi.org/10.1007/978-3-030-95484-0_22

research and development projects to shape future smart energy networks. The PNDC investigated the organisational aspects of cybersecurity to provide an improved understanding of the future energy system among PNDC members and beyond. This enabled an organisational and sectoral context to be brought to the technical solutions. Furthermore, this research facilitated the coming together of different experiences and understandings across the PNDC membership, such as IT skills adapting to an Operational Technology (OT) context and a synthesis of power systems and telecoms experience. Section 3 describes an assessment of current cyber security concerns within utility networks. Section 4 then proposes how the impact of different issues can be assessed, and Sect. 5 emphasises key aspects to improving the resilience of power networks.

## 1.1 Approach

This research involved bringing together different experiences to make clear the context of a changing energy sector. The changing role of Distribution Network Operators (DNO) was also considered as they would be evolving to include system operator responsibilities to balance power flows for their grid zones.

The research builds upon Hurst's work that recommended a holistic defence in depth approach after surveying different infrastructure security strategies. Proactive protection needs a broad view of the infrastructure, coordinated responses to disruptions and requires diverse information about systems, networks, devices and processes to model correct behaviour [1].

Key concerns and issues on achieving cybersecurity for future energy scenarios were evaluated through a workshop and interviews with PNDC industry partners. This included 20 people with cybersecurity responsibilities, in UK based operations, from the spread of organisations listed below.

- 5 energy companies
- 3 telecom service providers
- 2 suppliers of automation and smart grid equipment
- 2 consultants in security and risk.

A grounded theory approach was followed, combining insights from literature, relevant project experience and analysis of the discussions [2]. The workshop brought together IT security skills, OT engineers and telecoms experts to form the organisational context of a future Distribution System Operator (DSO). This enabled a backdrop of shared understanding for the ongoing development of cybersecurity implementations in the sector to be formed. Several round-table discussions, with different skillsets in each invited an open exploration of the issues. Bringing together stakeholders in this way to address sector specific issues with mutual cooperation and by going beyond organisational boundaries aligns with Burns' partnership approach [3]. The arising issues were then discussed as a whole workshop group and categorised into emerging themes that are outlined in Sect. 3. Interactions during the workshop and the experience of participants enabled the building of the analysis and the discovery of the categories [4].

The workshop output formed the basis of some follow-up interviews with each of the participating organisations. Interviews allowed time to further explore with in-depth discussion, using open questioning based on the themes and categories that arose during the workshop [4]. These interviews were conducted in a semi-structured manner to allow further sharing beyond what could be communicated in the group workshop setting. The use of anonymity during the interview stage, where stakeholders were less willing to share sensitive information in a group, provided a platform for gathering and analysing information anonymously and then acting on it collectively [3]. A multi-actor approach by listening and understanding different perspectives across industry was paramount to this research [5]. The compilation of workshop and interview findings later allowed PNDC members to select priority issues to set the focus for future cybersecurity projects at PNDC.

The emphasis of this exercise on the needs of DNO organisations was important due to their holding responsibility for the cybersecurity of their operations and services. While the focus needed to be on PNDC members due to this work leading into future work based at PNDC, it holds relevance to the energy sector in general and beyond the UK and to the necessity of ensuring an understanding of organisational context for more effective cybersecurity implementations.

## 2 Preparing for Future Energy Scenarios

With uncertainties about the impact of cyber security on organisations within the energy sector, exploring potential scenarios can help direct more effective preparations. Each scenario gives us a future vantage point from which to observe the present situation. The capacity to manage future uncertainties requires both learning from past attacks as well as consideration of different futures [6].

Table 1 shows different areas of activity that can be distinguished, from solving one-off problems to looking at longer term capability, using an exploratory mindset or achieving closure with decisions and actions. All four activities play a role in effective preparations.

"Systems cannot be constructed to eliminate security risk" [7] so it is essential that systems are designed to recognise, resist and recover from attacks. Longer term considerations and the ability to adapt to new threats are important for systems to sustain assurance over time. A continued adaptation is necessary to respond both to changes in threats and changes in functions or usage of the system that could enable an attack.

**Table 1.** Dimensions of purposeful activity [8]

| | Single activity problem solving | Ongoing activity surviving/thriving |
|---|---|---|
| Opening up exploration | What's going on? Making sense of the latest threat landscape | What's coming? Anticipation preparedness |
| Closure decisions | Developing a strategy to deal with cybersecurity | Organisational learning adapting to changes and new threats dynamic response |

This research focussed more on the opening up and exploratory dimension of Table 1 to provide an improved awareness and understanding of the situation and context of future energy networks and enable decisions to be made on the priorities and focus areas for future projects at PNDC.

## 2.1 Setting the Context

National Grid operates the transmission network in much of the UK. Its future energy scenarios (FES), shown in Fig. 1, offer a context to explore potential cyber security scenarios and impacts. Four different pathways are described towards net-zero carbon emissions, including consumer or system transformation as different ways to reach 2050 goals [9]. The FES will require an integrated whole system approach to manage a more complex picture of power flows and to coordinate demand with supply.

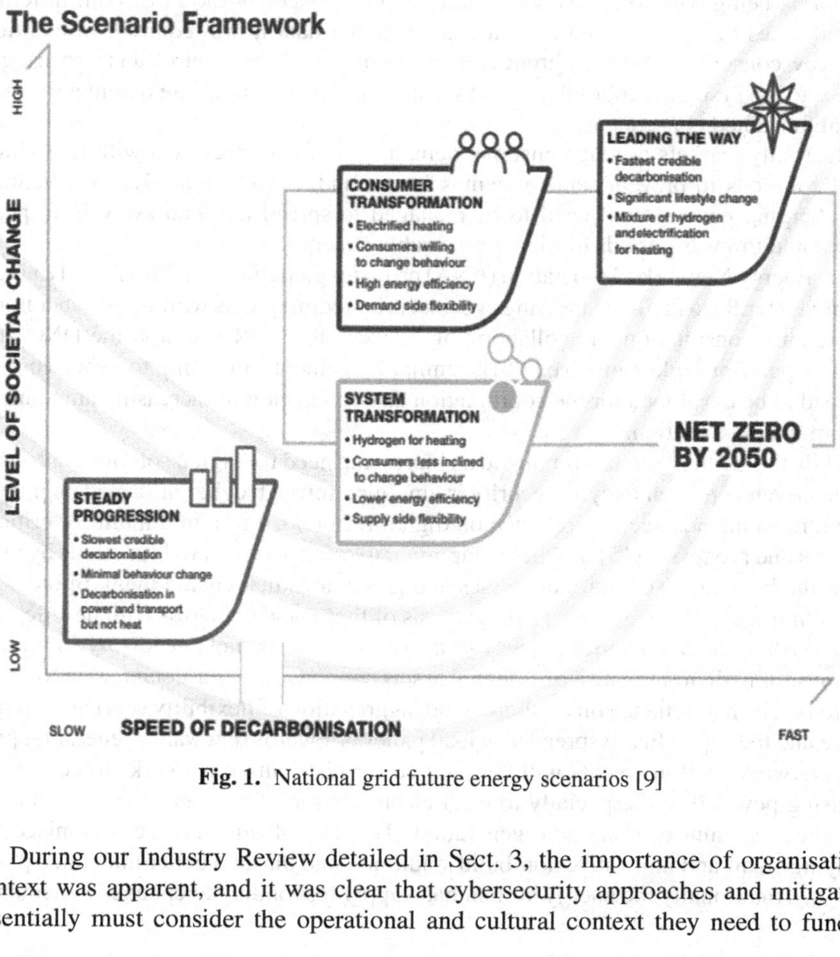


**Fig. 1.** National grid future energy scenarios [9]

During our Industry Review detailed in Sect. 3, the importance of organisational context was apparent, and it was clear that cybersecurity approaches and mitigations essentially must consider the operational and cultural context they need to function within. The real potential of a vulnerability is also highly contextual. "The real impact of a vulnerability is heavily dependent on the context surrounding the targeted device" [10]. Considering risks from an operational perspective as well as a security perspective ensures that cybersecurity risks are managed from an organisational understanding [11]. The wider engineering solution around it could be more important than the security solutions especially where there are security gaps. A vulnerable asset can be assessed based on its importance to the organisation using 'Environmental Metrics' to customise a vulnerability score by assigning a high medium or low value in terms of Availability Integrity Confidentiality [12].

A significant power outage in the UK in August 2019 emphasised the importance of adaptability and cooperation in operating a changing and complex power system [13]. Stronger and faster interactions are expected between different aspects of the energy sector, to obtain value from coordinating and optimising the whole system. The wide adoption of data-driven insights to manage a distributed energy system must be balanced with the necessary attention to cybersecurity and privacy. From a policy perspective, attention is being paid to securing consumer smart devices in the FES, both in terms of the devices themselves, and their interactions and data flows required. In addition to privacy concerns, where different actors and devices have control and can trigger changes to the system, a coordinated and secured approach within safe parameters must prevent unwanted consequences.

Electricity markets driving consumer demand with price incentives will necessitate digital solutions to prevent sudden swings in demand. For example, Electric Vehicle (EV) charging patterns will need to be managed to spread the load away from peak demand and towards periods of higher renewable generation.

The Energy Networks Association (ENA) provides guidelines for Distributed Energy Resources (DER) to facilitate meeting cybersecurity requirements with small generators. They require consultation and collaboration between the DER operator, the DNO and any third-party providers involved [14]. Similar agreements attending to cybersecurity will need to be developed for the coordination and connection of increasing amounts of offshore wind generation.

While these future scenarios point to an increasing need for digital solutions, a consequence driven approach to cybersecurity is emerging through cyber informed engineering that recommends keeping reliance on digital technology to a minimum for critical functions and processes [15]. It will be important to prioritise essential functions by protecting the hardware, software, processes and procedures that enable them, in order to prevent unwanted consequences [16]. Analysis of these new scenarios with new dependencies will identify potential impacts to avoid, where it is most necessary to reduce pathways for malicious control of essential assets and functions. Particular attention will need to be given to reliance on offshore wind, aggregation of flexibility services, energy storage and the capability to spread new load patterns towards renewable generation patterns. Network reinforcements will be required for distribution networks to cope with increasing power flows, especially to meet electrification of heat and transport, and to avoid the constraint of renewable generation. The cost of this "can be minimised by deploying smart and innovative non-build solutions" and through better integrated planning [9]. Traditionally the energy system had supply responding to changes in demand, the new scenarios put supply in charge and expect smart flexible demand to either use or store electricity when it is available. To prevent opening additional pathways to attack, cybersecurity must be embedded into these smart solutions.

All these FES will need the support of a highly interconnected control structure, and will also increasingly interact with natural gas, hydrogen and biofuels. Aggregated technologies on the demand side, responding to half hourly price signals, will require managing at street, local and regional level so that distribution networks protect system stability. A whole street of EVs responding to price signals, all drawing or all feeding back power to the system, could otherwise cause instability. Achieving Net Zero expects a "deep digitalisation of all energy assets" [17]. This will require secure solutions at all levels. "As new sources of flexibility come online, we will need their operational data" [17]. Information becoming available in more places could also be assisting adversaries to build a clearer view of the system. The transformed energy system will require "interaction between digital platforms, technologies and markets signals" and "interoperability across data, services and technologies" [17]. An increasingly interactive and interoperable energy system must be developed with cybersecurity in mind.

With this opening up of access to data and lots of pathways into networks, it is likely to become too much to monitor for anomalies without some simplification to effectively oversee the cybersecurity of such solutions. The integrity of data is essential where it is being used to control devices and system responses. An honest look at our reliance on complex digital solutions, and the recognition that we will have "combined technologies, delivering multiple services", "smart technologies, all digitally enabled" and "deployed at scale and throughout the energy system" [17] makes it clear that cybersecurity must be fully embedded into the journey to net zero. Where dependencies are greatest and to protect essential functionality, priority decisions will need to be made. An engineering perspective must find ways of defending an extensive attack surface such as keeping system capabilities within safe limits, while retaining the system orchestration that digitalisation brings.

# 3 Industry Review

A review was undertaken by PNDC of the main points of concern in cyber security in utility networks. The approach used is detailed in Sect. 1.1. The review started with a cybersecurity workshop attended by various energy sector actors, including DNOs, vendors and consultants. Follow-up meetings and discussions were then held with participants to build a full picture of the situation. This provided a thorough organisational context for ongoing design of cybersecurity improvements and to prioritise innovation projects at PNDC. The following sub-sections describe the emerging cyber security issues and requirements for these energy sector organisations.

## 3.1 Accessing Multiple Sites

There is a requirement for security of both local access to equipment within a substation's own network and remote access to substations over wide area networks. The need for remote access support for substations is required from third parties, vendors and external contractors. Corporate network access into substations was also essential, requiring an economical solution which meets the needs of different branches of the business, yet preserves security of the operational network.

There was a strong requirement for Identity and Access Management (IAM) capability, with a need for logging of actions, as well as control of who is able to access systems, and a facility for revocation of access, while considering the unique nature of an operational network and ensuring availability of systems. To avoid the introduction of complex security systems which slow down operations, operational networks often do not feature the same security features as corporate networks, such as 2-factor authentication. Introducing stronger verification of the identity of a party connecting to equipment, as well as the actions they are permitted to carry out, must consider the operational context of an always-on environment.

In a control room setting, it is difficult to switch the identity of the operator without shutting down and restarting the interface which is not appropriate for a real time environment. There are layers needed to the solution, and there is a different class of problem for unattended equipment.

For remote access there were issues with creating VPN tunnels into substations such that alternatives to VPN may need to be considered. A specific concern was how to manage cryptographic keys and VPN configurations, and in making coordination and management scale to the high number of substations sites.

There were different views on the extent of encryption and whether it is necessary for all communications to be encrypted or would authentication alone offer sufficient security for certain services. Grid protection applications, in particular, could require very fast, potentially sub-millisecond encryption to meet latency requirements.

There was a desire to look into "encrypted by default" communications within operational networks, provided suitable provisions are made for availability, reliability and performance. However, there was a concern with regard to the security and management of certificates and cryptographic keys, and ensuring the correct handling of issuance and revocation, to avoid any downtime or loss of functionality.

Specific technologies for linking sites were discussed, such as whether there were any security benefits to using MPLS over more traditional technologies. There was considerable concern about the widening cybersecurity issues caused by moving towards IP-based networks and IEC 61850 substations.

There are some unique challenges within operational networks which can make deployment of standard solutions more complex, such as most single-sign-on systems failing if the centralised authentication server fails or goes offline. It would be possible to build a more resilient solution using Public Key Infrastructure (PKI) technology, to securely authenticate parties through certificates issued on a regular basis, with no direct requirement for the authentication servers to remain online to permit remote access to systems during outages or other emergency scenarios. For log aggregation, the main priority would be ensuring provenance of the logs against tampering, while keeping bandwidth usage to a minimum for remote sites which have limited network link capacity available for log aggregation. PKI was seen as a potential approach to securing networks, although the risks of quantum computing advances were highlighted as DNOs – and regulators – traditionally expect relatively long-term deployments of equipment.

### 3.2 Securing Legacy Equipment and Future Networks

There is a significant challenge in managing legacy equipment as the network moves to a more integrated environment with inter-connected systems, especially as legacy equipment was often not designed with security in mind. Legacy devices frequently lack access control and other security measures, and assume the network is only available to fully trusted devices. It is not possible to change, modify or update legacy equipment to be compliant with newer security systems, and many older security protocols feature weaknesses which cannot be resolved other than by updating to a newer version of the protocol such as Transport Layer Security (TLS) protocol.

If legacy equipment has no access control, any party with access to the network to which that device is connected may interact with the equipment, and potentially carry out operations. To maintain the security of such devices, it is necessary to firstly identify these devices, and secondly ensure that they are isolated from other network traffic with network segmentation, and from remote users with VPN access, limiting access to nodes that specifically require it. Legacy equipment almost invariably has no logging or auditing capabilities, meaning that attempts to gain access to the equipment may not be detected. Building adequate secure capability around legacy systems is essential. Security monitoring is vital to stop attacks more quickly, identify suspicious access or traffic, and monitor configuration and authentication events.

Lifetime management of equipment is an issue, including ensuring suitable vendor support, particularly for embedded systems where security updates are not necessarily forthcoming a small number of years after release.

The practical security considerations of firmware updates on equipment in the field were also raised. There is a perceived risk of updating working equipment, due to the loss of availability while updating or other failure due to the update. However, software vulnerabilities present a serious risk to the security of the network, and insecure devices could be used as "pivot" points to explore other parts of the network, potentially exposing more critical systems to attackers. The risks of allowing non-updated devices to remain on the network needs to be evaluated, perhaps using penetration testing outcomes, versus the risks of carrying out an update (ideally remotely), and the impact on security and availability this may have. Another risk introduced through remote updates is the potential for an attacker to use this method to deploy a malicious update, indicating a requirement for remotely updateable devices to have suitable security in place to authenticate any updates issued.

With a large number of embedded systems deployed in the network, an interest was expressed in whitelisting technology, which could be used to constrain embedded devices to mitigate against malicious software or other attacks, by ensuring that only the specific software originally installed on the device would be able to execute.

To improve the integrity of the OT environment, there could be potential for the use of VPN tagging to monitor data flows and record log in access and operations on legacy equipment which may not currently have support for this.

### 3.3 Network Monitoring

The introduction of malicious equipment to a secure network is a security concern. Having the capability to monitor networks for the introduction of new devices, or changes to existing devices, would reduce cost and provide a more rapid response. Additionally, identification of specific unusual traffic is a potentially beneficial proactive measure, in order to attempt to gain early warning of unusual behaviour on a network, or of a device being compromised. The benefit of monitoring also extends to monitoring devices for important security updates, to ensure that each device is patched against any known vulnerabilities, and running the latest approved software revision. This process could be combined with targeted penetration testing to identify widely deployed devices which should be tested to ensure no obvious vulnerabilities are present. However, controlling and verifying devices present on networks is challenging given the numbers of devices involved.

There was a need to improve visibility of all devices connected to networks. Most large systems such as servers had agents installed, but no monitoring or control of the devices present, or how they are managed and patched.

The need to better understand the traffic experienced within SCADA networks was recognised. Concern was raised over how to correctly identify both "good" and "bad" traffic within a network, for intrusion detection and prevention systems. There were questions over when to stop traffic, and risk interrupting availability, versus permitting and then investigating after-the-fact, since detections systems are generally preferred for SCADA environments,

There was an interest in log aggregation for auditing and accountability of actions, which was felt to be a growing concern in the future with increasing remote access. There are challenges with limited bandwidth to some remote sites, and the need to ensure logs are transmitted securely.

The transition to IP-based networks brings about opportunities to improve resilience and availability by removing reliance upon centralised points of failure. This comes with significant alterations to network design and organisation, specifically around security. A distributed trust management approach would permit equipment to communicate only with other authorised devices, ensuring that any unauthorised devices introduced to networks would be unable to interfere with or communicate with authorised devices. Such an approach, without requiring a single centralised point of failure for authentication, was identified as a potential area for future work, particularly applying the concept of distributed trust in a non-product specific context.

### 3.4 Building Incident Response Capability

Capabilities to identify, respond and recover from a cyber-attack are limited at present. The current power system was not designed to handle the effects of a cyber-attack. It has been designed with n-1 redundancy as a goal, to handle the loss of generation or transmission assets. In the context of cyber security, there are many other scenarios to be prepared for. There is a need to develop faster detection of malicious or unpredicted activity and to design appropriate responses to potential cyber incidents.

Appreciating the differing context of an OT environment is crucial to handle cybersecurity in an appropriate way for an operational setting. The focus leans towards protecting systems and restoring operations. Incident responses must consider real-time and availability requirements. For example, control systems cannot be disconnected from the network if under attack like an office computer could be. Cyber-security responses appropriate for an OT environment are needed.

**Defining Responsibility.** Part of incident response will be to define the level of incident handling within an operator's capability and agree responsibilities within and across organisations. Operators need to decide what needs to be passed up to, for example, the National Cyber Security Centre (NCSC), or how to engage a response across supply chain organisations, so that an incident response structure can be agreed. Also, identifying where practical help may be needed to withstand an attack, especially over a long time period: e.g. a sustained Denial of Service attack for several days. An effective coordination of the response needs to also be established so that crisis management procedures are in place for cyber security. Previous cyber-attacks have highlighted the use of cascaded attacks to reduce the efficacy of responses. Crisis management must also consider how procedures would be implemented under degraded communications, or following the failure of communications infrastructure as a result of the attack.

To resolve attack situations, organisations will need to build a reliable and strong network of partners for incident response and recovery, as well as agreeing on escalation processes and responsibility levels within and between organisations.

### 3.5 Knowledge of Threats

With an uncertain picture of evolving threats, utilities are expected to prepare for unknown threats to their essential services. Concerns were raised over being without a formal threat landscape for operational networks. While the latest threat landscape is constantly evolving, intelligence gathering could indicate attack trends and future security risks and help to prepare for new scenarios. The potential for an interactive platform to share an evolving picture of threats was discussed. While there are clearly some challenges to producing an all-encompassing threat landscape model, it was felt that most work is being carried out "in the dark", with limited awareness of the types of attack techniques that could be faced.

Identifying various scenarios will aid the preparation of responses to cyber incidents. It is important to consider how vulnerabilities in digital components could cause failures across the grid and to consider different threat agents and types of attack. This will help to identify high impact scenarios and build up a picture of the potential scenarios that need to be prepared for to reduce the impact of attacks.

### 3.6 Electricity Sector Specifics

There is the risk of single site compromises cascading into a wider system threat and affecting other organisations as well. It was noted that the involvement of cross-DNO working groups, would be needed in these circumstances. Being unprepared for cyber incidents exposes the system to the risk of cascading effects which could result in a brownout or even blackout situation. There is also the risk of manipulation of or loss of control and monitoring systems. The ability for an attacker to exert control over large loads, or indeed a significant number of smaller loads, could adversely affect system balancing and lead to blackouts. Likewise, malicious control of generation could affect supply and cause instability.

**Real Time Performance.** There are technical challenges with securing protection communications, due to the need for ~ 4 ms response times, and the perception that this is difficult to achieve alongside secure communications. A cost/benefit and performance analysis was felt to be necessary for securing extensive distribution networks. The security risks to assets from secondary substation and below needs further investigation. The impact of encryption on performance and availability to discover where high speed encryption applications may be needed. Encryption, for example, could add cost, without providing sufficient benefit.

Active Network Management New technology such as Active Network Management (ANM) is presenting DNOs with new security challenges. ANM requires connections to both the primary control network and secondary telemetry networks, limiting the traditional approach of segregating these networks. With the potential introduction of servers and other equipment within substations, and wider deployment of connected monitoring equipment, itself vulnerable to attack and manipulation, a more ANM-oriented network is introducing new security and management requirements. This was considered important, due to the ability for ANM to interact with and control generation equipment on third party sites and networks.

### 3.7 Organisational Culture

Unwillingness to risk introduction of complexity which may otherwise impact on availability means that operational networks frequently lack the same security measures found on corporate networks, such as 2-factor authentication and other measures to ensure security during sign-in processes.

The challenge of management not being familiar with the currently deployed systems was also highlighted as a concern, given the significant changes in approach to security required with newer, more interconnected equipment. Another challenge identified was in keeping up with advances in IT, and security in general. The pace of change and developments, and the speed with which information about vulnerabilities may be disseminated makes it difficult for small cyber security teams to keep up to date with information. A need for training in cyber security was also highlighted, to ensure everyone who needs it has a strong basic knowledge of the essentials for securing systems. The ability for a 'small' mistake to completely compromise the security of an installation was a concern. An example given was of an engineer bridging the 'secure' operational side of the network to a WAN link using a patch cable while working on equipment. Knowing the organisational context that security solutions are to be implemented and maintained within gives a broader view of what is needed to build a security culture and more secure ways of working.

Overall governance of cybersecurity within the organisation as a whole needed some attention. Progress had been made in different business units but had resulted in different approaches and security policies, which would be better unified and coordinated. There was interest in establishing a broad governance and security architecture, to create a secure state to aim towards when deploying and designing systems.

IT/OT Integration The organisational boundaries between operational and corporate sides of IT provisions were also highlighted as being a concern – equipment not installed by IT and not connected to the corporate IT network was considered to be outside the responsibility of IT. Advances in corporate security (single sign-on, enforced 2-factor authentication etc.) had not been replicated on the operational network due to IT not having visibility of activity on the OT side.

It was recognised a new model for working was required to manage the increasing numbers of computer systems (such as servers) in operational networks. There was a desire for the IT teams to manage such systems, as this was more within their area of expertise, but this presented challenges such as providing access for corporate IT staff into substations.

Supply Chain Security Based upon the significance with which it was emphasised by all DNO members consulted, some of the largest risks to DNO operations appear to be posed by their supply chains, and by connections which are permitted from external third parties, operating outside the control of the DNO's business and security policies. Taking some measures to begin to increase the level of trust in suppliers and components is an important step.

Equipment vendors increasingly wish to have remote access abilities to provide support. This introduces risk if a supplier's internal procedures are insufficient to prevent abuse of this access, or if there are technical weaknesses in the implementation of the remote access system. Currently, such connections are established through VPN links, but with very little logging and auditing of the specific equipment connected to, and actions carried out. The number of external connections to controlled networks will increase, both due to practical and business reasons. Connections to third party generation sites are one such example, where it is necessary for relatively simple communications to take place over an external IP network. While best efforts are made to assume the worst-case when considering third party networks, there is clearly potential for compromise here. There would be security benefits in having the capability to segment access to only a particular type of equipment, or localised site, to reduce exposure of assets to those with remote access. Care should be taken around legacy devices and protocols being introduced to IP-based networks, to ensure they cannot be reached from untrusted areas of the network, such as incoming VPN connections and similar.

The reliance of DNOs upon their supply chain of suppliers, vendors and subcontractors was recognised as being a major limitation of current cybersecurity measures. Questions were raised on how to audit, assess and review the cybersecurity competencies of third parties, especially while considering implementation-specific requirements or validation of vendor claims. There is also the issue of the validation of the supply chains of the vendors themselves. A code of practice for suppliers and other third parties, covering their expected capability in cyber security, was highlighted as an important requirement going forward.

Within substations, a significant concern identified was in managing suppliers' understanding of substation implementations and preventing inappropriate hardware from being installed in substation environments, where it is left unmanaged with security issues. For example, features that may be disabled on a product may still leave functioning remnants, capable of communication and remote exploitation.

The trade-offs and challenges of embedded systems were also discussed, specifically around short support periods from Original Equipment Manufacturer (OEM), which are often only a few years. The need for significantly longer equipment lifespans, causing vulnerabilities and weaknesses to get "locked in" with no clear way to mitigate or resolve them without OEM involvement.

**Inter-Organisational Issues.** There is a need to define collective responsibility across interdependent organisations, in order to secure energy systems and to ensure all market players and applications have achieved an adequate level of cyber-security. Aiming for a consistent approach across organisations will require collaborative agreements on cyber security responsibilities and increasing cyber-awareness both within and between organisations. Considering suppliers and components that affect the criticality of an operator and understanding security requirements in different operational contexts will help to adapt countermeasures to different use cases. With a better understanding of appropriate countermeasures, DNOs can agree obligations with suppliers to implement technical or organisational security measures and make plans to ensure compliance with those obligations. This could include a classification of threats, risks and vulnerabilities that indicates how essential certain measures are and the level of implementation required depending on criticality for the operator.

### 3.8 Recognising the Shared Context

It was important to bring together a shared understanding of the future energy situation through this research activity with different players. Operational teams were getting to know new capability and new systems, learning an unfamiliar context. For example, keeping the power network stable involves controlling generation equipment on third party sites, managing Electric Vehicle (EV) charging patterns, so that power flows can be optimised within the constraints of the network. The resulting increase in complexity and data traffic, mean the availability and integrity of measurement data is essential to minimise unnecessary curtailment of generation. Agreement on cybersecurity requirements and code of conduct is also necessary between generators, DNOs, aggregators and other third-party providers.

The academic and industry experts participating in this research activity gained a closer understanding of the issues the DNOs face. This has provided a shared understanding from which to design more applicable cybersecurity solutions and deployments going forward. Our multi-actor approach was able to consider the wider engineering solution, beyond security, for wider protection from undesirable consequences, especially where security is lacking. Knowing the operational perspective allows cybersecurity to be managed from an understanding of the organisational context.

Achieving security across organisational boundaries arose as a significant issue across several topic areas, including cooperation during incident response. The collective responsibility across interdependent organisations requires an adequate cybersecurity level across all market players.

Painting the picture of both organisational and sectoral contexts provided a backdrop of understanding among different players for ongoing cybersecurity research projects at PNDC. A quarterly theme meeting continues to bring together members from different companies in the energy sector to further guide the research programme of PNDC.

## 4 Exploring Impact and Uncertainty

The FES all present an increased use of smart technology and therefore an increased exposure to cybersecurity risks. There are multiple dependencies on assurance decisions in the supply chain and across diverse actors. It is important to recognise and respond to risks across all interconnected stakeholders and elements so that threats are not missed at different points across those interactions. It is necessary to secure beyond just the critical components with everything interconnected and a wide set of roles and technologies supporting the system. An integrated system inherits the security limitations of each interacting component. Transparency of assurance actions will be necessary where there is dependency on the cybersecurity maturity level of other actors.

Attacks are inevitable and are constantly evolving. By establishing clear responsibility for assurance and effective coordination across stakeholders, a broader protection across people, processes and technology can be attained. This would be aided by effective measures to evaluate the assurance of all components and their interactions and make sure appropriate areas are addressed across all aspects of the socio-technical system.

An exploration of impacts and consequences in a power system context was carried out. Sharing an appreciation for potential consequences can give different stakeholders a reason to take the necessary action. Table 2 outlines a selection of potential impacts showing consequences of cyber events including data loss, data modification or unwanted control actions.

There may also be indirect or unintended consequences involved in the system's response to a threat. Considering the system functions and how particular workflows and stakeholders are affected by the sequence of the threat through the technology, people and processes can help to uncover potential consequences of a threat.

### 4.1 Impact Analysis

Consider the roles, processes and underlying IT and OT technologies involved in delivering energy system functions, the assets and actors involved at each step in a business process. The flow of activities can be mapped onto components and interactions to identify the assets and actors [18]. This will build a picture of the systems, devices, communications channels, internal and external actors etc. that are supporting the functions [15]. The expected 'deep digitalisation' of assets [9] correspondingly requires a deep enough knowledge of system operation to know all the sources of control and automation and potential access pathways for attackers. Detailing the assets that contribute to essential functions and their impact if unavailable or compromised and from where changes can be made to configurations and settings [15]. The scale involved also changes the threat exposure i.e. how many instances of the data or device there are and if an asset is centralised or distributed [18].

A functional example such as operating within network constraints requires the secure retrieval of data from the network for real-time information on thermal ratings and voltage stability. This may also require access to smart meter voltage data or power flow and voltage information at DER connections. The cybersecurity of a 3rd party data centre or cloud service could also be a part of this flow of information. Threats to

**Table 2.** Potential impacts of cyber attack [19, 20, 21]

| Event | Consequences |
|---|---|
| Temporary outages | Activation of load shedding tripping of protection communications outage causing delay in data transmission/control actions |
| Affecting synchronisation | Coordinating connection and re-connection of generators, without proper synchronisation could destroy generators |
| Resource unavailable | Denial of service attacks making a resource unreachable or unresponsive, and affecting data streams from devices e.g. phasor measurement data |
| Stealing data | Extracting confidential information social engineering to gain credentials Eavesdropping, sniffing IP packets, intercepting wireless transmission side-channel attack to infer cryptographic keys from unintended information leakage. Impacting customer privacy, passwords, unauthorised access to systems |
| Manipulation of data | Injecting false data, e.g. man-in-the-middle attack hiding true status from control centre modifying data e.g. tampering with sensor data to cause inappropriate load management resulting in unnecessary load shedding or generator trip out manipulating measurements undesired system behaviours |
| Unauthorised access | Access to private data identity spoofing, impersonating an authorised user e.g. man-in-the-middle attack, message replays intrusion affecting behaviour of system e.g. via open ports or malware |
| Sabotage | Embedding malware to launch an attack later |
| Asset replacement | Considerable lead times for replacing destroyed assets |
| Unintended consequences | Unknown consequences aggravated by evolving threats and interdependencies across diverse actors |

consider would include the unauthorised access or potential data manipulation of the SCADA monitoring and notifications of thermal or power flow constraints [22].

The resolution of network constraints being either demand led or generation led would require secure access to flexibility resources for service activation or dispatch. The cybersecurity of control actions in the actuation of DER, aggregator services or active customers would need to minimise the risk of inappropriate control actions or unauthorised access. The assessment of the operational performance of flexibility services could require cybersecurity performance to be included in their reliability metrics [22].

Mapping the entire thread of activity for energy system functions onto the supporting processes, assets and roles in this way presents the impact of threats on essential functions. The aim is to apply mitigations to protect these functions and minimise the impact of events.

## 5 Resilience Efforts

To improve resilience across interdependent actors, cybersecurity expectations and requirements appropriate to each actor will need to be defined and agreed for [22].

- Aggregators supplying services to the power grid via DSOs from assets on the distribution network.
- Active customers and developers exporting power to and importing power from the distribution network.
- Increasing volumes of Distributed Energy Resources with connection arrangements via distribution networks, the cybersecurity aspects of their operational role and their participation in markets via DSOs or aggregators.
- Combined approaches for supply chain actors to engage with multiple DSOs.
- Transmission connected demand and generation, with cybersecurity and resilience actions included in their connection agreements.

Resilience efforts across all actors need to include activities such as:

- Testing changes to assets for cybersecurity or operational impact before deployment.
- Managing access and identity across human and IoT actors.
- Involving stakeholders in threat and vulnerability management for access to a more thorough threat landscape.
- Coordinating incident response activity with appropriate external entities.
- Constructing evidence, contracts, and agreements with third parties.
- Assigning and managing cybersecurity responsibilities across personnel and all relevant stakeholders [23]

Each stakeholder will hold a different level of interest in contributing to system resilience and differing degrees of influence on the cybersecurity level of the system. Considering the relative positions of different stakeholders would reflect how best to engage each actor in required resilience actions. Only 26% of security issues can be addressed by technology alone, leaving 74% requiring people or policies to form a solution to these issues [24].

To know and measure operational resilience requires defined and implemented processes. Processes offer the context for how to achieve a resilience activity with specifics related to roles, technology and operations. The processes that contribute to resilience need to be performing well to build a confident state of readiness in the face of new and different threats and risks. The supporting assets and interactions that enable the functionality of smarter grids need to be cybersecure and reliable. Processes aiming for operational resilience need to be embedded within functional activities to improve the security and resilience of essential services [25].

Reporting on assurance actions across organisations may be necessary where there are dependencies on other actors to deliver a function or service. Preparing combined resilience actions and measures per function would help to define clearer responsibilities for assurance and effective coordination across stakeholders.

## 6 Conclusions

This work enabled a thorough observation of the cybersecurity situation for the energy sector by inviting insights from different perspectives to be shared. The energy system is evolving into a complex web of demand and supply across diverse actors. It will increasingly rely on the security of the information infrastructure supporting it, and the resilience of a digitalised operating environment. To make sense of the latest threat landscape requires a wider sharing of knowledge and awareness among all stakeholders for organisations to make better informed decisions and actions. To construct a picture of the latest operating conditions and vulnerabilities requires knowing the resilience of different assets and interactions that make up the functions of the energy system. Along the thread of activities required to deliver each function, a change in vulnerability in one area could increase the threat affecting other areas. The number of instances of a vulnerable component will affect the scale of threat a function is exposed to. Processes and measures that allow for a greater transparency of cybersecurity activities will encourage preparations and build the necessary trust across interconnected stakeholders. This will enable a more robust response to changing events on the system.

This paper has provided an investigation of cybersecurity issues and concerns for utilities to provide an organisational and future energy system context for the ongoing design of cybersecurity improvements. Methods and approaches have been recommended for improving resilience across interdependent actors and to minimise the impact and consequences of cyber-attack. With smart digital technology deployed at scale, cyber governance must provide an essential foundation for our future energy scenarios with the capability to, repeatedly and reliably, assure the integrity of interconnected systems and users.

This work led the way to future cybersecurity projects at PNDC including improving incident response capabilities, asset discovery on power communications networks, identification and analyses of vulnerabilities in network assets and penetration testing of electric power assets.

## References


1. Hurst, W., Merabti, M., Fergus, P.: A survey of critical infrastructure security. In: Butts, J., Shenoi, S. (eds) Critical Infrastructure Protection VIII. ICCIP 2014. IFIP Advances in Information and Communication Technology, vol. 441. Springer, Berlin (2014)
2. Glaser, B.G.: Theoretical sensitivity (1978)
3. Burns, M.: Participatory operational and security assessment on homeland security risks: an empirical research method for improving security beyond the borders through public/private partnerships. J. Transp. Secur. **11**, 85–100 (2018). https://doi.org/10.1007/s12198-018-0193-1
4. Charmaz, K.: Discovering chronic illness: using grounded theory. Soc. Sci. Med. **30**(11), 1161–1172 (1990)
5. Gjørv, G.H.: Security by any other name: negative security, positive security, and a multi-actor security approach. Rev. Int. Stud. **2012**(38), 835–859 (2012). https://doi.org/10.1017/S0260210511000751
6. Bradfield, R., Derbyshire, J., Wright, G.: The critical role of history in scenario thinking: Augmenting causal analysis within the intuitive logics scenario development methodology. Futures **77**, 56–66 (2016). https://doi.org/10.1016/j.futures.2016.02.002

7. Mead, N.R., Woody, C.C.: Cyber Security Engineering. Addison-Wesley, A Practical Approach for Systems and Software Assurance (2017)
8. Van der Heijden, K., Bradfield, R., Burt, G., Cairns, G. and Wright, G.: The sixth sense: Accelerating organizational learning with scenarios, John Wiley & Sons (2009)
9. National Grid ESO. Future Energy Scenarios (2021). https://www.nationalgrideso.com/future-energy/future-energy-scenarios/fes-2021
10. Dos Santos, D., Dashevskyi, S., Wetzel, J.: Amnesia: 33 How TCP/IP Stacks Breed Critical Vulnerabilities in IoT, OT and IT Devices. Forescout Research Labs (2021). https://www.forescout.com/research-labs/amnesia33/
11. Piccalo, M.: How to Use Asset Management as the Foundation for OT Network Segmentation, Forescout, 21 10 2019. https://www.forescout.com/company/blog/how-to-use-asset-management-as-the-foundation-for-ot-network-segmentation/. Accessed 26 July 2021
12. Forum of Incident Response and Security Teams. Common Vulnerability Scoring System version 3.1: Specification Document, June 2019. https://www.first.org/cvss/specification-document#Environmental-Metrics. Accessed 26 July 2021
13. OfGem. Investigation into 9 August 2019 power outage (2019). https://www.ofgem.gov.uk/publications-and-updates/investigation-9-august-2019-power-outage
14. Department for Business Energy and Industrial Strategy, "Distributed Energy Resources - Cyber Security Connection Guidance," Energy Networks Association (2020). https://www.energynetworks.org/industry-hub/resource-library/distributed-energy-resources-(der)-cyber-security-connection-guidance.pdf
15. Bochman, A.A., Freeman, S.: Countering Cyber Sabotage. CRC Press, Boca Raton (2021)
16. Bochman, A.: The End of Cybersecurity, Harvard Business Review https://store.hbr.org/product/the-end-of-cybersecurity/BG1803
17. National Grid ESO. Bridging the Gap to Net Zero March 2021. https://www.nationalgrideso.com/future-energy/future-energy-scenarios/bridging-the-gap-to-net-zero. Accessed 27 July 2021
18. European Commission. Data protection impact assessment for smart grid and smart metering environment 27 September 2018. https://ec.europa.eu/energy/topics/markets-and-consumers/smart-grids-and-meters/smart-grids-task-force/data-protection-impact-assessment-smart-grid-and-smart-metering-environment_en#dpia-template-and-users. Accessed 27 July 2021
19. Congrès International des Réseaux Electriques de Distribution, RESILIENCE OF DISTRIBUTION GRIDS WORKING GROUP, in International Conference on Electricity Distribution 31.05.2018. http://cired.net/cired-working-groups/resilience-of-distribution-grids
20. Liu, R., Vellaithurai, C., Biswas, S.S., Gamage, T.T., Srivastava, A.K.: Analyzing the Cyber-Physical Impact of Cyber Events on the Power Grid. IEEE Trans. Smart Grid **6**(5), 2444–2453 (2015). https://doi.org/10.1109/TSG.2015.2432013
21. Yang, Y., Littler, T., Sezer, S., McLaughlin, K. and Wang, H.F.: Impact of cyber-security issues on Smart Grid. In: 2nd IEEE PES International Conference and Exhibition on Innovative Smart Grid Technologies, pp. 1–7 (2011). https://doi.org/10.1109/ISGTEurope.2011.6162
22. Energy Networks Association. Open Networks Future Worlds. Developing change options to facilitate energy decarbonisation, digitisation and decentralisation, 31 July 2018 https://www.energynetworks.org/assets/images/Resource%20library/ON18-WS3-14969_ENA_FutureWorlds_AW06_INT%20(PUBLISHED).pdf. Accessed 27 July 2021
23. US Department of Energy. Office of Electricity, Electricity Subsector Cybersecurity Capability Maturity Model v. 1.1., February 2014. https://www.energy.gov/oe/downloads/electricity-subsector-cybersecurity-capability-maturity-model-v-11-february-2014. Accessed 27 July 2021
24. Cisco. Cisco 2018 Annual Cybersecurity Report. https://www.cisco.com/c/en_uk/products/security/security-reports.html#~more-reports

25. Allen, J.H., Curtis, P.D., Gates, L.P.: Using Defined Processes as a Context for Resilience Measures. Software Engineering Institute. Carnegie Mellon University, December 2011. https://apps.dtic.mil/sti/pdfs/ADA610464.pdf
26. Allen, J.: Measures for managing operational resilience. EDP Audit, Control, Secur. **44**(6), 1–6 (2011). https://doi.org/10.1080/07366981.2011.643192
27. Whyte, W.F.: Learning from the Field. A guide from experience, Sage Publications (1984)
28. Beech, N., Arber, A., Faithfull, S.: Restoring a sense of wellness following colorectal cancer: a grounded theory. J. Adv. Nurs. **68**(5), 1134–1144 (2012). https://doi.org/10.1111/j.1365-2648.2011.05820.x

# SMILE - Smart eMaIl Link Domain Extractor

Mattia Mossano(✉), Benjamin Berens, Philip Heller, Christopher Beckmann, Lukas Aldag, Peter Mayer, and Melanie Volkamer

Karlsruhe Institute of Technology, Karlsruhe, Germany
{mattia.mossano,benjamin.berens,philip.heller,christopher.beckmann, lukas.aldag,peter.mayer,melanie.volkamer}@kit.edu

**Abstract.** Phishing over email continues to be a significant threat, as such messages still end up in users' inboxes. Several studies showed that users rarely check the URL in the statusbar before clicking a link and that they have difficulties reading URLs. To support users, we propose SMILE (Smart eMaIl Link domain Extractor), a novel approach that provides the relevant information to distinguish between legitimate and phishing emails checking the links in them. Once applied, SMILE modifies all links in an email to contain the domain and top-level-domain of the URL behind them, e.g., "Click here" in an legitimate Amazon email is modified to "Click here [amazon.com]".

**Keywords:** Anti-phishing intervention · User support · URL analysis

## 1 Introduction

Phishing is still a growing threat, e.g., the Anti Phishing Working Group [6] shows that in 2020 the number of phishing websites doubled. Despite improved phishing detection tools, phishing emails still reach people's email inboxes. While there are various types of phishing emails, we focus on those containing dangerous links that could download malware or take victims to phishing webpages. Simple phishing emails can be detected through sender address or typos, but this is not the case for sophisticated attacks. Yet, all phishing emails with links can be identified through the URL behind each link. However, [23] showed that most people are not aware of this and [3] demonstrated that people have problems reading URLs correctly.

We propose SMILE, **S**mart e**M**a**I**l **L**ink domain **E**xtractor. SMILE checks the HTML code of an email to detect links and modifies them only to contain what we call a "SMILE-string". These strings are then the only clickable elements in the respective email. They can be the domain and top-level-domain (TLD) of the URL behind a link, an IP address, or include some subdomains (e.g., sites.google.com). This paper presents the SMILE concept and its working.


S. Katsikas et al. (Eds.): ESORICS 2021 Workshops, LNCS 13106, pp. 403–412, 2022.
https://doi.org/10.1007/978-3-030-95484-0_23

## 2 Related Works

There are various solutions to provide tool based anti-phishing support to users. Tools can, e.g., analyse and operate on malicious emails/websites content [1,16, 25], work on the DNS side [4,7,10] or identify malicious websites with machine learning [2,8,12]. They either block or warn users if the risk is above a predefined threshold. Yet, there is no 100% guarantee for detection. SMILE differs from them as it helps users to identify phishing emails, not block the latter.

Researchers have proposed in [5,18,20,22] two different solutions to support users to analyse emails URLs. In [18,20,22], the authors show a tooltip just-in-time and just-in-place with the URL behind links. Some parts of SMILE, namely the SMILE-string resolution and SMILE special cases (see Sect. 5), are based on [20,22]. In [5], the authors propose a chat-bot that helps users to decide the legitimacy of a link through text interactions. SMILE advantage over them is placing the relevant information (and only that) whenever an email is opened.

Valve's videogame digital distribution service, STEAM, employs a SMILE-like security feature on their forum. In [21] there are some examples of the forum text formatting, however, we found no official documentation explaining this security feature. Thus, we conducted some tests on their platform, shown in the Appendix (Fig. 3). Valve adds domain and TLD of the URL after the link itself, between square parenthesis, as normal text with darker font colour and smaller character size. The feature only applies to textual links but only those where the text is a URL which does not start with http/https. SMILE modifies textual links (with and without protocol), image links, short URLs, and moves the clickable element to the SMILE-string.

## 3 Background on Link-Types

Our interest are links in emails. Thus, we focus on the four ways to create them:

- *Anchor-Element*, also known as a-tag
- *Form-Element*, that can send data to a link given by the "action" attribute
- *Formaction-Attribute*, special form-elements with the "formaction" attribute
- *Area-Element*, enable areas in a (possibly transparent) image to be clickable

We would like to make these remarks: (1) The term "link" usually indicates only anchor-elements, but we use it for all four for simplicity. (2) Links can be created with JavaScript, but the common web mail services and clients [15] block it [9]. Thus, we do not consider it further. (3) From the users' point of view, form-elements and formaction-attributes are indistinguishable.

There are three *link-types* for anchor-element, form-element, and formaction-attribute: *Image*, *URL-like*, and *Misc* (e.g., "Click here"). Area-tag is only applicable for the link-type Image (as we consider its usage in the email context).

In summary, SMILE needs to cope with *ten different situations* (= 3 anchor-elements + 3 form-elements + 3 formaction-attributes + 1 area-element).

## 4 SMILE: General Idea

The general idea underlying SMILE is to enhance the transparency of every email link by substituting them with easy-to-read versions whenever the email is opened without further user action. After applying SMILE, the email contains textual links with the *SMILE-string*. This can be the domain and the TLD of the original link URL, an IP address, or include some subdomains (e.g., sites.google.com). The SMILE-string only provides the minimum information required to decide on a URL legitimacy (i.e., no automated URL analysis). Note, the statusbar is left untouched and it shows the entire URL on mouse-hover.

Our design principle has four motivations: (1) substituting every link at once saves time, as users do not have to check them independently (e.g., as with a tooltip). (2) Only placing the SMILE-string, instead of the URL, reduces the efficacy of phishing URLs with misplaced legitimate domains. (3) The relevant security indicator (SMILE-string) is in the email body, i.e., just-in-place, as recommended in [18]. (4) Limited information prevents conflicts/overlap with other tools, e.g., the solution in [22]: users wanting more information can combine SMILE with other tools. An example of an email modified by SMILE is shown in Fig. 1.

*Toggle Function.* SMILE might make complex emails unreadable. Thus, we implemented a toggle function to undo all substitutions on demand.

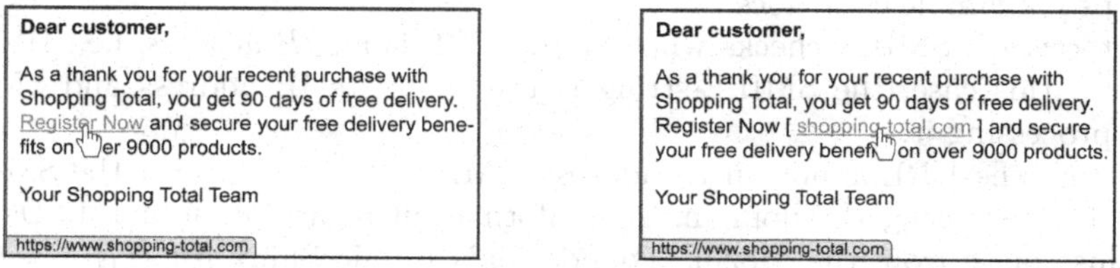


(a) Without SMILE (b) With SMILE

**Fig. 1.** Link in email, without and with SMILE.

## 5 SMILE: Algorithm

A high-level description of the algorithm is depicted in Fig. 2. Note, the credit for the processes described in "Resolve SMILE-string" (*short URL service*, *redirects*, *IP-address*, legitimate TLDs recognition and *punycode*) and "Resolve special case SMILE-string" (*programmed tooltips* and *dangerous files at cloud services*) goes to the authors of [20,22]. However, differently from TORPEDO, SMILE: (1) only shows the SMILE-string, not the entire URL, (2) adds the SMILE-string to the email text, not in a tooltip, (3) substitutions are situation based, and (4) substitutions are shown whenever the email is opened, not only on mouse-hover.

**Identify Link-Type.** First, SMILE searches for a link and identifies the link-type (see Sect. 3 for the different link-types).

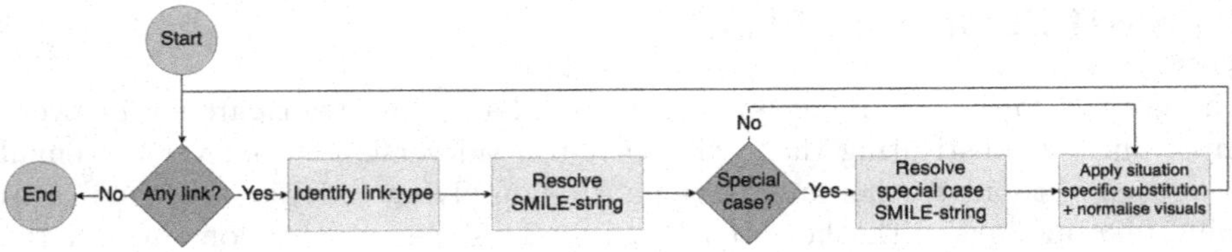


**Fig. 2.** Flow chart showing the algorithm behind SMILE.

**Resolve SMILE-String.** SMILE extracts the URL from the link and checks if it points to a known *short URL service* or a known *redirect service.* In these cases, the URL is meaningless to the user to determine whether it is a phishing one or not. SMILE resolves the final destination, if needed by repeatedly applying this step. Then, the resolved URL is set as actual URL.

For the *short URL service*, SMILE loads the headers of the service to check the target location following the HTTP 3xx server response. This can be a privacy issue, as it allows the link owner to get the user IP address Therefore, the users can configure SMILE to not send any request and to show domain and TLD of the short URL service.

For the *redirects*, SMILE resolves the URL from the path of the actual URL applying rules that recognise the structure used by known redirect services. For example, from google.de/url?url=https%3A%2F%2Fexample.com%2Fdocs to https://example.com/docs.

Afterwards, SMILE checks whether the URL is an *IP address*, i.e., IPv4 or IPv6. In this case, the SMILE-string is the complete IP address and SMILE stops processing it.

In case the URL is not an IP address, SMILE deduces from it the SMILE-string by extracting the domain. The information regarding actual TLDs and domains comes from the Mozilla Foundation's Public Suffix list [17] using the solution in the "publicsuffixlist.js" GitHub project [13].

Finally, SMILE checks the extracted SMILE-string for specific characters in the *Unicode character space.* This check is to prevent homographic techniques, i.e., using similar-looking characters from other character spaces in the domain or TLD, e.g., using a Cyrillic "e" for the domain "google.de". SMILE replaces non-ASCII characters in the SMILE-string with puny code, e.g., xn–googl-7of.de. This approach is already used in many programs, e.g., Google Chrome 51+ [11].

**Resolve Special Case SMILE-String.** SMILE addresses three special cases: (1) *programmed tooltips*, (2) *dangerous files at cloud services* and (3) *website creation and hosting tools.*

In the *first case*, the tooltip contains the legitimate URL for the link and is meant to distract users from the actual URL in the statusbar. If users do not know that a tooltip is not expected in a context, they can mistakenly consider the URL in the tooltip as a legitimate location, thus clicking on a fraudulent link. SMILE checks for programmed tooltips and blocks them from being displayed.

In the *second case*, phishers would store dangerous files at a cloud service and provide a link to them in the email. In this case, the SMILE-string alone might be misleading to users. Therefore, SMILE checks for the URL structure of well known cloud service providers (e.g., Dropbox, Google Drive, OneDrive). It then adds a warning before the SMILE-string link: "[Only click if you were expecting this email, as you are redirected to a cloud service:]".

In the *third case*, SMILE checks for well known website creation and hosting tools, e.g., Google Sites, Microsoft Azure. The SMILE string is then extended with the subdomain (e.g., sites.google.com) and a warning is added before the SMILE-string link: "[Only click if you were expecting this email, as you are redirected to a webpage that could have been set up by anyone:]".

**Apply Situation Specific Substitution + Normalise Visuals.** Each of the 10 situations identified in Sect. 3, is treated differently by SMILE:

- *Image link-type.* A link including an image as its first and only child. SMILE disable the link and adds the phrase "Image link:" above the image, followed by the SMILE-string between square parenthesis.
- *URL-like link-type.* A textual link appearing to be a URL. SMILE detects specific patterns (i.e., http, https, www, /) or a specific structure (i.e., *domain.tld*). Thus, SMILE works both on extended URLs, e.g., https://www.amazon.co.uk, and reduced ones, e.g., amazon.co.uk. In this case, SMILE substitutes the text content of the element with the SMILE-string.
- *Misc link-type.* Links whose content is neither an image nor URL-like, e.g., "Click here". To preserve the information in the misc type text, SMILE keeps the text but disables the link, i.e., it is just normal email text. SMILE adds the SMILE-string between square brackets as a new link right after this text.

These three link-types cover 9 of the 10 situations. The last situation are *maps with clickable areas over images.* SMILE adds a list of links above the image, analogously to the *Image link-type* described above. The map is then removed from the image to disable the clickable parts. This approach loses the original image area contextual information, but introduces a clear list of links.

Note that links created through form-elements and formaction-attributes (Sect. 3) do not show the URL behind them on mouse-hover. Without SMILE, the only way to check their URL is inspecting the HTML code of the webpage. However, since every SMILE-string is an anchor-element textual link, users can check their URL on mouse-hover, accessing otherwise hidden information.

Code examples in HTML for each of the ten situations are provided in the Appendix (Table 2). Examples of the substitutions can be seen in Table 1.

SMILE also normalises the font visuals. For example, it applies a minimum font size to prevent a too small to read SMILE-string and it checks for enough contrast with the background colour to make the SMILE-string easily legible.

## 6 Discussion

SMILE can work on both the receiving email server (*central approach*) or the email client, i.e., the software or app used by the user (*local approach*).

**Central Approach.** No user installation is required and SMILE is also available on mobile devices. However, the toggle function is either not available or users

**Table 1.** Examples of SMILE substitutions. Note, SMILE also works on buttons and button-like links, i.e., images of buttons and CSS modified anchor-elements.

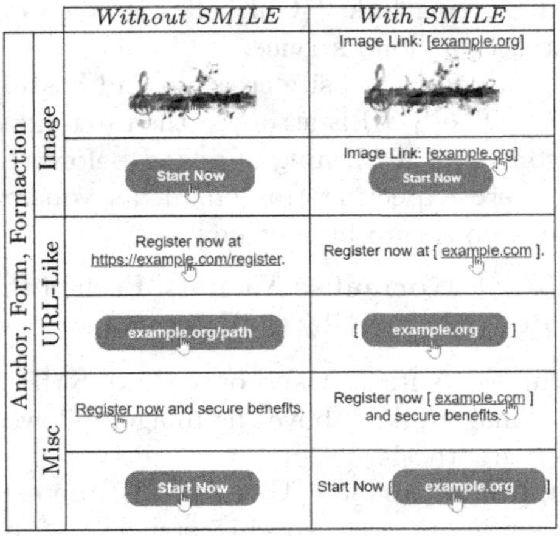


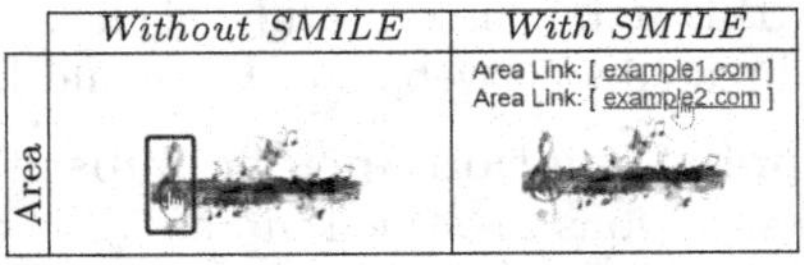


have to install an extension. Moreover, the DKIM authentication method has issues, as it uses digital signatures over the email body and any alteration leads to a client-side failed check. A workaround is for the server to perform the DKIM check and pass it on to the user, e.g., by changing the subject. End-to-end encryption mechanisms, e.g., PGP or S/MIME, can be used, but SMILE would not work, as the email text would not be accessible (i.e., encrypted).

**Local Approach.** DKIM authentication, end-to-end encryption and toggle function work. However, SMILE needs to be adapted to various email clients as an extension (i.e., add-on). Note, Outlook, Apple Mail and mobile clients require specific solutions.

As future work, we plan an evaluation of the SMILE concept, i.e., its effectiveness in different settings (e.g., mobile and desktop) as well as its performance in comparison to the tooltip proposed in [22]. This could be conducted in two ways: in a *non-interactive environment* and in an *interactive environment.* Both approaches have been used in the past (e.g., [14,19,22,24] used a non-interactive environment and [5,22] used an interactive one). We believe both options to be worthwhile, as each can potentially show different aspects. Hence, we plan to evaluate SMILE in both ways. Furthermore, we want to check SMILE in the real world to see how much the toggle function is required.

## 7 Conclusion

We propose SMILE, a new security intervention supporting users while detecting phishing emails. SMILE has various advantages over existing approaches: (1) it displays the relevant information immediately, not only on mouse-hover. (2) It only shows the SMILE-string, thwarting obfuscation techniques like subdomain-as-domain (e.g., google.com.domain.com). (3) It can work centrally (i.e., on the receiving email server) or locally (i.e., in the email client). As future work, we plan to conduct user studies to get empirical evidence of these advantages and to evaluate SMILE usability.

**Acknowledgements.** This work was supported by funding from the topic Engineering Secure Systems of the Helmholtz Association (HGF), by KASTEL Security Research Labs, by the Federal Ministry of Education and Research (BMBF) and the Baden-Württemberg Ministry of Science as part of the Excellence Strategy of the German Federal and State Governments, and by the Google Faculty Research Award 2019 for the Link-centric Phishing Warnings for Online Email Clients project.

# Appendix

**Table 2.** Examples in html code for every substitution situation. The *formaction* attribute for the *input* and *button* is optional. If no *formaction* attribute is given, the *action* attribute of the *form* is used.

| | *Without SMILE* | *With SMILE* |
|---|---|---|
| *Anchor* -Image | `<a href="https://example.org/"><img src="./example.png" /></a>` | `Image Link: [ <a href="https://example.org/">example.org</a> ]<br><img src="./example.png"/>` |
| *Anchor* -URL-Like | `<a href="https://www.example.org/path">https://sub.example.org/path</a>` | `[ <a href="https://www.example.org/path">example.org</a> ]` |
| *Anchor* -Misc | `<a class="button" href="https://example.org/">Start Now</a>` | `Start Now [ <a class="button" href="https://example.org/">example.org</a> ]` |
| *Form* -Image | `<form action="https://sub.example.com/path" method="POST">`<br>`<button type="submit"><img src="./example.png"/></button></form>` | `<form action="https://sub.example.com/path" method="POST">Image Link: [ <button type="submit">example.org</button> ]<br><img src="./example.png" /></form>` |
| *Form* -URL-Like | `<form action="https://sub.example.com/path" method="POST">`<br>`<button type="submit">https://sub.example.org/path</button>`<br>`<input value="https://example.org/" type="submit"/></form>` | `<form action="https://sub.example.com/path" method="POST">`<br>`[ <button type="submit">example.org</button> ]`<br>`[ <input value="example.org" type="submit"/> ]</form>` |
| *Form* -Misc | `<form action="https://sub.example.com/path" method="POST">`<br>`<button type="submit">Submit Now</button>`<br>`<input value="Submit Now" type="submit"/></form>` | `<form action="https://sub.example.com/path" method="POST">`<br>`Submit Now [ <button type="submit">example.org</button> ]`<br>`Submit Now [ <input value="example.org" type="submit"/> ]</form>` |
| *Formaction* -Image | `<form action="https://sub.example.com/path" id="form1"></form>`<br>`<button type="submit" formaction="https://example.com/path" form="form1"><img src="./example.png" /></button>` | `<form action="https://sub.example.com/path" id="form1"></form>`<br>`Image Link: [ <button type="submit" formaction="https://example.com/path" form="form1">example.org</button> ]<br><img src="./example.png" />` |
| *Formaction* -URL-Like | `<form action="https://sub.example.com/path" id="form1"></form>`<br>`<input type="submit" form="form1" value="https://page1.example.co.uk/path1" formaction="https://page1.example.co.uk/path1" />`<br>`<button type="submit" formaction="https://page2.example.de/path2" form="form1">https://page2.example.de/</button>` | `<form action="https://sub.example.com/path" id="form1"></form>`<br>`<input value="example.co.uk" type="submit" form="form1" formaction="https://page1.example.co.uk/path1" />`<br>`<button formaction="https://page2.example.de/path2" type="submit" form="form1">example.de</button>` |
| *Formaction* -Misc | `<form action="https://sub.example.com/path" id="form1"></form>`<br>`<input type="submit" form="form1" value="Submit Now" formaction="https://page1.example.co.uk/path1"/>`<br>`<button type="submit" form="form1" formaction="https://page2.example.de/path2" >Submit Now</button>` | `<form action="https://sub.example.com/path" id="form1"></form>`<br>`Submit Now [ <input value="example.co.uk" type="submit" form="form1" formaction="https://page1.example.co.uk/path1" /> ]`<br>`Submit Now [ <button type="submit" form="form1" formaction="https://page2.example.de/path2"> example.de</button> ]` |
| *Area* -Image | `<img src="./example.png" usemap="#map"/><map name="map">`<br>`<area shape=".." coords=".." href="https://example1.com/">`<br>`<area shape=".." coords=".." href="https://example2.com/"></map>` | `Area Link: [ <a href="https://example1.com/">example1.com</a> ]<br>`<br>`Area Link: [ <a href="https://example2.com/">example2.com</a> ]<br>`<br>`<img src="./example.png"/>` |

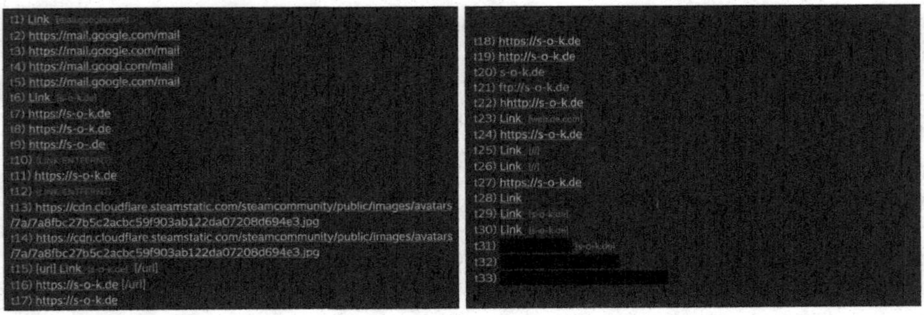


**Fig. 3.** Tests of Valve's STEAM forum formatting of links. The substitution is added only for some of them. T31, 32 and 33 use the "spoiler" function, that allows to obscure some of the text, then visible only through mouse-hover.

## References


1. Afroz, S., Greenstadt, R.: PhishZoo: detecting phishing websites by looking at them. In: International Conference on Semantic Computing, pp. 368–375 (2011). https://doi.org/10.1109/ICSC.2011.52
2. Al-Janabi, M., de Quincey, E., Andras, P.: Using supervised machine learning algorithms to detect suspicious URLs in online social networks. In: International Conference on Advances in Social Networks Analysis and Mining, pp. 1104–1111 (2017). https://doi.org/10.1145/3110025.3116201
3. Albakry, S., Vaniea, K., Wolters, M.K.: What is this URL's destination? Empirical evaluation of users' URL reading. In: Conference on Human Factors in Computing Systems (CHI), pp. 1–12 (2020). https://doi.org/10.1145/3313831.3376168
4. Ali, M., Nelson, J., Shea, R., Freedman, M.J.: Blockstack: a global naming and storage system secured by blockchains. In: USENIX Annual Technical Conference (USENIX ATC), pp. 181–194 (2016). https://www.usenix.org/conference/atc16/technical-sessions/presentation/ali
5. Althobaiti, K., Vaniea, K., Zheng, S.: Faheem: explaining URLs to people using a Slack bot. In: Symposium on Digital Behaviour Intervention for Cyber Security, pp. 1–8 (2018). https://vaniea.com/papers/aisb2018.pdf
6. APWG: Phishing activity trends report, 4th quarter 2020 (2021). https://docs.apwg.org/reports/apwg_trends_report_q4_2020.pdf
7. Bin, S., Qiaoyan, W., Xiaoying, L.: A DNS based anti-phishing approach. In: 2010 Second International Conference on Networks Security, Wireless Communications and Trusted Computing, pp. 262–265 (2010). https://doi.org/10.1109/NSWCTC.2010.196
8. Chiew, K.L., Chang, E.H., Sze, S.N., Tiong, W.K.: Utilisation of website logo for phishing detection. Comput. Secur. **54**, 16–26 (2015). https://doi.org/10.1016/j.cose.2015.07.006
9. Englehardt, S., Han, J., Narayanan, A.: I never signed up for this! Privacy implications of email tracking. Proc. Priv. Enhancing Technol. **2018**(1), 109–126 (2018)
10. Gastellier-Prevost, S., Gonzalez Granadillo, G., Laurent, M.: A dual approach to detect pharming attacks at the client-side. In: 4th IFIP International Conference on New Technologies, Mobility and Security, pp. 1–5 (2011). https://doi.org/10.1109/NTMS.2011.5721063

11. Google: Internationalized Domain Names (IDN) in Google Chrome (2021). https://chromium.googlesource.com/chromium/src/+/refs/heads/main/docs/idn.md
12. Hajgude, J., Ragha, L.: Phish mail guard: phishing mail detection technique by using textual and URL analysis. In: 2012 World Congress on Information and Communication Technologies, pp. 297–302 (2012). https://doi.org/10.1109/WICT.2012.6409092
13. Hill, R.: Public suffix list (2020). https://github.com/gorhill/publicsuffixlist.js
14. Lastdrager, E., Gallardo, I.C., Hartel, P., Junger, M.: How effective is anti-phishing training for children? In: Thirteenth Symposium on Usable Privacy and Security (SOUPS), pp. 229–239 (2017). https://www.usenix.org/conference/soups2017/technical-sessions/presentation/lastdrager
15. Litimus Email Analytics: Email client market share (2021). https://emailclientmarketshare.com/
16. Marchal, S., Armano, G., Grondahl, T., Saari, K., Singh, N., Asokan, N.: Off-the-hook: an efficient and usable client-side phishing prevention application. IEEE Trans. Comput. **66**, 1717–1733 (2017). https://doi.org/10.1109/TC.2017.2703808
17. Mozilla: Public Suffix List (2020). https://publicsuffix.org/
18. Petelka, J., Zou, Y., Schaub, F.: Put your warning where your link is: improving and evaluating email phishing warnings. In: Conference on Human Factors in Computing Systems (CHI), pp. 1–15 (2019). https://doi.org/10.1145/3290605.3300748
19. Reinheimer, B., et al.: An investigation of phishing awareness and education over time: when and how to best remind users. In: Sixteenth Symposium on Usable Privacy and Security (SOUPS), pp. 259–284 (2020). https://www.usenix.org/conference/soups2020/presentation/reinheimer
20. SecUSo: TORPEDO-Webextension (2021). https://github.com/SecUSo/TORPEDO-Webextension
21. Valve: Text formatting (2021). https://steamcommunity.com/comment/Recommendation/formattinghelp
22. Volkamer, M., Renaud, K., Reinheimer, B., Kunz, A.: User experiences of TORPEDO: TOoltip-poweRed Phishing Email DetectiOn. Comput. Secur. **71**, 100–113 (2017). https://doi.org/10.1016/j.cose.2017.02.004
23. Wash, R.: How experts detect phishing scam emails. In: Proceedings of the ACM on Human-Computer Interaction, pp. 1–28 (2020). https://doi.org/10.1145/3415231
24. Wen, Z.A., Lin, Z., Chen, R., Andersen, E.: What. Hack: engaging anti-phishing training through a role-playing phishing simulation game. In: Conference on Human Factors in Computing Systems (CHI), pp. 1–12 (2019). https://doi.org/10.1145/3290605.3300338
25. Zhou, Y., Zhang, Y., Xiao, J., Wang, Y., Lin, W.: Visual similarity based anti-phishing with the combination of local and global features. In: 13th International Conference on Trust, Security and Privacy in Computing and Communications, pp. 189–196 (2014). https://doi.org/10.1109/TrustCom.2014.28

# A Semantic Model for Embracing Privacy as Contextual Integrity in the Internet of Things (Short Paper)

Salatiel Ezennaya-Gomez[1](✉), Claus Vielhauer[2], and Jana Dittmann[1]

[1] Otto-von-Guericke University Magdeburg, Magdeburg, Germany
{salatiel.ezennaya,jana.dittmann}@ovgu.de

[2] Brandenburg University of Applied Sciences, Brandenburg, Germany
claus.vielhauer@th-brandenburg.de

**Abstract.** Due to the increasing number of complaints alleging privacy violations against companies to data protection authorities, the translation of business goals to system design goals and the subsequent consequences for customers' privacy poses a challenge for many companies. For this reason, there is a need to bridge the economics of privacy and threats to privacy. To this end, our work relies on the concept of privacy as contextual integrity. This framework defines privacy as appropriate information flows subjected to social norms within particular social contexts or spheres. In this paper, we introduce a preliminary version of a semantic model which aims to relate and provide understanding on how well-established business goals may affect their customers' privacy by designing IoT devices with permission access, data acquired by sensors, among other factors. Finally, we provide a use case application showing how to use the semantic model. The model aims to be an educational tool for professionals in business informatics during the modeling and designing process of a product which may gather sensitive data or may infer sensitive information, giving an understanding of the interaction of the product and its footprint with diverse actors (humans or machines). In the future, a further complete model of the presented may also target other groups, such as law enforcement bodies, as part of their educational training in such systems.

**Keywords:** Privacy · Contextual integrity · Internet of Things · Semantic model · Digital exclusion

---

The work results presented are related in part of the general approach to the MSCA-ITN-ETN - European Training Networks Programme under Project ID: 675087 ("AMBER - enhAnced Mobile BiomEtRics") and in part to educational purposes of the model to guide forensics to the project FINANzkriminalitaeT: MethodIsche Analyse von Bedrohungsszenarien fuer moderne Karten- und App-basierte Zahlungssysteme (FINANTIA; FKZ:13N15297) funded by the Bundesministerium fuer Bildung und Forschung (BMBF).


S. Katsikas et al. (Eds.): ESORICS 2021 Workshops, LNCS 13106, pp. 413–423, 2022.
https://doi.org/10.1007/978-3-030-95484-0_24

## 1 Introduction

In June 2021, the number of GDPR (General Data Protection regulation) fines were six hundred ninety-two, with an amount of nearly three hundred million euros [2]. These numbers may showcase many companies and how little they embrace Privacy-by-Design as part of their business and system design processes. One side of the many-sided problem is caused by how the applications and devices, which support Big Data business models, are designed to pursue those business goals. For these reasons, it is essential to bridge the economics of privacy, ethics in system design, and privacy risks and understand the cause-effect of business goals. We believe that this objective is achievable by embracing privacy as Contextual Integrity (CI) as part of the educational agenda for professionals of business informatics.

Our work is based on a well-established philosophical framework, called CI, introduced by Nissenbaum in [14], and previous work on semantic model literature reviews for privacy risks [5,8,10]. CI defines *privacy* as "appropriate information flows according to norms specific to social spheres or contexts" as described in [7]. The framework includes abstract concepts, such as societal values and stakeholders interests, bases for privacy's ethical legitimacy. It unifies multiple known concepts of privacy, e.g., security design aspects, including the concept of context(s) or spheres, and abstract factors, such as business relations and their influence in the behavior of applications and IoT devices, as stated in [7]. If the privacy norms are not respected, the situation leads to privacy violations, such as inferring sensitive attributes from social media posts even when these attributes are not revealed, and later on, using the extracted information for psychological advertising targeting individuals [6].

In the review presented by Benthall et al., in [7], the authors conclude by calling for actions on "designing systems that address the challenges of matching concrete situation with abstract spheres". They raised a set of research questions in their review on how computer science approaches CI: (RQ1) "how to be more technically precise about the nature of contexts in order to relate the definition given in CI with more concrete notions used by computer scientist?"; (RQ2) "how to apply the CI framework to IT systems which are designed to work across multiple contexts?" We aim to contribute to finding an answer to these questions by scoping the relations among every participant, from the individual(s) to businesses. Notably, in smart environment applications, where sensors and actuators interact with many users at once, e.g., in a videoconference or in a schoolroom, where it is hard to rely on individual privacy preferences and expectations [7]. For this reason, our objective is to design a semantic model capturing CI elements and privacy threats for IoT devices. The model aims to be an educational tool for professionals in business informatics during the modeling and designing process of a product (or device) which may gather sensitive data or may infer sensitive information, giving an understanding of the interaction of the product and its footprint with diverse actors (humans or machines). In the future, a further complete model of the presented may also target other groups, such as law enforcement bodies, as part of their educational training in such systems.

The document is structured as follows: In Sect. 2, the CI theory is briefly explained. Subsequently, in Sect. 3, a semantic model based on CI principles is presented, describing the methodology and introducing the model with a use case scenario. Finally, conclusions and discussion are in Sect. 4.

## 2 Background

This section briefly describes the CI theory. For a more detailed description and reasoning about it, we refer to Nissenbaum's work in [7,14,15].

Contextual Integrity (CI) is a benchmark theory of privacy based on law and societal norms introduced by Helen Nissenbaum in her book Privacy in context in [14]. CI defines privacy as *appropriate information flows* which are subjected to social norms within particular social contexts or spheres. Subsequently, informational privacy norms (or privacy norms) are mapped onto privacy expectation of the individuals. The norms are formed by five parameters: the *data subject*, the *sender* of the data, the *recipient* of the data, the *attribute* or *information type*, and *transmission principle*, which are the *information flow conditions* among parties such as, those that are well-known, *with data subject's consent, in confidence, required by law*, and *entitled by the recipient.*

Lastly, the author describes contextual ends, purposes, and values of society as the "essence" of the social context, legitimizing the norms mentioned earlier. Thus, when privacy norms are fulfilled, contextual integrity (i.e., privacy) is respected. Privacy norms are in line with the law as well as, with privacy expectations and social values. In legal contexts, there is a privacy violation when there is a violation of privacy laws. In CI, if defined privacy norms are not respected, the situation leads to privacy violations, such as inferring sensitive attributes from social media posts even when these attributes are not revealed, and later on, using the extracted information for psychological advertising targeting individuals [6].

In the literature, there are studies on how the users of smart home devices perceive privacy norms [4]. These studies help to understand how privacy expectations and contexts change while using those IoT devices. The results show that these expectations rely on user's trust in companies, business practices, among other factors, such as geopolitical situations.

## 3 A CI Semantic Model

Our goal is to design a semantic model introducing CI concepts in the IoT environment. It aims to provide another view on how related could be the elements of an agent (i.e., device or applications) to business purposes and privacy threats.

For the creation, we employed the seven steps of the 101 methodology described in [16], which are summarized into the following three steps: (1) knowledge acquisition and identification of the purpose of the ontology; (2) modeling the ontology, defining the classes and relations; (3) evaluation of the semantic model. The first step encompasses from the first to the third step of 101, which are *(step 1) determine the domain and scope of the ontology, (step 2) consider reusing existing ontologies, and (step 3) enumerate important terms in the ontology.* The second step groups *4 (Define the classes and the class hierarchy), 5 (Define the properties of classes-slots), 6 (Define the facets of the slots), and 7 (Create instances)* of the 101 methodology. Finally, the third is out of the scope of the 101 but is necessary for semantic modeling and evaluation. We achieved the first and second steps of the methodology, considering the third step as our future work. Nevertheless, we describe the model as a use case application in Subsect. 3.3.

### 3.1 Knowledge Acquisition and identification of the Purpose of the Semantic Model

Our knowledge is based on literature reviews presented in [5,8,10]. The authors identified some points in which semantic models in privacy fall short of identifying potential attributes, which can be detected/inferred from data types or different sources. As reviewed in [8], many ontologies have been proposed for semantic knowledge modeling for privacy. These ontologies range from those ensuring consent based on the legal framework (mainly focused on GDPR) to ontologies that define and relate online privacy risks, such as phishing. However, these proposals lack the issues mentioned above regarding the links between business goals and privacy violations. From the conclusions drawn in the review, we defined the following questions which the ontology aims to answer: (Q1) how are the attributes related to the purposes of the application(s) and the organization(s)? (Q2) what actions performed by agents in the IoT system may affect individual and others' attributes? Since the semantic model aims to answer questions related to privacy that need to be implemented and interpreted by human beings, we do not focus on having the best time responds while lunching a query, but rather to have consistencies in its answers.

### 3.2 Modeling the Ontology, Defining the Classes and Relations

In this subsection, we introduce our suggested semantic model by describing each of the top-level class nodes, their functional interrelations with other nodes in Fig. 1, and some of their subclasses or instances. Following 101 methodology recommendations, it is possible to reuse other semantic models connected through those top-level classes, e.g., *SecurityPrivacyIssues* for information security [11,12]. Figure 1 shows the core concepts of our semantic model.

**Agent.** An agent is an entity, i.e., *DataSubject* (active users and other individuals who are inactive users whose data are also part of the gathered dataset), *Organization, Embedded Organization, and OrganisationsDataReceivers* (other organizations which process data handed by another organization), who generates and creates other entities, such as *DigitalAgents* and *Embedded DigitalAgent* (e.g., mobile applications, trackers, third-party APIs). The agents may access several objects across the diagram, such as sensors, data generated by those sensors, and other smart devices. In addition, some of these agents may be linked to another class, called *Actors*, defined in the other data regulation semantic models, such as GConsent [17].

**Assets.** Assets are those essential elements for the existence of a relation between agents and essential to protecting with security mechanisms. They may be divided into two categories, *tangible assets* and *non-tangible assets*. Some subclasses are, e.g., *PhysicalSensors*, *TelemetryData*, and *ApplicationConnections*. The data are generated by data subjects and digital agents (e.g., an application), which interact with the data subjects or other digital agents. Some assets may contain instances from class *Attributes*.

**Actions.** They are activities that the agents can perform. Some actions or activities are mainly related to certain actors. For instance, an organization and embedded organizations could perform advertising tracking or traffic analysis using digital agents. Other actions, such as *SendReceiveStreams* or *Active Interaction* could be performed by some digital actors.

**Purposes.** The *Purposes* class defines the intentions for which an application is used. This class has three categories (overlapping sets) which are: *User, Business, and Application* which correspond to purposes of agents *DataSubject, Organization and Embedded Organization, and DigitalAgent and EmbeddedDigialAgent*. In addition, subclasses of purposes which contain more specific instances, among others, are *Education, Security (e.g., LockDoor), Health (e.g., DailySteps, DailyCalories), Office (e.g., ReadEmails), Banking (e.g., NFCPayment), Social Media (e.g., Tweets), and Entertainment*.

For instance, an application can be used for educational purposes, social media purposes, and security purposes, e.g., an app that teaches new languages has some security features (for unlocking the application using face and voice), including messaging with other users of the app. Therefore, the user's purposes are *education, security, and social media*. These purposes may coincide with the application purposes. Nevertheless, the set of application purposes may include more purposes, such as *IdentityFraudDetection, DeviceProfiling, Advertising*. Moreover, these application purposes may be part of a more extensive set of general business purposes which are also *Adversiting, FraudDetection, Adprofiling, DataModelsTrading, PartnerDataSharing, and SelfBusinessActivities*, among others.

**Attributes.** They are relevant features for the identification of individuals, their environment(s) (e.g., location, including special attributes, such as social background or race [19]), and the devices within the IoT system. These attributes can be either directly or indirectly extracted (i.e., inferred information) from a set of instances of *Assets*, e.g., data types. For example, they can be directly obtained by performing face and voice recognition while extracting a set of attributes available in live interactions or in pictures and audio stored in the device's local storage, previously permission access to storage should be granted. Also, they can be indirectly extracted from a set of assets and actions performed, e.g., audio background filtering or speaker detection performing knowledge discovery in the cloud.

**Transmission Principles.** This class is complex due to its interactions with other classes and subclasses. The class refers to the conditions that are created for the *transmission or gathering* of the data, e.g., protection mechanisms are applied to secure the data exchange with the user's consent, including to whom the data are sent, locations of the organization(s). Some of the subclasses of the class are *SecurityRequirements, LegalRequirements, AppliedProtectionMechanisms, DataSubjectConsent, and DataSubjectExpectations*, among others. The latter could have instances obtained from a list of user's expectations as a result of surveys in contextual privacy norms design by device manufacturers [4].

**Values.** As indicated by the CI theory, agents conduct their decisions and actions according to a series of ethical values and interests, which may be part of their established social norms. We understand that this class should cover social and individual's situations, for instance, current geopolitical situation of agents' region(s) where data are transferred. This class is the most abstract class of the model, and we believe that professionals in ethics and technology should define its instances. A starting point for this may be the core points established in a standard on ethics, and system design, such as the IEEE P7000 family [3]. This class is closed related to the *Transmission Principles* class since it governs the abstract principles of the transmission principles' instances.

**Security and Privacy Issues.** This class describes known and known-unknown security and privacy issues, which may pose security threats and privacy risks by the usage of extracted information from individuals' attributes from an active user or non-active user(s), actions performed, and relations among digital agents. The class has two non-disjoint subclasses, which are *Security Vulnerabilities* and *Privacy Threats*. They are non-disjoint classes since the former may also imply threats to privacy by exploiting a set of security vulnerabilities. Moreover, these subclasses can also be linked to more specific semantic models on privacy and security, e.g., based on ISO 27001, on legal compliant semantic models, and attack knowledge databases, such as ATT&CK of MITRE [1].

### 3.3 An Exemplary Use Case Application

The semantic knowledge model can be applied in the first stage of requirement analysis and definition in any software engineering design methodology found in the literature, e.g., agile or waterfall models. Within the requirement analysis step, use cases related to the technical functionalities of the product and privacy risks and law enforcement should also be described. For example, a person wears a smartwatch-fitness tracker in his workplace, connected to an app (or application) installed in the user's smartphone. Current smartwatches in the market are multi-purpose devices, i.e., a smartwatch could be used as a fitness tracker, a home assistant, among diverse usages. Hence, a list of high-level requirements for

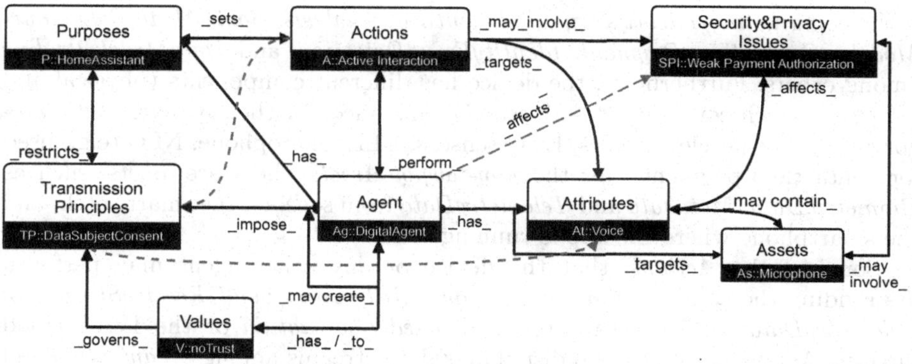


**Fig. 1.** The diagram showcases the relations and dependencies among classes. Below each class label, an exemplary instance is written, extracted from the use case in Subsect. 3.3. Black lines define direct relations, and blue dash lines show indirect implications between classes. (Color figure online)

the tandem smartwatch and its app could be (1) *the device must capture ECG and speech*; (2) *the smartwatch should be interoperable with an intelligent voice assistant (IVA) device and skills (third-party applications for smart home devices)*; (3) *the device can emulate a credit card for authorized contactless payments.*

In this example, the modeling starts breaking down the functional requirements for the identification of the classes. Starting from the *Agent* class, the *data subject* is the active user who wears the device; the class *organization(s)* is the company of the smartwatch and app, along with the *embeddedOrganization(s)* which offer the smartwatch services, its modalities, and other business purposes of the organization. These embedded organizations could be connected to the device via APIs or software development kits (SDKs) to develop the app and the smartwatch software. Subsequently, the primary piece of software of the device or smartwatch and the app are *digital agent(s)* which are created by the *organization(s)*, along with the trackers and third-party trackers (pieces of code that collects and send data) embedded in the used SDK or API, which are the *embeddedDigitalAgent(s)* created by *embeddedOrganization(s)*. Finally, another user could be present as a *(inactive) data subject(s)*, who may be further identified by applying specific actions on the acquired data.

On the other hand, the list of common *Purposes* for the category *user* and *business*, i.e., for the data subject and organization(s) are *Health* with instances, such as *DailySteps*, as a fitness tracker, *SmartHome* as a home assistant or IVA, and *Contactless-Payment* as a credit card emulator. Furthermore, there are more purposes for small functionalities, such as *social media*, whether sharing extracted information (e.g., hiking tracks and performance) while acting as a fitness tracker is possible. Moreover, apart from the aforementioned purposes that may have each agent, there are more purposes for the organization and the embedded organization(s), i.e., their business purposes, such as *marketing/advertising*, *IntelligentDataAnalysis*, *SocialMediaBehaviourModels*, *Contactless-Payment*, *IdentityFraudDetection*, and *DataModelsTrading* among others. Furthermore, the device has different components (physical and software) which constitute the *Assets*. For instance, for the *tangibleAssets* category, there are accelerometers, ECG sensors, BLE, microphone, NFC (e.g., used for contactless payment), for the *non-tabgibleAssets*, there are assets, such as *BiometricData*, *Metadata* and *TelemetryData* from sensors, the smartwatch, and the smartphone where the app is running.

Some of the *Actions*, that the device or any other agent may perform, are sending the collected data, e.g., *CaptureUtterance*, *Send/ReceiveStreams* of *TelemetryData* to either the app, *EmbeddedOrganization* or the IVA's cloud directly. Additionally, the app distributes data streams among *organization* and *embedded organization(s)* according to the list of purposes for both business and functionalities of the device. For instance, an organization embeds APIs that belong to financial companies or fintech in the app for conducting contactless payments. These APIs connect other applications and send information about a payment process, among other information, to their servers and fintech companies involved in the payment process. In addition, depending on the business purpose of the embedded organization, e.g., *Advertising*, the API may establish a connection to servers of another organization, called *X*, which is not involved in the payment process. This action triggers the installation of another *embedded digital agent* of the organization*X* in the user's device, as it is shown in a recent study on online payment traffic analysis in [9]. When the app has third-party trackers, i.e., one or more *embedded digital agent(s)*, at least technical/metadata data about the device where the app is installed, its functions, plus information about which app has invoked that tracker, are sent to these new embedded organization(s). Note that there are types of trackers (e.g., long-term tracker that lasts up to two years) that identify a user, which may pose a privacy threat.

From the data captured by the digital agent(s), some information is directly or indirectly extracted, which may correspond to instances of the *Attributes* class. One group of attributes may be those related to the data subject, e.g., attributes extracted from speech are *nationality*, *age*, *educational background*, *health condition*, *emotions*, and *gender* along with captured traits from other individuals. From technical information, such as access network state and connections, the location could be inferred.

The *TansmissionPrinciples* includes the so-called agreement conditions, which refers to the *LegalRequirements, DataSubjectConsent*, along with data subject's expectations fulfilled by surveys, which may be, e.g., *AppliedAdditionalObfuscation* on specific attributes that are found in a particular asset. Specifically, this particular transmission principle may be governed by an instance of the abstract class *Values*, such as *geopolitical situation* under which the transmission and process of information take place. Also, there could be instances from *Values* related to agents, e.g., *data subject* has *No Trust* on *Embedded Organisation.*

The semantic model can relate business purposes to individuals' privacy, answering *Q*1 and *Q*2 from the Subsect. 3.1 as follows. For example, for the

*Contactless-Payment* purpose, it is needed access to a set of tangible and non-tangible assets. These assets are, but not restricted to, *NFC sensor*, *payment data*, *telemetrydata* and *metadata*. These assets are also used for purposes, such as *IdentityFraudDetection* (for detecting payment fraud), *DataModelsTrading* (for selling models to merchants or other companies). From these datasets, attributes and subsequent user information can be inferred. From the *telemetrydata, payment data, and metadata*, the attributes of *location* of the user, and *language* used in the device can be obtained. Moreover, from these attributes, it is possible to know the educational background or nationality, as well as from purchased items, including the categorization of the merchant's marketplace, it is possible to infer attributes, such as *gender* or *sexual orientation*. Nevertheless, these attributes may imply a set of instances of the *Security and Privacy Issues* class. The aforementioned inferred attributes, along with specific actions performed by the organizations involved, may imply known privacy issues, such as knowing the user's residence district is possible to infer information about the ethnic group or economic status. This particular example is due to the digital agent of *Send/ReceiveStreams* of *payment data*, and to use the asset for *OnlineBehaviouralDataModelsTrading* as business purpose. Furthermore, known security vulnerabilities of physical assets, e.g.,*NFC sensor*, may pose privacy threats as well.

## 4 Discussion and Conclusions

In the presented paper, we have introduced a semantic model based on privacy as contextual integrity. One limitation of our semantic model is the lack of validation by privacy engineers. This point is expected to be solved in our future work. The other limitation is the creation of relationships among classes. For some exemplary cases of privacy issues, describing the relationships becomes a difficult task due to the complexity and dependencies between classes and instances. In addition, the model does not yet cover cases such as, identifying bystanders who have not given consent and are accidentally recorded and what mitigations should be employed to reduce privacy risks; however, they are not ruled out for the next stages of model development.

During the literature review and creation of the model, we encountered some privacy challenges in the field. One is the inferred information (extracted information of other individuals) not provided explicitly by a single user. However, it could be extracted from the user's data by knowledge discovery methods, which is mathematically described in [6] as a situated information flow theory. We believe that this challenge could be described in the semantic model by using instances of the classes *Asset, Actions, Attributes*, and *Security&PrivacyIssues* based on studies on knowledge discovery. The second is the description of the consequences of the privacy preferences of a social group, which may affect an individual's privacy preferences. This problem is called Digital Exclusion, and it is discussed in [18]. Unfortunately, this particular problem is not described in the semantic model yet. Such problems seem to be closer to an ethical and philosophic issue than a technical issue. Nevertheless, the use of technology affects these issues. For these reasons, the inclusion of socio-technological models as part of the design cycle of a technological product becomes essential to achieve systems that respect social norms and the integrity of individuals.

Bridging the gap between Nissenbaum's theory, in which privacy is understood as contextual integrity (CI), and IoT system design, we provide a preliminary version of a semantic model to understand what aspects may affect an individual's privacy using IoT devices. The model aims to be an educational tool for professionals in business informatics during the modeling and designing process of a product which may gather sensitive data or may infer sensitive information, giving an understanding of the interaction of the product and its footprint with diverse actors (humans or machines). Moreover, the model can be helpful for organizations that conduct a privacy impact assessment, research ethics in pervasive data, and developers to get information on where and what could impact individuals' privacy by relations among attributes, sensors, and actors. We believe that this model may also contribute to the initiative of the Software Bill of Material of the National Telecommunications and Information Administration of the US (NTIA) for enhancing transparency in software by including the influence of third-party software over users' privacy and privacy statements, along with security vulnerabilities [13].

In the future, a further complete model of the presented may also target other groups, such as law enforcement bodies, as part of their educational training in such systems. The presented paper is a theoretical proposal and is considered for future implementation and validation as future work.

## References


1. A definition of the mitre att&ck framework. https://attack.mitre.org/matrices/enterprise/. Accessed 12 July 2021
2. GDPR Fines Tracker & Statistics (2021), https://www.privacyaffairs.com/gdpr-fines/. Accessed 12 July 2021
3. Model process for addressing ethical concerns during system design (2021). https://ethicsinaction.ieee.org/p7000/. Accessed 16 Sept 2021
4. Abdi, N., Zhan, X., Ramokapane, K.M., Such, J.: Privacy norms for smart home personal assistants. In: Proceedings of the 2021 CHI Conference on Human Factors in Computing Systems (2021)
5. Badillo-Urquiola, K., Page, X., Wisniewski, P.: Literature review: Examining Contextual Integrity Within Human-Computer Interaction. SSRN 3309331 (2018)
6. Benthall, S.: Situated information flow theory. In: Proceedings of the 6th Annual Symposium on Hot Topics in the Science of Security. HotSoS 2019, Association for Computing Machinery, New York (2019)
7. Benthall, S., Gürses, S., Nissenbaum, H.: Contextual integrity through the lens of computer science. found. Trends® Priv. Secur. **2**(1), 1–69 (2017)
8. Ezennaya-Gomez, S.: Rethinking and privacy-knowledge and modeling-about and uncovering accepted and data collection and business and practices as privacy and risks. Technical Report FIN-03-2020, Otto-von-Guericke University Magdeburg, Germany (2020)

9. Ezennaya-Gomez, S., Kiltz, S., Kraetzer, C., Dittmann, J.: A semi-automated http traffic analysis for online payments for empowering security, forensics and privacy analysis. In: The 16th International Conference on Availability, Reliability and Security. ARES 2021, Association for Computing Machinery, New York (2021). https://doi.org/10.1145/3465481.3470114
10. Gharib, M., Giorgini, P., Mylopoulos, J.: Towards an ontology for privacy requirements via a systematic literature review. In: Conceptual Modeling, pp. 193–208. Springer International Publishing, Berlin (2017). https://doi.org/10.1007/978-3-642-34002-4
11. Halpin, H.: Semantic insecurity: security and the semantic web. In: PrivOn 2017 - Workshop Society, Privacy and the Semantic Web - Policy and Technology. vol. 1951, pp. 1–10. Vienna, Austria, October 2017
12. Herzog, A., Shahmehri, N., Duma, C.: An ontology of information security. Int. J. Inform. Secur. Privacy **1**(4), 1–23 (2007)
13. National Telecommunication Information Association, U.S.D.o.C.: Software bill of material (2021), https://www.ntia.gov/SBOM. Accessed 12 July 2021
14. Nissenbaum, H.: A contextual approach to privacy online. In: Digital Enlightenment Yearbook 2012, vol. 140, pp. 219–234 (2012)
15. Nissenbaum, H.: Respecting context to protect privacy: why meaning matters. Sci. Eng. Ethics **24**(3), 831–852 (2015). https://doi.org/10.1007/s11948-015-9674-9
16. Noy, N.F., McGuinness, D.L.: Ontology Development 101: A Guide to Creating Your First Ontology: Knowledge Systems Laboratory. Stanford University. Tech. rep, Stanford University (2001)
17. Pandit, H.J., Debruyne, C., O'Sullivan, D., Lewis, D.: GConsent - a consent ontology based on the GDPR. In: Hitzler, P., Fernández, M., Janowicz, K., Zaveri, A., Gray, A.J.G., Lopez, V., Haller, A., Hammar, K. (eds.) ESWC 2019. LNCS, vol. 11503, pp. 270–282. Springer, Cham (2019). https://doi.org/10.1007/978-3-030-21348-0_18
18. Rehak, R.: What does data protection actually protect? Why data protectionists must stop talking about individual privacy (2018). https://media.ccc.de/v/35c3-9733-was_schutzt_eigentlich_der_datenschutz. Accessed 12 July 2021
19. A requirement analysis for privacy preserving biometrics in view of universal human rights and data protection regulation. In: 2018 26th European Signal Processing Conference (EUSIPCO), pp. 548–552 (2018)

# Data Protection Impact Assessments in Practice
## Experiences from Case Studies

Michael Friedewald[1](✉), Ina Schiering[2], Nicholas Martin[1], and Dara Hallinan[3]

[1] Fraunhofer Institute for Systems and Innovation Research ISI, Karlsruhe, Germany
{michael.friedewald,nicholas.martin}@isi.fraunhofer.de
[2] Ostfalia University of Applied Sciences, Wolfenbüttel, Germany
i.schiering@ostfalia.de
[3] FIZ Karlsruhe – Leibniz-Institut für Informationsinfrastruktur, Eggenstein-Leopoldshafen, Germany
dara.hallinan@fiz-karlsruhe.de

**Abstract.** In the context of the project *A Data Protection Impact Assessment (DPIA) Tool for Practical Use in Companies and Public Administration* an operationalization for Data Protection Impact Assessments was developed based on the approach of *Forum Privatheit*. This operationalization was tested and refined during twelve tests with startups, small- and medium sized enterprises, corporations and public bodies. This paper presents the operationalization and summarizes the experience from the tests.

**Keywords:** Data Protection Impact Assessment · Privacy · General Data Protection Regulation · Standard Data Protection Model · Data protection goals · Risk management

## 1 Introduction

A central element of the General Data Protection Regulation (GDPR) is the risk based approach, which is aimed at addressing new technologies and complex services processing personal data. Examples are Internet of Things (IoT), mHealth and mobility applications where various sensors and Artificial Intelligence (AI) approaches are employed. Especially in the area of mHealth applications, special categories of personal data in the sense of Art. 9 GDPR are typically processed. Such services often contain products from several technology providers (hardware and software artifacts) and are composed of cloud services from various providers.

When considering the specific privacy risks in the context of a service, the controller needs to clarify whether the intended processing is likely to result in a high risk to the rights and freedoms of natural persons. In this case a Data Protection Impact Assessment (DPIA) according to Art. 35 (1) GDPR must be conducted. In guidance concerning the severity of privacy risks the Article 29 Data Protection Working Party proposed - in their Guidelines on Data


S. Katsikas et al. (Eds.): ESORICS 2021 Workshops, LNCS 13106, pp. 424–443, 2022.
https://doi.org/10.1007/978-3-030-95484-0_25

Protection Impact Assessment - several criteria which serve to define technologies as constituting a high risk: evaluation and scoring, automated-decision making with legal or similar significant effect, systematic monitoring, sensitive data, data processed on a large scale) [2,14].

The GDPR itself merely provides a minimum standard for carrying out a DPIA, as stipulated by Art. 35(7) GDPR. Accordingly, in recent years, data protections authorities [10,23], scientific consortia [12,27], standardisation bodies [25] and trade associations [17] have developed methodological frameworks for carrying out a DPIA. However, these methods differ considerably with regard to the procedure, the process and the interpretation of the abstract requirements of Art. 5 GDPR. As they are very abstract, their concrete implementation in practice is the responsibility of the respective institution.

For a substantial DPIA, the context in particular is very important since it makes a huge difference for the individual whether a service - e.g. a communication or collaboration service - is used in a normal business context or for the processing of health relevant personal data. Finally, the implementation of a DPIA is always a process involving many people - or at least it should be. It is a challenge to introduce people whose background is neither data protection law nor computer science to the questions and evaluation standards that are to be applied for a DPIA. Finally, in addition to the data protection requirements, in many cases there are other important requirements that have to be balanced against each other.

In this regard, we were interested in designing and testing a DPIA process that is generic enough to be used in all possible application areas, but also able to take into account the specifics of each area. The basis for this work was a methodology that we had developed prior to the applicability of the GDPR [3,18]. In a project funded by the German Ministry of Research and Education we then tested and refined this methodology. More specifically, we carried out a number of DPIAs in cooperation with companies and authorities using our methodology. This paper gives an insight into the experiences we had and the conclusions that can be drawn from them.

The rest of this paper is organized as follows: Sect. 2 briefly discusses some of the existing DPIA frameworks, their merits and shortcomings, then Sect. 3 outlines the methodology that we sought to validate. Sections 4 and 5 present and discuss the results from the empirical work. Section 6 concludes the paper.

## 2 Related Work

As the GDPR itself does not specify any specific operationalization for data protection impact assessments, stakeholders from different backgrounds have proposed approaches to fill this gap. Most of these methods are in principle suitable for fulfilling the requirements of Art. 35 GDPR [29,38]. The most important approaches come from data protection authorities. These are attractive for the data controllers because they are officially rubber-stamped.

The most popular methodological framework was developed by the *French Data Protection Authority CNIL* [10] based on the EBIOS risk management methodology of the French national IT security authority ANSSI.[1] In this approach, the assessment comprises of a highly structured and detailed but "checklist"-style query system that closely follows the legal text and inquires as to typical technical implementations – supported by a software tool. In this process, stakeholder consultation is not at the centre of the assessment. Rather, the input for the necessary analyses (on risk, proportionality, etc.) comes from the controller. The views of the data subjects are sought for the purpose of validating the results at the end of the process. In general, the CNIL operationalizes the DPIA as a compliance check of the GDPR and IT security requirements. Many other institutions, e.g. the German Association for Information Technology, Telecommunications and New Media BITKOM [17], have followed the CNIL in this approach.

The other influential DPIA framework was developed by the *Information Commissioner's Office ICO* in the United Kingdom [23] and adapted by other national DPAs [1]. In particular, this framework builds on the long-standing tradition of privacy impact assessments (PIAs), which have been used in the English-speaking world since the 1990s [7,40]. The most important offspring of the ICO approach is the ISO/IEC 29134 standard [25] – although this was adopted before the GDPR came into force and is therefore not fully compliant, ISO standards have a unifying effect and are readily used by (especially internationally operating) companies.

The ICO (and ISO) take a more reflexive and discursive approach, producing continuous text and asking more qualitative - and even organisational-sociological - questions (e.g. how to avoid "function creep", the creeping expansion of processing purposes). Such an approach is more flexible in addressing the characteristics of very different applications, but the results tend to be less precise and verifiable. Instead of a relatively static request for specific implementations and guarantees, there is a more discursive, often workshop-based development of damage scenarios. For this reason, consultation of data subjects has a much greater importance in all steps of the process. The biggest weakness, in our view, is that the principles in Art. 5 GDPR are not further operationalized. This means that, for example, difficult legal concepts such as lawfulness, fairness and appropriateness, which are usually unfamiliar to legal laypersons, have to be discussed with data subjects or other stakeholders.

This weakness was recognised by the German supervisory authorities which proposed a so-called standard data protection model (SDM) [11]. The SDM is a general concept relevant for the GDPR as a whole, rather than a DPIA framework in the strict sense. However, it contains important elements that can be used for the purpose of creating a framework for operationalizing the DPIA requirement. In particular, the SDM uses the concept of protection goals, developed by Rost, Pfitzmann and others [34], and places them - instead of the data protection principles from Art. 5 GDPR – at the centre of operationalization. Of course, the protection goals do not contradict the principles of Art. 5 GDPR.

[1] https://www.ssi.gouv.fr/en/guide/ebios-risk-manager-the-method/ (last accessed 25-07-2021).

On the contrary, as has been shown in [11], the protection goals completely cover the principles of Art. 5. However, they translate the principles into the language of IT-Security (from where the concept of "protection goals" was originally taken), presenting the principles in a concise and condensed form. The authors of this paper have developed their own DPIA framework based on their own preliminary work [3] using the SDM protection goals. The goal of our methodology is a process that effectively identifies relevant data protection risks in a participatory manner. In the following sections, we analyse our experience with this process and what needs to be considered in order to carry out a DPIA across a heterogeneous group of stakeholders.

Since services are of increasing complexity, controllers need detailed information about a service to carry out a DPIA. Therefore the DPIA methodology proposed by the Government of the Netherlands [31] contains a so-called umbrella DPIA where service providers implement a general DPIA, which can then be used as a basis for individual risk assessments based on a specific context. An example of such a generic DPIA is the DPIA for diagnostic data processing in Microsoft Windows 10 Enterprise [30].

Thus, although there is a plethora of available DPIA methods, there has not been much work to evaluate and compare them from a *practical* perspective, e.g. [38]. There are two main types of studies: Evaluations of approaches to implementing DPIA or sub-elements thereof [14,29] and studies on the notion of risk under the GDPR [15,19,21].

Finally, there are a number of publications presenting DPIA results for critical technologies such as facial recognition [6], COVID-19 contact tracing apps [5] or eHealth [26,35] that also report implementation experiences selectively [4].

## 3 Operationalization of DPIA[2]

The operationalization of the DPIA methodology presented below is structured as described in Table 1, where the central DPIA consists of the *DPIA preparation, execution* and *DPIA implementation* accompanied by the *initialization* and *sustainability* phase. An important aspect of a DPIA is responsibility. In general, the controller of data processing is responsible for performing a DPIA (Art. 35 (1) GDPR), potentially assisted by processors (Art. 28 (3)(f) GDPR). In addition the controller should seek the advice of the data protection officer (Art. 35 (2) GDPR). Participation of data subjects or their representatives is in general recommendable. Especially in relation to complex services, advice from processors or even technology providers may be helpful. During the case study, workshops with organizations in different roles, i.e. controller, processor or technology provider, were performed.

[2] A detailed description of the methodology can be found in [28].

**Table 1.** Overview of DPIA phases [28, p. 24]

| DPIA phase | Description |
|---|---|
| I. Initiation phase | – Threshold assessment: Clarify whether a DPIA is necessary |
| II. Preparation phase | – Description of the processing operations & collection of information,<br>– Planning of the execution phase |
| III. Execution phase | – Consultation of the data subject (or their representatives)<br>– Risk identification and analysis<br>– Risk assessment, mitigation measures, assessment of remaining risks<br>– Assessment of the necessity and proportionality<br>*In case of high remaining risks → consult with the supervisory authorities or abandon the processing* |
| IV. Implementation phase | – Implementation of the mitigation measures<br>– Test of the mitigation measures (where possible before the start of the processing)<br>– Proof of compliance with the GDPR<br>→ *Processing can go ahead* |
| V. Sustainability phase | – Monitoring<br>– Identification of deviations or changes<br>– Adjustments<br>*Depending on the size of deviations or changes → potentially repeat phases II. to IV.* |

### 3.1 Initialization Phase

In the first phase, the *initialization phase* the aim is to analyze whether a DPIA is necessary for a processing activity. The so-called "threshold analysis" is itself a first rudimentary risk assessment based on a few criteria, which – like the full DPIA – must be carried out before the processing of personal data starts. The records of processing activities (Art. 30(1) GDPR), the documentation of lawfulness (Art. 6 GDPR) and preliminary considerations of necessity and adequacy (Art. 5 GDPR) could serve as a basis for this initial step.

In this phase, the controller is obliged to consider whether the processing is likely to result in a high risk to the rights and freedoms of natural persons according to Art. 35 (1) GDPR. Besides the indications concerning processing activities in Art. 35 (3) GDPR, supervisory authorities should establish and communicate lists of processing activities which fulfill the relevant criteria (Art. 35 (4) and Art. 68 GDPR). In addition, the criteria of the Article 29 Data Protection Working Party should be considered [2]. The result of this threshold analysis should be documented.

In the context of the case studies, this initialization phase was conducted via preliminary communication with the organizations. In these preparatory

**Table 2.** Description of the processing operations and collection of information

| Aspect | Summary of preparation |
|---|---|
| Data subjects | – Data subjects<br>– Representatives (e.g. work council) |
| Organization | – Controllers<br>– Processors resp. joint controllers<br>– Other stakeholders in general<br>– Description of organizational structure |
| Data processing | – Description of personal data<br>– Documentation of data flows (e.g. in the form of a data flow diagram)<br>– (Intended) processes as context for data processing |
| Technical documentation | – Documentation of the (intended) technical implementation<br>– Technical infrastructure<br>– Existing or planned technical and organizational measures |
| Legal documents | – Contracts<br>– Work council agreements, etc. |

conversations, other relevant issues such as information gathering on processing operations were also discussed.

### 3.2 DPIA Preparation Phase

If during the initialization phase potentially high risks for the rights and freedoms of natural persons are detected, a full DPIA needs to be carried out.

The first step in the *DPIA preparation phase* according to Art. 35 (7)(a) GDPR is "a systematic description of the envisaged processing operations and the purposes of the processing, including, where applicable, the legitimate interest pursued by the controller". In addition to the records of processing activities, toward this end, information about the intended processing activities and the context of processing should be provided to facilitate the privacy risk assessment in the subsequent *DPIA execution phase* (see Table 2).

In addition the *DPIA execution phase* needs to be planned and a proposal for an adequate team assisting the controller performing the DPIA is needed.

An important aspect of this phase is the detection of all persons involved in, and affected by, the processing activities. Especially via the use of workflow management systems and meta data in general, customer data and the personal data of staff members is often collected - the latter potentially allowing performance control of work processes. In the case of IoT services such as smart homes, smart mobility services or even CCTV applications, beside the intended users, the personal data of friends, family members, employees, etc. may also be processed. For complex products or services which are part of the intended processing, details of processing are typically not completely documented and service providers, technology providers, human resources representatives, process experts or IT experts are helpful for clarifying details. An important tool is a data flow diagram to detect all stakeholders and interfaces with data transfers.

### 3.3 DPIA Execution Phase

The focus of the execution phase is the assessment of risks to the rights and freedoms of data subjects[3] (Art. 35 (7)(c) GDPR), the choice of measures to address the risks and to ensure the protection of personal data (Art. 35 (7)(d) GDPR) and the assessment of the necessity and proportionality of the processing operations in relation to the purposes (Art. 35 (7)(b) GDPR).

Based on the information collected in the *DPIA preparation phase* the DPIA team conducts the risk identification and analysis for risk assessment. At the start of the process, a common understanding of the intended processing is developed.

**Risk Identification.** The first goal is the identification of privacy risks. In the context of our case study an approach adapted from scenario analysis was used [24]. Based on the information about data subjects and personal data processed, scenarios incorporating potential harms to data subjects are identified via brainstorming. For these scenarios the information summarized in Table 3 is collected concerning the identified scenario in question (*damage scenario*). In addition, information about technical and organizational measures which are already present in the processing operation should be collected in parallel (*existing countermeasures*) as, typically, new processing activities are realized in the context of an existing IT landscape which employs standard security and privacy measures.

**Risk Analysis.** The next step is to analyze the identified risks from the viewpoint of the data subject. Instead of the abstract normative provisions in the GDPR, our methodology uses the data protection goals defined in the SDM as an assessment benchmark [11]. They are more suited to practical work because they translate the abstract norms into concrete system requirements. These are much better understood by people involved in a DPIA as they allow to establish a direct link to the functionality and implementation of the data processing to be assessed. The protection goals include:

- *Data Minimisation* stands for the principle of necessity, according to which no more personal data are to be processed than are needed to achieve the purpose.

[3] This means that not only the risks to the right to data protection (Art. 8 CFR) and the right to respect for private and family life (Art. 7 CFR) have to be considered, but also the other fundamental rights in the Charter [21]. In our test cases however, the focus was on data protection risks.

**Table 3.** Documentation of risk assessment

| Aspect | Description |
|---|---|
| Damage scenarios | – Description of the scenario<br>– Data subjects<br>– Personal data<br>– Involved actors/stakeholders<br>– Potential harm/damage for data subjects<br>– Elements triggering the harm/damage |
| Existing countermeasures | – Already existing technical and organizational mitigation measures |
| Data protection goals | *Describe how data protection goals are affected and prioritize the goals together with data subjects resp. representatives*<br>– Data Minimisation<br>– Availability<br>– Integrity<br>– Confidentiality<br>– Unlinkability<br>– Transparency<br>– Intervenability |
| Risk assessment | – Severity of the potential damage (minor, manageable, substantial, major)<br>– Likelihood (minor, manageable, substantial, major)<br>– Resulting Risk Level (low risk, normal risk, high risk) |
| Additional measures | *Also processing activities might be changed resulting in an adapted risk assessment*<br>– Additional mitigation measures<br>– Enhancement of existing measures |

- *Availability* refers to the requirement that personal data must be available and can be used properly in the intended process.
- *Integrity* stands for the requirement (a) that IT processes and systems continuously comply with specifications and (b) that the data to be processed remain intact, complete, and up-to-date.
- *Confidentiality* means that no person is allowed to access personal data without authorisation.
- *Unlinkability* is the requirement that data shall be processed and analysed only for the purpose for which they were collected.
- *Transparency* means that the data subject, system operators, and supervisory authorities must be able to understand the how and why of any data processing.
- *Intervenability* refers to the requirement that data subjects can actually exercise their rights of notification, access, rectification, blocking and erasure at any time.

Just as there are usually tensions between the interests of different stakeholders, the protection goals are not independent but influence each other. This means that not all protection goals can be fulfilled to the same extent. If complete confidentiality is guaranteed in a system, this means that access to certain data is restricted for certain actors, i.e. availability is limited. There is also a trade-off between integrity and intervenability, because integrity means that subsequent changes to data and processes are not allowed, while intervenability means that changes are allowed e.g. in the form of the right to rectification. Finally, there is also a conflict between transparency and unlinkability, as the former aims to increase the understanding of the actual data processing, e.g. by logging the actions of users and administrators, whilst the latter tries to avoid creation of such surplus knowledge [22, 39].

During the workshops the protection goals were well understood and helpful for participants describing their privacy perception and priorities in the context of a concrete scenario. When carrying out the assessment, consideration should also be given to which protection goals are most important to the data subjects and other stakeholders concerned in the context of the scenario. This can and will lead to a prioritisation of the protection goals in relation to each scenario.

**Risk Assessment.** After the analysis of risks, the likelihood of the occurrence of risks and the severity of consequent harm are estimated by the DPIA team. This is typically done from the subjective viewpoint of the data subjects on a scale ranging from *minor, normal, substantial, major*: As a rule, in data protection neither the severity of damage nor the likelihood of its occurrence can be meaningfully quantified. Instead, one should offer and document a valid and reasonable argumentation for how one decides to scale the different risks in terms of their likelihood and severity, based on the most objective criteria possible. The severity of the damage results from the physical, material, or non-material effects on data subjects. The reversibility of the damage should also be considered here (the more difficult, or costly in terms of time, money or effort, that reversibility is, the more severe the damage). Relevant too is the difficulty data subjects would face if they wanted to withdraw from the processing (including if they do not know about the processing in the first place), and how easy or difficult it would be for them to examine the processing themselves or have it examined in court. The more persons are "at the mercy" of processing, the greater the severity of possible damages connected to the processing. To assess the likelihood, it is useful to consider the motives and capabilities of the stakeholders as well as the effort needed to trigger the risk event and the robustness of existing mitigation measures.

The value of such a procedure leading to a purely qualitative classification lies in the fact that in the discourse either a consensual assessment is reached or a potential conflict is revealed. Both outcomes are useful for risk mitigation.

The result of the risk evaluation can be visualized in a risk matrix in order to gain an overview of existing privacy risks. There risks are roughly quantified as *low, normal or high.* In the context of a continuous improvement process, necessary additional, or adapted, technical and organizational measures are defined and/or the processing activities themselves are changed to reduce risks to the rights and freedoms of natural persons. The aim is to ensure the protection of personal data and to demonstrate compliance (Art. 35 (7)(d) GDPR). In addition, an assessment of the necessity and proportionality of the processing operations in relation to the purposes of processing is performed (Art. 35 (7)(b) GDPR).

The whole process, including information collected in the DPIA preparation phase, the result of the risk assessment and the measures defined to address risks, must be documented in a comprehensive DPIA report (Art. 35 (7) GDPR).

If the risks can be reduced to an acceptable extent - such that the intended processing is compliant with the GDPR - the processing can be implemented incorporating the defined measures. Otherwise, a prior consultation of the supervising authority is needed: the intended processing may have to be abandoned if the risks cannot be eliminated or at least reduced to an acceptable extent.

### 3.4 DPIA Implementation Phase

In this phase the measures defined in the DPIA report are implemented and the effectiveness of measures is tested and documented to the extent possible before the approval of GDPR compliance. For the monitoring of risks and effectiveness of defined measures, a monitoring and test concept has to be developed and implemented, including a comprehensive documentation of test results. It is advisable to integrate this monitoring into a data protection management system, which is ideally part of the organisation's risk management approach. After ensuring the compliance of processing activities with the GDPR, the processing can begin.

### 3.5 Sustainability Phase

During the operation of a system, the controller must continuously ensure that, in the context of the processing, the risks to the rights and freedoms of natural persons are adequately reduced. Therefore, risks and effectiveness of implemented measures have to be monitored based on the defined test concept.

In case of slight deviations to the envisaged processing, the risk assessment, the measures and the DPIA, can all be adjusted. If significant changes or operational differences occur, the controller needs to adapt phases II. to IV. in Table 1.

## 4 Methodology of the Case Studies

In 2018/19, we worked with twelve organisations (corporate and public) in conducting DPIAs using the methodology presented in Sect. 3. We have analysed real data processing operations as used by the partner organisations in their daily business.

The aim was to operationalize, test and adapt an earlier version of the presented DPIA approach [18] on the basis on the experience gained in these validation tests. In particular, we wanted to find out whether the framework works equally well in organisations of different sizes and from different sectors, or whether significant differences might exist. The sample of organisations (Table 4) finally included 3 start-ups or micro-enterprises, 2 SMEs, 5 large companies and 2 public administrations (cities). These came from different economic sectors and included for-profit and non-profit organisations. Although most technology providers are not obliged to carry out a DPIA under the GDPR, there is strong demand on the part of their clients for input and/or for collaboration. For this reason, we also conducted a validation workshop with an automotive supplier.[4]

**Table 4.** Number, role and sector of test candidates

| | Controller | Processor | Technology Provider |
|---|---|---|---|
| Mobility | | 1 | 1 |
| Health | 3 | 2 | |
| Telecommunications | | 1 | |
| Public authority | 2 | | |
| Retail | 2 | | |

The focus of the case studies was mainly on phases II. and III. of our framework and in particular on risk identification, analysis and assessment. The workshops lasted typically one full day per organization and were mainly composed of the following elements:

- Workshop preparation
  1. Decision about the processing activity to be considered in the workshop
  2. Collecting information about the processing activity based on a questionnaire/list of required information for the *DPIA preparation phase.*
- Workshop
  3. Finalization of the *DPIA preparation phase* in the first part of the workshop
  4. Privacy risk assessment of the *DPIA execution phase* in the second part of the workshop for selected risks.
  5. Final discussion and feedback

[4] It was interesting to note that organisations are often not aware that there might be joint controllership with a service or software provider and that these then also have to contribute to the DPIA.

The composition of the group of participants was quite diverse - and was varied as an element of the study concept. In all cases the data protection officer (or the responsible manager) was present. In addition, in most cases, representatives from IT (security) and people responsible for the processing were also involved. During workshops with startups, all members of the company usually took part as formal roles had often not been fully defined. In some workshops, especially in the retail and healthcare sector, employee representatives, and even data subjects or their representatives, were involved. In one workshop, representatives from (external) processors were also present because of the complexity of the service. Thus typically there was a mix of qualifications: the DPO in most cases has a legal and/or technical background, while the background of most others involved was not legal. Nevertheless, they were all experts in their field and needed to be taken seriously with regard to their professional principles and experiences.

Involving data subjects is a particular challenge, as they are usually not experts in any of the processing-related areas. However, they must be enabled to make an informed and sound assessment of the potential risks from their perspective. It is crucial that the person facilitating such a workshop does justice to all these aspects so as not to marginalise any viewpoint. This is a risk, especially in larger organisations that have already professionalised data protection. While they usually have sufficient knowledge about the provisions of the General Data Protection Regulation (GDPR), there is a tendency to focus on formal legal aspects (e.g. the existence of a legal basis for data processing), which is rather secondary to the risk perception of data subjects and other stakeholders.

For the evaluation of the workshops, there were two different roles in the study team. The first role was that of the auditor, who had to conduct the DPIA workshops as realistically as possible according to the methodology to be tested. The second role was that of the observer, who checked how the workshop participants responded to the auditor's questions, whether they were able to use the protection goals for the assessment and what kind of interaction took place between the workshop participants. For the evaluation of the workshop, the perceptions of the auditor(s) and the observer(s) were compared and changes were made in the workshop design. Such changes concerned, for example, the way the protection goals were presented or the order of the questions. The use of damage scenarios was also a result of this evaluation, as it became clear that a risk assessment is easier based on a tangible case than on an abstract description. Fortunately, no fundamental changes had to be made to the approach, so the methodology presented in Sect. 3 was basically confirmed.

## 5 Experiences from the Case Study

In the course of our validation tests, we have been able to gather a wide range of experience, (a) as to how prepared companies are to carry out DPIAs, (b) as to how understandable the assessment criteria are to stakeholders, and (c) how best to engage different stakeholders in the assessment process. Many of these experiences have already been taken into account in the process outlined in Sect. 3. In the following, however, we will highlight and discuss the most important findings from the different process phases.

### 5.1 General Aspects

During the interviews and workshops it was pointed out that processors of personal data, and even technology providers who only provide technologies without any additional service, are sensitized to the obligation of DPIAs. Customers of processors, and even technology providers, now demand information about the privacy risks of services and information about technical and organizational measures deployed in relation to services. In most of the tests, besides focusing on the DPIA itself, the test candidates also used the workshops for discussions and exchange of experiences concerning general aspects of data protection within the organization.

### 5.2 In the Initialization Phase

In recent years, there has been intense debate in the scientific community about when data processing is "is likely to result in a high risk to the rights and freedoms of natural persons" [13,19]. For practitioners this question is of little importance in the initialization phase. Rather, we experienced lively discussion in our workshops as to whether a DPIA was actually necessary for the selected processing. As there was a general fear of compliance violations and the corresponding fines, organisations tried to include a broad range of processing activities as requiring a DPIA to be on "the safe side". In such a situation, it was helpful in providing guidance, especially to those organizations that had hitherto given little attention to data protection issues, that the data protection authorities have compiled authoritative lists of processing operations which are always subject to the requirement to undertake a DPIA (aka "blacklists").

### 5.3 In the DPIA Preparation Phase

The actual *collection of information* in the DPIA preparation phase has not only shown the importance of a thorough analysis from the data subjects' perspective, but also how incomplete the knowledge of those in charge of the DPIA is about the details and context of the processing to be assessed. On the one hand risks are overlooked which emerge from scenarios beyond normal processing activities: the (rare) cases in which law enforcement and supervisory authorities gain access to data are also often not problematized. On the other hand, there is often still a lack of awareness that the greatest risks usually come from processing for the intended purposes and by authorised actors [16,33]. Instead, the focus is often on the malicious external attacker (aka "hacker").

Due to the increasing *complexity and modularisation of IT services* and the incorporation of cloud services and IT providers in general, it was an intricate task for many controllers to obtain the requisite information and understanding of their own processing activities. The involvement of processors is generally of utmost importance. It was promising that one SME which provided cloud services for companies as a processor demonstrated thorough data protection competencies and stated that data protection is a key selling point in its market. In the case of standard cloud services by international companies this would be difficult to realize. Another issue is the inherent agility of cloud services which are steadily changing. This is not always transparent to users. In this context compositional approaches towards DPIAs [36,37] and generalized DPIAs for services [30] should be further investigated.

As a thorough basis for assessing data protection risks, it is of utmost importance to involve not only the controller, IT security experts, and data protection experts, but also individuals with in-depth knowledge of domain-specific workflows and processing activities and their technical implementation. It is advisable to involve additional stakeholders or their representatives. This *heterogeneity of the working group* must be taken into account by a transparent methodological approach. In the first round of testing, we worked with interviews structured along the protection goals. In the interview-based workshops it turned out that, for people without deep knowledge in privacy and data protection, the privacy risks for data subjects in the context was not sufficiently clear. It proved more useful to carry out the assessment in a participatory way based on collaborative identification and analysis of scenarios (see Table 3) which might cause damage to data subjects.

One implication that emerged from the case studies was that concrete risks to data subjects were often a function of complex and highly domain- and use case-specific details of the particular processing activities. Domain/use case experts with deep knowledge of the details and context of the particular processing activity – but often limited knowledge of data protection – frequently provided crucial insights here, based on their deep "everyday knowledge" of the processing and its context. This suggests that one risk for conducting good DPIAs is excessively foregrounding the expertise and authority of data protection lawyers and professionals (who will usually have limited understanding of the use-case details and context), and downplaying the inputs and expertise of the domain professionals.

### 5.4 In the DPIA Execution Phase

The *choice of words* in the risk assessment in particular is very important for participants. In particular, terms with negative connotations from IT security - such as "attacker" or "source of risk" - almost lead to the exclusion of internal stakeholders in the following discussion. In their self-image, they do not perceive themselves as a "risk factor". In this regard it is necessary to meet them on the level of their core expertise. Choosing negative wording could potentially cause harm in scenarios where the purpose of the processing is only slightly extended and the parties involved act with the best intentions, i.e., do not intend to cause any harm. Thus more neutral terms such as "stakeholders", "triggers for the scenario" etc. are used to facilitate the brainstorming. Since IT security risks caused by external attackers have already been sufficiently considered in most cases, we have focused on scenarios triggered by internal actors.

Apart from internal attackers, internal data subjects such as employees were also not always in focus for the DPIA teams in the workshops. Often, privacy risks were mainly identified and analyzed from the point of view of external data subjects as customers, users or patients. *Risks for internal data subjects*, i.e. employees were considered as of lower priority. When employees such as data subjects are present, it is important to consider power inequalities in the DPIA team. Hence, it is advisable to incorporate work council members. Also, data subjects which are not directly customers, users or patients - e.g. friends and family - were often overlooked. Therefore, we mainly concentrated on these types of data subjects. It is important in DPIA execution to raise awareness concerning these data subjects.

For stakeholders who are involved as data subjects and who are not data protection experts, the concept of privacy is rather vague and is often misunderstood as restricted to confidentiality. We perceived during the workshops that the data protection goals allowed these stakeholders to formulate their personal privacy perceptions and priorities. Here, context is particularly important. For example, in the health care sector, availability and integrity of documented work processes and activities may be much more important to employees than confidentiality, whereas in HR data management, confidentiality and unlinkability are paramount. In other cases transparency and intervenability were stated as the most important goals. The fact that the protection goals are explicitly framed (and often graphically presented) as counterveiling principles that partially stand in tension to each other and can require balancing trade-offs proved particularly helpful in this case, as it seemed to give stakeholders (especially those without legal expertise) greater confidence to state which risks and protection goals in the particular use case were of paramount importance to them, and where tradeoffs to secure these were acceptable.

During the workshops in the *DPIA execution phase*, many participants asked for guidance through *checklists and risk catalogs*. Although the desire for checklists is understandable and their use has a practical value, the implementation of a DPIA must not become a purely mechanical checklist work-through exercise. Because the focus of a DPIA is to identify privacy risks in specific contexts where innovative technologies, etc. are used, it is important to explore risks beyond standardized lists. However, it may be useful to provide participants with illustrative examples to give them an idea of what is understood as risk for the purposes of the DPIA. In particular, it turns out that a small number of typical risks - largely independent of the application domain - occur again and again. These can be reused when similar processing activities in similar contexts are investigated and allow a transfer of results from DPIAs to the standard risk-based approach. Some examples that can serve as illustrations are provided in [9,18].

Stakeholders with an IT security background, in particular, questioned several times why, in our methodology, risks were assessed with a *qualitative risk assessment instead of quantitative approaches* as usually employed for security risks. It was important to point out that several privacy related risks are so-called "chilling effects" which always occur - e.g. people feel surveyed because of the existence of CCTV and therefore feel restricted with regard to exercising their right to protest [16,32]. In addition, in most cases it is not possible to state the cost of such an incident for the individual.

### 5.5 In the DPIA Implementation Phase

During our workshops we concentrated on the initiation, DPIA preparation and DPIA execution phases. But it was obvious that identifying and assessing the severity of a risk alone was not enough. For many controllers, the immediate question arose as to how a risk could best be addressed. At this point, well-maintained catalogs of reference measures are of great benefit. Fortunately, such catalogs have already been created by national supervisory authorities such as the CNIL [9] or the German Data Protection Conference.[5]

### 5.6 In the Sustainability Phase

An important point of discussion during the workshops was the question of how DPIAs can be updated on a regular basis. To this end, it would make sense to integrate DPIAs into the standard risk assessment and risk management processes of organizations, as suggested in [8,17,41].[6]

## 6 Conclusions

According to first experiences with DPIAs (and many years of experience with privacy impact assessments), it can be stated that DPIA is basically a good instrument to support decision-makers and developers, if it is not merely regarded as a compulsory exercise, but as a useful tool. The systematic identification of risks is a valuable basis for strategic action by implicated actors for the continuous improvement of products and services. It also provides an opportunity to evaluate potentially controversial data processing systems in relation to which a societal consensus is needed as to which risks should be acceptable and which should not. DPIA results can provide the basis for this.

But the potential of DPIAs will not unfold automatically. A broad and effective consultation of stakeholders and data subjects requires a relatively high level of time, organizational and material effort. The DPIA process developed as part of our work, and the methods and tools used to engage individuals from diverse backgrounds, are promising, but also made clear that additional issues need to be addressed:

---

5 https://www.datenschutz-mv.de/datenschutz/datenschutzmodell/ (last accessed 30-07-2021).

6 We have (anecdotal) evidence that this is a challenging task, as it requires a comprehensive modelling of the system landscape and data flows that does not exist in most organizations. Therefore, the solutions we know are either trivial or highly complex.

Any specialist knowledge required (in particular technical or legal) must be communicated to the participants in such a way that it can be understood by laypersons. In this context, attention must be paid to the effect of different formulations, which may unintentionally favor technophile participants or those with legal knowledge, for example. This is important not only from a normative point of view, but also from a practical perspective: it makes little sense to conduct a focus group, for example, without ensuring that all group members can also contribute.

Communication processes both among the participants, and between them and the organization, must be designed in such a way that communication barriers are reduced, misunderstandings are avoided, and, as far as possible, everyone can participate to the same extent. Furthermore it has to be taken into account that some of the participants in the DPIA can be the source of a data protection risk and the affected data subjects at the same time. Finally most participants are employees of an organisation or company and therefore have to act in accordance with what is in the best interests of the business. This can lead to tensions when they are supposed to assess risks in an unbiased way from the point of view of the people concerned. Again, this is both a functional and a practical imperative: stakeholder consultations dominated by a few participants are rarely appropriate. Here, the use of external facilitators with experience in consultation processes can be helpful.

Finally, it should not go unmentioned that a DPIA (like any formalized procedure) also specifies what must remain outside the scope of the assessment. For this reason, scientifically oriented DPIAs are useful, for example, for the area of research and development, even if they do not necessarily meet the requirements of the GDPR for a DPIA. They do, however, make it possible to integrate data protection issues into the risk management of technology producers and system operators. This can provide a balance, often missed in technology assessment, between the desire for normativity on the one hand and operationalization on the other [20].

**Acknowledgement.** This work was partially funded by the German Ministry of Education and Research under grant nos. 03VP03551, 03VP03553 and 16KIS0741K. Our thanks to Britta Mester (Datenschutz Nord GmbH) and Meiko Jensen (Kiel University of Applied Research) who contributed to the work presented in this paper.

## References

1. Agencia Española de Protección de Datos (AEPD), Madrid: Guía práctica para las Evaluaciones de Impacto en la Protección de los datos sujetas al RGPD (2018). https://www.aepd.es/sites/default/files/2019-09/guia-evaluaciones-de-impacto-rgpd.pdf
2. Article 29 Data Protection Working Party, Brussels: Guidelines on Data Protection Impact Assessments (DPIA) and determining whether processing is "likely to result in a high risk" for the purposes of Regulation 2016/679 (2017). http://ec.europa.eu/newsroom/document.cfm?doc_id=47711

3. Bieker, F., Friedewald, M., Hansen, M., Obersteller, H., Rost, M.: A process for data protection impact assessment under the European general data protection regulation. In: Schiffner, S., Serna, J., Ikonomou, D., Rannenberg, K. (eds.) APF 2016. LNCS, vol. 9857, pp. 21–37. Springer, Cham (2016). https://doi.org/10.1007/978-3-319-44760-5_2
4. Bisztray, T., Gruschka, N.: Privacy impact assessment: comparing methodologies with a focus on practicality. In: Askarov, A., Hansen, R.R., Rafnsson, W. (eds.) NordSec 2019. LNCS, vol. 11875, pp. 3–19. Springer, Cham (2019). https://doi.org/10.1007/978-3-030-35055-0_1
5. Bock, K., Kühne, C.R., Mühlhoff, R., Ost, M.R., Pohle, J., Rehak, R.: Data protection impact assessment for the corona app. https://doi.org/10.2139/ssrn.3588172
6. Castelluccia, C., Le Métayer, D.: Position paper: analyzing the impacts of facial recognition. In: Antunes, L., Naldi, M., Italiano, G.F., Rannenberg, K., Drogkaris, P. (eds.) APF 2020. LNCS, vol. 12121, pp. 43–57. Springer, Cham (2020). https://doi.org/10.1007/978-3-030-55196-4_3
7. Clarke, R.: Privacy impact assessment: its origins and development. Comput. Law Secur. Rev. **25**(2), 123–135 (2009). https://doi.org/10.1016/j.clsr.2009.02.002
8. Coles, J., Faily, S., Ki-Aries, D.: Tool-supporting data protection impact assessments with CAIRIS. In: 2018 IEEE 5th International Workshop on Evolving Security & Privacy Requirements Engineering (ESPRE), pp. 21–27. IEEE Computer Society, Los Alamitos, August 2018. https://doi.org/10.1109/ESPRE.2018.00010
9. Commission Nationale de l'Informatique et des Libertés (CNIL), Paris: Privacy Risk Assessment: Knowledge Bases (2018). https://www.cnil.fr/sites/default/files/atoms/files/cnil-pia-3-en-knowledgebases.pdf
10. Commission Nationale de l'Informatique et des Libertés (CNIL), Paris: Privacy Risk Assessment: Methodology (2018). https://www.cnil.fr/sites/default/files/atoms/files/cnil-pia-1-en-methodology.pdf
11. Conference of the independent data protection authorities of the Federal and State Governments of Germany: The Standard Data Protection Model: A method for data protection advising and controlling on the basis of uniform protection goals (2020). https://www.datenschutzzentrum.de/uploads/sdm/SDM-Methodology_V2.0b.pdf
12. De, S.J., Le Métayer, D.: Privacy Risks Analysis. Morgan & Claypool (2016). https://doi.org/10.2200/S00724ED1V01Y201607SPT017
13. Demetzou, K.: Data protection impact assessment: a tool for accountability and the unclarified concept of 'high risk' in the general data protection regulation. Comput. Law Secur. Rev. **35**(6), 105342 (2019). https://doi.org/10.1016/j.clsr.2019.105342
14. Demetzou, K.: Processing operations 'likely to result in a high risk to the rights and freedoms of natural persons': lessons to be learned from national authorities' DPIA 'blacklists'. In: Antunes, L., Naldi, M., Italiano, G.F., Rannenberg, K., Drogkaris, P. (eds.) APF 2020. LNCS, vol. 12121, pp. 25–42. Springer, Cham (2020). https://doi.org/10.1007/978-3-030-55196-4_2
15. van Dijk, N., Gellert, R., Rommetveit, K.: A risk to a right: beyond data protection impact assessments? Comput. Law Secur. Rev. **32**(2), 286–306 (2016). https://doi.org/10.1016/j.clsr.2015.12.017
16. European Data Protection Supervisor, Brussels: Accountability on the Ground Part II: Data Protection Impact Assessments and Prior Consultation (2019). https://edps.europa.eu/node/4582_env
17. Federal Association for Information Technology, Telecommunications and New Media (BITKOM), Berlin: Risk Assessment & Data Protection Impact Assessment - Guide (2017). https://www.bitkom.org/sites/default/files/file/import/170919-LF-Risk-Assessment-ENG-online-final.pdf

18. Friedewald, M., et al.: Datenschutz-Folgenabschätzung: Ein Werkzeug für einen besseren Datenschutz. Fraunhofer ISI, Karlsruhe (2017). https://www.forum-privatheit.de/wp-content/uploads/Forum-Privatheit-WP-DSFA-3-Auflage-2017-11-29.pdf
19. Gellert, R.: Understanding the notion of risk in the General Data Protection Regulation. Comput. Law Secur. Rev. **34**(2), 279–288 (2018). https://doi.org/10.1016/j.clsr.2017.12.003
20. Grunwald, A.: Technology assessment or ethics of technology? Reflections on technology development between social sciences and philosophy. Ethical Perspect. **6**(2), 170–182 (1999). https://doi.org/10.2143/EP.6.2.505355
21. Hallinan, D., Martin, N.: Fundamental rights, the normative keystone of DPIA. Eur. Data Prot. Law Rev. **6**(2), 178–193 (2020). https://doi.org/10.21552/edpl/2020/2/6
22. Hansen, M., Jensen, M., Rost, M.: Protection goals for privacy engineering. In: SPW 2015: Proceedings of the 2015 IEEE Security and Privacy Workshops, pp. 159–166. IEEE, Washington (2015). https://doi.org/10.1109/SPW.2015.13
23. Information Commissioner's Office (ICO), Wilmslow, UK: Guide to the General Data Protection Regulation (GDPR) (2021). https://ico.org.uk/media/for-organisations/guide-to-data-protection/guide-to-the-general-data-protection-regulation-gdpr-1-1.pdf
24. ISO/IEC 27001:2013(E): Information technology - Security techniques - Information security management systems - Requirements. International Standardisation Organisation, Geneva (2013)
25. ISO/IEC 29134:2017(E): Information technology - Security techniques - Guidelines for privacy impact assessment. International Standardisation Organisation, Geneva (2017)
26. Iwaya, L.H., Fischer-Hübner, S., Åhlfeldt, R.M., Martucci, L.A.: Mobile health systems for community-based primary care: identifying controls and mitigating privacy threats. JMIR Mhealth Uhealth **7**(3), e11642 (2019). https://doi.org/10.2196/11642
27. Kloza, D., et al.: Towards a method for data protection impact assessment: making sense of GDPR requirements. d.pia.lab Policy Brief 1/2019, VU Brussels, Brussels (2019). https://doi.org/10.31228/osf.io/es8bm
28. Martin, N., Friedewald, M., Schiering, I., Mester, B.A., Hallinan, D., Jensen, M.: The Data Protection Impact Assessment according to Article 35 GDPR: A Practitioner's Manual. Fraunhofer Verlag, Stuttgart (2020). http://publica.fraunhofer.de/dokumente/N-590015.html
29. Martin, N., Schiering, I., Friedewald, M.: Methoden der Datenschutz-Folgenabschätzung: Welche Unterschiede bieten die verschiedenen methodischen Ansätze? Datenschutz und Datensicherheit - DuD **44**(3), 154–160 (2020). https://doi.org/10.1007/s11623-020-1242-z
30. Mas, S., Terra, F.: DPIA Office 365 ProPlus version 1905. Data protection impact assessment on the processing of diagnostic data. Ministry of Justice and Security, The Hague. https://www.rijksoverheid.nl/binaries/rijksoverheid/documenten/rapporten/2019/06/11/data-protection-impact-assessment-windows-10-enterprise/DPIA+Office+365+ProPlus+spring+2019+22+July+2019+public+version.pdf
31. Ministerie van BZK, The Hague: Model gegevensbeschermings-effectbeoordeling rijksdienst (PIA). https://www.rijksoverheid.nl/binaries/rijksoverheid/documenten/rapporten/2017/09/29/model-gegevensbeschermingseffectbeoordeling-rijksdienst-pia/model-gegevensbeschermingseffectbeoordeling-rijksdienst-pia.pdf

32. Raab, C., et al.: Effects of surveillance on civil liberties and fundamental rights in Europe. In: Wright, D., Kreissl, R. (eds.) Surveillance in Europe, pp. 259–318. Routledge (2015). https://doi.org/10.4324/9781315851365
33. Rost, M.: Risiken im Datenschutz. Vorgänge: Zeitschrift für Bürgerrechte und Gesellschaftspolitik **57**(1/2), 79–91 (2018)
34. Rost, M., Pfitzmann, A.: Datenschutz-Schutzziele - revisited. Datenschutz und Datensicherheit **33**(6), 353–358 (2009). https://doi.org/10.1007/s11623-009-0072-9
35. Todde, M., Beltrame, M., Marceglia, S., Spagno, C.: Methodology and workflow to perform the data protection impact assessment in healthcare information systems. Inform. Med. Unlocked **19**, 100361 (2020). https://doi.org/10.1016/j.imu.2020.100361
36. Van Landuyt, D., Sion, L., Dewitte, P., Joosen, W.: The bigger picture: approaches to inter-organizational data protection impact assessment. In: Boureanu, I., et al. (eds.) ESORICS 2020. LNCS, vol. 12580, pp. 283–293. Springer, Cham (2020). https://doi.org/10.1007/978-3-030-66504-3_17
37. Vandercruysse, L., Buts, C., Dooms, M.: Practitioner's corner: beyond data controllership: merits of a generic DPIA by hardware and technology suppliers. Eur. Data Prot. Law Rev. **6**(1), 133–136 (2020). https://doi.org/10.21552/edpl/2020/1/18
38. Vemou, K., Karyda, M.: An evaluation framework for privacy impact assessment methods. In: 12th Mediterranean Conference on Information Systems, MCIS 2018, Corfu, Greece, 28–30 September 2018. AISeL (2018). https://aisel.aisnet.org/mcis2018/5
39. Wolf, G., Pfitzmann, A.: Properties of protection goals and their integration into a user interface. Comput. Netw. **32**(6), 685–700 (2000). https://doi.org/10.1016/S1389-1286(00)00029-3
40. Wright, D., De Hert, P. (eds.): Privacy Impact Assessment. Springer, Dordrecht (2012). https://doi.org/10.1007/978-94-007-2543-0
41. Wright, D., Wadhwa, K., Lagazio, M., Raab, C., Charikane, E.: Integrating privacy impact assessment in risk management. Int. Data Priv. Law **4**(2), 155–170 (2014). https://doi.org/10.1093/idpl/ipu001

# 2nd Cyber-Physical Security for Critical Infrastructures Protection (CPS4CIP 2021)

# CPS4CIP 2021 Preface

The CPS4CIP workshop is a forum for researchers and practitioners working on cyber-physical security for critical infrastructures protection that supports finance, energy, health, air transport, communication, gas, and water. The secure operation of critical infrastructures is essential to the security of nations and, in an increasingly interconnected world, of unions of states sharing their infrastructures in order to develop their economies; it is also essential to public health and safety. Security incidents in critical infrastructures can directly lead to a violation of users' safety and privacy, physical damage, interference in the political and social life of citizens, significant economic impact on individuals and companies, and threats to human life while decreasing trust in institutions and questioning their social value. Because of the increasing interconnection between the digital and physical worlds, these infrastructures and services are more critical, sophisticated, and interdependent than ever before. The increased complexity makes each infrastructure increasingly vulnerable to attacks, as confirmed by the steady rise of cyber-security incidents, such as phishing or ransomware, and cyber-physical incidents, such as physical violation of devices or facilities in conjunction with malicious cyber activities. To make the situation even worse, interdependency may give rise to a domino effect with catastrophic consequences on multiple infrastructures.

To address these challenges, the workshop aims to bring together security researchers and practitioners from the various verticals of critical infrastructures (such as the financial, energy, health, air transport, communication, gas, and water domains) and rethink cyber-physical security in the light of the latest technological developments (e.g., cloud computing, blockchain, big data, AI, Internet of Things) by developing novel and effective approaches to increase the resilience of critical infrastructures and the related ecosystems of services.

The workshop has attracted the attention of the critical infrastructures protection research communities and stimulated new insights and advances with particular attention to the integrated cyber and physical aspects of security in critical infrastructures. The 2nd International Workshop on Cyber-Physical Security for Critical Infrastructures Protection (CPS4CIP 2021) was held online. The workshop was organized in conjunction with the 26th European Symposium on Research in Computer Security (ESORICS 2021), held in Darmstadt, Germany, during October 4–8, 2021. The format of the workshop included two keynotes and technical presentations. The workshop was attended by around 28 people.

The workshop received seven submissions, of which one was withdrawn and six were sent for review, from authors in four distinct countries. After a thorough peer-review process, four papers were selected for presentation at the workshop. The review process focused on the quality of the papers, their scientific novelty, and their applicability to the protection of critical financial infrastructure and services, and the acceptance rate was 67%. The accepted articles represent an interesting mix of techniques for resilience, security threat, vulnerability, and malware detection. The workshop was proactive with one important and stimulating keynote on "Analysing the Impact of Software Supply Chain Vulnerabilities on Critical Infrastructure". The technical presentations were by followed by presentations of preliminary project results from seven H2020 projects from the ECSCI cluster, CyberSANE (Cyber Security Incident Handling, Warning and Response System for the European Critical Infrastructures - https://www.cybersane-project.eu/), EnergyShield (Integrated Cybersecurity Solution for the Vulnerability Assessment, Monitoring and Protection of Critical Energy Infrastructures - https://energy-shield.eu/), ENSURESEC (securing the e-commerce ecosystem from cyber, physical, and cyber-physical threats - http://www.ensuresec.eu/), PRECINCT (a collaborative ecosystem platform for increased resilience of connected critical infrastructures - www.precinct.info), SOTER (human factors in cybersecurity - https://soterproject.eu/), SPHINX (a universal cyber security toolkit for the healthcare industry - https://sphinx-project.eu/), and 7SHIELD (a holistic framework to protect ground segments of space systems against cyber, physical, and natural complex threats - https://www.7shield.eu/).

The workshop was supported by various ECSCI (European Cluster for Securing Critical Infrastructures) projects (https://www.finsec-project.eu/ecsci), mainly FINSEC (www.finsec-project.eu/), ANASTACIA (www.anastacia-h2020.eu/), CyberSANE (https://www.cybersane-project.eu/), DEFENDER (https://defender-project.eu/), EnergyShield (https://energy-shield.eu/), ENSURESEC (http://www.ensuresec.eu/), FeatureCloud (https://featurecloud.eu/), IMPETUS (https://www.impetus-project.eu/), InfraStress (www.infrastress.eu/), PHOENIX (https://phoenix-h2020.eu/), RESISTO (www.resistoproject.eu/), SAFECARE (www.safecare-project.eu/), SATIE (http://satie-h2020.eu), SealedGRID (https://www.sgrid.eu/), SecureGas (www.securegas-project.eu/), SmartResilience (http://www.smartresilience.eu-vri.eu/), SOTER (https://soterproject.eu/), SPHINX (sphinxproject.eu/), and STOP-IT (stop-it-project.eu/). The workshop was also supported by two national projects, NORCICS (https://www.ntnu.edu/norcics) and RESTABILISE4.0 (http://www.restabilise4-0.it/). The organizers would like to thank these projects for supporting the CPS4CIP 2021 workshop.

Finally, the organizers of the CPS4CIP 2021 workshop would like to thank the CPS4CIP 2021 Program Committee, whose members made the workshop possible with their rigorous and timely review process. We would also like to thank the Fraunhofer Institute for Secure Information Technology and the National Research Center for Applied Cybersecurity ATHENE in Darmstadt, Germany, for hosting the workshop and the ESORICS 2021 workshop chairs for valuable help and support.

November 2021

Habtamu Abie
Silvio Ranise
Luca Verderame
Enrico Cambiaso
Rita Ugarelli
Gabriele Giunta
Isabel Praça
Federica Pascucci

# Organization

## General Chairs

| | |
|---|---|
| Habtamu Abie | Norwegian Computing Center, Norway |
| Silvio Ranise | University of Trento and Fondazione Bruno Kessler (FBK), Italy |

## Program Committee Chairs

| | |
|---|---|
| Luca Verderame | University of Genoa, Italy |
| Enrico Cambiaso | National Research Council (CNR), Italy |
| Rita Ugarelli | SINTEF, Norway |
| Gabriele Giunta | Engineering Ingegneria Informatica, Italy |
| Isabel Praça | GECAD/ISEP, Portugal |
| Federica Pascucci | Roma Tre University, Italy |

## Program Committee

| | |
|---|---|
| Dieter Gollmann | Hamburg University of Technology, Germany |
| Sokratis Katsikas | Norwegian University of Science and Technology, Norway |
| Javier Lopez | University of Malaga, Spain |
| Fabio Martinelli | IIT-CNR, Italy |
| Einar Arthur Snekkenes | Norwegian University of Science and Technology, Norway |
| Omri Soceanu | IBM Research, Israel |
| Stamatis Karnouskos | SAP Research, Germany |
| Reijo Savola | VTT Technical Research Centre of Finland, Finland |
| Alessandro Armando | University of Genoa, Italy |
| Federica Battisti | University of Padua, Italy |
| Alessio Merlo | University of Genoa, Italy |
| Cristina Alcaraz | University of Malaga, Spain |
| Giovanni Livraga | University of Milan, Italy |
| Gustavo Gonzalez-Granadillo | Atos Spain, Spain |
| Shouhuai Xu | University of Texas at San Antonio, USA |
| Christos Xenakis | University of Piraeus, Greece |
| Mauro Conti | University of Padua, Italy |

# Resilience Quantification for Critical Infrastructure: Exemplified for Airport Operations

Corinna Köpke[1](✉), Kushal Srivastava[1], Natalie Miller[1], and Elena Branchini[2]

[1] Fraunhofer Institute for High-Speed Dynamics, Ernst-Mach-Institut, EMI, Am Klingelberg 1, 79588 Efringen-Kirchen, Germany
Corinna.Koepke@emi.fraunhofer.de

[2] Società per Azioni Esercizi Aeroportuali (SEA), Linate Airport, Segrate, Italy
elena.branchini@seamilano.eu

**Abstract.** In the EU-H2020 project SATIE (Security of Air Transport Infrastructure of Europe), a security toolkit is developed to protect airport infrastructure from various cyber-physical threats. One of these tools is the Impact Propagation Simulation (IPS) which is designed to estimate impacts of incidents in an airport and thus to quantify the system's resilience under varying conditions. IPS consists of two main engines, i.e. a network model and an Agent-Based-Model (ABM). Exemplified for Malpensa airport in Milan, a specific cyber-physical threat scenario is analyzed and the resilience of the impacted systems is discussed.

**Keywords:** Resilience · Airport · Impact propagation

## 1 Introduction

Resilience management and quantification is a development that is based on classical risk assessment approaches like the nine-step resilience management process [7], which is an extension of the ISO 31000:2018 [8] from risk management to resilience. Resilience, as a concept, recognizes the vitality of the critical infrastructure and works in a variety of different ways to maintain the functioning of these systems before, during and after a crisis event. To this end, the resilience of the infrastructure can be represented by a resilience cycle [4,13] and [6]. The resilience cycle consists of five phases, i.e. (1) prepare, which prepares also for the unexpected, (2) prevent to avoid the worst impact, (3) protect the most vulnerable and critical, (4) respond to serious situations and (5) recover fast and learn from it.

The resilience of airport infrastructure has been studied in various previous works. In [3], airport networks are based on graph theory and resilience strategies are suggested based on adaptive and permanent modifications to the topology of air traffic. Further, airport network resilience is analyzed in [2] by considering both structural and dynamical aspects. Based on the topology, four metrics are


S. Katsikas et al. (Eds.): ESORICS 2021 Workshops, LNCS 13106, pp. 451–460, 2022.
https://doi.org/10.1007/978-3-030-95484-0_26

suggested for quantifying the performance, i.e. departure delay, system delay, punctuality and a general resilience index derived from various attributes of the resilience curve. In [11], malicious attacks in smart airports are discussed. Different types of threats in the cyber-domain are highlighted and mitigation is suggested in the form of cyber-security best practices and resilience measures. The resilience of global air transportation networks is investigated in [12] with emphasis on different attacking strategies motivated by the topology of the graph. Functional robustness is assessed by e.g. overall unaffected passengers, available operational routes, the size of connected components and algebraic connectivity. In [5], the impact of a global health crisis on resilience and the recovery of airports is analyzed. Resilience quantification is derived using performance-based methods such as aircraft movements, passenger throughput, and freight throughput.

Here, a different modelling approach is followed as compared to the literature presented above. The systems under consideration are involved from the entry of the passengers in the airport to the departure of their flights. The physical topology of these components is not considered, rather their inter-dependencies are modeled using edges in the network and the focus is on consequences of failures and associated cascades. In this context, the Impact Propagation Simulation (IPS) is presented which is part of the toolkit developed in the EU-H2020 project SATIE (Security of Air Transport Infrastructure of Europe). The IPS consists of two main simulation engines, i.e. a network model and an Agent-Based Model (ABM) which have been presented previously e.g. in [9] and [10]. The ABM is employed in this work to visualize the considered threat scenario and the impact specifically on the passengers. On the other hand, the network model is used to estimate the impact of the scenario on the network representation of the airport, to assess cascading effects and to quantify the systems' resilience (see Fig. 1).

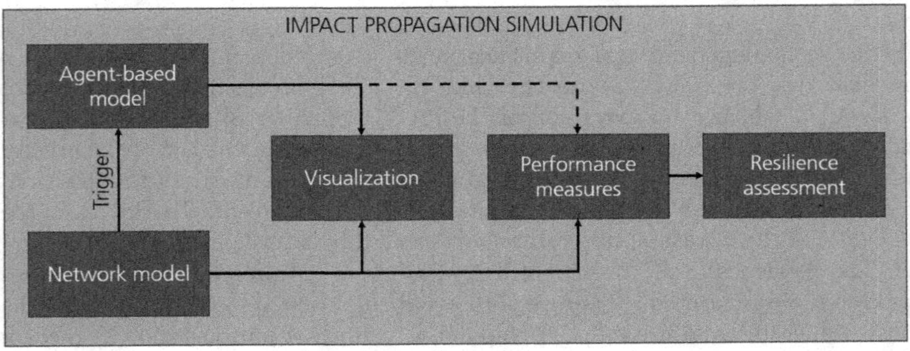


**Fig. 1.** IPS architecture. The network model triggers the ABM. Both tools visualize the airport with different levels of detail. Performance measures can be defined-here, only demonstrated for the network model-to assess the system's resilience.

The structure of the paper is the following. First, in Sect. 2 the threat scenario is presented and modeled using (i) the ABM and (ii) the network model. In Sect. 3, results of the impact propagation simulation in the network model and the ABM are visualized and discussed. Further, resilience indicators are introduced. Finally, in Sect. 4 the findings are summarized and an outlook is provided.

## 2 Scenario and Model

The hypothetical scenario that is considered in this work is located in Malpensa airport in Milan. It is assumed that initiated by social engineering, an attacker gains access to a workstation in the airport network. From there two systems are manipulated, i.e. (i) the gate assignments and (ii) the aircraft stand assignments. These cyber-attacks might not only lead to physical consequences for the passengers and airport personnel but also to huge organizational impacts. All logistical mechanisms that depend on on- and off-loading of an aircraft will be disturbed such as personal assignment to gates, bus allocations, and also the baggage-handling system.

### 2.1 Network Model

The network model in Fig. 2 presents the network topology of the considered airport systems. Nodes in the graph represent assets of the airport such as buildings, rooms, servers, workstations but also personnel and passengers. The threat scenario is visualized by highlighting the attacked nodes which in this case is a specific workstation, the gate assignment and the aircraft stand assignment $N = \{37, 32, 33\}$ which are attacked at the times $T = \{10, 15, 20\}$ min, respectively. Starting from these three nodes, the cascade propagates the damage through the network depending on the interconnections between the nodes.

The network model requires the specification of several parameters presented in Table 1. One of these parameters is the propagation probability. It represents the opposite of the level of protection of the infrastructure in a generic way. Here, this propagation probability is assumed initially to be 75% which means that only very little measures are in place to stop a threat from propagating and thus the corresponding level of protection is low. Technically, a propagation probability of 75% means that the impact on one node of the network model propagates to a connected node if a random number drawn from a uniform distribution between 0 and 1 is smaller than 0.75. Another parameter, the restoration time is regenerated randomly for every asset in the beginning of each iteration from a normal distribution and controls the time an asset takes to recover after being impacted. The same approach is used to specify the impact delay for each asset which controls the time it takes until the propagated threat becomes effective for this asset.

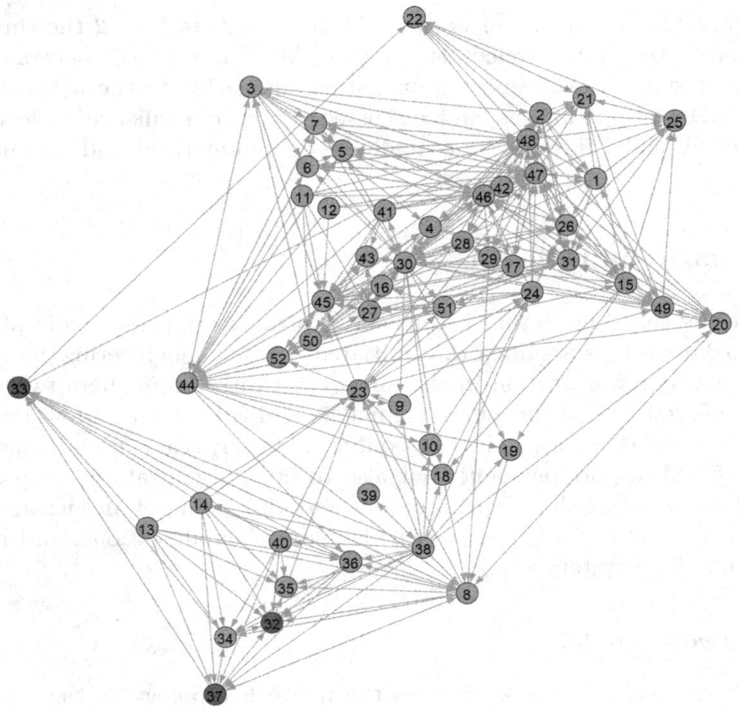


**Fig. 2.** Network topology of the airport assets. The attacked nodes are highlighted in red. (Color figure online)

**Table 1.** Network model specifications

| Parameter | Value |
|---|---|
| Iterations | 100 |
| Time steps | 300 |
| Time step length | 1 min |
| Propagation probability | 75% |
| Mean of restoration time | 60 min |
| Standard deviation of restoration time | 10 min |
| Mean of impact delay time | 10 min |
| Standard deviation of impact delay time | 1 min |

In the IPS, if specific nodes of the network model are affected by an attack, the ABM is triggered to assess the impact specifically on the passengers in more detail.

### 2.2 Agent-Based Model

To simulate the impact of the described scenario on the passengers, ABM can be used. Generally, ABM is a bottom-up modeling approach that starts by defining agents and their properties [14]. In the context of airports and in the IPS ABM, agents represent passengers. Agent properties along with simulation settings are given in Table 2.

**Table 2.** ABM agent parameters and simulation specifications

| Parameter | Value |
|---|---|
| Non-Schengen agent velocity mean | 1.5 m/s |
| Schengen agent velocity mean | 2.5 m/s |
| Agent velocity standard deviation | 0.5 m/s |
| Agent size | 0.8 m |
| Distance between agents | Agent size + 0.8 m |
| Distance to obstacles | Agent size/2 + 0.5 m |
| Simulation time steps | 2000 |
| Time step length | 1 s |
| Spawn rate | 1 agent every 4 time steps |
| Initial number of agents | 25 |

The next step in developing an ABM is the definition of internal rules [14]. The distance between agents, the distance to obstacles and the definition that passengers after the security are not allowed to re-enter the landside are examples for such rules. An environment with agents following these rules, leads to an emergent system behavior that finally can be analyzed.

## 3 Simulation Results

In this section, the simulation results for the described scenario and the modeling approaches are presented.

### 3.1 Resilience Curves

To quantify the system's resilience, a performance measure needs to be defined. Here, the number of well-functioning assets has been chosen. Note, this is the most basic graph-based performance measure but also a very intuitive one for interpretation. Using all parameters and attacked nodes as input for the simulation, produces resilience curves which are presented in Fig. 3(a). The uncertainty of the results originates from the randomly generated restoration times, impact delays and the propagation probability. These three factors lead to the deviations between the 100 iterations. In some very rare cases, the system does not recover and instead drops into a second low performance period. This is due to the high connectivity of the network topology.

(a) 75% of probability for propagation.

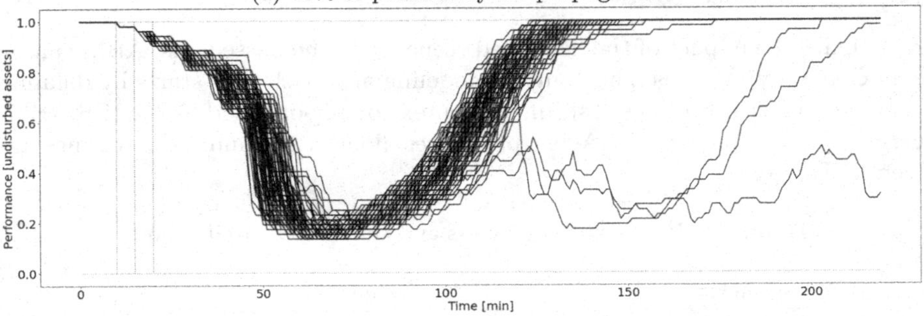


(b) 25% of probability for propagation.

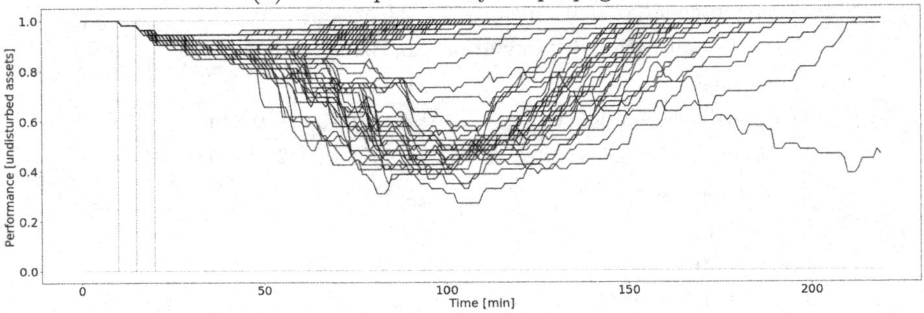


**Fig. 3.** Resilience curves for 100 repeated simulations with different impact propagation probabilities. The three initial attacks are presented with red dotted vertical lines at the times of occurrence. A performance of 1.0 stands for 100%.

The assumption of a 75% chance for impact propagation was quite arbitrary which motivated a comparative study with different values. Under the assumption of more effective security measures in place, the impact propagation probability should be reduced. Thus, in the second step a 25% probability was chosen to estimate the system's resilience. The results are presented in Fig. 3(b). The reduction in propagation leads to a smaller overall impact but the results are more diverse and the uncertainty in each time-step is increased.

Further, especially in Fig. 3(a) the re-impacting of some assets can be observed in the curves that present two performance minima. This effect is due to the large number of connections between the assets and circular dependencies as presented in Fig. 2. It means that an asset that is impacted in the simulation and in the process of recovery cannot be impacted during that time. But as soon as it has fully recovered it can be impacted again still triggered by the cascade of the initial attacks.

### 3.2 Resilience Indicators

To further quantify and compare the difference in resilience when the propagation probability varies, resilience indicators are introduced, i.e. the area below the curves and the minimum values observed for the curves. A similar approach is presented in [1] where the equivalent of the minimum values observed would be the so-called recovery effectiveness. The area below the curve is a very general measure for resilience and summarizes several characteristics of the system behavior.

The larger the area and the larger the minimum value, the more resilient the system is. Resilience indicators have been estimated for four different propagation probabilities $P = \{100, 75, 50, 25\}\%$. The results are presented in Fig. 4.

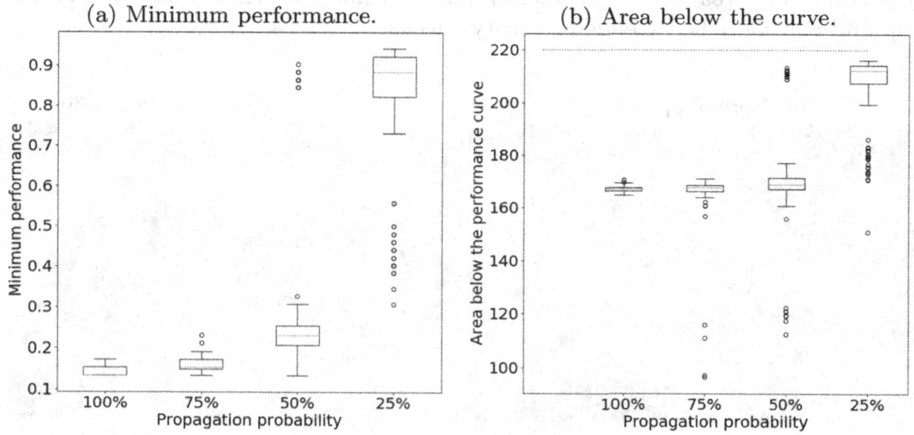


**Fig. 4.** Resilience indicators for 100 repeated simulations and four different impact propagation probabilities. The horizontal line in the box is the median. The upper and lower outer bounds of the box represent the upper and lower quartile. The whiskers present all data within 1.5 times the interquartile range and the circles are outliers. In (b), the horizontal dotted red line presents the maximum area to be expected when the system is not impacted. The measurement unit is performance times minute. (Color figure online)

The results suggest that a protection against threat propagation that reduces the probability of propagation to 50% does not change the results significantly in comparison to no protection (100% of propagation). Only with 25%, a significant change in the system's resilience can be observed. The visually assessed increase in uncertainty when the impact propagation is reduced can also be observed in Fig. 4 with an increased number of outliers in the 50% and 25% case.

The system's behavior under varying propagation probabilities, is very network specific and needs to be studied in more detail. Further, security measures need to be implemented in the simulation specifically for each asset to produce meaningful results for the airport under consideration. For simplicity, here this very general level of protection represented by the propagation probability has been assumed to model the implementation of safety and security measures in the infrastructure. However, a more realistic model should consider the type of asset each node represents and specifically modify the node properties dependent on which measure has been implemented such as e.g. redundancies in place, the ability to be isolated or to be switched to manual operation in case of failure.

### 3.3 Agent-Based Simulations

The consequence of the described scenario for passengers simulated using the ABM is presented in Fig. 5. Parts of the non-Schengen terminal area is presented with the passport control counters. Normally, only non-Schengen passengers enter this area who are typically not in a hurry as they plan for a longer trip and consider the extended security checks.

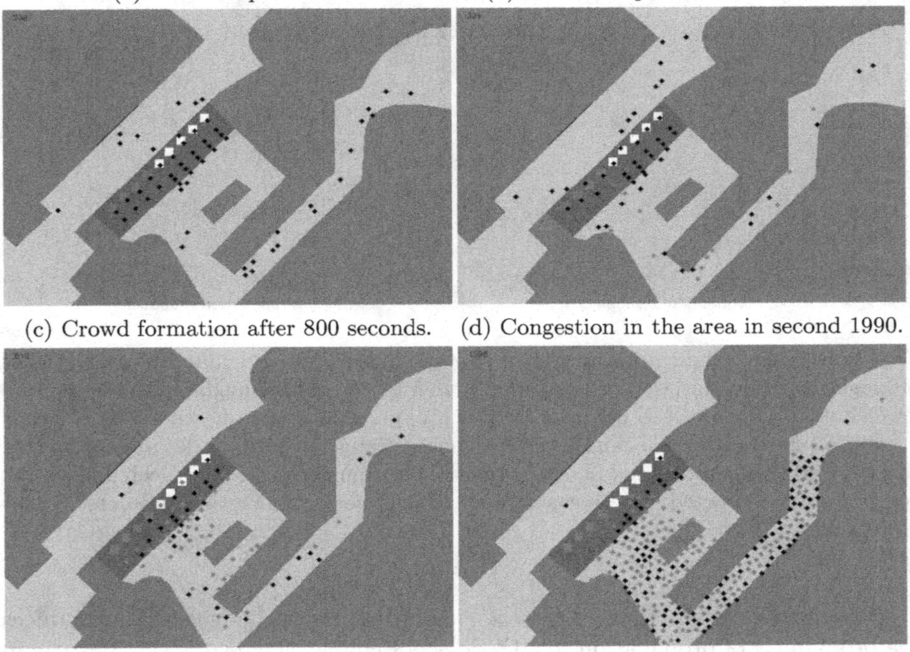

(a) Normal operation. (b) Gate manipulation in second 300.

(c) Crowd formation after 800 seconds. (d) Congestion in the area in second 1990.

**Fig. 5.** Visualization of the impact of the gate changes on the passengers during four different time steps estimated by the ABM. Black dots present the non-Schengen passengers and red dots the Schengen passengers. (Color figure online)

However, during the threat scenario considered in this work, Schengen passengers are sent to gates in the non-Schengen area. They are in a hurry as they have to walk longer distances and were surprised by this change in gates. The different behavior of the two groups of passengers is reflected in different walking speeds (see Table 2). During the scenario when both types of passengers are sent to the same area for the passport check, a crowd is forming because of the additional passengers. Additionally, most of the Schengen passengers are rejected at the counters and sent the same way back which finally leads to a huge congestion.

More details on the ABM and analysis approaches of the acquired data, can be found in previous work [9,10]. Here, the ABM is used for visualization purposes only and the data is not further analyzed.

## 4 Conclusion

In this work, the resilience of airport systems has been assessed considering a specific cyber-physical attack scenario of gate and aircraft stand assignment manipulation. The analysis has been performed using the IPS which has been developed as part of the SATIE toolkit. The ABM has been used to visualize the threat scenario and the network model is employed to estimate the airport's resilience. Repeated simulations with different impact propagation probabilities have been compared to study the impact of potential safety and security measures to reduce the probability of propagation and thus cascading effects.

As the study is very generic, the results cannot suggest the implementation of specific measures for the airport under consideration. They have to follow various standards and regulations and need to be very carefully placed into a more realistic simulation environment. However, as not only the assets of critical infrastructure such as airports are highly interconnected but also different kinds of critical infrastructure are dependent on each other, the generic study performed in this work sheds some light on the issues of systems with many connections. Impact propagation can lead to the re-impacting of assets that were already broken during one simulation when enough connections exist. Further, the reduction of the propagation probability with safety and security measures might reduce the overall impact and increase the resilience but at the same time the uncertainty which makes predictions more difficult.

**Acknowledgement.** This project has received funding from the European Union's Horizon 2020 research and innovation programme under grant agreement No 832969. This output reflects the views only of the author(s), and the European Union cannot be held responsible for any use which may be made of the information contained therein. For more information on the project see: http://satie-h2020.eu/.

## References

1. Cho, J.H., Xu, S., Hurley, P.M., Mackay, M., Benjamin, T., Beaumont, M.: STRAM: measuring the trustworthiness of computer-based systems. ACM Comput. Surv. (CSUR) **51**(6), 1–47 (2019)

2. Clark, K.L., Bhatia, U., Kodra, E.A., Ganguly, A.R.: Resilience of the US national airspace system airport network. IEEE Trans. Intell. Transp. Syst. **19**(12), 3785–3794 (2018). https://doi.org/10.1109/TITS.2017.2784391
3. Dunn, S., Wilkinson, S.M.: Increasing the resilience of air traffic networks using a network graph theory approach. Transp. Res. Part E Logistics Transp. Rev. **90**, 39–50 (2016)
4. Edwards, C.: Resilient nation demos (2009)
5. Guo, J., Zhu, X., Liu, C., Ge, S.: Resilience modeling method of airport network affected by global public health events. Math. Probl. Eng. **2021** (2021). https://doi.org/10.1155/2021/6622031
6. Hiermaier, S., Hasenstein, S., Faist, K.: Resilience engineering-how to handle the unexpected. In: 7th REA Symposium, p. 92 (2017)
7. Häring, I., et al.: Towards a generic resilience management, quantification and development process: general definitions, requirements, methods, techniques and measures, and case studies. In: Linkov, I., Palma-Oliveira, J.M. (eds.) Resilience and Risk. NAPSC, pp. 21–80. Springer, Dordrecht (2017). https://doi.org/10.1007/978-94-024-1123-2_2
8. Risk management - guidelines. Standard, International Organization for Standardization, Geneva (2018). https://doi.org/10.3850/978-981-14-8593-0_4026-cd
9. Köpke, C., et al.: Security and resilience for airport infrastructure. In: Baraldi, P., Di Maio, F., Zio, E. (eds.) Proceedings of the 30th European Safety and Reliability Conference and the 15th Probabilistic Safety Assessment and Management Conference, pp. 1191–1198. Research Publishing, Singapore (2020)
10. Köpke, C., et al.: Impact propagation in airport systems. Cyber Phys. Secur. Crit. Infrastruct. Prot. **12618**, 191–206 (2020). https://doi.org/10.1007/978-3-030-69781-5_13
11. Lykou, G., Anagnostopoulou, A., Gritzalis, D.: Smart airport cybersecurity: threat mitigation and cyber resilience controls. Sensors **19**(1), 19 (2019). https://doi.org/10.3390/s19010019
12. Sun, X., Gollnick, V., Wandelt, S.: Robustness analysis metrics for worldwide airport network: a comprehensive study. Chin. J. Aeronaut. **30**(2), 500–512 (2017). https://doi.org/10.1016/j.cja.2017.01.010
13. Thoma, K.: Resilien-Tech: Resilience by Design: a strategy for the technology issues of the future. Herbert Utz Verlag (2014)
14. Van Dam, K.H., Nikolic, I., Lukszo, Z.: Agent-Based Modelling of Socio-Technical Systems. ABSS, vol. 9. Springer, Dordrecht (2012). https://doi.org/10.1007/978-94-007-4933-7

# Severity Level Assessment from Semantically Fused Video Content Analysis for Physical Threat Detection in Ground Segments of Space Systems

Gerasimos Antzoulatos(✉), Georgios Orfanidis, Panagiotis Giannakeris, Giorgos Tzanetis, Grigorios Kampilis-Stathopoulos, Nikolaos Kopalidis, Ilias Gialampoukidis, Stefanos Vrochidis, and Ioannis Kompatsiaris

Information Technologies Institute (ITI), Centre for Research and Technology Hellas (CERTH), Thermi, Thessaloniki, Greece
{gantzoulatos,g.orfanidis,giannakeris,tzangeor,grigstat,nikokopa, heliasgj,stefanos,ikom}@iti.gr

**Abstract.** Disaster risks related to natural hazards are evolving gradually, albeit accelerating over time, the human-made and cyber threats are changing rapidly exploiting the increasing progress in technologies and the complex, highly interlinked, modern environment of critical infrastructures. Therefore, as these threats have been intensifying, the actions to strengthen the resilience of critical infrastructures should be step up, by understanding their complex systems as well as the multi-risks nature. In this landscape, the aim of this work focuses to propose a framework enables to identify potential human-made threats, generated by using physical means, and captured by heterogeneous sources (CCTVs, UAVs etc.). Advanced machine learning techniques provide analysis of events and useful information, which are fused semantically and estimate the severity level of the potential attack, serving the needs for real-time monitoring and mitigating the risk.

**Keywords:** Risk assessment · Critical infrastructures · Human-made threats · Video-based object detection · Face detection and recognition · Knowledge-based representation · Severity level estimation

## 1 Introduction

Nowadays, the crisis panorama has changed and diversify increasingly from "traditional" crises generated by natural hazards to technology-driven crises generated by cyber-attacks, or a combination of them [8,9]. The unexpectedly large scale of the extreme natural events in terms of their severity and frequency, the trans-boundary and cross-sectoral nature of new or unprecedented crises, compose a challenging and changing landscape in disaster and risk management [2]. In Global Assessment Report on Disaster Risk Reduction 2019, has

This work has been supported by the EC-funded H2020-883284 7SHIELD project.


S. Katsikas et al. (Eds.): ESORICS 2021 Workshops, LNCS 13106, pp. 461–476, 2022.
https://doi.org/10.1007/978-3-030-95484-0_27

been underlined the need to move beyond the conventional definition for the disaster risk, re-examine and re-assess the risk, by taking into consideration the pluralistic nature of it: in multiple dimensions, at multiple scales and with multiple impacts [7]. Furthermore, the rise of new technologies, from one side intensifies the potential threats and attacks and from the other, provides empowered solutions to address them and strengthen the resilience in human societies and Critical Infrastructures (CI). Recent technological innovations like IoT, 5G, unmanned aircraft vehicles, and artificial intelligence have brought immense benefits and contributed further efficiencies to CI operations. However, they have posed serious threats facilitating the malicious actors interested in disrupting CI operations. Particularly, in the CIs which are becoming increasingly complex, automated, and interconnected, thereby new vulnerabilities have been introduced exposing them to malicious physical activities [8,9,13].

Object detection is considered one of the fundamental fields of computer vision. The detectors can be roughly divided into 2 categories: the two phase ones and the single-phase ones. The former include an extra sub-network which is responsible for proposing bounding boxes. The more prestigious work in the former category is Faster R-CNN [19] while for the latter category are Single Shot Detector (SSD) [17] and You Only Look Once detector (YOLO) [18] (which has actually spawn a family of detectors). The two-phase detectors are considered more robust and effective but also less efficient while the single-phase ones are lighter, more efficient and less effective. Over the years new architectures have emerged which attempt to combine the best of the practices proposed. Such a work is EfficientDet [25] which is based on an efficient backbone, EfficientNet [24] and a bi-directional intra-level feature fusion.

For activity recognition also the focus is on deep learning techniques, since they provide the state-of-the-art performances. One of the first attempts was the Two-stream algorithm [22] which combines two different streams (visual and depth streams in order to increase performance and collect features from both spectra. Also, another monumental work is 3D ResNet [11] which tries to adopt the success of ResNet networks [12] to temporal spectrum by expanding 2D ResNets to the temporal dimension also.

Face recognition depends heavily on deep learning methodologies to achieve significant boost in performance. In this class of algorithms, deep feature extractors are used to generate face representations, tuned for pose and illumination invariance, from the plethora of the available training data rather than from low-level hand-crafted features. Siamese networks for deep metric learning were proposed in the work of [4], which was one of the initial attempts to leverage deep learning. A Siamese network works by extracting features separately from two modes (inputs), with two identical CNNs, taking the distance between the outputs of the two CNNs as dissimilarity. In a similar fashion with face detection works, facial parts were processed separately in cascade networks, as in the work of [23]. Soon after, the focus shifted heavily towards improving the deep metric learning methodology, which led to significant performance improvements [6]. Experimentation with novel face similarity measures dominates the undertaken effort in these works. Moreover, discriminant face representations are characterized by smaller maximal intra-class distance and minimal inter-class distance in the embedding space, thus, novel CNN loss functions are meticulously explored as well, in order to find the most appropriate for the task.

Although the application of Machine Learning methodologies to tackle specific problem areas in disaster risk management dates back to a recent couple of decades, however, significant challenges still need to be addressed [13]. Machine Learning methods have penetrated in a descriptive and/or predictive manner in all the phases of disaster/crisis management, contributing in various ways to the assessment of the hazard, exposure and vulnerability from natural and human-made disasters [27]. Hence, one of the main challenges concerns the lack of required training data which limits the utilisation of the machine learning algorithms to be trained in order for the latter to be able to predict or assess the risk of a crisis event. Motivating by this gap, the proposed annotation tool aims to involve the experts in the Satellite ground segments domain, by mapping their experience and knowledge into the characterisation of hypothetical extreme physical (natural or human-made) events in terms of their severity and impact.

The continuous growth of semantic web technologies provides several ontology-based approaches in several domains. For this task, the categorisation of the domains includes the events and observations, the crisis management and the cyber-physical threats and vulnerabilities. In particular some representative ontologies for each domain respectively, that influenced the process and the methodological approach for our framework include SSN [5] and SOSA [15] for mapping of sensors and their observations, properties and features of interest; MMF [10] an ontology developed in the context of managing sensor assignment to mission; finally MOAC [16] and SoKNOS [1] with wide field of application in crisis management and response. Our ontological representation is tailored to the protection of ground segments of space systems.

In this work, we focus on the detection and monitoring of physical threats generated by human-made malicious activities on ground segments of space systems. The potential attacks are classified and assessed in terms of their severity level and potential consequences in the ground segments, supporting in this way the decision-making processes to mitigate the risks. Machine learning advances are the core aspect of our approach as innovative deep-learning methodologies analyse multimedia content from videos, aiming to detect malicious objects and suspicious activities of identified and potentially unauthorised persons in restricted areas. Finally, the semantic fusion of information leads to the real-time monitoring and assessment of the potential attack's severity level are carried out by utilising machine learning methods. Due to the lack of adequate annotated datasets in automatic risk assessment supervised methods, we propose an annotation tool that aims to engage the community of users and experts in the domain of the protection of ground segments of space systems.

## 2 Methodological Framework for Physical Attack Detection and Response

In this work, our intention is to highlight some aspects of the above framework, especially those that detect physical attacks, fuse semantically the identified malicious events, and assess the severity level of those attacks. The proposed framework combines tools (*Detection Layer*) for detection and recognition of objects, faces, and activities from video-based content, that obtained from surveillance systems (CCTVs cameras) or cameras on the UAVs. After the detection, the generated alerts of the events are combined, homogenised and semantically indexed in the Knowledge Base (*Fusion Layer*). The enriched information is propagated to the Crisis Classification module which is responsible to estimate the severity level of the event and propagate the results to the CI operators (*Decision Layer*) to support decision-making and mitigation actions for timely response to the physical threat. In Fig. 1 the workflow of information as well as the interactions between modules in various levels are illustrated. In the following subsections a more detailed description of the functionalities of each module is exhibited.

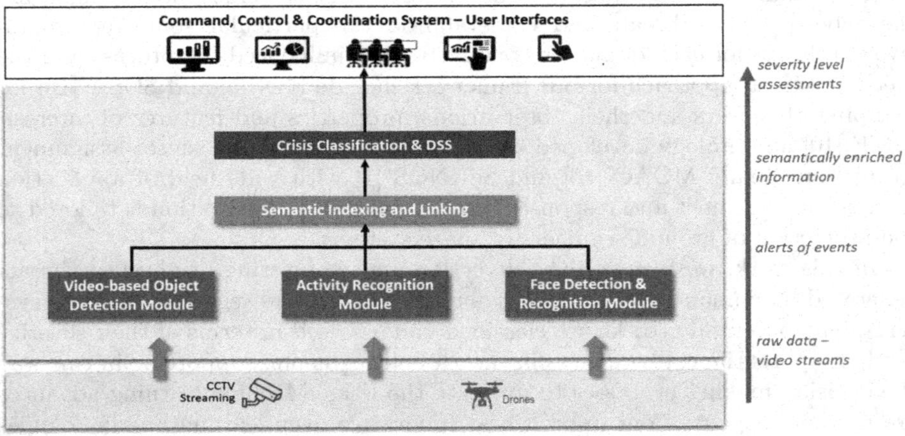


**Fig. 1.** The proposed decision support framework

### 2.1 Video-Based Object Detection and Activity Recognition

The surveillance of ground segments of space systems is a vital issue for their secure and seamless operation since new threats seem to arise and some of them especially focusing on those infrastructures. A huge asset to the latter is the visual understanding of the surrounding area. The Video-based Object Detection (VOD) and Activity Recognition (AR) modules are efforts to aid towards this aim.

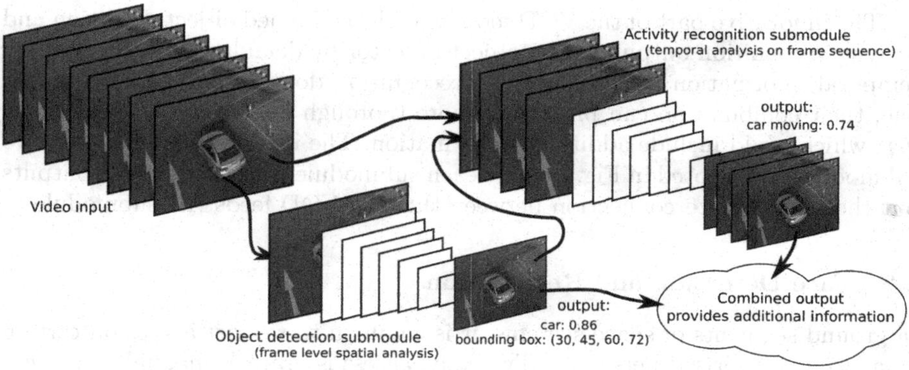


**Fig. 2.** High-level view of combined VOD-AR architecture

First, the VOD module utilise deep learning techniques in order to visually locate and identify the objects of interest inside the ground segment of space systems. The input of the module are video streams which are being processed by large in width but mainly in depth networks. The analysis provide the system with an initial interpretation of the monitored area regarding the objects appearing in it. Although, the initial analysis is performed on a frame level, an interconnection with consecutive frames is also provided, augmenting the capabilities of the system to clearly isolate true threats from false positive ones. The actual outcome of the VOD module is a group of bounding boxes around each detected object of interest accompanied by a confidence score, which reveals how certain is the network for this detection, and label to denote the class the object belongs to. Since each detection is performed on a specific frame a spatio-temporal association of the detected objects across consecutive frames can be deducted, and, this correlation can be further feed to the relevant AR module. AR module is responsible for identifying an activity given a specific frame span (or equivalently a time span and a video from where the temporal boundaries can be deducted). Thus, VOD can function as a trigger for AR module if certain conditions are met. Such conditions could be a combination of objects being detected, such as a person and an object like a bag, a vehicle to specific location etc. Of course, in a more generic mode, all detected objects involving in potential activities could be forwarded to the AR to decide the existence of any potential harmful and suspicious activity. Summarising, the output of the Video-based Object detection is:

- Awareness of surroundings via detected objects and individuals
- Bounding boxes and class label for each instance of interest

while for Activity Recognition, the output is:

- Awareness of surroundings via recognized activities
- Label for each activity along with the participating objects

The innovative part of the VOD module is the combined object detection and activity recognition output. Since, object detector by default do not involve any temporal information and the activity recognition do not consider any spatial one, their combination can produce a more thorough analysis of the surroundings which could include additional information. The idea of combining the two submodules is decipted in Fig. 2 where each submodule produces its own outputs but their is also interconnection between them as VOD feeds AR submodule.

### 2.2 Face Detection and Recognition

In ground segments of space systems, it is common to restrict access on certain areas to unauthorised personnel. Typically, access is granted manually by security guards, or with electronic access control systems via identity cards. However, these control mechanisms may be vulnerable to identity fraud attacks. For example, someone could get access to a building or an area by using a lost or stolen card. Therefore, the traditional solutions, when used alone, cannot guarantee maximum security. Our solution is designed to assist in access control systems using automatic facial recognition.

The Face Detection and Recognition (FDR) module ensures that restricted access to facilities is under secure control. At the same time, this module may also assist in intrusion detection systems, by notifying about unauthorised access to areas of interest. Within this objective, Satellite Ground Segments and general Critical Infrastructure are protected from hazardous activities of unauthorised trespassers while the corresponding personnel and their daily activities are also secured.

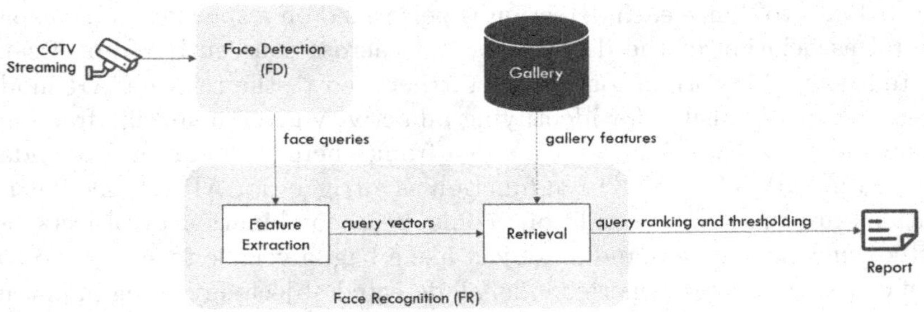


**Fig. 3.** High-level FDR architecture

The overall approach of FDR is naturally split into its two cooperating tasks and is shown in Fig. 3. The module is initialized with a video stream and it is designed to process single video frames in a serial processing pipeline (one after another). Processing begins on the Face Detection (FD) component. FD is responsible to detect patches inside the input frame where faces are tightly enclosed. The acquired face patches are instantly characterized as unknown and are immediately provided to the Face Recognition (FR) component for further processing. FR takes additional input from a pre-existing gallery of known faces and tries to match the detected faces with the ones from the gallery. The gallery images belong to authorized personnel with unrestricted access in the area covered by the CCTV camera. After the recognition process, detailed reports can be produced with the detection and recognition metadata, e.g., alarm notifications of potential unauthorised access, list of recognised identities with attached timestamps for monitoring access to critical assets, enhanced video data with bounding boxes showing the detected faces for visualisation in command and control dashboards, etc.

## 2.3 Semantic Indexing and Linking

The Knowledge Base (KB), is a knowledge representation model for semantically representing concepts relevant to the cyber-physical threats. The goal of the KB framework is to research and develop technologies for semantic content and sensor input modeling, integration, reasoning and question answering.

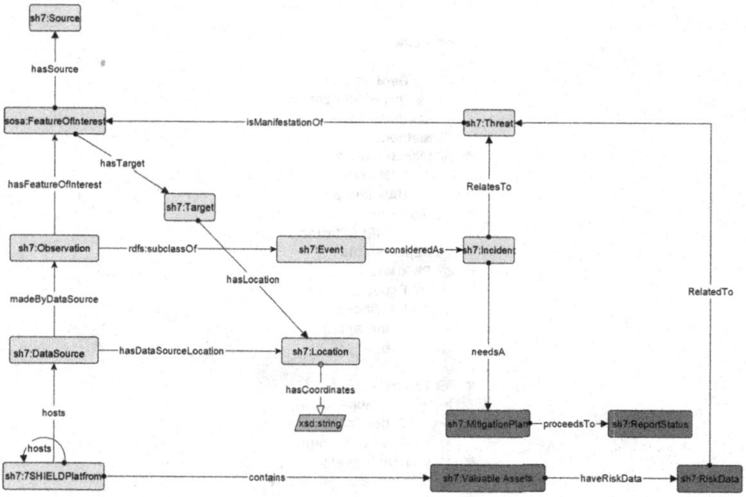


**Fig. 4.** High Level overview of 7SHIELD ontology

The models that are created will constitute for the reasoning mechanisms taking into account the ontology vocabulary and infrastructure for capturing and storing information related to the 7SHIELD[1] application domain, such as: (a) Observation and Events (e.g. data collection from face recognition/detection,

[1] https://www.7shield.eu.

multimodal automated surveillance, drone detection), (b) C/P security (e.g. cyber detection, correlation services output), (c) Mitigation and response plans (e.g. First responder teams, UAV neutralisation). The 7SHIELD Knowledge Base (KB), can be also called 7SHIELD ontology modelling, will be described below. The 7SHIELD ontology was based on Semantic Sensor Network (SSN) ontology and the OWL language was used. As we can see from the picture the 7SHIELD ontology at a high level the classes and its entities that it consists of:

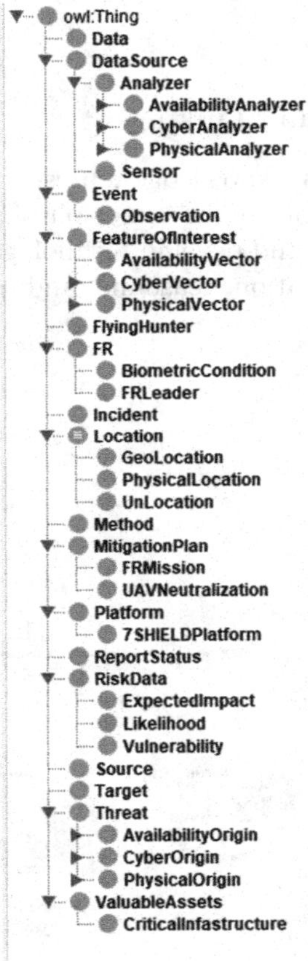


**Fig. 5.** List of classes as they are viewed in protege

- **Data Source**: This class represents data that have been analyzed and a result has been extracted
- **Event**: This class represents one of the primaries of the overall data model of the information sharing environment. Event is an abstract entity which has a subclass, the Observation

- **Location**: This class represents the place or position that something is in or where something happens. The class is further divided into 3 subclasses (PhysicalLocation, GeoLocation, Unlocation).
- **Target**: This class represents an object of attention or attack.
- **7SHIELD Platform**: This class hosts other entities, particularly Sensors, Detectors, Samplers
- **Report Status**: Its purpose is to make a report when trigger from an event.

Finally, the purpose of the data converter module is to receive JSON data as input and accordingly form the TURTLE Resource Description Framework (RDF) data as output, for mapping them the RDF triplestore. The JSON data should be in the appropriate format in order to be converted to semantic data (RDF triplets).

### 2.4 Crisis Classification and DSS Module

The main goal of the Crisis Classification (CRCL) & DSS module (Fig. 6) is to enhance the decision-making processes, by providing real-time assessments of the severity level of an ongoing physical and/or cyber-attack in critical satellite and ground segments. To achieve this goal, a multi-level fusion approach is developed which encompass methodologies for Information and Decision fusion.

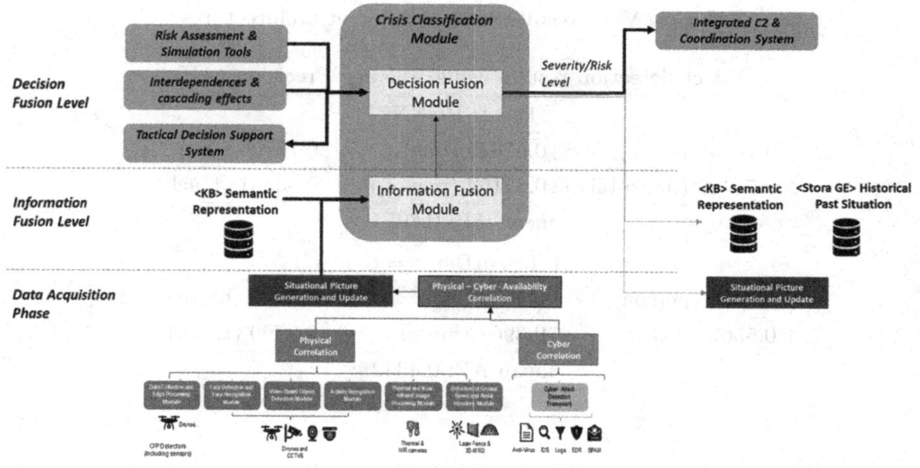


**Fig. 6.** CRCL module in 7SHIELD framework

At the *Information Fusion* level, the real-time (or "near" real-time) information, generated by the fusion of heterogeneous data from detection modules, is analysed by utilised machine learning techniques that are able to estimate the severity level of a malicious event. Then, at the *Decision Fusion* level, decision-making approaches will be tailored aiming to enrich the outcomes of the Information Fusion level semantically with information extracted from Knowledge Base. Hence, this process will estimate accurately, interpret and provide assessments in terms of the severity level and classify the crisis events generated by P/C attacks. This approach and the CRCL module are easily adjustable to fuse information from various available modules depending on the field of application.

## 3 Experimental Validation and Evaluation

### 3.1 Evaluation of the Detection Layer

**Visual Object Detection for Activity Recognition.** We have been experimenting with various object detection models in order to achieve a working solution. First, a Faster R-CNN two-phase detector model has been trained on a specially collected dataset. This model can detect 6 classes: a UAV class, a Car class, a Bus class, a Truck class (which also include Van instances), a combined Motorcycle/Bicycle class, and a Person class. We have also experimented with a lighter (but less effective) model, namely an EfficientDet ($\phi = 0$) model, which also included 6 classes (but with a few differences): a Car class, a Bus class, a Truck class, a Bicycle class, a Motorcycle class, and a Person class.

**Table 1.** VOD results using 2 different architectures

| Object detection results using Average Precision (AP) | | |
|---|---|---|
| Faster RCNN | | |
| 0.75330 (UAV) | 0.57315 (bus) | 0.75726 (car) |
| 0.73409 (moto-bike) | 0.82152 (person) | 0.53351 (truck) |
| mean AP: 0.6954 | | |
| EfficientDet $\phi = 0$ | | |
| 0.4563 (person) | 0.4668 (car) | 0.3438 (bicycle) |
| 0.5562 (bus) | 0.3968 (motorcycle) | 0.3790 (truck) |
| mean AP: 0.4332 | | |

As a first note for the results in Table 1, the results are not completely comparable since they include somehow different classes. Nevertheless, it is clear that the two-fold detector (Faster R-CNN) seems to perform better in the core detection part. The reported Average Precision values are much higher than its counterpart EfficientDet. On the other hand regarding the efficiency of the model EfficientDet is much lighter and faster by one order of magnitude. Regarding the results for AR submodule it is not so easy to be evaluated because they are highly dependent to the output of the VOD submodule.

**Face Detection and Recognition.** The experiments in this section were conducted with the aim to (a) deploy deep learning face detection and recognition models as a means of testing the development platform, (b) replicate and confirm the published evaluation results on public benchmarks and (c) make performance comparisons and draw conclusions about the state-of-the-art. For each task, three approaches were selected to represent the current state-of-the-art landscape, i.e., for face detection, (i) TinyFaces [14], (ii) PyramidBox [26], (iii) DSFD [28] and for face recognition, (i) Facenet [20], (ii) PFE [21], (iii) Arcface [6]. Each one was evaluated in a benchmark dataset, appropriate for the task. Specifically, for face detection the WIDER FACE benchmark was selected, and for face recognition the LFW.

WIDER FACE [29] is a face detection benchmark dataset. It contains over 30000 images which mostly show people participating in various activities of everyday life based on 61 event classes. The human faces appear with a high degree of variability in scale, pose and occlusion. For each event class, predefined splits consisting of 40%/10%/50% of the total amount of data exist as training, validation and testing sets respectively.

**Table 2.** Face detection state-of-the-art evaluation

| Method | Wider face AP (%) |
|---|---|
| TinyFaces (2017) [14] | 90.7 |
| PyramidBox (2018) [26] | 94.3 |
| DSFD (2019) [28] | 95.5 |

The Labelled Faces in the Wild (LFW) [3] dataset is a database of face photographs designed for studying the problem of unconstrained face recognition. The data set contains more than 13,000 images of faces collected from the web. The people that appear in this dataset are known public figures like politicians, athletes, actors, musicians and other various celebrities.

**Table 3.** Face recognition state-of-the-art evaluation

| Method | LFW accuracy (%) |
|---|---|
| Facenet (2015) [20] | 99.4 |
| PDE (2019) [21] | 99.6 |
| Arcface (2019) [6] | 99.7 |

The evaluation metric for face detection is Average Precision. It is taken by calculating the area under the Precision-Recall curve. Precision is defined as the proportion of true positives (TP) out of all the detected faces and Recall as the proposition of true positives out of all the annotated faces. In other words, precision measures the accuracy of the detector and recall measures its ability to retrieve the existing faces. Whether a bounding box detection counts as a

TP is decided based on its overlap with a ground truth box. The overlap is measured by the Intersection over Union (IoU) threshold. Thus, detected faces must have a good alignment with true faces in order to be considered correct. The Precision and Recall metrics are calculated for every alignment threshold (from most relaxed to most strict) to draw the Precision-Recall curve. The evaluation metric for face recognition is Accuracy. The dataset is split to 10 equal parts, where the first 9 are used for cross validation in order to select the optimal distance threshold to achieve top accuracy. The 10th part is the test set from which pairs of queries are given and the model decides if they belong to the same person or not. This is a standard strategy for evaluating face verification models, but it is also a good indicator of face recognition performance as well.

Tables 2 and 3 show the performance comparison of face detection and recognition SoA methods respectively. There is an overall good agreement with published results, with maximum deviation at 0.3%. Regarding face detection performance in WIDER FACE, the three methods achieve high average precision, especially the more recent approaches. From the ones that focus on leveraging surrounding face context, the PyramidBox is the most superior. Regarding face recognition performance in LFW, all methods perform extremely well, which may indicate both superior performance of SoA and dataset saturation.

### 3.2 Validation of the Fusion Layer

We also present the metrics about the current version of the 7SHIELD ontology, we used the OntoMetrics tool, an online framework that evaluates the ontology based on predefined metrics. The following tables present the results of the aforementioned process. The Fig. 7 contains the base metrics which show the quantity of the ontology; numbers of triples, classes, object and datatype properties and individuals.

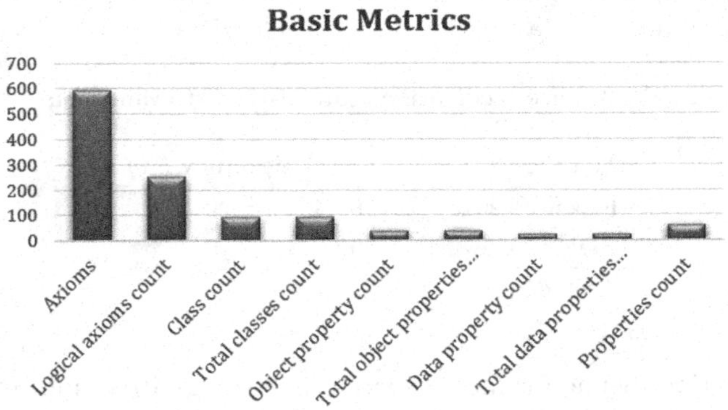


**Fig. 7.** Basic ontology metrics

### 3.3 Annotation Tool for the Validation of the Decision Layer

As mentioned above, the main issue in the utilisation of Machine Learning techniques is the lack of annotated datasets, namely datasets that assess the severity level of an attack with the specific characteristics of the attack (physical or cyber). To overcome this, we designed and developed the Annotation tool that aims to capture the knowledge and experience of experts in a qualitative, simple, fast and user-friendly way. The main idea of this tool is to generate scenarios of physical/cyber attacks in specific locations/assets in pilot sites and request experts to characterize those scenarios in terms of likelihood of the attack and potential consequence of it. Combining these two concepts we can assess the severity level.

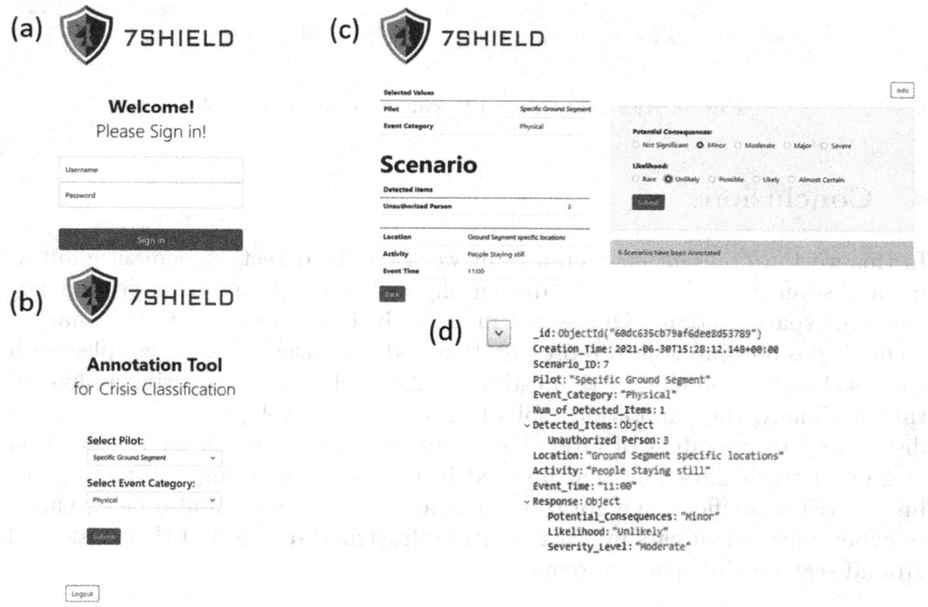


**Fig. 8.** Annotation tool; (a) Login page, (b) Selection page, (c) Main page, (d) MongoDB

Annotation Tool is a Web Application. The users can access it through a web browser with an active network connection. The users must first login, using the credentials that were given to them. Then, at the selection screen, the specific Satellite Ground Segment and the Event Category (cyber or physical) can be selected. Based on this selection random scenarios are generated. The hypothetical scenario is represented under the "Scenario" tag. The users, after studying the random parameters, must select a "Potential Consequence" and a "Likelihood" value. Then, the annotated scenario can be submitted and stored online in the MongoDB database. Automatically, the process continues and the next non-annotated scenario appears. Finally, the estimation of the "Severity level" is carried out, by relying on the risk matrix (Fig. 9), that adjusts to the project's needs.

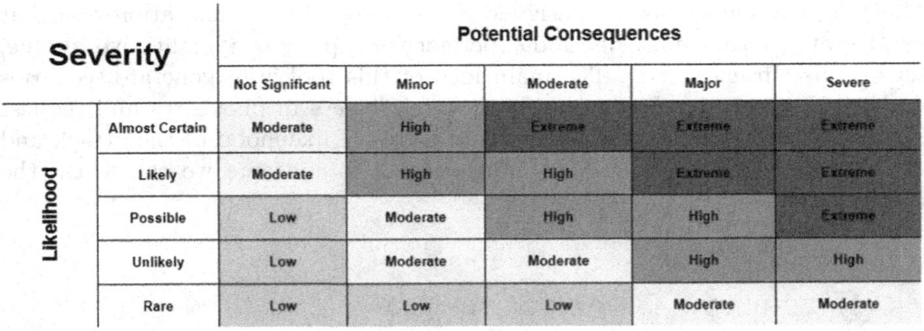

| Severity | Not Significant | Minor | Moderate | Major | Severe |
|---|---|---|---|---|---|
| Almost Certain | Moderate | High | Extreme | Extreme | Extreme |
| Likely | Moderate | High | High | Extreme | Extreme |
| Possible | Low | Moderate | High | High | Extreme |
| Unlikely | Low | Moderate | Moderate | High | High |
| Rare | Low | Low | Low | Moderate | Moderate |



**Fig. 9.** Risk matrix used to calculate severity level

# 4 Conclusions

In this work we present an overall framework for the detection, semantic indexing and severity level estimation during physical attack scenarios in ground segments of space systems. Our set of modules includes not only visual analysis technologies but ontological representation and semantic indexing, coupled with a crisis classification module that estimates the level of severity during a physical threat. Finally, the annotation tool which has been developed is planned to be distributed to operators of ground segments of space systems for the creation of ground truth data that will be used in training, validating and testing the future crisis classification algorithms. The annotation tool will also be extended to cyber/physical threats in other critical infrastructures beyond the considered ground segments of space systems.

# References

1. Babitski, G., Bergweiler, S., Grebner, O., Oberle, D., Paulheim, H., Probst, F.: SoKNOS – using semantic technologies in disaster management software. In: Antoniou, G., et al. (eds.) ESWC 2011. LNCS, vol. 6644, pp. 183–197. Springer, Heidelberg (2011). https://doi.org/10.1007/978-3-642-21064-8_13
2. Baubion, C.: OECD Risk Management: Strategic crisis management 23 (2013). https://doi.org/10.1787/5k41rbd1lzr7-en
3. Belhumeur, P.N., Jacobs, D.W., Kriegman, D.J., Kumar, N.: Localizing parts of faces using a consensus of exemplars. IEEE Trans. pattern Anal. Mach. Intell. **35**(12), 2930–2940 (2013)

4. Chopra, S., Hadsell, R., LeCun, Y.: Learning a similarity metric discriminatively, with application to face verification. In: 2005 IEEE Computer Society Conference on Computer Vision and Pattern Recognition (CVPR 2005), vol. 1, pp. 539–546. IEEE (2005)
5. Compton, M., et al.: The SSN ontology of the W3C semantic sensor network incubator group. J. Web Seman. **17**, 25–32 (2012). https://doi.org/10.1016/j.websem.2012.05.003
6. Deng, J., Guo, J., Xue, N., Zafeiriou, S.: ArcFace: additive angular margin loss for deep face recognition. In: Proceedings of the IEEE/CVF Conference on Computer Vision and Pattern Recognition, pp. 4690–4699 (2019)
7. United Nations International Strategy for Disaster Reduction: Global Assessment Report on Disaster Risk Reduction 2019. United Nations (2019). https://doi.org/10.18356/f4ae4888-en, https://www.un-ilibrary.org/content/books/9789210041805
8. EC: Overview of natural and man-made disaster risks the European union may face (2020). https://ec.europa.eu/echo/sites/default/files/overview_of_natural_and_man-made_disaster_risks_the_european_union_may_face.pdf
9. EY: Evaluation study of council directive 2008/114 on the identification and designation of european critical infrastructures and the assessment of the need to improve their protection (2019). https://op.europa.eu/en/publication-detail/-/publication/118dcd3d-b041-11ea-bb7a-01aa75ed71a1. https://doi.org/10.2837/864404
10. Gomez, M., et al.: An ontology-centric approach to sensor-mission assignment. In: Gangemi, A., Euzenat, J. (eds.) EKAW 2008. LNCS (LNAI), vol. 5268, pp. 347–363. Springer, Heidelberg (2008). https://doi.org/10.1007/978-3-540-87696-0_30
11. Hara, K., Kataoka, H., Satoh, Y.: Can spatiotemporal 3d CNNs retrace the history of 2d CNNs and imagenet? In: 2018 IEEE/CVF Conference on Computer Vision and Pattern Recognition (CVPR), pp. 6546–6555 (2018). https://doi.org/10.1109/CVPR.2018.00685
12. He, K., Zhang, X., Ren, S., Sun, J.: Deep residual learning for image recognition. In: 2016 IEEE Conference on Computer Vision and Pattern Recognition (CVPR), pp. 770–778 (2016). https://doi.org/10.1109/CVPR.2016.90
13. Hegde, J., Rokseth, B.: Applications of machine learning methods for engineering risk assessment - a review. Safety Sci. **122**, 104492 (2020). https://doi.org/10.1016/j.ssci.2019.09.015
14. Hu, P., Ramanan, D.: Finding tiny faces. In: Proceedings of the IEEE conference on computer vision and pattern recognition, pp. 951–959 (2017)
15. Janowicz, K., Haller, A., Cox, S.J., Le Phuoc, D., Lefrançois, M.: Sosa: a lightweight ontology for sensors, observations, samples, and actuators. J. Web Seman. **56**, 1–10 (2019). https://doi.org/10.1016/j.websem.2018.06.003
16. Limbu, M., Wang, D., Kauppinen, T., Ortmann, J.: Management of a crisis (MOAC) vocabulary specification (2012). http://observedchange.com/moac/ns/ (zuletztbesuchtam:29-07-2014)
17. Liu, W., et al.: SSD: single shot MultiBox detector. In: Leibe, B., Matas, J., Sebe, N., Welling, M. (eds.) ECCV 2016. LNCS, vol. 9905, pp. 21–37. Springer, Cham (2016). https://doi.org/10.1007/978-3-319-46448-0_2
18. Redmon, J., Divvala, S., Girshick, R., Farhadi, A.: You only look once: unified, real-time object detection. In: 2016 IEEE Conference on Computer Vision and Pattern Recognition (CVPR), pp. 779–788 (2016). https://doi.org/10.1109/CVPR.2016.91

19. Ren, S., He, K., Girshick, R.B., Sun, J.: Faster R-CNN: towards real-time object detection with region proposal networks. IEEE Trans. Pattern Anal. Mach. Intell. **39**, 1137–1149 (2015)
20. Schroff, F., Kalenichenko, D., Philbin, J.: FaceNet: a unified embedding for face recognition and clustering. In: Proceedings of the IEEE conference on computer vision and pattern recognition, pp. 815–823 (2015)
21. Shi, Y., Jain, A.K.: Probabilistic face embeddings. In: Proceedings of the IEEE/CVF International Conference on Computer Vision, pp. 6902–6911 (2019)
22. Simonyan, K., Zisserman, A.: Two-stream convolutional networks for action recognition in videos. CoRR abs/1406.2199 (2014). http://arxiv.org/abs/1406.2199
23. Sun, Y., Wang, X., Tang, X.: Deeply learned face representations are sparse, selective, and robust. In: Proceedings of the IEEE conference on computer vision and pattern recognition, pp. 2892–2900 (2015)
24. Tan, M., Le, Q.: EfficientNet: Rethinking model scaling for convolutional neural networks. In: Chaudhuri, K., Salakhutdinov, R. (eds.) Proceedings of the 36th International Conference on Machine Learning. Proceedings of Machine Learning Research, vol. 97, pp. 6105–6114. PMLR (2019)
25. Tan, M., Pang, R., Le, Q.V.: Efficientdet: scalable and efficient object detection. In: 2020 IEEE/CVF Conference on Computer Vision and Pattern Recognition (CVPR), pp. 10778–10787 (2020). https://doi.org/10.1109/CVPR42600.2020.01079
26. Tang, X., Du, D.K., He, Z., Liu, J.: Pyramidbox: A context-assisted single shot face detector. In: Proceedings of the European Conference on Computer Vision (ECCV), pp. 797–813 (2018)
27. Wagenaar, D., et al.: Invited perspectives: how machine learning will change flood risk and impact assessment. Natural Hazards Earth Syst. Sci. **20**(4), 1149–1161 (2020). https://doi.org/10.5194/nhess-20-1149-2020
28. Wang, C.Y., Liao, H.Y.M., Wu, Y.H., Chen, P.Y., Hsieh, J.W., Yeh, I.H.: Cspnet: a new backbone that can enhance learning capability of CNN. In: Proceedings of the IEEE/CVF conference on computer vision and pattern recognition workshops, pp. 390–391 (2020)
29. Yang, S., Luo, P., Loy, C.C., Tang, X.: Wider face: a face detection benchmark. In: Proceedings of the IEEE conference on computer vision and pattern recognition, pp. 5525–5533 (2016)

# Diminisher: A Linux Kernel Based Countermeasure for TAA Vulnerability

Ameer Hamza[1(✉)], Maria Mushtaq[3], Khurram Bhatti[1], David Novo[2], Florent Bruguier[2], and Pascal Benoit[2]

[1] ECLab, Information Technology University, Lahore, Pakistan
mscs18020@itu.edu.pk
[2] LIRMM, Univ. Montpellier, CNRS, Montpellier, France
[3] LTCI, Télécom Paris, Institut Polytehcnique de Paris, Paris, France

**Abstract.** TSX Asynchronous Abort (TAA) vulnerability is a class of Side-Channel Attack (SCA) that allows an application to leak data from internal CPU buffers through asynchronous Transactional Synchronization Extension (TSX) aborts that are exploited by the recent Microarchitectural Data Sampling (MDS) attacks. Cross-core TAA attacks can be prevented through microcode updates where CPU buffers are flushed during Operating System (OS) context switching, but there is no solution to our knowledge that exists for hyper-threaded TAA attacks in which the attacker leaks data from sibling hardware threads through asynchronous abort. In this work, we have proposed Diminisher, a Linux kernel-based detection and mitigation solution for both hyper-threaded and cross-core TAA attacks. Diminisher can be logically divided into three phases, i.e., scheduling, detection, and mitigation. Diminisher is a lightweight tool to prevent TAA vulnerability. The novelty lies in the methodology that we propose enabling easy extensions to cover other hyper-threaded attacks for which no satisfactory solutions exist yet. Diminisher detects and mitigates the TAA attacks around 99% of the time at a low-performance overhead of 2.5%.

**Keywords:** Side-channel attacks · Intel's x86 Architecture · Linux Kernel · Intel TSX · Hyper-threading · Caches

## 1 Introduction

Side-Channel Attacks (SCA) have gained a lot of popularity in the last decade, and there are a variety of threatening attacks [6–9,20–22] that are proposed in the recent past. One of the most recent developments in the SCA domain is the advent of transient execution attacks [20–22] in which the attacker leaks the data by exploiting speculative and out-of-order execution. The Microarchitectural Data Sampling (MDS) vulnerability [4–8] is derived from the same class of transient execution attacks where data is leaked speculatively from internal CPU buffers. Data leakage through SCA is also widespread in virtualized


S. Katsikas et al. (Eds.): ESORICS 2021 Workshops, LNCS 13106, pp. 477–495, 2022.
https://doi.org/10.1007/978-3-030-95484-0_28

environments [37–39] where many users are bound to share the same physical hardware in the form of Virtual Machines (VMs). SCA can be prevented at various levels including hardware layer, kernel layer, and the application layer. Kernel-based/OS-based mitigation for SCA is more convenient due to additional privileges and the kernel ability to access all hardware resources. One of the drawbacks of hardware-based mitigation is that it requires modifications in hardware, which makes it inconvenient to implement. Moreover, userspace based mitigation techniques suffer from lack of privileges and the lack of access to the system resources.

Recent MDS attacks like Zombieload [7], RIDL [8] and CacheOut [6] exploit the TAA vulnerability [2] that allows unprivileged speculative access to leak data from internal CPU buffers by using asynchronous aborts within an Intel TSX transaction. This vulnerability is present on all Intel CPUs that ship with Intel TSX extension [31], which is added to aid hardware-based locking. The TAA vulnerability, when initially proposed, allows applications to leak data from either cross-core or hyper-threaded core scenarios. Moreover, leaking data from a sibling hardware thread is easier to exploit due to the same physical socket sharing between logical cores.

Intel proposed a microcode update where they used the legacy VERW instruction to overwrite the internal CPU buffers, which Linux uses during context switching to mitigate cross-core TAA attacks [11,12]. However, this mitigation is not viable for hyper-threaded TAA attacks, where data can be leaked well before context switching [12]. The only workaround that Intel has suggested for this is to either turn off hyper-threading or disable Intel TSX extensions. However, both of these options serve a considerable performance penalty, i.e., Intel hyper-threading provides a performance boost up to 30% [32] and similarly, the Intel TSX provides a performance boost up to 40% [36].

In this work, we propose Diminisher, a Linux kernel-based detection and mitigation solution for the TAA vulnerability. To our best knowledge, there is no prior work published on TAA mitigation. This paper represents the first step towards full TAA mitigation. Our proposed model is divided into three phases, i.e., scheduling, detection, and mitigation. Scheduling utilizes the Intel hyper-threading feature to schedule Linux kernel threads on all available cores in the system to detect the TAA vulnerability on the sibling hardware threads. Detection is performed by monitoring the features that cause TSX abort, which is followed by the mitigation phase. We have proposed two different techniques for mitigation, in the first technique, we terminate execution of the attacker's process. Alternatively, in the second technique, we replace the vulnerable instructions in the attacker's address space. Since the kernel is the most privileged software in the system, it is advantageous to handle runtime detection and mitigation in the kernel space. Diminisher is loaded as a Linux kernel module and covers the scope of the TAA vulnerability [6–8]. In this paper, we make three main contributions:

1. We present Diminisher, a Linux kernel-based countermeasure for hyper-threaded and cross-core TAA vulnerability.

2. We demonstrate the capability of Diminisher to detect and mitigate the TAA vulnerability with high accuracy, low-performance overhead, low latency, and high scalability.
3. We demonstrate that the Diminisher is resilient to the noise generated by the system under various loads.

Diminisher successfully mitigates the TAA vulnerability around 99% of the time at a performance overhead of 2.5%. We have tested our solution under various system load scenarios. In Diminisher, the scheduling and mitigation phases are generic, but the detection phase is specific to the TAA vulnerability. We have designed a scalable solution to enhance it for other hyper-threaded attacks as future work. To add support for a new side-channel attack in Diminisher, only the detection part needs to be updated by analyzing the features according to the nature of the attack. For instance, to add support for Flush+Reload attack [9] in Diminisher, kernel threads can be facilitated to monitor the number of cache flushes by reading the hardware performance counters [24–30], considering the attacker is leaking the data from a sibling hyper-threaded core.

The rest of the paper is organized as follows: Sect. 2 provides the necessary background to demonstrate the TAA vulnerability. Section 3 describes the methodology for Diminisher. Section 4 demonstrates the experimental results. Section 5 elaborates the discussion and finally, we conclude our paper in Sect. 6.

## 2 Background

### 2.1 Intel TSX

To support transactional memory for speeding up multithreaded applications, Intel introduced Transaction Synchronization Extensions (TSX) as part of the x86 instruction set for hardware transactional memory [13], which is introduced in the Haswell Architecture. TSX allows memory transactions to be set up through XBEGIN and XEND instructions and the code is placed between these instructions to execute transactionally. Transactions are either committed or aborted, committed to the CPU only when all instructions within a transaction are completed successfully. When a transaction is aborted, the microarchitecture state is rolled back to the previous point, i.e., before the transaction, and all executed operations within the transaction are reverted. Transaction aborts can be caused due to various reasons; most commonly, due to memory address conflicts with the sibling hardware thread, where the other sibling hardware thread tries to read or modify the same address used in the transaction. Some instructions and system events like SMIs also abort the transaction [13]. Moreover, the amount of data accessed within a transaction should not exceed L1 and last level cache, respectively [14].

### 2.2 LFB

Line Fill Buffers (LFBs) are internal CPU buffers along with load and store buffers to keep track of L1 cache misses at the cache line level. LFB entry is allocated for each L1 data cache miss to retrieve data from higher-level cache. This is implemented to avoid cache line stall when multiple load and store misses happen on the same cache line. Instead, waiting happens within the LFB entry until data is retrieved [10,15]. Despite fetching data from L1 data cache, there also exists an undocumented path, where data evicted from the L1 data cache occasionally ends up inside the Line Fill Buffers (LFBs) [6].

### 2.3 TAA Vulnerability

A cache line conflict during a clflush operation is one of the reasons for the TSX transaction to abort [1]. Reading the same address that is recently flushed by the clflush instruction causes a TSX abort. In TSX Asynchronous Aborts (TAA) [2,6–8], the attacker first flushes the address and then attempts to read the data from the flushed cache line, which causes the transaction to abort. However, the processor already allocates an LFB entry for the load instruction just before the faulting load. When the transaction aborts, the load instruction is allowed to proceed speculatively with data from LFB. Since the load is never completed, the load proceeds with the stale value from LFB, which might be the previous memory address loaded by the victim, allowing the attacker to sample LFB data [2,3]. The processor state reverts back to a point before the transaction, but this leaves a footprint in the cache that can be retrieved by a timing attack such as Flush + Reload [9]. Figure 1 depicts the TAA vulnerability where the attacker process is continuously leaking the secret data that is accessed by the victim process through the faulting load.

The TAA vulnerability is exploited by multiple MDS attacks [6–8]. RIDL [8] leaks the data from LFBs and mainly focuses on hyper-threaded attacks where the attacker leaks the data from sibling hardware threads as the victim accesses it. RIDL implemented a TAA attack to recover passwords from Linux `/etc/shadow` file by passively listening to all LFB entries and matching the data with previous observations. By this approach, RIDL was able to recover 26 characters from the shadow file after 24 h. Zombieload [7] extends the RIDL findings to show leakage even without faulting loads. Zombieload also demonstrates LFB leakage from the Cascade architecture, which Intel claimed to be the first MDS-resistant architecture. Zombieload argued that the leakage from TAA is negligible and limited to 0.1 bytes per second. CacheOut [6] also leaks data from LFB but provides an attacker the additional control over LFB entries by selecting the cache line with leakage rate peeks out at 2.85 KiB/s. CacheOut claimed itself to be the first attack to mount the TAA on Whiskey Lake that Intel shipped with MDS mitigation at the hardware layer. In the TAA vulnerability [6–8], the data is leaked from the internal CPU buffers. To address the buffer leakage issue in existing CPUs, Intel released a microcode update that

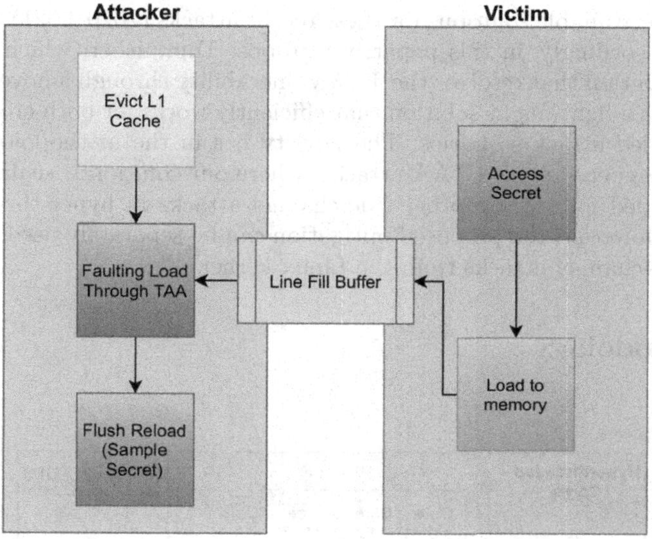


**Fig. 1.** TAA vulnerability

reused the legacy VERW instruction to clear the CPU buffers. Operating Systems (OS) like Linux, issue the VERW instruction on each context switch to flush entries in CPU buffers [11,12]. According to Intel, Whiskey Lake architecture contains the hardware mitigation for MDS attacks, but CacheOut claims to mount a TAA attack due to its ability to select the entry in LFB [6].

However, for hyper-threaded TAA attacks, the buffer overwrite countermeasure is not sufficient as hyper-threading provides the attacker an opportunity to mount the TAA attack well before context switching. Intel suggested that TAA can be mitigated by ensuring only trusted code is ever executed in the sibling threads [8]. However, this strategy introduces nontrivial complexity, as it requires scheduler modifications as well as synchronization at system call entry points. It is also insufficient to protect sandbox applications and SGX enclaves. As a last resort for TAA mitigation in hyper-threaded environments, Intel proposed to disable either the hyper-threading or the TSX component, but both of these options come at the cost of substantial performance overhead [32,36].

OS-based solutions for side-channel attacks are widespread. Hardware performance counters keep track of all system-level activities like cache hits, cache misses, branch misprediction, etc., which is the reason that they are widely used for SCA detection [24–30,40,41]. SmokeBomb [18] protects the sensitive code by manipulating the cache lines in such a way that the attacker is not able to leak the sensitive data. StealthMem [19] is a solution to mitigate cache-based SCA in a cloud environment by locking the cache lines. However, none of the OS-based solutions are proposed for the TAA vulnerability. There are some inspirations from SOA which can be opted for mitigation in OS-based solutions [16,17].

Thus, the available solutions for these recent attacks (2020–2021) are not satisfactory. Accordingly, in this paper, we propose Diminisher, which is the first OS-based solution that resolves the TAA vulnerability through a novel approach. Diminisher is a lightweight solution that efficiently works for both cross-core and hyper-threaded attack scenarios. The novelty lies in the methodology that we propose for hyper-threaded TAA attacks, where our solution is scalable enough to be expanded for various other side-channel attacks in hyper-threaded environments. Moreover, the proposed mitigation can be separately used to mitigate most of side-channel attacks from the Linux kernel.

## 3 Methodology

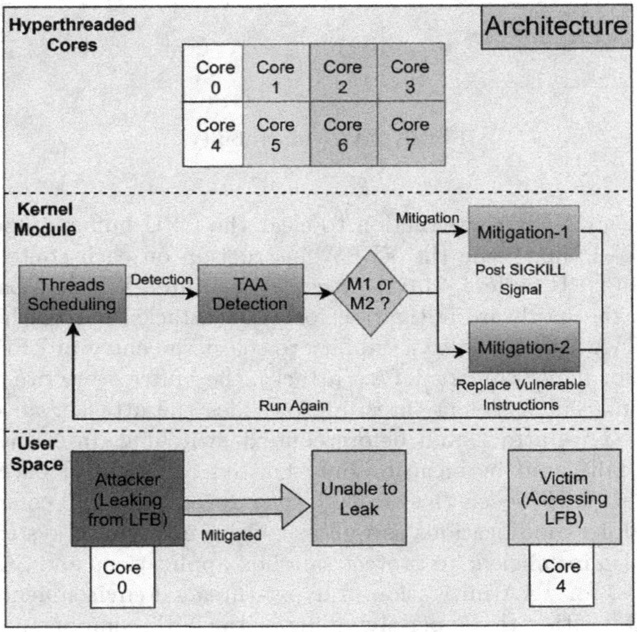


**Fig. 2.** System methodology

Our proposed methodology is illustrated in Fig. 2. The upper part of Fig. 2 shows the hyper-threaded core architecture, where the same color cores represent sibling cores, i.e., Core-0 shares the same physical socket with Core-4, Core-1 with Core-5, and so on. The middle part of Fig. 2 represents the architecture of Diminisher, which is logically separated into three phases, i.e., scheduling, detection, and mitigation. Scheduling relies on Intel hyper-threading in which the kernel threads schedule on all available cores in the system. Once scheduled, the next phase is detection which is performed by monitoring the TAA aborts. After the successful detection, the final phase is the mitigation. For mitigation, we have proposed two approaches, i.e., SIGKILL to the attacker's process, and the vulnerable instructions replacement. The lower part of Fig. 2 represents the userspace layer, where the attacker mounts a TAA attack by running on the victim's sibling hardware thread. However, as soon as the Diminisher is scheduled on Core-4, it detects the TAA attack mounted on Core-0 and instantly applies the mitigation, which prevents the attacker to leak any further data.

## 3.1 Scheduling

Diminisher loads as a Linux kernel module and relies on Intel hyper-threading for scheduling. Hyper-threading is a hardware innovation that allows more than one hardware thread to run on the same physical socket to aid parallel processing through multi-threaded applications [32]. Since hyper-threaded cores share the same physical socket, if an attacker's process is scheduled on one logical core, and one of the kernel threads is scheduled on its sibling hardware thread, that kernel thread can detect the vulnerable process by analyzing the attacker's execution patterns.

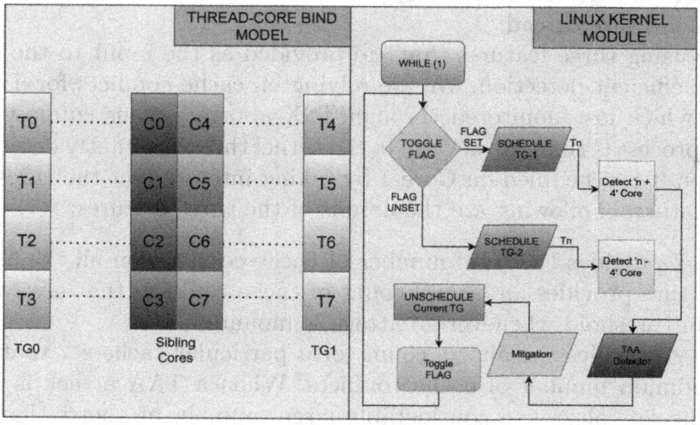


**Fig. 3.** OS-Based scheduling

As shown on the left-hand side of Fig. 3, we have affined separate kernel threads (T0 to T7) to all available logical cores (C0 to C7) in the system. C0 and C4 belong to the same physical socket, and so on. Hence, a kernel thread running on C0 may analyze the application's execution patterns running on C4. Since we have four physical cores and eight logical cores in our test machine, we have spawned eight kernel threads (T0 to T7) that are associated with the logical cores (C0 to C8). We have divided the kernel threads into two groups, i.e., thread-group-0 (TG0) and thread-group-1 (TG1). T0 to T3 are assigned to TG0, whereas T4 to T7 are assigned to TG1.

The scheduling algorithm is based on a Boolean flag which makes two thread groups (TG0 and TG1) to toggle. We schedule TG0 on C0–C3 and detect the attacker's processes on the sibling cores (C4–C7) for a time quantum. Once the time quantum is expired, we toggle the boolean flag which lets TG1 to execute, and TG0 has to wait. This alternate switching is maintained as long as the kernel module is loaded, as shown on the right-hand side of Fig. 3. The scheduling algorithm that we have proposed monitors all cores efficiently with the condition that the processor must support Intel hyper-threading technology.

### 3.2 Detection

After scheduling, the second phase is a TAA attack detection. Detection is performed by monitoring the number of cache conflicts observed by a kernel thread that is caused due to the sibling hyperthreaded core. In the kernel thread, we continuously mount the TSX transactions to check for cache conflicts, considering that the attacker is running on its sibling hyperthreaded core to leak the data through a TAA attack. If the kernel thread observes a large number of cache conflicts that exceed our calculated threshold, which will be discussed in Sect. 4.2, then the detection module decides that the TAA attack is mounted on its sibling hardware thread.

We are using three features that are provided as the input to the detection module for efficient detection. We are relying on cache conflicts for TAA-based detection, which are monitored through TSX aborts. Let us suppose that the attacker's process is running on Core-0, the kernel thread instantly detects a TAA attack when it is scheduled on Core-4 by taking into account the thresholds for all three features. Following are the details of the three features:

1. Feature-1 provides the total number of cache conflicts on all the cache sets. This feature provides an overall count of cache conflicts that always exceeds a certain threshold whenever an attack is mounted.
2. Feature-2 provides the aborts count for a particular cache set that observes the maximum number of cache conflicts. When a TAA attack is mounted, few cache sets observe a considerably larger number of aborts than the rest of the cache sets, which are exploited in this feature.
3. Feature-3 provides the aborts count for a cache set that observes minimum cache conflicts. This feature provides a measurement for the cache set that is least affected by a TAA attack, as some cache sets observe a lesser number of conflicts than the rest of the cache sets when the TAA attack is mounted.

The proposed detection framework is reliable because it takes all three features into account, and then it also takes at least 3 consecutive detection decisions to conclude that the system is under attack, thus reducing the chances of false positives. We have calculated separate thresholds for each of the features which will be discussed in Sect. 4.2.

**Detection Implementation.** Algorithm 1 presents the abstract pseudocode for the TAA detection.

**Algorithm 1:** TAA Attack Detection

```
abrt ← 0, no_abrt ← 0, abrt_per_set[SETS] ← 0, samples ← 0
while samples ≤ 50000 do
    for set ← 0 to 64 by 1 do
        Begin_TSX_Transaction();
        Access_All_Ways(set);
        End_TSX_Transaction();
        if ABORT_REASON_CACHE_CONFLICT then
            abrt ← abrt + 1;
            abrt_per_set[set] ← abrt_per_set[set] + 1;
        else if NO_ABORT then
            no_abrt ← no_abrt + 1;
    samples ← samples + 1;
    Sleep_Detection();
if ((abrt / no_abrt)*50000 ≥ F1_THRESHOLD &&
Get_Max(abrt_per_set) ≥ F2_THRESHOLD &&
Get_Min(abrt_per_set) ≥ F3_THRESHOLD) then
    /* Attack Detected */
    return 1;
/* No-Attack Detected */
return 0;
```

We are collecting 50,000 samples for each detection, which is a hypothetical limit that is decided after performing the bulk of experimentation. If we go below this limit, we must compromise on accuracy. Similarly, going above this limit increases the latency. Hence, 50 thousand samples are suitable for the TAA detection. For every detection sample, we check for cache conflicts in each of the cache sets. For this, we start the TSX Transaction, access all ways of a particular cache set, and end the transaction. If we get a TSX abort due to cache conflict, the abort count and per set abort count are incremented, otherwise we increment no abort count. After each sample, we suspend the kernel thread to avoid CPU starvation. After collecting all samples, the detection framework makes a valid detection decision by taking into account the measurements of all three features as a mandatory requirement.

### 3.3 Mitigation

Mitigation is the final phase of our proposed solution. We have proposed two approaches for mitigation that are specific to the Linux kernel and rely on the Linux process descriptor. Our proposed mitigations are not dependent on any hardware resource or a TAA vulnerability, thus, can be used as an independent solution to mitigate most of the side-channel attacks from the Linux kernel. Following are details of the proposed mitigations:

### 3.4 Mitigation-1 (SIGKILL to the Attacker's Process)

Linux kernel has control over all userspace processes running in the system including their execution state. After the successful detection, we post a SIGKILL signal from the kernel thread to terminate the execution of the attacker's process.

Algorithm 2 shows the pseudocode for mitigation-1. After getting the task list of the attacker's processes, we lock the task structure and send the SIGKILL signal to the userspace attacker's process. As soon as the attacker application gets the SIGKILL signal, it has no choice but to terminate its execution. Finally, we unlock the task structure and conclude the mitigation. The termination of vulnerable applications avoids any further leakage.

**Algorithm 2:** Mitigation-1 (SIGKILL to Vulnerable Process)

```
if Is_TAA_Detected() then
    task_struct ← Get_Task_Struct();
    Task_Lock(task_struct);
    ret ← Send_SIG_KILL_Signal(task_struct);
    Task_Unlock(task_struct);
    if ret == SUCCESS then
        /* Killed vulnerable process */
        return 1;
    /* Unable to kill vulnerable process */
    return 0;
```

### 3.5 Mitigation-2 (Instruction Replacement)

In Linux, each of the instructions that a userspace process executes reside in the code section of the process descriptor. In this mitigation technique, we parse the code section of the attacker's process and check for the vulnerable instructions that cause the attack. As discussed in Sect. 2.1, XBEGIN and XEND instructions are used to mount the transaction in the case of a TAA attack, i.e., both these instructions are vulnerable in our scenario. Thus, we replace XBEGIN and XEND instructions with the NOP instructions. A NOP instruction in Intel ISA is a harmless instruction that does not update the program flow, which makes it the best choice for the replacement.

Algorithm 3 presents the pseudocode for mitigation-2. We first iterate through the process list to get the task structure of the vulnerable process for the detected core. Afterwards, we acquire the task lock to avoid any race condition and get the userspace pages for the text section of the detected process. Subsequently, we map the user pages to the kernel space, followed by the examination of vulnerable instructions by parsing the code section. For the TAA case, we look for XBEGIN and XEND instructions. We replace all vulnerable instructions with NOP instructions to mitigate the attack. Finally, we unmap the kernel mapping and release the task lock and return.

**Algorithm 3:** Mitigation-2 (Vulnerable Instruction Replacement)

```
if Is_TAA_Detected() then
    task_struct ← Get_Task_Struct();
    Task_Lock(task_struct);
    user_pages ← Read_Text_Section(task_struct);
    text_ptr ← Map_Kernel_Space(user_pages);
    for i ← 0 to code_size by 1 do
        if text_ptr[i] == VULNERABLE_INSTRUCTION then
            Replace_To_NOP(text_ptr[i]);
            ret ← SUCCESS;
    Unmap_And_Release_Pages(user_pages);
    Task_Unlock(task_struct);
    if ret == SUCCESS then
        /* Replaced Vulnerable Instruction */
        return 1;
    /* Unable to find Vulnerable Instruction */
    return 0;
```

The overall mitigation framework deals with two key challenges; firstly, the possibility of innocent processes being killed due to false positives, and secondly, the possibility that the attacker figures out the presence of mitigation. The first issue is dealt with by a high accuracy detection framework that yields minimum false positives, while for the second challenge, we further improve the mitigation process using the instruction replacement feature as discussed in this section.

# 4 Experimental Results

## 4.1 System Model

We have tested the proposed solution on Intel's Core i7-6700 CPU running on Linux Ubuntu 18.04.5 LTS with kernel version 5.4.0-74 at 3.40-GHz. Our threat model is an open-source TAA attack code that leaks the data from sibling hardware threads. The attack is mounted with all the latest mitigation in place for both BIOS and the Linux kernel. The results are obtained by running the TAA attack 25,000 times on different hardware cores and relying on the Diminisher to detect and mitigate the TAA attack.

We observed some variation in the readings for the loaded system compared to the idle system. We call the system loaded when there are 100+ userspace processes running, although we could not reproduce the loaded system scenario with standard stress tester tools. For the loaded system, we executed 40+ Google Chrome tabs, each running YouTube videos, video players, Skype call with video and screen sharing, and various other applications. For the idle system, no additional userspace applications were running except the Diminisher module, attacker process, and the victim process.

### 4.2 Detection Threshold

As a first step, we calculated the detection thresholds for each of the features. Figure 4, 5 and 6 show detection thresholds for all three features. The right-hand side of each graph shows the stable readings for the idle system scenario. We hardly get any abort when no TAA attack is mounted for the idle system scenario and in the case of the TAA attack, we mostly get constant readings. In the case of a TAA attack mounted on an idle system, Fig. 4 shows a constant reading line at around 150 value, Fig. 5 shows some variation around 700 value, and the Fig. 6 shows some variations at around 280 value.

In the left-hand graph of Fig. 4, the variations in the readings can be seen for the loaded system. There are quite a few aborts in the case of no TAA attack scenario as cache conflicts are higher when a lot of applications are running in parallel, which causes transactions to abort. If we specifically talk about Fig. 4, after analyzing both loaded and idle graphs, we chose a lower bound of 90 from the loaded scenario, when no attack is mounted, and chose the upper bound of 150 from the idle scenario, where the TAA attack is mounted. Between the lower bound and upper bound, it is safe to detect the attack, so we choose a mid-value of 120 for the feature-1 detection threshold. Similarly, for feature-2 and feature-3, we have calculated the detection thresholds as 500 and 200, respectively, by analyzing Fig. 5 and Fig. 6. Since the behaviors of attack and no attack are quite discernible, a simple threshold determination is very helpful to detect the attack even in load conditions. We have calculated the offline thresholds for all system loads and used the calculated thresholds for the run-time detection.

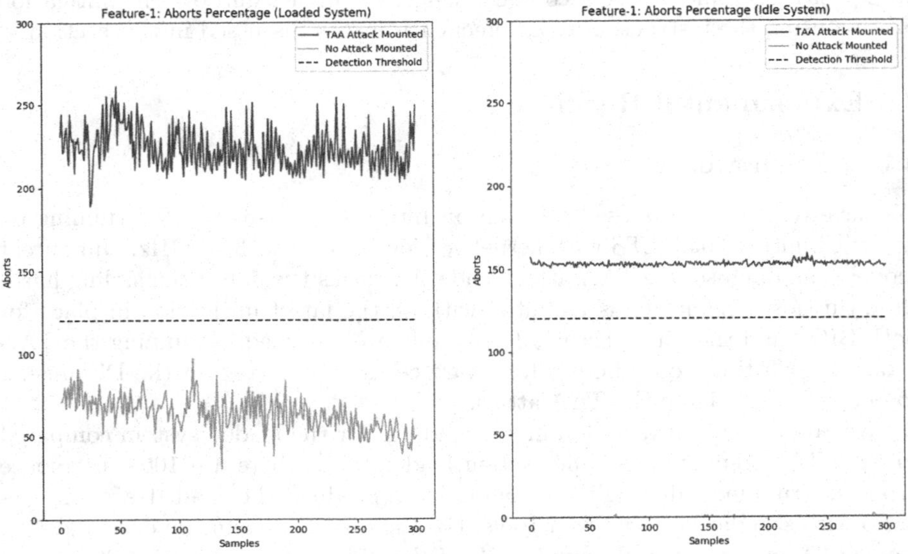


**Fig. 4.** Feature-1 Threshold detection

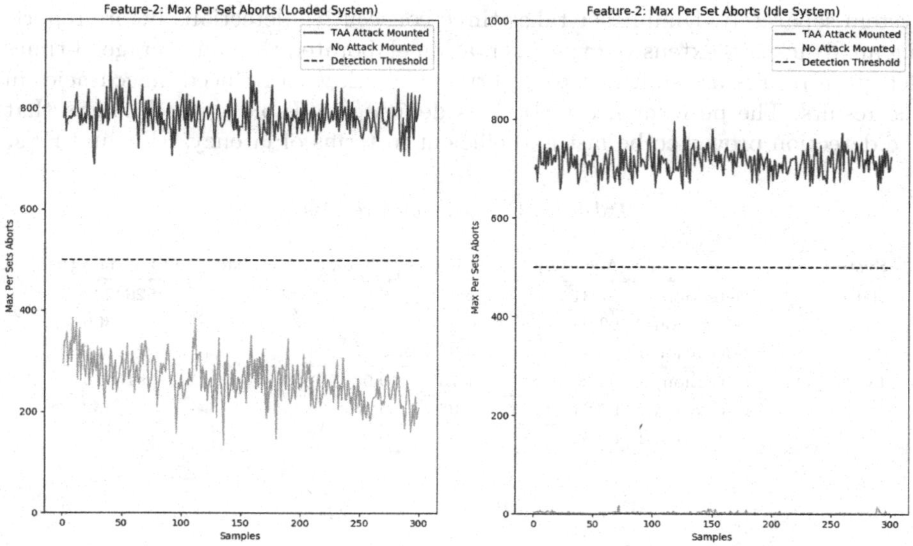


**Fig. 5.** Feature-2 Threshold detection

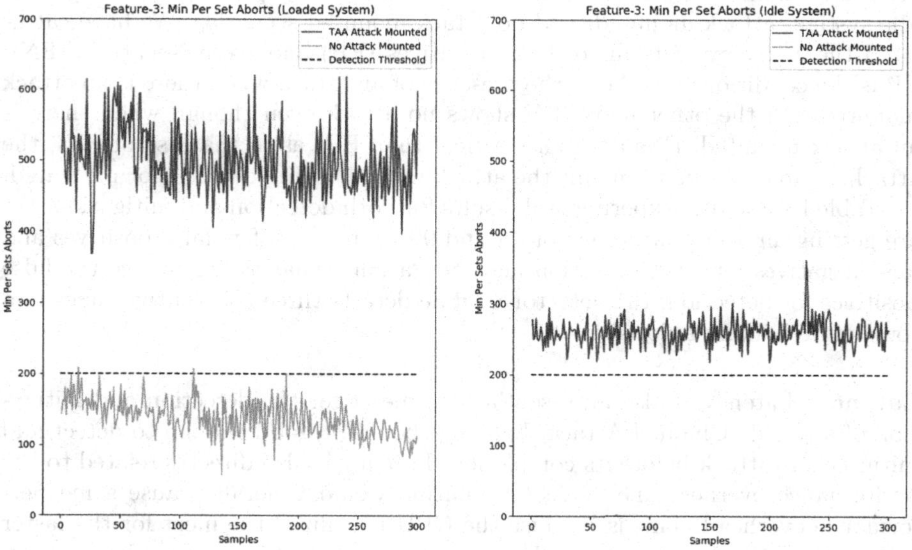


**Fig. 6.** Feature-3 Threshold detection

### 4.3 Results

We have evaluated the proposed solution for both detection and mitigation as shown in Table 1. The readings are taken for the loaded system and idle system separately. Diminisher takes three consecutive detections before reporting an attack and extensive experimentation elaborated that on average, 3-times detection results are sufficient to report the attack with reduced inaccuracies in the results. The performance metrics as depicted in Table 1, which shows that the detection proved to be fast and efficient in terms of latency, FPs, and FNs.

**Table 1.** Experimental results

| System state | Type | Accuracy (%) | FP (%) | FN (%) | Overhead (%) | Latency (us) |
|---|---|---|---|---|---|---|
| IDLE | Detection | 97.31 | 2.64 | 0.03 | 2.5 | 5264232 |
| | Mitigation-2 | 99.94 | 0.03 | 0 | | 306 |
| | Mitigation-1 | 99.85 | 0.03 | 0.18 | | 86 |
| LOADED | Detection | 98.26 | 1.73 | 0.03 | 2.5 | 6916110 |
| | Mitigation-2 | 99.91 | 0.03 | 0.06 | | 452 |
| | Mitigation-1 | 99.82 | 0.03 | 0.21 | | 106 |

**Accuracy.** Accuracy is the most convenient way to measure the effectiveness of any runtime detection tool. We have used percentages to demonstrate the accuracy results. We have used the same number of samples for loaded-system, idle-system, attack-mounted, and no attack-mounted scenarios. We have calculated the accuracy in terms of False Positives (FP) and False Negatives (FN). FP is the condition that shows the presence of an attack when there is no attack mounted. On the other hand, FN shows no attack even though when there is an attack mounted. FNs are more critical than FPs as in the case of FNs, the attacker can continue to mount the attack without being detected or mitigated.

Table 1 shows the experimental results for both detection and mitigation. We are getting an overall accuracy of around 99% with very few false positives and false negatives for both detection and mitigation scenarios. To reduce the false positives for detection, the detector module detects three consecutive times in a row before making a decision.

**Latency.** Latency is also an essential parameter for the detection and mitigation of any Side-Channel Attack. Latency should be good enough to detect and mitigate the attack before its completion. Latency is also directly related to the performance overhead, i.e., a faster solution would generally cause some performance overhead. This is because the CPU is utilized the most for the faster solutions, which depletes the CPU resources for general-purpose tasks.

The TAA attack is slower by nature as it takes around 24 h to leak the root password for the RIDL attack as discussed in Sect. 2.3. Therefore, latency is not a very big concern for us. Detection takes around 5 s in idle conditions and around 7 s when the system is loaded. Moreover, our proposed mitigation techniques are significantly faster, i.e., mitigation-2 takes around 500 uS on average as we have to parse the code section, whereas mitigation-1 is even quicker as we just have to post a SIGKILL signal to the vulnerable process.

**Overhead.** Another important design parameter for scheduling and mitigation tools is the performance overhead. The runtime detection tools should keep the overhead minimum, i.e., there should be no significant effect on general-purpose applications running in the system. Furthermore, the adaptability and scalability of the scheduling and mitigation solution are highly dependent on the performance overhead. As discussed earlier, going more fine-grained would result in a faster response but that comes at the cost of higher performance overhead.

We measure the performance overhead based on the CPU utilization after loading the kernel module. The performance overhead of Diminisher is very low, i.e., 2.5% on average. The low system overhead is because we do not let kernel threads to run continuously for all the samples, instead we unschedule the threads after we do a single round of detection on the whole L1 cache. We also did not find performance degradation for any user-space application while Diminisher was loaded.

## 5 Discussion

Experimental results show that the Diminisher efficiently detects and mitigates the TAA vulnerability with 99% accuracy at 2.5% of performance overhead. Moreover, 2.5% overhead is acceptable as it does not cause any performance degradation in the overall system and Diminisher has a very low count of false positives and false negatives. Threshold-based detection proves to be useful to counter the noise under system load as we perform offline analysis for both the loaded system and the idle system cases to select the appropriate threshold. Since we already know the thresholds for both the load/noise case and idle case, detecting in between the two limits helps us to mitigate the noise. Diminisher is equally effective for both cross-core and hyperthreaded core scenarios.

As discussed in Sect. 3 there is no prior mitigation proposed for the TAA vulnerability except for the Intel microcode update, however, the microcode update is not effective for hyper-threaded TAA attacks. There are some proposed mitigations for SCAs, e.g., Jonathan Behrens [33] proposed a mitigation for transient attacks and proposed a novel kernel design that is safe for the process to expose. SmokeBomb [18] and StealthMem [19] proposed the mitigations for cache-based Side Channel attacks, but no mitigation is proposed for hyper-threaded TAA attacks or MDS attacks. Hyper-threaded attacks are hard to mitigate because of the sibling core architecture, due to which there is no satisfactory solution for such attacks until now. Therefore, it is usually suggested to disable the hyper-threading feature to promote secure computing [34].

Diminisher successfully accomplishes all three objectives that were discussed in Sect. 2 with the following novelties:

- Diminisher resolves the TAA vulnerability with very promising results of over 99% accuracy at 2.5% latency.
- Diminisher can efficiently mitigate hyper-threaded TAA attacks and it is scalable enough to be expanded for other hyper-threaded attacks.

- Proposed mitigation techniques can be used independently to mitigate most of the SCAs from the Linux kernel.
- The mitigation-2 technique helps to reduce DOS attacks as the attacker is unable to figure out the presence of the mitigation framework in the case of this technique.
- Since kernel-based solutions are more autonomous than userspace due to higher privileges, Diminisher effectively detects and mitigates the userspace applications from kernel space.
- We provide simplicity, i.e., Diminisher is simply loaded as a kernel module and does not require any change in kernel code.

Although the proposed solution efficiently resolves the TAA vulnerability, there are some possible improvements that we would like to discuss. Firstly, the TAA detection phase is slower and takes between three and five seconds on average due to the collection of a large number of samples and the detection functionality, which utilizes an iteration of three consecutive detections. Secondly, the CPU buffer monitoring can be added to make TAA detection more robust, which can also help to detect other MDS attacks. Lastly, Diminisher is limited to kernel space only, i.e., it cannot mitigate cross VM SCAs, which can be opted as an extension to this work.

As a future work, we are planning to extend Diminisher to cover other side-channel attacks. The proposed module is efficient in terms of scalability, i.e., more Side-Channel Attacks like Flush+Reload, Prime+Probe, etc., can be added to our module, and for that, only the detection phase needs to be updated according to the type of attack. We were able to successfully run recent transient execution attacks including Spectre [20], Meltdown [21], and Foreshadow [22] in our environment, and Diminisher can be expanded for such attacks as a future work. Diminisher can also be expanded to the hypervisor layer to mitigate cross VM SCAs. There can also be some work done to make the current solution more efficient, i.e., detection latency improvement, feature addition, and performance improvement.

## 6 Conclusion

In this paper, we have proposed a solution for the TAA vulnerability that works very efficiently at a low-performance overhead of around 2.5% and the accuracy of over 99%. Furthermore, the experimental results depict that there are very few false positives and false negatives in the case of both detection and mitigation. Generally, hyper-threaded attacks are hard to mitigate since multiple logical cores share the same physical socket, and an attacker using one hyper-threaded core can leak data from its sibling hardware thread without being noticed by the OS. With the proposed solution, we can efficiently mitigate hyper-threaded and cross-core TAA attacks, and the solution is scalable enough to mitigate other attacks with some modification in the detection phase. The proposed mitigations can also be used as standalone mitigation techniques for future research.

## References


1. Intel. Intel 64 and IA-32 Architecture Software Developer's Manual, Vol. 3 (3A, 3B & 3C): System Programming Guide (2016)
2. Intel. Deep Dive: Intel Transactional Synchronization Extensions Asynchronous Abort, January 2021. http://www.software.intel.com/content/www/us/en/develop/articles/software-security-guidance/technical-documentation/intel-tsx-asynchronous-abort
3. Intel. Deep Dive: Intel Analysis of Microarchitectural Data Sampling, May 2021. http://www.software.intel.com/content/www/us/en/develop/articles/software-security-guidance/technical-documentation/intel-analysis-microarchitectural-data-sampling
4. Moghimi, D., Lipp, M., Sunar, B., Schwarz, M.: Medusa: Microarchitectural data leakage via automated attack synthesis. In: USENIX Security, August 2020
5. Canella, C., et al.: Fallout: leaking data on Meltdown-resistant CPUs. In: CCS (2019)
6. Schaik, S.V., Minkin, M., Kwong, A., Genkin, D., Yarom, Y.: CacheOut: leaking data on intel cpus via cache evictions. In: IEEE Symposium on Security and Privacy (SP) (2021)
7. Schwarz, M., et al.: ZombieLoad: cross-privilege-boundary data sampling. In: CCS (2019)
8. van Schaik, S., et al.: Rogue in-flight data load. In: IEEE SP (2019)
9. Yarom, Y., Falkner, K.: Flush+Reload: a high resolution, low noise, L3 cache side-channel attack. In: USENIX Security (2014)
10. Cache memory system having data and tag arrays and multi-purpose buffer assembly with multiple lines buffers. US Patent 5,680,572, July 1996
11. Linux Kernel: Microarchitectural Data Sampling (MDS) mitigation April 2021. http://www.kernel.org/doc/html/latest/x86/mds
12. Linux Kernel: TAA - TSX Asynchronous Abort April 2021. http://www.kernel.org/doc/html/latest/admin-guide/hw-vuln/tsx_async_abort
13. Intel TSX Overview January 2021. http://scc.ustc.edu.cn/zlsc/tc4600/intel/2016.0.109/compiler_c/common/core/GUID-FB2F2539-18F5-4D5A-B814-F29FD0C32326
14. Intel 64 and IA-32 architectures optimization reference manual, June 2016
15. Akkary, H., et al.: Methods and apparatus for caching data in a nonblocking manner using a plurality of fill buffers. US Patent 5,671,444, October 1996
16. Chiappetta, M., Savas, E., Yilmaz, C.: Real time detection of cache- based side-channel attacks using hardware performance counters. J. Appl. Soft Comput. **49**, 1162–1174 (2016)
17. Mushtaq, M., Novo, D., Bruguier, F., Beniot, P., Bhatti, M.K.: TransitGuard: an OS-based defense mechanism against transient execution attacks. In: 26th IEEE European Symposium (ETS 2021), May 2021
18. Cho, H., et al.: SmokeBomb: effective mitigation against cache side-channel attacks on the ARM architecture. In: MobiSys 2020: Proceedings of the 18th International Conference on Mobile Systems, Applications, and Services, June 2020
19. Kim, T., Peinado, M., Mainar-Ruiz. G.: STEALTHMEM: system-level protection against cache-based side channel attacks in the cloud. In: Proceedings of the 21st USENIX Security Symposium (Security), Bellevue, WA, pp. 189–204 (2012)
20. Kocher, P., et al.: Spectre attacks: exploiting speculative execution. In: IEEE SP (2019)

21. Lipp, M., et al.: Meltdown: reading kernel memory from userspace. In: USENIX Security (2018)
22. Van Bulck, J., et al.: Foreshadow: extracting the keys to the Intel SGX kingdom with transient out-oforder execution. In: USENIX Security (2018)
23. Goktus, E., Razavi, K., Portokalidis, G., Bos, H., Giuffrida, G.: Speculative probing: hacking blind in the spectre era. In: CCS 2020: Proceedings of the 2020 ACM SIGSAC Conference on Computer and Communications Security, October 2020
24. Wang, X., Karri, R.: Reusing hardware performance counters to detect and identify kernel control flow modifying rootkits. IEEE TCAD **35**, 485–498 (2016)
25. Demme, J., et al.: On the feasibility of online malware detection with performance counters. In: ISCA (2013)
26. Tang, A., Sethumadhavan, S., Stolfo, S.J.: Unsupervised anomaly based malware detection using hardware features. CoRR (2014)
27. Alam, M., et al.: Performance counters to rescue: a machine learning based safeguard against micro-architectural side-channel attacks. Crypt. ePrint Arch. (2017). https://eprint.iacr.org/2017/564
28. Chiappetta, M., Savas, E., Yilmaz, C.: Real time detection of cache-based side-channel attacks using hardware performance counters. Appl. Soft Comput. **49**, 1162–1174 (2016)
29. Torres, G., Liu, C.: Can data-only exploits be detected at runtime using hardware events?: A case study of the heartbleed vulnerability. In: HASP, pp. 2:1–2:7 (2016)
30. Zhang, T., Zhang, Y., Lee, R.B.: Cloudradar: a real-time side-channel attack detection system in clouds. In: RAID (2016)
31. Intel TSX Overview, January 2021. http://software.intel.com/content/www/us/en/develop/documentation/cpp-compiler-developer-guide-and-reference/top/compiler-reference/intrinsics/intrinsics-for-intel-advanced-vector-extensions-2/intrinsics-for-intel-transactional-synchronization-extensions-intel-tsx/intel-transactional-synchronization-extensions-intel-tsx-overview
32. Intel Hyperthreading, June 2021. https://www.intel.com/content/www/us/en/gaming/resources/hyper-threading
33. Behrens, J., Cao, A., Skeggs, C., Belay, A.,Kaashoek, M.F., Zeldovich, N.: fficiently mitigating transient execution attacks using the unmapped speculation contract. In: 14th USENIX Symposium on Operating Systems Design and Implementation (2020)
34. Mushtaq, M., Mukhtar, M.A., Lapotre, V., Bhattic, M.K., Gogniat, G.: Winter is here! A decade of cache-based side-channel attacks, detection & mitigation for RSA. Inf. Syst. **92**, 101524 (2020)
35. Weisse, O., et al.: Foreshadow-NG: breaking the virtual memory abstraction with transient out-of-order execution (2018). https://foreshadowattack.eu/foreshadowNG.pdf
36. Yoo, R.M., Hughes, C.J., Lai, K., Rajwar, R.: Performance evaluation of intel transactional synchronization extensions for high-performance computing. In: 14th USENIX SC 2013: Proceedings of the International Conference on High Performance Computing, Networking, Storage and Analysis (2013)
37. Xu, Y., Bailey, M., Jahanian, F., Joshi, K., Hiltunen, M., Schlichting, R.: An exploration of L2 cache covert channels in virtualized environments. In: Proceedings of the 3rd ACM Workshop on Cloud Computing Security Workshop, Ser. CCSW 2011, pp. 29–40. ACM, New York (2011). http://doi.acm.org/10.1145/2046660.2046670

38. Yarom, Y., Falkner, K.: FLUSH+RELOAD: a high resolution, low noise, L3 cache side-channel attack. In: Proceedings of the 23rd USENIX Conference on Security Symposium, ser. SEC2014, pp. 719–732. USENIX Association, Berkeley (2014). http://dl.acm.org/citation.cfm?id=2671225.2671271
39. Zhang, Y., Juels, A., Reiter, M.K., Ristenpart, T.: Cross-VM side channels and their use to extract private keys. In: Proceedings of the 2012 ACM Conference on Computer and Communications Security, ser. CCS 2012, pp. 305–316. ACM, New York (2012). https://doi.org/10.1145/2382196.2382230
40. Mushtaq, M., Akram, A., Bhatti, M.K., Chaudhry, M., Lapotre, V., Gogniat, G.: NIGHTs-WATCH: a cache-based side-channel intrusion detector using hardware performance counters. In: Proceedings of the 7th International Workshop on Hardware and Architectural Support for Security and Privacy, New York, June 2018, pp. 189–204 (2018)
41. Mushtaq, M., et al.: WHISPER: a tool for run-time detection of side-channel attacks. IEEE Access, **8**, 83 871–83 900 (2020)

# The Rise of ICS Malware: A Comparative Analysis

Yassine Mekdad[1(✉)], Giuseppe Bernieri[2], Mauro Conti[2], and Abdeslam El Fergougui[1]

[1] Laboratory of Computer Networks and Systems, Moulay Ismail University of Meknes, Meknes, Morocco
y.mekdad@edu.umi.ac.ma, a.elfergougui@umi.ac.ma

[2] Department of Mathematics, University of Padua, Padua, Italy
{bernieri,conti}@math.unipd.it

**Abstract.** Cyber attacks against Industrial Control Systems are one of the major concerns for worldwide manufacturing companies. With the growth of emerging technologies, protecting large-scale Critical Infrastructures has become a considerable research topic in the past decade. Nowadays, software used to monitor Industrial Control Systems might be malicious and cause harm not only to physical processes but also to people working in industrial environments. To that end, integrating safety and security in Industrial Control Systems requires a well-developed understanding of malware-based cyber attacks.

In this paper, we present a comparative analysis framework of ICS Malware in a bi-layered approach: A cyber threat intelligence layer based on the ICS cyber kill chain and a hybrid analysis layer based on a static and dynamic analysis of ICS malware. We evaluated our proposed method by experimenting five well-known ICS malware: Stuxnet, Havex, BlackEnergy2, CrashOverride, and TRISIS. Our comparative analysis results show different and similar strategies used by each ICS malware to disrupt the ICS environment.

**Keywords:** Industrial control system · Malware · Cyber attack · Hybrid analysis · ICS cyber kill chain

## 1 Introduction

The industrial revolution in the 21st century has created a plethora of cyber-physical attacks against plants and critical infrastructures. They are one of the significant threats to the public and private sectors. The ICS threat landscape has changed thoroughly, and the adversaries are becoming increasingly numerous [10,21]. The CIA security characteristics, known as Confidentiality, Integrity, and Availability, are the most crucial goals of cybersecurity. In contrast, their priority level differs from the Information Technology (IT) to the Operation Technology (OT) networks. The principal concern of IT is data protection, while safety and


S. Katsikas et al. (Eds.): ESORICS 2021 Workshops, LNCS 13106, pp. 496–511, 2022.
https://doi.org/10.1007/978-3-030-95484-0_29

availability are OT's priorities. Targeting Critical Infrastructures (CIs) such as power plants or gas pipelines damages industrial devices, physical processes and exposes people working in the manufacturing industry to safety issues. Therefore, the safety and security of ICSs turned out into a high level of importance for the industrial environment. Malware targeting industrial plants are becoming bolder with a destructive capability to damage industrial devices [17]. Legacy industrial control systems are known to be insecure since they are not built with a security-by-design approach. The convergence between IT and OT networks and the robust integration of the Industrial Internet of Things (IIoT) exposes ICS systems to potential cyber attacks [2].

Nowadays, ICS environments are prone to hardware and software vulnerabilities due to their lack of basic security requirements. Detecting malicious intrusion activities in ICS environments is a complex process to handle. In particular, ICS malware targeting specific industrial devices, also known as *ICS-tailored malware*. Identifying these types of illegitimate ICS software is a challenging task for industrial companies and ICS security teams. Moreover, understanding modern ICS malware requires advanced knowledge of the supporting infrastructure. Therefore, the adversaries have a broader window to compromise ICS devices because each cyber attack targets a particular ICS device. To help identify the behavior of these types of malicious intrusion activities, we are motivated to investigate existing ICS-tailored malware in the wild over the past decade through a comparative analysis.

In this context, prior works cover different aspects related to modeling and analysis of malicious industrial intrusions [4,5,13,16,22]. However, existing works cannot illustrate the detailed analysis of ICS malware attacks. Ani et al. [5] reviewed the cybersecurity issues in critical industrial infrastructure, the authors provided a taxonomical presentation of ICS cybersecurity issues and potential mitigation techniques. Similarly, in [13], the authors presented a comprehensive analysis of cyber security issues for ICS. In particular, different adversarial ICS threats, attacks, and existing solutions to secure such systems. Alladi et al. [4] presented case studies on major ICS attacks in the last 20 years. For each of these attacks, the authors described the attack methodology used and suggested potential mitigation techniques. In [16], the authors carried out a comparative analysis of three malware targeting operational technology systems. However, the authors only considered finding similar attack properties at a high level between ICS malware and discussed possible mitigation strategies based on these similarities. However, they did not consider each ICS malware's unique characteristics and behaviors, and their proposed method to prevent similar cyber attacks in the future cannot guarantee that the threats will be fully identified.

To the best of our knowledge, we provide an exhaustive comparative analysis framework of ICS malware for the first time. Our work also introduces a taxonomy of ICS malware that provides a systematic approach to categorize the malicious intrusion activity in the ICS environment. During our analysis, we explore five well-known ICS-tailored malware: *Stuxnet*, *Havex*, *BlackEnergy2*, *CrashOverride*, and *TRISIS*. Moreover, we provide a security analysis evaluation to learn about the similarities and differences between ICS malware. Our proposed comparative framework can develop a set of expectations for future ICS malware-based cyber attacks. Furthermore, we believe that learning from previous ICS cyber attacks can help to provide a better defense mechanism for ICS cybersecurity.

**Research Questions.** Throughout our paper, we emphasize the practical usefulness of comparing ICS malware by answering the following research questions:

- *RQ1. What is our understanding of the existing ICS malware threats and their development during the past decade?*
- *RQ2. How do the adversaries operate in OT networks?*

We present the core of our comparative framework in two layers: the *Cyber Threat Intelligence Layer* and the *Hybrid Analysis Layer*. In the *Cyber Threat Intelligence Layer*, we comparatively model existing ICS malware using the ICS Cyber Kill Chain model [6]. In the *Hybrid Analysis Layer*, we analyze each ICS malware's main features and behaviors. Then, we provide a set of comparative analysis to describe and explain the consequences of ICS malware-based cyber attacks.

**Contribution.** The novelty and contributions of our work are summarized as follows:

- We develop an original comparative analysis framework for ICS malware in a bi-layered approach: the *Cyber Threat Intelligence Layer* and the *Hybrid Analysis Layer*.
- We provide a classification of ICS malware based on the targeted system.
- We evaluate our proposed framework for five well-known ICS malware in the past decade: *Stuxnet*, *Havex*, *BlackEnergy2*, *CrashOverride*, and *TRISIS*.
- From the outcomes of our results, we provide a set of comparative analysis to understand the strategies used for each ICS malware.

**Organization.** The remainder of this paper is organized as follows. In Sect. 2, we provide an overview of the fundamental concepts of cyber threat intelligence and malware analysis for industrial environments. In Sect. 3, we present our method for a comparative analysis of ICS malware. Then, we evaluate our proposed framework using five experimental ICS malware in Sect. 4. Finally, Sect. 5 concludes the paper.

## 2 Background

In the manufacturing industry, the Purdue Model [29] is the reference model of IT and OT, illustrating the architecture of ICS. The Purdue model consists of five zones: Enterprise Zone, demilitarized Zone, Manufacturing Zone, Cell/Area Zone, and Safety Zone, including six levels of operations across these zones. The systems with similar functions or requirements are in the same zone with different levels [23]. Different characteristics between the IT environment and control systems environment open new security challenges to professionals and organizations, leading to various attacks [14]. According to Kaspersky Lab's Industrial CERT report [9], industrial malware are exponentially growing, and organized cyber attacks are increasingly common. Consequently, their detection becomes difficult. The same laboratory confirmed that the risk of chance infections between computers on corporate networks and those on industrial networks are equal [20]. In this section, we state the background of cyber threat intelligence for the industrial environment that is useful to understand the *Cyber Threat Intelligence Layer* of our proposed framework (Sect. 2.1). Then, we overview the fundamental concepts of industrial malware analysis (Sect. 2.2).

## 2.1 Cyber Threat Intelligence for Industrial Environment

To protect critical infrastructures from potential cyber attacks, we need to understand the life cycle of malicious intrusion activity. Cyber threat intelligence is the process of gathering a complete understanding of a cyber threat posed by an adversary. Different approaches enable the description and characterization of such threats in the ICS environment. Examples include the ATT&CK for ICS knowledge base model that consists of understanding the tactics and techniques used by an adversary within an ICS network [3], and the ICS cyber kill chain model [6], which is an extension of the cyber kill chain for IT networks [19]. In our paper, we rely on the ICS cyber kill chain. It is a two-stage-based ICS threat model that describes an ICS malware intrusion. The first stage of an ICS cyber attack represents a cyber intrusion preparation stage and consists of five phases that could be mapped to a traditional cyber kill chain [19]. These phases are: (i) planning, (ii) preparation, (iii) Cyber intrusion, (iv) management and enablement, and (v) development and execution. Based on the knowledge gained in the first stage, the adversary can develop and test a capability over an infrastructure to execute the ICS attack against the victim. The second stage is a mapping of the first stage of the ICS Cyber Kill Chain. It represents an ICS attack development and execution and consists of three phases: (i) attack development and tuning, (ii) validation, and (iii) ICS attack.

## 2.2 Industrial Malware Analysis

The growth of ICS malware-based cyber attacks triggered the need to analyze ICS malware samples. However, performing such analysis in industrial networks might not guarantee their safety and could accidentally harm third parties. Therefore, we have to guarantee a *safe*, *controlled* and *isolated* environment for exploring ICS Malware behaviors. Cybersecurity researchers from both academia and industry can rely on sandboxing technology to satisfy these conditions. It provides a better security mechanism to analyze ICS malware behaviors.

To that end, we rely on two different approaches to analyze ICS malware [24]: Static analysis and Dynamic analysis. The static analysis aims to gather static-related information of ICS malware without its execution. We use the control flow and data flow analysis to conclude the functionality of the malware. We apply different techniques to extract static ICS features: String analysis, reverse engineering and fingerprinting. However, the standalone static feature extraction is not effective in analyzing the complete behavior of ICS malware. The second approach is dynamic analysis, and it is an efficient way to identify the functionality of a malicious process. The dynamic analysis focuses on gathering dynamic-related information of the ICS malware during its execution. Dynamic analysis techniques include function call analysis, execution control such as debugging, flow tracking, and tracing. In addition, we can supervise and monitor the network traffic and monitor the interaction of the ICS malware with the executing environment. In our framework, we use sandboxing technology to analyze our ICS malware samples. Moreover, we leverage both static and dynamic analysis to increase the performance and accuracy of extracting hybrid ICS malware features.

## 3 A Framework for Comparative Analysis

In this section, we present our comparative analysis framework for ICS malware. We define the proposed methodology in a bi-layered approach for a set of $n$ industrial malware, and Fig. 1 illustrates these layers. We model in the *Cyber Threat Intelligence Layer* (Sect. 3.2) the industrial malware using the ICS Cyber Kill Chain model. Afterward, we perform in the *Hybrid Analysis Layer* (Sect. 3.3) a static and dynamic analysis for the given ICS malware. Then, we handle both results from these layers to a comparative analysis process (Sect. 3.4).

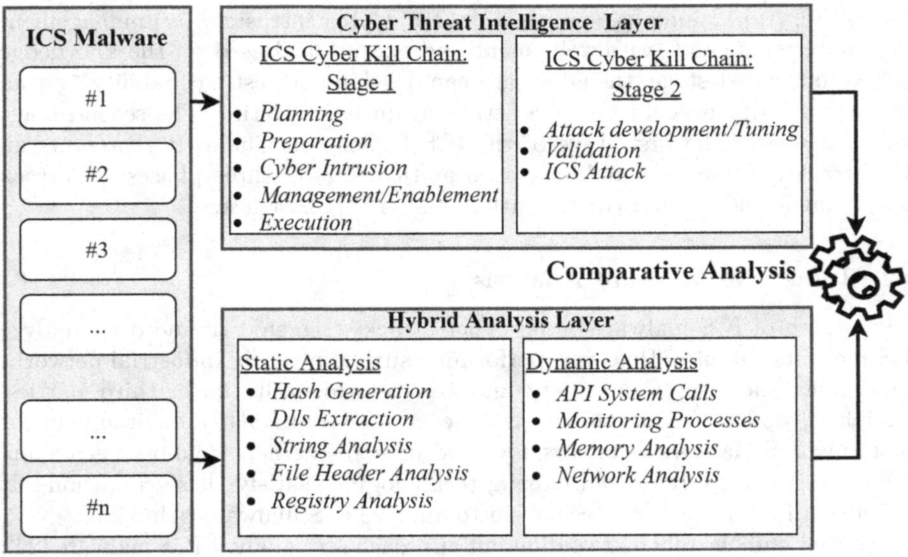


**Fig. 1.** Proposed comparative framework for ICS malware

### 3.1 ICS Malware Classification

The increased number of ICS malware in the wild has attracted research interest for the scientific community [18,28]. Therefore, the most common way to understand ICS malware is to classify them by targeted systems [1]. As depicted in Fig. 2, we categorize ICS malware in two broad categories: *Non-Targeted ICS malware* and *Targeted ICS malware.*

*Non-Targeted ICS malware* are not designed to target and gain access to ICS environments. Their structure is similar to classical malware, and they mainly target the IT network operating in an ICS environment. However, with the convergence of the IT and OT networks, the non-targeted ICS malware could indirectly compromise the OT networks and disrupt the ICS's normal state.

The main functionality of *Targeted ICS malware* is to gain a foothold in the industrial environment. In this case, the adversaries target the ICS operators by delivering ICS-themed malware or ICS-tailored malware. ICS-themed malware are disguised as legitimate ICS software such as Human Machine Interface (HMI) installers, and they are available from public internet domains. ICS-themed malware are specifically designed to fool the ICS operators and infiltrate the OT network. Recently, there have been very few public cases of ICS-themed malware [1].

An interesting category of ICS malware intrusions includes *ICS-tailored malware.* They are designed to target particular components of the ICS-related environments, such as Programmable Logic Controllers (PLCs) and Safety Instrumented Systems (SIS). In addition, it is challenging to detect ICS-tailored malware because they exploit vulnerabilities of a specific ICS-product. However, ICS-tailored malware are costly in development, and the adversary needs proper ICS knowledge to develop such malware.

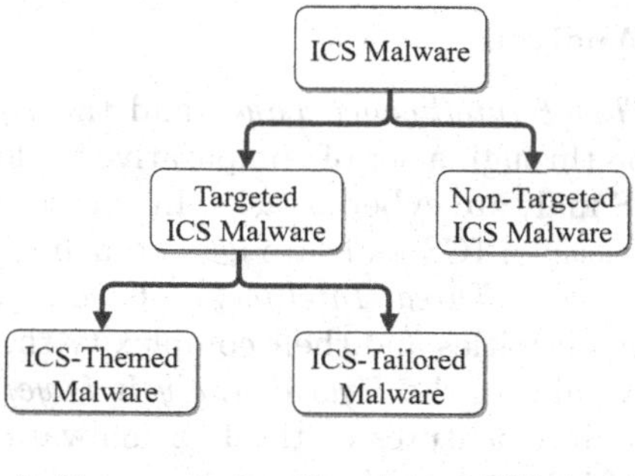


**Fig. 2.** Proposed classification of ICS malware

### 3.2 Cyber Threat Intelligence Layer

The *Cyber Threat Intelligence Layer* aims to understand the adversary's tactics, techniques, and procedures to target a victim. We model each of $n$ industrial malware using the two stages of the ICS Cyber Kill Chain [6]. In the first stage, we explore the cyber intrusion preparation and execution of the malicious activity. We categorize this stage as an intelligence operation that an adversary performs to gather important information about the ICS environment. In the second stage, we analyze the ICS cyber attack development and execution through different activities. In this stage, the adversary can deploy his capabilities to compromise the industrial processes.

### 3.3 Hybrid Analysis Layer

For a set of $n$ ICS malware, we perform in the *Hybrid Analysis Layer* a static and dynamic analysis in a black box setting to gather information about the industrial intrusion activity [24]. We use COTS (Commercial-Off-The-Shelf) malware analysis solution enabling the hybrid analysis, namely Cuckoo Sandbox [7]. It is an open-source automated malware analysis solution that includes static and dynamic analysis of malicious code inside an isolated environment. Cuckoo can analyze different malicious files, trace API calls and the general behavior of the malware, dump and analyze the network traffic, and perform advanced memory analysis. By combining both static and dynamic analysis, we increase the rate of feature extraction. In static analysis, we dissect the ICS malware to extract static features such as Dynamic Linked Libraries (DLLs), file headers, and registries. Then, we perform dynamic analysis to investigate ICS malware behaviors and functionalities. In the dynamic analysis, we extract dynamic features to generate the execution graph for each ICS malware. Dynamic features are extracted by monitoring the processes and analyzing the dropped files. Network analysis can also be applied during dynamic execution to capture malicious packets. The main functionality of the *Hybrid Analysis Layer* is to gather the maximum of information associated with the behavior of ICS malware.

### 3.4 Comparative Analysis

Based on the *Cyber Threat Intelligence Layer* and the *Hybrid Analysis Layer*, we present and describe through a set of comparative tables the similarities and differences between ICS malware cyber attacks. In this process, we compare and evaluate each characteristic of ICS malware using our framework to understand their behaviors. In the *Cyber Threat Intelligence Layer*, we compare the industrial malicious intrusion activities and their complexity through different phases of the ICS Cyber Kill Chain. In the *Hybrid Analysis Layer*, we analyze the relationship between the hybrid features of the ICS malware to gather knowledge about the occurrence of industrial cyber attacks.

## 4 Evaluation and Results

In this section, we overview the industrial malware used in this paper and present the results of our comparative analysis. In our study, we consider $n = 5$, and we evaluate our comparative analysis framework for five well-known ICS Malware obtained from public sources.

### 4.1 Experimental Industrial Malware

We devote this subsection to describe the experimental ICS malware used in our comparative framework. In particular, *Stuxnet*, *Havex*, *BlackEnergy2*, *CrashOverride*, and *TRISIS*.

**Stuxnet.** It was the first public ICS malware discovered in 2010. It has a physical payload capable of destroying a nuclear enrichment center and is one of the most sophisticated malware with several features and components [15]. It is also a worm that exploited four 0-days in Windows machines and targeted industrial devices by reprogramming their PLCs (Programmable Logic Controllers). From a high-level structure, the malware contains three main modules: a worm executing the payload attack, a link file for automatic execution of propagated copies of the worm, and a rootkit for hiding malicious files and processes. We consider Stuxnet as the first well-known PLC rootkit.

**Havex.** As part of an espionage campaign, *Havex* is a Remote Access Trojan (RAT). It targets energy grid operators and impacts thousands of critical infrastructures over the United States and Europe [25]. Given the wide-scale of its targets, *Havex* used three principal attack vectors shifted over time: Watering hole attack, email spear Phishing, and trojanizing software downloaded from ICS vendors [8].

**BlackEnergy2.** It is a malware family expanded over time from an HTTP-based botnet for DDoS (Distributed Deny of Service) attacks to a plugin-based malware with a robust modular architecture [26]. *BlackEnergy2* targeted industrial control systems and was involved in the recent Ukraine power grid attack. It contains exploits for particular types of HMI (Human-Machine Interface) applications such as Siemens SIMATIC and GE CIMPLICITY. The structure and flow of *BlackEnergy2* is a dropper that uses rootkit/process-injection capabilities. The *BlackEnergy2* framework provides extra functionalities for network scanning, fraud, and cyber-espionage. It relies on local files execution, self-updates with C&C servers, downloading/executing remote files, and die or destroy commands execution.

**CrashOverride.** It is also known as Industroyer. It is more sophisticated than *BlackEnergy2. CrashOverride* is the first ICS malware designed to attack industrial protocols used in electrical substations [11]. It is a modular malware that supports four different ICS protocols. The main backdoor is one of the core components of *CrashOverride*. It provides access to the industrial environment. The initial backdoor installs the launcher module inside the infected system and enables four payloads targeting specific industrial communications protocols (IEC 60870-5-101, IEC 60870-5-104, IEC 61850, and OLE for Process Control Data Access).

**TRISIS.** It is the first ICS malware targeting Schneider Electric's Triconex safety instrumented system (SIS) [12]. It compromises the security of SIS by enabling the replacement of ladder logic. Using possible social engineering techniques, the adversaries injected the main dropper of *TRISIS* to the engineering workstation of SIS with logging capabilities. Afterward, they obtained a direct interaction and remote control of the targeted SIS device, leading to compromise its safety. It is worth mentioning that *TRISIS* functionality depends on a full understanding of Triconex Safety Instrumented Systems.

### 4.2 Cyber Threat Intelligence Layer Evaluation

In what follows, we evaluate our five ICS malware using the ICS cyber kill chain model [6]. Across both ICS cyber kill chain stages, we comparatively analyze different malicious threat actors and their operations in IT and OT networks.

**ICS Cyber Kill Chain - Stage 1.** We map the first stage of the cyber threat intelligence layer to the classical cyber kill chain [19]. Then, we evaluate our industrial malware by comparing different malicious activities for each phase across the first stage of the ICS cyber kill chain.

During the *planning and reconnaissance phase*, each adversary conducts his way of gathering information from the victim given different types of industrial targets. In the *Stuxnet* case, the adversaries stole two valid digital certificates, then conducted a reconnaissance of the potential computing environment in the facility, such as the design documents of the ICS target network. For *Havex* cyber attack, the attackers gathered information and collected documents of the targeted victims and their ICS vendors. Whereas in *TRISIS* and *BlackEnergy2* malware, the adversaries conducted an open-source intelligence of the targeted IT and OT Network. In the *CrashOverride* cyber attack, the planning and reconnaissance phase is unknown. However, given the modular architecture and design of *CrashOverride*, we believe that the adversaries gathered knowledge about the industrial protocols used in the victim's electric power systems [27].

In the *preparation phase*, the adversaries performed various types of attacks by weaponizing specific files containing an exploit or targeting potential victims inside the facility. Stuxnet attackers have possibly purchased 0-days from the black market [30]. Then, they developed the *Stuxnet* Windows Rootkit and the *Stuxnet* PLC Rootkit. Afterward, they signed their malicious code with the two previous valid digital certificates to evade antivirus detection [30]. Alternatively, *Havex* and *BlackEnergy2* adversaries performed a spear-phishing mail attack by sending malicious PDF in mail attachments to the victim. The *BlackEnergy2* malware infiltrated the ICS environment easily while *Havex* malware needed an additional delivery method. Moving forward, *Havex* adversaries compromised energy-related websites of victim's ICS vendors using a watering hole attack and redirected the victim to another compromised website hosting the hello exploit kit. Finally, they accessed the ICS vendor's websites and injected the malicious code into legitimate software updates. In the *CrashOverride* attack, the adversaries leveraged a phishing campaign to capture sensitive ICS credentials. The *TRISIS* attackers performed a different approach by reverse-engineering the SIS software of targeted victims and developing the corresponding ICS malware.

Throughout the *cyber intrusion phase*, the main objective is to gain initial access to the victim's network. In the *Stuxnet* cyber attack, the adversaries delivered the malware using an insider by infecting a third party who has access to the victim's facility. The removable drive was then used as support for the delivery to spread *Stuxnet* over the LAN network (MS10-061 and MS08-067 vulnerability). Once *Stuxnet* propagates inside the industrial facility (MS10-046 vulnerability), it infects a specific device of SIMATIC Field PG (Industrial Programming Device for PLCs). Then, *Stuxnet* installs the Windows Rootkit (MS10-73 and MS10-92). With stolen VPN credentials, *BlackEnergy2* attackers infected HMIs victims through the crafted archive in the email attachment. The capabilities of *BlackEnergy2* include downloading and executing remote files, executing local files, updating the malware, and die on command. Similarly, *CrashOverride* attackers created an attacker account using the stolen VPN credentials and consequently pivoting to the ICS environment. For the *Havex* case, the victim downloads either the PDF in mail attachments or the trojanized software. In the *TRISIS* cyber attack, the delivery method developed by the adversaries is still unknown.

In the *management and enablement phase*, the adversary establishes a command and control process to ensure his persistence and therefore update and execute the malicious code. *Stuxnet* connects to a Command and Control server for updating and executing the malicious code. For *Havex*, the command and control nodes are established between the adversary servers and the victim. In the *CrashOverride* case, the attacker account is operational and connected to the control systems. The *BlackEnergy2* adversaries used privilege escalation and lateral movement inside the network to enable the command and control servers. However, in the TRISIS cyber attack, the command and control process is still unknown.

In the *execution phase*, which is the last phase of the first stage of the ICS cyber kill chain, the adversary already has the knowledge and capability to compromise the OT network. *Stuxnet* injected the PLC rootkit after finding the suitable Industrial Programming Device. Then, infected the machines outside the target organization. *Havex* software modules are installed and executed: the OPC scanning module and the network scanning module. The adversary gathers the victim's system information through the OPC standard. The *CrashOverride* malware remotely pivoted to the ICS through the historian, a centralized database in the control system. The *BlackEnergy2* malware established authenticated access to the SCADA workstations. For *TRISIS*, the adversary identified and had access to the target system, which is ready to communicate with the SIS.

**ICS Cyber Kill Chain - Stage 2.** In the second stage of the ICS cyber kill chain, the adversary performs the ICS attack development and execution using the knowledge and capabilities acquired from the first stage. We mention that although *Havex* malware is not designed to disrupt or destroy industrial systems, the data collected from the victim's industrial devices could help design and develop specific cyber attacks. Therefore, we consider Havex as a Stage 1 malware-based intrusion attack.

In the *attack development and tuning phase*, the adversary develops a tailored capability to target specific ICS devices. *Stuxnet's* adversaries developed the latest version of the malware, while in the *CrashOverride* cyber attack, the adversaries developed an electric transmission protocol capable of compromising electric power systems. The malicious actors of *BlackEnergy2* developed a backdoor for remote administration of SCADA workstations. For *TRISIS*, the attackers developed the malware with logic and ladder replacement. Then, they disguised the *TRISIS* malware as Trilogger (Software for analyzing SIS logs). During the *validation phase*, the adversary tests his capability on a similar ICS scenario to validate his malicious intrusion. However, this phase is challenging and requires the acquisition of costly ICS devices. Moreover, identifying the validation phase for ICS malware is very difficult due to the complexity of the cyber attacks and the availability of evidence.

In the *ICS attack phase*, the adversary disrupts and compromises the ICS environment. *Stuxnet* sends updates through the Command and Control servers and modifies the code in the PLCs. Afterward, the ICS attack is executed by slowing down and speeding up the motor to different rates at different times, causing the centrifuge overpressure. The *BlackEnergy2* adversaries executed the ICS cyber attack by opening the circuit breakers through the HMIs, which led to the power outage across multiple substations. The *CrashOverride* attackers created a malicious service to compromise configuration files of HMIs, impacting the electric grid operations. For the *TRISIS* cyber attack, the ICS malware targets the memory location and uploads the initializing code. Then *TRISIS* uploads and replaces the logic ladder, entering the SIS into a fail-safe mode.

### 4.3 Hybrid Analysis Layer Evaluation

This layer aims to perform a hybrid analysis for the given ICS malware samples. And thus, through static and dynamic analysis. First, we extract the static features of each ICS malware. Then we gather knowledge about the behavior of our ICS malware samples using dynamic analysis.

**Static ICS Malware Analysis.** For each ICS malware sample, we extracted the imported dynamic linked libraries. Analyzing such libraries helps us understand each ICS malware's behavior during the execution of the malicious code. We found that `KERNEL32.dll` is a very common DLL used by our samples. It contains core functionality such as manipulation of files, memory, hardware, and access. *Stuxnet* uses more linked libraries than other ICS malware. However, all of them except *TRISIS* have some similar DLLs such as `SHELL32.dll` and `USER32.dll` libraries. `SHELL32.dll` is a Windows shell commonly used for API functions and loaded into the main memory, while `USER32.dll` contains Windows API functions related to the user interface. We found that *TRISIS* imports only two DLL files: `MSVCR90.dll` and `KERNEL32.dll`. `MSVCR90.dll` is a part of Windows out-of-box experience, mainly used to setup a process and initiate a configuration to prepare the users for the first use of a specific software product (Schneider's Triconex SIS software). On the other hand, *Havex* is the only ICS malware that imports `GDI32.dll` and `COMCTL32.dll` libraries. Indeed, Havex uses `GDI32.dll` to export Windows Graphics Device Interface (GDI) functions for possible spear-phishing through PDFs. These functions are also used by `COMCTL32.dll` which is responsible for standard Windows controls. A particular characteristic of BlackEnergy2 is the import of `WINHTTP.dll`, resulting that *BlackEnergy2* uses essential system files. Furthermore, given its predecessor, an HTTP-based botnet, we can state that *BlackEnergy2* operates under the Windows HTTP services. *CrashOverride* leverages cryptographic messaging functions using `CRYPT32.dll` to encrypt its malicious industrial communications through the ICS network.

**Dynamic ICS Malware Analysis.** We explore the behavior of our ICS malware samples by executing them in a safe, controlled, and isolated environment using the Cuckoo sandbox solution [7]. Then, we generate the execution graph of each ICS malware sample and compare the percentage of their execution across different categories. In Table 1, we report the percentage of each ICS malware execution by categories.

**Table 1.** Dynamic graph execution for each ICS malware

| Categories (%) | **S** | **H** | **B** | **C** | **T** |
|---|---|---|---|---|---|
| Exception | 1.08 | 0 | 0 | 0.18 | 1.43 |
| Resource | 0 | 0.52 | 0 | 0.36 | 4.29 |
| Process | 25.27 | 2.79 | 31.43 | 5.83 | 8.57 |
| System | **51.61** | 5.36 | **41.43** | 31.33 | 31.43 |
| Registry | 9.14 | 17.02 | 11.43 | **35.52** | **50** |
| File | 4.3 | 5.88 | 10 | 6.74 | 2.86 |
| Synchronisation | 6.99 | **66.14** | 5.71 | 4.55 | 1.43 |
| Object linking | 0 | 0.22 | 0 | 0 | 0 |
| User interface | 1.61 | 1.94 | 0 | 0 | 0 |
| Services | 0 | 0.03 | 0 | 0 | 0 |
| Network | 0 | 0.09 | 0 | 15.48 | 0 |

**S**: Stuxnet **H**: Havex **B**: BlackEnergy2 **C**: CrashOverride **T**: TRISIS

The dynamic ICS malware analysis shows that the high execution of *Stuxnet* and *BlackEnergy2* occurs in the operating system, while *CrashOverride* and *TRISIS* have high execution in the registry. In particular, *TRISIS* attack was focused on Schneider Electrics Triconex safety instrumented system (SIS). The high execution of the malware was in the registry. For the *Stuxnet* case, we explain the high execution on the system because most of the vulnerabilities exploited by *Stuxnet* targeted ICSs through the operating system. On the opposite, a low percentage of *Havex* execution is on the system because *Havex* targets the victims using cyber-espionage against energy suppliers. The results gathered through dynamic execution shows that each ICS malware targets a specific category of execution. Therefore, we are facing tailored ICS cyber attacks.

We summarize the main characteristics of each ICS malware in Table 2. We remark that the size of malicious code is decreasing, and bypassing antiviruses is no more a challenge for ICS malware authors. Moreover, ICS malware-based cyber attacks target specific industrial devices. We also remark that industrial malware with a physical payload do not perform actions on files and registries.

**Table 2.** Comparison of ICS Malware characteristics

| | **S** | **H** | **B** | **C** | **T** |
|---|---|---|---|---|---|
| Size | 1.2 MB | 2.4 MB | 717.0 KB | 10.5 KB | 21.0 KB |
| Date of disclosure | July, 2010 | February, 2013 | October, 2014 | June, 2017 | December, 2017 |
| Type | Worm | RAT | Trojan | Backdoor | TRISIS malware |
| Number of 0-Days | 5 | 0 | 0 | 0 | 1 |
| Number of rootkits | 3 | 0 | 1 | 0 | 1 |
| Targeted systems | Siemens Simatic S7-300 PLC | ICS Software | HMIs products of ICS | ICS Protocols for electrical engineering and power system automation | Schneider Electric's Triconex SIS |
| Payload type | Physical | Software | Software | Software | Physical |
| Targeted countries | Iran | USA and Europe | Asia and Europe | Ukraine | Saudi Arabia |
| Antivirus Bypass | Two certificates (Realtek and Jmicron) | Certificate looks like signed by IBM | code obfuscation | N/A | N/A |
| File modification | No | Yes | Yes | No | No |
| File deletion | No | Yes | No | Yes | No |
| Registry modification | No | yes | No | No | No |
| Registry deletion | No | yes | No | No | No |
| Number of sections | 7 | 5 | 5 | 5 | 4 |
| Number of imported Dlls | 16 | 8 | 8 | 7 | 2 |
| Number of functions | 3359 | 79 | 164 | 46 | 74 |

**S**: Stuxnet **H**: Havex **B**: BlackEnergy2 **C**: CrashOverride **T**: TRISIS

On the other hand, the number of 0-days and rootkits decreased in the past decade. Additionally, the number of imported DLLs and functions used by each ICS malware decreased, thus confirming the lightweight process of industrial malware. The comparative results show that malware authors are lightweighting their malicious code while maintaining physical damage to ICSs.

### 4.4 Security Discussion

The interconnection between IT and OT networks brings new security challenges for industrial practitioners, such as ICS malware-based cyber attacks. Therefore, we need a better understanding of the general behavior of these cyber attacks. The necessity to adopt ICS cybersecurity standards such as IEC 62443, BSI Grundschutz, and VDI/VDE 2182 cannot entirely prevent the ICS environment from being compromised. Indeed, the experimental results of our study showed that most of existing ICS malware in the wild target specific industrial devices or software: *Stuxnet* (Siemens Simatic S7-300 PLC), *TRISIS* (Schneider Electric's Triconex SIS), *Havex* (ICS software), *BlackEnergy2* (HMI products). Therefore, each organization must consider a specific defense-in-depth strategy according to its existing ICS architecture. Moreover, since most ICS Malware are IT-based malware, they infect corporate networks before infecting the industrial ones. To that end, We can claim that ICS Malware are built upon the combination of inside knowledge, advanced skills, and vast resources. From the outcome of our investigation, it is possible to indicate that future ICS malware-based cyber attacks will likely focus on specific industrial devices. Therefore, the authors of ICS malicious code will easily evade most of the existing defense mechanisms in IT and OT networks.

## 5 Conclusions

In our work, we presented the first comparative analysis framework of ICS Malware cyber attacks in a bi-layered approach. We have comparatively analyzed five well-known ICS malware from two different points of view: A *Cyber Threat Intelligence Layer* and a *Hybrid Analysis Layer*. The evaluation of our comparative analysis framework demonstrated that performing a cyber threat intelligence is helpful to understand the general behavior of ICS malware. On the other hand, the hybrid ICS malware analysis reinforces our study to correlate the obtained results. Furthermore, our investigation can help to develop a standardized set of expectations for the next generations of ICS malware-based cyber attacks. We can use our approach to ascend from case studies to general theoretical models. Our comparative analysis framework for ICS malware demonstrates that the best defense mechanism is to use proven security best practices for ICS cybersecurity and learn from previous cyber attacks.

## References

1. Malware in Modern ICS: Understanding Impact While Avoiding Hype. https://www.powermag.com/malware-in-modern-ics-understanding-impact-while-avoiding-hype/
2. Alcaraz, C.: Secure interconnection of IT-OT networks in industry 4.0. In: Gritzalis, D., Theocharidou, M., Stergiopoulos, G. (eds.) Critical Infrastructure Security and Resilience. ASTSA, pp. 201–217. Springer, Cham (2019). https://doi.org/10.1007/978-3-030-00024-0_11

3. Alexander, O., Belisle, M., Steele, J.: Mitre ATT&Ck® for Industrial Control Systems: Design and Philosophy. The MITRE Corporation, Bedford (2020)
4. Alladi, T., Chamola, V., Zeadally, S.: Industrial control systems: cyberattack trends and countermeasures. Comput. Commun. **155**, 1–8 (2020)
5. Ani, U.P.D., He, H.M., Tiwari, A.: Review of cybersecurity issues in industrial critical infrastructure: manufacturing in perspective. J. Cyber Secur. Technol. **1**(1), 32–74 (2017). https://doi.org/10.1080/23742917.2016.1252211. https://www.tandfonline.com/doi/abs/10.1080/23742917.2016.1252211
6. Assante, M., Lee, R.: Information Security Reading Room The Industrial Control System Cyber Kill Chain. Sans Institute, pp. 1–22 (2015). www.lockheedmartin.com/content/dam/lockheed/data/corporate/documents/LM-White-Paper-Intel-Driven-Defense.pdf
7. Bremer, J.: Cuckoo Sandbox - open source automated malware analysis (2013). https://media.blackhat.com/us-13/US-13-Bremer-Mo-Malware-Mo-Problems-Cuckoo-Sandbox-WP.pdf
8. Byrum, S.: InfoSec Reading Room the Impact of the Sarbanes Oxley Act on IT (2003). https://www.sans.org/reading-room/whitepapers/casestudies/impact-sarbanes-oxley-act-security-1344
9. De Souza, M.E.: An alternative to the variation of the fine structure constant. Phys. Essays **24**(4), 472–474 (2011)
10. Dragos: The ICS Landscape and Threat Activity Groups, pp. 11–45 (2020), https://dragos.com/wp-content/uploads/The-ICS-Threat-Landscape.pdf
11. Dragos Inc.: CRASHOVERRIDE: Analysis of the Threat to Electric Grid Operations. Technical report (2017). https://www.dragos.com/wp-content/uploads/CrashOverride-01.pdf
12. Dragos Inc.: TRISIS Malware-Analysis of Safety System Targeted Malware. Dragos, pp. 1–19 (2017). https://www.energy.senate.gov/public/index.cfm/files/serve?File_id=40B2ED59-D34E-47C3-B9E2-1E8D030C5748
13. Drias, Z., Serhrouchni, A., Vogel, O.: Analysis of cyber security for industrial control systems. In: 2015 International Conference on Cyber Security of Smart Cities, Industrial Control System and Communications, SSIC 2015 - Proceedings (2015). https://doi.org/10.1109/SSIC.2015.7245330. https://ieeexplore.ieee.org/abstract/document/7245330/
14. Fabro, M.: Control Systems Cyber Security: Defense-in- Depth Strategies Control. Idaho National Laboratory, USA, pp. 1–30, May 2007. https://www.osti.gov/biblio/923499
15. Falliere, N., Murchu, L.O., Chien, E.: W32. Stuxnet Dossier, Symantec Security Response, Version 1.4, February 2011. Symantec Security Response 4 February, pp. 1–69 (2011), 20 September 2015
16. Geiger, M., Bauer, J., Masuch, M., Franke, J.: An analysis of black energy 3, Crashoverride, and Trisis, three malware approaches targeting operational technology systems. In: IEEE International Conference on Emerging Technologies and Factory Automation, ETFA 2020, September, pp. 1537–1543 (2020). https://doi.org/10.1109/ETFA46521.2020.9212128
17. Ginter, A.: The Top 20 Cyber Attacks Against Industrial Control Systems. Waterfall, stronger than firewalls, May, p. 3 (2018). https://waterfall-security.com/20-attacks/
18. Hemsley, K.E., Fisher, E.: History of Industrial Control System Cyber Incidents. INL/CON-18-44411-Revision-2, December, pp. 1–37 (2018). https://www.osti.gov/servlets/purl/1505628

19. Hutchins, E., Cloppert, M., Amin, R.: Intelligence-driven computer network defense informed by analysis of adversary campaigns and intrusion kill chains. In: 6th International Conference on Information Warfare and Security, ICIW 2011, July 2005, pp. 113–125 (2011)
20. Kaspersky Lab: Threat Landscape for Industrial Automation Systems in H1 2020. ICS Cert, pp. 1–27 (2020). https://ics-cert.kaspersky.com/reports/2020/09/24/threat-landscape-for-industrial-automation-systems-h1-2020/#_Toc49782409
21. Lab, K.: Threat landscape for industrial automation systems in the second half of 2020. AO Kaspersky Lab, 1997–2017, pp. 1–12 (2021). https://ics-cert.kaspersky.com/wp-content/uploads/sites/6/2017/03/KL-ICS-CERT_H2-2016_report_FINAL_EN.pdf
22. Mekdad, Y., Bernieri, G., Conti, M., Fergougui, A.E.: A threat model method for ICS malware: the TRISIS case. In: Proceedings of the 18th ACM International Conference on Computing Frontiers, pp. 221–228 (2021)
23. Obregon, L.: Information security reading room secure architecture for industrial control systems. SANS Instit. InfoSec GIAC (GSEC) Gold Certification **1**, 1–27 (2020)
24. Or-Meir, O., Nissim, N., Elovici, Y., Rokach, L.: Dynamic malware analysis in the modern era–a state of the art survey. ACM Comput. Surv. **52**(5), 1–48 (2019). https://doi.org/10.1145/3329786
25. Rrushi, J., Farhangi, H., Howey, C., Carmichael, K., Dabell, J.: A Quantitative Evaluation of the Target Selection of Havex ICS Malware Plugin, December 2015. https://pdfs.semanticscholar.org/18df/43ef1690b0fae15a36f770001160aefbc6c5.pdf
26. Shrivastava, S.: Analysis Report BlackEnergy-Malware for Cyber-Physical Attacks Malware for Cyber-Physical Attacks, May 2016. http://itrust.sutd.edu.sg
27. Slowik, J.: Anatomy of an attack: Detecting and defeating Crashoverride. Virus Bulletin 2018 Montreal, June 2017, pp. 1–23 (2018). https://www.virusbulletin.com/uploads/pdf/magazine/2018/VB2018-Slowik.pdf
28. Slowik, J.: Evolution of ICS Attacks and the Prospects for Future Disruptive Events. Ph.D. thesis (2019). https://www.dragos.com/resource/evolution-of-ics-attacks-and-the-prospects-for-future-disruptive-events/
29. Williams, T.J.: The Purdue enterprise reference architecture. Comput. Ind. **24**(2–3), 141–158 (1994). https://doi.org/10.1016/0166-3615(94)90017-5
30. Zetter, K.: Countdown to Zero Day: Stuxnet and the Launch of the World's First Digital Weapon. Broadway Books, New York (2014)

# 1st International Workshop on Cyber Defence Technologies and Secure Communications at the Network Edge (CDT&SECOMANE 2021)

# CDT&SECOMANE 2021 Preface

The increasing digitalization of the public and private sectors emphasizes the reliance on network and information systems on everyday life. Their pervasive interconnectedness is expanding the attack surface for malicious cyber activities. It is of particular interest to analyze which cyber defence technologies could lead to an information advantage, enabled in part by network-centric architectures and enhanced data fusion approaches. The instrumentalization of this advantage must consider a resilient communications infrastructure at the network edge. This edge is the last physical or logical boundary where all the external network integrations and interfaces happen. According to the new EU Cybersecurity Strategy, it will be critical that the Member States increase their ability to prevent and respond to cyber threats on such surfaces, which highlighted the need to boost the development of state-of-the-art cyber defence capabilities through different EU policies and instruments. A clear example of these intentions can be observed in the degree of ambition inherent in the European Defence Fund (EDF) on related topics, as with the case of the previous European Defence Industrial Development Programme (EDIDP), which demands cooperation between partners thorough a cross-sectorial and multi-stakeholder community. On the other hand, achieving the EU's digital strategic autonomy and thus digital sovereignty have become priorities, which require an overarching vision of the information and communications technology landscape and prompt necessary research priorities on related topics, where cyber defence stands out and demands joint multi-sectorial efforts. Theses urgent actions together with the emergence of innovative concepts in the field of secure communications, notably at the network edge, evidences a necessary coordination and synchronization to balance common interests and dual use endeavors. In this context, most of the EU cybersecurity and cyber defence forums are currently not cross-sectorial and therefore it is difficult to find dual-use related discussions to engage the civil and military research community.

In this context, the 1st International Workshop on Cyber Defence Technologies and Secure Communications at the Network Edge (CDT&SECOMANE 2021) aimed to close this gap by opening a forum where both communities exchange information for a mutual benefit. Hence, the 26th European Symposium on Research in Computer Security (ESORICS 2021) community could openly contribute and participate in cyber defence and secure network dual-use related discussions contributing to enrich and enlarge participation. The result is a collection of high-quality scientific contributions from leading-edge researchers in academia and industry, showing the latest research results in the targeted fields. This volume contains revised versions of the selected papers that were presented at CDT&SECOMANE 2021.

December 2021

Jorge Maestre Vidal
Marco Antonio Sotelo Monge
Salvador Llopis Sánchez
Gregorio Martínez Perez
Nicolai Stoianov
Roumen Daton Medenou Choumanof

# CDT&SECOMANE 2021 Organization

## General Chairs

| | |
|---|---|
| Jorge Maestre Vidal | Indra, Spain |
| Marco Antonio Sotelo Monge | Indra, Spain |
| Salvador Llopis Sánchez | Universitat Politecnica de Valencia, Spain |
| Gregorio Martínez Perez | University of Murcia, Spain |
| Nicolai Stoianov | Bulgarian Defence Institute, Bulgaria |
| Roumen Daton Medenou Choumanof | Indra, Spain |

## Program Committee

| | |
|---|---|
| Gerardo Ramis Pasqual de Riquelme | Indra, Spain |
| Ángel Leonardo Valdivieso Caraguay | Escuela Politécnica Nacional, Ecuador |
| Marco Manso | PARTICLE, Portugal |
| Joaquin Garcia-Alfaro | Telecom SudParis, France |
| Victor Villagrá González | Universidad Politécnica de Madrid, Spain |
| Giovanni Comande | Scuola Superiore Sant'Anna, Italy |
| Sergio Mauricio Martínez Monterrubio | Universidad Internacional de la Rioja, Spain |
| Alberto Huertas Celdran | University of Zurich, Switzerland |
| Lorena Isabel Barona López Escuela | Politécnica Nacional, Ecuador |
| Harald Schmidt | Fraunhofer FKIE, Germany |
| Marta Irene García Cid | Indra, Spain |
| Álvaro Luis Martínez | Auren, Spain |

# Framework Proposal to Measure the Stress as Adversarial Factor on Cyber Decision Making

David Sandoval Rodríguez-Bermejo[1,3], Jorge Maestre Vidal[2(✉)], and Juan Manuel Estévez Tapiador[3]

[1] Tarlogic, Madrid, Spain
david.sandoval@tarlogic.com
[2] Indra, Madrid, Spain
jmaestre@indra.es
[3] Universidad Carlos III de Madrid, Madrid, Spain
jestevez@inf.uc3m.es

**Abstract.** There are several factors that make cyber operations stressful, which include their complexity, unpredictability, and a continuum of decisions involving high risk and fast cost-benefit reasoning. Thus, in this context, defining a working methodology or framework to assess and quantify the impact of stress during decision making can be extremely useful both in real operations and in cyber exercises (to enhance decision making skills). Defining this framework is not a trivial task due to the complexity of stress and the innumerable subjective nuances associated with it, which correspond to the characteristics of each individual.

This paper presents stress understood as a disease and introduces the main current biometric systems that allow inferring and quantifying the stress level of an individual. Secondly, the main methodologies that allow to evaluate the stress level of a person are presented. Thirdly, a framework composed of five stages (monitoring, visualization, risk management, evaluation, decision making) is defined to model and standardize a methodology for assessing the level of stress in cyber-operations. Fourthly, a validation scenario is proposed to test the proposed framework. Finally, the procedure for the use of the methodology is defined and future directions for the continuation of this research are proposed.

**Keywords:** Cyber decision making · Stress as adversarial factor · Evaluation methodologies · Cyberoperations · Biometric systems

## 1 Introduction

Nowadays we live in a world in constant change where digitalization processes are becoming more and more important and are being taken to all levels of industry.

This research has received funding from the European Defence Industrial Development Programme (EDIDP) under the grant agreement Number EDIDP-CSAMN-SSC-2019-022-ECYSAP (European Cyber SituationalAwareness Platform).


S. Katsikas et al. (Eds.): ESORICS 2021 Workshops, LNCS 13106, pp. 517–536, 2022.
https://doi.org/10.1007/978-3-030-95484-0_30

Thus, in this new interconnected world, the factor of human decisions takes on a critical nuance due to the impact of the repercussions that bad decisions can entail.

Regardless of whether we work in military or industrial domains, the cognitive domain is directly dependent on the human factors that underpin the decisions made. Among the main causes that negatively affect the decision-making process, the following prevail: lack of information, stress and anxiety [1]. Although it is true that there is a strong interrelation between these factors, stress is the main risk associated with making bad decisions.

In the context of cybersecurity, due to the high level of digitization in today's society, operator stress [2], is a common, persistent and disabling effect of cyber operations and a major risk factor for performance, safety and employee burnout; which propagates through the cyber decision loop and requires in-depth related investigative action. Hence, as stated in [3] "*the process of decision making in and of itself can be stressful, such as when a decision involves high risk and its outcome is uncertain. Thus, the relationship between stress and decision making can be bidirectional because stress may affect the quality of the decision and also be evoked by the decision-making process*". In addition to this relationship between stress and decision making, a third variable comes into play: information. While possessing information is critical in any sector, this dimension takes on greater importance in the military context [4].

Thus, in the military context, a new concept appears called cybersituational awareness and defined in [5] as a process that allows us to perceive the elements of the environment within a spatial and temporal context in order to be able to infer their meaning and predict the projection of their state in the near future [6]. Among the possible methodologies existing in the current literature, what is known as Boyd's cycle or OODA loop (observe-oriented-decide-act) predominates to model acquisition process of cybersituational awareness. Originally designed to support decision-making in uncertain and chaotic environments, Boyd's cycle adapts the scientific method to solve the problems of identifying, selecting and executing countermeasures (or safeguards). Hence, the observation phase resembles the acquisition of preliminary factual knowledge; the guidance-decision stage seeks to propose the best hypothesis in the face of an incident; and, finally, the action stage aims to test and contrast the assumed hypothesis [7].

The objective of this paper is to present a framework to assess and quantify the level of stress to which cybersecurity professionals are subjected in their daily activities and how this stress affects the acquisition of cybersituational awareness and the decision-making process.

The paper is structured in seven sections that address a general introduction to stress, biometric systems and assessment methodologies (Sect. 2); the design principles on which the work is based (Sect. 3); the proposed framework (Sect. 4); the case study to validate the framework (Sect. 5); the challenges and opportunities detected (Sect. 6) and some final conclusions (Sect. 7).

## 2 Background

In this section, stress is approached from three different perspectives. First, stress as a disease is presented, exposing the main models that coexist today as well as the physiological responses of this state. Secondly, the different families of biometric systems that allow the quantification of physiological responses in order to detect the state of stress are introduced. Thirdly, the different existing methodologies to induce stress and to quantify the effort or mental load are presented.

### 2.1 The Stress as a Disease

Despite being one of the most widespread diseases today, stress continues to be studied by many professionals in the areas of medicine and psychology. Due to its complexity, the causes that trigger it and its effects are still not well known, and there are different theories about its origin [8]. Among the most extended currents stand out the theories based on: the response [9,10], the stimulus [11], the interaction [12,13] and the process [8].

In this paper we will use the model proposed in [8], which understands stress as a process made up of seven stages (psycho-social demands, cognitive assessment, stress response, coping, personal characteristics, social support and health status) that are related to each other through mediation and modulation relationships.

On the other hand, regarding the physiological responses associated with stress, we must distinguish two important moments. In the first instance, during what is known as the shock phase, the organism adopts a defensive posture to protect itself from the action of the noxious agent (tachycardia, decrease in temperature, decrease in blood pressure and loss of tone). In a second moment, during what is known as the counter shock phase, the organism undergoes a complementary response to the previous phase, producing an equivalent response of opposite sign (hypertension, hyperglycemia and hyperthermia).

It is especially interesting to study the physiological response experienced by the facial region. In the face of a threat or situation of high effort, the body must provide the muscles with a greater quantity of nutrients. For this purpose, blood flow is increased and, consequently, the facial temperature increases. The areas corresponding to the periorbital [14] and supraorbital [15] regions have a greater predisposition to increase temperature to minimize the effect of stressors. For this purpose, blood flow is redirected from the cheek area [16] to the area of the ocular musculature. In this way, the cheeks are cooled and the ocular areas are warmed. In turn, the increase in temperature and, therefore, in blood flow, contributes to minimize ocular response times.

Thus, from a biological point of view, thermal changes are mainly observed through changes in subcutaneous vasoconstrictors and body sweating. In a threatening situation, epinephrine is released into the bloodstream reducing its blood volume. In this way, the human body protects itself against excessive blood loss. On the other hand, when the threat is the threat, there is a muscular relaxation accompanied by a gradual increase in temperature, a consequence of parasympathetic recovery.

All these indicators will be extremely useful to quantify the physiological response using different biometric systems and to identify a stress situation in the person.

## 2.2 Biometrics Systems to Measure the Stress

Faced with an unfavorable situation involving a high level of stress or anxiety, people tend to experience different physiological responses depending on their life experience, their coping strategies and their ability to minimize stressors. Having an external monitoring system to quantify the physiological response can help to train the response to certain stressful situations and to enhance these types of skills.

There is a wide range of biometric devices that can be classified into different categories depending on the type of response they measure. These families focus on the quantification of changes in heart rate, skin conductivity, brain activity, temperature, and changes in biometrics based on facial expressions.

Among the devices focused on quantifying heart rate variations, three types of solutions predominate (HRV, ECG, plethysmography). These solutions, based on the measurement of cardiac changes allow us to know firsthand the state of stress or anxiety suffered by an individual [17,18]. With the current proliferation of wereables, these solutions are really affordable although their accuracy is not too high.

In a situation of anxiety or high stress [19], people often experience sweating and an increase in average temperature. This biological response acts as a defense and allows the individual to react more quickly in an attempt to deal with the situation. To quantify this type of response, GSR devices provide an inexpensive but inaccurate and noise-prone solution.

Among the systems based on quantifying brain activity, EEG solutions predominate. These systems have good temporal resolution and are extremely useful for studying cognitive load [20] and emotions based on the activation of different regions of the brain. From the activation of different regions of the brain. Currently, the line of brain-computer interfaces (BCI) is becoming very relevant and has an extremely high potential.

In the field of facial biometrics, we are currently working on different lines of research such as ocular analysis (eye arrangement [21], pupil dilation [22] or eye tracking [22]); thermal response of the face [23]; speech analysis and recognition; or the study of facial microexpressions.

To conclude this section, it is necessary to comment that since not all users respond in the same way (from a physiological point of view) to the same event, it is necessary to make an important effort to study and calibrate this type of devices (regardless of the selected technology) in order to identify the user's expected footprint or type of response and to obtain conclusive results.

### 2.3 Evaluation Methodologies

This section reviews the main existing methodologies to: induce stress; to quantify the level of cognitive load and to quantify the degree of acquired cybersituational awareness.

**Stress Induction Systems.** In [24,25] it is presented an exhaustive review of some of the many techniques or approaches existing today to induce stress in an artificial and controlled way in a person is presented. This type of methodologies allow us to study the stress response of a person in an experimental or laboratory environment with the aim of being able to extract valid results from our study.

Among the most used techniques are the Stroop test [26], the social stress test [27] and the arithmetic stress test [28]. It is important to emphasize that, although these methodologies are standardized, the effect that they generate on people depends on numerous factors among which the coping of each person introduced in the previous section stands out.

*Stroop's test* originally proposed in [29], is a test widely used [30] as a generator of psychological stress. In [26] it is demonstrated that this test fulfills the four basic criteria or physiological changes necessary to induce stress: increase in the sensation of distress; stimulation of the adrenal sympathetic system (increasing adrenaline levels); activation of the fight-flight mechanism and changes at the cognitive-neuronal level. In [30] and [31] the validity of this stress system is demonstrated by contrasting the (active) confrontation of the stress situation (of the threat) with the changes of the heart rate and the cardiovascular reactivity.

*Trier social stress test (TSST)* [27]. It is a test that is characterized by forcing a person to speak for 10 min in front of a relatively large audience. In [27], this approach was shown to satisfy the four basic criteria.

*Arithmetic stress test.* It is another widely used approach to stress generation. In this line, there are many different tests (mathematical tests, puzzles, questionnaires to measure IQ, etc.) that allow generating stress levels with different intensities as in [32,33].

**Mental Effort (or Cognitive Load) Measurement Systems.** In the area of cyber-situational awareness it is important to assess and try to quantify in some way the level of cognitive load or effort that a person has during the decision stage. In this context, a new line of research emerges (human cognitive load) [34] to measure and explore the interaction of people with other individuals and systems [35]. Thus, evaluating cognitive effort allows us to quantify the cost associated with performing a cognitive task in order to predict the performance of the operator and/or the system [36]. Numerous studies have shown that both the excess and lack of cognitive load can slow down the decision-making process, as well as decrease the effectiveness of the same [37]. Generally, the increase in mental effort is associated with different external circumstances that generate an increase in the level of anxiety or stress in the individual.

The Fig. 1 schematically represents the typical decision-making process (in line with Boyd's cycle). It takes into account both the changes in context and the impact of these changes on the mental effort supported by the individual.

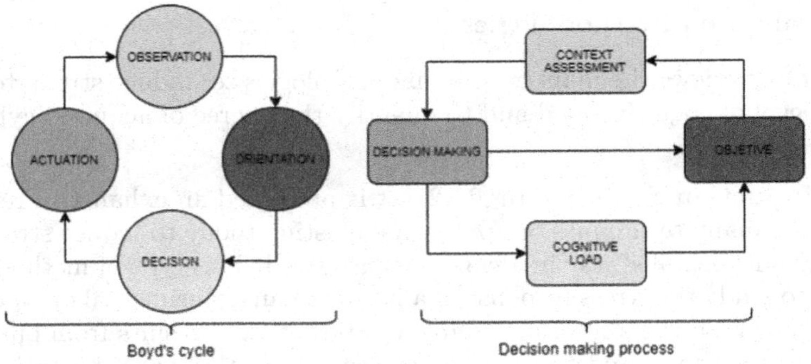


**Fig. 1.** Stages of the decision making process

To maximize the benefit obtained in the decision-making process, it is necessary to rigorously and consistently evaluate the mental effort supported by the decision-maker. In this line of work, different approaches arise to study both the cognitive load and the level of knowledge acquired during the decision-making process. Among the most widespread solutions, they stand out: the SUS [38]; the NASATLX [39]; the SWAT [40]; the WP [41]; the RSME [42]; or the SWDT [43] among others.

In addition to the studies presented previously, there are two methodologies [44] of special relevance that apply to the operational and military context, whose purpose is to know both the level of cognitive load and the capacity to assimilate information and, in short, the situational awareness acquired before (SAGAT) and after (SART) the execution of the mission.

The first methodology, SAGAT [45], consists of a preliminary mission assessment and focuses on quantifying the skills and knowledge acquired by the individual during the planning phase. On the other hand, the SART [46] methodology focuses on the study of the awareness of the situation acquired by the individual after the mission and applies extraordinarily well to the interests of our work.

**Methodologies for Evaluating Acquired Cyber-Situational Awareness.** The SART methodology [46] is a subjective a posteriori qualification technique widely used in operational and military contexts to measure the degree of knowledge that an operator possesses when making decisions or, what is the same, it measures if these decisions have been made with knowledge of cause and with the minimum of possible interference, for example, all those caused by a stress situation. The methodology is quantified from ten dimensions grouped into three different domains: the attention demanded (AD), to measure the degree of attention required by the context; the attention paid (AP), to measure how right are the decisions taken according to the level of stress/mental capacity of the person who takes them in a given moment; and the understanding (U), to measure how much of the information that reaches the user is being processed and understood correctly).

Each of the dimensions (regardless of the domain to which they are associated) is quantified using a numerical scale defined between 1 (little) and 7 (lot). The final degree of the cyber-situational awareness adquired (DCSA) during the operation is calculated as $DCSA = U - (AD - AP)$. Typically, this value is usually normalized to a scale between 0 and 100.

## 3 Design Principles

This paper aims to address the current need for a proven framework to assess the impact of stress in the context of cybersecurity. Although it is true that it can be used for both industrial and military purposes, it is more focused on military environments where the impact of the decisions taken and stress play a more critical role in most situations.

In addition to the evaluation of the impact of stress, the evaluation of the degree of cybersituational awareness acquired during the exercise will also be assessed.

The proposed model is purely theoretical and could not be put into practice due to the limitations of the COVID19.

The main and secondary objectives, functional requirements and limitations of the work are detailed in more detail below.

- **Main objective.** To define a framework to assess the impact of stress on cyberexercises and decision making.
- **Secondary objective.** To be able to use the framework as a complementary system to improve decision making for cybersecurity professionals under high stress conditions.
- **Functional requirements.** To have a working environment (validation scenario) on which to perform the cyber exercises; have a list identifying the possible risks associated with the working environment in order to be able to better perform the decision-making process.
- **Limitations.** Due to COVID-19 restrictions, it has not been possible to test this methodology on an experimental basis; it is expected that the methodology will be tested with an initial battery of 50 users.

## 4 Framework

This section proposes the action protocol on which to execute the framework; a block model of the proposed system/framework and the interrelationship between the different blocks and the cybersituational awareness acquisition process based on Boyd's cycle.

### 4.1 Action Protocol

This section describes the proposed performance protocol to obtain the database to evaluate the decision-making process performed by the study participant under stress conditions.

Due to people react differently to the same stimulus, it is necessary to perform a previous calibration to calibrate the biometric acquisition device to the study participant. Once the devices have been calibrated, the protocol can be executed.

#### 4.1.1 Protocol Acceptance Requirements

For the calibration process and the application of the proposed work protocol, it is necessary to include a series of restrictions to define which people can participate in the study and under what circumstances they should/can leave the study. In addition, it is necessary to contemplate a series of environmental restrictions to homogenize the acquisition of data for all participants. These requirements are described below according to different criteria.

**Inclusion criteria:** no chronic diseases or psychiatric history; age between 18 and 55 years; knowledge and/or experience related to the area of application of the study.

**Exclusion criteria:** diagnosis of psychiatric or neurological disorder; use of psychotropic drugs or psychotropic substances of any kind; use of tobacco, alcohol or nervous system excitatory substances (caffeine, theine, etc.) 8 h before the test; excessively high signs of stress; if the participant considers that he/she has a higher baseline stress level than usual.

**Sufficient conditions for exclusion after starting the study:** at the subject's request; presenting adverse reactions; presenting a clinical condition that could modify some of the parameters measured.

**Requirements for taking the test:** no consumption of any psychotropic substance in the last 24 h prior to the study; wake up at least two hours before the test; eat a light breakfast and low-sugar food; no alcohol in the 12 h prior to the study; no smoking or caffeine in the 8 h prior to the test; no strenuous exercise before the time of the study; and preferably wear comfortable clothing.

**Regarding environmental conditions:** the temperature of the room should be adequate (22–25 °C); air flows directed towards the test area (doors and windows) should be avoided; and constant illumination should be maintained.

#### 4.1.2 System Calibration

The system calibration protocol has been designed to recreate stress situations similar to those the subject might encounter on a daily basis in order to calibrate the stress detection system. Specifically, the protocol focuses on three key stages: the Stroop test, a memory test and a mathematical reasoning test. In addition, we will have an initial contact stage (Acclimatization) and a final stage of return to the basal state (Recovery).

The order of the proposed stages is critical and must be respected at all costs since the Stroop test allows a high amount of stress to be generated in the subject that will be maintained (at least in a residual way) during the rest of the test. With this test, the aim is to recreate a stressful situation of high intensity in order to calibrate this type of responses. In the memorization stage, the aim is to quantify the retention capacity that a person has in a stressful situation.

Finally, in the stage of logical-mathematical reasoning, the aim is to measure the critical reasoning capacity of a person subjected to high stress.

A more detailed description of the protocol is given in the Annex Table 1. This template should be used by the tester to collect the results obtained during the test.

#### 4.1.3 Cyber-Situational Awareness Questionnaire

With the objective of quantifying the degree of cyber-situational awareness acquired during the evaluation methodology, a transposition of the SART methodology detailed in Table 2 [46] is proposed as a template to be used in the Proof of Concept.

For each of the different dimensions you must answer from 1 (little) to 7 (a lot) to the questions proposed in the evaluation methodology of the degree of cyber-situational awareness acquired. Subsequently, the values provided for each of the domains will be grouped from their respective dimensions and the degree of cyber-situational consciousness acquired will be calculated with the mathematical expression presented.

### 4.2 Framework Architecture

The system architecture proposed to validate the evaluation methodology is modular and is subdivided into the following blocks: monitoring; risk management; decision support system; evaluation; and system visualization. The relationship between the different components of the system is presented in Fig. 2.

It is important to emphasize that this architecture is a generic design and, therefore, all components can be replaced by others based on a different technology stack (see Sect. 2.2) as long as they maintain a similar performance at a high level.

**Monitoring.** This block, together with the display block, corresponds to the observation stage of Boyd's cycle. Its objective is to monitor and diagnose the system in order to provide the most complete and realistic image of it. To do this, this module will use different monitoring tools such as SIEM or IDS as well as other applications for data processing and representation.

Regarding the relationship of this first block with the rest of the system, we can observe how it impacts directly on the visualization module and on the biometric evaluator module, feeding them with the complete vision of the current situation of the system.

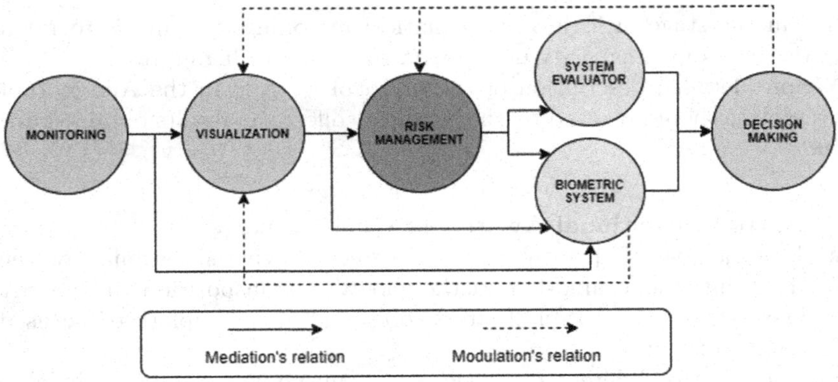


**Fig. 2.** Framework architecture

**Visualization.** The visualization module seeks to present the information obtained by the monitoring component in an attractive and useful way for the user, so that he can work with it easily. This component can reuse the visualization capabilities provided by the own systems used in the previous stage (SIEM, IDS, etc.) or offer a new view from other tools such as the technology stack ELK [47].

As regards the relationship with the other components, this module provides the risk management module with an enriched and aggregated view of all the information collected during the monitoring phase.

To enrich this information, the visualization component is modulated by the evaluation components (biometrics and system), so that it can change the views according to the existing demands in the system from a technical (of the system itself) and human (of the biometrics module) point of view.

An example of the change in behavior of this module would be the following: let's suppose that the operator is monitoring a system in a SOC and starts receiving a high number of alerts that make his stress level skyrocket. To make his work easier, the biometric evaluation module informs the visualization module of the operator's current status, which results in a reduction of the low-level alerts that reach the operator so that he can focus correctly on the problem and gradually reduce his stress level.

**Risk Management.** This component receives information on the current state of the system through the display module. It is important to emphasize that the information obtained is related both to the technical level (of the system) and to the human level (operator/biometrics).

From the information obtained, an assessment of the existing threats can be made, studying which assets are affected and which are the possible safeguards to be adopted. Thus, it is possible to pre-select a safeguard and send that information to the evaluation modules to assess the goodness of that decision.

**Evaluation.** The evaluation component corresponds to the decision stage of Boyd's cycle. Its objective is to assess whether or not the safeguards adopted in the previous stage are adequate in light of the current situation of the system or, in other words, whether we are making the best decision. To do this, the component is divided into two smaller ones according to the information they handle

*System Evaluation.* This component seeks to somehow simulate the impact that applying the selected safeguard would have on the system. Ideally, it should be used as an impact calculator so that a set of safeguards can be consulted and, based on evaluation criteria defined by the user, these can be evaluated to obtain the most appropriate one at each moment. This evaluation will be sent to the decision-making component that will be responsible for carrying out our choice.

*Biometric Evaluation.* This component is the most critical of all and constitutes the main and differentiating element of the proposed solution in relation to the existing commercial solutions today for the identification, management and mitigation of threats.

As has been commented throughout this work, the human factor in decision making is very critical. Being able to correctly assess the decision-making capacity that a person has at a given time can have a high impact on the repercussions of their actions. Therefore, this component must be able to monitor the current state of the person to evaluate and assess the goodness of their decision.

As can be seen in the Fig. 2, this component impacts directly on decision making (like the evaluation system) but also mediates the scope of the visualization module allowing it to adapt to the needs of the operator, such as the level of stress.

**Decision Making.** It constitutes the last component of the system and corresponds to the performance stage of Boyd's cycle. The objective of this component is to allow the user to choose which decision to make based on the previously selected safeguards and the assessment made by the evaluation component (on a technical and human level).

As can be seen in Fig. 2, the impact of this component on the system is quite high, mediating the behavior of visualization and risk management, by modifying the context from the decisions made.

## 5 Case of Study

### 5.1 Validation Scenario

To validate the evaluation methodology proposed in this work, a small use case is proposed to simulate the work that should be performed by a person in charge of monitoring and responding to incidents that appear in a simulated environment with a topology similar to the one proposed in the Fig. 3.

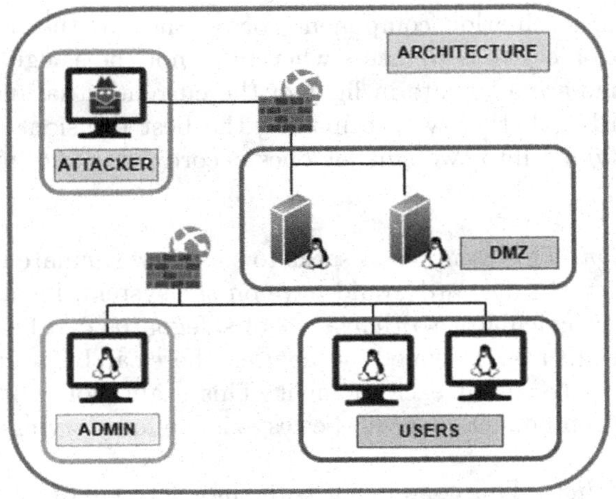


**Fig. 3.** Validation scenario

The demonstration scenario will be a simple environment (as shown in Fig. 3) in which there will be 2 server machines hosting a set of web applications and distributed network service. These machines will be located in the DMZ of the system. In addition, in the network topology, two other sub-nets of interest can be distinguished, one to host user equipment and the other for the administrator's equipment. Finally, all systems will be protected with 2 levels of firewall and it is assumed that notification systems will be deployed in all of them to monitor the status of the equipment and detect new threats (SIEM environments, IDS, NIDS, etc.).

### 5.2 Vulnerabilities List

The vulnerabilities have been grouped into two classes according to the nature of the machines. On the one hand, we will have a set of vulnerabilities that will affect user machines and, on the other hand, we will have vulnerabilities whose scope is more related to web and server environments. The following are some examples of vulnerabilities belonging to these two classes.

*Attacks to User Machines:* attacks to user machines [48]; attacks due to misconfigurations; privilege escalation through capabilities; privilege escalation through the sudoers configuration; path hijack; and weak passwords.

*Web Server Attacks:* Remote Code Execution; Remote File Inclusion; Path Traversal; XSS Attacks; disclosure of information via Robots.txt; disclosure of information via Server-status; CookieHttpOnly based attacks.

### 5.3 Methodology Application Proposal

As shown in Fig. 3, the validation process will involve two kind of users: the system administrator (study participant) and an attacker who will be responsible for carrying out a series of predefined attacks that the administrator will have to deal with and repel. To maintain tension during the exercise and make it more attractive to the participants, a gamification strategy will be adopted so that points will be obtained for each attack avoided and/or threats neutralized.

On the other hand, to homogenize the data acquisition process of the study (analogous to the calibration protocol proposal), minimizing the interaction with the test subject is very important. Therefore, it is proposed to automate the attacks so that all study participants can face the same scenario under equal conditions.

The steps that should be followed in order to obtain conclusive results that would allow us to validate the proposed methodology are presented below:

1. The participant must be submitted to the calibration protocol presented in Sect. 4.1. The proposed templates for data collection should be used (see Table 1). Among these data, it is very important to collect the socio-demographic part in order to be able to elaborate a profile of the participants in the study.
2. The topology of the scenario, the rules and the objectives of the proof of concept will be explained to the participant by means of a video. In addition, a pre-analysis will be provided with indications (safeguards) to be performed in case of some of the attacks already foreseen. Not all previously presented vulnerabilities will have an associated safeguard.
3. The cyber-exercise whose topology is shown in Fig. 3 will be performed, in which the participant will acquire the role of system administrator and will have to repel the attacks carried out by the attackers.
4. At the end of the exercise the participant will be provided with a questionnaire similar to the one presented in Table 2 to assess the degree of cybersituational awareness acquired during the cyber-exercise. The questions presented in that template are extensible and can be further tailored to the exercise proposed.
5. With all the data obtained, the proposed methodology will be validated and the pertinent conclusions will be drawn.

## 6 Challenges and Opportunities

Among the main challenges to be faced when implementing this framework and continuing with this line of research are the following:

- **Degree of user acceptance.** This is the first challenge to solve and is related to the distrust that users have of being monitored by biometric systems. There is a natural suspicion among users who fear being penalized or even fired if it is shown that any of their errors could have been prevented or mitigated or if it is shown that they do not perform adequately under stressful situations.
- **Biometric device selection.** It will be necessary to properly choose the biometric devices that will profile the user's response. Depending on the devices chosen, their degree of intrusiveness, their accuracy, their noise tolerance, etc., we will have to make more effort in the calibration process, in the post-processing of the data, etc. The intrusiveness of the devices is directly related to the degree of user rejection.
- **Calibration process.** It constitutes the third challenge to be solved and is probably one of the most complicated to resolve. As has been mentioned throughout this work, not all people respond in the same way from a physiological point of view to the same stressor agent. Therefore, it is necessary to identify the user's response pattern in order to adapt the results to this pattern and thus obtain conclusive results.
- **Testing of the proposed methodology.** It is necessary to generate a sufficiently large dataset that allows us to validate the proposed methodology, thus giving it added value.
- **Real-world application.** After validating the methodology and testing its usefulness in simulated or training environments, it will be necessary to take the solution to the next level of maturity and include it in real operational environments. Of particular relevance are all those solutions related to rapid response centers (CERTs) and military environments. To reach this level of maturity, we will have to overcome the previous challenges and develop a framework that can be integrated with the systems currently used by our customers.

## 7 Conclusions

This work has reviewed the main lines of research related to cybersituational awareness, decision making and stress, highlighting the close relationship between these three areas and how they constitute a whole in the context of cybersecurity.

The proposal contained in the paper seeks to reflect a need currently existing in the market and to propose a theoretical solution as to how it should be solved. Due to COVID-19 limitations, it has not been possible to implement this solution and obtain a dataset generated with real users.

As future lines of research it is proposed to implement the proposed framework and test it with a small number of users (50–60) to draw some initial conclusions in order to see in which lines of research to make more efforts. It is also proposed to play with different technologies of biometric systems and even combine technology families to see which of them have a greater acceptance by the user, greater accuracy...

To conclude, it should be noted that the applications of this type of solutions in military environments can lead to significant improvements in cyber operations, improving the decision making process and the stress tolerance of cyber operators through different simulations and training exercises through which they are provided with adequate feedback that allows them to improve as professionals.

**Acknowledgment**

European Commission

This research has received funding from the European Defence Industrial Development Programme (EDIDP) under the grant agreement Number EDIDP-CSAMN-SSC-2019-022-ECYSAP (European Cyber Situational Awareness Platform).

**Disclaimer.** The contents reported in the paper reflect the opinions of the authors and do not necessarily reflect the opinions of the respective agencies, institutions or companies.

# Appendix

**Table 1.** Appendix A - Biometric calibration template

**Socio-demographic data**

1. **Id:** ______
2. **Role:** __________
3. **Name:** __________
4. **Surname:** __________
5. **Age:** ____
6. **Sex (M/F):** __

**Acclimation**

1. Do you consider that you are currently under a higher level of stress than usual? (1. No, 2. Yes). ____
2. If yes, please indicate the main reason(s) you consider to cause such stress (e.g., family reasons, studies, job-related, personal situation, etc.): __________
3. Indicate your current level being 0 no stress at all and 100 absolutely stressed. _____

**Stage II: Stroop's test**

1. **Nº of successes:** ____
2. **Perceived stress level (0 to 100)** _____

**Stage III: Memorization**

- **Story 1:** Many /of the children/ of a school /in northern /Lilliput/ were killed /or seriously injured/ and others /seriously hurt/ when a bomb/ exploded/ in the village school./ The children/ were blown/ over a ravine/ up a hill/ a considerable distance/ from the school./ Only two children/ were unharmed.

1. **Nº of memories S1 (min 10)** _____
2. **Perceived stress level at the end of the test (from 0 to 100)** ____

**Stage IV: Logical-mathematical reasoning**

- Sequence to be followed by the subject. *1022, 1009, 996, 983, 970, 957, 944, 931, 918, 905, 892, 879, 866, 853, 840, 827, 814, 801, 788, 775, 762, 749, 736, 723, 710, 697, 684, 671, 658, 645, 632, 619, 606, 593, 580, 567, 554, 541, 528, 515, 502, 489, 476, 463, 450, 437, 424, 411, 398, 385, 372, 359, 346, 333, 320, 307, 294, 281, 268, 255, 242, 229, 216, 203, 190, 177, 164, 151, 138, 125, 112, 99, 86, 73, 60, 47, 34, 21, 8, -5, -18, -31, -44*

1. **Number of errors** _______
2. **Last value reached** _____
3. **Perceived stress level at the end of the test (from 0 to 100)** ______

**Stage V: Recovering**

Answer from 1 (a little) to 5 (a lot) according to your perception of your current state.

1. **I feel palpitations** ____
2. **I feel my mouth dry** ____
3. **I feel a stiff neck.** ____
4. **I feel short of breath, I sigh frequently.** ____
5. **I feel I sweat** ____
6. **I feel chills** ____
7. **I feel like I have nerves in my stomach.** ____
8. **I feel my face blushing** ____
9. **I feel dizzy** ____
10. **I make a lot of mistakes** ____
11. **I don't want to talk** ____
12. **I feel angry** ____
13. **I feel that I am easily distracted or do not concentrate.** ____
14. **I feel on the edge** ____
15. **I feel annoyed by everything** ____
16. **I don't feel motivated to do things** ____
17. **I feel I get impatient easily** ____
18. **I feel agitated and/or restless** ____

**Table 2.** Appendix B - SART template

**Attention Demanded (AD)**

- **Level of situation's stability degree**
  - **Question (Q):** Is the current situation prone to sudden changes (7) or does it seem to remain stable (1)?
  - **Response (R):** ______
- **Level of situation's variability**
  - **Q:** How many variables are changing in the current context? Are there a high number of factors that change (7) or do they tend to remain unchanged (1)?
  - **R:** ______
- **Level of situation's complexity level**
  - **Q:** How would you rate the degree of complexity of the situation: are there many interrelated components or circumstances (7) or is the situation simple and straightforward (1)?
  - **R:** ______

**Attention Paid (AP)**

- **Excitement level**
  - **Q:** How alert do you feel you are right now? Do you consider your level of arousal to be high (7) and are you ready for the activity you are doing or, on the contrary, do you maintain a low level of alertness (1)?
  - **R:** ______
- **Cognitive capacity available**
  - **Q:** How much cognitive capacity do you have in the current situation to deal with many variables? (7, a lot of capacity; 1, you have nothing to spare).
  - **R:** ______
- **Concentration level**
  - **Q:** How focused are you right now? Are you concentrating on many aspects of the situation (7) or just one (1)?
  - **R:** ______
- **Attention level**
  - **Q:** How much is your attention divided in the current situation? Are you concentrating on many aspects of the situation (7) or just one (1)?
  - **R:** ______

**Understanding (U)**

- **Amount of information**
  - **Q:** How much information have you obtained about the situation? Have you been able to receive and understand a great deal of knowledge (High) or very little (Low)?
  - **R:** ______
- **Degree of information quality**
  - **Q:** How reliable is the information obtained and how good (high, 7; low, 1) is it?
  - **R:** ______
- **Level of familiarity**
  - **Q:** How familiar are you with the situation, do you feel you have a lot of relevant experience (7) or is it a new situation (1)?
  - **R:** ______

**Degree of the cybersituational awareness adquired (DCSA:** $U - (AD - AP)$**)**

- AP: __________
- AD: __________
- U: __________
- **DCSA:** __________

## References

1. Sandoval Rodríguez-Bermejo, D., Maestre Vidal, J., Estévez Tapiador, J.: The stress as adversarial factor for cyber decision making. In: The 16th International Conference on Availability, Reliability and Security, pp. 1–10 (2021)

2. Dykstra, J., Paul, C.L.: Cyber operations stress survey (COSS): studying fatigue, frustration, and cognitive workload in cybersecurity operations. In: 11th USENIX Workshop on Cyber Security Experimentation and Test (CSET 2018), Baltimore, MD, August 2018. USENIX Association (2018). https://www.usenix.org/conference/cset18/presentation/dykstra
3. Wemm, S.E., Wulfert, E.: Effects of acute stress on decision making. Appl. Psychophysiol. Biofeedback **42**(1), 1–12 (2017). https://doi.org/10.1007/s10484-016-9347-8
4. Maestre Vidal, J., Sotelo Monge, M.A.: Denial of sustainability on military tactical clouds. In: 15th International Conference on Availability, Reliability and Security (ARES), Dublin, Ireland, pp. 1–9, August 2020
5. Endsley, M.R., Selcon, S.J., Hardiman, T.D., Croft, D.G.: A comparative analysis of SAGAT and SART for evaluations of situation awareness. In: Proceedings of the Human Factors and Ergonomics Society Annual Meeting, vol. 42, pp. 82–86. SAGE Publications, Los Angeles (1998)
6. Maestre Vidal, J., Sotelo Monge, M.A.: Framework for anticipatory self-protective 5G environments. In: 14th International Conference on Availability, Reliability and Security (ARES) (2019)
7. Maestre Vidal, J., Sotelo Monge, M.A.: A novel self-organizing network solution towards crypto-ransomware mitigation. In: 13th International Conference on Availability, Reliability and Security (ARES) (2018)
8. Belloch, A., Bonifacio, S., Francisco, R.: Manual de psicopatología (2008)
9. Selye, H.: The Stress of Life. McGran-Hill Book Company, New York (1956)
10. Cannon, W.B.: The wisdom of the body, New York (1932). Harvey's work with bodily circulation looms over this book. In his chapter "Feedback and Oscillation," Norbert Wierner redefined homeostasis in terms of information: cybernetics, or control and communication in the animal and the machine, (Cambridge, Mass., 1961), esp, pp. 114–15 (1932)
11. Cox, T.: Stress: a review of theories, causes and effects of stress in the light of empirical research (1978)
12. Lazarus, R.S., Folkman, S.: Stress, Appraisal, and Coping. Springer, New York (1984)
13. Lazarus, R.S.: Coping theory and research: past, present, and future. In: Fifty Years of the Research and Theory of RS Lazarus: An Analysis of Historical and Perennial Issues, pp. 366–388 (1993)
14. Levine, J.A., Pavlidis, I., Cooper, M.: The face of fear. The Lancet **357**(9270), 1757 (2001)
15. Puri, C., Olson, L., Pavlidis, I., Levine, J., Starren, J.: StressCam: non-contact measurement of users' emotional states through thermal imaging. In: CHI 2005 Extended Abstracts on Human Factors in Computing Systems, pp. 1725–1728 (2005)
16. Merla, A., Romani, G.L.: Thermal signatures of emotional arousal: a functional infrared imaging study. In: 2007 29th Annual International Conference of the IEEE Engineering in Medicine and Biology Society, pp. 247–249. IEEE (2007)
17. Ballinger, B., et al.: DeepHeart: semi-supervised sequence learning for cardiovascular risk prediction. arXiv preprint arXiv:1802.02511 (2018)
18. Mousavi, S., Afghah, F., Razi, A., Acharya, U.R.: ECGNET: learning where to attend for detection of atrial fibrillation with deep visual attention. In: 2019 IEEE EMBS International Conference on Biomedical & Health Informatics (BHI), pp. 1–4. IEEE (2019)

19. Mundell, C., Vielma, J.P., Zaman, T.: Predicting performance under stressful conditions using galvanic skin response. arXiv preprint arXiv:1606.01836 (2016)
20. Hernandez-Ortega, J., Daza, R., Morales, A., Fierrez, J., Ortega-Garcia, J.: edBB: biometrics and behavior for assessing remote education. arXiv preprint arXiv:1912.04786 (2019)
21. Mequanint, E., Zhang, S., Forutanpour, B., Qi, Y., Bi, N.: Weakly-supervised degree of eye-closeness estimation. In: Proceedings of the IEEE International Conference on Computer Vision Workshops (2019)
22. Minadakis, G., Lohan, K.: Using pupil diameter to measure cognitive load. arXiv preprint arXiv:1812.07653 (2018)
23. Sandoval Rodríguez-Bermejo, D., Ugena, A.M.: Diseño e implementación de un sistema para la detección del estrés mediante redes neuronales convolucionales a partir de imágenes térmicas. Master's thesis, Universidad Politécnica de Madrid (2019)
24. Skoluda, N., et al.: Intra-individual psychological and physiological responses to acute laboratory stressors of different intensity. Psychoneuroendocrinology **51**, 227–236 (2015)
25. Hou, X., Liu, Y., Sourina, O., Tan, Y.R.E., Wang, L., Mueller-Wittig, W.: EEG based stress monitoring. In: 2015 IEEE International Conference on Systems, Man, and Cybernetics, pp. 3110–3115. IEEE (2015)
26. Tulen, J.H.M., Moleman, P., Van Steenis, H.G., Boomsma, F.: Characterization of stress reactions to the Stroop Color Word Test. Pharmacol. Biochem. Behav. **32**(1), 9–15 (1989)
27. Kirschbaum, C., Pirke, K.-M., Hellhammer, D.H.: The 'Trier Social Stress Test'-a tool for investigating psychobiological stress responses in a laboratory setting. Neuropsychobiology **28**(1–2), 76–81 (1993)
28. Poh, C.H., et al.: The effect of antireflux treatment on patients with gastroesophageal reflux disease undergoing a mental arithmetic stressor. Neurogastroenterol. Motil. **23**(11), e489–e496 (2011)
29. Stroop, J.R.: Studies of interference in serial verbal reactions. J. Exp. Psychol. Gen. **121**(1), 15 (1992)
30. Šiška, E.: The stroop colour-word test in psychology and biomedicine. Acta Universitatis Palackianae Olomucensis. Gymnica **32**(1), 45–52 (2002)
31. Payne, J.D., Nadel, L., Allen, J.J.B., Thomas, K.G.F., Jacobs, W.J.: The effects of experimentally induced stress on false recognition. Memory **10**(1), 1–6 (2002)
32. Smeets, T., Cornelisse, S., Quaedflieg, C.W.E.M., Meyer, T., Jelicic, M., Merckelbach, H.: Introducing the Maastricht Acute Stress Test (MAST): a quick and non-invasive approach to elicit robust autonomic and glucocorticoid stress responses. Psychoneuroendocrinology **37**(12), 1998–2008 (2012)
33. Yuenyongchaiwat, K.: Cardiovascular response to mental stress tests and the prediction of blood pressure. Indian J. Psychol. Med. **39**(4), 413 (2017)
34. Longo, L.: Experienced mental workload, perception of usability, their interaction and impact on task performance. PLoS ONE **13**(8), e0199661 (2018)
35. Young, M.S., Brookhuis, K.A., Wickens, C.D., Hancock, P.A.: State of science: mental workload in ergonomics. Ergonomics **58**(1), 1–17 (2015)
36. Cain, B.: A review of the mental workload literature. Technical report, Defence Research And Development Toronto, Canada (2007)
37. Xie, B., Salvendy, G.: Review and reappraisal of modelling and predicting mental workload in single-and multi-task environments. Work Stress. **14**(1), 74–99 (2000)
38. Brooke, J.: SUS: a 'quick and dirty' usability, p. 189. Usability Evaluation in Industry (1996)

39. Hart, S.G.: NASA-task load index (NASA-TLX); 20 years later. In: Proceedings of the Human Factors and Ergonomics Society Annual Meeting, vol. 50, pp. 904–908. Sage Publications, Los Angeles (2006)
40. Reid, G.B., Nygren, T.E.: The subjective workload assessment technique: a scaling procedure for measuring mental workload. Adv. Psychol. **52**, 185–218 (1988)
41. Tsang, P.S., Velazquez, V.L.: Diagnosticity and multidimensional subjective workload ratings. Ergonomics **39**(3), 358–381 (1996)
42. Zijlstra, F.R.H.: Efficiency in work behaviour: a design approach for modern tools (1995)
43. Vidullch, M.A., Ward, G.F., Schueren, J.: Using the subjective workload dominance (SWORD) technique for projective workload assessment. Hum. Factors **33**(6), 677–691 (1991)
44. Salmon, P.M., et al.: Measuring situation awareness in complex systems: comparison of measures study. Int. J. Ind. Ergon. **39**(3), 490–500 (2009)
45. Endsley, M.R.: Direct measurement of situation awareness: validity and use of SAGAT. In: Situation Awareness Analysis and Measurement, vol. 10, pp. 147–173 (2000)
46. Taylor, R.M.: Situational awareness rating technique (SART): the development of a tool for aircrew systems design. In: Situational Awareness, pp. 111–128. Routledge (2017)
47. Elasticsearch B.V.: ELK stack (2020). https://www.elastic.co/es/elk-stack
48. Maestre Vidal, J., Sotelo Monge, M.A.: Obfuscation of malicious behaviors for thwarting masquerade detection systems based on locality features. Sensors **20**(7), 2084 (2020)

# Measuring the Impact of Tactical Denial of Sustainability

Pedro Ramón y Cajal Ramo[1,2], Jorge Maestre Vidal[1], and Marco Antonio Sotelo Monge[1,3(✉)]

[1] Indra, Digital Labs, Avenida de Bruselas, 35, 28108 Alcobendas, Madrid, Spain
{pjramon,jmaestre,masotelo}@indra.es
[2] Universidad Rey Juan Carlos, C/ Tulipán, s/n, 28933 Móstoles, Madrid, Spain
[3] Faculty of Computer Science, University of Murcia, Campus de Espinardo s/n, 30100 Murcia, Spain

**Abstract.** The adoption of the latest advances in Information and Communication Technologies (ICT) at the military operational edge raises promising points of disruption, emphasizing significant improvements in decision support, information sharing, and situational awareness acquisition. Among these, tactical clouds are perceived as necessary assets for achieving information and cyberspace sovereignty, serving as backbone for other cyber functionalities and their connectivity to the kinetic world. However, the attacks against the sustainability of tactical clouds, commonly referred to as Tactical Denial of Sustainability attacks (TDoS), pose one of the challenges that is mostly attracting the attention of the research community, mainly due to its asymmetric nature and cross-domain implications. Hence, the TDoS concept has been conceptually explored and analyzed through vignettes and case of study; but to date no previous work has addressed the problem of its measurement and quantification. With the aim of their understanding, this paper presents a research work that addressed the problem of identifying and analyzing mission-centric Measures of Effectives (MOEs), Measure of Performance (MOPs) and quantitative/qualitative Performance Indicators (PI) able to detect and assess TDoS situations. These measurements embrace capacity, technological, socio-cognitive and energetic aspects, discussing their possible application at offensive and defensive thinking.

**Keywords:** Cloud computing · Cyber defence · Denial of sustainability · Operational assessment · Risk management

## 1 Introduction

The rapid development and consolidation of emerging and disruptive technologies (EDT) comes hand in hand with the digitalization of society and the means of production, thus affecting all sectors and aspects of life. This resulted in the coining and popularization of the expression Society 5.0 [8], which beyond the


S. Katsikas et al. (Eds.): ESORICS 2021 Workshops, LNCS 13106, pp. 537–556, 2022.
https://doi.org/10.1007/978-3-030-95484-0_31

cross-sectional sharing of knowledge and information achieved by the 4.0 concept, emphasizes the role of the cyber persons as human operators on the cyberspace [14]. In line with the social and industrial developments, the adoption of the latest advances in Communication and Information Systems (CIS) at the military operational edge raises promising points of disruption, emphasizing significant improvements in decision support, information sharing, and situational awareness acquisition. As suggested by the NATO Emerging and Disruptive Technology Implementation Roadmap for the next decade [16], and recently agreed at the NATO Summit in Brussels [15]: "The speed of technological change has never been higher, creating both new opportunities and risks in the security environment and to the way NATO operates. We (NATO) are determined to preserve our technological edge, and ensure Alliance interoperability, in order to maintain the credibility of our deterrence and defence posture". Among these, the tactical clouds are perceived as necessary assets for achieving information and cyberspace sovereignty, serving as backbone for other cyber functionalities and their dependencies. Consequently, the cloud computing paradigm bring unique capabilities to the tactical edge, prompting end-to-end communication and tactical synchronization between commander and effectors, allowing to increase and smart allocate computational resource for high priority operational missions thorough automatic scaling and expandability by design [2]; and enabling layered Big Data and Artificial Intelligence, the latter serving the rapid analysis of the situation and support decision-making. But the development, maintenance and operation of tactical cloud is not exempt of challenges concerning synchronization and orchestration, operability, constant adaptation to changes in the CIS ecosystem, or the smart balancing of features and adjustment of the desired performance indicators against their counterpart [37]. According to [5] the defence sector must prepare across all disciplines to embrace the capabilities enabled by tactical clouds, where the biggest challenges will not be technological but related with changes in the culture that drives their design, deployment and operation. This results in a cross-disciplinary challenges that puts the person in the middle, and which affects their sustainability at all dimensions: technological, operational, socio-cognitive, doctrine, resource optimization, etc. In this context, the attacks against the sustainability of tactical clouds, commonly referred to as Tactical Denial of Sustainability (TDoS), pose holistic challenges that due to their asymmetric nature and cross-domain implications, are recently attracted the attention of the research community mostly [12,25].

As indicated in [12], "the TDoS situations target to impact on the tactical level of war by jeopardizing the sustainability of the capabilities provisioned by the tactical clouds, so they embrace tactical-level actuations focused on jeopardizing the decisions and actions that shall originally create advantages when in contact with or in proximity to the enemy". By exploiting the cross-disciplinary inherent in tactical clouds, they threatened hybrid dimensions mostly referring to the economics, safety, security, energy efficiency or socio-technical features of the supported missions; being the Economic Denial of Sustainability (EDoS) attack vectors the most referred in the bibliography [26]. On these grounds, the TDoS concept has been conceptually explored and analyzed through vignettes and case of study; but to date no previous work has addressed the problem of its measurement and quantification [12]. With the aim of facilitate their understanding, this paper presents a research work that addressed the problem of identifying and analyzing mission-centric Measures of Effectives (MOEs), Measure of Performance (MOPs) and quantitative/qualitative Performance Indicators (PI) which shall be able to detect and assess TDoS situations. These measurements embrace capacity, technological, socio-cognitive and energetic aspects; being proposed a framework for their unification and possible application at offensive and defensive thinking. The most differentiating aspects of the research presented in this paper are enumerated below.

- A review of the recent contributions and state-of-the-art on tactical denial of sustainability has been conducted, summarizing key concepts, trends, challenges, and opportunities
- A reference model for mapping the cross-domain indicators of TDoS is presented, which describes the horizontal and vertical dependencies between the scoped dimensions (technical/capabilities, cognitive and energy) and planes (Mission-level, CIS-Level)
- A base set of Measures of Effectiveness (MOE), Measures of Performance (MOP) and Performance Indicators (PI) for TDoS assessment has been identified and analyzed. The proposed measures are mission-centric, so they are consistent with the current military culture and doctrines.
- In-depth discussions and reflection on TDoS assessment is spread throughout the paper, concluding in guidelines and recommendation for TDoS assessment applied at offensive and defensive military thinking scenarios.

The paper is organized into eight sections, being the first of them the present introduction. Section 2 reviews the state of the art on the digitalization of the military sector, tactical denial of sustainability and mission-centred operational assessment. Section 3 summarized the design principles of the conducted research, including objectives, assumptions, hypothesis, and limitations. Section 4 defines and analyzes a base set of MOEs, MOPs and PIs for operational-based TDoS assessment on military operations. Section 5 for socio-cognitive aspects and Sect. 6 for technical features. Section 7 analizes the measurements in terms of military thinking. Finally, Sect. 8 highlights the achieved conclusions and most promising future research lines.

## 2 Background

### 2.1 Threatening the Sustainability of the Digital Tactical Edge

Throughout the last decades, cutting-edge technological advances have emerged spanning several areas of our society. The digitalization phenomena have led to not only transformations in the underlying ICT supporting the business processes of the value chain, but also transformations in the human factor involvement in the cyber-space. Among the areas of disruptive immersion of ICT is also the defence sector in the road to attain combat capabilities to cope with forthcoming next-generation warfare scenarios [25]. The technological landscape has shifted to a high complex scenario where several emerging trends have converged in the digitalization race in defense. Such is the case of artificial intelligence and data analytics for assisting commanders in the decision-making process, advanced network communication systems with growing presence of IP-based platforms, Human-computer interaction and immersive systems or a bunch of virtualization-based solutions to extend the capabilities of physical resources [18]. The latter playing a critical role in today's "on-demand" service provisioning models, moving the "everything as a service" principle exploited by cloud computing ahead in several areas of presence. With that principle in mind, the tactical cloud pursues the rollout of digital capabilities embracing those for logistic coordination, intelligence, surveillance, and reconnaissance, in support of kinetic tactical operations [27]. However, having a purely centralized cloud is far from being effective in the tactical domain since accessing the digital capabilities offered from a centralized datacenter is constrained by the surrounding environment of the end user location, which can be multi-hop and miles-away distant from the central datacenter, being subjected to adverse (sometimes hostile) conditions in the operational edge as is the case of Delayed, Intermittent and Low-bandwidth (DIL) environments [3].

The orchestration of digital capabilities in the tactical edge is thereby crucial to provide critical communications and service delivery closer to the end user, leveraging the computing, storage, and networking capabilities of the technological assets in proximity, at one-hop in the best case [6]. The tactical edge supports heterogeneous communication protocols, mobile networks based on different waveforms, efficient use of processing and communication nodes and, more importantly, the scalability of the computational resources [23]. Regardless of the tactical edge location, the pooling of physical resources and the abstraction of physical resources should be leveraged in the maximum possible extent, paving the way for an elastic provisioning of on-demand digital capabilities orchestrated in proximity to the end-user. Managing the end-to-end communications from the tactical cloud is closely bound to cutting-edge technologies like Network Function Virtualization (NFV), Software-defined Networking (SDN), Cloudlets or Ground-Centric Networking (GCN) harmonized to drive self-management capabilities, commonly referred as Self-organizing Networks (SON) [9]. NFV is a paradigm where conventional hardware-based networking functions (e.g. load balancers, firewalls, proxies) are decoupled from the underlying hardware and represented as virtualized instances that can be dynamically orchestrated across different locations in the tactical edge. NFV deployments require high levels of automatism and programmability of the network when facing the configuration of multiple traffic flows for chaining virtualized functions, which is provided by SDN [17]. In a software-defined network the functions of the control plane are logically centralized in the SDN controller which interfaces with software applications that ultimately steer the forwarding nodes in the data plane. The synergy of NFV and SDN allows the optimization of the network traffic reducing complexity of the network management whilst boosting self-organizing capabilities as widely addressed by emerging architectures like 5G or by the tactical cloud itself [10]. Moving digital capabilities closer to the tactical edge poses a trade-off between the availability high processing capacity on the central cloud versus the communication delay/latency reduction stem from deploying services at the edge. For this reason, keeping the SWAP (Space, Weight and Power) ratio in acceptable conditions becomes critical to preserve the sustainability of the physical and virtual infrastructure on which tactical capabilities are deployed. Nevertheless, the advantages of allocating services in the tactical edge outnumber the drawbacks of having a unique-centralized cloud as they boost the chances for an end operator to execute a mission smoothly but brings other security concerns into stage, among them, threats towards the sustainability of the tactical edge. In this line, recent research has been conducted to elaborate a thorough definition of the Tactical Denial of Sustainability (TDoS) delving into its formalization and cases of study, which has grounds on the Economical Denial of Sustainability (EDoS) concept widely covered by the literature, and the research presented here deepens into their assessment from the eyes of military operations aligned to the NATO doctrine.

### 2.2 Assessment of Military Operations

Operation assessment (OA) refers specifically to the process used during planning and execution to measure progress toward accomplishing tasks, creating conditions or effects, and achieving objectives. During the process staff monitors key factors that can influence operations and provide the commander with the information needed for decisions. As one can guess, assessment and learning enable incremental improvements to the commander's operational approach to the campaign. The aim is to understand the problem and develop effective actions to address it. Once the problem is understood and the needs for success are identified, means to assess effectiveness and the related information requirements that support assessment must be followed. This feedback becomes the basis for learning, adaptation, and subsequent adjustment [32]. OA is a continuous process that measures the overall effectiveness of employing force capabilities during military operations. It involves monitoring and evaluating the current situation and progress toward mission completion. Assessments can help determine whether a particular activity contributes to progress with respect to a set of standards or desired objective or end state [34]. Therefore, maintaining and securing this activity is crucial for the mission, nevertheless, in today's operations, due to the high dependency of communications on digital systems, an especial effort must be shown to reduce this human-induced vulnerability. OA depends on the correct and efficient functioning of cyberspace making its protection a priority. Key OA metrics and indicators can be included in the Commanders Critical Information Requirements (CCIRs) process to provide timely support to the planning and execution decisions. These include measures of effectiveness (MOEs), measures of performance (MOPs) and indicators. Which are developed at all levels of the mission to track progress towards accomplishment [35]. MOEs help answer the question, "Are we creating the effect(s) or conditions in the OE that we desire?" MOPs help answer the question, "Are we accomplishing tasks to standard?". More precisely, an MOE is a measurement of results/effects/purpose accomplishment (change in system state). It's more subjective and there's no direct control over items measured by it. They focus on the results or consequences of task execution and provide information that guides decisions to take additional or alternate actions. Additionally, MOE assess the impact of actions of behaviour, capability, operational environment but does not measure task performance. The metrics used must be relevant, measurable, responsive (sensible to change), resourced, scientific, objective (reducible to quantity), independent and auditable. On the other hand, a MOP is a measurement of activity or action/task accomplishment. It's more objective and focuses on answering: Are the actions being executed as planned? What amount of effort is being input into a situation? At the most basic level, every soldier assigned a task maintains a formal or informal checklist to track task completion. The items on that checklist are MOP. At battalion level and above, command posts monitor MOP for assigned tasks [20]. They measure actions necessary to achieve the end state, objectives, DCs and effects. They can be expressed as speed, payload, range, time-on-station, frequency, or other distinctly quantifiable performance features. They measure the status of own-force actions, but does not measure the changes that result from those actions (MOE). Therefore, there's direct control over items measured by the MOP. Finally, in order to facilitate the tracking of progress, the use of indicators is recommended. FM 3-07 [4] describes them as items of information that provide insight into an MOE or MOP. An indicator is an event that serves as evidence that an effect is being accomplished or, for an MOP, that an output outcome is being achieved. MOE, MOP and Indicators must be repeatedly measured over time to determine changes in system states/progress and it's essential to identify MOE and MOP thresholds prior to any data gathering activity. On a cautionary note, it's not recommended to link MOPs with MOEs. Doing things right does not necessarily mean you are doing the right things [32].

## 3 Design Principles

This section presents the key considerations adopted during the conducted research, which describe the objectives, premises, operational requirements and constraints.

### 3.1 Tactical Denial of Sustainability Threats

This research adopts the TDoS definition cited in the Introduction and referenced from [12]. Accordingly, let the state A that models the expected operability of a digital capability deployed at the military operational edge, if the B real observation on the field is inconsistent with A, so the maintenance cost of A and/or the number of technical instances that enable A is/are significantly higher than in B due to malicious intervention, it is possible to conclude that a

TDoS vector is impacting on the covered capabilities. According to [25] there are different vectors able to jeopardize a tactical cloud sustainability, raging from technical (e.g. EDoS attacks, fraudulent resource consumption vulnerabilities, conventional malware and remote control software, etc.), up to physical but less likely situations, such as over-stimulation of sensors, exposure to environmental factors (heat, water, etc.), electromagnetic emanation, etc. But despite previous work, the state of the art reveals virtually nothing quantitative/qualitative about TDoS impact dimensions or how to measure and assess such situations, which is the focus of the main motivation of this paper.

### 3.2 Research Objectives and Hypothesis

The main objective of the conducted research has been to act as spearhead in the materialisation of pragmatic solutions against TDoS threats, thus exploring and discussing its impacts in different battlefield dimensions while analysing how they can be quantitative/qualitative measured. This has been expected to be fulfilled by addressing the following secondary goals: 1) Identification of the most relevant operational dimensions for TDoS assessment; 2) creating list of candidate MOEs, MOPs and PIs for TDoS evidence measurement; 3) developing a unified framework for their correlation and joint consideration; and 4) widely discuss the implications of TDoS assessment at military-thinking, the latter demanding strong consistencies with the existing operational assessment doctrines and field manuals.

### 3.3 Premises and Operational Requirements

The research has been addressed by addressing the following operational baseline:

1. Doctrinal aspects have been taken into account from a NATO and European perspective, as well as the recommendations for just war set out in the Tallinn manifesto [20] and similar reflections. The proposed operational assessment discussions and measurements are aligned with JDN 1-15 [33] and related notes from the EU region.
2. The tactical cloud concept referred thorough the research is based on application of paradigms like edge computing, cloudlets, network virtualization, etc. and their principles inherited from the dual domain [22], to their tactical application during military conflict and emergency situations.
3. The intended impact of TDoS attacks is expected to go beyond the depletion and/or misuse of resources, thus this research exploring more concrete defence-level objectives such as their ability to weaken the commander's decision-making flexibility, jeopardize the surprise factor of an operation, or demoralisation of troops at socio-cognitive level.
4. The conducted research adopted a mission-centred perspective, where each analysis, valuation, cyber terrain identification or horizontal/vertical propagation directly assumes the characteristics of a mission, its objectives, and the breakdown of tasks and Courses of Action (CoA) that elaborate it.

5. Although this research has the tactical cloud concept as its gravitational centre, the assessment of TDoS situations has taken into account its escalation to the different battle levels: strategic, operational, tactical and technological; so it is possible to properly study the TDoS implications at cross-side dimensions like economic, politics, regulations, ethics, etc.
6. In analogy with [25], it is assumed that TDoS targets military Digital Tactical Capabilities as entry attack surfaces. They are considered as the result of the adoption of the technological enablers that support the digitalization of the tactical edge, thus including services, networks, virtualizations, software repositories, cross-domain policies, etc.

### 3.4 Assumed Limitations and Constraints

In order to narrow down the scope of the research work and its understanding, the following limitations/constraints has been intentionally postponed for further research, so their implications in terms of TDoS measurements shall be reviewed a posteriori:

1. The research undertaken does not cover and has not taken into account the safeguarding aspects of the process of capturing and reporting indicators.
2. As a continuation of the previous bullet, it is worth mentioning that the possible use of counter-intelligence techniques, adversarial artificial intelligence [11] or data poisoning has also not been taken into account [7,13]; therefore, the authors have not explored cases in which an adversary might try to "force" situations in its favour derived from decisions made on intentionally manipulated indicators.
3. Considerations related to the presence of private, protected or sensitive information have not been taken into account when identifying and developing measures. Neither the possibility of dealing with different indicators according to the level of protection of sensitive information manageable by the level of risk and criticality of the mission [36].
4. The technical and tactical feasibility of capturing and processing the introduced measurements have not been addressed. Therefore, this research assumes an omniscient view of the operational environment that will require to be particularised as real options for its application lead to more in-depth analysis and lessons learned.
5. The paper does not delve into the management of uncertainty when measuring and analyzing TDoS indicators. However, it is understood that their treatment is inherent to real sampling, thus opening up a wide range of options for future research oriented to their stochastic treatment via data mining and decision support research outcomes [1].
6. The conducted research ignored the country-specific and cultural differences between armies, military agencies and cyber defence related actors. Given the available bibliography, it is therefore possible to assume bias towards the NATO/EU vision but without going into details at country or regional level. Based on this, it should be emphasised that the views of the authors

are their own, and that any bias will originate in the bibliographic sources they consulted, and not in intentional attempts to generate biased opinions or technological perspectives.

### 3.5 Overall Vision

As the mission-centric cyber situational awareness related bibliography suggests [12], the conducted research explored both mission level and CIS level dimensions, which correlation is semantically illustrated at Fig. 1.

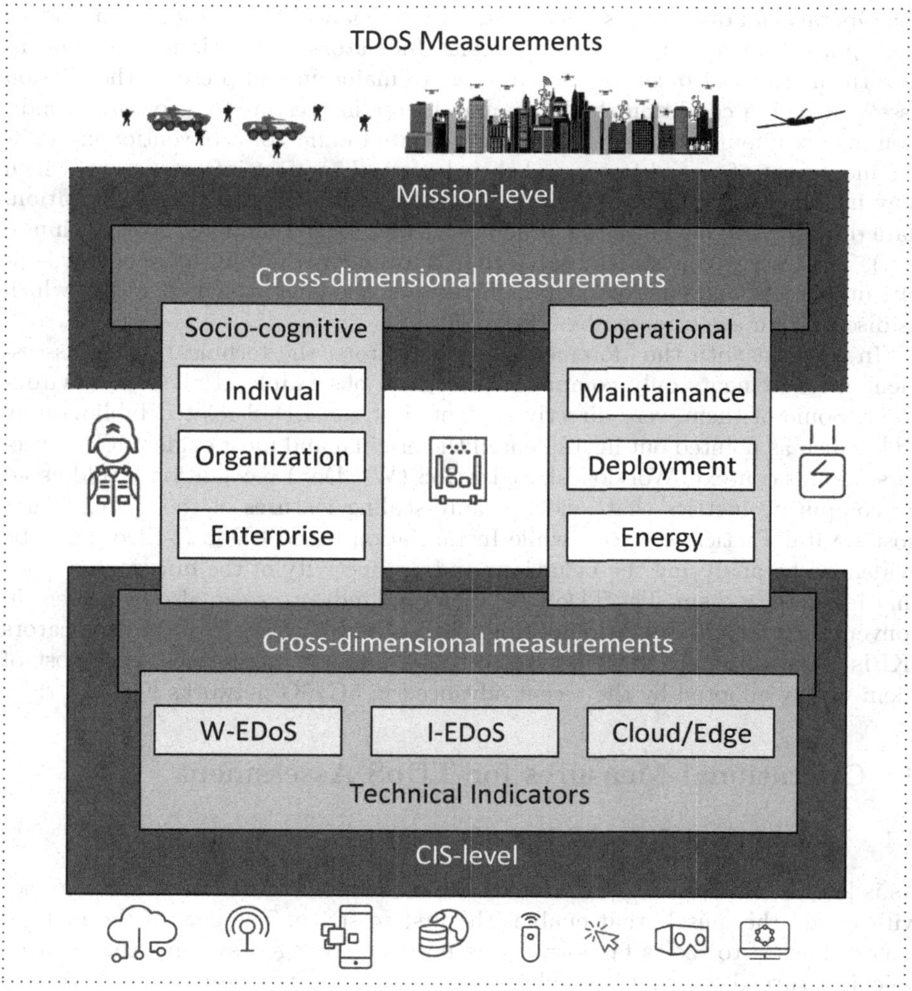


**Fig. 1.** Studied measurement dimensions for TDoS assessment.

Accordingly, Socio-cognitive and Operational observation shall be visible at both mission level and its CIS dimensions (in the second case, taggled to the cyber person concept [30]). Socio-cognitive aspects are linked to the [21] human physical experience, perceived job performance, perceived fairness of appraisal, social relationships, and emotional aspects of the mission supported by Digital Tactical services. They are differentiated as suggested in [30] and discussed in [24]: Enterprise, Organizational and Individual. The first refers to the army human capital lifecycle management (recruiting, trusting, educating, etc.); the second to accelerating communication, decision-making, and DOTMLPF-P integration for military human resource management [25]; and the third to the independent actions of each individual within the army. On the other hand, the Operational dimensions refers to the Maintenance, Deployment and Energy concepts within the supported operations. Indicators about Maintenance facilitate the assessment of situations targeting to maintain and preserve the mission assets in such a condition that they may be readily restored to operable condition in a minimum time [5]. Deployment related indicators conventionally refer the movement of armed forces and their logistical support infrastructure, which may include kinetic assets but also cybernetic actions (e.g. service reallocation, data distribution, instantiation of new services, virtual functions, host machines, etc.). The Energy concept embraces all features mainly linked to the energy supply, utilisation, and environmental efficiency of the operational edge [28], which as discussed in are targeted by TDoS [25].

In contrast with the aforementioned indicators, the technical TDoS assessment measurements only comprise indications observable at the CIS environment. Some of them were directly presented at the EDoS related bibliography [26], which as pointed out in [12], entail the original and most evident TDoS vectors. In this context, Workload-based EDoS (W-EDoS) recognition is addressed by computing metrics that evidence auto-scaling features of the systems that host Digital Tactical services; while Instantiation-based EDoS (I-EDoS) can be evidenced by analyzing the behaviour and productivity of the functions/service that instantiate them. The TDoS Technological indicators can also be present in conventional Cloud/Edge Computing metrics and Key Performance Indicators (KPIs), like efficiency, security, connectivity, latency, intelligence, etc. most of them widely adopted by the recent advanced in 5G/6G networks [9].

# 4 Operational Measures for TDoS Assessment

## 4.1 Maintenance Related Factors

As is known, maintenance will remain the cornerstone of readiness and logistics will remain the muscle that enables the first to strike. The goal of the maintenance effort is to fix as far forward as possible damaged systems that can be quickly returned to a unit in combat-ready condition. Its phases normally consist of inspecting, servicing, lubricating, and adjusting. Among the many possible ones, for its analysis and verification the following measures are proposed (Table 1).

**Table 1.** Maintenance related measurements for TDoS assessment.

| MOE | MOP | Indicator |
|---|---|---|
| 1. Maximize asset availability<br>2. Enhanced equipment maintenance<br>3. Consistent critical asset availability<br>4. Efficient and effective MRO<br>5. Reduce unpredicted risk<br>6. Maintain service reliability<br>7. Minimize transportation requirements<br>8. Deal with unexpected work<br>9. Improve flexibility<br>10. Reduce maintenance cost<br>11. Reduce latency sensitiveness | % of automatism<br>Nº of quality controls<br>Personnel/material adequacy<br>Nº of dedicated facilities/assets<br>Nº of assets restored<br>Frequency of tasks<br>Nº of Internal Defensive Measures (IDM)<br>Nº of Defensive Response Actions (DRA) | Equipment<br>Weather<br>Stock<br>Audit trail<br>Failure Rate<br>Time |

### 4.2 Deployment Related Factors

Deployment refers to activities required to move military personnel and materials from a home installation to a specified destination. It also refers to the placement in battle formation or appropriate positions within operational areas. The related indicators must study kinetic assets but also cybernetic actions in order to have a clear picture of the deployment needs (Table 2).

**Table 2.** Deployment related measurements for TDoS assessment.

| MOE | MOP | Indicator |
|---|---|---|
| 1. Maximize CIS availability<br>2. Reduce deployment cost<br>3. Consistent critical asset availability<br>4. Effective and efficient logistics<br>5. Reliable and redundant capabilities<br>6. Reduce local resistance<br>7. Improve data distribution<br>8. Support mobility | Speed<br>Nº of prioritized tactical services<br>Nº of avenues of withdrawal<br>% of Cloud stability<br>Nº of enemy obstacles destroyed<br>Nº of new services<br>Nº of host machines | Timescale/schedule<br>Feasibility analysis<br>Failure Rate<br>Risk threshold<br>Territory |

### 4.3 Energy Related Factors

Energy's primary objectives are mission assurance and creation of decisive advantage on the battlefield. It combines concern for energy economics and affordability with a desire for environmental protection and assured energy security. The intention is to create the desired levels of performance, range and readiness whilst environmental regulations are followed [19]. For these reasons energy measurements and indicators are of vast importance (Table 3).

**Table 3.** Energy related measurements for TDoS assessment.

| MOE | MOP | Indicator |
|---|---|---|
| 1. Maintain connectivity<br>2. Improved orchestration<br>3. Improved scalability of the ICT resources<br>4. Reduce resource intensiveness<br>5. Effective resource management<br>6. Sustainable development<br>7. Restore optimal system performance | Nº of controlled tactical nodes<br>% Cloud availability<br>Nº of incidents<br>% of connectivity<br>Personnel/material adequacy<br>Nº of systems restored | Money<br>Weather<br>People<br>Timescale/schedule<br>Supply<br>% of proximity |

# 5 Socio-cognitive Measures for TDoS Assessment

## 5.1 Individual Related Factors

Throughout combat operations the individuals within the force will routinely make discretionary judgments and take appropriate action. They must be prepared and given the adequate material and environment to endure their tasks correctly. Cyberspace is often full of unexpected situations and therefore individuals need to be capable to react appropriately. Some measurements to assess this capacity are recommended (Table 4).

## 5.2 Organization Related Factors

The objective of any military mission is to achieve the expected outcome in a planned and effective manner. To this end, it is essential that rapid and stable communication is maintained to enable timely decision-making. Successful manpower management supports both attack and defence, provides the opportunity to maintain a steady rhythm and encourages the retention of initiative.

**Table 4.** Individual related measurements for TDoS assessment.

| MOE | MOP | Indicator |
|---|---|---|
| 1. Enhance skill acquisition | % completed educational level | Productivity |
| 2. Improve vigilance and threat detection | Work experience | Well-being |
| 3. Improve situation awareness | Specificity of tasks | Confidence |
| 4. Emotional control | Nº of threats detected | |
| 5. Reduce cognitive overload | Nº of COA accomplished | |
| 6. Maintain ability to use Tactical Cloud | | |
| 7. Maintain action proximity | | |
| 8. Regain initiative | | |

**Table 5.** Organization related measurements for TDoS assessment.

| MOE | MOP | Indicator |
|---|---|---|
| 1. Controlled target reachability | Nº of targets reached | Success |
| 2. Controlled propagation | % of desired effects | Speed |
| 3. Proactive and open communication | Nº of COA accomplished | Level of trust |
| 4. Fighting spirit development | Nº of deception tactics | Risk threshold |
| 5. Maintain Battle Rhythm | % of mission accomplishment | Latency |
| 6. Unrelented pressure | % of facts/suppositions | |
| 7. Exacerbate enemy disorganization | Nº of dedicated facilities/assets | |
| 8. Enhanced resilience | % of automatism | |
| 9. External information integration | | |

### 5.3 Enterprise Related Factors

The army human capital lifecycle management binds individual members together in a common moral purpose to do the right thing for the right reason in the right way [29]. It provides standards, accepted and upheld by all members, to sustain trust. This is of special importance for the military profession given the lethality inherent in its expertise. The pursuit of expert knowledge, of honourable work, camaraderie and value of service should be motivated and measured (Tables 5 and 6).

**Table 6.** Enterprise related measurements for TDoS assessment.

| MOE | MOP | Indicator |
|---|---|---|
| 1. Enable and maintain operational assessment<br>2. Improved training/education<br>3. Enhanced and specific recruiting process<br>4. Credibility and transparency<br>5. Attitude/opinion/behavioral changes | % of Cloud availability<br>Nº of educational tasks<br>Personnel/material adequacy<br>Level of specialization<br>Expenses on education | Timeframe<br>Failure Rate<br>Money<br>Opinion |

# 6 Technical Measures for TDoS Assessment

Due to the tight relationship between the technical layout and the principles of "on-demand" service delivery, the main substrates of the technical layout are analyzed from the standpoint of the broader cloud/edge platforms. They, differentiating three levels of intervention: infrastructure, platform and application.

## 6.1 Infrastructure Related Factors

Infrastructure factors bring the first building block of the underlying technological assets. Proper operational conditions are vital at this level since their availability is rather limited when supporting the deployment of tactical services in the edge (Table 7).

**Table 7.** Infrastructure-related measurements for TDoS assessment.

| MOE | MOP | Indicator |
|---|---|---|
| 1. Higher energy consumption<br>2. Increased downtime<br>3. Higher operational costs.<br>4. Increased hardware maintenance<br>5. Hardware life-time<br>6. Performance per Watt<br>7. SWAP (Space, Weight and Power) ratio | Network throughput<br>Disc utilization<br>CPU utilization<br>Power consumption<br>Operation cost<br>Heating overhead<br>Number of pooled nodes<br>RTT delay | Money units<br>Temperature<br>Cost<br>Time<br>% Occupation<br>Failure Rate<br>Bytes per second |

## 6.2 Virtualized Platform Related Factors

As the digital capabilities are not directly bind to physical elements, the intermediate virtualized platform provides an abstraction of general-purpose computing, storage and networking capacities and the orchestration of virtualized functions at the tactical edge. Therefore, threatening its sustainability compromises the operational performance of both, the subjacent hardware and the services running on top (Table 8).

**Table 8.** Virtualized-platform related measurements for TDoS assessment.

| MOE | MOP | Indicator |
|---|---|---|
| 1. Processing overhead of virtual CPUs<br>2. Increased downtime<br>3. Higher configuration time<br>4. Higher number of virtualized entities<br>5. Scaling thresholds violations<br>6. Traffic burden<br>7. Low VNF productivity<br>8. Increased convergence time | Available memory<br>Processing nodes overhead<br>Disc consumption<br>Nº of running instances or containers<br>I/O requests per time unit<br>Virtual link's delay<br>Virtual links throughput<br>% NFVI availability<br>Network coverage<br>Handover requests | Time<br>Failure Rate<br>Money<br>Log entries<br>Audit trails<br>Bytes per second |

### 6.3 Service-Related Factors

Digital services are the core elements ultimately supporting defence forces when courses of actions are planned and executed. Their primary role demand operational conditions matching the expectations of commanders as first-line sensing, decision-making and actuation elements intended to accomplish the mission goals. Understood as streamlined virtual entities, digital services' sustainability must comply with the desired service levels conditions on which the following indicators shall be considered (Table 9):

**Table 9.** Service-related measurements for TDoS assessment.

| MOE | MOP | Indicator |
|---|---|---|
| 1. Service-level non-compliance<br>2. Delayed Service Response time<br>3. Unexpected service behaviour<br>4. Service down-time<br>5. Cluster size increment<br>6. Persistent connected users<br>7. Over scaled service<br>8. Billing increments | % CPU demand per VNF<br>% RAM demand per VNF<br>Cache hit/miss rate<br>Latency<br>Cluster occupation<br>% Service availability<br>Service cost<br>Nº connected users<br>Service reachability | Time<br>Availability Rate<br>Money<br>Audit trails<br>Opinion<br>Success rate<br>Signal intensity |

## 7 Considerations at Military Thinking

Offensive action is the key to achieving decisive results. Commanders conduct the offense to defeat enemy forces or gain control of terrain to produce the effects required. Circumstances may require defending; however, tactical success normally requires shifting to the offense as soon as possible. The offense is the ultimate means commanders have of imposing their will on enemy forces. When conducting the offense Commanders seize, retain, and exploit the initiative. The main characteristics to be exploited in order to success are audacity, concentration, surprise and tempo. If these are studied and promoted the Commander will be able to manoeuvre forces to advantageous positions and regain the initiative. Furthermore, an adequate offensive thinking must have the willingness to take bold risks and dispel uncertainty by acting decisively. Opportunities must be exploited, and continuous pressure must be shown to seize the initiative. A competent offensive thinking must focus on adjusting tempo to create opportunities, reduce friendly vulnerabilities and deny the enemy forces to rest or synchronize their combat power. On the other hand, a defensive operation pretends to defeat an enemy attack, gain time, economize forces, and develop conditions favourable for offensive or stability operations (ADP 3-0). The inherent strengths of the defence are the defender's ability to occupy positions before an attack and use the available time to improve those defences. Even during combat, a defending force takes the opportunities afforded by lulls in action to improve its positions and repair combat damage [31]. Furthermore, defensive thinking aggressively seeks ways of attriting and weakening enemy forces before close combat begins. Forces must pressure the enemy to manoeuvre into a position of disadvantage and attack them at every opportunity. Additionally, disruption, flexibility, manoeuvre, mass concentration, operations in depth, preparation, and security are characteristics that should be considered in defensive thinking in order to regain the initiative and seek to transition to the offense.

### 7.1 TDoS Assessment at Offensive Thinking

TDoS attack capabilities shall create fires in and thorough cyberspace, occasionally leading to physical alterations and deriving in cascading and collateral effects in the rest of kinetic warfare domains. These actions shall typically aim on jeopardizing the sustainability of adversary digital tactical capabilities or triggering first-order sustainability effects to initiate carefully controlled circuitous situations at strategical, operational or tactical levels. In this sense, offensive TDoS assessment must measure the ability to degrade, disrupt, destroy or manipulate enemy Cloud capability, as well as the capacity to cause deception, decoying, conditioning, spoofing, and other similar effects. Furthermore, the principal aspirations embedded in offensive thinking shall include the idea of getting inside the enemy's decision cycle, attacking adversary sensing grids, attacking an adversary's long-range strike systems, rapidly attriting adversary forces and forcing horizontal escalation. Finally, TDoS may force adversarial capabilities to distribute over the theatre of operations and/or move from specific terrains, so allies can exploit the triggered situation for reorient their efforts and address high-value regions. Socio-technical TDoS actions and attacks reducing the autonomy, energy or digital resources of the tactical cloud and/or its sensors grids entail promising support for these actions.

### 7.2 TDoS Assessment at Defensive Thinking

The adoption of a defensive thinking posture may be subject to different conditions, including military superiority, tactical restrictions or strict Rules of Engagement (ROE). As occurs with conventional cyber situations, attackers have the advantage of surprise, and plenty of time to gather the cyber threat intelligence needed to success on the TDoS actions (discovery of vulnerabilities, customization of exploits, etc.). The goal of tactical cloud defence is to defeat the threat of a specific adversary and/or return the cloud or the affected digital tactical services to a secure and functional state. According to the NATO JP3-20 [2], defensive actions on tactical clouds may entail Internal Defensive Measures (IDM), Defensive Response Actions (DRA), or the combination of both of them at owned or ally cyberspace. The idea focuses on preventing the fraudulent scaling of the computational resources expenditures while removing and isolating those that may contribute to the horizontal propagation of the threats. Active defence against TDoS shall focalize on the sources of the hostile activities and block, trace and neutralize them. All the actions exposed are heavily supported by proper digital tactical capabilities deployed at the edge by a Tactical Cloud. In this context, the concept of Tactical Denial of Sustainability (TDoS) includes two raw technical variations: Maintenance-based Tactical Denial of Sustainability (U-TDoS) and Deployment-based Tactical Denial of Sustainability (D-TDoS); and their horizontal/vertical socio-technical propagations as Enterprise (E-TDoS), Organizational (O-TDoS) and Individual (I-TDoS) levels. It's also revealed the close synergy between TDoS and energy efficiency situations, as well as how the latter may jeopardize the tactical availability of tactical clouds [8].

## 8 Conclusions

As it is known, the adoption of the latest advances in Communication and Information Systems (CIS) at the military operational edge raises promising points of disruption, affirming significant improvements in decision support, information sharing, and situational awareness acquisition. More precisely, tactical clouds are now perceived as necessary assets for achieving information and cyberspace sovereignty, serving as backbone for other cyber functionalities and their connectivity to the kinetic world. Nowadays, attacks against the sustainability of tactical clouds, referred to as Tactical Denial of Sustainability attacks (TDoS), pose one of the greatest risks for mission accomplishment and for this reason they must be carefully monitored during operation assessment.

Throughout this research a mission-centric and CIS approach have been presented to tackle this matter. Focusing the study on the identification of

Measures of Effectives (MOEs), Measure of Performance (MOPs) and quantitative/qualitative Performance Indicators (PI) able to detect and assess TDoS situations. These measurements embrace capacity, technological, socio-cognitive, technical and energetic aspects, discussing their possible application at offensive and defensive thinking. Socio-cognitive (Enterprise, Organizational and Individual) and Operational (Maintenance, Deployment and Energy) observation shall be visible at both mission level and CIS dimensions. This is of great importance due to the cross-domain implications; the horizontal and vertical dependencies between the scoped dimensions and planes; and the danger of undesired propagation. The maintenance of reliable cloud capability is essential to regain the initiative, succeed both offensively and defensively and maintain the credibility of our deterrence and defense posture. Therefore, it is necessary to develop and monitor measures and indicators to demonstrate that the tactical cloud will be able to cope with forthcoming next-generation warfare scenarios and will have the capacity to produce the effects required. Future lines of research are clearly meant to extend the conceptualization, formalization and validation of the proposed measurements.

## Disclosure

The contents reported in the paper reflect the opinions of the authors and do not necessarily reflect the opinions of the respective agencies, institutions or companies.

**Acknowledgements**

European Commission

This research has received funding from the European Defence Industrial Development Programme (EDIDP) under the grant agreement Number EDIDP-CSAMN-SSC-2019-022-ECYSAP (European Cyber Situational Awareness Platform).

## References

1. Barbosa-Póvoa, A.P., da Silva, C., Carvalho, A.: Opportunities and challenges in sustainable supply chain: an operations research perspective. Eur. J. Oper. Res. **268**(2), 399–431 (2018)
2. Barrett, D., Mansfield, A.: The challenge and opportunities of standing on cloud - finding our warfighting advantage. Cyber Defense Rev. **4**(1), 15–22 (2019)
3. Bergh, A.: The final destination: Building test bed apps for DIL environments. In: 2015 IEEE 81st Vehicular Technology Conference (VTC Spring), pp. 1–5. IEEE (2015)
4. Caldwell IV, W.B., Flournoy, M., Brimley, S., Davidson, J.: The US Army Stability Operations Field Manual: US Army Field Manual No. 3–07. University of Michigan Press (2009)

5. Cook, A., Janicke, H., Smith, R., Maglaras, L.: The industrial control system cyber defence triage process. Comput. Secur. **70**, 467–481 (2017)
6. Dolui, K., Datta, S.K.: Comparison of edge computing implementations: fog computing, cloudlet and mobile edge computing. In: 2017 Global Internet of Things Summit (GIoTS), pp. 1–6. IEEE (2017)
7. Duvenage, P., Sithole, T., von Solms, B.: Cyber counterintelligence: an exploratory proposition on a conceptual framework. Int. J. Cyber Warf. Terror. (IJCWT) **9**(4), 44–62 (2019)
8. Fukuyama, M.: Society 5.0: aiming for a new human-centered society. Jpn. Spotlight **1**, 47–50 (2018)
9. Gui, G., Liu, M., Tang, F., Kato, N., Adachi, F.: 6G: opening new horizons for integration of comfort, security, and intelligence. IEEE Wirel. Commun. **27**(5), 126–132 (2020)
10. Kaur, K., Mangat, V., Kumar, K.: A comprehensive survey of service function chain provisioning approaches in SDN and NFV architecture. Comput Sci. Rev. **38**, 100298 (2020)
11. Maestre Vidal, J., Sotelo Monge, M.: Obfuscation of malicious behaviors for thwarting masquerade detection systems based on locality features. Sensors **20**(7), 2084 (2020)
12. Maestre Vidal, J., Sotelo Monge, M.A.: Denial of sustainability on military tactical clouds. In: Proceedings of the 15th International Conference on Availability, Reliability and Security, pp. 1–9 (2020)
13. Maestre Vidal, J., Sotelo Monge, M.A., Martínez Monterrubio, S.M.: EsPADA: enhanced payload analyzer for malware detection robust against adversarial threats. Future Gener. Comput. Syst. **104**, 159–173 (2020)
14. NATO: Allied joint doctrine for cyberspace operation (AJP-3.20) (2020). https://www.gov.uk/government/publications/allied-joint-doctrine-for-cyberspace-operations-ajp-320
15. NATO: Brussels summit communiqué (2021). https://www.nato.int/cps/en/natohq/news_185000.htm
16. NATO: Emerging and disruptive technologies (2021). https://www.nato.int/cps/en/natohq/topics_184303.htm?
17. Poularakis, K., Iosifidis, G., Tassiulas, L.: SDN-enabled tactical ad hoc networks: Extending programmable control to the edge. IEEE Commun. Mag. **56**(7), 132–138 (2018)
18. Rodriguez-Bermejo, D.S., Medenou, R.D., de Riquelme, R.P., Vidal, J.M., Torelli, F., Sánchez, S.L.: Evaluation methodology for mission-centric cyber situational awareness capabilities. In: Proceedings of the 15th International Conference on Availability, Reliability and Security, pp. 1–9 (2020)
19. Samaras, C., Nuttall, W.J., Bazilian, M.: Energy and the military: convergence of security, economic, and environmental decision-making. Energy Strategy Rev. **26**, 100409 (2019)
20. Schmitt, M.N.: Tallinn Manual 2.0 on the International Law Applicable to Cyber Operations. Cambridge University Press, Cambridge (2017)
21. Smaliukiene, R., Bekesiene, S.: Towards sustainable human resources: how generational differences impact subjective wellbeing in the military? Sustainability **12**(23), 10016 (2020)
22. Smith, W., et al.: Cloud computing in tactical environments. In: Military Communications Conference (MILCOM), pp. 882–887. IEEE (2017)

23. Solozabal, R., Sanchoyerto, A., Atxutegi, E., Blanco, B., Fajardo, J.O., Liberal, F.: Exploitation of mobile edge computing in 5G distributed mission-critical push-to-talk service deployment. IEEE Access **6**, 37665–37675 (2018)
24. Song, S.C.: A systems analysis of the us army's human dimension strategy. In: Proceedings of the International Annual Conference of the American Society for Engineering Management, pp. 1–10. American Society for Engineering Management (ASEM) (2018)
25. Sotelo Monge, M.A., Maestre Vidal, J.: Conceptualization and cases of study on cyber operations against the sustainability of the tactical edge. Future Gener. Comput. Syst. **125**, 869–890 (2021)
26. Sotelo Monge, M.A., Maestre Vidal, J., Martínez Pérez, G.: Detection of economic denial of sustainability (EDoS) threats in self-organizing networks. Comput. Commun. **145**, 284–308 (2019)
27. Sotelo Monge, M.A., Maestre Vidal, J., Medenou Choumanof, R.D.: Adaptive mitigation of tactical denial of sustainability. In: The 16th International Conference on Availability, Reliability and Security, pp. 1–9 (2021)
28. Thomas, D., Shankaran, R., Orgun, M., Hitchens, M., Ni, W.: Energy-efficient military surveillance: coverage meets connectivity. IEEE Sens. J. **19**(10), 3902–3911 (2019)
29. US Army: Army doctrine reference publication no. 1: The army profession (2015). https://irp.fas.org/doddir/army/adrp1.pdf
30. US Army: The army human dimension strategy (2015). https://caccapl.blob.core.usgovcloudapi.net/web/character-development-project/repository/human-dimension-strategy-2015.pdf
31. US Department of the Army: ADP 3–90 Offense and Defense (2019). https://irp.fas.org/doddir/army/adp3_90.pdf
32. US Joint Chiefs of Staff: Commander's handbook for assessment planning and execution (2011). https://www.jcs.mil/Portals/36/Documents/Doctrine/pams_hands/assessment_hbk.pdf
33. US Joint Chiefs of Staff: Joint doctrine note 1–15: Operations assessment (2015). https://www.hsdl.org/?view&did=761727
34. US Joint Chiefs of Staff: Joint publication 3.0 on joint operations (2018). https://www.jcs.mil/Portals/36/Documents/Doctrine/pubs/jp3_0ch1.pdf
35. US Joint Chiefs of Staff: Joint publication 5.0 on joint planning (2020). https://www.jcs.mil/Portals/36/Documents/Doctrine/pubs/jp5_0.pdf
36. Vacca, A., Onishi, H.: Drones: military weapons, surveillance or mapping tools for environmental monitoring? The need for legal framework is required. Transp. Res. Procedia **25**, 51–62 (2017)
37. Yang, H., et al.: Dispersed computing for tactical edge in future wars: vision, architecture, and challenges. Wirel. Commun. Mob. Comput. **2021** (2021)

# A Mathematical Framework for Evaluation of SOAR Tools with Limited Survey Data

Savannah Norem(✉), Ashley E. Rice, Samantha Erwin, Robert A. Bridges, Sean Oesch, and Brian Weber

Oak Ridge National Laboratory, Oak Ridge, TN 37830, USA
noremsa@ornl.gov

**Abstract.** Security operation centers (SOCs) all over the world are tasked with reacting to cybersecurity alerts ranging in severity. Security Orchestration, Automation, and Response (SOAR) tools streamline cybersecurity alert responses by SOC operators. SOAR tool adoption is expensive both in effort and finances. Hence, it is crucial to limit adoption to those most worthwhile; yet no research evaluating or comparing SOAR tools exists. The goal of this work is to evaluate several SOAR tools using specific criteria pertaining to their usability. SOC operators were asked to first complete a survey about what SOAR tool aspects are most important. Operators were then assigned a set of SOAR tools for which they viewed demonstration and overview videos, and then operators completed a second survey wherein they were tasked with evaluating each of the tools on the aspects from the first survey. In addition, operators provided an overall rating to each of their assigned tools, and provided a ranking of their tools in order of preference. Due to time constraints on SOC operators for thorough testing, we provide a systematic method of downselecting a large pool of SOAR tools to a select few that merit next-step hands-on evaluation by SOC operators. Furthermore, the analyses conducted in this survey help to inform future development of SOAR tools to ensure that the appropriate functions are available for use in a SOC.

**Keywords:** SOAR tools · User study · Cybersecurity

## 1 Introduction and Background

The term *security operations center* (SOC) refers to the subteam of an organization's IT department tasked with maintaining the network's cyber health—the

This manuscript has been co-authored by UT-Battelle, LLC, under contract DE-AC05-00OR22725 with the US Department of Energy (DOE). The US government retains and the publisher, by accepting the article for publication, acknowledges that the US government retains a nonexclusive, paid-up, irrevocable, worldwide license to publish or reproduce the published form of this manuscript, or allow others to do so, for US government purposes. DOE will provide public access to these results of federally sponsored research in accordance with the DOE Public Access Plan (http://energy.gov/downloads/doe-public-access-plan).


S. Katsikas et al. (Eds.): ESORICS 2021 Workshops, LNCS 13106, pp. 557–575, 2022.
https://doi.org/10.1007/978-3-030-95484-0_32

confidentiality, integrity, and availability of the enterprise's data and systems. SOCs are now equipped with a widespread collection of data from a vast array of sensors feeding logs, alerts, and raw data to a security information and event management system (SIEM). SIEMs and back-end infrastructure generally provide SOCs customizable, real-time dashboards and rapid data query. However, the process of identifying incidents, responding appropriately, and documenting findings remains to be done by the operators. The SIEM, along with the many other SOC tools, can only provide limited awareness, leading to extended threat detection and response times and reduced ability to prevent or quickly mitigate an attack [1,2].

Further, SOC efficiency suffers due to time spent documenting findings, collecting evidence across an array of sources, and completing other administrative-type procedures [3]. Security orchestration, automation, and response (SOAR) tools—the term coined by Gartner in 2017 [3]—are the newest generation of software tools designed to enable SOC operators to more efficiently and uniformly detect and address cybersecurity threats. While orchestration and automation are often marketed together, they do have distinct functions and can be distinguished [2] as follows: *orchestration* specifically refers to the integration of separate tools with different functions into a single platform to streamline and accelerate the investigation of a threat; *automation* refers to reducing the manual effort required by SOC operators during investigation and threat response phase [4]. SOAR tools aim to help by automating parts of an investigation and helping SOC operators prioritize alerts to investigate. A SOAR tool has the following defining capabilities: (1) ingests a wide variety of SOC data, (2) assists in prioritizing, organizing, and displaying the data to the users, (3) allows customizable workflows or "playbooks" to standardize SOC procedures, (4) provides automation to expedite the SOC's procedures, (5) integrates with a ticketing system, and (6) facilitates collaboration of operators, potentially in disparate geographic locations or networks. The capabilities of a SOAR tool are observed with the integration of a SOAR mechanism to secure energy microgrids—wherein the tool collects and contextualizes security data from multiple sources in the microgrid, performs an overall sweep of the system to identify present vulnerabilities, and initialize or engage a response to detected threats [5].

SOAR tools are a transformational and centerpiece tool for a SOC promising measurable gains in effectiveness and efficiency; as such, they require substantial investments. In addition to monetary costs, configuration depends on standardizing and codifying workflows, and incurring technological and organizational debt. Hence, efforts to find the right SOAR tool for a SOC are warranted, yet because SOAR tools are so new, there is little research assessing their usability or the degree to which they improve SOC operators' ability to respond to threats. This work will provide an in-progress report on the first-ever user study to assess and compare user preferences of SOAR tools with the aim of downselecting to a smaller number of tools to be extensively tested. Our goal is to provide scientific assistance to an organization to winnow the wide variety of SOAR tools to the best one for the organization's needs.

A first step for evaluating SOAR tools, and the focus of this work, is down-sampling the variety of tools to a subset worthy of the costly hands-on evaluation without discarding a potentially desired tool. We describe both our experimental design methodology and anonymized results—as a prerequisite, SOAR vendors agreed to providing licenses and support for this study in exchange for anonymity of their results and participation—of actual SOC operators evaluating 11 market-leading SOAR tools based on vendor-supplied technological overviews. Previous work has used game theory to aid in decisions of mid-size enterprises on cyber-security tools [6], or conducted user studies questioning users why they do (not) employ specific cybersecurity measures [7]. Yet none of this work addresses how users perceive current market leading tools that are available to them.

In terms of understanding usability of SOAR tools, this work aids in understanding what defining capabilities are most desired by SOC operators and how this affects their preferences. Our unique pipeline provides a method for narrowing down to only the tools that are most preferred by SOC operators. This pipeline's many unique and modular components could be applicable to future user studies, in particular: statistical simulations to quantify confidence of results under varying number of participants; a novel algorithm for optimizing participant assignments; a framework for optimizing combinations and variants of multi-criteria recommender system (for predicting missing ratings) to the data at hand that outperforms the previous versions; an evaluation of supervised regressors for predicting overall ratings from aspect ratings is provided (and verifies that this is a needed step as it greatly out-performs predictions from the recommender system); many methods for ranking the tools based on the data are provided side-by-side including a novel application of PageRank to convert ratings data to ranking data; statistical analyses that investigate correlations present. To assist the community in reusing any of these methods, code will be released here once open-source copyright is gained.

In summation, this work will present a novel pipeline of ingesting sparse data and using a mathematically sound method to fully populate the matrix of data. Novel methods are then applied to create multiple views of data along with the statistical relevance of demographic factors. This paper will fill a gap in knowledge where we start with a survey of what the users of these tools actually want, and will proceed to an in depth user study of what the tools deliver. We first present our methods, beginning with study design and progressing through our algorithms and machine learning techniques for handling missing data and predicting overall ratings. We then detail our use of PageRank for rank aggregation, along with statistical methods to analyze demographic impact on user responses.

## 2 Methodology

In total, 11 SOAR tools are included in this study. Before the study, operators were asked to provide an ordered ranking of the defining capabilities (listed in the SOAR definition above) in order of importance. Participants watched two vendor-prepared videos, one that gives of their tool and one that provides a demonstration. We provided general guidelines regarding the videos, wherein the overview must include information on the technical approach of the tool (architecture, deployment, algorithms, etc.) as well as the novelty of the tool. We requested that the demonstration video provide an introduction to the platform with examples of users viewing events, using playbooks, collaborating, along with capabilities to automatically populate tickets and orchestrate multiple incidents. Participants then provided per-capability Likert scale ratings (1 to 5), an overall tool rating, and ranked all tools viewed.

### 2.1 Data Collection

**Survey Design.** Prior to the survey in which the operators evaluated the tools in this study, we collected information from the operators about which defining capabilities of SOAR tools are most important to them. Four SOCs participated in this preliminary conversation and informed the questions we asked in our Internal Review Board[1] approved full survey. The capabilities in question included: the ability to rank/sort alerts so that high priority alerts are emphasized, ability to automate common tasks, easy of playbook creation and modification, ability to provide a unified experience across geographic locations, ability to ingest disparate data sources, and ability to pre-populate alerts and tickets with additional context. These same aspects were the criteria by which the operators evaluated the SOAR tools. For each question, answers followed the 1–5 Likert scale, with an additional option for "Can't Tell".

Before the set of SOAR tool videos and surveys were administered, a set of demographic questions were posed to each participant including how long they had been in their role, what their role was, the level of familiarity they had with each specific SOAR tool, and finally, asking them to rank by importance the defining capabilities of a SOAR tool.

After viewing all SOAR tool videos and completing the per-tool surveys, users were asked to rank the tools they had reviewed. The survey was provided online via a secured website to protect the sensitive nature of both SOAR tool privacy videos as well as information provided by SOC analysts. The full survey can be found in Table 4.

**How Many Participants to Recruit?** In general, unless the differences between the groups are rather extreme, small sample sizes do not yield enough statistical power. We begin this study by choosing an appropriate sample size to ensure validity of the results. We design and run a simple (two-tool, single-rating) simulation to quantify the sensitivity of statistical significance to number of participants. Although our actual user study will include several tools and ratings, this simple exercise will be sufficient to provide quantifiable reasoning about the number of participants to target.

For the simulation, we consider two scenarios in which a pair of tools are rated on the Likert scale: (1) a pair of tools are rated differently (tool 2 preferred to tool 1) and (2) a pair of tools are rated the same (no preference for tool 1 over tool

[1] The IRB works to ensure the rights of participants in any human subject study are fully protected.

2, or vice versa). We sample $m = 5, 10, \ldots, 40$ participants' overall ratings of the two tools—one overall rating sampled per user per tool–from two distributions over sample space $\{1, 2, \ldots, 5\}$. We then compare results of different hypothesis tests that assess whether the ratings are sampled from the same distribution.

First, we examine the number ($m$) of pairwise tool reviews needed to have confidence that tool 2 is preferred over tool 1 given distribution means of $\mu = 3.65$ and $\mu = 2.93$, and variances of $\sigma^2 = 1.17$ and $\sigma^2 = 0.923$ for tool 2 and tool 1, respectively. Second, we examine the number of reviews needed to tell with confidence that tool 2 is preferred equally to tool 1 by using the same distribution ($\mu = 3.65, \sigma^2 = 1.17$) for both. In both scenarios, we run the simulation 100 times and for each compute a two-sided $t$ test. We use Welch's $t$ test assuming variances are not equal for the first scenario.

Next we convert the Likert data to binary data using a threshold of 2.5 such that $(1, 2 \mapsto 0; 3, 4, 5 \mapsto 1)$, and with a threshold of 3.5 where $(1, 2, 3 \mapsto 0; 4, 5 \mapsto 1)$. We compute the $z$-score on difference of means, a $\chi^2$ test with Yates' correction on the difference in proportions of 0 and 1s, and two binomial tests (first hypothesis is tool 2 is sampled from tool 1's distribution, second is vice-versa) for each. The statistical tests in this section were designed based on Loveland [8] and applications of Sauro and Lewis [9].

Our results (Table 1) confirm that more reviews provide higher, or at least negligibly worse, percentages of correct conclusions in all cases. Our results show that the $z$ test and Binomial test under both thresholds are poor at identifying when tools are the same, whereas the $\chi^2$ test with threshold of 2.5 is poor at telling when they are different. However, the $t$ test has good performance in both scenarios, as does the $\chi^2$ test with threshold of 3.5, so we use these results for our target number. These estimates are based only on the specific distributions used in the two scenarios (which may not match real-world data we obtain), but are reasonable assumptions to provide a quantitative approach to reasoning how many operators are needed.

**Table 1.** For each simulated number of participants, the table reports the percent of the simulations for which the hypothesis test confirmed the two tool's data were different. For example, a result of 0.67 implies that test provided at least 95% confidence that the tool 2 rating was different from the tool 1 rating in 67% of the simulations. For the $z$-, $\chi^2$-, and Binomial tests, Likert values $\{1, \ldots, 5\}$ are converted to binary $\{0, 1\}$ using thresholds 2.5, then 3.5. Both results are given in the form of (%{thresh = 2.5}, %{thresh = 3.5}). Since these tests were testing the null hypothesis that the ratings were sampled from the same distribution, higher (lower) percentages in the top (bottom) half when the distributions were different imply high (low) performance by the test, respectively.

| #reviews/pair | | 10 | 15 | 25 | 30 | 35 | 40 |
|---|---|---|---|---|---|---|---|
| Different | $z$ test | (0.88, 0.96) | (0.89, 0.99) | (0.95, 1.0) | (0.97, 1.0) | (0.98, 1.0) | (0.98, 1.0) |
| | $\chi^2$ test | (0.04, 0.23) | (0.06, 0.37) | (0.17, 0.71) | (0.24, 0.81) | (0.29, 0.88) | (0.34, 0.91) |
| | Bin. test | (0.36, 0.68) | (0.42, 0.8) | (0.57, 0.93) | (0.63, 0.97) | (0.66, 0.97) | (0.71, 0.99) |
| Same | $t$-test | 0.04 | 0.05 | 0.05 | 0.03 | 0.05 | 0.06 |
| | $z$-test | (0.73, 0.82) | (0.79, 0.86) | (0.81, 0.89) | (0.83, 0.89) | (0.86, 0.91) | (0.86, 0.91) |
| | $\chi^2$-test | (0.0, 0.02) | (0.0, 0.01) | (0.01, 0.03) | (0.01, 0.01) | (0.01, 0.02) | (0.02, 0.02) |
| | Bin.-test | (0.1, 0.18) | (0.13, 0.18) | (0.19, 0.19) | (0.2, 0.21) | (0.2, 0.17) | (0.23, 0.21) |

We presented these statistical results to the sponsor organization allowing them to quantifiably reason about the balance between their operator's time and statistical power of the results desired. Note that there are 11 total tools, and thus [11 choose 2] = 55 unique pairs of tools, and secondly that each participant will be asked to rate eight of 11 tools to respect their time, yielding [8 choose 2] = 28 pairwise reviews. Thus, 1,650 desired total desired pairwise reviews divided by 28 pairwise reviews per participant yields a target of 59 participants. After being presented with this information along with Table 1 our sponsoring organization decided that nineteen participants was sufficient.

**How to Assign Reviews to Each Participant?** Since we only will require 8 of 11 tools to be reviewed by each participant, the problem of which 8 tools to assign to each participant arises because the assignment of tools to reviewers affects how many pair reviews we obtain. We seek to maximize the number of reviews for every pair of tools given a fixed number of participants. Further, the algorithm must accommodate more/less participants than is desired to accommodate optimistic/realistic participation.

Note that independent of the assignment, for $n$ total tools, $m$ participants, and $l$ reviews per participant there will be an average of $\mu := m \times [l \text{ choose } 2]/[n \text{ choose } 2]$ ratings of each pair of tools. Our assignment algorithm seeks to find $m$ different $l$-tuples of tools so that each pair of tools occurs in as close to $\mu$ of the tuples as possible (each pair is assigned to exactly $\mu$ participants). For our case ($m = 59, l = 8, n = 11$) we seek $\mu = 59 \times 28/55 \sim 30$ reviews for each pair.

For each $l$-tuple, we enumerate the [$l$ choose 2] pairs in the $l$-tuple, and for each pair, we track the number of times that tuple has already occurred. Initially all counts are 0, and we define the score for the $l$-tuple as the sum of these tallies. While the set of assignments is less than $m$, the algorithm sorts all $l$-tuples by score, and picks the next participant's assignment uniformly at random from those $l$-tuples with minimal score, then updates the tallies and scores of all $l$-tuples. Once an assignment is given (a list of $m$ total $l$-tuples), we define the assignment error as the average absolute difference of the number of pairwise assignments from $\mu$. Although this algorithm may not find an optimal assignment, it is usually close. We set $m$ larger than the desired number of users, to optimistically accommodate over-recruitment, and run the algorithm 100 times (10 s), keeping only the best assignment. Since the recruitment in practice yielded only 19 participants, we note that because the algorithm is greedy, using the first 19 assignments is also close to optimal. In our case of $n = 11, m = 59, l = 8$, we have $\mu = 30.0\overline{36}$, and the resulting assignment produced 6 pairs with 29, 41 pairs with 30, and 8 pairs with 31 reviews for an average error of $\sim$0.28.

**Sentiment Analysis.** After watching the videos for each tool, participants were asked to complete the free response question, "Is there anything else about this tool that you would like to share?" The problem for analyzing this feedback is it is text, i.e., not numerical. In order to convert text feedback into a numerical rating, our algorithm takes the average of two sentiment analyzers, VADER[2] [10], which provides a polarity score based on heuristics leveraging sentiWordnet [11], and roBERTa[3] [12], a sentiment analyzer that uses BERT [13] and is trained on sentiment-labeled tweets to produce a polarity score. The average of these scores provides a polarity (in $[-1,1]$), which we map to $[1,5]$ Likert scale. Finally, we included a check for similarity of the VADER and roBERTa scores, manually inspecting if they differed more than .5, which never occurred herein. Overall, the free responses are parsed into strings and converted to a Likert value using sentiment analysis, which can be analyzed similar to the other numeric feedback.

### 2.2 Predicting Missing Ratings

Since operators recruited for this survey were assigned a subset of the tools to review, this means that we have missing data since every operator did not complete the survey for each tool. This section provides a linear progression of previous research that informs our approach followed by our algorithm for filling in missing values to populate a complete dataset. Our contributions include providing a simple Bayesian technique for computing similarities dependent on unseen ratings and a method to optimally weight multiple predicted ratings, which, at least on our data, outperforms previous methods. Consider a vector, $\vec{r}(u,t,:)$, that comprises the ratings assigned by user $u$ to tool $t$; i.e., $\{\vec{r}(u,t,i)\}_{u,t,i}$ is a tensor, $\vec{r}$ with the third dimension representing the ratings.

**Relevant Recommender System Literature.** Breese et al. [14] considers the single-criteria problem where $\vec{r}(u,t,:) = r(u,t)$ is a scalar, equiv. $r$ is a matrix. Unknown values are defined as follows,

$$\vec{r}(u,t,:) := \frac{1}{\sum_{v\in\text{Users}} \texttt{sim}(u,v)} \sum_{v\in\text{Users}} \texttt{sim}(u,v)\vec{r}(v,t,:) \tag{1}$$

where $\texttt{sim}(u,v)$ is a similarity measure of users $u$ and $v$ computed with a standard similarity measure (e.g., cosine, inverse Euclidean, Pearson correlation) applied to the vector of ratings from $u$ and $v$ on the set of items both users rated.

Adomavicius and Kwon (AK) [15] extend this framework to multi-criteria ratings where $\vec{r}(u,t)$ is a vector with $\vec{r}(u,t,n)$ user $u$'s overall rating of tool $t$ on the $n^{th}$ aspect. Setting a distance on rating vectors, $d_R(\vec{r}(u,t,:),\vec{r}(v,s,:))$, AK defines the distance between two users, $u,v$, as $d_U(u,v) = \sum_{t\in T_{u,v}} d_R(\vec{r}(u,t),\vec{r}(v,t,:))/|T_{u,v}|$,where $T_{u,v} :=$ {tools $t$ rated by both $u$ and $v$}. The similarity of two users is simply an inverse function of their distance such that $\texttt{sim}(u,v) := 1/(1+d_U(u,v))$. Notably, the general framework is symmetric in users and items; hence, item similarity could just as easily produce predicted missing values. Finally, for each missing aspect rating ($j = 1,...,n-1$), the output

[2] https://www.nltk.org/_modules/nltk/sentiment/vader.html.
[3] https://huggingface.co/cardiffnlp/twitter-roberta-base-sentiment.

$\vec{r}(u,t,j)$ is predicted according to Eg. 1, supervised learning techniques are suggested for learning $\vec{r}(u,t,n)$ from the aspect ratings $\{\vec{r}(u,t,j) : j = 1,...,n-1\}$. The progression of the research literature diverged from these "instance-based" methods to develop "model-based" methods, e.g., [16–18], which seek Bayesian network models that include latent variables designed to encode clusters of similar users and of items. Results of Sahoo et al. [18] conclude that model-based methods excel (in precision-recall balance and in precision-rank balance) when $\vec{r}$ is sparse (common, e.g., in online marketplaces with a huge inventory of items), whereas, the instance-based method of AK excels for dense $\vec{r}$, which is the case in this study.

**Predicting Aspect Ratings.** For each user, $u$, and for each tool, $t$, we have a vector of numeric responses $\vec{r}(u,t,:)$ of length eight, with the first seven entries as the aspect ratings—the six questions on the SOAR tool's capabilities and the numerically-converted text comments field—and the last entry the overall rating by user $u$ for tool $t$. Hence, $\vec{r}$ is a stack of eight $19 \times 11$ matrices. As each user was assigned a minimum of eight tools (of 11 total), on average we expect 3 tools $\times$ 8 ratings missing, leaving a whole vector $\vec{r}(u,t,:)$ empty. In addition to empty entries due to how tools were assigned, some entries were empty due to an operator leaving a question blank for a tool that they were assigned to evaluate. In all there were approximately one third missing values. Following the results of Sahoo et al. [18], we use the AK workflow with tailored modifications.

From our data we define and compute three different similarities. Each produces predictions for all unknown values following Eq. 1, and we learn an optimal convex combination of the three as our prediction. The first two similarities are simply the user similarity $\texttt{sim}_U(u,v)$ and tool similarity $\texttt{sim}_T(s,t)$ from the ratings matrix. To compute these, we first need a distance on the rating vectors. We use $\ell^p$ distance and test four distances, $p = 0, 1, 2, \infty$, where $p = 0$ denotes counting the number of unequal entries in the two input vectors. For our implementation, we define $\texttt{sim}_U(u,v) := \exp\left(-\|\vec{r}(u,:,:) - \vec{r}(v,:,:)\|_p\right)$, and $\texttt{sim}_I(s,t) := \exp\left(-\|\vec{r}(:,s,:) - \vec{r}(:,t,:)\|_p\right)$.

When computing $\texttt{sim}_U$, the original work of AK ignored items that were not rated by both users. We tested both the naive rating distances against a Bayesian version. To compute the Bayesian distance between two vectors that may be missing values, we simply marginalize over a uniform distribution on the set of all possible missing values, (uniform on $\{1,...,5\}$). Upon training we will have eight ratings distances to consider parameterized by $p \in \{0,1,2,\infty\}$ and each using the naive or Bayesian approach.

Recall from Sect. 2.1 our survey asked each participant to rank the aspects of a SOAR tool in advance of seeing and rating any of the tools. This is valuable information for understanding each user's preferences, and we take this into account by providing a second user similarity (third similarity in total) from this data, which in turn provides a prediction of unknown ratings. We simply define $\texttt{sim}_{U_{rank}}(u,v) = (1+\texttt{kendalltau}(u,v))/2$ where the function **kendalltau** computes the Kendall Tau correlation [19] of the two users' aspect rankings.

As kendalltau$(u, v) \in [-1, 1]$ this similarity achieves its minimum of $-1$ with opposite rankings input, and maximum of 1 with identical rankings input.

Let $\vec{r}_U, \vec{r}_I$, and $\vec{r}_{U_{rank}}$ denote the populated tensors with previously missing values now predictions from $\texttt{sim}_U, \texttt{sim}_T, \texttt{sim}_{U_{rank}}$, respectively. Define the unknown ratings as $\vec{r} := (1 - a - b)\vec{r}_U + b\vec{r}_I + a\vec{r}_{U_{rank}}$, where $a \in [0, 1]$, and $b \in [a, 1]$ are weight parameters to be learned. To learn the parameters, we grid search over $a, b, p$ and across using naive vs. Bayesian ratings distances. For each set of parameters, we compute the macro-averaged error over a 20-fold cross validation to find the most accurate combination. We use 20-fold cross validation so that each fold has only 5% known but hidden values used for testing.

Our optimal parameters were found to use the Bayesian ratings distance computation with $p = 1$, $a = 0.2$, and $b = 0.2$, which exhibited the (lowest) average error of 0.682. Since we used a grid search, the previous methods (non-Bayesian distances, using only a single similarity) are included in the results, and hence our advancements to provide greater accuracy than previous methods.

**Predicting Overall Ratings.** While overall ratings were included in the predictions above, we suspect (as AK [15] suggests) that overall ratings are more accurately predicted from the seven aspect ratings (for that tool by that user). To this end, we test a wide variety of supervised machine learning algorithms for regressing the overall ratings from the corresponding learning algorithms on a held out test set.

After creating fully populated ratings for each aspect of each tool for each user, we first take the data that has a user-given overall ranking. We use this populated data to train and test ten machine learning regression algorithms. We then do a five-fold cross-validation on each model to determine which has the smallest error. We use the results from the model that produced the lowest average mean squared error (MSE) across the five folds. The model with the lowest MSE is then trained on all the available user given rankings. We then use the predicted aspect ratings to predict the overall rating.

## 2.3 PageRank

Using the predicted overall rating, we developed a directed graph. Each vertex of the directed graph represents a tool. The edges between each node are drawn with an arrow, where the arrow points to higher rated tools based on each user. For example, if a user rated Tool A: 5; Tool B: 3; Tool C: 1, there would be directed edges as follows: $C \to B$, $C \to A$, $B \to A$. In cases where a user rates tools with the same number, no edges are drawn between those tools that would indicate which one is higher rated. In the case of duplicate links, the edges become weighted. A single edge has a weight of 1, if the directed edge is duplicated then 1 is added to the weight for every duplicate. If the converse directed edges is added, then 1 is deducted from the weight of the edge. This method was particularly applicable because we considering filling in missing data in a pairwise fashion, and this algorithm compares the tools pairwise.

After developing a weighted directed graph, we use the PageRank algorithm to measure the importance of each node [20]. To implement the PageRank algorithm we used the NetworkX PageRank link analysis toolbox [21].

### 2.4 Statistical Analyses

When we interpret results, we need to consider them in the context of certain demographics if it is shown that these factors have an impact on how operators are rating these SOAR tools. Through these univariate and multivariate analyses, we sought to determine the strength of four relationships:

1. Tool rating and operator experience (in years)
2. Tool rating and operator occupation (security operator or other)
3. Tool rating and operator familiarity with the tool
4. Tool rating and perceived video quality by the operator

We employed three tools to conduct these analyses: linear regression, Kruskal-Wallis Test, and multivariate analysis of variance (MANOVA). Each of these methods are described briefly below.

**Linear Regression.** For each tool, we regressed its overall rating onto years of experience the operator has. After a line is fit to the data, Wald's Chi-Squared Test is to determine whether years of experience has an impact on the rating of the tool. Here, the null hypothesis is that the slope of the line that we fit to the data is zero, indicating that there is no relationship at all between years of experience and tool rating. Based on a 5% error rate, a sufficiently small $p$-value ($<0.05$) from Wald's Chi-Squared Test indicates that the slope of the best fit line is *not* zero and there is likely a relationship between the variables.

**Kruskal-Wallis.** In our analysis of the impact of tool familiarity on tool rating, we sought to address the question "Do users assign higher ratings to tools with which they have more familiarity?" Familiarity had five categories that users could mark for the tools they reviewed: *Currently use it often, Used it at least once, Used it often in the past, Heard of it, Never heard of it.*

For this analysis, we use a non-parametric Kruskal-Wallis test to compare the median overall tool scores of each of these five groups. All tool scores from every group are put into a single vector and sorted in ascending order. The tools are then ranked by their position in order from $1...n$, where $n$ is the number of observations. For each of the five group, a sum of the ranks from each of its observations are calculated. These sums, along with the sample size and number of groups, are used to calculate an $H$ statistic. The $H$ statistic then gets compared to a critical chi-squared value at a certain error rate. Should the $H$ statistic be greater than the critical value, the null hypothesis ("the medians of these five groups are the same") is rejected in favor of the alternate hypothesis ("the medians of the five groups are not the same").

A Kruskal-Wallis Test was also performed to answer the question "Does perceived video quality impact tool ratings?" After watching the overview and demonstration videos about the tools, users specified whether they felt the video was *Great, Okay, Terrible.*

**MANOVA.** We use a MANOVA test to determine whether a user's occupation impacts how they rated tools, and whether certain occupations preferred specific tools. MANOVA is useful for testing the effects that one explanatory variable (occupation) has on two or more dependent variables (ratings of tools 1–11) and compares the means of multiple dependent variables across two or groups.

# 3 Results

## 3.1 Results from Raw Data

Survey results were collected from four different SOCs, for a total of 19 SOC operators and 158 reviews (10–17 reviews per tool). The survey had two sections: evaluation of what users wanted most out of a SOAR tool (*aspect ratings*), evaluation of how users scored each of their assigned SOAR tools on these aspects, and how they ranked them in order of preference (*tool ratings and rankings).*

**Tool Results.** Each SOC operator watched a tool overview video and a tool demonstration video. Following completion of the video reviews, the operators completed our survey that asked questions about each aspect of the tool, provided an overall tool ranking (1: most preferred), and then rated (scored) all of the tools (1: lowest score).

Before investigating individual tools, we asked each operator to rank six aspects, or tasks that a SOAR tool could perform, in order of descending importance. In Fig. 1, we plot how many times each tool was ranked in each position. In this grouped bar chart, we see that playbooks are ranked first by ten operators, indicating that operators prioritize playbooks and workflows that are easy to manage. In second place, most operators voted that automating common tasks was important, followed by pre-populating tickets in third and ranking alerts in fourth. Fifth and sixth places are less clear, but we can conclude the last two places are reserved for collaboration ability and ingestion of data from various sources.

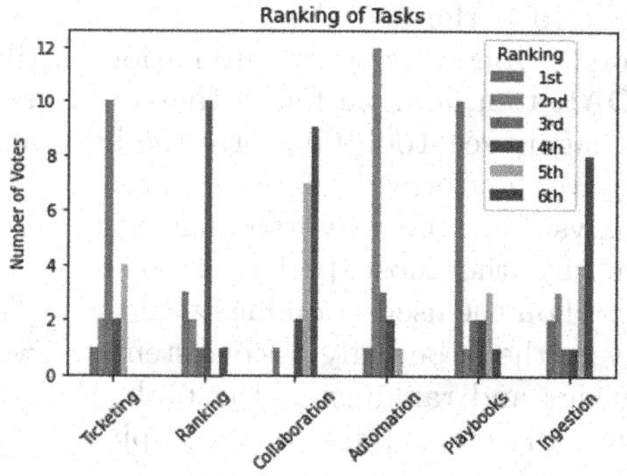

**Fig. 1.** Each aspect's rank of importance from 1 (very important) to 6 (not important)

**Aspect Ratings.** Before investigating individual tools, we asked each operator to rank six aspects, or tasks that a SOAR tool could perform, in order of descending importance. In Fig. 1, we plot how many times each tool was ranked in each position. In this grouped bar chart, we see that playbooks are ranked first by ten operators, indicating that operators prioritize playbooks and workflows that are easy to manage. In second place, most operators voted that automating common tasks was important, followed by pre-populating tickets in third and ranking alerts in fourth. Fifth and sixth places are less clear, but we can conclude the last two places are reserved for collaboration ability and ingestion of data from various sources.

In Fig. 2, we note that Tool 6 is scored the highest on average with a mean rating of 4.36 out of 5. Contrarily, Tool 7 is rated the lowest on average with a mean rating of 3.27. Operators ranked playbook management as the most important aspect (Fig. 1) and the tools received an average score of 3.56 on this aspect. Tool 9 performed the best on their playbook aspect, and scored a 4.07, while Tool 10 performed the worst. Operators rank automation as the second most important feature of a SOAR tool, and we found that on average our tools received a rating of 3.75. We again see Tool 9 perform the best, and Tool 7 perform the worst.

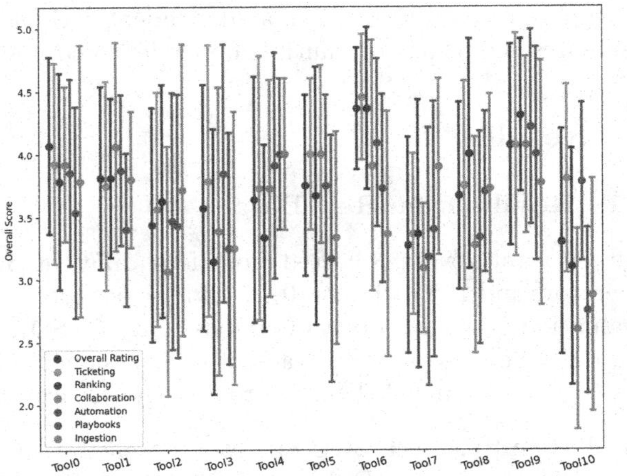


**Fig. 2.** Summary of all of the raw survey scores. Each tool is on the X-axis, and the score is on the Y-axis. The unique colors represent a specific aspect of the survey.

We performed a PageRank analysis on the tool rankings to identify the most preferred tool based on the user's rankings alone, given the seemingly inconsistent ratings and rankings of the tools. The directed PageRank graph (Fig. 3) is based on user rankings, and we note that Tool 6 has the most inward weights, which indicates that most users ranked this tool as the best. Analogously, we see Tool 0 has the most outward weights, indicating that most users ranked this tool last.

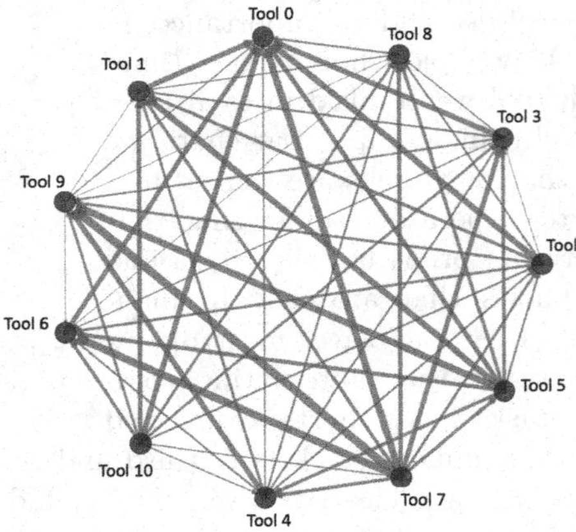


**Fig. 3.** PageRank graphical network from raw data.

## 3.2 Results from Populated Data

The following results are derived from the populated data, or the data for which we have filled in all the missing aspect ratings and used these to predict the missing overall ratings. With the populated data, we have a total of 197 complete tool reviews.

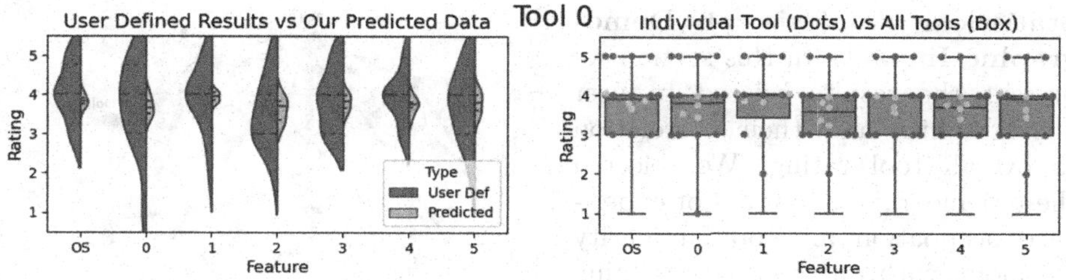


**Fig. 4.** Tool 0 score summary based on user defined results and predicted results. In the left panel, the distribution of the user defined results (green) and the predicted results (red). In the right panel, comparison of the results (green/red dots, respectively) with the average scores across all tools (grey box plot). (Color figure online)

**Predicted Responses.** In Fig. 4 we highlight how our predicted responses compare the user defined responses in this single example of Tool 0. Analogous plots are available for each tool. In Fig. 4 (left), the green region is the user-defined ratings for the six aspects and the overall score of the tool. The red region is the predicted ratings for the overall score and aspects our algorithm filled in for missing user responses. Importantly, our predicted values fall well within in the middle quartiles, indicating that our predictions are not skewing the overall tool ratings. In Fig. 4 (right), we compare the results of all of the tools to the responses for the individual tool. The green/red dots are the user-defined/predicted scores.

**Table 2.** Ten machine learning algorithms compared based on cross validation mean squared error.

| Model | MSE |
|---|---|
| SGD | 0.2733 |
| Bayesian Ridge | 0.2735 |
| Kernel Ridge | 0.2736 |
| Linear Regression | 0.2762 |
| Support Vector | 0.3567 |
| Random Forest | 0.3786 |
| Gradient Boost | 0.3887 |
| CatBoost | 0.4375 |
| AK Modeling | 0.7379 |
| Elastic Net | 0.7623 |

After having a complete user profile, we used 10 machine learning regression algorithms to predict an overall tool score (Table 2). Because Stochastic Gradient Descent Regression had the highest accuracy, we used this algorithm to complete the missing values in the overall scores.

As previously mentioned, some users *rank* tools differently then how they have *rated* them, and we implement PageRank to account for these discrepancies (see Fig. 5). As we did on the raw data with missing values, we create the same directed graph for the populated data to identify the most preferred tool using only rankings. Following the pipeline we now have a complete picture of user overall scores of a tool and how that translates to user tool rankings. When calculating the overall rankings with our predicted data, we assume users rank tools based on the overall score they give a tool. If a user gives 2 tools the same overall score we then deflect to the initial tool ranking. As with the raw data, we find Tool 6 to be the most preferred tool and Tool 7 to be the least preferred tool using the populated data.

**Statistical Analysis of Demographic Impact.** In this section we present the results related to user demographics and their correlation to overall tool rating. We selected these demographics—years of experience, occupation, and tool familiarity —, along with one factor pertaining to video quality, because these demographics are most likely to influence tool ratings and rankings. First, we note in Fig. 6 that there is no relationship between a tool's rating and the years of experience a user has. Similarly, we find that a user's occupation has no impact on tool rating, with no discernible preference for one tool over another by users of specific occupation. As such, we need not consider the effects of these factors moving forward.

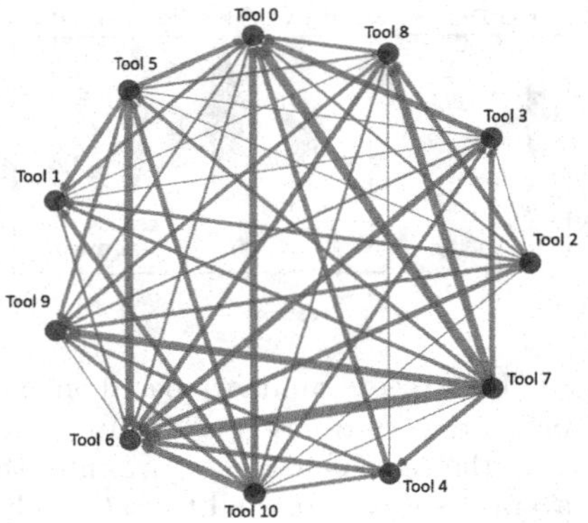


**Fig. 5.** PageRank graphical network from populated data based on ML algorithms.

However, we did identify two factors that did correlate to how a tool was rated (Fig. 7). The first factor we found that influences tool rating is the familiarity a user has with a tool. We found that tools were generally rated higher by users when the user had used the tool before. The second of these was perceived quality of the submitted video. In this case, tools with higher quality videos were subsequently rated higher. It is not necessarily true that a low quality video is related to a tool's performance, and caution must be taken to ensure that the best tools are selected to move to Phase 2. Similarly, we need to account for the fact that if an operator is familiar with a tool then they likely will rate it higher.

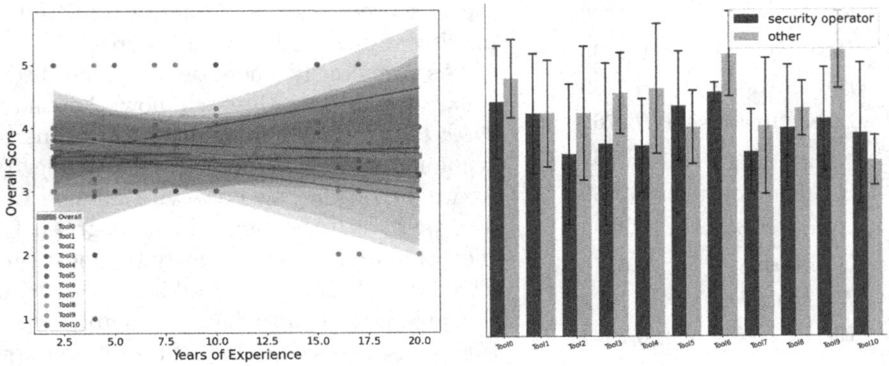


**Fig. 6.** There is no relationship between operator years of experience or occupation and how a tool was rated. This confirms that there is no decision bias based on experience or occupation, and even operators with similar backgrounds have different visions for SOCs.

### 3.3 Overall Results

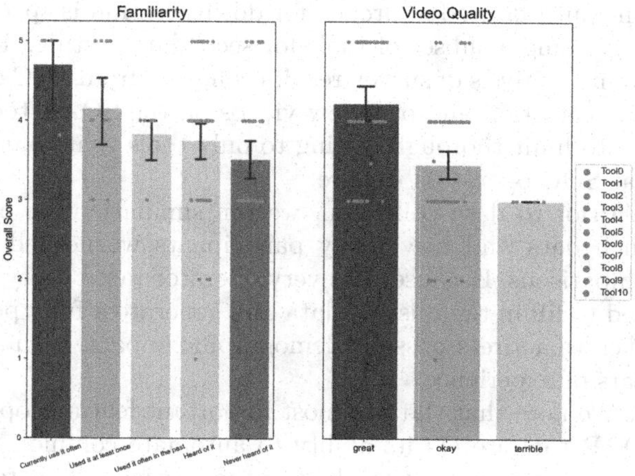


**Fig. 7.** In the left panel we see there is a relationship between overall score and user familiarity. In the right panel we see a relationship between video quality and overall score.

We have two sets of data, the raw data with missing values and the populated data, and we have two ways of evaluating tool preferences, ratings and rankings. As previously mentioned, there were some discrepancies in how a user rated the tool and how a user ranked the same tool. Here, we present the results of four analyses we implemented to determine tool preferences (Fig. 8 and Table 3). Note that the first two columns are from the raw data, and the last two columns are from the populated data.

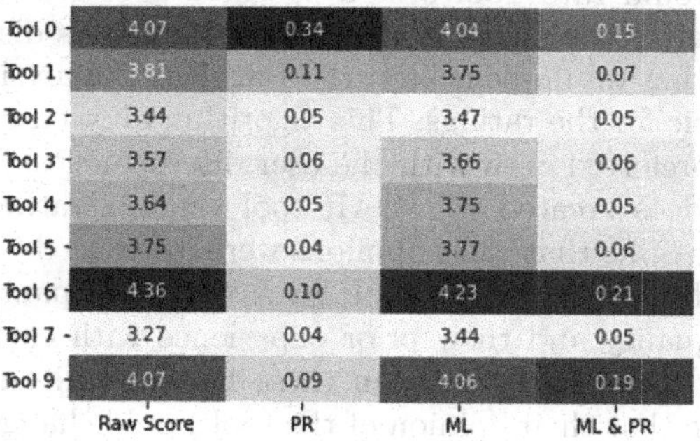
Tool 0 4.07 0.34 4.04 0.15
Tool 1 3.81 0.11 3.75 0.07
Tool 2 3.44 0.05 3.47 0.05
Tool 3 3.57 0.06 3.66 0.06
Tool 4 3.64 0.05 3.75 0.05
Tool 5 3.75 0.04 3.77 0.06
Tool 6 4.36 0.10 4.23 0.21
Tool 7 3.27 0.04 3.44 0.05
Tool 9 4.07 0.09 4.06 0.19
Raw Score
PR
ML
ML & PR

**Fig. 8.** Heat map summary of all four methods used to report or derive overall ratings of the tools. Raw score: average of user-defined ratings; PR: average of overall ratings derived from PageRank algorithm on the raw data; ML: average of overall ratings derived from machine learning predictions on populated data; ML + PR: average of overall ratings derived from machine learning and PageRank algorithm on populated data.

We note that in every analysis, Tool 7 was the bottom performer, and for three out of four analyses, we note that Tool 2 is the second to last performer. Similarly, Tool 6 is the top performer in three out of four cases, and only dropping to a lowest preference of third place in the PageRank analysis on raw data. It is worth noting, too, that for three of the four analyses, we have the same tools in the top three places: Tool 0, Tool 6, and Tool 9. The middle placements shuffle around considerably, but the top performers remain consistent.

## 4 Discussion

In this work, we (1) provide a summary of features operators value in a SOAR tool, and (2) develop a method for down-selection when survey data is limited.

Our multi-faceted approach for downselection is specifically applicable here, for progressing a subset of tools for secondary testing. This approach was centered around analysis of survey results collected from SOC operators after they viewed demonstration and overview videos on the SOAR tools. The goal of the survey was to limit thorough testing to only tools that contained many of the features that SOC operators require.

Prior to data collection, we ran simulations to obtain an estimate for how much data and how many participants we needed to have statistically valid comparisons. Because not every operator rated every tool, machine learning was used to fill in the missing data and generate a fully populated dataset. Care was taken to address possible demographic impact, such as operator occupation and years of experience.

We note that the two most important features operators are looking for in a SOAR tool are (1) its ability to automate common tasks and (2) functionality of playbooks. More than half of the participants voted that playbooks were the most important aspect of a SOAR tool, followed by task automation, ticketing, and ranking of alerts in a clear second, third, and fourth order, respectively. This survey, even with its limitations, provides a starting point for SOAR tool vendors to focus their efforts on aspects that are most beneficial to SOC function.

Another survey aspect that affected our analysis of operator preferences were the discrepancies between how an operator rated tools vs ranked tools. For example, in many instances operators would rate Tool 0 at a 5/5 and Tool 1 at a 3/5, but then would rank Tool 1 better than Tool 0. Due to the numerous discrepancies between ranking and rating we implemented the PageRank analysis algorithm to develop a scoring metric for the ratings. This algorithm allowed us to predict which node is the most preferred even with the user discrepancies.

Because participants viewed videos created by SOAR tool vendors rather than using the tools directly, it is possible that their opinions were influenced by either video quality or prior knowledge of a particular tool. We asked participants to provide their opinion of video quality and their prior experience with each tool in our survey, and we discuss correlations between these factors and our results in Sect. 3.2. It is also possible that their opinion of the tool would change if they had the opportunity to use it in an operational context, which is the next phase of our research. However, the largest limitation to our study was the number of participants. We recognize that in an ideal world we would have had more participants, however given the information we found about how many participants would provide what confidence, our sponsor determined they were satisfied with nineteen for this phase of down-selecting.

Based on this analysis, we are equipped to identify a subset of these 11 tools that will be thoroughly tested. Operators will use these tools in several realistic scenarios and will be asked to complete a survey after regarding their experience. Furthermore specific performance metrics will be collected to measure the improvement to efficiency and effectiveness by usage of SOAR tools in a SOC. While this framework was developed in the context of SOC survey responses and downselecting a large sample, the impacts of this study are far-reaching. In general the framework we present provides designers of user studies with the ability to quantify the statistical power of their analyses based on their sample size, and furthermore provides a reliable method of populating missing user data. If there are multiple methods of evaluation, such as scores and ranking, we demonstrate a novel method of reconciling differences between the two for a more clear interpretation and meaningful results.

**Acknowledgements.** Special thanks to Jeff Meredith for assisting with the website. The research is based upon work supported by the Department of Defense (DOD), Naval Information Warfare Systems Command (NAVWAR), via the Department of Energy (DOE) under contract DE-AC05-00OR22725. The views and conclusions contained herein are those of the authors and should not be interpreted as representing the official policies or endorsements, either expressed or implied, of the DOD, NAVWAR, or the U.S. Government. The U.S. Government is authorized to reproduce and distribute reprints for Governmental purposes notwithstanding any copyright annotation thereon.

# A Appendix

**Table 3.** Four methods used to report or derive overall ratings of the tools. Raw score: average of user-defined ratings; PR: average of overall ratings derived from PageRank algorithm on the raw data; ML: average of overall ratings derived from machine learning predictions on populated data; ML + PR: average of overall ratings derived from machine learning and PageRank algorithm on populated data.

| Raw score [1 – 5] | PR [0 – 1] | ML [1 – 5] | ML + PR [0 – 1] |
|---|---|---|---|
| Tool 6 (4.363) | Tool 0 (.341) | Tool 6 (4.23) | Tool 6 (.207) |
| Tool 9 (4.071) | Tool 1 (.114) | Tool 9 (4.06) | Tool 9 (.192) |
| Tool 0 (4.071) | Tool 6 (.097) | Tool 0 (4.04) | Tool 0 (.146) |
| Tool 1 (3.813) | Tool 9 (.085) | Tool 5 (3.77) | Tool 1 (.070) |
| Tool 5 (3.750) | Tool 3 (.057) | Tool 4 (3.75) | Tool 5 (.061) |
| Tool 4 (3.636) | Tool 2 (.052) | Tool 1 (3.75) | Tool 3 (.055) |
| Tool 3 (3.571) | Tool 4 (.048) | Tool 3 (3.66) | Tool 4 (.054) |
| Tool 2 (3.438) | Tool 5 (.043) | Tool 2 (3.47) | Tool 2 (.046) |
| Tool 7 (3.273) | Tool 7 (.042) | Tool 7 (3.44) | Tool 7 (.046) |

**Table 4.** Survey questionnaire given to the SOC operators. The survey was delivered electronically and included 4 pre-survey questions, 10 questions about the specific tools (including their aspects), and 1 question about the overall ranking. All ratings questions were scored 1–5, with 1 being the worst and 5 being the best. On the two ranking questions, the operators ranked their most preferred aspect/tool as 1 and their least preferred as the highest value.

| Question # | Question type | Question |
|---|---|---|
| 1 | Pre-Survey | How familiar are you with SOAR tools? |
| 2 | Pre-Survey | Which of these best fits your role? |
| 3 | Pre-Survey | How many years have you been in that role? |
| 4 | Pre-Survey | Please rank the following capabilities in order of importance, with 1 being the most important and 7 being the least important in your SOC |
| 1 | Familiarity | How familiar are you with this tool? |
| 2 | Quality | What do you think of the quality of these videos? |
| 3 | Overall score | What is you overall impression of this tool? |
| 4 | Ranking | Does the tool present and prioritize data in a way that is beneficial? |
| 5 | Ingestion | Do you think this tool could effectively ingest the data in your SOC? |
| 6 | Playbooks | Does the tool provide steps (playbook, workflow) that guide tier 1 or junior analysts through common tasks? |
| 7 | Ticketing | Does the tool automate tasks in a way that would increase efficiency? |
| 8 | Collaboration | Does the tool enable multiple analysts to effectively collaborate (simultaneously)? |
| 9 | Automation | Does the tool enable a hand off of investigations (for example, between two shifts or across SOCs)? |
| 10 | Free response | Is there anything else about this tool that you would like to share? |
| N/A | Overall ranking | Please rank the tools that you reviewed by order of preference, where 1 indicates the tool that you would most like to see used in your SOC. You can drag and drop the tool names to reorder them |

## References


1. Goodbye SIEM, hello SOARX: Network Security, p. 20 (2019)
2. Islam, C., Babar, M.A., Nepal, S.: A multi-vocal review of security orchestration. ACM Comput. Surv. **52**(2), 1–45 (2019)
3. Brewer, R.: Could SOAR save skills-short SOCs? Comput. Fraud Secur. **2019**(10), 8–11 (2019). https://www.sciencedirect.com/science/article/pii/S136137231930106X
4. Trull, J.: Top 5 best practices to automate security operations (2017). https://www.microsoft.com/security/blog/2017/08/03/top-5-best-practices-to-automate-security-operations/

5. Dutta, S.D., Prasad, R.: Cybersecurity for microgrid. In: 23rd International Symposium on Wireless Personal Multimedia Communications (WPMC) (2020)
6. Fielder, A., Panaousis, E., Malacaria, P., Hankin, C., Smeraldi, F.: Decision support approaches for cyber security investment. Decis. Support Syst. **86**, 13–23 (2016)
7. Dupuis, M., Geiger, T., Slayton, M., Dewing, F.: The use and non-use of cybersecurity tools among consumers. In: Proceedings of the 20th Annual SIG Conference on Information Technology Education (2019)
8. Loveland, J.L.: Mathematical justifcation of introductory hypothesis tests and development of reference materials, p. 133
9. Sauro, J., Lewis, J.R.: Quantifying the User Experience: Practical Statistics for User Research. Elsevier Morgan Kaufmann, New York (2012)
10. Hutto, C., Gilbert, E.: VADER: a parsimonious rule-based model for sentiment analysis of social media text. In: Proceedings of the International AAAI Conference on Web and Social Media, vol. 8, no. 1 (2014)
11. Baccianella, S., Esuli, A., Sebastiani, F.: SENTIWORDNET 3.0: an enhanced lexical resource for sentiment analysis and opinion mining. In: Lrec, vol. 10, no. 2010, pp. 2200–2204 (2010)
12. Barbieri, F., Camacho-Collados, F., Anke, L.E., Neves, L.: TweetEval: unified benchmark and comparative evaluation for tweet classification. In: Proceedings of the 2020 Conference on Empirical Methods in Natural Language Processing: Findings, pp. 1644–1650 (2020)
13. Devlin, J., Chang, M.-W., Lee, K., Toutanova, K.: BERT: pre-training of deep bidirectional transformers for language understanding. In: NAACL-HLT, vol. 1 (2019)
14. Breese, J.S., Heckerman, D., Kadie, C.: Empirical analysis of predictive algorithms for collaborative filtering. In: Proceedings of the Fourteenth Conference on Uncertainty in Artificial Intelligence, pp. 43–52 (1998)
15. Adomavicius, G., Kwon, Y.: New recommendation techniques for multicriteria rating systems. IEEE Intell. Syst. **22**(3), 48–55 (2007)
16. Hofmann, T., Puzicha, J.: Latent class models for collaborative filtering. In: IJCAI, vol. 99, no. 1999 (1999)
17. Si, L., Jin, R., Flexible mixture model for collaborative filtering. In: Proceedings of the 20th International Conference on Machine Learning (ICML-03), pp. 704–711 (2003)
18. Sahoo, N., Krishnan, R., Duncan, G., Callan, J.: The halo effect in multicomponent ratings and its implications for recommender systems: the case of Yahoo! movies. Inf. Syst. Res. **23**(1), 231–246 (2012)
19. Knight, W.R.: A computer method for calculating Kendall's Tau with ungrouped data. J. Am. Stat. Assoc. **61**(314), 436–439 (1966)
20. Page, L., Brin, S., Motwani, R., Winograd, T.: The PageRank citation ranking: Bringing order to the web. Technical Report, Stanford InfoLab (1999)
21. Hagberg, A., Swart, P., Chult, D.S.: Exploring network structure, dynamics, and function using NetworkX, Los Alamos National Lab (LANL), Los Alamos, NM (United States), Technical Report (2008)

# Author Index

Printed in the United States
by Baker & Taylor Publisher Services